Introduction to

A Way of Life

5th Edition

Ted M. Preston, Ph.D.
Rio Hondo College

A Local Source Textbook™ Company

Introduction to Philosophy: A Way Of Life (5th Ed.)

Table of Contents

Preface to 5th edition

The 5th edition of this book comes with several changes, some minor, and several quite significant. Minor changes are too numerous and probably too trivial to mention. Slight additions or altered wording occur throughout. I have provided a more lengthy and detailed treatment of psychological egoism in the ethics chapter, as well as an expanded and revised explanation of both subjectivism and cultural relativism. The entirety of the "Enchiridion" by Epictetus has been added to the chapter on philosophical therapy, and both chapters on philosophy of religion, as well as the political philosophy chapter, have received significant expansions. Most significantly, I have added two entirely new chapters on "personal identity."

Acknowledgments

The first edition of this textbook was published in 2009, and since that time I have been blessed with the opportunity to write a text for Ancient Philosophy, Philosophy of Religion, Ethics, Political Philosophy, and now four further editions of this book.

Writing has been a joy, not a job—and my primary inspiration remains the same as it was in 2009: to produce quality texts that are accessible to my students both in terms of cost as well as content. My students have been both the inspiration and the living laboratory that make these books possible. Their questions, confusions, and moments of clarity have helped me to refine my explanations and ideas, and continue to do so. So, to my students, for whom I write: thank you.

I would like to thank my colleague Dr. Adam Wetsman for his vision of Gnutext, and making all of these books possible. I would also like to thank Professor Brian Brutlag for challenging me and collaborating with me in ways that resulted in my chapter on the politics of identity. I would finally like to thank my friend and colleague Professor Scott Dixon for his (Aristotelian) friendship, helpful feedback, and countless philosophical conversations over the years. Finaly, I would like to thank my wife and partner, Dr. Portia Alexandria Jackson Preston, for her love, support, and feedback.

Introduction

Comprehension questions you should be able to answer after reading this introduction:

1. *What does each of the following mean, in the context of philosophy: Metaphysics, epistemology, logic, value theory / axiology?*
2. *What time periods does each of the following include: Ancient philosophy, Medieval philosophy, Modern philosophy, Contemporary philosophy?*
3. *Describe the "ancient" approach to philosophy, as offered in this introduction.*
4. *What does each of the following mean?*
    a. *Areté*
    b. *Askesis*
    c. *Bios*
    d. *Ergon*
    e. *Eudaimonia*
    f. *Logos*
    g. *Philosophy*
    h. *Telos*
    i. *Technē*

This is a book meant to introduce you to the study of philosophy. If you are taking an introductory philosophy class, it's safe to assume that many (if not most) of you do not yet know what philosophy is. Or, perhaps you have an idea of what philosophy is, but one in need of correction.

To begin with, I would like to distinguish *philosophy* from one's "personal philosophy."

Do you have a personal philosophy? If so, describe it in a few sentences:

A personal philosophy is some belief, or value, or set of beliefs and values, that tends to guide your approach to life, and can sometimes be captured in a catchy slogan. Possible examples of a personal philosophy include (but are certainly not limited to) the following:

- Do unto others as you would have them do unto you.
- YOLO ("you only live once")
- Live, and let live.
- Live according to Nature.
- *Carpe Diem* ("seize the day")
- Manners: I will be humble, respectful, and courteous above all. Peace: I will observe the way of peace and teamwork. Drive: I will practice with all the drive that I have, and strive for more than I think I have. Courage: I will have true courage in all facets of life. Self-Improvement: I will strive for individual achievement for the benefit of others.

Whether or not you have a personal philosophy worked out at this stage in your life, and regardless of its content, as important as your personal philosophy is, it is not the same thing as philosophy itself—although I think there is, or at least *should be*—an important connection between the two. To see why, let's consider just one of the examples from above: "YOLO."

Presumably, those who embrace "you only live once" as a personal philosophy try to live their lives fully, are willing to take risks, and emphasize the present moment. After, "you only live once" so you had better enjoy the only life you will ever have!

What if that's not true?

That is, what if it is *false* that you "only live once?" What if there is an afterlife? What if we are reincarnated under some system of karma? What if we are judged on the basis of how we lived this (one) Earthly life, but will spend eternity in Heaven or Hell as a result of that judgment. These two (general) possibilities are believed to be true by *billions* of people. Living today.

To put it bluntly, "YOLO" might be terrible advice if its basic premise (i.e., that this life is the only experience we will ever have) turns out to be false. It stands to reason, then, that it is quite important to determine (as best we can) whether or not that premise is true.

The discipline of philosophy is a means by which to do exactly that. As we will throughout the course of this book, philosophy helps us to determine what is true and false (and what those terms even mean in the first place), how we can tell, what the possibilities are for what might be true or false in the first place, and helps us to consider and evaluate a variety of possible values in our efforts to not only come up with a personal philosophy that seems true, but then to put that personal philosophy into practice.

Those efforts will occupy us for the remainder of the book. But, before we delve so deeply, we should first establish just what philosophy is, and what it meant to do for us.

Philosophy

There are a variety of ways in which to chop up the philosophical landscape, and these ways tend to correspond to the different approaches an instructor might take to teaching an introduction to philosophy course. Some instructors (including myself) like to organize and teach topically. That is, we divide philosophy into sub-categories, and teach a little bit from each one. There are several ways to divide up the topics covered by philosophy. Some people (like myself) prefer four broad categories, while others prefer five, six, or even more categories. To be honest, it doesn't matter all that much. The point of identifying these sub-divisions of philosophy is to provide some shared vocabulary, and a shared sense of important themes. My own preferred method of dividing up philosophical themes is as follows:

1. Metaphysics: an investigation into the ultimate nature of reality itself.
2. Epistemology: an investigation into the nature of knowledge
3. Logic: an investigation into reason and argumentation
4. Value theory/axiology: an investigation into the nature of those things to which we assign value

Starting with **metaphysics**, I'll now provide just a little bit more detail for each. As mentioned, metaphysics concerns the ultimate nature of reality, beyond what the physical sciences can tell us. Once physics has done all it can accomplish, there remain "deep" questions about reality that are not necessarily subject to empirical verification or testing.

Metaphysics is as old as philosophy itself. One of the central concerns of the pre-Socratic philosophers (the "first philosophers") was to understand the "first principle:" that which gives structure and explanation to everything we observe. Their answers were varied and sometimes amusing, from our privileged vantage point thousands of years later.

Thales thought that reality was, ultimately, water. Democritus proposed "atoms." Many of these philosophers were materialists, in that they believed that the "first principle" was physical. Later philosophers, such as Plato, endorsed a dualistic understanding of metaphysics, according to which some things were physical, but other things were non-physical (mental, spiritual). This is a basic metaphysical distinction. Is reality, ultimately, purely physical? Matter and energy governed by the laws of physics? Or, is there something about reality not reducible to a purely physical description? Something "spiritual," or "mental?"

Our answer to that most basic metaphysical question leads naturally to many others. What is the ultimate nature of a person? Purely physical? A biological machine? A sophisticated animal? Or, is there something about us that is different, something "spiritual" or "mental?" Our answer to those questions immediately informs our understanding of our own behavior (a critical issue in the free will debate). It also contributes to our understanding of the nature of mind (is the "mind" merely a *brain,* or something "more?"), the nature of life and death, the possibility of an afterlife, etc. Many issues in the philosophy of religion also fall into this large and fascinating category of metaphysics.

Epistemology concerns the nature of knowledge. Just as old as metaphysics, philosophers have long agonized over whether knowledge is possible, and, if possible, what it means to know something (as opposed to merely believing something). The skeptics argued that knowledge was unattainable, while other philosophers across the centuries sought to demonstrate that it is attainable.

Another epistemological concern is the nature of truth. Is there any such thing as "the Truth? Objective truth? Absolute truth? Or, is truth always a matter of perspective? The sophist Protagoras claimed that "man is the measure of all things," and that truth is always a matter of perspective. Others, such as Plato, claimed that Truth is something objective and independent of our perspectives, and that the task of philosophy is to help us arrive at that Truth.

With both metaphysical and epistemological issues, arguments have been employed by philosophers at least since Thales. Argument and reasoning are perhaps the most distinguishing features of philosophy. Philosophy does not rely on tradition or appeals to authority to prove a point—philosophers *prove* their points. Such attempts involve arguments and the exercise of reason, and this is the domain of **logic**. Logical issues include methods of reasoning, in general, different kinds of argument (e.g., deductive and inductive), and how we evaluate the quality of arguments in terms of their validity, soundness, absence of fallacies, etc.

Finally, numerous issues in philosophy involve value judgments. What is morally right, and morally wrong? Morally good, and bad? Ethics, of course, is the obvious domain of such questions. Some philosophers believe that moral rightness and wrongness are relative to individuals or communities, while others believe that objective values exist instead. Political questions arise in this category as well. What justifies the existence of the State (government)? Are laws merely local conventions, or can laws themselves be just or unjustness when compared to a "higher" standard? When (if ever) is civil disobedience morally acceptable, or war? Finally, even aesthetic value may be considered within this category. What is art? What is beauty? All such questions may be considered under the category of **value theory (axiology)**.

As mentioned, the point of these categories is to have a shared vocabulary, a shared familiarity with central themes. As we explore specific issues throughout this book, try to identify into which category they best belong—but don't agonize over it. The point is not to fetishize these categories, but to become comfortable within the philosophical landscape.

I previously mentioned different approaches of organizing and teaching philosophy. We have already discussed the topical approach. A second approach is historical. Just as we may divide philosophy up into central themes, we can also divide it up into four major historical periods.

- Ancient: 6th century B.C.E. to 3rd century C.E. (roughly): this period includes the beginning of Western philosophy, starting with the pre-Socratics (such as Pythagoras, Parmenides, Thales, etc.), moving through the sophists and Socrates, to Socrates' student Plato, Plato's student Aristotle, and continuing through the Stoics (e.g., Epictetus, Marcus Aurelius, etc.), Epicurus, the Skeptics, and neo-Platonists such Plotinus.

- Medieval: 4th century C.E. to 14th century C.E. (roughly): this period was heavily influenced by the Catholic Church's control of scholarship and education during this historical period, and includes such great thinkers as Saint Augustine (who "Christianized" Plato), Saint Anselm, Saint Aquinas (who "Christianized" Aristotle), the friar Ockham, etc.

- "Modern": 15th century C.E. to 19th century C.E. (roughly). This "Renaissance" period is, in many respects, a reaction against some of the systems of thought constructed during the Medieval period. It includes philosophers such as Hobbes, Locke, Descartes, Spinoza, Leibniz, Hume, and Kant, among others.

- "Contemporary": 20th century C.E. to now. Finally, the contemporary period of philosophy is everything from the end of the Modern period until today. Just as the Modern period was often a reaction against the Medieval, the Contemporary period has been, in many respects, a reaction against the Modern. Anyone living and doing philosophy today (such as Martha Nussbaum, or Peter Singer) is included in this category, as are late-greats such as Nietzsche, Wittgenstein, Heidegger, Sartre, and Foucault (among others).

As with the topical divisions of philosophy, the point of these historical divisions is not to agonize over which philosopher belongs where, but rather to gain a shared sense of these major periods of thought, and a shared sense of vocabulary.

I've provided a brief glimpse of the sorts of things philosophers think about, but haven't yet properly explained what philosophy *is*. Philosophy, literally speaking, is the "love of wisdom." That, by itself, might not be terribly informative. After all, you might ask, what is meant by "wisdom?" A nice, official dictionary definition is that wisdom is the "quality or state of being wise; knowledge of what is true or right coupled with just judgment as to action; sagacity, discernment, or insight." That's pretty decent, but given the philosophical context, the term needs a bit more explanation.

The philosophy that is studied in the West is grounded, in large part, on the traditions, definitions, and values of its acknowledged founders: wise persons of the ancient Mediterranean civilizations. Typically, one thinks of the Greeks and Romans. So, let us get a taste of what some of these ancient Greeks and Romans actually said about philosophy.

> *Most people imagine that philosophy consists in delivering discourses from the heights of a chair, and in giving classes based on texts. But what these people utterly miss is the uninterrupted philosophy which we see being practiced every day in a way which is perfectly equal to itself.... Socrates did not set up a grandstand for his audience and did not sit upon a professorial chair; he had no fixed timetables for talking or walking with his friends. Rather, he did philosophy sometimes by joking with them, and finally by going to prison and drinking poison. He was the first to show that at all times and in every place, in everything that happens to us, daily life gives us the opportunity to do philosophy.*[1]

This quotation from Plutarch gives us a nice introduction to the character and significance of Socrates. Rather than thinking of "doing philosophy" in terms of standing in front of people and lecturing from a book (in other words, what *I* do for a living!), Plutarch reminds us that Socrates

[1] Plutarch, Whether a Man Should Engage in Politics When He Is Old.

did neither. He had no fixed schedule, no classroom, and no textbook. He talked with friends and strangers alike, and (arguably) his finest demonstration of philosophy was how he died. Daily life provides occasion for philosophy, and everything we do is an opportunity to practice it. This is undoubtedly in sharp contrast to a vision of philosophy consisting of reading books and arguing about their contents! Instead, philosophy was seen as a practical pursuit, capable of providing practical benefit.

> *Vain is the word of a philosopher which does not heal any suffering of man. For just as there is no profit in medicine if it does not expel the diseases of the body, so there is no profit in philosophy either, if it does not expel the suffering of the mind.*[2]

Here, Epicurus is employing the (common, at that time) medical analogy for philosophy. We all recognize that there are diseases and injuries of the body, and a skill and understanding pertaining to those injuries and diseases: medicine. Similarly, there are "diseases and injuries" of the "soul," and a skill and understanding relevant to those ailments: philosophy. Just as we think medicine has failed to do its job if our symptoms don't improve (where improvement is possible), so too did ancient philosophers think philosophy had failed to do its job if our lives were not made better as a result of our practicing philosophy. To put it bluntly, if practicing philosophy showed no positive change in your life, provided no improvements, then you weren't doing it right!

> *I think there is no one who has rendered worse service to the human race than those who have learned philosophy as a mercenary trade.*[3]

Here, the Stoic Seneca is distinguishing genuine philosophers—those who pursue philosophy for the sake of wisdom and living an excellent life—from intellectual mercenaries such as the Sophists. The Sophists were notorious for demanding payment for their instruction, and for their general willingness to argue any position if the price was right. But, for Seneca and other philosophers, philosophy was no game or sport, nor even an intellectual diversion.

> *Philosophy is no trick to catch the public; it is not devised for show. It is a matter, not of words, but of facts. It is not pursued in order that the day may yield some amusement before it is spent, or that our leisure may be relieved of a tedium that irks us. It moulds and constructs the soul; it orders our life, guides our conduct, shows us what we should do and what we should leave undone; it sits at the helm and directs our course as we waver amid uncertainties. Without it, no one can live fearlessly or in peace of mind. Countless things that happen every hour call for advice; and such advice is to be sought in philosophy.*[4]

Philosophy was not, for Seneca, merely a mentally stimulating exercise—it was the means by which we navigate life's challenges, find direction, and, ultimately, seek to live a better life.

With a few quotations behind us, setting the tone, I now want to take a "vocabulary break" and introduce you to several terms that will help us to refine our understanding of philosophy, as it was conceived in Greece and Rome.

- *Areté* (ἀρετή): human excellence/goodness/virtue
- *Askesis* (ἄσκησις): spiritual exercise/training/practice
- *Bios* (bioß): way of life/manner of living
- *Ergon* (ἔργον): product/deed/action
- *Eudaimonia* (εὐδαιμονία): well-being/flourishing/happiness
- *Logos* (λόγος): rational explanation/theory/argument/principle
- Philosophy (φιλοσοφία): love of wisdom

[2] Epicurus, Extant Remains, Fragments.

[3] Seneca, Letters to Lucilius.

[4] Ibid.

- *Telos* (τέλος): end/purpose/goal
- *Technē* (τέχνη): art/craft/skill/expertise

Starting (at least) with Socrates, philosophy (φιλοσοφία) was conceived as a skill/art (τέχνη), whose goal (τέλος) was instilling excellence/virtue (ἀρετή) in its practitioner, and thereby achieving flourishing/happiness (εὐδαιμονία). Like other skills, philosophy requires both theoretical understanding (λόγος) as well as training (ἄσκησις) in order that the philosophy be manifested in action (ἔργον) and transform one's life (*bioß*). The Stoic Epictetus does a wonderful job of illustrating this view of philosophy by means of two different analogies.

> *Those who have learned the principles and nothing else are eager to throw them up immediately, just as persons with a weak stomach throw up their food. First digest your principles, and then you will surely not throw them up this way. Otherwise they are mere vomit, foul stuff and unfit to eat. But after you have digested these principles, show us some change in your governing principles that is due to them; as the athletes show their shoulders as the results of their exercising and eating.*[5]

> *A carpenter does not come up to you and say, "listen to me discourse about the art of carpentry," but he makes a contract for a house and builds it...Do the same thing yourself. Eat like a man, drink like a man...get married, have children, take part in civic life, learn how to put up with insults, and tolerate other people.*[6]

Epictetus has provided us analogies with athletics and carpentry—both being skills (τέχνη). In the first quotation, Epictetus is describing the behavior of every person I have ever known (myself included) when first studying philosophy. At first, students of philosophy become fascinated with whichever philosopher they happen to be reading at the time, and are eager to quote from him (or her), and to demonstrate their understanding of the text or philosopher in question. Usually, there is very little actual understanding involved, just regurgitation. Or, to use Epictetus' colorful imagery: "vomiting."

The mark of philosophical understanding, for Epictetus, is not the ability to recite passages from a philosopher, or even to summarize arguments, but rather the effect that the philosophy has had on the student's life and behavior.

We evaluate the skill of an athlete not by how well she can *talk about* basketball, but by how well she *plays*. If someone merely *tells* us that he is a great dancer, that is far less persuasive than demonstrating some dancing. Talk is cheap for aspiring MMA fighters. Get in the cage and win a fight!

The next quotation offers the same theme. An excellent carpenter isn't one who can speak well about carpentry, but rather someone who can actually work well with wood. If I want to hire a carpenter to build a gazebo for me, I'm far less interested in his lectures on carpentry than with some examples of his previous work.

When it comes to philosophy, the best demonstration of your philosophical progress is not you *telling* me about it, but the way you live an excellent life.

> *If philosophical theories seduce you, sit down and go over them again and again in your mind. But never call yourself a philosopher, and never allow yourself to be called a philosopher.*[7]

Those for whom philosophy is merely a mental exercise have missed the point of philosophy, according to Epictetus, and he doesn't want them to use the term "philosopher" for themselves. Perhaps they are philologists (lovers of words), but they are not philosophers (lovers of wisdom).

"Love of wisdom" is the literal meaning of philosophy, in the original Greek. Philosophers,

---

[5] Epictetus, *Discourses*, III.21.

[6] Ibid.

[7] Ibid.

therefore, were lovers of wisdom. But, just what is this "wisdom?"

Remember, philosophy has been described as a skill, analogous with medicine or carpentry or athletics. This helps us to understand what was meant by wisdom, at the time. "Wisdom," in the original philosophical conception, is the skill of knowing-how-to-live-well. Philosophers are those who love, and pursue, that know-how.

Wisdom, in this sense, is thought to correlates with age and experience. Aristotle thought that you couldn't really do philosophy until you were around the age of 40. I don't think there's anything magical about that age, but his point is, I suspect, less controversial or objectionable than it might originally appear.

In order to get a sense of what the world is like, what life is like, what and who you are, and how best to navigate life's challenges, you need to have lived some life! You need to have experienced relationships, tragedies and triumphs, etc. We don't expect a ten year old to understand love, or the meaning of life. This is no insult to ten year olds—just a common sense recognition that they probably lack the perspective with which to have an informed view of such things. Exceptions are possible, of course. We do credit some young people with being wise, but we have an expression for that. The person is "wise beyond her years." This indicates that we don't usually expect young people to be wise, but if they have had a lot of significant life experiences packed into their years, they could be. At the same time, age is no guarantee of wisdom either. It's possible to be an old fool!

Wisdom is associated with experience, and less so with formal education, but we need to be careful here. This is by no means to suggest that education is unimportant, but rather just to recognize that wisdom is not identical to IQ, nor magically conferred by a degree. Just because someone is very smart, and has a string of fancy degrees after her name, is no guarantee that she knows how to live an excellent life. Education and understanding, though, are nevertheless essential to doing philosophy.

Although a common understanding of philosophy at the time, emphasized deeds over words, and although Epictetus claimed that the better demonstration of philosophy was in our actions rather than our ability to talk about philosophy, this was by no means an indicator that we could somehow get by without theoretical understanding. In a quotation in which Epictetus rehearses a conversation with a student who wants to skip over the education/understanding, and get straight to the practical stuff, Epictetus makes this point clear. I have added some words in brackets to provide further clarity.

> *Tell me then about what I should talk to you: about what matter are you able to listen?—About good and evil [ETHICS]. — Good and evil in what? In a horse? No. Well, in an ox? No. What then? In a man? Yes. Do we know then what a man is [METAPHYSICS], what the notion is which we have of him, or have we our ears in any degree practised about this matter? But do you understand what nature is? [METAPHYSICS] or can you even in any degree understand me when I say, I shall use demonstration to you? How? Do you understand this very thing, what demonstration is, or how any thing I, demonstrated, or by what means; or what things are like demonstration, but are not demonstration? [LOGIC] Do you know what is true or what is false? [EPISTEMOLOGY] What is consequent on a thing, what is repugnant to a thing, or not consistent, or in-consistent? But must I excite you to philosophy, and how? Shall I show to you the repugnance in the opinions of most men, through which they differ about things good and evil, and about things which are profitable and unprofitable, when you know not this very thing, what repugnance (contradiction) is?*[8]

Let us suppose that we agree with Epictetus

[8] Epictetus, *Discourses* II.24.

(and his peers) that philosophy is a skill aimed at producing an excellent life and, ultimately, happiness. How can any of us expect to figure out the recipe for a good life if we haven't figured out what we are, as humans, and therefore what would count as a good life in the first place? For example, your basic metaphysical understanding of "human" will make a big difference with regard to what you think is good *for* humans. If you have a purely naturalistic worldview, and believe that humans are rational animals wrought by the same evolutionary forces that produced every other animal on Earth, you will develop a certain kind of understanding of what would count as a good life as a rational animal. On the other hand, if your worldview includes the existence of God, and a belief in an afterlife for the non-physical soul, you will presumably have a different view. To put it bluntly, the sorts of things that might be valuable if this earthly life is the only existence we'll ever have might amount to "nothing" against the backdrop of an eternal life, and what counts as a good life for a theist might be profoundly different than what counts as a good life for an atheist. In other words, metaphysics matters. You need to acquire a sense of "reality," and how it operates, in order to come up with your value system.

Of course, in order to know what reality is like, we need to know what knowledge is, and how it can be acquired (if at all). This means we need to do some epistemology. And, the various arguments concerning both epistemology and metaphysics are *arguments*. We are in no position to assess those arguments unless we understand logic and reasoning, in general. This is just to say that there are no "short cuts" in philosophy. Countless contemporary self-help gurus peddle their books promising to guide you to the good life, but how many of them have actually done the *work* necessary to back up that pledge? One hopes that their vision of the good life is actually built upon a foundation that includes metaphysics, epistemology, and logical reasoning.

While the pay-off in philosophy is the transformation of our deeds and our lives into something excellent, we need to develop the *understanding* necessary for that transformation to occur. To return to our analogy, a carpenter needs to understand the mechanics and principles that explain *why* wood needs to be joined using certain techniques and tools, and certain angles, *why* certain structures support weight while others don't—but ultimately the carpenter has to take that understanding and go build something.

Take your philosophical understanding, and then go build an excellent life.

Books like this one, and courses (like mine) that tend to use books like this one, can only promote the "understanding" component (λόγος) of philosophy. The deeds are up to you.

With regard to that understanding, I'll offer some guidance concerning the primary source readings provided in this text. At the end of every chapter you will find one or more reading selections pertaining to the main topic of that chapter. These are excerpts from books or dialogues written by some of the finest minds from the history of Western philosophy, spanning from the 4th century (BCE) to the 20th century (CE).

Although I like to think that my own summaries and introductions are illuminating, engaging primary source materials is an essential part of studying philosophy. You will discover that (with a few exceptions), I have not provided specific summaries or explanations of these texts. There is a reason for that.

Engaging the readings yourself, grappling with the arguments, and coming to your own understanding (λόγος) is one of the primary tasks of philosophy. If you're taking a philosophy course using this book, your instructor will undoubtedly offer assistance along the way, but it's important to meet with these thinkers, your mind to their minds, and participate in the great conversation that we call philosophy. It's also important to remember that we all stand on the shoulders of those who came before us. To remain ignorant of their ideas and achievements, and to attempt to "reinvent the wheel" ourselves, is inefficient at best, and intellectually dishonest and disrespectful, at worst.

Lucius Annaeus Seneca (4 BCE – 65 CE) was a Roman Stoic who was not only a philosopher, but a politician, writer, and tutor/advisor to the Emperor Nero. A prolific and talented writer, his letters to Lucilius Junior (the procurator of Sicily) serve as "essays in disguise." Though they are thought to be genuine letters, it is also believed they were intended for publication, and served as a new medium with which Seneca could deliver his ideas. In the two letters provided below, Seneca provides his views on the role and value of philosophy.

Lucius Annaeus Seneca
On Philosophy, the Guide of Life

Chapter XVI

1. It is clear to you, I am sure, Lucilius, that no man can live a happy life, or even a supportable life, without the study of wisdom; you know also that a happy life is reached when our wisdom is brought to completion, but that life is at least endurable even when our wisdom is only begun. This idea, however, clear though it is, must be strengthened and implanted more deeply by daily reflection; it is more important for you to keep the resolutions you have already made than to go on and make noble ones. You must persevere, must develop new strength by continuous study, until that which is only a good inclination becomes a good settled purpose. **2.** Hence you no longer need to come to me with much talk and protestations; I know that you have made great progress. I understand the feelings which prompt your words; they are not feigned or specious words. Nevertheless I shall tell you what I think, – that at present I have hopes for you, but not yet perfect trust. And I wish that you would adopt the same attitude towards yourself; there is no reason why you should put confidence in yourself too quickly and readily. Examine yourself; scrutinize and observe yourself in divers ways; but mark, before all else, whether it is in philosophy or merely in life itself that you have made progress. **3.** Philosophy is no trick to catch the public; it is not devised for show. It is a matter, not of words, but of facts. It is not pursued in order that the day may yield some amusement before it is spent, or that our leisure may be relieved of a tedium that irks us. It moulds and constructs the soul; it orders our life, guides our conduct, shows us what we should do and what we should leave undone; it sits at the helm and directs our course as we waver amid uncertainties. Without it, no one can live fearlessly or in peace of mind. Countless things that happen every hour call for advice; and such advice is to be sought in philosophy.

4. Perhaps someone will say: "How can philosophy help me, if Fate exists? Of what avail is philosophy, if God rules the universe? Of what avail is it, if Chance governs everything? For not only is it impossible to change things that are determined, but it is also impossible to plan beforehand against what is undetermined; either God has forestalled my plans, and decided what I am to do, or else Fortune gives no free play to my plans." **5.** Whether the truth, Lucilius, lies in one or in all of these views, we must be philosophers; whether Fate binds us down by an inexorable law, or whether God as arbiter of the universe has arranged everything, or whether Chance drives and tosses human affairs without method, philosophy ought to be our defence. She will encourage us to obey God cheerfully, but Fortune defiantly; she will teach us to follow God and endure Chance. **6.** But it is not my purpose now to be led into a discussion as to what is within our own control, – if foreknowledge is supreme, or if a chain of fated events drags us along in its clutches, or if the sudden and the unexpected play the tyrant over us; I return now to my warning and my exhortation, that you should not allow the impulse of your spirit to weaken and grow cold. Hold fast to it and establish it firmly, in order that what is now impulse may become a habit of the mind.

7. If I know you well, you have already been trying to find out, from the very beginning of my letter, what little contribution it brings to you. Sift the letter, and you will find it. You need not wonder at any genius of mine; for as yet I am lavish only with other men's property. - But why did I say "other men"? Whatever is well said by anyone is mine. This also is a saying of Epicurus: "If you live according to nature, you will never be poor; if you live according to opinion, you will never be rich." **8.** Nature's wants are slight; the demands of opinion are boundless. Suppose that the property of many millionaires is heaped up in your possession. Assume that fortune carries you far beyond the limits of a private income, decks you with gold, clothes you in purple, and brings you to such a degree of luxury and wealth that you can bury the earth under your marble floors; that you may not only possess, but tread upon, riches. Add statues, paintings, and whatever any art has devised for the luxury; you will only learn from such things to crave still greater.

9. Natural desires are limited; but those which spring from false opinion can have no stopping-point. The false has no limits. When you are travelling on a road, there must be an end; but when astray, your wanderings are limitless. Recall your steps, therefore, from idle things, and when you would know whether that which you seek is based upon a natural or upon a misleading desire, consider whether it can stop at any definite point. If you find, after having travelled far, that there is a more distant goal always in view, you may be sure that this condition is contrary to nature. Farewell.

XLVIII. On Quibbling as Unworthy of the Philosopher

1. In answer to the letter which you wrote me while travelling, - a letter as long as the journey itself, - I shall reply later. I ought to go into retirement, and consider what sort of advice I should give you. For you yourself, who consult me, also reflected for a long time whether to do so; how much more, then, should I myself reflect, since more deliberation is necessary in settling than in propounding a problem! And this is particularly true when one thing is advantageous to you and another to me. Am I speaking again in the guise of an Epicurean? **2.** But the fact is, the same thing is advantageous to me which is advantageous to you; for I am not your friend unless whatever is at issue concerning you is my concern also. Friendship produces between us a partnership in all our interests. There is no such thing as good or bad fortune for the individual; we live in common. And no one can live happily who has regard to himself alone and transforms everything into a question of his own utility; you must live for your neighbour, if you would live for yourself. **3.** This fellowship, maintained with scrupulous care, which makes us mingle as men with our fellow-men and holds that the human race have certain rights in common, is also of great help in cherishing the more intimate fellowship which is based on friendship, concerning which I began to speak above. For he that has much in common with a fellow-man will have all things in common with a friend.

4. And on this point, my excellent Lucilius, I should like to have those subtle dialecticians of yours advise me how I ought to help a friend, or how a fellow man, rather than tell me in how many ways the word "friend" is used, and how many meanings the word "man" possesses. Lo, Wisdom and Folly are taking opposite sides. Which shall I join? Which party would you have me follow? On that side, "man" is the equivalent of "friend"; on the other side, "friend" is not the equivalent of "man." The one wants a friend for his own advantage; the other wants to make himself an advantage to his friend. What *you* have to offer me is nothing but distortion of words and splitting of syllables. **5.** It is clear that unless I can devise some very tricky premisses and by false deductions tack on to them a fallacy which springs from the truth, I shall not be able to distinguish between what is desirable and what is to be avoided! I am ashamed! Old men as we are, dealing with a problem so serious, we make play of it!

6. "'Mouse' is a syllable. Now a mouse eats its cheese; therefore, a syllable eats cheese." Suppose now that I cannot solve this problem; see what peril hangs over my head as a result of such ignorance! What a scrape I shall be in! Without doubt I must beware, or some day I shall be catching syllables in a mousetrap, or, if I grow careless, a book may devour my cheese! Unless, perhaps, the following syllogism is shrewder still: "'Mouse' is a syllable. Now a syllable does not eat cheese. Therefore a mouse does not eat cheese." **7.** What childish nonsense! Do we knit our brows over this sort of problem? Do we let our beards grow long for this reason? Is this the matter which we teach with sour and pale faces?

Would you really know what philosophy offers to humanity? Philosophy offers counsel. Death calls away one man, and poverty chafes another; a third is worried either by his neighbour's wealth or by his own. So-and-so is afraid of bad luck; another desires to get away from his own good fortune. Some are ill-treated by men, others by the gods. **8.** Why, then, do you frame for me such games as these? It is no occasion for jest; you are retained as counsel for unhappy mankind. You have promised to help those in peril by sea, those in captivity, the sick and the needy, and those whose heads are under the poised axe. Whither are you straying? What are you doing?

This friend, in whose company you are jesting, is in fear. Help him, and take the noose from about his neck. Men are stretching out imploring hands to you on all sides; lives ruined and in danger of ruin are begging for some assistance; men's hopes, men's resources, depend upon you. They ask that you deliver them from all their restlessness, that you reveal to them, scattered and wandering as they are, the clear light of truth. **9.** Tell them what nature has made necessary, and what superfluous; tell them how simple are the laws that she has laid down, how pleasant and unimpeded life is for those who follow these laws, but how bitter and perplexed it is for those who have put their trust in opinion rather than in nature.

I should deem your games of logic to be of some avail in relieving men's burdens, if you could first show me what part of these burdens they will relieve. What among these games of yours banishes lust? Or controls it? Would that I could say that they were merely of no profit! They are positively harmful. I can make it perfectly clear to you whenever you wish, that a noble spirit when involved in such subtleties is impaired and weakened. **10.** I am ashamed to say what weapons they supply to men who are destined to go to war with fortune, and how poorly they equip them! Is this the path to the greatest good? Is philosophy to proceed by such claptrap and by quibbles which would be a disgrace and a reproach even for expounders of the law? For what else is it that you men are doing, when you deliberately ensnare the person to whom you are putting questions, than making it appear that the man has lost his case on a technical error? But just as the judge can reinstate those who have lost a suit in this way, so philosophy has reinstated these victims of quibbling to their former condition. **11.** Why do you men abandon your mighty promises, and, after having assured me in high-sounding language that you will permit the glitter of gold to dazzle my eyesight no more than the gleam of the sword, and that I shall, with mighty steadfastness, spurn both that which all men crave and that which all men fear, why do you descend to the ABC's of scholastic pedants? What is your answer?

Is this the path to heaven?

For that is exactly what philosophy promises to me, that I shall be made equal to God. For this I have been summoned, for this purpose have I come. Philosophy, keep your promise!

12. Therefore, my dear Lucilius, withdraw yourself as far as possible from these exceptions and objections of so-called philosophers. Frankness, and simplicity beseem true goodness. Even if there were many years left to you, you would have had to spend them frugally in order to have enough for the necessary things; but as it is, when your time is so scant, what madness it is to learn superfluous things! Farewell.

Chapter 1
Epistemology

Comprehension questions you should be able to answer after reading this introduction:

1. *What is "epistemology?"*
2. *What is the definition of "knowledge?"*
3. *What is a "claim?" What does it mean to say that a claim has a "truth-value?"*
4. *What is an argument?*
5. *What does it mean for an argument to be "valid?"*
6. *What does it mean for an argument to be "sound?"*
7. *Why is the soundness of arguments often difficult to establish?*
8. *What is the principle of charity?*
9. *What are the two justification questions we ask when presented with a new piece of information?*
10. *How is "truth" understood by each of the following: epistemic relativism, pragmatism, correspondence theory?*
11. *What do skeptics believe about knowledge? Why?*
12. *What is the distinction between "appearance" and "reality," and how does it make skepticism possible?*
13. *Explain how each of the following is intended to work as an argument for skepticism:*
    a. *argument from the unreliability of the senses*
    b. *argument from dreaming*
    c. *argument from insanity*
    d. *evil demon argument*
14. *What does "cogito ergo sum" mean, and why did Descartes think that it defeated skepticism?*

As you learned in the introductory chapter, philosophy is the love of wisdom, traditionally understood as the pursuit of knowing-how-to-live-well. Since philosophy is concerned with *knowledge*, it's important for us to get a sense of what knowledge is, in the first place.

Epistemology, the focus of this chapter, is the study of knowledge. Believe it or not, there's some pretty serious debate concerning how best to understand "knowledge." Some, for example, believe that we can never possess knowledge. Classical skeptics fit this description. Others believe that "knowledge" is never more than personal perspective. Despite the plurality of views, there is a generally accepted definition of knowledge that seems to work for most people, in most cases. There are some complications, of course, and some disagreements here and there, but, for the most part, Plato's understanding of knowledge is pretty good. In his dialogue, the *Theaetetus*, Plato has the character Socrates (his real life mentor and friend) explore the proper definition of knowledge. The most promising candidate that emerges is that knowledge is "justified, true belief." Or, as Plato puts it, "true belief with an account."

Why should we accept Plato's definition? Plato is a giant in Western Philosophy, to say the least. A student of Socrates himself, Plato (428/427 BCE—348/347 BCE) founded the first institution of higher education (an "Academy") in the Western world. He also developed very impressive accounts of virtually every major topic of philosophical interest. Indeed, the 20th century philosopher Alfred North Whitehead said of Plato and Philosophy:

> *The safest general characterization of the European philosophical tradition is that it consists of a series of footnotes to Plato. I do not mean the systematic scheme of thought which scholars have doubtfully extracted from his writings. I allude to the wealth of general ideas scattered through them...*

Still, just because a definition comes from Plato doesn't *automatically* make it correct. To assume so is a fallacy—an "appeal to authority." The reason why (most of us) use this definition is because it seems like a pretty good one! You'll soon see why.

Knowledge: justified, true belief

Plato's definition has three components, each of which requires a little bit of explanation.

1. Belief

It is generally accepted that in order to know something, one must also believe it. It seems odd to say that I know Barack Obama is the current U.S. President, but that I don't believe that he is. Note that the reverse is not also true. We are quite comfortable with the idea that someone can believe something without also knowing it. For example, at the moment I'm writing this sentence, I believe my mother is at her home, but I wouldn't claim to *know* that she is. It's entirely possible that I'm not remembering her schedule accurately, and that she's volunteering somewhere. Or, perhaps she's on an errand? As we can see, to know something, one must also believe it, but one can believe without knowing.

An easy way to think of the relationship between belief and knowledge, in this sense, is with the language of a "promotion." We believe all kinds of things, but some of the things we believe have a special quality to them. These beliefs earn a "promotion," and a new title: knowledge. What is this quality that earns the belief a promotion to knowledge? As it turns out, this quality is the other two parts of our definition of knowledge: justification, and truth.

Before delving into justification, we'll spend a little more time on belief and complicate matters by asking what a belief *is*. A good chunk of my doctoral dissertation was devoted to just that question, but, once again, that level of analysis and expertise is not needed for our own purposes right now. At the minimum, we can simply talk about what form beliefs take in our language, so that we may easily identify them in speech and writing.

Very simply, beliefs appear in the form of "claims." *Claims* are statements, assertions, or propositions (different terms meaning roughly the same thing), and, due to that fact, have what is called a "*truth-value.*" To say that a claim has a truth-value is simply to say that it must be either true or false (if true, then its truth-value is true; if false, then its truth-value is false). Note that we do not need to know *which* truth-value applies to a claim to know that it is a claim. Consider the examples below.

Claims

You are reading this sentence right now.

Barack Obama is the current U.S. president.

There is intelligent life elsewhere in the universe.

Not Claims

What time is it?

Please shut the door.

Ouch.

Remember, a claim is a statement that has to be either true or false (even if we're not sure which it is). You either are, or you are not, reading this book right now. Barack Obama either is, or is not, the current U.S. President. You're probably pretty confident about those two. What about life elsewhere in the universe? Well, you probably aren't certain either way. But (and this is the important part), we know that there either is, or there is not, intelligent life elsewhere in the universe. In other words, that claim has a truth-value, even though we don't know (for sure, right now) if that value is "true" or if it is "false."

Now, consider the other column of examples. What time is it? True or false? You probably had to reread those sentences just now, and my question probably still doesn't make any sense. There's a reason for that. "What time is it?" is not the sort of thing that can be either true or false. Neither is "Please shut the door." Neither is "ouch." None of those has a truth-value, because none is a claim, and therefore none is a belief. Why does this matter? Because claims are the building blocks of arguments, and arguments form the core of what we study and what we do in philosophy.

For most of us, if you want to start an "argument" at a family dinner, we should bring up either politics or religion or some sort of moral issue. That is not usually, however, what an "argument" means in the context of philosophy.

An argument is an attempt to establish the truth of a claim (the conclusion) by offering evidence (premises) in support of that claim. No name-calling, no chair-throwing, no raised voices—not even any presumption of disagreement. In a philosophical context, an argument is not a fight, but simply an attempt to make a point, using evidence, and following certain rules of reason.

Although we don't usually encounter arguments in the following format (except in philosophy courses), all arguments at least implicitly have the same general form:

Premise$_1$
Premise$_2$
Conclusion

Please note that we have not yet specified any particular content for that argument. That is because arguments can be about *anything*. Any time you try to persuade someone to believe anything at all, on the basis of some kind of reason/evidence, you are offering an argument. Also note that although there were two premises in the generic argument above, there is nothing special about that number. You might have only a single premise (piece of evidence), or you might have a hundred premises, or any other number whatsoever. So long as you have at least one piece of evidence, at least one reason to believe that the conclusion is true, you have provided an argument.

Every philosophical essay that you read in this book (or any other) is an argument, or at least contains arguments. What all arguments have in common is that they are attempts to prove that a claim (the conclusion) is true, by offering other claims (premises) as evidence. Note that both the conclusion of an argument and all the premises in an argument, are *claims*. This is not a trivial observation! Every (proper) piece of every argument is a claim. Therefore, every (proper) piece of every argument has a truth-value—which is what makes argument evaluation possible.

However, although some professional philosophers will sometimes write out their arguments in obvious "premise$_1$, premise$_2$, therefore conclusion" format, most philosophical readings are not so blatantly reader-friendly. Philosophical arguments will be made in the context of paragraphs, essays, chapters, or even entire books. As we read, then, our job is to identify the main point the author seems to be trying to make. This is the conclusion. Then, we must try to identify all of the supporting points the author provides in defense of that conclusion. These are the premises. Once we have identified the conclusion and premises, we are prepared to evaluate the argument.

I hope it's obvious that not all arguments are created equal. Just because you have offered a reason to believe something is true doesn't mean you have provided a *good* reason, or even a relevant one. Consider the following example:

Argument (A)
Egg yolks are high in cholesterol.
High cholesterol is associated with increased

risk of heart disease.

Therefore, abortion is morally wrong.

Argument (A) is laughably bad, and I'm sure you realize that, but it's important to recognize *why*. Here, some standard "critical thinking/logic" vocabulary might help. Arguments are (generally) evaluated in terms of their validity, and soundness. Both of those words (valid, sound) have specific meaning in the context of argument, and both (especially validity) have different uses in everyday speech. For example, you might hear someone say "that's a valid point." What that person means is that you have made a good point. In that usage, valid means something like "good," or "apt," or "true." That is not what "valid" means for our purposes, though.

Validity

A deductive argument is valid if the conclusion necessarily follows (logically) from the premises. Another way of putting that idea is that an argument is valid when, *if* the premises are true, the conclusion must also be true. Or, an argument is valid if it's impossible for the conclusion to be false, *if* all the premises are true.

You might have noticed that I italicized the word "if" in a couple of places. There's a good reason for that. When we assess an argument's validity, it's a hypothetical exercise. We're not making any claim that the premises are, in fact, true—we're just asking what would happen *if* the premises are true. Consider the following:

1. All humans are mortal.
2. Preson is human.
3. Therefore, Preston is mortal.

Is this argument "valid," according to our definition? To find out if it is, ask yourself the following: *if* all the premises are true, must the conclusion also be true? *If* it's true that all humans are mortal, and *if* it's true that Preston is a human, then, must it also be true that Preston is mortal? The answer, of course, is "yes." Therefore, this is a valid argument. This indicates that there is the right kind of logical relationship between the premises and conclusion, there is a relationship of structural relevance between them. We haven't yet established that the premises are, in fact, true (that's a later step), but we have established that *if* they are true, the conclusion is as well. That is very important. Let's reconsider example (A) from above:

Argument (A)

1. Egg yolks are high in cholesterol.
2. High cholesterol is associated with increased risk of heart disease.
3. Therefore, abortion is morally wrong.

We're now in a position to articulate the "badness" of this argument: it's not valid. Undoubtedly, you experienced an intuitive recognition that there was something deeply flawed with the argument. Presumably, you recognized that eggs, cholesterol, and heart disease risks have nothing to do with whether or not abortion is morally wrong! There isn't the right kind of relationship between those premises, and the conclusion. If we consider this in terms of validity, the problem becomes clear.

Is it possible for it to be true that egg yolks are high in cholesterol, and true that high cholesterol is associated with increased risk of heart disease, and yet for it to be false that abortion is morally wrong? Of course that's possible! So, if, for some weird reason, you try to prove the moral wrongness of abortion by appealing to the cholesterol content of eggs, you will fail in grand, embarrassing fashion. Even if all your evidence is proven to be true, you still will not have proven that your conclusion ("abortion is morally wrong") is true.

Soundness

If validity appeals to the hypothetical truth of the premises, soundness refers to their actual truth. *An argument is "sound" when it is both valid and all its premises are, in fact, true.* Notice that in order for an argument to be sound, it must first already be valid. You can imagine an implicit checklist for argument evaluation:

- ☐ Is the argument valid?
- ☐ Is the argument sound?

Only if we can "check the first box" do we bother to consider whether the argument is sound. Let's go back to one of our earlier examples:

1. All humans are mortal.
2. Preston is a human.
3. Therefore, Preston is mortal.

Is the argument valid? Yes, it is (as established above).

✓ Is the argument valid?
☐ Is the argument sound?

Since it's valid, we can now move on to consider its soundness. Are all of the premises, in fact, true? To be honest, the question of "truth" opens Pandora's proverbial box. What does "truth" mean? What does it take for something to be true, let alone known to be true? You could spend an entire career as a philosophy professor focusing solely on the concept of "truth," and still have plenty of questions remaining. We will not spend entire careers on the concept of truth, but we will spend some time later in this chapter on several different interpretations of what it means for a claim to be true. For now, however, let's set aside the murky notion of "truth" and assume (for the sake of argument) that we know what it means for a claim to be true. Even so, how can we tell if a particular claim is, in fact, true?

Obviously, not all claims will be easily verifiable as true. While we might be fairly confident that it is true that egg yolks are high in cholesterol, some truth-values (unfortunately, probably the ones we tend to care the most about—truth-values for claims about morality, religion, politics, etc.), might be especially difficult to establish.

Do aliens exist, or not? Hard to say, since we haven't explored the entire universe just yet. Is abortion immoral? Hard to say, since there's so much disagreement, and so many compelling arguments that can be given on both sides. Does God exist? Hard to say, since there are compelling arguments on both sides of the debate, and legitimate debate as to what does or could count as evidence for God's existence in the first place....

Recognizing that some claims will be difficult to establish, let us return to a relatively easy argument just to complete our discussion of "soundness."

1. All humans are mortal.
2. Preston is human.
3. Therefore, Preston is mortal.

In order for this argument to be sound, it has to be valid, and all of its premises must be true. We've already established that it's valid. Are its premises, in fact, true? Does the claim that "all humans are mortal" seem to be true? If we interpret "mortal" in its usual sense ("liable or subject to death"), then it does, in fact, appear to be true. That all humans are subject to death seems to be true, like it or not. What about the second premise? Is it, in fact, true that Preston (the author of this book) is a human? Again, if we're assuming the usual sense of "human" ("a member of the genus *Homo* and especially of the species *H. sapiens*"), then it would appear that Preston being human is true as well. Given that both premises are, in fact, true, we have established that the argument is not only valid, but sound.

✓ Is the argument valid?
✓ Is the argument sound?

If you have established that an argument is sound, you have proven that the conclusion is true. It doesn't get any better than that! Unfortunately, whenever we're dealing with serious, important arguments, it's usually pretty challenging to establish that the argument is sound. Consider another argument for the wrongness of abortion:

<u>Argument (B)</u>

1. Murder is morally wrong.
2. Abortion is murder.
3. Therefore, abortion is morally wrong.

You should know the routine by now:

- ☐ Is the argument valid?
- ☐ Is the argument sound?

If it's true that murder is morally wrong, and it's also true that abortion is murder, must it also be true that abortion is morally wrong? Yes, this is a valid argument. Is it sound? Perhaps, but this is far from obvious. Murder, by its usual definition, is the unjustified killing of an innocent person, so I suspect *most* people would agree that premise 1 is true.[9] Premise 2 is going to be much more controversial, though. Is abortion the unjustified killing of an innocent person? People who argue that abortion is (at least sometimes) morally acceptable will usually argue either that the fetus is not a "person," or that the killing is justified (or both). Such persons would not grant the truth of premise 2, and would not recognize the argument as sound, even though it is valid.

Let's take a moment to summarize the ground we've covered so far. An argument is an attempt to prove some point by appealing to reasons that support that point. In order for an argument to be a good argument, it needs to at least be valid, and preferably sound as well. For an argument to be valid, it needs to be the case that if all the premises are true, the conclusion has to be true as well. For it to be sound, all the premises must, in fact, be true.

Some of you might have wondered about one of the sentences in that previous paragraph: "in order for an argument to be a good argument, it needs to at least be valid, and preferably sound as well." Perhaps that sentence made you pause, and ask something like "why only *preferably* sound? Why doesn't the argument have to be both valid and sound in order to be good?" If you wondered about that, good for you!

Ideally, of course, good arguments *will* be *both* valid and sound. But, if we insist that an argument be sound in order to be "good," we might be setting the bar so high that few, if any, arguments are "good." This is because, as we have already seen, soundness can be difficult and controversial to establish. Consider one more argument:

Argument (C)

1. If God does not exist, objective moral values and duties do not exist.
2. Objective moral values and duties do exist.
3. Therefore, God exists.

This is actually one of the more famous arguments for God's existence known as the "moral argument." For our purposes, though, let's just consider our checklist:

- ☐ Is the argument valid?
- ☐ Is the argument sound?

If both premises are true, must the conclusion also be true? Yes—and this shouldn't be surprising. Any of the "major" arguments for God's existence, the arguments that have withstood the test of time (often centuries, if not millennia), are presumably going to be valid—otherwise they would have been abandoned long ago.

- ✓ Is the argument valid?
- ☐ Is the argument sound?

Now that we know it's valid, is it sound? Is it, in fact, true that if God does not exist, objective moral values and duties do not exist? Is it, in fact, true that objective moral values and duties do exist? Those who use the moral argument for God's existence will offer reasons to accept both premises as true. If you find those reasons compelling, you will presumably conclude that both premises are, in fact, true—in which case you will conclude that the argument is sound. But, if you think the reasons are not compelling, you will instead conclude that the premises are not true—in which case you will conclude that the argument is not sound. Or, perhaps some of you, even after serious consideration, will come to the honest conclusion that you're just *not sure* if those premises are true—in which case you will conclude that you don't know whether the argument is sound.

[9] In fairness, there might even be disagreement as to the truth of *this* premise!

- ✓ Is the argument valid?
- ? Is the argument sound?

That the soundness of this (or any other of the major arguments for, *or against*, God's existence) is in question should not be surprising. Remember: if an argument is sound, its conclusion *is, in fact, true*. So, if an argument for God's existence can be shown to be sound, that would mean that it is, in fact, true that God exists—and that this has been proven! Conversely, if an argument against God's existence were shown to be sound, it would mean that God has been proven not to exist. Had either of these events occurred, you probably would have heard about it! Similarly, if the soundness of various arguments concerning moral issues could be easily established, you would think that there would no longer be any debate about things like abortion, eating meat, the death penalty, etc. The fact that people still passionately debate these issues should tell us something about the difficulty in establishing the soundness of those sorts of arguments. Don't be discouraged, though. Just because it's difficult to establish the soundness of these sorts of arguments doesn't mean that there's no point in evaluating them, nor does it mean that we will be unable to say anything evaluative or interesting about them. Even if we're not *sure* if argument B is sound, it's clearly a better argument for the wrongness of abortion than the one referencing the risks of high cholesterol (argument A)!

One important element of (honest) argument evaluation is what's known as the *"principle of charity."* Basically, we want to be "charitable" when evaluating arguments—especially if we're inclined to disagree with them.

It's all too easy to develop a "straw man" interpretation of someone else's position, and then dismiss it as foolish, fallacious, or misguided. The fact of the matter is that people don't tend to view their own arguments as foolish. This doesn't mean they aren't, but in order to perform an honest evaluation of an argument, we need to present it in its best possible light. We must put ourselves in the position of the person who presented the argument, consider the argument in the strongest possible way (given the original author's intentions), and then evaluate the argument, so charitably constructed. This is a good approach to evaluating arguments, in general, but it's especially apt in the context of considering formal philosophical arguments in a book like this one.

The sorts of arguments and theories we will consider have stood the test of time. They're considered in this book for a reason. No matter what your personal views happen to be, it's uncharitable to casually dismiss "the other side" as fools offering lousy arguments. You might well conclude that "their" arguments fail, but to be justified in that conclusion you need to consider those arguments charitably, in their best light.

2. Justification

Having just spent a lot of time on arguments, and determining their validity and soundness, let us now turn to (perhaps) the most critical component of argument evaluation: justification.

Justification is probably the most critical aspect of this process because it is the process by which we attempt to determine whether claims (e.g., premises or conclusions) are (in fact) true, and therefore whether arguments are good arguments, and therefore whether or not we can "know" whether the conclusion of an argument is true.

Justification is probably the most controversial element of this definition, primarily because we can bicker over what, exactly, counts as sufficient justification. Again, this is a very complicated subject, but this is not an extended treatment of epistemology, so we can get by with a basic understanding of the key ideas.

To say that knowledge requires justification is simply to say that you can only "know" something on the basis of good reasons. If I present you with a jar filled with marbles, and you guess there are 457 marbles in the jar (just pulling a number "out of the air," at random), and, with a startled look on my face, I tell you that there are, in fact, 457 marbles in the jar, we wouldn't want to say that you *knew* the number of marbles in the jar at the time you guessed. We call it a guess for a reason! You didn't know, but you took a shot at it, and happened to get lucky. That's not knowledge; it's a lucky guess.

Sometimes, we like to distinguish "believing" from "knowing" by making explicit appeals to how much justification we have for the belief in question. I claimed to believe that my mother was at home, because I have reason to think that she is. However, my confidence in those reasons is pretty low, so I don't think I have sufficient justification to claim to *know* that she's at home.

As I mentioned, justification can be a thorny issue. How can we tell when we have enough justification to claim that we know something, as opposed to merely believing it? As with many questions in philosophy, there's no obvious, uncontroversial answer to that question. We can, however, talk about ways in which our beliefs are justified, and the degree to which our beliefs are supported by evidence. Here is a small sample of the kinds of questions that are relevant when we're evaluating justification.

1. *To what extent is the belief supported by good reasons and compelling evidence from reliable sources?*

Is the belief in question supported by your own first-hand observations? Or, is it in conflict with your own observations? If you're receiving your evidence from another source, how reliable is that source? How credible is the source? Does the source have any relevant expertise? Is there any reason to be biased?

2. *To what extent is the belief consistent with other (justified) beliefs I have?*

We each have, at our disposal, what we may call our "background knowledge," or "background information, or our "worldview." Whatever we want to call it, it is that vast collection of everything we have heard, seen, read, and otherwise learned, throughout our lives. This collection is everything we know (or think we know) about the world and how it works.

Every time we are confronted with a piece of information, we automatically and instantly evaluate it against our background knowledge. If the new information seems to "fit" with our background knowledge, we're likely to accept it as true. If it does not fit, however, if the claim is surprising to us, we're likely to hesitate and to demand more justification before accepting it as true. For example, if I were to claim that I drove home on the Southbound 605 freeway at 5 PM on a Thursday afternoon, and the freeway was wide open, with hardly any cars on it at all, anyone living in Southern California (that is, anyone for whom the 605 freeway, on a weekday, at 5 PM, is part of their background knowledge/worldview) would immediately doubt what I'm saying. Why? Because her understanding of the world and how it works is that Southern California freeways are jammed at that time of day.

When it comes to justification, then, we'll want to know if the belief is consistent with other things that we know about the world and how it works. If the belief is consistent, so far, so good. If it is not, then we'll naturally be skeptical, and we'll require further evidence before accepting the belief.

We always need to be aware, however, that our own background knowledge can be flawed. For example, it used to be part of most people's worldview that the Sun revolved around the Earth. Now, it's part of our worldview that it's the Earth that moves relative to the Sun. Background knowledge is subject to revision. So, *the mere fact that a piece of information conflicts with your understanding of the world does not automatically mean that the claim is false. It's possible that it's true, and that it's your understanding that needs revision.* Obviously, the more you know, the better equipped you are to evaluate claims, and to be accurate in your evaluations.

We can put all these considerations together by comparing two claims.

1. "I believe that, someday, my body will die, because (bodily) death is the natural end of living."
   - Question: To what extent is the belief supported by good reasons and compelling evidence from reliable sources?
   - Answer: Ample evidence is supplied every day, every time someone dies.

Obituaries, news stories about deaths, and personal experiences and memories of people (and every other animal on Earth) dying all serve as evidence.

- Question: To what extent is the belief consistent with other (justified) beliefs I have?
- Answer: The claim is consistent with the complex web of our beliefs involving the natural sciences. Biology and history both inform our worldview, and our worldview certainly includes bodily death.

2. "I believe that I will win the lottery this week."
   - Question: To what extent is the belief supported by good reasons and compelling evidence from reliable sources?
   - Answer: Excluding the possibility of cheating, there is no compelling evidence to indicate I will win. Indeed, it's unclear what could possibly count as evidence of this in the first place.

   - Question: To what extent is the belief consistent with other (justified) beliefs I have?
   - Answer: The claim that I will win the lottery conflicts with our understanding of probability in general, and with our experience of lotteries, in particular.

When we compare these examples, we can detect a sharp contrast. The first claim (concerning bodily death) is so strongly justified as to constitute knowledge. If you disagree with this, and deny that you know that your body will die someday, you probably think it's impossible to know *anything*. That's not necessarily a bad thing. There is a respectable and ancient school of thought called "Skepticism" that regards knowledge as impossible to obtain. You'll learn more about skepticism later. The second example (me winning the lottery) is so poorly justified as to be little better than wishful thinking—certainly not knowledge.

3. Truth

Having discussed beliefs and justification, what about truth? It is generally accepted that one can't know something that is false. I can't know (as of 2014) that George Washington is the current U.S. President—because he isn't!

Note that we can *think* that we know all kinds of things, and then discover that we were mistaken. In those cases, we never *really* knew what we believed we knew at all. This is complicated, but only a very basic understanding is needed for our purposes. In summary, if we really do know something, it must be something that is true.

What does it mean for something to be true? Once again, this is a complicated issue, but, once again, we can avoid needless complications by focusing just on some key concepts. Though there are several ways of understanding truth, we can focus on just a few that seem useful.

Epistemic Relativism

Epistemic relativism claims that truth is "relative" to the observer. Or, to put it a bit more famously, truth is a matter of perspective. Truth depends on one's point of view.

Now, at a certain level, this is obvious and unobjectionable. Most everyone would agree that there are certain kinds of claims we can make, certain kinds of judgments, that are merely expressions of personal opinion, or personal taste. One's favorite color, or whether or not one likes a band, or whether or not one likes spicy food—all such things seem to be matters of perspective. I like spicy food. My mother doesn't. She's not "wrong" or "mistaken" about spicy food—she just has different taste preferences. I really like the band "Switchfoot." I'm sure some people couldn't bear them (as hard as that is for me to believe). Again, no one is in error over such matters.

We call these sorts of claims "subjective claims." When we're dealing with subjective claims, there is no one right point of view, no single correct answer to the questions involving subjective claims. In cases of disagreement, it's not the case that someone must be wrong. Also, in cases of disagreement, there's little that can be accomplished from debate. I can sing the praises of spicy food for hours, but my mother will never be convinced of the truth of my claims and change her mind. This isn't because she's stubborn, it's because she just doesn't like spicy food! Her opinion on this matter is no better, or worse, than my own. It's just different.

So far, there's nothing terribly interesting or controversial about epistemic relativism. Where epistemic relativism does become controversial, however, is when we realize that the theory claims that *all* truths are relative in the way that subjective claims are.

If you stop to reflect on that for a moment, you can start to see how extraordinary that claim really is (whether true, or not). If all "truths" are matters of perspective, and if no perspective is inherently any more privileged than any other, then everyone is always "right" about everything.

You believe the Earth is a sphere. I believe it's flat (I don't, really). Assuming each claim represents our own respective opinions, why would your opinion be any more "right" than mine? In a sense, we're both right—even though we're making mutually exclusive claims. I think George W. Bush is the current U.S. President (I don't believe that either). That's my opinion, and I'm entitled to it, and your opinion isn't any more accurate than mine. "But," you might counter, "no one else shares your opinion, while lots of people share mine." Fine. That just means your opinion is more popular—it doesn't mean it's more accurate.

If all truth is subjective, then all truth is like my taste in music. If 99% of the world population couldn't stand Country music, but I loved it, my opinion that Country music is great would be no less legitimate than the nearly six billion who disagree—it would just be a lot less popular. If this sounds counter-intuitive to you, this idea that there are no "right answers" and that *all* truth is merely a matter of perspective, then I think you're on to something....[10]

To make matters even more interesting, consider this: "all truth is relative" is a claim. That means it's either true, or it's false. If it's false, then we obviously have no good reason to entertain it any further. If, on the other hand, it's true that all truth is relative, then that very claim is itself only relatively true. That is, it's just a matter of opinion, a matter of perspective. In that case, if I disagree, then my opinion is no worse, no less correct, than that of those who embrace epistemic relativism. To sum this up, either "all truth is relative" is a relative truth, or it's not-relative. If it's relative, then it's merely an opinion that is no "more true" than an opposing opinion. If it's not-relative, then not all truth is relative, and the claim refutes itself. That's usually a bad thing, when a claim refutes itself. What's more, the basic motivation that inspires epistemic relativism appears to presuppose the *falsity* of epistemic relativism.

Consider the following examples and inferences:

- Two people taste the same chocolate cake. One thinks it's overly sweet. The other thinks it could stand to be sweeter. Therefore, the sweetness of the chocolate is merely a matter of individual perspective. There is no "Truth" regarding its sweetness.
- I look at a flower and perceive it to be yellow. A bee looks at the same flower and perceives it to be blue with a red center. Therefore, the appearance of the flower is a matter of individual perspective. There is no "Truth" regarding the appearance of the flower.

Such common sense differences in perspective seem to suggest that epistemic relativism might be the correct way to understand truth. However, if one considers carefully these examples, it will soon be clear that these examples do *not* imply that "*all* truth is relative"—indeed they presuppose something very different. Epistemic relativism is driven by the force of the relativity of perception. That is, because it is such

[10] Or, at least that's *my* perspective.

a common experience for people to perceive "the same thing" in very different ways, it's easy to conclude that truth is relative. Be careful, though! The relativity of perception, even if true, doesn't imply that *all* truth is relative. Some truths must be held absolute in order for the relativity to make any sense.

Reconsider the chocolate cake. Two people taste the same cake with different results. Therefore, perception is relative. What is not thought relative in this example, however, is the existence of the cake, the tasters, and the world in which both cake and tasters exist. The same sorts of presuppositions apply to the flower example.

The bee and I perceive the flower with different results, but what is *not* thought relative is the existence of the flower itself, the bee, myself, and the reality in which all three of us reside.

In order to even make sense of the relativity of perception, one must presuppose that it is "True" that observers exist, and that a reality exists that may be perceived differently. The commonsense observation that initially gives rise to relativism is that the "real world" exists, that perceivers (such as you, me, and the bee) exist, but that we experience the "real world" in different ways.

Even if it's true that perceptions vary, that perceptions are relative, that certainly doesn't entail that *all truth* is relative. Indeed, it's arguable that it *cannot* entail that conclusion, if one accepts that relativity of perception implies absoluteness of perceivers and the world that is being perceived. Full-fledged epistemic relativism seems, then, to suffer from the threat of internal inconsistency. If epistemic relativism is a problematic way to understand truth, we'll have to consider some alternatives.

Correspondence Theory

Consider the following statements:

- The claim that George W. Bush is the current U.S. President is true if and only if he really is the current U.S. President.
- The claim that there are exactly 457 marbles in the jar is true if and only if there really are exactly that many marbles (457) in the jar.
- The claim that there is life on Mars is true if and only if there really is life on Mars.

Are these statements reasonable? If you think so, you're probably sympathetic to what is known as the correspondence theory of truth.

According to correspondence theory, a claim is true if it "corresponds" to the way things really are in the world, if the claim "matches up" with reality, if it "maps on" to how the world actually is. This is the most stringent of all the approaches to understanding truth because it claims that there is a way that the universe "really is," and our claims are true, or not, depending on whether they match up with the world. This is the approach implicitly employed by most people, whether they realize it or not.

Imagine that you intercept a fellow student on the way to class, and she tells you that the class has been cancelled. Has she told you the truth? What would you need to know in order to make that assessment? Simply this: you would need to know if the class really had been cancelled. If it had, her statement was true. If it had not, her statement was false. Her claim either "corresponded" to the world, or it didn't.

Obviously, not all of our claims will be so easily verifiable. Some truth claims (unfortunately, probably the ones we tend to care the most about—claims about morality, religion, politics, etc.), might be especially difficult to establish because we might not know how "the world is" concerning that particular subject. Do aliens exist, or not? Hard to say, since we haven't explored the entire universe just yet. Is abortion immoral? Hard to say, since there's so much disagreement, and so many compelling arguments that can be given on both sides. What correspondence theorists will claim is that even if we're not sure what the answers to some of these difficult questions are, we nevertheless can be confident that there are answers—not merely opinions—out there for us to discover.

Coherence Theory

Correspondence theorists say that a claim is true when its content matches up to reality. With regard to empirical claims, it might be obvious how this would apply. For example, the truth of the claim "there is water on Mars" would seem to depend upon whether or not there really is water on Mars! But, we use the word "true" in other contexts as well. For example, logicians say it is true that "B" may be inferred from the pairing of "A" and "A→B." What would it mean to say that this corresponds to reality? What is this "A" that's out there in the universe? Let alone this mysterious "A→B!"

In at least some cases, it appears that "correspondence" doesn't really capture what we mean by "true." Those who embrace the coherence theory of truth believe that claims are true when they "cohere" with a system of other statements, when they are consistent with our background information (our worldview). This approach is often thought to be a response to perceived weaknesses and "blind spots" of the correspondence theory, such as those described above.

Take the example of logic. When a logician says that it is true that "B" may be inferred from the pairing of "A" and "A→B," what the logician means is that, *given the rules of logic* (in this case, "modus ponens"), "B" may be derived from the combined claims of "A," and "A→B." That is, deriving "B" is a legitimate "move." No one "cheated."

Or, consider a particular move in the game of chess. According to the rules of chess, bishops may only move diagonally across the board. If you pick up a bishop and move it just one square to the left, you have made a move that violates the rules of chess. It is "true" that bishops may only move diagonally—but this doesn't affirm anything about "the world," it just "coheres" with a set of larger claims: the rules of chess.

The most enthusiastic coherence theorists claim that it is not merely in logic and geometry where we best understand "truth" in terms of coherence with an already accepted system of claims, but that this is the best understanding of truth in *all* cases.

Consider claims about the past, for example. What would it mean to say that it is true that the American Declaration of Independence was adopted by the Continental Congress on July 4th, 1776? When we say that that is "true," there is nothing "out there" in reality, to which that claim corresponds. Instead, we say that it is true because that claim "coheres" with many other accepted claims, because it fits with our understanding of the world and how it works. That claim is consistent with documents, the testimony of history books, the testimony of history professors, etc. In other words, it "coheres" with a larger body of accepted claims.

Or, what could it mean to say that it is true that bachelors are unmarried men other than, given what we mean by the words "bachelor," and "men," and "married," a bachelor is, *by definition* an unmarried man? This is what is known as an analytic truth, or an *"a priori"* truth: something that is true just by virtue of the meaning of the words involved.

Coherence theory certainly seems to be a good way to understand "truth" when we're dealing with analytic statements ("bachelors are unmarried men"), or axiomatic systems such as logic or math, but it seems to me that coherence theorists have confused justification with truth if they extend their interpretation beyond those kinds of claims.

The extent to which a claim coheres with the larger body of accepted claims (our background information), is the extent to which the claim is *justified*, and (in large part) determines the confidence we have that the claim is true. But, whether or not it is true that aliens from outer space exist seems to depend on whether or not there really are aliens out there in the universe (correspondence). The extent to which a particular claim about aliens is *justified* will be based, in part, by how well the claim coheres with one's worldview (coherence), and also, in part, by how much reliable evidence is provided in its favor. Coherence is absolutely relevant to justification, and certainly the right way to understand axiomatic systems and analytic truths, but doesn't stand as a strong candidate for our understanding of truth, in general.

Pragmatism

A pragmatist approach to truth is something somewhat in-between the "rigidity" of the correspondence theory and the perspectivism of epistemic relativism. As one might gather from its title, truth is understood in terms of its usefulness. There are various terms and phrases that help to illustrate what this means.

- Truth is what "works" for us.
- Truth "bears fruit."
- Truth is "productive."

As William James expresses it, in *The Meaning of Truth*: "Any idea that helps us to deal, whether practically or intellectually, with either the reality or its belongings, that doesn't entangle our progress in frustrations, that FITS, in fact, and adapts our life to the reality's whole setting, will agree sufficiently to meet the requirement. It will be true of that reality."

Other ways James tried to express this notion of truth include the following:

- "truth happens to an idea."

- "Any idea upon which we ride, so to speak; any idea that will carry us prosperously from any one part of our experience to any other part, linking things satisfactorily, working securely, simplifying, saving labor, is true for just so much, true in so far forth, true instrumentally."

- "The individual...meets a new experience that puts them to a strain. Somebody contradicts them; or in a reflective moment he discovers that they contradict each other; or he hears of facts with which they are incompatible; or desires arise in him which they cease to satisfy. The result is an inward trouble to which his mind till then had been a stranger, and from which he seeks to escape by modifying his previous mass of opinions...until at last some new idea comes up which he can graft upon the ancient stock. This new idea is then adopted as the true one. It preserves the older stock of truths with a minimum of modification, stretching them enough to make them admit the novelty, but conceiving them in ways as familiar as the case leaves possible. [A radical] explanation, violating all our preconceptions, would never pass as a true account...We would scratch around industriously till we found something less eccentric. The most violent revolutions in an individual's beliefs leave most of his old order standing."

Truth is going to be evaluated in terms of the usefulness or practical consequences of holding a claim to be true. For example, it is very "useful" for me to believe that the ground will continue to support my weight, barring very unusual circumstances. Indeed, without that belief, I can't imagine how I'd get by on a daily basis. Imagine if you were to think it false that the ground will continue to support your weight? Do you intend to remain immobile for the rest of your life, from fear of falling through the ground? I also find it terribly useful to believe that I need food to survive. If I deny that claim, I'm going to run into some serious problems in just a few days. It's very productive for me to believe I can't walk through walls. It's not at all productive for me to believe that I can. Get the idea?

Bear in mind that what is "pragmatic" is not simply whatever my own opinion happens to be. I can believe that I can walk through walls until the day I die, but it's hard to imagine a time in which that belief would ever be helpful. I could believe that you don't exist, and are simply a figment of my imagination, but that won't be very "helpful" when I am forced to interact with you in life.

I used to work in a locked placement psychiatric facility. Some of the clients held there had some (tragically) interesting beliefs. One woman believed her breasts were made of Styrofoam. A man believed snakes were (continually) emerging from the tile floor. Another man believed he was an employee of the hospital. None of those beliefs "worked" for them. Indeed, we might think that sometimes beliefs are so unproductive that to hold them is to be what we call "insane," or "irrational." So, the standards of pragmatism are certainly more stringent than those of epistemic relativism. At the same time, its standards are "looser" than those of the correspondence theory.

The pragmatist approach allows for revision of what is true, as new beliefs become more "useful" than previous beliefs. For example, it used to be quite "useful" to believe that the sun revolved around the earth. For one, it helped to explain why that big yellow ball appeared to move across the sky each day (we still talk about the sun "rising" and "setting"). Once a geocentric model of the universe was worked out, the theory also allowed humans to track and predict the motions of other celestial bodies, and even aided in navigation. However, the geocentric model became increasingly complicated as astronomers attempted to refine their predictive powers and to account for the mystery of "retrograde motion" in the planets.[11] Eventually, a heliocentric model emerged as an alternative—and a far more efficient, far more elegant, and just plain superior model when it came to predicting the motions of celestial objects. The geocentric model was replaced by the heliocentric model because believing that the Earth revolves around a (relatively) fixed Sun is more "useful." For a time, it was "true" that the Sun revolved the Earth, but now the reverse is true instead.

It's more useful to believe that mental illness is caused by a brain disorder than demonic possession. If patients are provided drugs that stabilize their brain chemistry, their symptoms improve. This is typically not the case when an exorcism is performed, or when a hole is drilled in the skull to release the demon. Someday, a different understanding of mental illness might replace the medical model if it proves to be more "fruitful."

In summary, the pragmatist approach does claim standards more rigorous than those of epistemic relativism, but allows for a more flexible interpretation of truth than that offered by the correspondence theory.

Skepticism

Skepticism is a school of thought with a very old and distinguished pedigree. It is also often misunderstood. Many people think that a skeptic is simply a nay-sayer—someone who will disagree with whatever she hears just to be difficult. In fact, true skeptics are much more modest, and will be largely indistinguishable from non-skeptics.

At the heart of skepticism is the belief (based on how things appear to the skeptic) that it is never possible to be certain of anything. Even that belief is not thought to be certain—it just appears to be the case. If we can never be certain of anything, a skeptic will think that we can never claim to "know" anything, since we will always lack sufficient justification to go from belief to knowledge. Why would anyone be skeptical in this way? The reasons are better than you might initially suspect.

Skeptics will point out that our perceptions are often flawed, or limited. This is obviously the case if someone is near-sighted, blind, or deaf. It's also the case, however, that every single human being appears to be limited, at the very least, to the part of the light spectrum that we are able to see. Look at the image of the dandelion below. What color is it? (Or, if your book is in black and white, what color would you expect a dandelion to be?) Yellow, right? Notice the bee on the flower? Because insects, like bees, access a different portion of the spectrum of energy (the UV portion), the flower is more likely to appear

[11] A very nice illustration (animation) of this can be found here: http://www.lasalle.edu/~smithsc/Astronomy/retrograd.html

"white", with a purplish patch right in the center. From our perspective, flowers that are a single color actually often light up like a "bulls-eye" to insects.[12] Now ask yourself this question: "What does the flower *really* look like?" Is it yellow? Or is it blue with a red center? Is the bee wrong? Or are you? How can you both be right?

Rub the top of a desk or table. It probably feels smooth, but look at it under a powerful microscope and you'll see a rough and jagged surface. Is the surface *really* smooth, or rough? A skeptic will say of such things, "I don't pretend to know what the flower 'really' looks like. It appears to be yellow to me right now, so I'm going to call it yellow. But, I'm not claiming that the flower really is yellow. For that matter, I can't know for sure that you actually exist. I might be dreaming right now. Or hallucinating. Or mentally ill. It doesn't seem that way. By all appearances, other people exist, so I'm going to operate on that assumption, but I could be wrong. So, I don't claim to know anything. I simply go by appearances, and leave false and unjustifiable confidence for others...."

There are *many* other arguments skeptics can offer that are meant to inspire doubt as to whether or not we can know anything with certainty. To go through all, or even most, would be too much of a tangent. Suffice it to say, we're keenly aware that we can be mistaken about all sorts of things, and quite often at that. If our senses, and our judgments, are known to be fallible, the skeptic would suggest we be more reluctant to claim to know anything. After all, we used to "know" that the Sun revolved around the Earth, and children "know" there's a Santa Claus, and you and I "know" that certain flowers are yellow.

Descartes: The Rationalist in Skeptic's Clothing

Rene Descartes (pronounced: "ruh-nay day-cart") is one of the most famous and respected philosophers of the Western tradition. A true renaissance man, he was an accomplished philosopher, scientist, and mathematician. He was also, by all accounts, a pious Catholic. During his lifetime, academic skepticism experienced a resurgence of popularity. Skepticism was threatening for a man like Descartes. After all, skepticism claims that we can never know anything with certainty. This would include scientific claims, mathematical claims, and religious claims. One of Descartes primary aims, then, was to prove skepticism wrong, to establish that knowledge is, in fact, possible. To prove this point, he employed an interesting (and ironic) strategy: adopt skepticism.

Descartes was not entirely hostile to skepticism. He recognized the value of subjecting our beliefs to scrutiny, and not falling prey to naïve beliefs or unwarranted superstitions. Indeed, he went so far as to claim that everyone, at some point in his or her life, should question everything they had believed up to that point, put every belief to the test, and continue on only with those beliefs that had survived the trial.

To defeat skepticism, Descartes put all his own beliefs to the test, using the most potent skeptic techniques he could muster. His goal was to question everything, and see if anything survived that process. If anything did, it would establish that knowledge is possible, because it would show that there are some things (or some thing) that can't be doubted. Obviously, he couldn't doubt every one of his beliefs, one at a time. He would die long before he made any meaningful progress. Instead, he would subject his beliefs to doubt in broad categories, by employing a handful of skeptical arguments. It's important to remember, though, that although Descartes adopts skeptical techniques, his ultimate goal was to *defeat* skepticism.

His method of "radical doubt" is to call into question all of his beliefs, in large groups. He does so with a series of arguments meant to inspire

---

12 An excellent website, with numerous vivid photographs showing exactly these sorts of differences, can be found at the following URL: http://www.naturfotograf.com/UV_flowers_list.html (All rights are reserved by the photographer, Bjørn Rørslett, and I can only hope that the URL is still valid at the time you're reading this).

doubt. One is rooted in the unreliability of the senses, another in the vivacity of dreams, another in the compelling nature of delusions, and the final argument even postulates the existence of an evil, deceptive demon! Each argument is presented below, in a formal fashion, with all claims numbered.

These arguments appear in Descartes *Meditations*. Understand that he meant for them to be genuine meditations. He reflected upon each argument, considering it carefully, and allowing it to chip away at his confidence in his beliefs. Ideally, you will follow along in similar fashion yourself.

Radical Doubt

The Argument from the Unreliability of the Senses

1. Most of my beliefs are based on the senses.
2. The senses have deceived me in the past.
3. It is reasonable to doubt something which has deceived me.
4. Therefore, most of my beliefs are open to reasonable doubts.

Descartes' point here is simple, but easily misinterpreted. He is not claiming that our senses always deceive us. No skeptic (not even a pretend one, like Descartes) could claim that. Why? To assert that our senses always deceive us is to make a knowledge claim, and skeptics can't make *any* knowledge claims. After all, to claim (with confidence) that our senses are mistaken requires one to know what the world is really like—and that's just what the skeptics deny is possible. So, all Descartes is doing here is pointing out that sometimes the senses deceive us, and, at the time, we usually aren't aware of that fact.

Examples of sense-deception are countless. Think of all the times you thought you saw something, but it turned out to be something else? Or thought you heard something, but it turned out to be something else? Think about optical illusions. Isn't it amazing that something so small as the sun can provide all that heat and light for our planet? I mean, it's about the size of a quarter!

That's ridiculous, of course. You know perfectly well that the sun is very large—or at least astronomers tell us it is. But, my eyes tell me it's very small. In other words, my senses are deceiving me!

If there is someone in your life, a friend or family member, and you have caught that person lying to you, isn't it the case that you never trust them again the way you used to? Trust, once lost, is difficult to regain. This doesn't mean that this person has lied to you about everything, or that this person will lie to you about everything in the future, but the problem is that this person has established himself as a liar. A precedent has been set.

"You've lied to me before, how do I know you haven't lied to me about other things, too? Or that you won't lie to me again?"

"I promise never to lie to you again."

"Is *that* a lie, too?"

Our senses are like that lying friend. It's not as though the argument is that everything our senses have ever told us is a lie, but how many lies have we failed to catch? If we know that our senses are at least sometimes deceptive, it should cause us to question the veracity of our beliefs based on sense-testimony—and that includes a lot of beliefs! Think about it: how much of what you believe and think you know about the world is based off of what you see, hear, touch, smell, etc.? How many of those beliefs are subject to reasonable doubt?

The Argument from Dreaming

1. There are no internal criteria by which one can distinguish dreaming from waking sense experiences.
2. Dream experiences are usually false.
3. Therefore, any of my waking experiences could be false.
4. Therefore, all (or most) of my beliefs could be false.

This argument is a lot of fun, once it's understood. Ask yourself this very simple question: have you ever had a dream that was so vivid that, at the time, you didn't know it was a dream and thought it was real?

Almost everyone can answer "yes" to that question. Some dreams are so realistic that they produce actual physical effects in us, such as sweating, racing pulse, etc. The power of this argument lies in the realization that, while we are having one of those vivid dreams, we don't know that it's a dream. At the same time, most of us are confident that what happens in dreams isn't real. For example, it would be hard to find someone who, upon having a dream in which she committed a crime, would feel obligated to go turn herself in to the police. It was "just a dream," after all.

If, during those dreams, you don't know that you're dreaming, how do you know you're not dreaming right now? Perhaps you're having a wonderful, amazing dream in which you're reading a philosophy text? Perhaps I'm having a dream in which I'm writing one.

Again, don't misunderstand this argument. No one is claiming that you are always dreaming. That would be to make a knowledge claim. Instead, the skeptic argument is that you could be dreaming and, if you were, you wouldn't be aware of that fact. If so, all kinds of things that you believe are might instead have been the result of dreams. How many of me "memories" are actually just memories of things I dreamt about? Maybe some things I think I learned in school were actually things I "learned" in dreams? Once again, a huge percentage of my beliefs, and yours, can be doubted thanks to this argument.

The Argument from Insanity

1. Delusional beliefs are unwarranted.
2. People holding delusional beliefs do not usually recognize them as delusional (at the time).
3. Any number of my beliefs might be delusional, and I would not recognize them as such.
4. Therefore, any number of my beliefs might be unwarranted.

I used to work as a counselor at a locked-placement psychiatric hospital. The residents there were all seriously mentally ill adults. Nearly all suffered from delusions. I use the word "suffer" intentionally. There is nothing amusing about delusions. They produce great suffering and tragedy in the lives of those who have them. Why? Because profoundly mentally ill people usually don't recognize that their delusions are delusions. They believe they are real, or represent a real image of the world.

One poor man who constantly believed that snakes were crawling out of the floor reacted accordingly: with fear. The man who believed he was not a patient, but an employee of the hospital, would become understandably upset when he was not allowed to go home at the end of the day. Those suffering from paranoid delusions, who believed that various forces were conspiring against them, were constantly anxious and fearful of their (imagined) powerful enemies. What made the situation so especially tragic is that the man who believed he was an employee, and not a patient, believed so (seemingly) with just as much confidence as I had in my belief that he was a patient.

The application of this argument is simple, if not disturbing: how do you know you're not mentally ill right now, and that all sorts of things that you believe aren't, in fact, delusions?

Perhaps your whole life is one grand delusion, and you're actually restrained and living in a psychiatric hospital right now? If that were the case, and your present perception of reality were delusional, you wouldn't be aware of that fact, after all....

Again, don't misinterpret the skeptic: he's not claiming that we're all mentally ill and everything you believe is a delusion. That would be to make a knowledge claim! Instead, he's claiming that you *could* be suffering from delusions, and wouldn't be able to tell the difference, with certainty. If any number of our beliefs could be delusional, and we wouldn't be able to tell which ones were delusional, and which were not, we have yet another reason to be skeptical.

The Argument from the "Evil Demon"

1. There could be a powerful "evil demon"

deceiving me.

2. If there were such a demon, then I could be mistaken in all my beliefs.
3. Therefore, all my beliefs could be mistaken.

This is the most powerful of the skeptical arguments. In fact, with this one, no other is needed.

Descartes imagines that his entire life could be a lie. Everything he thinks he knows could be an illusion. Even seemingly indubitable truths, like the claim that 2 + 2 = 4 could be a lie. How?

Perhaps Descartes is presently being deceived by a very powerful evil demon. Perhaps he is not a 17th century Frenchman, but is, instead, in hell, and this evil demon is causing him to believe (falsely) that he is living a life as a French scholar.

Perhaps, right now, you are not wherever you think you are, reading this text, but are instead being deceived into thinking that you are by this evil demon?

If you don't like the "evil demon" thought experiment, substitute the "Matrix." Perhaps none of your life is real, and you are, in fact, floating in a bunch of goo, providing bio-electric energy to countless machines that pacify you by stimulating your brain into generating the vast and complex delusion that is your life.

One more time, don't misunderstand this argument. Descartes is not claiming that there is an evil demon, and that he (or anyone else) is being deceived in such a manner. He's introducing that *possibility*, and recognizing that if that *were* the case, any or all of his beliefs could be a lie, and he would not be able to tell the difference. In that case, nothing survives the skeptic's challenge. Or so it would seem....

Doubt Defeated: Cogito Ergo Sum

Descartes was no skeptic, but he did do a very convincing job of pretending to be one. By the end of his process of radical doubt, it's hard to see how we could be certain of *anything*—but Descartes thinks he can be. The one thing that survives the skeptic process is possibly the most famous slogan in Western philosophy—a quotation so famous that almost everyone has heard it (though few fully understand it): *Cogito Ergo Sum.*

Cogito ergo sum—I think, therefore I am (or, I think, therefore I exist). What does this mean, and why is it significant? Many assume Descartes was trying to prove his own existence. He wasn't. He was trying to prove that knowledge is possible, and he was confident that the "cogito" accomplished that. How? Simple.

Try to doubt that the cogito is true. Seriously. As a thought experiment, right now, try to convince yourself that you do not exist.

You failed, didn't you? Of course you did. If it wasn't obvious why, ask yourself this: who was doing the convincing?

Obviously, in order to try to convince yourself of something, you have to exist at the time you're trying to convince yourself! Similarly, Descartes recognized that it was impossible for him to doubt the truth of the cogito, at least whenever he thought about it, because the very act of thinking about it proved that he was existing at that time. Moreover, the truth of his existence, whenever he's thinking, survives every single skeptical argument.

- Argument from the unreliability of the senses: in order to be deceived by the senses, he has to exist.
- Argument from dreaming: in order to be deceived by a dream, he has to exist.
- Argument from insanity: in order to suffer from delusions, he has to exist.
- Evil demon argument: in order to be deceived by an evil demon, he has to exist.

In other words, in order to believe anything, true or false, he has to exist at the time. He can't doubt his own existence (whenever he's thinking) because the very act of doubt establishes his existence. That he exists (when thinking) is something that he can't doubt, no matter how hard he tries. If he can't doubt it, he's *certain* that it's true. If he's certain, that's knowledge—and that means knowledge is possible. Even if he only knows one thing ("cogito ergo sum"), he knows *something*, and that means that the skeptic's claim that knowledge is impossible is mistaken.

Admittedly, at this point, Descartes doesn't

know very much—just the brute fact of his own existence. He goes on to try to prove much more than that, but that effort is far too much of a tangent given our current agenda. The basic point to grasp is that Descartes has offered what most take to be a very convincing argument against the most aggressive strains of skepticism.

Conclusion

Epistemology is a broad, deep, and complicated sub-discipline of philosophy. When we ask "what is truth?" Or, "what is knowledge?" We are, indeed, asking questions both difficult and profound.

It is not expected that you have formulated your own answers to these questions just yet! Instead, try to understand the nature and importance of the questions themselves, and try to understand and appreciate the broad attempts to address these questions that we've already considered (i.e., epistemic relativism, correspondence theory, pragmatism, and skepticism).

Bear in mind, as you consider other philosophical issues in other chapters of this book, that whatever philosophical questions we pose, epistemology lurks in the background. For example, if someone claims that we have no free will, is she making a knowledge claim? What would it mean for that statement to be "true?" What counts as evidence? How would we *know*?

Exercises for Wisdom and Growth

1. List 5 things that you think you know, and another 5 that you believe, but that you wouldn't claim to know. What do you think is the difference between the examples in your "know" set, and those in your "belief" set?
2. What does it mean to "know" something? If you had to define "knowledge" in one sentence, what would your definition be?
3. Do you consider yourself a skeptic? About what sorts of things? Why? Are there good reasons for people to be skeptics? Can skepticism be taken too far?
4. Is truth simply a matter of opinion? A matter of perspective? Why would someone believe this to be true? What if my opinion is that 2 + 2 = 5? Does it make sense to say that 2 + 2 = 5 is my "truth?"
5. Skeptics require that we be 100% certain (couldn't possibly be mistaken) about something in order to claim to *know* it. Do you agree with that standard? When you say that you know something, do you mean that you couldn't possibly be mistaken? If not, what *do* you mean?

Bertrand Russell (18 May 1872 – 2 February 1970) was a prominent British philosopher, logician, and mathematician. He also happened to be from an important aristocratic family (making him the 3rd Earl Russell). This selection is from Russell's larger work, Problems of Philosophy. Much as I prefer to do in my own book, Russell began his treatment of philosophy, in that book, with some epistemology. Russell acknowledges the legitimate challenge presented by skepticism, and demonstrates how the distinction between appearance and reality makes skepticism possible. He then explores some of the further implications of this distinction: if, for example, all we ever perceive are appearances (as distinct from a thing's reality), how can we be certain that there even is a "reality" underlying the "appearance?" Though Russell was not, himself, a skeptic (let alone an idealist), he nevertheless offers a powerful presentation of the plausibility of skepticism. I recommend that you actually play along with Russell towards the beginning of the reading, and find an object in your environment (table, or anything else) to examine. If you follow Russell's reasoning with a perception of your own, his argument will be easier to appreciate.

Bertrand Russell
Problems of Philosophy

Chapter 1, Appearance and Reality

IS there any knowledge in the world which is so certain that no reasonable man could doubt it? This question, which at first sight might not seem difficult, is really one of the most difficult that can be asked. When we have realized the obstacles in the way of a straightforward and confident answer, we shall be well launched on the study of philosophy -- for philosophy is merely the attempt to answer such ultimate questions, not carelessly and dogmatically, as we do in ordinary life and even in the sciences, but critically after exploring all that makes such questions puzzling, and after realizing all the vagueness and confusion that underlie our ordinary ideas.

In daily life, we assume as certain many things which, on a closer scrutiny, are found to be so full of apparent contradictions that only a great amount of thought enables us to know what it is that we really may believe. In the search for certainty, it is natural to begin with our present experiences, and in some sense, no doubt, knowledge is to be derived from them. But any statement as to what it is that our immediate experiences make us know is very likely to be wrong. It seems to me that I am now sitting in a chair, at a table of a certain shape, on which I see sheets of paper with writing or print. By turning my head I see out of the window buildings and clouds and the sun. I believe that the sun is about ninety-three million miles from the earth; that it is a hot globe many times bigger than the earth; that, owing to the earth's rotation, it rises every morning, and will continue to do so for an indefinite time in the future. I believe that, if any other normal person comes into my room, he will see the same chairs and tables and books and papers as I see, and that the table which I see is the same as the table which I feel pressing against my arm. All this seems to be so evident as to be hardly worth stating, except in answer to a man who doubts whether I know anything. Yet all this may be reasonably doubted, and all of it requires much careful discussion before we can be sure that we have stated it in a form that is wholly true.

To make our difficulties plain, let us concentrate attention on the table. To the eye it is oblong, brown and shiny, to the touch it is smooth and cool and hard; when I tap it, it gives out a wooden sound. Any one else who sees and feels and hears the table will agree with this description, so that it might seem as if no difficulty would arise; but as soon as we try to be more precise our troubles begin. Although I believe that the table is 'really' of the same colour all over, the parts that reflect the light look much brighter than the other parts, and some parts look white because of reflected light. I know that, if I move, the parts that reflect the light will be different, so that the apparent distribution of colours on the table will change. It follows that if several people are looking at the table at the same moment, no two of them will see exactly the same distribution of colours, because no two can see it from exactly the same point of view, and any change in the point of view makes some change in the way the light is reflected.

For most practical purposes these differences are unimportant, but to the painter they are all-important: the painter has to unlearn the habit of thinking that things seem to have the colour which common sense says they 'really' have, and to learn the habit of seeing things as they appear. Here we have already the beginning of one of the distinctions that cause most trouble in philosophy -- the distinction between 'appearance' and 'reality', between what things seem to be and what they are. The painter wants to know what things seem to be, the practical man and the philosopher want to know what they are; but the philosopher's wish to know this is stronger than the practical man's, and is more troubled by knowledge as to the difficulties of answering the question.

To return to the table. It is evident from what we have found, that there is no colour which preeminently appears to be the colour of the table, or even of any one particular part of the table -- it appears to be of different colours from different points of view, and there is no reason for regarding some of these as more really its colour than others. And we know that even from a given point of view the colour will seem different by artificial light, or to a colour-blind man, or to a man wearing blue spectacles, while in the dark there will be no colour at all, though to touch and hearing the table will be unchanged. This colour is not something which is inherent in the table, but something depending upon the table and the spectator and the way the light falls on the table. When, in ordinary life, we speak of the colour of the table, we only mean the sort of colour which it will seem to have to a normal spectator from an ordinary point of view under usual conditions of light. But the other colours which appear under other conditions have just as good a right to be considered real; and therefore, to avoid favouritism, we are compelled to deny that, in itself, the table has any one particular colour.

The same thing applies to the texture. With the naked eye one can see the gram, but otherwise the table looks smooth and even. If we looked at it through a microscope, we should see roughnesses and hills and valleys, and all sorts of differences that are imperceptible to the naked eye. Which of these is the 'real' table? We are naturally tempted to say that what we see through the microscope is more real, but that in turn would be changed by a still more powerful microscope. If, then, we cannot trust what we see with the naked eye, why should we trust what we see through a microscope? Thus, again, the confidence in our senses with which we began deserts us.

The shape of the table is no better. We are all in the habit of judging as to the 'real' shapes of things, and we do this so unreflectingly that we come to think we actually see the real shapes. But, in fact, as we all have to learn if we try to draw, a given thing looks different in shape from every different point of view. If our table is 'really' rectangular, it will look, from almost all points of view, as if it had two acute angles and two obtuse angles. If opposite sides are parallel, they will look as if they converged to a point away from the spectator; if they are of equal length, they will look as if the nearer side were longer. All these things are not commonly noticed in looking at a table, because experience has taught us to construct the 'real' shape from the apparent shape, and the 'real' shape is what interests us as practical men. But the 'real' shape is not what we see; it is something inferred from what we see. And what we see is constantly changing in shape as we, move about the room; so that here again the senses seem not to give us the truth about the table itself, but only about the appearance of the table.

Similar difficulties arise when we consider the sense of touch. It is true that the table always gives us a sensation of hardness, and we feel that it resists pressure. But the sensation we obtain depends upon how hard we press the table and also upon what part of the body we press with; thus the various sensations due to various pressures or various parts of the body cannot be supposed to reveal directly any definite property of the table, but at most to be signs of some property which perhaps causes all the sensations, but is not actually apparent in any of them. And the same applies still more obviously to the sounds which can be elicited by rapping the table.

Thus it becomes evident that the real table, if there is one, is not the same as what we immediately experience by sight or touch or hearing. The real table, if there is one, is not immediately known to us at all, but must be an inference from what is immediately known. Hence, two very difficult questions at once arise; namely, (1) Is there a real table at all? (2) If so, what sort of object can it be?

It will help us in considering these questions to have a few simple terms of which the meaning is definite and clear. Let us give the name of 'sense-data' to the things that are immediately known in sensation: such things as colours, sounds, smells, hardnesses, roughnesses, and so on. We shall give the name 'sensation' to the experience of being immediately aware of these things. Thus, whenever we see a colour, we have a sensation of the colour, but the colour itself is a sense-datum, not a sensation. The colour is that of which we are immediately aware, and the awareness itself is the sensation. It is plain that if we are to know anything about the table, it must be by means of the sense-data -- brown colour, oblong shape, smoothness, etc. -- which we associate with the table; but, for the reasons which have been given, we cannot say that the table is the sense-data, or even that the sense-data are directly properties of the table. Thus a problem arises as to the relation of the sense-data to the real table, supposing there is such a thing.

The real table, if it exists, we will call a 'physical object'. Thus we have to consider the relation of sense-data to physical objects. The collection of all physical objects is called 'matter'. Thus our two questions may be re-stated as follows: (1) Is there any such thing as matter? (2) If so, what is its nature?

The philosopher who first brought prominently forward the reasons for regarding the immediate objects of our senses as not existing independently of us was Bishop Berkeley (1685-1753). His Three Dialogues between Hylas and Philonous, in Opposition to Sceptics and Atheists, undertake to prove that there is no such thing as matter at all, and that the world consists of nothing but minds and their ideas. Hylas has hitherto believed in matter, but he is no match for Philonous, who mercilessly drives him into contradictions and paradoxes, and makes his own denial of matter seem, in the end, as if it were almost common sense. The arguments employed are of very different value: some are important and sound, others are confused or quibbling. But Berkeley retains the merit of having shown that the existence of matter is capable of being denied without absurdity, and that if there are any things that exist independently of us they cannot be the immediate objects of our sensations.

There are two different questions involved when we ask whether matter exists, and it is important to keep them clear. We commonly mean by 'matter' something which is opposed to 'mind', something which we think of as occupying space and as radically incapable of any sort of thought or consciousness. It is chiefly in this sense that Berkeley denies matter; that is to say, he does not deny that the sense-data which we commonly take as signs of the existence of the table are really signs of the existence of something independent of us, but he does deny that this something is nonmental, that it is neither mind nor ideas entertained by some mind. He admits that there must be something which continues to exist when we go out of the room or shut our eyes, and that what we call seeing the table does really give us reason for believing in something which persists even when we are not seeing it. But he thinks that this something cannot be radically different in nature from what we see, and cannot be independent of seeing altogether, though it must be independent of our seeing. He is thus led to regard the 'real' table as an idea in the mind of God. Such an idea has the required permanence and independence of ourselves, without being -- as matter would otherwise be -- something quite unknowable, in the sense that we can only infer it, and can never be directly and immediately aware of it.

Other philosophers since Berkeley have also held that, although the table does not depend for its existence upon being seen by me, it does depend upon being seen (or otherwise apprehended in sensation) by some mind -- not necessarily the mind of God, but more often the whole collective mind of the universe. This they hold, as Berkeley does, chiefly because they think there can be nothing real -- or at any rate nothing known to be real except minds and their thoughts and feelings. We might state the argument by which they support their view in some such way as this: 'Whatever can be thought of is an idea in the mind of the person thinking of it; therefore nothing can be thought of except ideas in minds; therefore anything else is inconceivable, and what is inconceivable cannot exist.'

Such an argument, in my opinion, is fallacious; and of course those who advance it do not put it so shortly or so crudely. But whether valid or not, the argument has been very widely advanced in one form or another; and very many philosophers, perhaps a majority, have held that there is nothing real except minds and their ideas. Such philosophers are called 'idealists'. When they come to explaining matter, they either say, like Berkeley, that matter is really nothing but a collection of ideas, or they say, like Leibniz (1646-1716), that what appears as matter is really a collection of more or less rudimentary minds.

But these philosophers, though they deny matter as opposed to mind, nevertheless, in another sense, admit matter. It will be remembered that we asked two questions; namely, (1) Is there a real table at all? (2) If so, what sort of object can it be? Now both Berkeley and Leibniz admit that there is a real table, but Berkeley says it is certain ideas in the mind of God, and Leibniz says it is a colony of souls. Thus both of them answer our first question in the affirmative, and only diverge from the views of ordinary mortals in their answer to our second question. In fact, almost all philosophers seem to be agreed that there is a real table. they almost all agree that, however much our sense-data -- colour, shape, smoothness, etc. -- may depend upon us, yet their occurrence is a sign of something existing independently of us, something differing, perhaps, completely from our sense-data whenever we are in a suitable relation to the real table.

Now obviously this point in which the philosophers are agreed -- the view that there is a real table, whatever its nature may be is vitally important, and it will be worth while to consider what reasons there are for accepting this view before we go on to the further question as to the nature of the real table. Our next chapter, therefore, will be concerned with the reasons for supposing that there is a real table at all.

Before we go farther it will be well to consider for a moment what it is that we have discovered so far. It has appeared that, if we take any common object of the sort that is supposed to be known by the senses, what the senses immediately tell us is not the truth about the object as it is apart from us, but only the truth about certain sense-data which, so far as we can see, depend upon the relations between us and the object. Thus what we directly see and feel is merely 'appearance', which we believe to be a sign of some 'reality' behind. But if the reality is not what appears, have we any means of knowing whether there is any reality at all? And if so, have we any means of finding out what it is like?

Such questions are bewildering, and it is difficult to know that even the strangest hypotheses may not be true. Thus our familiar table, which has roused but the slightest thoughts in us hitherto, has become a problem full of surprising possibilities. The one thing we know about it is that it is not what it seems. Beyond this modest result, so far, we have the most complete liberty of conjecture. Leibniz tells us it is a community of souls: Berkeley tells us it is an idea in the mind of God; sober science, scarcely less wonderful, tells us it is a vast collection of electric charges in violent motion.

Among these surprising possibilities, doubt suggests that perhaps there is no table at all. Philosophy, if it cannot answer so many questions as we could wish, has at least the power of asking questions which increase the interest of the world, and show the strangeness and wonder lying just below the surface even in the commonest things of daily life.

Rene Descartes (31 March 1596 – 11 February 1650) is one of the most famous and studied philosophers of the Western tradition. His most well-known work is his "Meditations", from which you have an excerpt. The following text demonstrates Descartes' method of radical doubt, by which he calls into question everything he thinks he knows. He does this by a series of skeptical arguments that includes an argument questioning the reliability of sense testimony, an argument that considers the implication of dreaming and another of mental illness, and finally an argument that considers the possibility that he has been systematically deceived about everything at the hands of an evil demon. Note that these were meant as actual meditations. Ideally, the reader will participate in the process just as Descartes did. By the end of this first Meditation, the reader might conclude that Descartes is a committed skeptic, and find plenty of reasons to agree with him. In the second selection, however (Meditation 2), Descartes reveals his true agenda: to prove that knowledge is possible, and that the skeptics are mistaken. He does so by establishing that he knows he exists—at least whenever he is thinking.

Rene Descartes, *Meditations*

Meditation I, Of the Things of Which We May Doubt

1. SEVERAL years have now elapsed since I first became aware that I had accepted, even from my youth, many false opinions for true, and that consequently what I afterward based on such principles was highly doubtful; and from that time I was convinced of the necessity of undertaking once in my life to rid myself of all the opinions I had adopted, and of commencing anew the work of building from the foundation, if I desired to establish a firm and abiding superstructure in the sciences. But as this enterprise appeared to me to be one of great magnitude, I waited until I had attained an age so mature as to leave me no hope that at any stage of life more advanced I should be better able to execute my design. On this account, I have delayed so long that I should henceforth consider I was doing wrong were I still to consume in deliberation any of the time that now remains for action. To-day, then, since I have opportunely freed my mind from all cares [and am happily disturbed by no passions], and since I am in the secure possession of leisure in a peaceable retirement, I will at length apply myself earnestly and freely to the general overthrow of all my former opinions.

2. But, to this end, it will not be necessary for me to show that the whole of these are false--a point, perhaps, which I shall never reach; but as even now my reason convinces me that I ought not the less carefully to withhold belief from what is not entirely certain and indubitable, than from what is manifestly false, it will be sufficient to justify the rejection of the whole if I shall find in each some ground for doubt. Nor for this purpose will it be necessary even to deal with each belief individually, which would be truly an endless labor; but, as the removal from below of the foundation necessarily involves the downfall of the whole edifice, I will at once approach the criticism of the principles on which all my former beliefs rested.

3. All that I have, up to this moment, accepted as possessed of the highest truth and certainty, I received either from or through the senses. I observed, however, that these sometimes misled us; and it is the part of prudence not to place absolute confidence in that by which we have even once been deceived.

4. But it may be said, perhaps, that, although the senses occasionally mislead us respecting minute objects, and such as are so far removed from us as to be beyond the reach of close observation, there are yet many other of their informations (presentations), of the truth of which it is manifestly impossible to doubt; as for example, that I am in this place, seated by the fire, clothed in a winter dressing gown, that I hold in my hands this piece of paper, with other intimations of the same nature. But how could I deny that I possess these hands and this body, and withal escape being classed with persons in a state of insanity, whose brains are so disordered and

clouded by dark bilious vapors as to cause them pertinaciously to assert that they are monarchs when they are in the greatest poverty; or clothed [in gold] and purple when destitute of any covering; or that their head is made of clay, their body of glass, or that they are gourds? I should certainly be not less insane than they, were I to regulate my procedure according to examples so extravagant.

5. Though this be true, I must nevertheless here consider that I am a man, and that, consequently, I am in the habit of sleeping, and representing to myself in dreams those same things, or even sometimes others less probable, which the insane think are presented to them in their waking moments. How often have I dreamt that I was in these familiar circumstances, that I was dressed, and occupied this place by the fire, when I was lying undressed in bed? At the present moment, however, I certainly look upon this paper with eyes wide awake; the head which I now move is not asleep; I extend this hand consciously and with express purpose, and I perceive it; the occurrences in sleep are not so distinct as all this. But I cannot forget that, at other times I have been deceived in sleep by similar illusions; and, attentively considering those cases, I perceive so clearly that there exist no certain marks by which the state of waking can ever be distinguished from sleep, that I feel greatly astonished; and in amazement I almost persuade myself that I am now dreaming.

6. Let us suppose, then, that we are dreaming, and that all these particulars--namely, the opening of the eyes, the motion of the head, the forth-putting of the hands--are merely illusions; and even that we really possess neither an entire body nor hands such as we see. Nevertheless it must be admitted at least that the objects which appear to us in sleep are, as it were, painted representations which could not have been formed unless in the likeness of realities; and, therefore, that those general objects, at all events, namely, eyes, a head, hands, and an entire body, are not simply imaginary, but really existent. For, in truth, painters themselves, even when they study to represent sirens and satyrs by forms the most fantastic and extraordinary, cannot bestow upon them natures absolutely new, but can only make a certain medley of the members of different animals; or if they chance to imagine something so novel that nothing at all similar has ever been seen before, and such as is, therefore, purely fictitious and absolutely false, it is at least certain that the colors of which this is composed are real. And on the same principle, although these general objects, viz. [a body], eyes, a head, hands, and the like, be imaginary, we are nevertheless absolutely necessitated to admit the reality at least of some other objects still more simple and universal than these, of which, just as of certain real colors, all those images of things, whether true and real, or false and fantastic, that are found in our consciousness (cogitatio),are formed.

7. To this class of objects seem to belong corporeal nature in general and its extension; the figure of extended things, their quantity or magnitude, and their number, as also the place in, and the time during, which they exist, and other things of the same sort.

8. We will not, therefore, perhaps reason illegitimately if we conclude from this that Physics, Astronomy, Medicine, and all the other sciences that have for their end the consideration of composite objects, are indeed of a doubtful character; but that Arithmetic, Geometry, and the other sciences of the same class, which regard merely the simplest and most general objects, and scarcely inquire whether or not these are really existent, contain somewhat that is certain and indubitable: for whether I am awake or dreaming, it remains true that two and three make five, and that a square has but four sides; nor does it seem possible that truths so apparent can ever fall under a suspicion of falsity [or incertitude].

9. Nevertheless, the belief that there is a God who is all powerful, and who created me, such as I am, has, for a long time, obtained steady possession of my mind. How, then, do I know that he has not arranged that there should be neither earth, nor sky, nor any extended thing, nor figure, nor magnitude, nor place, providing at the same time, however, for [the rise in me of the perceptions of all these objects, and] the persuasion that these do not exist otherwise than as I perceive them ? And further, as I sometimes

think that others are in error respecting matters of which they believe themselves to possess a perfect knowledge, how do I know that I am not also deceived each time I add together two and three, or number the sides of a square, or form some judgment still more simple, if more simple indeed can be imagined? But perhaps Deity has not been willing that I should be thus deceived, for he is said to be supremely good. If, however, it were repugnant to the goodness of Deity to have created me subject to constant deception, it would seem likewise to be contrary to his goodness to allow me to be occasionally deceived; and yet it is clear that this is permitted.

10. Some, indeed, might perhaps be found who would be disposed rather to deny the existence of a Being so powerful than to believe that there is nothing certain. But let us for the present refrain from opposing this opinion, and grant that all which is here said of a Deity is fabulous: nevertheless, in whatever way it be supposed that I reach the state in which I exist, whether by fate, or chance, or by an endless series of antecedents and consequents, or by any other means, it is clear (since to be deceived and to err is a certain defect) that the probability of my being so imperfect as to be the constant victim of deception, will be increased exactly in proportion as the power possessed by the cause, to which they assign my origin, is lessened. To these reasonings I have assuredly nothing to reply, but am constrained at last to avow that there is nothing of all that I formerly believed to be true of which it is impossible to doubt, and that not through thoughtlessness or levity, but from cogent and maturely considered reasons; so that henceforward, if I desire to discover anything certain, I ought not the less carefully to refrain from assenting to those same opinions than to what might be shown to be manifestly false.

11. But it is not sufficient to have made these observations; care must be taken likewise to keep them in remembrance. For those old and customary opinions perpetually recur-- long and familiar usage giving them the right of occupying my mind, even almost against my will, and subduing my belief; nor will I lose the habit of deferring to them and confiding in them so long as I shall consider them to be what in truth they are, viz, opinions to some extent doubtful, as I have already shown, but still highly probable, and such as it is much more reasonable to believe than deny. It is for this reason I am persuaded that I shall not be doing wrong, if, taking an opposite judgment of deliberate design, I become my own deceiver, by supposing, for a time, that all those opinions are entirely false and imaginary, until at length, having thus balanced my old by my new prejudices, my judgment shall no longer be turned aside by perverted usage from the path that may conduct to the perception of truth. For I am assured that, meanwhile, there will arise neither peril nor error from this course, and that I cannot for the present yield too much to distrust, since the end I now seek is not action but knowledge.

12. I will suppose, then, not that Deity, who is sovereignly good and the fountain of truth, but that some malignant demon, who is at once exceedingly potent and deceitful, has employed all his artifice to deceive me; I will suppose that the sky, the air, the earth, colors, figures, sounds, and all external things, are nothing better than the illusions of dreams, by means of which this being has laid snares for my credulity; I will consider myself as without hands, eyes, flesh, blood, or any of the senses, and as falsely believing that I am possessed of these; I will continue resolutely fixed in this belief, and if indeed by this means it be not in my power to arrive at the knowledge of truth, I shall at least do what is in my power, viz, [suspend my judgment], and guard with settled purpose against giving my assent to what is false, and being imposed upon by this deceiver, whatever be his power and artifice. But this undertaking is arduous, and a certain indolence insensibly leads me back to my ordinary course of life; and just as the captive, who, perchance, was enjoying in his dreams an imaginary liberty, when he begins to suspect that it is but a vision, dreads awakening, and conspires with the agreeable illusions that the deception may be prolonged; so I, of my own accord, fall back into the train of my former beliefs, and fear to arouse myself from my slumber, lest the time of laborious wakefulness that would succeed this quiet rest, in place of bringing any light of day, should prove inadequate to dispel the

darkness that will arise from the difficulties that have now been raised.

Meditation II, Of the Nature of the Human Mind;

...

1. The Meditation of yesterday has filled my mind with so many doubts, that it is no longer in my power to forget them. Nor do I see, meanwhile, any principle on which they can be resolved; and, just as if I had fallen all of a sudden into very deep water, I am so greatly disconcerted as to be unable either to plant my feet firmly on the bottom or sustain myself by swimming on the surface. I will, nevertheless, make an effort, and try anew the same path on which I had entered yesterday, that is, proceed by casting aside all that admits of the slightest doubt, not less than if I had discovered it to be absolutely false; and I will continue always in this track until I shall find something that is certain, or at least, if I can do nothing more, until I shall know with certainty that there is nothing certain. Archimedes, that he might transport the entire globe from the place it occupied to another, demanded only a point that was firm and immovable; so, also, I shall be entitled to entertain the highest expectations, if I am fortunate enough to discover only one thing that is certain and indubitable.

2. I suppose, accordingly, that all the things which I see are false (fictitious); I believe that none of those objects which my fallacious memory represents ever existed; I suppose that I possess no senses; I believe that body, figure, extension, motion, and place are merely fictions of my mind. What is there, then, that can be esteemed true? Perhaps this only, that there is absolutely nothing certain.

3. But how do I know that there is not something different altogether from the objects I have now enumerated, of which it is impossible to entertain the slightest doubt? Is there not a God, or some being, by whatever name I may designate him, who causes these thoughts to arise in my mind? But why suppose such a being, for it may be I myself am capable of producing them? Am I, then, at least not something? But I before denied that I possessed senses or a body; I hesitate, however, for what follows from that? Am I so dependent on the body and the senses that without these I cannot exist? But I had the persuasion that there was absolutely nothing in the world, that there was no sky and no earth, neither minds nor bodies; was I not, therefore, at the same time, persuaded that I did not exist? Far from it; I assuredly existed, since I was persuaded. But there is I know not what being, who is possessed at once of the highest power and the deepest cunning, who is constantly employing all his ingenuity in deceiving me. Doubtless, then, I exist, since I am deceived; and, let him deceive me as he may, he can never bring it about that I am nothing, so long as I shall be conscious that I am something. So that it must, in fine, be maintained, all things being maturely and carefully considered, that this proposition (pronunciatum) I am, I exist, is necessarily true each time it is expressed by me, or conceived in my mind.

Chapter 2
Ethics

Comprehension questions you should be able to answer after reading this introduction:

1. *What are altruistic motivations?*
2. *What are egoistic motivations?*
3. *What is the difference between a descriptive theory and a prescriptive theory?*
4. *What is psychological egoism? What does it claim about human motivation?*
5. *Why would psychological egoism, if true, have such a significant impact on our understanding of ethics?*
6. *What are some possible problems for (objections to) psychological egoism?*
7. *What are subjective claims? What are objective claims?*
8. *How do "Simple Subjectivists" understand moral claims? What makes a moral claim "true," according to subjectivism? How do Emotivists understand moral "claims?"*
9. *What do subjectivists mean when they say moral claims are neither analytically true nor empirically verifiable? Why would this be an argument for moral claims being subjective, rather than objective?*
10. *What do subjectivists mean when they say that moral claims are "conventional," rather than objective?*
11. *If subjectivism is true, can anyone ever be mistaken about a moral value judgment? Why or why not?*
12. *If subjectivism is true, how would we have to understand a person's moral "progress" (or regress)?*
13. *If subjectivism is true, how would we have to interpret claims that some people (e.g., Martin Luther King Jr.) were morally better than other people (e.g., Osama Bin Laden)?*
14. *If subjectivism is true, how must we understand "disagreement" on moral issues? How will moral conflict be resolved?*
15. *What makes something morally right or wrong, according to cultural relativism?*
16. *What is meant by an "observation of cultural differences?" Why is this not necessarily identical to cultural relativism?*
17. *Explain Benedict's argument concerning "normality" and "morality." What is she trying to prove? How might someone try to refute her argument?*
18. *What is the "argument from tolerance" and how does it show a mistaken understanding of cultural relativism, if actually used to support CR?*

19. *Why is it that CR can't require universal toleration or respect for diversity? If CR is true, how would we have to understand cross-cultural comparisons on moral issues?*
20. *If CR is true, how would we have to understand the moral status of moral reformers, at the time of their reform efforts?*
21. *Why is the claim the "culture" is a "vague concept" a possible problem for CR?*
22. *What does James Rachels mean when he suggests that some "cultural differences" are actually just different manifestations/expressions of the same moral values?*
23. *Why does Rachels think that there are some universal moral values, found in every culture? What does he offer as examples? How does he try to prove this?*
24. *What are Lewis' criticisms of CR?*

When one first studies ethics, it might not be immediately obvious what one is "doing." Are you training yourself to be a morally better person? Possibly—but not necessarily. The study of ethics doesn't entail moral "self-improvement."

The reality is that the vast majority of us (including you, I presume) are already morally-motivated persons. That is simply to say that you already have a sense of what is right or wrong, that you already have a "conscience," that you are already (generally) motivated to be a good person. If that is not the case, this course is unlikely to help you, sociopath that you are!

Clearly, there are many different interpretations of what is morally good or bad, and to say that each of us already has a sense of what is morally right and wrong is certainly not to say that we can never be mistaken about such judgments, but that most of us are already concerned with "morality," at least, is a given. If not, it is unlikely that a formal study of ethics will change that.

Ethics, by the way, is the formal study of moral concepts and moral decision-making. Ethics concerns the study of questions such as, but not limited to, the following:

- How do we know what is morally right, or wrong?
- Is there any such thing as an "objective" moral code?
- Is "selfishness" a virtue, or a vice?
- Is abortion morally acceptable?
- Am I morally obligated to donate a portion of my resources (such as time or money or effort) to those "worse off" than me?

These are all interesting questions, and there are many more besides. Our focus, of necessity, will be much more limited. If you find this material interesting, I encourage you to continue your study, perhaps by reading books, or taking courses, focusing specifically on ethics. For our purposes, we will focus on one very specific cluster of topics that I label "challenges" to ethics." They are "challenges" in that each one of them, if taken seriously, will require a significant revision of what is likely a common, and maybe even a "common sense," understanding of the project of ethics itself.

Ethics is the formal study of moral principles, decision making, right and wrong behavior, virtue and vice, etc. It concerns what we should, or should not, do. To even speak in terms of what we *should* do presupposes that we have a choice. This is why the free will debate is so intimately bound to ethics. It is a curious thing to tell me that I should not lie if it is literally impossible for me to tell the truth. A taken-for-granted principle in ethics is that "ought implies can." That is, if I ought to do X, it must be possible for me to do X; and, if I ought to refrain from X, that must be possible for me to refrain from doing X.

One of the first "challenges" to ethics we will consider is what sorts of moral obligations might apply to us. To begin, it will be useful to distinguish two basic kinds of motivation: altruistic, and egoistic.

Altruism: acting for the benefit of others; acting for the sake of others; foregoing some benefit for oneself so that another may enjoy a benefit instead

Egoism: acting for self-benefit; acting from self-interest; promoting one's own good (possibly at the expense of another's)

Presumably, the most morally relevant of those two types of motivations is the altruistic variety. After all, it's easy to think of moral obligations that involve acting for the benefit of others. The most obvious examples involve anything charitable. Giving money to help the poor instead of spending on something for yourself, or donating time to work for the good of others (instead of using that time for your own benefit), are both examples of altruistically motivated actions. Whether or not a particular altruistic behavior is morally required of us would, of course, be subject to interpretation and debate, but the mere idea that we are all, at least sometimes, morally obligated to put other people's interests ahead of our own seems uncontroversial.

What if altruistically motivated behavior is impossible, though?

Psychological Egoism

Psychological egoism is a *descriptive theory* of human nature. That is, rather than making recommendations (as we find in *prescriptive theories*), it seeks merely to describe the nature of something—in this case, human motivation. As such, it claims to be empirical and scientific.

According to psychological egoism (henceforth referred to as PE), every single human being, without exception, is always driven solely by egoistic motivations. Altruism is an illusion, a myth. Even those actions that we *believe* to be altruistic in intention actually serve self-interest—otherwise, they would not be performed.

A very early account of PE is found in Plato's *Republic*, as presented by Glaucon (Plato's half-brother, in real life). It is important to note that Plato was not himself a psychological egoist. At most, a character (Glaucon) in one of Plato's dialogues (*Republic*) promotes PE, sort of. . . .[13]

In seeking to explain the nature and origin of justice, Glaucon appeals to the myth of Gyges' ring. According to this myth, a shepherd named Gyges is tending his flock one day, when an earthquake splits the ground. He explores the fissure and discovers a large tomb in the shape of a horse. Inside, he finds the body of a giant. The dead giant is wearing a ring. Gyges takes the ring. The shepherd-turned-grave robber discovers that this is no ordinary ring. When he manipulates the ring a certain way, he becomes invisible! When he twists it back, he becomes visible once more. After mastering the ring, he arranges to have himself sent as the representative of his village to the royal court. Once there, he uses to power of the ring to murder the king and claim power for himself.

Before we come to any harsh judgments against Gyges, Glaucon recommends a thought experiment. Imagine there are two such magic rings, each of which renders the wearer invisible. These days, we might need to get a little more sophisticated. Perhaps you suppose that even invisible persons might still leave behind fingerprints, or hair samples, or other means by which a clever forensic investigator could identify a perpetrator. They're magic rings. We can make

[13] A footnote for those truly interested: not even Glaucon endorses PE. He finds himself in the awkward position of wanting to believe that morality and justice are intrinsically valuable, and worthy for their own sake, but concerned that this might not be true. So, he plays the role of a devil's advocate, arguing in favor of a selfish view of human nature and justice in the hopes that Socrates will leap into the conversation and prove him wrong.

them do whatever we want! Suppose the rings render the wearer invisible, magically cloaks any heat signatures, erases fingerprints, eliminates DNA evidence, etc.

Now, give one of the two rings to someone whom you regard as tremendously virtuous and just. Give the other to someone quite the opposite: a vicious and unjust jerk. What, do you suppose, each would do with the ring?

Glaucon believes that both the "just" and the "unjust" would come "at last to the same point." That is, they would each, eventually, do the same thing: whatever it is that each wanted.

To make matters more interesting, give yourself one of the rings. What would *you* do? Be honest!

If your answer includes anything you would not already do right now, without the ring, you have confirmed Glaucon's point (and his fear). If you would do something *with* the ring, that you would not do *without* it, it suggests that the reason why you refrain from that action now is not any commitment to moral principles, but fear of getting caught and punished. Remove the fear, and watch out....

The outcome of Glaucon's thought experiment provides a possible insight into human nature. If it is true that any one of us would ultimately and inevitably abuse the power of Gyges' ring, then the reason why most of us usually obey the rules and "play nice" with one another is fear. Although we would like to be able to do whatever we want, to whomever we want, whenever we want, we recognize that such behavior just isn't possible. None of us is Superman.

However powerful a given individual might be, she isn't bulletproof (to put it bluntly). No matter how wealthy, how powerful, how well-connected, each one of us is all-too-human, and all-too-vulnerable. Realizing that, and wishing to minimize the risk we face from others, we make mutual promises to "play nice." I won't rob you so long as you don't rob me. I won't kill you, so long as you don't kill me. We surrender some of our own power, and our own freedom, when we make those promises, but in exchange for that we gain security.

We behave ourselves because it is in our self-interest to do so. If it were no longer necessary, no *longer* in our self-interest (e.g., if we had Gyges' ring), we would no longer be inclined to "play nice."

Notice that the common theme in both cases is the same: self-interest. When we obey the law, it is because we perceive it is in our self-interest to do so. When we instead break the law, it is because we perceive it is in our self-interest to break it, instead.

These are understandable and even inevitable behaviors, according to psychological egoism. *According to PE, each person always pursues her own self-interest, without exception.* We can't help but do so. We're "wired" to always pursue our own self-interest. If this is true, it has profound implications for our understanding of moral obligation. The following argument illustrates why.

1. Everyone always acts from self-interest (PE).
2. If one can't do something, one is not obligated to do it ("ought implies can").
3. Altruism requires putting others' interests ahead of our own.
4. Altruism is therefore impossible (from lines 1 and 3).
5. Altruism is therefore never required (from lines 2 and 4).

Notice just how significant this is, if true. Every major ethical system in the world (with the notable exception of ethical egoism) claims that altruism is at least sometimes required of us. I'm confident that no matter what your own approach to ethics is, you believe that at least *sometimes* the morally right thing to do is to put another person's interests ahead of your own.

PE says that to do so is impossible.

You and I are *incapable* of putting other people first. Since it's impossible for us, we are never obligated to put others first. Therefore, we never have a moral obligation to behave altruistically. That means every major ethical system in the world (except for ethical egoism) is mistaken. Unless you happen to be an ethical egoist, you will need to revise your understanding of moral obligation.

If PE is true, it clearly has a profound impact on ethics. But, *is* it true? Should we believe it is? Why would anyone? The most often provided reason is because it appears that PE can provide an egoistic explanation for any action whatsoever, no matter how altruistic it might appear on the surface.

I'm going to pretend to be a psychological egoist, and set the bar very high, right from the beginning: I'm going to prove that Mother Teresa was selfish.[14]

"Mother Teresa was selfish?" you might ask.

"Certainly," I reply.

She was a nun, right? That suggests she took her religion pretty seriously. She believed in heaven and hell. As a Roman Catholic, she likely placed even greater emphasis on "works" (as opposed to faith alone) than would Protestants. In her own words: "I heard the call to give up all and follow Christ into the slums to serve Him among the poorest of the poor. It was an order. I was to leave the convent and help the poor while living among them."

On the very reasonable assumption that she believed that her actions in this world would impact her prospects in the next, the cost-benefit analysis is embarrassingly simple: a few decades of service and sacrifice in exchange for an eternity of indescribable bliss. This is easy math! By living "altruistically," Mother Teresa was promoting her own Salvation. Maybe she even didn't even have to wait in line to get into Heaven....

What's more, she was a celebrity, and not merely well-known, but beloved and admired by millions, if not billions, of people. That probably felt pretty good! She actually won the Nobel Peace Prize is 1979, and was "beatified" by the Catholic church in 2003. She needs just one more miracle attributed to her intercession, and she will be declared a Saint, as well.

Finally, by her own description, she was happy! "Poverty for us is a freedom. It is not mortification, a penance. It is joyful freedom. There is no television here, no this, no that. But we are perfectly happy." She was happy in her life. She was happy being poor. She was happy serving others.

To sum up, by serving the sick and the poor, Mother Teresa became famous and beloved, she made herself happy, and she engineered an eternity of reward for herself. Was she motivated by self-interest? So it would seem! And, if someone like Mother Teresa falls prey to egoistic interpretation, how much more easily do the rest of us? It seems that everyone (even Mother Teresa) is always driven by self-interest.

Summary (so far):

It appears to be a fact that people do indeed act for the sake of self-interest. That is, it's not difficult to think of examples where it is obvious that people acted for their own benefit, sometimes at the expense of others. It also appears that any action can be explained in terms of self-interest (e.g., Mother Teresa "serving" the poor). PE offers itself as an explanatory theory to account for those facts: all people necessarily (and exclusively) act from self-interest.

We now face the following question: is this explanatory theory (PE) the only, or at least the best, way to understand human behavior? If the answer is "yes," then we would have good reason to accept PE, and consequently accept the serious implications it would have on our understanding of ethics. If the answer is "no," however, then we may reject both PE and its serious implications. We have reviewed reasons to think PE is true, so we will consider some reasons to reject it.

---

[14] For those who aren't familiar with Mother Teresa: she was a globally-recognized Catholic nun who spent most of her life in India. She founded the "Missionaries of Charity" that included over 4,500 nuns and is active in over 130 countries. The organization runs hospices and homes for people with HIV/AIDS, leprosy and tuberculosis. It also operates soup kitchens, dispensaries and mobile clinics, child and family counseling programs, and orphanages and schools. Nuns of the order must take (and adhere to) vows of chastity, poverty and obedience, as well as a fourth vow: to give "wholehearted free service to the poorest of the poor."

Possible Problems for PE

Possible Problem #1: the "post hoc ergo propter hoc" fallacy

"Post hoc ergo propter hoc" is a Latin phrase. Roughly translated: "after the fact, therefore because of the fact."

The post hoc fallacy is an abuse of what is otherwise a perfectly legitimate form of causal inference. As I write this sentence, I first tap a key, then a letter appears on the monitor. Therefore, tapping the key causes the letter to appear. Nothing weird or presumptuous about that piece of reasoning! First one thing happens (tapping the key), then another thing happens (a letter appears), therefore the first thing (tapping) causes the second thing (appearing). Try a different example, though. I had some eggs for breakfast. Later in the day, the Dow Jones Industrial Average lost several hundred points. Therefore, my eating eggs caused the Dow to lose hundreds of points. Who would have guessed that my dietary practices exerted so much terrible influence over the U.S. economy?

They don't, of course—and I'm sure you recognize that it's silly to think that just because one thing happened first (eggs for breakfast), and then something else happened later (Dow loss), the two are somehow causally connected. When such a causal connection is hastily drawn, we have an example of the post hoc fallacy.

This kind of fallacious reasoning can occur not just with respect to causes, but also with *reasons*. For example, prior to obtaining full time employment at Rio Hondo College, I taught at several campuses, usually in the same academic terms. Some semesters, I taught at CSU Long Beach, Cal Poly Pomona, *and* UC Riverside. A typical day might involve starting in Long Beach and teaching there, then driving to Riverside and teaching a class there, then driving to Pomona to teach another class, and returning home to Long Beach to collapse from exhaustion, grade exams, prep for the next day, or whatever else seemed most appropriate. As a result of all that commuting, I burned up a lot of gasoline. It would be a mistake, though, to think in the following way:

1. Professor Preston drove to work.
2. As a result, he burned gasoline.
3. Therefore, he drove in order to burn gasoline.

I assure you that burning gas was not my goal. If I could have avoided it, I would have. My goals were many (e.g., to earn a paycheck, to advance my career, to do what I love, etc.), but burning gas was not among them. Just because an action produced a particular outcome (and a predictable one, at that) does not mean that the action was done *for the sake of* that outcome.

How does this apply to PE, you might wonder? Psychological egoists note that Mother Teresa helped the poor. As a consequence, she was made happy, became famous, and possibly earned herself eternal reward. Therefore, she helped the poor *for the sake of* her own happiness, fame, and eternal reward.

This is possibly true, of course, but may we simply *assume* it to be true? Just because helping others made her happy, does that mean she did it *in order* to promote her own happiness? Are we justified in assuming that to be the case, when we weren't justified in assuming that I commuted for the sake of burning gas? Isn't it possible (simply *possible*) that she helped the poor for some other reason (e.g., because it was the right thing to do, or because she thought it was God's will), and, as a result of her actions, she was made happy—but that her own happiness wasn't her goal? Consider (and compare) the following charts:

Table A

Action	Result	(inferred) Goal
Help the poor	Feel happy	Feel happy
Commute	Burn gas	Burn gas

Table B

Action	Result	(inferred) Goal
Help the poor	Feel happy	Do the right thing
Commute	Burn gas	Earn a paycheck

PE seems to assume that the egoistic explanation, represented in (A), is the correct explanation—but assuming and proving are two very different things. One might also assume that I commuted in order to burn gas! But, the critic of PE might allege that just as the correct explanation of my commuting is something other than burning gas (e.g., earning a paycheck), so too might the correct explanation of Mother Teresa's behavior be something other than self-interest. In other words, the explanation offered in (B) could be the correct kind of explanation. Unless a reasonable causal connection can be traced and *demonstrated*, it appears that PE is possibly guilty of the post hoc fallacy.

Can such a causal connection be demonstrated? Seemingly not. Consult your own experience. How often do you perform an action with your goal being "to satisfy self-interest?" Isn't it, instead, usually the case that your goal is something else altogether, and that when you achieve *that* goal, your self-interest is (at least sometimes, somehow conceived) served?

For example, suppose you buy your mother a nice present for Mother's Day, and she is visibly happy when you give it to her. You then feel proud and happy, and have a wonderful Mother's Day with her. Presumably, you could not have felt "proud and happy" if you had not desired to make your mother happy with the gift. If you couldn't care less about that, why would her happiness have made you proud and happy yourself? Implicitly, then, your desire was to make your mother happy—*that* is what you were pursuing. To have experienced happiness when your desire was satisfied, you had to have a desire other than your own happiness! If so, this suggests that it is not the case that *all* our actions are motivated by our own happiness, or self-interest. Rather, our actions seem to be motivated by all kinds of other desires, and when those desires are satisfied we often experience happiness or the fulfillment of our self-interest as a *result*.

Possible problem #2: Unfalsifiability

PE is often regarded as very convincing (at least initially) because it seems capable of providing an egoistic explanation for *any and every* action whatsoever.

Example	Egoistic Explanation
Helping the poor	Feeling self-rightous
Donating to charity	Tax Deduction
Risking your life for another	Avoiding survivor's guilt
Donating a kidney to a friend	Adulation for being a hero

On the surface, at least, this might seem like an incredible strength of the theory. No matter what example you provide, a psychological egoist can show how it is motivated by self-interest, even if this requires appealing to subconscious motivations.

You think you helped the poor because it was the "right thing to do," but really you did it to feel good about yourself. Don't think so? Well, that should come as no surprise. It's in your self-interest to not think of yourself as selfish, and instead to think of yourself as truly generous and charitable. If you were honest with yourself, though, and dug deeply enough into the layers of your motivation, you would eventually uncover your own self-interest. Don't think so? You obviously haven't delved deeply, and honestly enough, yet. Keep up the soul-searching! When may you stop? When you finally realize that your motivation was self-interested, of course!

Do you sense the problem, yet? Taken to this extreme, PE's explanatory power is quickly revealed to be falsifiable. This is not a virtue for a theory. If there is no possible way to disprove the theory, no possible counter-example that can be provided, the theory is unfalsifiable. This is another way of saying that it is unverifiable, untestable.

This is a not a good thing for a theory of human nature, for a theory that claims to be an explanatory theory, for a theory that cloaks itself in the language of science. In science, if a hypothesis is not testable, it is not scientific. End of discussion.

If the hypothesis that all human acts are egoistic is not testable (because it is not falsifiable), it is not scientific. End of discussion. Proponents of PE may *assume* that all our motivations are egoistic, they may *assert* that all our motivations are egoistic, but assuming and asserting and not at all the same thing as *proving*.

Possible Problem #3: Defining "self-interest"

PE claims that all our motivations are egoistic, that we always act in our own self-interest. By now, you're probably wondering what, exactly, that means. After all, "acting in self-interest" may mean any number of things, some of which being more plausible than others. Let us consider some possible meanings of "self-interest." For each candidate, we will consider both its meaning and whether, if true, it would rule out altruistic motivations.

1. We always do what is best for us.

Perhaps "self-interest," as understood by PE, means that we always do what is best for ourselves. If this were true, then altruistic motivations would be impossible, given that we always do what is best for ourselves. That rules out putting what is best for another first, if so doing would not be best for you as well. But, does it seem to be true that "we always do what is best for ourselves?"

It's clear that we do *not* always do what is best for ourselves. Sometimes we behave foolishly, recklessly, and dangerously. Sometimes we ruin our lives by making stupid mistakes. Sometimes the damage isn't so dire, but we recognize our errors all the same. Clearly, we do not always do what is best, even for ourselves. So, if this is what PE means by "self-interest," PE would be mistaken.

2. We always do what we *think* is best for us.

This seems to be a more plausible candidate, as it allows for honest mistakes. Perhaps we always do what *seems* to be best, but it turns out, in retrospect, that we were wrong. "I thought that cheating on the exam would be best for me, but it turns out I was mistaken. I had no idea the professor was so skilled at catching cheaters...."

This candidate is also a clear threat to altruistic motivations, since (like #1) it rules out ever acting in such a way that benefits another unless you *think* it's also best for yourself.

While this interpretation is more plausible than #1, it still seems false. If you're anything like me, you've had experiences in which you've said to yourself something along the lines of:

> "I know I shouldn't do this, but...."
> "I know I'm going to regret this...."
> "I know this is a bad idea, however...."

It seems to be the case that we sometimes do something while fully aware of the fact that it's not smart, or wise, or healthy, or prudent, or even the least bit a good idea. But, we do it anyway. If so, it would appear that it is not the case that we always do even what we *think* to be best.

3. We always do what we want most to do, all things considered.

This seems most plausible of all. Perhaps what PE boils down to is that we always do what we most want, and sometimes what we most want is pretty stupid, or harmful, or reckless. For example, a smoker wants to quit, and knows she should, but she continues smoking anyway. How can we understand that? Simply: although she wanted to quit, she wanted another cigarette even more. A person wants to lose weight, but still doesn't begin to exercise or control caloric intake. Explanation? Although he wants to lose weight, he wants to enjoy food and avoid strenuous exercise even more. What about when the smoker finally quits? Simple: at that point, her desire to quit was stronger than her desire to smoke. Whatever it is that we do, it's what we most wanted to do—otherwise, we'd have done something else.

So far, so good. A critic might wonder, however, just how it is that we discern what we most want to do. How can such things be identified? Easily, according to this interpretation of PE. We simply identify the action performed. We can identify what we most want, retroactively, by observing behavior. The mere fact that we perform an action X is evidence that what we most wanted was to do X---otherwise, we'd have done Y (or Z, etc.). Closer inspection, however, reveals this understanding to be problematic—circular, in fact. Consider the following:

1. We always do what *we most want to do.*

Now, what is it that we most want to do? What does that phrase mean?

2. What we most want to do, is *whatever it is that we actually do* (otherwise, we would have done something else).

So, "what we most want to do" is understood to be "what we actually do." If this is correct, I should be able to substitute "what we actually do" for "what we most want to do" wherever I find it expressed (such as in statement #1 above). Behold.

3. We always do what we actually do.

Brilliant! Obviously true. Also trivially true. Meaninglessly true. "We always do what we actually do?" How about simplifying that expression?

4. We do what we do.

This is what is called a "tautology." A tautology involves a repetition of meaning, saying (essentially) the same thing, but using different words—especially when the additional words fail to provide additional clarity. Of course it is true that "we do what we do." The problem is that this tells us nothing interesting. It's a safe assumption that all intentional human action is motivated by *some* sort of desire, that we perform actions on the basis of *some* sort of motivation. But, does it seem accurate to identify every and any desire or motive with "self-interest?"

> *"In assessing whether an action is self-interested, the issue is not whether the action is based on a desire; the issue is what kind of desire it is based on. If what you want is to help someone else, then your motive is altruistic, not self-interested." (James Rachels)*

PE claims that all actions are motivated by self-interest, that all motivations are egoistic. This seems obviously false, if we understand "self-interest" to mean something like "putting yourself first, at the expense of others." One can immediately begin to generate counter-examples: charitable giving, the life and work of Mother Theresa, sacrificing your own life to save another's, etc. Given the categorical nature of PE, all it takes is a single counter-example to refute the theory. In order to defeat these sorts of counter-examples, PE must be understood in such a way that even examples like those can be understood as egoistically motivated. This requires stretching the meaning of "self-interest" so as to incorporate every possible action whatsoever. Concepts are kind of like gum, though: the more you stretch it, the weaker and more transparent it becomes. Concepts have meaning not only by what they include, but also by what they *exclude*. Stretch a concept so that *nothing* is excluded, and *everything* is included, and the concept ceases to have meaning!

For example, in sports, the "MVP" is literally *the* "most valuable player." "The most" is a superlative term. By definition, only one member of the team can be the MVP. Imagine that a well-intentioned Little League coach is trying to increase the self-esteem of his players, and at the annual awards banquet announces that *every* player is the MVP that year. What does "MVP" now mean? When every player is the MVP, all MVP means (now) is "player." The word has literally lost its meaning, by being misapplied—no matter how well-intentioned the gesture might have been.

As another example, pretend you are an anthropologist, and you are visiting a recently discovered tribe of people called "Prestonians," where the inhabitants speak "Prestonian" due to the pervasiveness of the word "Preston" in their language. You are trying to learn this language, and a member of the Preston tribe points to what you call a tree, and says "Preston." He then points to what you call a dog and says "Preston." He points to another tribesman punching someone in the face and says "Preston," then points to a local couple kissing passionately: "Preston." He later points to a woman giving birth and says "Preston," and then to a man who just died of a heart attack: "Preston." After several days, you realize that everything he points to, he calls "Preston," and whenever you attempt to ask him a question in your own language, with the additional use of pointing and hand gestures, he always pauses, seems to reflect, and then answers "Preston."

What does the word Preston mean, in his language? You don't have the slightest clue, do you? *Everything* seemed to be "Preston"—which made it impossible for you to discern what the word *actually means.*

In the same way, psychological egoists point to "everything" and call it "egoistic," or "selfish." Saving a life? Selfish. Taking a life? Selfish. Helping the poor? Selfish. Hurting the poor? Selfish. Going to class? Selfish. Skipping class? Selfish. Given this usage, "selfish" or "self-interested" has no more meaning than does "Preston!" If "Preston" means "everything," it actually means *nothing.* So too with selfishness, or self-interest.

PE has an easy way to fix this problem: tighten up the meaning of self-interest so that "acting from self-interest" ceases to imply a tautology. If PE does this, the "definitional" problem can be resolved—but it is soon replaced by a new problem: it is no longer anything close to obvious that all actions really are motivated by self-interest!

It is possible that even seemingly heroic actions are motivated by self-interest, but is it plausible? Think about what this would mean. On September 11th, 2001, 346 firefighters were killed. They were moving into the World Trade Towers, while everyone else was trying to get out. PE does provide a possible explanation for their seemingly heroic behavior: self-interest. Perhaps they wanted to feel like heroes. Perhaps they didn't want to avoid losing their jobs, or being scorned by their peers for cowardice. In any event, PE claims their motivations must have been self-interested. On September 12th, 2001, USA Today reported that two men (Michael Benfante and John Cerqueira) spent an hour carrying an unnamed woman who used a wheelchair down 68 flights of stairs, at clear and obvious risk to their own life. PE offers an explanation for why they did so: self-interest (somehow conceived). Millions of ordinary citizens donated money, and time, and blood for the relief effort after 9-11. Why did they all do so? Self-interest, according to PE.

When I was a senior in high school, my father lost his job due to "downsizing." He ended up finding another job, but there's a story behind it. My dad had been a broadcast engineer for most of his working life. He had left a position as the Director of Engineering at a television station to take a sales job with a large company. He sold the broadcasting equipment he had used, purchased, and knew so much about in his capacity as an engineer. Much earlier in his career, he had worked for a boss he disliked very much—so much so that he took another job in another State to get away from him. Years later, that same boss became the boss of the television station my dad had left when he took the sales position. Then, he was "downsized" from his sales position, and found himself unemployed, and wondering how he was going to support his family. As I mentioned, he did find another job—an entry level engineer position at his old television station. He was the lowest seniority person in the very same department that he used to manage. He was working beneath the same guys that he used to supervise—and his boss was the *same guy* that inspired him to move across the country just to get away from him. Only as an adult now myself, can I appreciate how humbling that must have been for him: to have to take a job from a man he disliked, and did not respect; to have once been the manager, and to then be the "low man on the totem pole," with the worst shifts and the least seniority. What I found out from him decades later, but had never known before, was that he had been offered *another* job. It would have required us to move, however, and he refused to move during my senior year in high school. He knew how disruptive that would be to me socially, and emotionally, and (more importantly) academically. I was a good student, and was poised to be the first person in our immediate family to go to college, and one of only a handful in our entire extended family. He didn't want to mess things up for me. So, instead, he humbled himself and essentially started over in his career working for a man he despised. It seems to me that he acted *selflessly*, for my sake—certainly not for his own. However, the psychological egoist must interpret his actions as having been motivated by his own self-interest.

It is possible that self-interest is the explanation for all those actions, and for any other you or I might imagine. Since PE is unfalsifiable, we can't, of course, know with certainty whether those actions (or any other) really are motivated by self-interest. So, all you and I can do is try to figure out what seems to make the most sense. If, based on your experience of the world and how it works, it appears to you that PE offers the best explanation of human behavior, including the examples above, then PE is probably a compelling theory to you. On the other hand, if it appears to you that humans are at least sometimes capable of genuine altruism, that not every action is motivated by self-interest, then you will probably reject PE.

Subjectivism

As I hope you recall from our critical thinking chapter, a "claim" (in this context) is simply a statement, an assertion, a proposition. One of the features of claims is that they have a "truth value." This is just a fancy way of saying that a claim must be either true or false, even if we're not sure which one it is. For example, "Ted Preston is a philosophy professor" is a claim. That claim is either true, or it isn't. If you have no idea who Ted Preston is (or to which Ted Preston I refer), you might not be sure whether it is a true statement, but you can be confident that it's either true or it's false. If you have enough information, you might be confident as to which one of those two truth values is accurate. But, what is it that would make the claim true (or false)? How would we know? The answer depends upon the kinds of claims we're talking about.

We may divide claims into two basic categories: objective claims, and subjective claims. Objective claims concern facts, while subjective claims concern opinion. If a claim is objective, its truth or falsity is independent of whatever I believe or desire. It is sometimes said that "facts don't discriminate." If it is a fact that 2 + 2 = 4, then it is true that 2 +2 = 4 even if I believe that 2 + 2 = 17, even if my deepest desire is that 2 + 2 = 17. Bluntly, it doesn't matter what I believe or desire. If it is a fact that 2 + 2 = 4, then the truth of that claim applies equally to every person at every time and at every place. If I disagree, I am just plain mistaken. If a billion people disagree, then a billion people are mistaken.

Error is possible when we're dealing with objective claims. In fact, one of the ways to figure out if a claim is objective is to ask yourself what it would mean if two or more people disagreed about the claim. If their disagreement indicates at least one of the people is mistaken, that's a pretty good sign that the claim is objective. If I think that 2 +2 = 17, and you think that it equals 4, that's an indicator that one of us mistaken (or maybe both of us are mistaken, and the correct answer is some third option that neither one of us came up with).

Subjective claims, in contrast, concern opinions and personal taste preferences. Disagreement does not indicate error. If I think a meal is delicious, and you think it's too spicy, it's not the case that one of us is "wrong" about the meal. If I love the band "Switchfoot," and you can't bear to listen to them, it's not the case that one of us is in error. Opinions are indexed to particular people, at particular times and places. The truth or falsity of a subjective claim is "up to me" in a meaningful sort of way—unlike the truth or falsity of objective (factual) claims.

One of the kinds of claims we make—indeed, one of the most important kinds of claims we can make—are moral claims. Moral claims are simply assertions involving some moral issue. "Eating meat is wrong." "War is never justifiable." "Abortion is wrong." "Premarital sex is morally acceptable." These are all examples of moral claims. What we now have to address is whether moral claims are subjective, or objective? Are moral claims more like answers to math problems, or more like food preferences? First, consider a visual representation that applies if moral claims

are *objective*

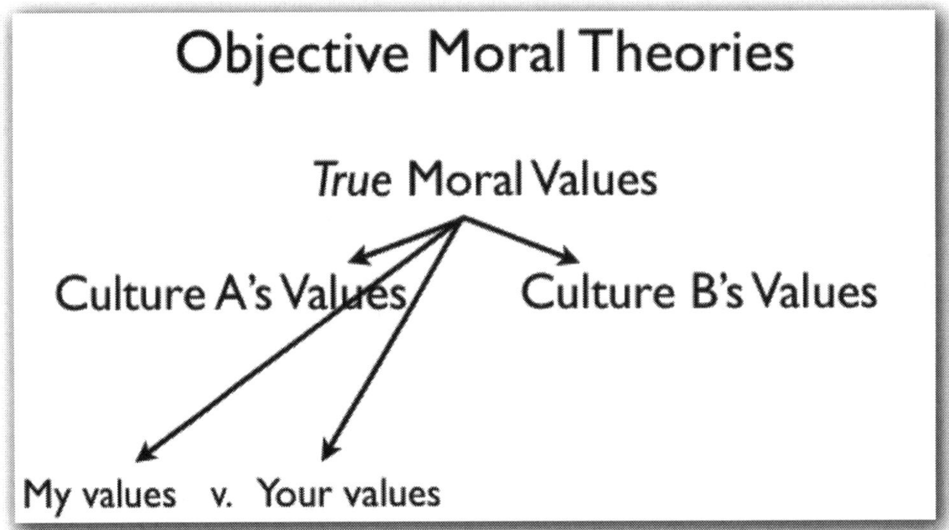

If moral claims are objective, then they appeal to facts (as opposed to opinions). I am going to begin an extended analogy that should resonate with most of you: tests and answer keys.

An answer key for a test is a version of the test that includes all of the correct answers. When a student takes a test for which there is an answer key, the student's answers are compared to the answer key for grading purposes. Consider the following mathematical example.

X + 3 = 5

Solve for X.

My answer: X = 1
Your answer: X = 2
Answer key: X = 2

The correct answer (i.e., the answer found in the answer key) is that X = 2. Your answer was 2. You got it right. My answer was 1. I got it wrong. As mentioned a few paragraphs ago, before we even looked at the answer key, we had reason to believe at least one of us was wrong. After all, we gave two different answers to the same math problem. It was possible that neither one of us got the correct answer, but what wasn't possible was that *both* of us got the correct answer.

If moral claims are objective, then there are moral *facts*. As facts, they apply equally to all people at all times. Facts don't discriminate. These moral facts are our moral "answer key." We can imagine that we are all continually engaged in a process of moral "test-making." Each day, by virtue of what we do, or fail to do, we are morally tested. As communities, too, we are being "tested" by virtue of the laws, policies, and actions we take (or fail to take) as communities. What determines whether an action taken by either an individual or by a community is morally correct? The "answer key."

If, for example, it is a moral fact that killing innocent people is morally wrong, then if you and I give two different "answers" to that same moral "question," one of us right, and the other wrong (here's a hint: whichever one of us is a murderer, is wrong). If a particular culture allows, let alone perpetrates, the killing of innocent people, then that culture is *wrong* on that particular issue. Obviously, there is room for plenty of spirited debate as to just which moral values are "facts" belonging in the universal moral answer key, but what any objective approach to ethics will have in common is the belief that there is such an answer key, even if we don't fully agree as to its contents.

According to a subjectivist approach to morality, moral claims are matters of personal opinion. As such, there is no "fact" that validates some opinions, but refutes others. Very simply, if I believe something is morally wrong, then, for me, it is morally wrong. If you believe differently, then it's not wrong for you. If you and I disagree, it's not the case that one of us is mistaken—we simply have different opinions on the matter.

If subjectivism is true, then moral claims share the same (or at least a similar) status as other claims indicating personal preference or perspective. A comparison of objective and subjective claims might make this clearer, as well as make clear one of the significant implications of subjectivism.

Objective claims	Subjective claims
• 2+2 = 4 • Bachelors are unmarried men • The final two Democratic presidential candidates in 2016 are Hillary Clinton and Bernie Sanders • The director of *The Hateful Eight* is Quentin Tarantino • Bacon is usually made from pork • Abortion is the intentional termination of a pregnancy	• Math is boring • It's better to be a bachelor than married • Bernie Sanders is the better Presidential candidate • The Hateful Eight was awesome! • Bacon is delicious. • Abortion is morally wrong.

One of the observations we can make about these groupings is that all of the examples of objective claims are either "analytic" claims or are empirically verifiable.

An analytic claim is a claim that is true (or false) by definition, by the very meaning of the words it contains. 2 + 2 = 4 is an analytic claim. Given the meaning of two, four, plus, and equals, we know that it is true that 2 + 2 = 4. The same is also true of our second example: bachelors are unmarried men. That is simply the definition of a bachelor. Assuming you know what the word means, you know that it is true that bachelors are unmarried men, "by definition." The final example from the objective column is also an analytic claim. Abortion just is the intentional termination of a pregnancy.

The remaining examples of objective claims are not true by definition, but can be demonstrated to be true (or false) with a little bit of research and effort. Simply by checking to see which were the final two candidates for the Democratic party in 2016 on primary ballots and in Democratic debates allows us to verify that the claim is true. Similarly, we can check the film credits for *The Hateful Eight* using resources such as "imdb" allows to verify who directed that film.[15] Finally, a survey of bacon production, or even a simple examination at a grocery store, would allow us to verify that most bacon is pork (as opposed to turkey, for example).

Now turn to the examples of subjective claims, and notice a stark contrast: they are neither analytic claims nor empirically verifiable. Starting with the claim that math is boring, regardless of whether *you* find math to be boring, you undoubtedly recognize that there is nothing inherent to our very concept of math that renders it boring (unlike being unmarried being inherent to our concept of a bachelor), nor is there any way to "prove" that math is boring. Even if you survey thousands of people, and discover that most people describe math as boring, all you have proven is that "*most people surveyed describe math as boring*," not that math *is* boring.

With regard to whether it's better to be

15 http://www.imdb.com/title/tt3460252/?ref_=nv_sr_1

married or a bachelor, once again we would all recognize that responses will vary. Some people love being married, others love being single—and neither preference is either analytically true nor empirically verifiable as "correct." So, too, with preferring Bernie Sanders to Hillary Clinton, whether or not *The Hateful Eight* was "awesome," and even whether or not bacon is delicious.

Last, but certainly not least, what about that claim that abortion is morally wrong? This is clearly a moral claim (i.e., a claim concerning a moral issue), and some subjectivists will say that, like those other claims, it is neither analytic nor capable of empirical verification. This leads us to an official argument for moral subjectivism.

Moral claims are not objective because moral claims aren't provable

1. Objective claims must be either analytic claims or empirically verifiable.
2. Moral claims are not analytic claims.
3. Moral claims are not empirically verifiable.
4. Therefore, moral claims are not objective claims.
5. Therefore, moral claims are subjective claims.

Let us now consider the argument, one line at a time. As with any subject in philosophy, the first premise is subject to disagreement.[16] However, that objective claims must be either analytic or empirically verifiable is a widely-accepted understanding of objective claims, and will be our working definition, given our limited purposes.

The second and third premises are much more important and interesting. The second premise claims that moral claims are not analytic claims. That is, they are not inherently true or false in the way that "bachelors are unmarried men" is inherently true, and "Ted is a married bachelor" is inherently false.

Consider the moral claim that it is wrong to steal. You might agree with that statement. You might think it is "obviously" true. However, you probably also acknowledge that if someone disagrees, and asserts that it is *not* wrong to steal (perhaps because they have a particular understanding of "property" and "property rights?"), that person has not uttered a literal logical contradiction. You might think that person is mistaken, but the person hasn't said something literally incoherent—unlike someone who says a bachelor is married. Even in cases of passionate disagreement, such as between "Pro-Life" and "Pro-Choice" camps, there is no notion that the "other side" believes something literally incoherent and logically impossible. If you agree with this reasoning, then this indicates that moral claims are not *analytic* claims, not true (or false) *by definition*.

The third premise claims that moral claims are not empirically verifiable. To return to our example of theft, supporters of this argument would say that there is no way to *prove* that stealing is wrong (or disprove it). After all, what test could someone propose that would *prove* the wrongness of stealing?

You could certainly prove the financial impact of stealing, or you could verify what someone (e.g., the thief, or the victim) *said* about stealing, or you could try to document the ownership of the item in question to determine whether a theft actually occurred, or you could verify that the act was indeed a violation of the law simply by consulting the laws in the place where the act occurred—but what verifiable fact or feature of reality corresponds to the *wrongness* of the stealing? Some subjectivists answer that there is no such verifiable fact or feature, and therefore moral claims are not empirically verifiable.

If objective claims must be either analytic, or empirically verifiable, and if moral claims are neither, then it seems to follow from that that moral claims are not objective. If they are not objective, but are, nevertheless, claims, then what remains for them is to be *subjective* claims.

Another argument for subjectivism relies upon the judgment that moral claims are not "natural." That is, they do not come from "Nature,"

16 Indeed, an amusing possible criticism of this claim is that it is, itself, neither analytic nor empirically verifiable, and therefore not an objective claim, according to its own standards.. . .

but are rather the product of human conventions, and are therefore arbitrary and subjective, as opposed to objective.

Moral claims aren't objective because they are merely conventional

By way of analogy, consider the game of chess. In chess, there are certain rules that govern the movement of the pieces. Rooks can only move forward and backward, or from side to side. Bishops can only move diagonally. Knights can only move in "L" shapes. If I try to move a Knight one space directly forward, I have broken one of the rules of chess—but the rules themselves are completely conventional and arbitrary. There is nothing "natural" and necessary about chess. Human beings happened to invent a game, and came up with a handful of arbitrary rules that govern it. Unlike the "rules" (i.e., Laws) of Nature, though, they are optional and arbitrary. Gravity, in contrast, is neither arbitrary, conventional, nor optional.

Some subjectivists will argue that moral "laws" (rules) are far more like the rules of chess than like the Laws of Nature, and for that reason are subjective rather than objective. Or, to put it a bit differently, natural laws are descriptive (i.e., they tell us how things in nature will behave) whereas moral claims are prescriptive (i.e., they tell us how moral agents *should* behave).

1. Natural Laws are descriptive, not prescriptive
2. Moral claims, though, are prescriptive.
3. Therefore, moral claims are not natural/objective but are conventional/subjective.

In support of the first premise, note that we recognize that natural laws don't make recommendations, but instead describe, explain, and predict. For example, Newton's law of Universal Gravitation claims that "any two bodies in the universe attract each other with a force that is directly proportional to the product of their masses and inversely proportional to the square of the distance between them." There is nothing to be recommended here. Newton wasn't suggesting how bodies should behave, but describing how they do behave. There are no value judgments in that description.

Even when we describe the behavior of other living things, we don't imply any sort of value judgments, but merely offer amoral descriptions of their behavior.

> *"A hawk that seizes a fish from the sea kills it, but does not murder it; and another hawk that seizes the fish from the talons of the first takes it, but does not steal it - for none of these things is forbidden."*[17]

The comparison here is interesting. The behavior of a hawk taking a fish from another hawk and a human taking a fish from another human are outwardly the same—or at least very similar. Why is one "taking" and the other "stealing?" Chimpanzees are somewhat notorious among primatologists for killing other (rival) chimps.[18] Most of us, however, would call that behavior "killing" rather than "murder"—and even if we use the word "murder" we would probably acknowledge that we are using the word differently than when we use it with human actions. If, by chance, you think chimps are sufficiently self-conscious that such killing really *is* murder, then switch my example to a black widow spider killing and eating her mate, and now ponder how killing became murder when it reached the chimpanzee.

What, though, justifies our different judgment? Why is it "killing" if a chimpanzee ends the life of another chimpanzee through violence, but "murder" if a human does the same thing to another human? From a purely naturalistic perspective, humans are primates just as are chimpanzees, after all. . . .

At this point, the subjectivist could say that it is clear that Nature does not prohibit killing. In fact, killing (in the form of predation) is a *necessity*

[17] Richard Taylor, Ethics, Faith, and Reason, pp.14.
[18] http://www.bbc.com/news/science-environment-29237276

for a great many species! Killing fellow humans is "wrong" not because "Nature" says so, but because humans have said so. In effect, we have set up some "rules" for a "game," and one of those more common rules is that we're not (usually) allowed to kill one another. There is, however, nothing "natural" about that rule any more than there is something "natural" about the rules of chess. We can easily imagine different rules for human behavior just as we can imagine different rules for chess. Accordingly, given the difference between moral claims and Natural Laws, we should recognize moral claims as arbitrary, conventional prescriptions rather than objective descriptions.

Consider, now, the implications of this, if true. Given the subjective nature of moral claims, some will focus on the "rules" of the "games" we create as communities, and identify morality in terms of those collective rules. We will consider this interpretation in the form of cultural relativism in a later section.

Others, though, will question the validity of the "game" itself, and emphasize the arbitrary nature of those rules. If the moral rules are "arbitrary," what could make one rule more legitimate than another? There are a lot of different ways to play Poker. In some versions, the Joker is in play, and is "wild"—meaning it can stand for any card you want. Or, in some versions, it can only stand for specific cards. Or, some people don't include the Joker at all.

Which of those variations is "true" Poker? Who has the authority to make such a judgment? Maybe some people like playing Poker without a Joker, and others like playing with the Joker being wild. Which of those groups is "right?" Does that question even make any sense? How could one style of play somehow be more "correct" than the other, if we acknowledge that the rules of Poker are completely arbitrary and products of human convention to begin with?

Now imagine that we consider moral "rules" (i.e., moral claims) in the same way. There are many different styles of "play," representing many different personal preferences. If you and I disagree about some particular moral issue, neither one of us is "mistaken." For one of us to be mistaken, there would need to be some sort of independent "answer key" against which we could compare our own values.

What or who could provide that "answer key?" Someone else? Why should her opinion count for more than our own? What about majority opinion? Isn't that just popularity?

Just because lots of people enjoy Country Music doesn't mean someone is mistaken for not liking it. Similarly, just because more people like to play Poker without the Joker than with it doesn't mean that those who like playing with the Joker are mistaken—they're just outnumbered.

What about appealing to the law? This sounds like an appeal to the "rules of the game." But, given the arbitrariness of those rules in the first place, no one could be "mistaken" if they prefer, instead, to substitute their own "house rules." Of course, if you're playing Poker at someone else's table, you might be bound to play by their rules, but that doesn't mean your own version of the game is "wrong." It might well be prudent of you to play by the rules of your host, but that is just a practical consideration, and in no way implies that your host's rules are somehow more correct than your own! If the only sources to which we may appeal are other humans, the question remains: why would one human's values be somehow more authoritative, more morally accurate, than another's?

Recall that, if moral claims are subjective, then the truth-value of a moral claim is not a "fact," nor is it "absolute" in any sense, but is, instead, a matter of personal perspective. Musical preferences, favorite colors, and favorite foods are easy and obvious examples of those sorts of claims. But, is my belief that it's wrong to torture babies for fun the same kind of claim as my belief that triple-cream brie is the best kind of cheese? Just a matter of perspective? Merely personal opinion? A matter of taste?

If you and I disagree about spicy food, we tend to think that's not a big deal. I'll eat spicy food, and you won't. Everyone's happy. But, what if I think it's OK for me to steal your identity and charge a bunch of merchandise in your name? I keep all the stuff, and you get stuck with the bill. You find out it was me, and you come complaining:

You: "Hey, Ted! What's wrong with you? Why did you steal my credit card and buy all that stuff for yourself? I just got a huge credit card bill in the mail?"

Me: "Um, I wanted the stuff, and I also didn't want to pay for it myself. Seemed like a pretty good way to handle that particular problem. . . ."

You: "But you can't just steal my credit card because *you* want something and don't want to have to pay for it! That's *wrong*!"

Me: "No it's not. . . ."

You: "What are you talking about? Of course it is!"

Me: "I don't think it is—and I would appreciate it if you would drop that self-righteous tone. The way you're speaking to me, it's as if you think your opinion concerning identity theft is somehow better, or more accurate, than mine. How arrogant. . . ."

At this point it will be helpful to distinguish two kinds of moral subjectivism: "simple subjectivism," and "emotivism."

Simple Subjectivism

Simple Subjectivism is the view that has been lurking in the background for this entire section, thus far. According to Simple Subjectivism, moral claims are matters of opinion, rather than fact. They are subjective, rather than objective. Moral claims are indicators of personal preference or taste, and are therefore more similar to a claim concerning whether I liked a movie than to a claim concerning who directed the movie. According to Simple Subjectivism, being opposed to abortion is more like offering your opinion about a painting than answering a math problem. Because moral claims appeal to opinions rather than facts, there are no "right" answers to our moral questions. Instead, something is morally right or wrong (to me) just to the extent that I *believe* it is, and if you should disagree with me, your opinion is no more (or less) correct than my own.

Emotivism

Although Emotivists agree with subjectivists that moral claims are about the individual/subject rather than the act/object (i.e., subjective, rather than objective), Emotivists go even further. Emotivists wouldn't even say that moral claims are subjective claims. Rather, they believe that moral "claims" are not *claims* at all! Instead, they are indicators of positive or negative emotional attitudes only.

For example, according to emotivists, if I say that "murder is morally wrong," I haven't reported any fact about murder (i.e., its wrongness). Instead, I have expressed my own negative *attitude* about murder. Famously, this is sometimes referred to as the "boo/hurrah!" interpretation of moral claims. Today, we might replace "boo" with ☹ and "hurrah" with ☺. As A.J. Ayer put it:

> *The presence of an ethical symbol in a proposition adds nothing to its factual content. Thus if I say to someone, 'You acted wrongly in stealing that money,' I am not stating anything more than if I had simply said, 'You stole that money.' In adding that this action is wrong I am not making any further statement about it. I am simply evincing my moral disapproval of it. It is as if I had said, 'You stole that money,' in a peculiar tone of horror, or written it with the addition of some special exclamation marks. The tone, or the exclamation marks, adds nothing to the literal meaning of the sentence. It merely serves to show that the expression of it is attended by certain feelings in the speaker.*
>
> *If now I generalize my previous statement and say. 'Stealing money is wrong.' I produce a sentence which has no factual*

meaning - that is, expresses no proposition which can be either true or false, it is as if I had written 'Stealing money! ! ' - where the shape and thickness of the exclamation marks show, by a suitable convention, that a special sort of moral disapproval is the feeling which is being expressed. It is clear that there is nothing said here which can be true or false.

Subjectivism and emotivism are similar, but not identical. According to subjectivism, an action is morally right (to me) simply if I approve of it. Moral claims are simply statements concerning a person's approval or disapproval of an action.

To claim that "eating meat is morally wrong" is just a way of that person saying "I don't approve of eating meat." This claim has a truth value. It is either true, or false. It is true if that person really does disapprove of eating meat (i.e., she is telling the truth), and it is false if she doesn't really disapprove of eating meat (i.e., she is lying).

Emotivists, in contrast, deny that there is any sort of claim being made at all, preferring instead to interpret so-called moral claims as mere expressions of a *feeling*—and feelings are neither true or false.

Whether or not someone is *experiencing* a particular feeling can be interpreted as true or false. If someone asks if you are sad, and you say "yes," your implied statement of "I am feeling sad" is true if you really are sad, or false if you're lying. But, while the statement *about* your sadness can be true or false, the *sadness itself* can't be. For emotivists, moral claims aren't statements about our feelings, but the actual "emoting" of the feeling itself.

With either of these versions of subjectivism, the impact on our understanding of ethics, moral claims, and the weight of moral obligations would be tremendous. But, is either interpretation true, or at least compelling?

We will now consider some possible criticism of moral subjectivism so you can decide, for yourself, whether it's the best interpretation of moral claims.

Possible problems for subjectivism

What most of these possible problems will have in common is that they involve "intuition tests." In a previous chapter, we addressed how we process new pieces of information. As you might recall, we each have, at our disposal, what we may call our "background knowledge," "background information," or our "worldview." Whatever we want to call it, it is that vast collection of everything we have heard, seen, read, and otherwise learned, throughout our lives. This collection is everything we know (or think we know) about the world and how it works. Every time we are confronted with a piece of information, we automatically and instantly evaluate it against our background knowledge. If the new information seems to "fit" with our background knowledge, we're likely to accept it as true. If it does not fit, however, if the claim is surprising to us, we're likely to hesitate and to demand more justification before accepting it as true.

Each of the possible problems for subjectivism we will consider involves an implication of subjectivism. Some of the possible problems will rely on the Simple Subjectivism interpretation, and others will apply more to Emotivism, but in each case the strategy is the same: "if subjectivism is true, then [something else] is also true." That "something else" is being presented as a "possible problem," in the following way: each implication of subjectivism is a new piece of information. It either fits nicely with your worldview, sounding "right"—in which case you are likely to accept it as true, and this indicates that you might well be a subjectivist. On the other hand, this new piece of information might conflict with your worldview, and sound "wrong"—in which case you are likely to reject it as false, or at least be skeptical and demand some convincing evidence before revising your worldview.

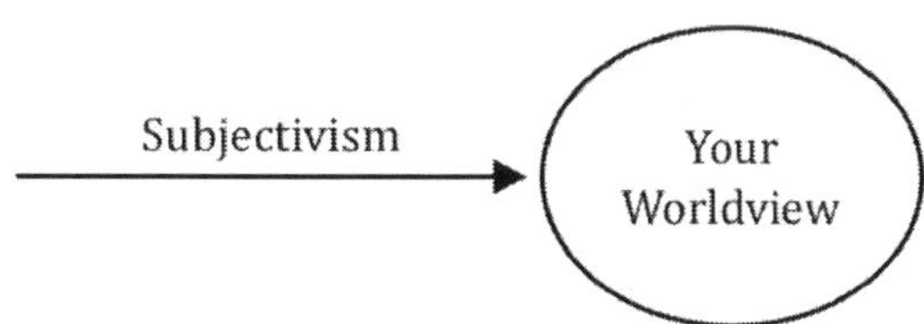

If any of these implications conflicts with your worldview, that doesn't necessarily mean that subjectivism is *false*, of course, but it would indicate that subjectivism *seems* at least unlikely to be true, given your understanding of the world and how it works.

Possible problem #1: Simple Subjectivism is counter-intuitive because no one is ever "mistaken" about moral value judgments

We can now consider a possible (and disturbing) possible problem arising from Simple Subjectivism: no one is ever "wrong"—at least not in any strong sense.

Professor Emeritus Harry Jaffa (from my own Alma Mater, Claremont McKenna College), penned a fictionalized account of a conversation between the serial killer Ted Bundy and one of his victims, "Laura." Jaffa has admitted that it was "composed on the same principle as the speeches in Thucydides' History of the Peloponnesian War, attributing to each speaker the words that fit his character and the circumstances in which he spoke." In other words, he made it up—but in a way that he thought was at least consistent with the character of Bundy. Though I can't express enough how much I disagree with Professor Jaffa on certain subjects, he has managed to make the crux of a subjectivist understanding of morality clear in this dialogue. A brief excerpt follows:

> *Bundy: I recognize that your life and your freedom are very valuable to you, but you must recognize that they are not so valuable to me. And if I must sacrifice your life and freedom to mine, why should I not do so? The unexamined life was not worth living to Socrates. And a life without raping and murdering is not worth living to me. What right do you—or does anyone—have, to deny this to me?*
> *Laura: But rape and murder are wrong. The Bible says they are wrong, and the law says they are wrong.*
> *Bundy: What do you mean by wrong? What you call wrong, I call attempts to limit my freedom. The Bible punished both sodomy and murder with death. Sodomy is no longer regarded as a crime, or even as immoral. Why then should murder—or rape?...*
> *I want you to know that once upon a time I too believed that God and the moral law prescribed boundaries within which my life had to be lived. That was before I took my first college courses in philosophy. Then it was that I discovered how unsophisticated—nay, primitive—my earlier beliefs had been. Then I learned that all moral judgments are "value judgments," that all value judgments are subjective, and that none can be proved to be either "right" or "wrong." . . . And I quickly discovered that the greatest obstacle to my freedom, the greatest block and limitation to it, consisted in the insupportable "value judgment" that I was bound to respect the rights of others. I asked myself, who were these "others"? Other human beings, with human rights? Why is it more wrong to kill a human animal than any other animal, a pig or a sheep or a steer? Is our life more to you than a hog's life to a hog? Why should I be willing to sacrifice my pleasures more for the one than for the other? Surely, you would not, in this age of scientific enlightenment, declare that God or nature has marked some pleasures as "moral" or "good" and others as "immoral" or "bad?"*

Jaffa's point is pretty simple: if moral truth is relative to the individual, then, strictly speaking, Bundy isn't *wrong* (as in, "incorrect") to believe that raping and murdering is a fine form of entertainment.

I disagree with Bundy, of course, and so do

you (I hope!). But, if moral claims are subjective, then all that means is that we have a different *opinion* about rape and murder than he does. Our opinion is neither better, nor worse, than Bundy's—in much the same way that someone who dislikes spicy food isn't "wrong" (whatever I might believe about their taste preferences). Similarly, someone who believes it's acceptable to have sex with young children isn't "wrong" according to a subjectivist approach. Such a person's opinion is no doubt quite unpopular, but "unpopular" isn't the same thing as "wrong."

I like garlic. For the most part, you can't put too much garlic in food as far as I'm concerned. Garlic ice cream is a feature at the Gilroy Garlic Festival, and can be purchased at the garlic-themed "Stinking Rose" restaurant in Los Angeles. Despite my love of garlic, I have never been excited about garlic ice cream. To be honest, garlic ice cream doesn't sound very appealing to me at all, though there are clearly some people who *do* like garlic ice cream—after all, the makers wouldn't bother making it if no one bought it!

I don't think those garlic ice cream enthusiasts are mistaken. If they like garlic ice cream, how can they be wrong about that? At the same time, those garlic ice cream fans must recognize that their ice cream preference is not very popular. They shouldn't be surprised when they can't find garlic ice cream in the freezer section of the grocery store, or at Baskin-Robbins. Instead, such venders cater to much more popular taste preferences such as mint chip, cookies and cream, etc. That doesn't mean that those of us who prefer mint chip are "correct" and those who prefer garlic ice cream are "incorrect"—but it does mean that we're in the majority, that our preference is more popular, and that our preference is much more likely to be honored in our community.

If subjectivism is true, then Ted Bundy's preference for rape and murder is like another person's preference for garlic ice cream. He was not "mistaken," but his view was unpopular, and he was outnumbered by those of us who believe rape and murder are wrong. That helps to explain why rape and murder are illegal, and why he was punished (executed!) once he was caught.

None of that indicates that he was *mistaken* about rape and murder, though. If Simple Subjectivism is true, none of us can be "mistaken" about any moral claim, no matter what example we might conjure.

People who like garlic ice cream aren't mistaken. That's just what they like. Is that true of pedophiles as well? Are we willing to think of "I like garlic ice cream" and "I like raping children" as the same kinds of claims? I'm being intentionally provocative here, because it's essential that we understand what it means if subjectivism is the proper way to understand morality. It's possible that moral truths really are simply matters of personal opinion. I don't personally think that is true, but it's *possible*. If that's the case, "morality," as most of us commonly understand it, doesn't exist—and this is why Simple Subjectivism is presented as a "challenge" to ethics.

Critics of Simple Subjectivism will point out that we do not, in fact, regard all opinions as equally true. This is evident, according to the critic, by the fact that we recognize areas of expertise, and experts whose views are regarded as more credible and authoritative as a result of that expertise.

Consider the following examples:

Subject	Expert
Medicine	Medical Doctor
Nutrition	Nutritionist
Carpentry	Carpenter
Botany	Botanist
Chemistry	Chemist
Physics	Physicist
Philosophy	Philosopher

I'll start with a deeply personal example. If you don't believe that my understanding of philosophy, on the basis of my several degrees (B.A., M.A., and Ph.D.), years of experience (more than 20 years at the time of this writing), and "accolades" (e.g., being a tenured professor, and having published multiple articles and textbooks, etc.), is any more informed than your own, why on Earth are you bothering to read this book, or take my class? What is the point of education, in general, if every student is equally informed as his or her teacher?

Let's make it more absurd. Why bother going to the doctor when you are sick and injured? If all opinions are equal, your own opinion about your medical condition is just as good as that doctor's!

Those astrophysicists who have spent studying the universe and who are debating whether or not this universe is situated within a broader multiverse? Their views are no better informed than the random person who has never studied that stuff a day in his or her life. . . .

You don't accept that as true, of course—and this is the critics point. In actual practice, we don't really believe that "all opinions are equal," but instead recognize that some people know what they're talking about, and others don't. Socrates himself criticized epistemic relativism (and moral subjectivism) thousands of years ago:

> *Why, that all those mercenary individuals, whom the many call Sophists and whom they deem to be their adversaries, do, in fact, teach nothing but the opinion of the many, that is to say, the opinions of their assemblies; and this is their wisdom. I might compare them to a man who should study the tempers and desires of a mighty strong beast who is fed by him—he would learn how to approach and handle him, also at what times and from what causes he is dangerous or the reverse, and what is the meaning of his several cries, and by what sounds, when another utters them, he is soothed or infuriated; and you may suppose further, that when, by continually attending upon him, he has become perfect in all this, he calls his knowledge wisdom, and makes of it a system or art, which he proceeds to teach, although he has no real notion of what he means by the principles or passions of which he is speaking, but calls this honourable and that dishonourable, or good or evil, or just or unjust, all in accordance with the tastes and tempers of the great brute. Good he pronounces to be that in which the beast delights and evil to be that which he dislikes; and he can give no other account of them except that the just and noble are the necessary, having never himself seen, and having no power of explaining to others the nature of either, or the difference between them, which is immense (Republic, 493a-c).*

In other words, these intellectual mercenaries know nothing of good or evil, justice or injustice. Instead, they merely *observe* what actually happens in the world, what people seem to like and dislike, and *proclaim* those things to be good or bad, just or unjust.

If we recognize that this sort of relativism is rife with problems in a non-moral context (e.g., think about what it would mean for it to be "just a matter of opinion" that humans require oxygen to survive), why should we entertain the notion in moral contexts?

The question we must now consider is whether moral claims concern a matter of possible expertise ("morality"), in which case we would presumably recognize that some people are better informed than others, and that not all views are equally good. Or, if we reject that, then we are presumably treating moral claims as mere indicators of personal taste. I might recognize that some people might be experts at "baking," and are certainly better informed than I am when it comes to how best to bake a cake, but I don't recognize that anyone else is somehow more informed than I am about what sort of cake I like! If you've gone to culinary school, your understanding of how to bake a red velvet cake is probably better informed than my own, but it makes no sense to suggest that you know better than I do regarding whether or not I *like* red velvet cake.

Herein lies the intuition test: based upon your worldview, is "morality" more like a skill that allows for expertise ("e.g., "baking"), or is it more like a personal taste preference ("red velvet cake is my favorite")?

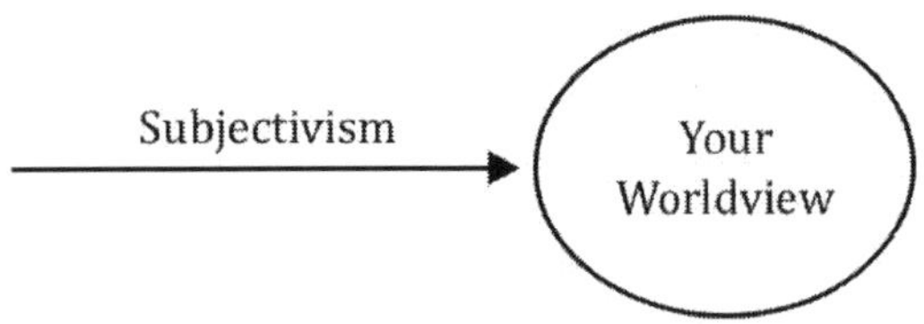

Possible problem #2: Simple Subjectivism is counter-intuitive because of how it interprets language use

This possible problem might sound mysterious and abstract, but it's really not very complicated. Language is a rich and sophisticated tool with which we may accomplish many things. We use language in a lot of different ways, and we intend different sorts of things when we use language.

Sometimes, when we make a claim (whether spoken or written), all we are intending to do is to express a personal preference or experience. For example, if I tell you that "*The Martian* was a good movie," it's very likely that all I am intending to do is to convey the fact that I liked the movie. In fact, if someone had to "translate" my claim using other words, but conveying the same meaning, that person might very well just translate it as "Ted liked *The Martian*."

As another example, suppose I go to see my doctor, and he refers me to an oncologist—a doctor who specializes in cancer diagnosis and treatment. Suppose that, after some tests, that oncologist says to me, "You have cancer." Presumably, the intention of my oncologist is not at all the same as with my first example. She's not saying anything at all like "I like cancer," or even "I don't like cancer." She's not offering an indicator of her personal preference at all. Instead, she is intending to provide a medically-accurate, *factual* diagnosis of my medical condition.

She is not intending to offer a mere *opinion*. Presumably, she regards that diagnosis as a medical *fact*. Given her presumed expertise, I am going to treat it as a fact, and certainly not as a mere personal perspective than is no more informed than anyone else's! Even if I seek a "second opinion," that doesn't mean that I think her diagnosis is "just an opinion." It means that I want a second doctor to double-check the tests, and to confirm the diagnosis, just in case any mistakes were made. In the same sort of way, if you complete a math problem, and you ask for someone to check your work, it's not because you think that answers to math problems are merely matters of opinion! Instead, you want something else to verify that your answer is correct.

Here is another example of a claim, but this time concerning a moral issue. "Abortion is the ending of pregnancy by removing a fetus or embryo before it can survive outside the uterus." If I offer a claim like that, it seems pretty clear that my intention is to define abortion. What I am hoping to accomplish is to convey the meaning of abortion, in the literal sense of what an abortion *is*.

Finally, let us consider the claim that "Abortion is morally wrong." As with all the other examples, we need to ask what is being intended by this claim, and how else might we "translate" it.

Simple Subjectivists seem to be assuming that the intention behind that claim is to convey personal taste preference, and therefore an accurate "translation" would be "I don't like abortion." Alternatively, an Emotivist would say my intention is to express "Abortion! ☹" Certainly, those are possible interpretations of what's going on, but are they the only ones? The best ones?

Some critics of Simple Subjectivism will claim that an expression of personal preference is not the only intention someone might have, or even the most common one. Or, when applied to Emotivism, that our intention is not always, or even primarily, merely to convey a feeling. Instead, someone who is claiming "abortion is morally wrong" might be intending to accurately describe an objective feature of a particular act; in this case, abortion. If so, the accurate "translation" would *not* be "I don't like abortion," or "Abortion ☹," but something like "abortion has the property of being morally wrong."

It's a statement of the obvious to point out that when someone tells us something, that person is offering his or her opinion—but it doesn't necessarily follow from that that the person is therefore offering something that is *only* subjectively true, nor that the intention is to offer a *mere* opinion. We can agree, without controversy, that if someone makes a claim (and the person is being sincere, as opposed to deceptive), that person is *at least* offering an opinion. What remains to be seen is whether it's possible to offer anything more: a fact.

In addition, with regards to the Emotivist interpretation, someone who claims that "abortion is wrong" might well have a negative feeling about it, but that doesn't necessarily mean that all they are doing is expressing that feeling. They might possibly have the negative feeling, but have it because they have determine that there is an objective feature of abortion (i.e., its "wrongness") that *causes* them to have that negative feeling. Or, someone might conclude that abortion is morally wrong, but not have any sort of feeling about it at all. It seems *possible* that someone could dispassionately believe that abortion is wrong, after all.

Which seems more accurate to you? That all moral claims are intending merely as expressions of personal taste (or expressions of feelings), or that at least some moral claims are intended as an accurate description of an objective property of a particular act?

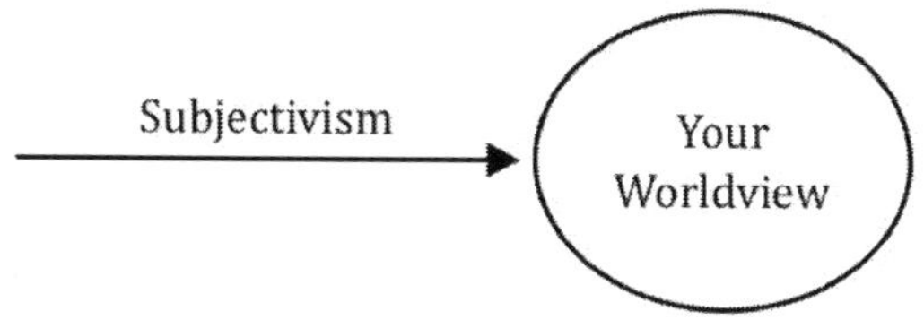

Possible problem #3: subjectivism is counter-intuitive because it doesn't allow for objective moral progress or regress in individuals

A third possible problem with subjectivism is what it does to our notions of moral progress and regress. In actual practice, we speak about people becoming morally better or worse people over time. "He's really turned his life around!" "What happened to Jane? She used to be such a good person?" What would such statements mean from a subjectivist perspective?

Stanley "Tookie" Williams was executed by the State of California in 2005. His impending execution was covered extensively in the California media not only because executions are infrequent in California, but also because Tookie had become a bit of a celebrity, and had numerous actual celebrities lobbying for a stay of execution. Although several different arguments were offered for why he should not be executed, one particular argument was, by far, employed most often: Tookie had "reformed."

Although he was convicted of several murders from 1979, and although he was a co-founder of the notorious Crips gang, his supporters claimed that he had transformed himself while in prison, and was no longer the man he used to be. He had become a morally better person, and didn't deserve to die (at least not any more).

> *"I no longer participate in the so-called gangster lifestyle, and I deeply regret that I ever did . . . I vow to spend the rest of my life working toward solutions."*
>
> —William's 1997 open apology for his gang activities.

What would it mean to say that Tookie was a better person in 2005 than he was in 1979? Better how? By what standard? By *whose* standard? Remember, if moral truths are subjective, his beliefs and values in 1979 were not *wrong* (mistaken). Whatever he believed was right, *really was* right (for him).

In 2005, he allegedly possessed a different set of values. Those values were neither better nor worse than his values from 1979. They were simply different.

If you think he had become a better person, then, according to Simple Subjectivism, that's simply *your* opinion. One can imagine that some of his still-dedicated Crips associates might disagree. Or, according to Emotivism, if you think he became a morally better person, that just indicates that you have a more positive emotional response to him now than you had (or would have had) in the past.

From a subjectivist perspective, to say that Tookie became a better person is to say something like the following:

- "*I* like Tookie a lot more than I used to."
- "*I* wouldn't have wanted to hang out with Tookie in 1979, but I would have in 2005."
- "*I* didn't have much in common with Tookie back in 1979, but now I do."
- "Tookie would have made me uncomfortable back in 1979, but now I feel good about him and his values."

Only if morality is *not* simply a matter of opinion, only if there is some non-subjective notion of truth behind it, can we have any strong notion of people becoming better or worse over time. Perhaps progress and regress are merely matters of perspective, but if you disagree and think there is a more powerful sense in which people can become morally better or worse, then you presumably disagree with the claims of subjectivism.

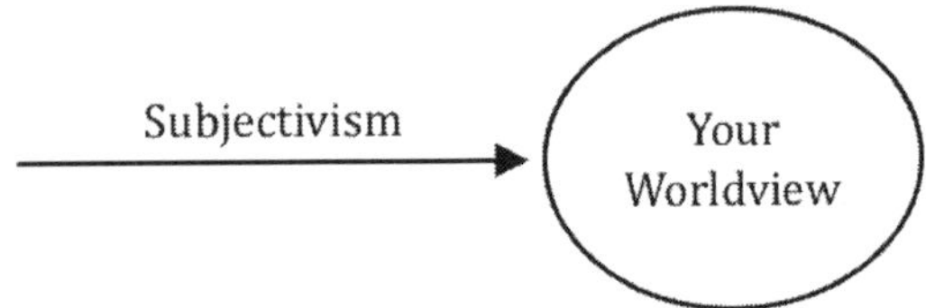

Possible problem #4: subjectivism is counter-intuitive because it doesn't allow for objective moral comparisons between individuals.

We've just seen how subjectivism can't provide strong comparisons of the *same* person over time. Now we can see how it also can't provide for strong comparisons of *different* people at the *same* time.

Consider these two men:

Now consider these two quotations. One is attributed to each man. I'll let you make an educated guess as to who is responsible for each quotation. . . .

> *"The pieces of the bodies of infidels were flying like dust particles. If you would have seen it with your own eyes, you would have been very pleased, and your heart would have been filled with joy."*

> *"Nonviolence is the answer to the crucial political and moral questions of our time; the need for mankind to overcome oppression and violence without resorting to oppression and violence. Man must evolve for all human conflict a method*

which rejects revenge, aggression and retaliation. The foundation of such a method is love."

Shameless moral imperialist that I am, I'm going to boldly proclaim that MLK was morally superior to bin Laden. I'm even going to assume that most of you agree. What would that mean, though, given a subjectivist framework? It certainly could *not* mean that King was morally better in any "objective sense"—after all, there is no such thing as moral objectivity from the point of view of the subjectivist. Instead, it must mean that my own *personal opinion* (yours too, presumably) is that King was morally superior.

That's just *my* opinion, though, and one that is no more or less correct than that of the most zealous fan of al-Qu'aida or bin Laden. If someone else thinks bin Laden to be the morally superior man, he or she is not "wrong"—we just have different moral taste preferences. To say that MLK is the better man is really just an indicator of my own values, as opposed to any claim about some moral truth—at least not any truth that is more than mere opinion.

Using Emotivism instead, to say that MLK is morally superior to OBL would just mean that I have a positive feeling about MLK and a negative feeling about OBL—or at least my feelings about MLK are more positive than those about OBL. Or, to put it succinctly: MLK ☺ but OBL ☹.

One must grant, in all fairness and honesty, that the subjectivists *could* be right. It might be the case that all our moral judgments are simply expressions of personal opinion (or personal feelings), and nothing stronger than that. You must ask yourself, in light of what is *possible*, if it's also *probable* that subjectivism is true. Are we incapable of any stronger moral comparison than the expression of our personal tastes? Is proclaiming King to be the morally better man the same kind of claim as pronouncing Switchfoot to be the best contemporary rock band?

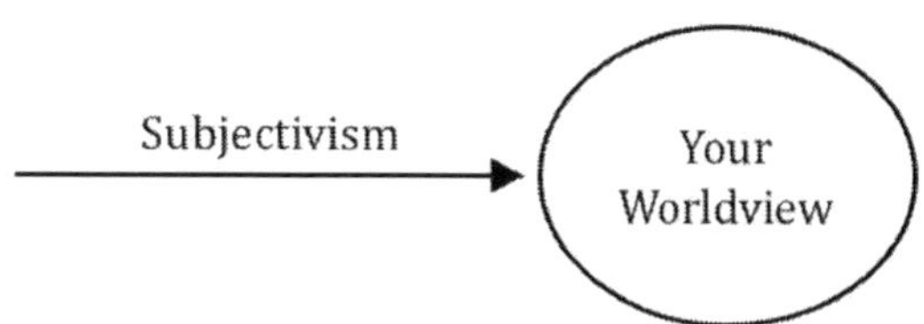

Possible problem #5: subjectivism is counter-intuitive because moral conflict must be resolved by appeals to power, rather than truth

One final (potentially disturbing) implication of subjectivism: if all moral judgments are mere expressions of personal opinion, and if no opinion can claim the mantle of truth, then moral disagreements cannot be resolved by appealing to the truth. Indeed, some subjectivists would deny that disagreement on moral claims is even possible!

Such subjectivists believe that there can be no such thing as contradictory moral claims. For example, the Pro-Life and Pro-Choice crowds aren't actually declaring contrary beliefs, according to this interpretation, but are instead expressing different emotional attitudes about abortion. Obviously, the Pro-Life people have a negative emotional attitude about abortion, while the Pro-Choice people have a positive emotional attitude about reproductive choice. It would be misguided, though, to think that one of the two groups could ever, somehow, be proven to be "right." No party to the pseudo-debate can be proved to be either "right" and the other "wrong" because there is nothing objectively right or wrong, or objectively true or false about our moral "claims." As the Emotivist AJ Ayer put it:

> *Another man may disagree with me about the wrongness of stealing, in the sense that he may not have the same feelings about stealing as I have, and he may quarrel with me on account of my moral sentiments. But he cannot, strictly speaking, contradict me. For in saying that a certain type of action is right or wrong, I am not making any*

> *factual statement, not even a statement about my own state of mind. I am merely expressing certain moral sentiments. And the man who is ostensibly contradicting me is merely expressing his moral sentiments. So that there is plainly no sense in asking which of us is in the right. For neither of us is asserting a genuine proposition.*

In a non-moral context, if I claim that a painting is "beautiful," I'm not declaring any objective fact about the painting, but simply indicating my own positive attitude towards the painting. I like the painting. It appeals to me. The beauty isn't something objective in the painting, but rather something subjective about me and my experience of the painting—otherwise, everyone would think the painting is beautiful.

Similarly, if subjectivism is correct, then claiming that "abortion is immoral" is not a declaration of any objective fact (about which someone else could be mistaken), but merely an indicator of the speaker's own attitude towards abortion (i.e., a negative attitude), or else an indicator of a negative feeling ("abortion ☹"). If that is the case, there is no genuine disagreement possible when it comes to abortion, or any other moral issue.

If you and I disagree on an objective matter, disagreement indicates error. If I claim that Barack Obama was the 42nd President of the United States, and you claim that George W. Bush was the 42nd President of the United States, at least one of us must be mistaken, since only one person could have been the 42nd President.[19] However, if I claim that George W. Bush is handsome and you claim that he is not, it is entirely consistent that both of us can be correct, since we are not actually contradicting each other. Note the comparison:

Objective Claim	Subjective Claim
Barack Obama was the 42nd President	*I* think GW Bush is handsome
George W Bush was the 42nd President	*You* think GW Bush isn't handsome

The claims in the first column can't be both be true at the same time, but the claims in the second can certainly both be true at the same time. This indicates, to subjectivists, that moral disagreement doesn't involve anything like the simultaneous utterance of contradictory claims, but merely the simultaneously different personal attitudes about something experienced by two different people.

Earlier in this chapter, we considered a criticism of subjectivism based on language use. The complaint was that our use of moral claims doesn't seem to be merely an indicator of personal taste preference, but that sometimes we are honestly trying to argue for or against a position. Ayer recognizes this experience, and has an interpretation to account for it (underlining added for emphasis).

> *This may seem, at first sight to be a very paradoxical assertion. For we certainly do engage in disputes which are ordinarily regarded as disputes about questions of value, But, in all such cases, we find, if we consider the matter closely, that the dispute is not really about a question of value, but about a question of fact. When someone disagrees with us about the moral value of a certain action or type of action, we do admittedly resort to argument in order to win him over to our way of thinking. But we do not attempt to show by our arguments that he has the 'wrong' ethical feeling towards a situation whose nature he has correctly apprehended. What we attempt to show is that he is mistaken about the facts of the case. We argue that he has misconceived the agent's motive: or that he has misjudged the effects of the action, or its probable effects in view*

[19] Actually, in that case both of us would be mistaken, since Bill Clinton was the 42nd President. Congratulations to those of you paying attention!

> *of the agent's knowledge; or that he has failed to take into account the special circumstances in which the agent was placed. Or else we employ more general arguments about the effects which actions of a certain type tend to produce, or the qualities which are usually manifested in their performance. We do this in the hope that we have only to get our opponent to agree with us about the nature of the empirical facts for him to adopt the same moral attitude towards them as we do. And as the people with whom we argue have generally received the same moral education as ourselves, and live in the same social order, our expectation is usually justified.*

For a different example, consider moral opposition to homosexuality. Some people believe that homosexual behavior is immoral, while others seemingly disagree. But, according to Ayer, they're not *really* "disagreeing." What could this mean?

Recall the following: "When someone disagrees with us about the moral value of a certain action or type of action, we do admittedly resort to argument in order to win him over to our way of thinking. But we do not attempt to show by our arguments that he has the 'wrong' ethical feeling towards a situation whose nature he has correctly apprehended. What we attempt to show is that he is mistaken about the facts of the case."

Consider how much effort has been made on both sides of the sexuality debate to determine whether or not homosexuality is a "lifestyle choice" or whether people are "born that way." 2016 Presidential candidate Ben Carson stirred some controversy when he argued that homosexuality is a choice "because a lot of people who go into prison go into prison straight -- and when they come out, they're gay. So, did something happen while they were in there? Ask yourself that question."[20] The American Psychological Association disagrees, claiming that "most people experience little or no sense of choice about their sexual orientation."

Why would it matter whether or not homosexuality is a choice? Presumably because most people (or most Americans, at least) think that it is unfair to condemn someone for something over which they have no control. If homosexuality is no more a choice than is heterosexuality, then to condemn homosexual activity between consenting adults while endorsing heterosexual activity between consenting adults might seem unfair, or even arbitrary.

One of the reasons Gay-rights activists have argued so consistently for the acceptance that homosexuality is not a lifestyle choice is so that an analogy with the American Civil Rights movement can be made. To discriminate against African-Americans on the basis of their skin color (something that was not a choice) is now regarded as unfair and unacceptable by most Americans. If sexuality is similar to skin color by virtue of being something we are born with, then discrimination on the basis of sexuality could also be argued to be unfair and unacceptable. On the other hand, if someone could prove that there is no biological basis for sexual orientation, if it could be proven that people choose their attractions, then the analogy breaks down, and other analogies are possible:

> *We never, ever judge someone on who's going to heaven, hell. That's the Almighty's job. We just love 'em, give 'em the good news about Jesus—whether they're homosexuals, drunks, terrorists. We let God sort 'em out later, you see what I'm saying?*[21]

In this quotation, "Duck Dynasty" patriarch Phil Robertson compares homosexuals to drunks and terrorists. Just as people choose to drink to excess (and that is wrong), and others choose to

---

[20] http://www.cnn.com/2015/03/04/politics/ben-carson-prisons-gay-choice/

[21] http://entertainment.time.com/2013/12/18/duck-dynasty-star-compares-gay-people-to-drunks-terrorists-and-prostitutes/

commit acts of terrorism (and that is wrong), so too do some people choose to engage in homosexual activity (and that is wrong). People are no more born to be gay than they are born to be terrorists, according to this logic.

Ayer would interpret the disagreement between these two camps as not actually being a disagreement about the rightness or wrongness of homoxesuality, which is merely a subjective preference, but instead a disagreement about the objective nature of sexual orientation. Similarly, disagreement about abortion is really disagreement about the objective fact as to whether or not a fetus is an innocent person with rights, analogous to adult humans, that are protected under the law.

Ayer thinks that, in most cases, we are confident enough that our "neighbors" have sufficiently similar emotional attitudes that our so-called disagreements on moral issues can be resolved simply by settling some objective matter (e.g., whether or not homosexuality is a "lifestyle").

But what if that's just not true? What if our emotional attitudes are quite different, and resolving the relevant facts wouldn't dissolve the dispute (underlining added for emphasis)?

> *But if our opponent happens to have undergone a different process of moral 'conditioning' from ourselves, so that, even when he acknowledges all the facts, he still disagrees with us about the moral value of the actions under discussion, then we abandon the attempt to convince him by argument. We say that it is impossible to argue with him because he has a distorted or undeveloped moral sense; which signifies merely that he employs a different set of values from our own. We feel that our own system of values is superior, and therefore speak in such derogatory terms of his. But we cannot bring forward any arguments to show that our system is superior. For our judgment that it is so is itself a judgment of value, and accordingly outside the scope of argument. It is because argument fails us when we come to deal with pure questions of value, as distinct from questions of fact, that we finally resort to mere abuse.*

Here, Ayer is describing scenarios in which "the other side" just plainly doesn't "see" things the same way we do, and we have concluded that there is nothing we can do to change that. If a Pro-Life advocate opposes abortion because he believes that an Almighty God has implanted an immeasurably valuable soul in the fetus from the very instant of conception, and that no appeal to women's rights, reproductive autonomy, or the biological development of a fetus' nervous system could possibly dissuade him from that conclusion, what is the Pro-Choice advocate to do?

The truth of the presence or absence of a soul in the fetus is not subject to empirical verification, and is either accepted on Faith, or not. For the subjectivist, there is no "truth" concerning the moral status of the abortion itself other than the truth or falsity of someone's personal attitudes about abortion. Truth, it may be said, has no role to play in this dispute.

If truth can't be used to settle moral conflict and debate, what can? If you and I disagree about some moral issue, and it's impossible (even in principle) for either one of us to establish who is correct (or at least closer to the truth), then what will resolve the conflict? The only thing left: power.

Thrasymachus, in Plato's *Republic*, argued famously that "might makes right."

> *"I declare justice is nothing but the advantage of the stronger." (Republic 338c)*

Rather than viewing morality and justice as anything lofty and noble, a much simpler (and more cynical) interpretation is offered: the people in charge get to make the rules. Whatever they say is right, is, for all practical purposes, "right." One of the perks of being the most powerful person is that you get to enshrine your own personal values into law and custom—at least until someone more powerful comes along with a different set of values.

From the standpoint of subjectivism, those of us who think it abhorrent to have sex with a child don't have "better" values than a pedophile. We're not "right." What we are, is more powerful, if for no other reason than because we are more numerous. It just so happens that the no-sex-with-children crowd gained control at some point in our history, and has remained more populous and more powerful than the percentage of our population who think it acceptable to have sex with children. We have no (objective) moral advantage over them, but we can force them to follow our values rather than theirs. After all, if they refuse, we'll throw them in jail.

Returning to our abortion example, neither side is "correct" or "incorrect," but in an ostensibly democratic society like the United States of America, whichever side can generate more votes and elect candidates that agree with them will have more power, and will "win."

Once again, the subjectivist could reply that, like it or not, that's just how things are. Moral judgments are all matters of personal opinion (or expressions of feelings), and the values supported by our laws and customs are not superior (in any strong, objective sense) to those values we label deviant.

Moral disagreement *could*, in fact, always be a power struggle, and is only ever resolved by force (social, or physical). That's possible, but does it seem to be true? Is there nothing more to your value judgments than opinion, or feelings? No way to resolve disagreement than by force? Can we only ever hope to be the most powerful, as opposed to the most right? Is it ever possible for someone to have no power, but nevertheless be *right*? If subjectivism is the best way to understand morality, it truly does require a radical revision of our understanding of morality, a revision that many of you might find untenable.

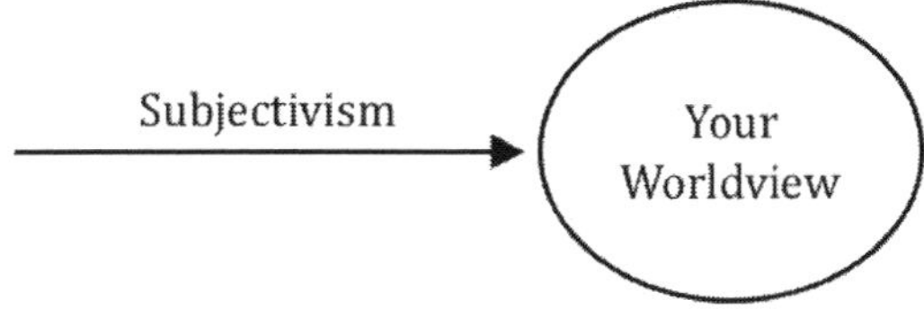

Cultural Relativism

Some are uncomfortable with the radical individualism entailed by subjectivism, but nevertheless agree that moral value judgments are matters of opinion, rather than fact. For those that continue to resist what we'll call an "objective" understanding of morality, the most logical alternative to subjectivism is cultural relativism (sometimes called ethical relativism).

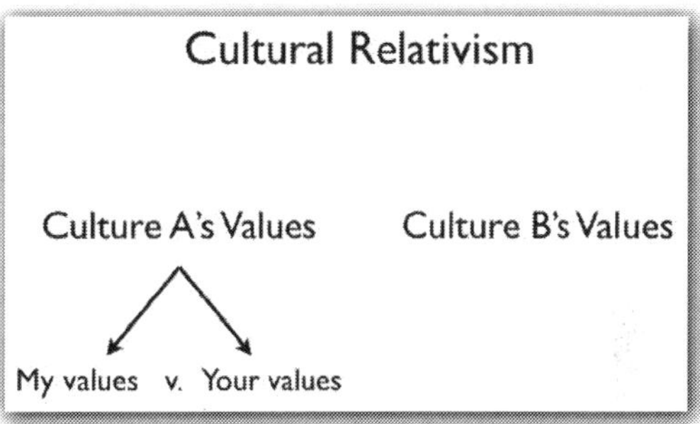

Consider the image above. It represents the kinds of judgments and comparisons possible according to cultural relativism. No such image was provided for subjectivism, in our previous section, since, if subjectivism is true, no comparisons of values are possible anyway—at least not anything other than a "taste test."

Cultural relativism (hereafter: CR) operates on just the same assumptions as subjectivism with one notable difference: whereas subjectivism claims that moral judgments are matters of personal opinion, and gain whatever legitimacy they have from the endorsement of the individual, CR claims that morality is a matter of *collective* judgment.

What is right and wrong is determined by the prevailing values of a given community. You've probably heard the expression, "when in Rome, do as the Romans do." Assuming this is meant as more than just practical advice, this is an expression of CR.

According to CR, what is morally right and morally wrong is established by the dominant values of a given culture. This allows for moral judgments and comparisons concerning individuals—at least within the same community.

The standard we would use for such judgments would be the dominant values of the culture in question. Each culture provides its own "answer key" for its own community. For example, in the United States, an adult male marrying a 9 year-old girl would not merely be considered morally wrong, he would be prosecuted for a sex crime! Thus, because the dominant cultural values of the U.S. frown upon such marriages, it is morally wrong to marry 9 year old girls in the U.S. Not so, elsewhere, however.

Tihun, a 9 year old Ethiopian girl, was arranged to marry a 19 year old Orthodox Church deacon by her father. This is not an aberration. According to UN and Ethiopian statistics, in some parts of Ethiopia almost 90 percent of the local girls are married before age 15 (technically, it is against Ethiopian law to marry anyone under the age of 18, but the punishment is a $12 fine, is rarely enforced, and is generally ignored by the conservative population.). "'In truth, if a girl reaches 13, she is already too old to be married,' declares Nebiyu Melese, 54, Tihun's wiry farmer father. 'I know some people say this is uncivilized. But they don't live here. So how can they judge?'" (reported By Paul Salopek, Chicago Tribune foreign correspondent, published December 12, 2004)

"How can they judge?" According to CR, we can't—at least not with any special credibility. Because CR claims, like subjectivism, that there is no set of "true" moral values that apply to all people, everywhere, and at all times, there is no *objective* standard (no universal answer key) with which to judge the values of a culture.

From *within* a given culture, one may (and should) employ the values of that culture, and individuals can (and should) be judged according to those standards. In the U.S., if you marry a 9 year old and I don't, I'm a morally superior person than you are (on that one issue, at least) because my values and behavior are more in harmony with those prescribed by our culture. Outside of our own culture, however, we are in no position to judge.

Why would anyone accept this view? There are several reasons, and not all of them are based on mistakes. One that *does* rest on a mistake, however, involves the *observation of cultural differences* throughout the world.

One need not be especially well-traveled, or cosmopolitan, to know that different cultures have different practices, and (seemingly) different values. Certain examples are obvious. Australian aborigines eat the "witchety grub" and consider it a welcome delicacy. Most Americans would only eat grubs if on a reality TV show. Americans eat meat with reckless abandon (171 pounds per person, in 2011, according to the U.S. Department of Agriculture), but Indian Hindus abstain from eating meat.[22]

It is not only our diets that vary, from one culture to the next. Marriage practices, sexual taboos, notions of masculinity and femininity, notions of "family," clothing practices, funerary practices, and many other activities vary. One need not be a world traveler to know this, just watch PBS or National Geographic.

Some cultural relativists, such as Ruth Benedict, observe these cultural differences, and make something morally significant out of it. Benedict claims that standards of normalcy and deviance vary from one culture to the next.

---

[22] "He who desires to augment his own flesh by eating the flesh of other creatures lives in misery in whatever species he may take his birth." (Mahabharat 115.47—for those unfamiliar, the Mahabharat is one of two major Sanskrit epics of ancient India. It is also an important part of Hindu mythology. Thus, quoting sections and verses from the Mahabarat is analogous to quoting from chapter and verse from the Christian Bible.)

The above picture shows former President George Herbert Walker Bush walking hand-in-hand with Saudi King Abdullah. In the United States, this is an interesting event, because in the U.S. it isn't "normal" for grown (heterosexual) men to hold hands. That is, when we see two adult men holding hands, we assume they are homosexual, and that their hand-holding means basically the same thing as when straight men and straight women hold each other's hands. Even for straight allies, men holding hands is seen as a sub-cultural practice for homosexuals—there's been little, if any, infiltration of this practice into the (straight) mainstream culture. The practice, and its meaning, however, is quite different in the Saudi culture. Men hold hands as a display of friendship, not as a display of a romantic relationship.

"We" give a "high-five," "they" hold hands.

Americans eat with forks, the Chinese eat with chopsticks.

American men wear pants, traditional Scotsmen wear kilts. Different strokes for different folks....

Most of us are willing to acknowledge that certain practices vary from one culture to the next, and that each is a *legitimate* practice. That is, it's hard to find someone who would claim, in any serious tone, that it's "wrong" to eat with chop-sticks, Chinese or not, and that eating with a fork is the only morally legitimate means to transport food to one's mouth. Benedict goes quite a bit farther than this, though, by claiming not only that "normalcy" varies (legitimately) from one culture to the next, but also that "normal" and "morally good" are synonymous terms. In other words, when we say that something is morally good, what we're really saying is that the practice in question is what we consider "normal," and if we label something to be morally bad, that's just another way of saying it's "weird." A slight bit of logic allows us to see the implication of this.

1. What is considered "normal" varies (legitimately) across cultures.
2. Therefore, there is no single standard of normalcy for humankind.
3. "Normal" and "morally good" are synonymous terms.
4. Therefore, there is no single standard of moral goodness for humankind.

A few points require immediate attention.

1. It is far from obvious that "normalcy" and "morality" are, in fact, synonymous terms—at least not across the whole range of practices deemed either normal/deviant, or good/bad.

For example, it's possible that there are practices deemed normal or abnormal that we don't regard as having any moral significance whatsoever. Talking to oneself in public is seen as "weird" in the U.S. culture, and is often assumed to be a sign of mental illness, but it's not obvious that it would also be considered morally wrong. Piercing one's face is still considered "extreme," despite the increasing popularity of body piercings, but it's not easy to find someone who would claim that those who do so have committed a moral offense.

Similarly, it's not obvious that we would all agree that certain practices, deemed immoral, are of the same type as those we also deem "abnormal." Child-rape is certainly considered deviant, and perceived as "weird," but the act seems to be more than *just* "weird." Intentionally urinating on oneself in public is weird. Very weird, in fact. Is raping a child just very, very weird? Very, very, very weird? Or, are some acts *qualitatively different*, such that they no longer fit into our categories or normalcy/deviancy, but require their own (distinct) category: good/evil?

If we consider the Venn diagram below, it seems possible that certain actions (e.g., extensive facial piercings) might be considered "abnormal/deviant" within a community, but *not* considered immoral. In fact, every time I survey my students and ask them if having facial piercings is morally wrong, almost no one ever says "yes"—though nearly everyone acknowledges that it is outside the "norm." Other actions might be considered "immoral," but are not abnormal in the sense of unusual or atypical. For example, pre-marital sex is the "norm" in the United States. The overwhelming majority of Americans has sex before marriage, across most demographic groups—but many (even if grudgingly) consider pre-marital sex to be (technically) morally wrong. Here we have an example of something "normal" (as in "common") but possibly immoral. Some actions, though, are generally considered to be *both* abnormal *and* immoral. Pedophilia is certainly outside the norm, but also widely regarded as morally wrong.

On the "positive" side, certain actions are "normal" in the United States (e.g., shaking hands as a form of greeting), but without necessarily attributing any moral "goodness" to the act. Other actions are regarded as possibly morally good (e.g., abstaining from pre-marital sex—chastity), but are not the norm. Still other actions might be regarded as both the "norm" as well as being morally good (e.g., honesty).

We can dispute particular examples, but the key question to ask is whether this preceding discussion, in general, seems plausible? If the relationship depicted in the Venn diagram seems plausible, then it would indicate that "normal" and "moral," while related, are *not* synonymous terms.

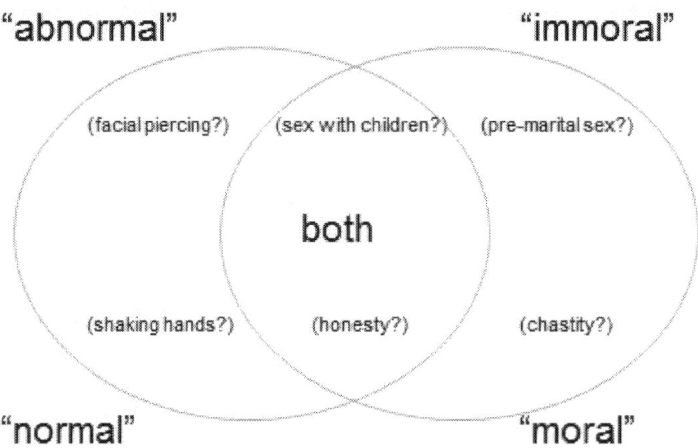

2. As James Rachels has argued, the mere fact of difference does not mean that there are no values that apply to all people, everywhere. The observation of cultural differences is consistent with *both* CR *and* objective approaches to ethics. Therefore, the fact of cultural differences is not automatically support for CR.

In cases of difference, a relativist will conclude that there are no universal values. Someone who believes morality is objective will look at those same differences and conclude that at least one of the cultures is *mistaken*.

Consider an analogy: if two people come up with two different answers to the same math problem, we would be foolish to leap to the conclusion that both of them are correct, or (more foolish still) that there is no "correct" answer at all. Much more plausibly, we would infer that at least one of those persons (and maybe both!) is mistaken and came up with the wrong answer.

Similarly, just because two different cultures come up with two different "answers" to the same (moral) question, that doesn't necessarily mean that both cultures are equally morally correct or that no "correct" answer exists. It's possible that one culture is mistaken. It might be *difficult to discern* who is right, and who is wrong, but there is nothing logically inconsistent with looking at two cultures, one of which prosecutes the rapist when a woman is raped, the other of which stones the woman to death for adultery, noting the different responses, and concluding that one of them is in error. My own vote is against stoning rape survivors. . . . What's the point? Simply this: the fact of cultural differences, by itself, is *not necessarily* an indicator of the truth of CR.

Cultural differences alone do not require one to accept CR, but there might well be other reasons to do so. One reason is a general skepticism that a universal moral code could ever be agreed upon. After all, that there is deep division on numerous moral issues (e.g., abortion, the death penalty, homosexuality, etc.), is obvious. One might think that agreement will never be reached and take that as a sign that no such set of universal values could exist. That might be true, but it's a hasty conclusion.

Even if humanity never does come to consensus on the requirements of morality, that might say far more about our own limitations than about the actual status of moral values. Humans might never fully understand the laws of Nature, or the true origin of the universe, but that doesn't mean that there is no explanation, no right answer—just none that *we* can reach. Moreover, even if it's true that we can never know (with certainty) the truth concerning our moral obligations, that doesn't mean that we can't *make progress* towards the truth, that we can't come ever closer to a full and accurate ethical theory.

An additional reason someone might embrace CR is a result of rejecting its perceived alternative: objective ethical theories.[23] This approach is presumably well-intentioned, and is rooted in a recognition that, for most of recorded history, "tribes" have usually assumed their own moral superiority over their neighbors.

In the West, we have a long and bloody history of European (and eventually, American) powers taking notice of a group of people, taking note of how different those people are, judging that to be different is to be "wrong" and in need of "correction," and then using that judgment to justify campaigns of invasion, colonization, exploitation, and even genocide.

If "savages" engage in morally inferior practices, then one is doing them a "favor" by "correcting" them. After all, they're being made "better." Since *our* way is the only *right* way, they should be made to dress like us, marry like us, speak like us, worship like us, govern like us, and so on.

Many of us, looking back on history, and even on contemporary policies and practices, are repulsed by the cruelties and atrocities that were perpetrated by virtue of the self-righteous assumption of one's own moral superiority. If the inspiration for such actions is the belief that there is one set of true moral values (undoubtedly, one's own!), then a *rejection* of such an assumption might prevent such actions. CR is seen as the tolerance-producing alternative to objective ethics, and is sometimes, for that reason, embraced. This "argument from tolerance" may be formulated as follows:

The Argument from Tolerance

1. If morality is culturally relative, then there is no independent basis for criticizing the moral values of any other culture.
2. If there is no independent way of criticizing any other culture, then we ought to be tolerant of the moral values of other cultures.
3. Morality is culturally relative.
4. Therefore, we ought to be tolerant of the moral values of other cultures.

---

[23] Cynics might call this the "liberal guilt argument" for CR.

If this argument works, then from cultural relativism we may derive that we ought to be tolerant of other cultures.

Tolerance is a good thing, right? Not necessarily! Ask yourself this question: is there any limit as to what should be tolerated? And what does it even mean to be "tolerant?" Does it mean to let people do whatever they want? Does it allow for judgment, but not intervention? Does it just mean we have to be "polite" when judging others? Which of the following should be (or should have been) "tolerated?" What would it mean to "tolerate" such practices?

- South African apartheid.
- Nazi mass-extermination of Jews.
- The Armenian genocide perpetrated by Turkey?
- The Cherokee "Trail of Tears?"
- The thousands of African-Americans lynched in the American South?[24]
- The internment of Japanese-Americans during WWII?
- Female Genital Mutilation that currently affects approximately 2 million girls each year?
- The harvesting of organs from executed criminals in China?
- Saddam Hussein's gassing of Kurdish villages?
- Beheadings and crucifixion of "infidels" by ISIS?

(If you don't know what some of these examples refer to, look them up!)

A first problem with the argument from tolerance is that it's not at all obvious that tolerance is always a good thing. It certainly seems to be the case that some practices, and some values, should *not* be tolerated. Which values fit into that category will be subject to spirited debate, of course, but it does seem that such a category exists.

A second problem with the argument from tolerance is a problem of internal consistency. Premise 1 seems uncontroversial, but premise 2 requires a close examination.

Premise 2 claims that "we" ought to be tolerant. Two words are significant: "we," and "ought." Notice that "ought" is a value-term. To say that we ought to do something is to make a prescriptive claim. We *should* be tolerant. It's *good* to be tolerant. It's *right* to be tolerant. Who, exactly, are "we" who are being told that "we" *ought* to be tolerant? There are three possibilities:

1. "We" are all of humanity—all people, in all places, at all times.
2. "We" are people from the same culture as the person making the argument.
3. "We" are people from a different culture than that of the person making the argument.

No matter which is intended (1-3), a problem emerges. Let's work backwards. If (3), then we are from a *different* culture than that of the person urging us to be tolerant. Why should we listen to her? Her values might be right for her own people, but they don't apply to us. If CR is true, we should heed the moral requirements of our own culture, and not hers.

If (2), then she is speaking to us as a peer. Now we must figure out what the values of our (shared) culture happen to be. Is tolerance, in fact, a dominant value in our culture? If so, then we *should*, in fact, be tolerant (whatever that means), but *not because of her argument.* We should be tolerant because that is what our cultural values prescribe. She's merely "preaching to the choir."

On the other hand, what if our culture is not tolerant? What if we come from an imperialist culture that believes that other cultures' values are savage and wrong? In that case, according to CR, we should be *in*tolerant! In fact, that tolerance-promoting troublemaker is actively encouraging us to be immoral by going against the values of our culture. This is something no self-aware, self-respecting cultural relativist could prescribe!

If (1), then she is claiming that there is at least one value (tolerance) that applies to all people,

[24] At least 3,400 from 1882-1968.

everywhere, at all times. That flatly contradicts a central feature of CR: namely, that there are *no* values that apply to all people, everywhere, at all times. She has contradicted herself and supplied the counter-example to her own theory. How embarrassing for her!

None of this means that a cultural relativist cannot, or will not, be tolerant. Instead, it simply demonstrates that tolerance is not a necessary consequence of CR. Indeed, anyone who alleges that CR *does* require, or even recommend, toleration reveals that he simply has not correctly understood CR!

Consider an analogy: suppose I were to tell you that my favorite thing about soccer (in America, soccer—football everywhere else in the world) is the fact that any player, at any time, can pick up the ball with his or her hands and run with it.

If you know anything about soccer, you immediately realize that I do not, given the fact that most players are *not* allowed to use their hands during the game. My comment is no commentary on soccer, but rather on my own *misunderstanding* of soccer.

Similarly, if someone tells me how CR requires (or even promotes) tolerance or respect for diversity, I immediately realize that this is no commentary on CR, but rather an indicator of that person's *misunderstanding* of CR.

According to CR, you should be tolerant only if that is what your culture demands, and if a culture is intolerant, that culture is not "wrong" for being so. This indicates a very important feature of CR: *CR does not take a stance on any moral issue whatsoever*. Instead, it provides a decision-making procedure with regard to the moral rightness or wrongness of whatever example we might entertain: "ask your culture."

This is simple to illustrate. According to CR, all moral values are relative to a particular culture. Therefore, CR (itself) does not indicate that abortion is morally acceptable (or unacceptable). Instead, it claims that the rightness or wrongness of abortion will depend upon the culture in question. In some cultures, abortion is morally wrong, but in others cultures it is acceptable. Similarly, CR takes no stance on the death penalty. The death penalty will be morally acceptable in some cultures, and unacceptable in others. Slavery is neither morally right nor wrong according to CR—but it will be morally right (or wrong) in *particular cultures*. So, too, with homosexual sex acts, human sacrifice, eating meat, pre-marital sex, etc.

Toleration and/or respect for diversity are moral values like *any other* just mentioned. CR does not endorse, or reject, toleration or respect for diversity. Instead, according to CR, the rightness or wrongness of toleration will depend upon the culture in question. CR does not—and can't—require toleration, though a particular culture *might*.

One final time, the preceding discussion is neither an indictment of CR, nor of toleration, but is simply meant to illustrate that the idea that CR somehow requires or promotes toleration is a *myth*. There might well be good reasons to endorse CR as an ethical theory, but the belief that it requires or promotes tolerance should not be one of them.

Possible Problems with CR

We now know that CR claims that all moral values are relative to particular cultures, and we have considered several reasons why someone might think this interpretation is correct (e.g., a general skepticism concerning universal moral values, a (misguided) association of CR with tolerance, or Benedict's argument concerning normalcy and morality). As we have done with both PE and subjectivism, we will now consider some reasons to reject CR, and enable you to make your own assessment.

Ultimately, CR is potentially vulnerable to the very same criticisms that were leveled against subjectivism, but adjusted to reflect CR's emphasis on collective values as opposed to personal opinion. Also, just as with subjectivism, most of these possible problems amount to "intuition tests" in which a new piece of information (an implication of CR) is evaluated against your worldview.

Possible problem #1: CR allows no objective stance from which to evaluate other cultures' values.

Much as subjectivism does not allow moral comparisons of individuals (beyond expressions of our own personal opinions), CR is incapable of strong cross-cultural comparisons.

Consider the Taliban. Prior to the U.S. led overthrow of the Taliban (2001), the laws and practices of Afghanistan drew considerable international criticism. Here are a few examples:

- Public executions, including stonings, were common.
- Kite-flying (a "frivolous" activity) was outlawed.
- TV, music, and the internet were banned (to remove "decadent" Western influences).
- Men were *required* to wear beards.
- Girls were forbidden to attend school.
- Women could not be examined by male doctors.
- Women could no longer work *as* doctors (think about what these last two mean for women's health care under the Taliban).
- Women could not leave the home without a male escort.
- "Idolatrous" art was destroyed--such as the giant statues of Buddha (constructed 2nd and 3rd centuries A.D., destroyed in 2001).

Much more recently (and similarly), the practices of ISIS (or ISIL)[25] have drawn international criticism. Public executions, including stonings and crucifixions occur "daily" in ISIS-controlled parts of Syria, women are lashed if not sufficiently "covered," international journalists are beheaded on camera, and (interestingly enough, given the context of this book) philosophy has been banned as a form of blasphemy.[26]

If CR is true, then the practices of the Taliban (or ISIS) are neither better nor worse than those of any other culture—just "different." Of course, the U.S. overthrow of the Taliban could not be condemned either, so long as it was consistent with the dominant values of U.S. culture. Moreover, neither the Taliban (or ISIS) nor the U.S.-led overthrow could be judged by other cultures—after all, they have no privileged position from which to judge the U.S. any more than the U.S. has a privileged position from which to judge the Taliban.

Perhaps this is accurate, and no community is ever in a position to judge another. If so, though, we must face a radical revision of our common practices, since we do, in fact, tend to condemn cultures such as Nazi Germany, the Taliban, and apartheid-era South Africa. Many countries condemn the actions of ISIS. Is there *any* behavior, *any* cultural practice, from *any* period in human history that you think is just plain *wrong*, period? Slavery? Human sacrifice? Child rape? Genocide? Anything at all?

If there is even one act, practice, or behavior that you think is always morally wrong, regardless of time, place, or opinion, you have an intuitive disagreement with CR. If you think condemnation that is more than a mere expression of collective taste is possible, then you would have reason to reject CR.

Possible problem #2: Moral reformers are always morally "wrong."

According to CR, the right thing to do is, by definition, whatever one's culture tells one to do. Since the dominant values of one's culture are the ultimate arbiter of morality (the "supreme court" of morality, as it were), there is nothing to which one can appeal that is "higher" than one's culture. You can never go "over the head" of your culture in the event that you disagree with its values. So where does that leave reformers?

A reformer, by definition, is trying to change her culture. All reformers detect something about their culture that they think is morally wrong, or unjust, and they try to change it. According to CR,

[25] "Islamic State of Iraq and al-Sham," or the "Islamic State of Iraq and the Levant," respectively.

[26] http://www.cnn.com/2014/09/04/world/meast/isis-inside-look/index.html?hpt=hp_t1

though, *it is not the individual's judgment* that establishes what is right and wrong; *it is the collective judgment of the entire culture as expressed in its dominant values.*

By definition, then, someone who is trying to change the values of the culture is trying to change what is "right." That makes them *wrong*, doesn't it?

Both Martin Luther King Jr. and Rosa Parks were icons of the American Civil Rights era. Both fought against racism and segregation laws. Both were also criminals, by definition, since they deliberately disobeyed segregation laws, and both were arrested for their "offenses." Both believed that the values of their culture, at the time, were wrong, and in need of correction. But who were they to challenge the values of their culture? By offering a set of values different from that of their culture, at the time, weren't they morally in the wrong, by definition? And yet, don't we tend to have precisely the *opposite* view of reformers, at least in retrospect?

When Rosa Parks died in 2005, her body was displayed in the Capitol Rotunda. The tribute, which requires an act of Congress, has taken place only 31 times in this country's history. Those receiving this rare honor include President Abraham Lincoln and several other Presidents, eight members of Congress, and two Capitol police officers slain at their posts, among a handful of others.[27] President Bill Clinton delivered a eulogy for her. In it, he said that she made us a "better people, and a better country."

If CR is true, what could it mean that she made us "better?" The segregationist values prior to the Civil Rights Movement were not "wrong," after all—just "wrong" given our *current* dominant values.

Much as individuals cannot get morally better or worse, in any strong sense, from a subjectivist perspective, neither can cultures get morally better or worse over time from the perspective of CR. Cultures become "different," but their former values were not "wrong;" they were "right," at the time. This aspect is especially fascinating considering how often proponents of CR condemn the "imperialist" practices of their own culture! If CR is true, on what grounds can they complain about their own culture's values?

In fairness, the advocate of CR could reply in the following way: "when we complain about our own culture, our complaint is that the practices of our culture are not consistent with its values. So, too, with reformers in general. What reformers do is appeal to the already existing values of their culture that are not being honored, to some extent."

Using the example of the Civil Rights Movement, a relativist could say that King and others appealed to the values of equality, brotherhood, freedom, and dignity that were already found in Christianity and in the political philosophy that shaped our government and society. When King advocated equality, he was not introducing some new, alien value into the culture, but was simply pointing out that U.S. society was not living up to its very own ideals, by virtue of the rampant discrimination at the time. Indeed, the advocate of CR could argue that had those basic values of equality, freedom, opportunity, and the like not already been present in the culture, the Movement could have never taken hold and been successful. *If* that's true, then Civil Rights activists were not "in the wrong," but were, instead, champions of the actual cultural values of the United States. Historians will be better prepared to address this issue, but it seems (to me) overly generous to think that racism and segregationism were not expressions of the dominant values at the time, considering how pervasive and enduring racism, and its legacy, has proven to be. Anti-"race-mixing" laws were not overturned by the Supreme Court until 1967. Lest one think such laws were regional only, found in the deep South alone, bear in mind that California's anti-miscegenation law was not overturned by a California Supreme Court until 1948, a mere seven years prior to the beginning of the Civil Rights Movement.

---

[27] If you are interested in a full and up-to-date listing, check the following URL: http://www.aoc.gov/nations-stage/lying-state

Let us suppose, however, for the sake of argument, that interpreting successful reform movements (such as the Civil Rights Movement, for example) as cases where reformers were actually appealing to pre-existing cultural values is plausible. This approach nevertheless seems limited, however, in that it would appear that a culture could never undergo a radical transformation from within. Social change would always need to be somehow consistent with already existing and honored values. Any radical change would have to be understood in terms of an "invasion" of a foreign value, and in terms of that initially-"wrong" value "vanquishing" and ultimately replacing the native values, much as a foreign usurper may claim a throne. Small changes might be understood as a somewhat different application of an already dominant value, while major change must come from the outside. Major changes, at the least, and the advocates of major change, would have to be considered "wrong," at the time.

This produces a potentially counter-intuitive evaluation of moral reformers—at least those advocating "major" change. In trying to change the "right" values of their culture, moral reformers are always "wrong." If they succeed, and their own values become dominant later on, they will be hailed as moral visionaries, in retrospect. But, in their own time, they are moral villains.

Perhaps that's just "how it is." We must acknowledge the possibility that our own perception that a culture (including our own) has gotten morally better or worse over time is just an expression of the bias of our own time and place. *We* think segregation laws are wrong because, in our own time, they are considered wrong. Had we been born (Caucasian, presumably) a half-century ago, though, we would have likely thought differently. Perhaps, at the time, we would have been "right."

On the other hand, if you have any strong intuition that cultures really *do* get morally better or worse over time (e.g., that a culture that abandons slavery has become objectively morally better than it had been), and that such judgments are not mere expressions of current collective opinion, then you presumably have a hard time accepting the implications of CR. What is certain is that CR requires a radical revision of our everyday notions of cultural moral progress and regress.

Possible problem #3: "Culture" is a vague concept.

You've perhaps noticed that I've tossed around words like "we" and "our" quite a bit in these past few pages. I've been speaking of U.S. culture, on the reasonably safe assumption that the overwhelming majority of you are Americans, or at least reside in the U.S., but to speak of the U.S. culture as if it were some obvious and monolithic thing is problematic. Just what is a "culture," anyway?

Merriam-Webster defines "culture" as "the customary beliefs, social forms, and material traits of a racial, religious, or social group." This is extraordinarily vague, and maybe even hopelessly so. To see why this is a problem, think of yourself, and your own social context. How do you self-identify, according to the following criteria?

Race/ethnicity
National origin
Gender
Sexual orientation
Ability/disability
Socio-economic status
Religious affiliation (atheist, agnostic, or secular humanist are each acceptable responses to this)
Generation (e.g., "baby-boomer," "Gen-X," "Gen-Next.")
Citizenship status
State, county, and city of residence
Group memberships (e.g., fraternal orders, Freemasons, etc.)

This is a partial list, to be sure, but serves to illustrate the possible problem. If you live on a small, remote island in which everyone comes from the same ethnic stock, belongs to the same religious tradition, and shares the same values, the identification of your culture is probably pretty simple. I, however, live in Southern California, and it's hard to imagine a more diverse, pluralistic region than L.A. County. According to the U.S. Census Bureau, in 2010, the following was true of the people of L.A. County:[28]

RACE	People	%
American Indian and Alaska Native	72,828	0.7
Asian	1,346,865	13.7
Filipino	322,110	3.3
Japanese	102,287	1.0
Korean	216,501	2.2
Vietnamese	87,468	0.9
Other Asian [1]	145,842	1.5
Asian Indian	79,169	0.8
Black or African American	856,874	8.7
Chinese	393,488	4.0
Cuban	41,350	0.4
Mexican	3,510,677	35.8
Native Hawaiian and Other Pacific Islander	26,094	0.3
Native Hawaiian	4,013	0.0
Guamanian or Chamorro	3,447	0.0
Samoan	12,115	0.1
Other Pacific Islander	6,519	0.1
Puerto Rican	44,609	0.5
White	4,936,599	50.3
Two or More Races	438,713	4.5

With respect to religion, the Association of Religion Data Archives tracked over 100 different denominations/faith traditions in 2010 within L.A. County, from the American Baptist Association to Zoroastrians.[29] That's over a hundred different faith traditions in only one county, of one region, of one state, in the United States.

I (and probably you, as well) live in a diverse, pluralistic society. Why does this matter so much? CR tells us that what determines moral rightness and wrongness is the dominant values of one's culture—but what is my culture? What is yours? Which values are the dominant ones?

If you're considering the moral permissibility of an abortion, for example, isn't it possible that you might get one answer if you live in Salt Lake City, Utah, and another if you live in San Francisco, California? One answer if you are Catholic, and another if you are Episcopalian? One answer if you

[28] More detail information is available here: http://factfinder2.census.gov/faces/tableservices/jsf/pages/productview.xhtml?src=bkmk

[29] More detail information is available here: http://www.thearda.com/rcms2010/r/c/06/rcms2010_06037_county_name_2010.asp

live in L.A. County, another if you live in Orange County (both within the State of California)? One answer if your family has just immigrated to the U.S., and another if your ancestors arrived on the Mayflower? One answer if you were born between 1940 and 1960 ("Baby-Boomer"), another if you were born between 1961 and 1981 ("Generation X"), and still another if you were born after 1982 ("Generation Y"/"Generation Next")?

Just how big and influential does a group have to be to count as a culture? As of 1995, the North American Man/Boy Love Association (N.A.M.B.L.A.) boasted a membership of 1,100. Is that enough to constitute a culture (one that advocates what the rest of us call pedophilia and pederasty, but a "culture" nonetheless)? If it is not a culture, why not? How large must a "social group" be to count as a culture? If it is a culture, then, according to CR, are its values just as legitimate as any others'? How do we handle the fact that the N.A.M.B.L.A. "culture" (or perhaps sub-culture) is found within other, broader cultures in which "man-boy love" is condemned as child rape?

From which group does one get one's values? Do we just pick for ourselves which group's values we'll adopt and value? If so, isn't that just subjectivism?

Whatever other challenges CR faces, a key feature of any ethical theory is its ability to provide a decision-making procedure, a method for resolving what to do when faced with a difficult ethical decision. If CR fails to provide this decision-making procedure, due to the vagueness of the very concept of "culture," then it fails as an ethical theory.

"Just consult the laws of the land," one might reply. "If it's against the law, then it's morally wrong according to your culture." This is probably too simplistic, though, given the fact that we recognize a distinction between what is legal/illegal and what is right/wrong. Lying, in most contexts, is not illegal, but is nevertheless generally regarded as wrong. African-Americans sitting at certain lunch counters was illegal at one time in the U.S., but most of us would deny that doing so was also morally wrong. Indeed, the very fact that we have a concept of "just" *and* "unjust" laws tells us that legality and morality, while usually overlapping, are not always the same thing. This is just one more challenge for this already besieged approach to ethics, but I'm not done yet!

All other challenges to CR aside, if one can establish that there are, in fact, at least some values that are found in all societies, at all times, and in all places, then such a finding would lend much credence to the claim that at least *some* moral values are universal, and that CR is false. James Rachels has attempted to provide a compelling argument that this is so.

James Rachels: Universal Moral Values

Rachels proposes that there is more moral "universality" across cultures than we might initially recognize. One reason for this is because cultures might manifest the same underlying value in different ways, given contingent historical, geographical, climatic, and other circumstances.

For example, throughout most of the U.S., the dead are buried below ground, but in New Orleans, they are buried above ground. Why? New Orleans is below sea-level, and has a high water table. Graves fill with water, and caskets float, creating an unhealthy, as well as deeply disturbing, result.[30] This is an example of how geography can influence the *manifestation* (burial below v. above ground) of the *same underlying value* (honor the dead). Other cultures cremate. Ancient Egyptians mummified their dead. All believed it to be morally right to honor the dead, but due to different circumstances, they demonstrated that belief in different ways.

As another example, consider child-rearing. Some cultures adopt the so-called "nuclear family" (mom, dad, and 2.5 kids under the same roof). Others prefer extended families (multiple

30 http://www.experienceneworleans.com/deadcity.htm

generations in the same home), and still others embrace communal child-rearing in which responsibility for caring for the young is shared by the larger community, including non-blood relatives.

There is any number of explanations for why one culture might manifest its child-care in one fashion, while a different culture does so in another, but the allegation is that the underlying value is the same, even though the manifestation is different.

The moral value that the young should be cared for is, in fact, one of a handful of values that Rachels claims that all cultures must have, if they are to survive as a culture. It is thus a *universal* (non-relative) value. Consider the alternative.

Try to imagine a culture in which no moral value was placed on caring for the young. There is no stigma, no shame, no pressure, no laws associated with child-rearing. How could such a culture persist? In order to survive, a culture must produce new members who will survive long enough to continue its traditions, and then create the next generation themselves. Although people care for children in a variety of formats, we struggle to even *imagine* a culture that does not care for them at all.

As another example, Rachels claims that no culture could survive if it did not have some prohibition against murder. Try to imagine what it would be like to live in a society in which no positive value was placed on innocent life, and in which there was nothing wrong with killing innocent people. What an anxiety-filled existence! How could such a culture avoid self-destruction?

As a final example, consider honesty. Rachels claims that all cultures, in order to survive as cultures, must endorse honesty and condemn deception. Why? Consider the alternative. If there was no stigma attached to deception, and no expectation of honesty, under normal circumstances, why would you ever believe what other people tell you? What you read? What you hear? Why would you assume the words you're reading right now are sincere and accurate? Why go to school, if it's just as likely that your instructors are lying as they are not? Why read the newspaper (or, more likely, internet news sources), if it's no worse for it to be filled with lies than the truth? Clearly, without an expectation of honesty, there's no basis for trust. Without trust, there's no basis for cooperation, and without cooperation, there is no society—not even family units can survive without trust-enabled cooperation. Obviously, people can and do lie, but this is the exception, rather than the rule. Imagine trying to get through your day if it was just as likely that everyone you met was lying to you as that they were telling the truth!

If Rachels is correct, then this is a major accomplishment. Though we might bicker as to just *which* moral principles and values are necessary for any society to survive (and are, therefore, "universal"), it would appear that there are some that fit that description. If so, then CR is wrong with respect to its claim that all values are relative, and that none is universal. That, at the very least, is a very important start for the rest of our process, in that it would allow us to operate on the assumption that (at least some) moral claims are objective.

If at least some moral claims are objective, then it's possible to make strong, meaningful comparisons of individuals, and of entire cultures. What will be the standard by which such comparisons are possible? The set of true moral values that apply to all people, everywhere, at all times.

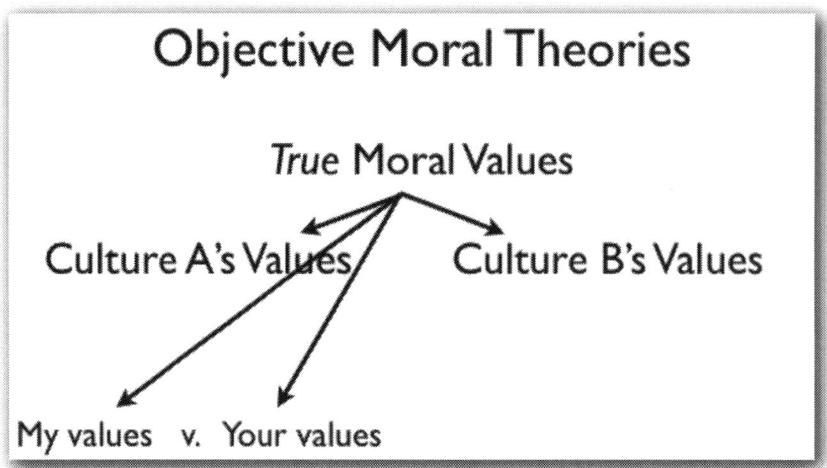

C.S. Lewis

Although his reasons are very different from those of James Rachels, C.S. Lewis agrees that there are universal (objective) moral values.

Lewis starts from what he takes to be the universal recognition of objective moral "rights" and "wrongs." This is evident, he thinks, from the fact that we all tend to *judge* the behavior of others (and ourselves). We really do think that some actions are good, and others bad—and morally so, not merely so in terms of what's prudent. We really do think that some actions are virtuous, and others vile, and that some people are heroes, and others villains. Although our particular examples might vary, we all engage in this general behavior. In addition, we have behavioral expectations of others, and we are upset when people violate them. We all think there are certain things that people just shouldn't do, and we get upset with them if they do it anyway. Spouses shouldn't be unfaithful. Friends shouldn't lie to you. Politicians shouldn't accept (or expect) bribes. Your neighbor shouldn't steal from you. No one should molest your child. And so forth. We don't merely blithely announce our expectations, and then shrug when they're violated, as though it didn't matter. We are offended, indignant, outraged, betrayed, hurt. . . With respect to our own behavior, when someone else accuses *us* of violating moral norms, we usually try to make excuses for the behavior, if we don't outright confess—thereby implying the need for an explanation in the first place. Compare the following hypothetical exchanges:

> You: "Hey! Don't cut in line in front of me."
> Me: "My friend has been saving my spot."

> You: "Hey! Don't cut in line in front of me."
> Me: "I'll do whatever I want!"

While there certainly are some people who flout convention, and are unashamed to do, we tend to judge those people very harshly—sometimes going so far as to label them sociopaths. Most of us play by the rules, try to justify our actions if we're caught "bending" them, get upset with others when they break them, and all the while at least implicitly acknowledge the existence of "the rules" in the first place. The implicit premise here seems to be that we all know that there exist certain (objective) moral principles.

Lewis is aware that not everyone would so readily agree to that claim, and he anticipates (and addresses) several possible objections. A first, obvious, objection is the theory of cultural relativism itself. But, just as Rachels argued that there are fewer differences in values across cultures as there might appear, Lewis makes a similar point.

> *Think of a country where people were admired for running away in battle, or*

> *where a man felt proud of double-crossing all the people who had been kindest to him. You might just as well try to imagine a country where two and two made five. Men have differed as regards what people you ought to be unselfish to-whether it was only your own family, or your fellow countrymen, or everyone. But they have always agreed that you ought not to put yourself first. Selfishness has never been admired. Men have differed as to whether you should have one wife or four. But they have always agreed that you must not simply have any woman you liked.*

Indeed, Lewis echoes most of the objections we have thus far considered. With regard to the fact that, if CR is true, there is no objective stance from which to evaluate or criticize any culture's values or practices, Lewis draws on his own experience of facing the threat of the Nazis in his lifetime. The Nazis were, for him, an example of a people and a cultural program gone *wrong*, and the mere fact that some Nazis might have thought differently doesn't change that fact. "People may be sometimes mistaken about [morals], just as people sometimes get their sums wrong; but they are not a matter of mere taste and opinion any more than the multiplication table."

A related objection was that, if CR is true, moral reformers are, paradoxically, always morally wrong. And yet, as Lewis points out, people *do* argue that reform is possible, and desirable.

> *If no set of moral ideas were truer or better than any other, there would be no sense in preferring civilised morality to savage morality, or Christian morality to Nazi morality. In fact, of course, we all do believe that some moralities are better than others. We do believe that some of the people who tried to change the moral ideas of their own age were what we would call Reformers or Pioneers-people who understood morality better than their neighbours did.*

Another objection to the existence of objective moral values, very much in the spirit of CR, is that "morality" is merely social conditioning produced by our education and upbringing. Lewis, however, replies that *how* something is learned doesn't necessarily indicate its ultimate source or status (e.g., we learn the multiplication tables at school without this implying that math is merely a human convention). "But," the skeptic might wonder, "why think that morality is objective in a way analogous to math?" Because, says Lewis, the "Moral Law" is (generally, at its core) the same across cultures, whereas mere convention (e.g., which side of the road one drives on) is not.

Returning to his arguments against CR, Lewis reiterates that we do, in actual practice, hold some cultural norms to be "better" or "worse" than others (e.g., Nazis are worse!), and alleged differences in values are often just differences in matters of fact. We have already rehearsed this point about alleged differences in values being just differences in local expressions of those values previously in this chapter, but Lewis uses an interesting example that's worth quoting: witch burning.

> *I have met people who exaggerate the differences, because they have not distinguished between differences of morality and differences of belief about facts. For example, one man said to me, 'Three hundred years ago people in England were putting witches to death. Was that what you call the Rule of Human Nature or Right Conduct?' But surely the reason we do not execute witches is that we do not believe there are such things. If we did-if we really thought that there were people going about who had sold themselves to the devil and received supernatural powers from him in return and were using these powers to kill their neighbours or drive them mad or bring bad weather, surely we would all agree that if anyone deserved the death penalty, then these filthy quislings did. There is no difference of moral principle here: the difference is simply about matter of fact. It*

may be a great advance in knowledge not to believe in witches: there is no moral advance in not executing them when you do not think they are there. You would not call a man humane for ceasing to set mousetraps if he did so because he believed there were no mice in the house.

A different sort of objection to the claim that morality is objective brings us back to the evolutionary understanding of morality previously considered by our appeals to Dawkins and Rachels. Perhaps "morality" is just our evolution-produced "herd instinct," just one instinctive drive amongst other instinctive drives? Lewis replies that desires are not identical to our sense of obligation with respect to those desires. For example, my awareness that I *ought* to be forgiving is not at all the same as a *desire* to be forgiving. Indeed, often our desires are in sharp contrast to our sense of obligation. Moreover, Lewis thinks that it makes little sense to understand moral prescriptions as impulses or desires amongst others, as he can identify no particular impulses or desires that the "Moral Law" tells us always to restrain or to pursue. Indeed, our sense of moral obligation seems to be a different sort of thing *by which we judge between* desires and impulses.

Supposing you hear a cry for help from a man in danger. You will probably feel two desires-one a desire to give help (due to your herd instinct), the other a desire to keep out of danger (due to the instinct for self-preservation). But you will find inside you, in addition to these two impulses, a third thing which tells you that you ought to follow the impulse to help, and suppress the impulse to run away. Now this thing that judges between two instincts, that decides which should be encouraged, cannot itself be either of them. You might as well say that the sheet of music which tells you, at a given moment, to play one note on the piano and not another, is itself one of the notes on the keyboard. The Moral Law tells us the tune we have to play: our instincts are merely the keys.

Nor does it seem plausible, according to Lewis, that morally good behavior is merely socially useful behavior (e.g., what's needed for community flourishing, as Rachels might argue). According to Lewis, morally good behavior *is* socially useful, but that doesn't explain its purpose (in a non-circular way), since being "socially useful" *is* of those behaviors we label "good."

If a man asked what was the point of playing football, it would not be much good saying 'in order to score goals,' for trying to score goals is the game itself, not the reason for the game, and you would really only be saying that football was football-which is true, but not worth saying. In the same way, if a man asks what is the point of behaving decently, it is no good replying, 'in order to benefit society,' for trying to benefit society, in other words being unselfish (for 'society' after all only means 'other people'), is one of the things decent behaviour consists in; all you are really saying is that decent behaviour is decent behaviour.

While Lewis and Rachels agree, then, on the existence of universal moral values, they very much disagree as the nature of the source and grounding of those values. For Rachels, our objective moral values arise as dispositions to behave that promoted our survival, and are, indeed, necessary for human survival and flourishing in communities. For Lewis, the ultimate source of those moral values is a transcendent, morally perfect God—though his defense of that claim is beyond the scope of this chapter, or even this book.

Although we have seen two critiques of CR from Rachels and Lewis, it's important to make three concessions:

1. Some differences are probably so significant that they're not best understood as merely different manifestations of the same underlying values. For example, someone might

claim that marriage is one way of expressing the value that human sexuality should be constrained, and Female Genital Mutilation (FGM) is simply another. I, for one, find the practices different enough that I doubt they express the same value at all. This is certainly subject to debate. The point, at this stage, though, is simply to acknowledge that it would be too easy, and too sloppy, to gloss over the genuine and controversial differences between various cultural practices by suggesting that they are just different manifestations of the same value. While there might be more universality than there appears, there's probably also less universality than we might wish were the case.

2. Both subjectivism and CR have something worthwhile to offer. There is certainly a category of value judgments that we make that is best understood using the subjectivist model. Our judgments concerning aesthetic preferences, for example, music, art, food, and so on, all very reasonably seem to be nothing more (or less) than expressions of personal opinion. They can, and should, be understood through the subjectivist lens.

There is another category of values and behaviors that seem to be based on cultural standards, and is both more than mere personal opinion, and less than a universal moral value. Once again, the exact content of this category is probably difficult to articulate, but things like expectations of behavior in particular settings (e.g., how to behave with respect to greetings, when visiting holy sites, when a guest in someone's home, etc.) are probably examples.

3. A lesson to be learned from both subjectivism and CR is to be cautious of hasty assumptions and self-righteousness. It's all too easy to presume one's own view of the world, and one's own values, are the absolute truth and worthy of promulgation. History is filled with the tragic consequences of such assumptions. Both subjectivism and CR give us reason to slow down, restrain our arrogant tendencies, and pay careful attention to what other individuals, and other communities, have to say.

Where both go too far, however, is in thinking that no truth is possible, that there are no right answers at all, that no meaningful comparisons and judgments are possible, and that no individual (or group) ever does wrong (in any strong sense beyond our own personal or collective opinion).

Indeed, there's a dangerous irony lurking behind both theories: the subjectivist judgment that all values are mere opinions is *itself* a mere opinion (according to its own standards), yet is offered as a rule for all; and the CR view that all values are relative to one's culture is also usually (implicitly, and mistakenly) offered as a reason for all people to be accepting, respectful, and tolerant, of other culture's values, even when some cultures clearly value doing just the opposite.

Exercises for Wisdom and Growth

1. What is your favorite flavor of ice cream? Your favorite musical group? Is the death penalty morally justifiable? What about unprotected sex without telling your partner you're HIV positive? Do you think the last few questions are similar to first few questions? Why, or why not?
2. Find someone in your life with whom you disagree concerning some moral issue (e.g., abortion, illegal immigration, the death penalty). Have a respectful, but spirited conversation with that person. Do you believe that you are "right," and the other person is mistaken? Or, do you simply believe that you're both right? What would it mean for you to both be right? What's the point of discussion, in that case?
3. What is your "culture?" Describe it, and its influences, as thoroughly as you're able. Be sure to consider possible cultural elements as race, gender, religion, nationality, sexual orientation, generation, and (dis)ability. Describe specific moral recommendations made by your culture (e.g., prohibiting pre-marital sex). List at least 5. Do you obey these recommendations? Discuss why, or why not. Do you agree with your culture's values? Why, or why not?
4. Find someone with a different cultural background (e.g., different ethnic category, religion, national origin, generation, etc.). Discuss and compare the prevailing values of your respective cultures. In what ways are they similar, and in what ways are they different? Have a respectful discussion concerning your differences. What, if anything, do you conclude from this experience?
5. Immerse yourself in another culture. Assuming that extensive travel is not a possibility, simply go to a part of your town that is "foreign" to you, considering your own cultural identification (e.g., "Little China," "Korea Town," the Yacht Club, a Bollywood film festival, a Gay Pride festival, etc.). Be conscious of your feelings, and judgments. What are they? How different are "those people?" How similar?

Plato (424 BCE – 328 BCE) is a very well-known ancient Greek philosopher and student of the possibly more well-known Socrates. Because Socrates wrote nothing himself, most of what we think we know about Socrates comes from the writings of others, most notably Plato. Socrates appears as the main character in numerous Platonic dialogues, including "The Republic", from which you have two excerpts. In this dialogue, Socrates is discussing the nature of justice with several other persons. In the first excerpt (from Book 1 of the Republic), Socrates is debating Thrasymachus. Thrasymachus argues that justice is simply the will of the stronger, that "might makes right." Socrates presses Thrasymachus on this, forcing him to acknowledge seeming contradictions and counter-examples, in an attempt to establish that there is a standard of justice that transcends the interests of the stronger, and that injustice is never more "profitable" than justice. In the second excerpt (Book 2), the conversation continues. Thrasymachus has withdrawn, but Glaucon has taken his place. Glaucon argues that justice is a necessary inconvenience that we agree to in the style of a social contract. This agreement is accepted by virtue of the fact that none of us has sufficient power to behave as we truly desire without fear of consequences. The Myth of Gyges' Ring is offered as evidence in support of this. Note that this brief section provides an incredibly early account of both the social contract approach to political philosophy, as well as the theory of human motivation known as psychological egoism.

Plato
The *Republic*

Book I

Socrates - Polemarchus – Thrasymachus

He roared out to the whole company: What folly. Socrates, has taken possession of you all? And why, sillybillies, do you knock under to one another? I say that if you want really to know what justice is, you should not only ask but answer, and you should not seek honour to yourself from the refutation of an opponent, but have your own answer; for there is many a one who can ask and cannot answer. And now I will not have you say that justice is duty or advantage or profit or gain or interest, for this sort of nonsense will not do for me; I must have clearness and accuracy.

I was panic-stricken at his words, and could not look at him without trembling. Indeed I believe that if I had not fixed my eye upon him, I should have been struck dumb: but when I saw his fury rising, I looked at him first, and was therefore able to reply to him.

Thrasymachus, I said, with a quiver, don't be hard upon us. Polemarchus and I may have been guilty of a little mistake in the argument, but I can assure you that the error was not intentional. If we were seeking for a piece of gold, you would not imagine that we were 'knocking under to one another,' and so losing our chance of finding it. And why, when we are seeking for justice, a thing more precious than many pieces of gold, do you say that we are weakly yielding to one another and not doing our utmost to get at the truth? Nay, my good friend, we are most willing and anxious to do so, but the fact is that we cannot. And if so, you people who know all things should pity us and not be angry with us.

How characteristic of Socrates! he replied, with a bitter laugh;--that's your ironical style! Did I not foresee--have I not already told you, that whatever he was asked he would refuse to answer, and try irony or any other shuffle, in order that he might avoid answering?

You are a philosopher, Thrasymachus, I replied, and well know that if you ask a person what numbers make up twelve, taking care to prohibit him whom you ask from answering twice six, or three times four, or six times two, or four times three, 'for this sort of nonsense will not do for me,'--then obviously, that is your way of putting the question, no one can answer you. But suppose that he were to retort, 'Thrasymachus, what do you mean? If one of these numbers which you interdict be the true answer to the question, am I falsely to say some other number which is not the right one?--is that your meaning?'--How would you answer him?

Just as if the two cases were at all alike! he said.

Why should they not be? I replied; and even if they are not, but only appear to be so to the person who is asked, ought he not to say what he thinks, whether you and I forbid him or not?

I presume then that you are going to make one of the interdicted answers?

I dare say that I may, notwithstanding the danger, if upon reflection I approve of any of them.

But what if I give you an answer about justice other and better, he said, than any of these? What do you deserve to have done to you?

Done to me!--as becomes the ignorant, I must learn from the wise--that is what I deserve to have done to me.

What, and no payment! a pleasant notion!

I will pay when I have the money, I replied.

Socrates - Thrasymachus - Glaucon

But you have, Socrates, said Glaucon: and you, Thrasymachus, need be under no anxiety about money, for we will all make a contribution for Socrates.

Yes, he replied, and then Socrates will do as he always does--refuse to answer himself, but take and pull to pieces the answer of some one else.

Why, my good friend, I said, how can any one answer who knows, and says that he knows, just nothing; and who, even if he has some faint notions of his own, is told by a man of authority not to utter them? The natural thing is, that the speaker should be some one like yourself who professes to know and can tell what he knows. Will you then kindly answer, for the edification of the company and of myself?

Glaucon and the rest of the company joined in my request and Thrasymachus, as any one might see, was in reality eager to speak; for he thought that he had an excellent answer, and would distinguish himself. But at first he to insist on my answering; at length he consented to begin. Behold, he said, the wisdom of Socrates; he refuses to teach himself, and goes about learning of others, to whom he never even says thank you.

That I learn of others, I replied, is quite true; but that I am ungrateful I wholly deny. Money I have none, and therefore I pay in praise, which is all I have: and how ready I am to praise any one who appears to me to speak well you will very soon find out when you answer; for I expect that you will answer well.

Listen, then, he said; I proclaim that justice is nothing else than the interest of the stronger. And now why do you not me? But of course you won't.

Let me first understand you, I replied. Justice, as you say, is the interest of the stronger. What, Thrasymachus, is the meaning of this? You cannot mean to say that because Polydamas, the pancratiast, is stronger than we are, and finds the eating of beef conducive to his bodily strength, that to eat beef is therefore equally for our good who are weaker than he is, and right and just for us?

That's abominable of you, Socrates; you take the words in the sense which is most damaging to the argument.

Not at all, my good sir, I said; I am trying to understand them; and I wish that you would be a little clearer.

Well, he said, have you never heard that forms of government differ; there are tyrannies, and there are democracies, and there are aristocracies?

Yes, I know.

And the government is the ruling power in each state?

Certainly.

And the different forms of government make laws democratical, aristocratical, tyrannical, with a view to their several interests; and these laws, which are made by them for their own interests, are the justice which they deliver to their subjects, and him who transgresses them they punish as a breaker of the law, and unjust. And that is what I mean when I say that in all states there is the same principle of justice, which is the interest of the government; and as the government must be supposed to have power, the only reasonable conclusion is, that everywhere there is one principle of justice, which is the interest of the stronger.

Now I understand you, I said; and whether you are right or not I will try to discover. But let me remark, that in defining justice you have yourself used the word 'interest' which you forbade me to use. It is true, however, that in your definition the words 'of the stronger' are added.

A small addition, you must allow, he said.

Great or small, never mind about that: we must first enquire whether what you are saying is the truth. Now we are both agreed that justice is interest of some sort, but you go on to say 'of the stronger'; about this addition I am not so sure, and must therefore consider further.

Proceed.

I will; and first tell me, Do you admit that it is just for subjects to obey their rulers?

I do.

But are the rulers of states absolutely infallible, or are they sometimes liable to err?

To be sure, he replied, they are liable to err.

Then in making their laws they may sometimes make them rightly, and sometimes not?

True.

When they make them rightly, they make them agreeably to their interest; when they are mistaken, contrary to their interest; you admit that?

Yes.

And the laws which they make must be obeyed by their subjects,--and that is what you call justice?

Doubtless.

Then justice, according to your argument, is not only obedience to the interest of the stronger but the reverse?

What is that you are saying? he asked.

I am only repeating what you are saying, I believe. But let us consider: Have we not admitted that the rulers may be mistaken about their own interest in what they command, and also that to obey them is justice? Has not that been admitted?

Yes.

Then you must also have acknowledged justice not to be for the interest of the stronger, when the rulers unintentionally command things to be done which are to their own injury. For if, as you say, justice is the obedience which the subject renders to their commands, in that case, O wisest of men, is there any escape from the conclusion that the weaker are commanded to do, not what is for the interest, but what is for the injury of the stronger?

Nothing can be clearer, Socrates, said Polemarchus.

Socrates - Cleitophon - Polemarchus - Thrasymachus

Yes, said Cleitophon, interposing, if you are allowed to be his witness.

But there is no need of any witness, said Polemarchus, for Thrasymachus himself acknowledges that rulers may sometimes command what is not for their own interest, and that for subjects to obey them is justice.

Yes, Polemarchus,--Thrasymachus said that for subjects to do what was commanded by their rulers is just.

Yes, Cleitophon, but he also said that justice is the interest of the stronger, and, while admitting both these propositions, he further acknowledged that the stronger may command the weaker who are his subjects to do what is not for his own interest; whence follows that justice is the injury quite as much as the interest of the stronger.

But, said Cleitophon, he meant by the interest of the stronger what the stronger thought to be his interest,--this was what the weaker had to do; and this was affirmed by him to be justice.

Those were not his words, rejoined Polemarchus.

Socrates - Thrasymachus

Never mind, I replied, if he now says that they are, let us accept his statement. Tell me, Thrasymachus, I said, did you mean by justice what the stronger thought to be his interest, whether really so or not?

Certainly not, he said. Do you suppose that I call him who is mistaken the stronger at the time when he is mistaken?

Yes, I said, my impression was that you did so, when you admitted that the ruler was not infallible but might be sometimes mistaken.

You argue like an informer, Socrates. Do you mean, for example, that he who is mistaken about the sick is a physician in that he is mistaken? or that he who errs in arithmetic or grammar is an arithmetician or grammarian at the me when he is making the mistake, in respect of the mistake? True, we say that the physician or arithmetician or grammarian has made a mistake, but this is only a way of speaking; for the fact is that neither the grammarian nor any other person of skill ever makes a mistake in so far as he is what his name implies; they none of them err unless their skill fails them, and then they cease to be skilled artists. No artist or sage or ruler errs at the time when he is what his name implies; though he is commonly said to err, and I adopted the common mode of speaking. But to be perfectly accurate, since you are such a lover of accuracy, we should say that the ruler, in so far as he is the ruler, is unerring, and, being unerring, always commands that which is for his own interest; and the subject is required to execute his commands; and therefore, as I said at first and now repeat, justice is the interest of the stronger.

Indeed, Thrasymachus, and do I really appear to you to argue like an informer?

Certainly, he replied.

And you suppose that I ask these questions with any design of injuring you in the argument?

Nay, he replied, 'suppose' is not the word--I know it; but you will be found out, and by sheer force of argument you will never prevail.

I shall not make the attempt, my dear man; but to avoid any misunderstanding occurring between us in future, let me ask, in what sense do you speak of a ruler or stronger whose interest, as you were saying, he being the superior, it is just that the inferior should execute--is he a ruler in the popular or in the strict sense of the term?

In the strictest of all senses, he said. And now cheat and play the informer if you can; I ask no quarter at your hands. But you never will be able, never.

And do you imagine, I said, that I am such a madman as to try and cheat, Thrasymachus? I might as well shave a lion.

Why, he said, you made the attempt a minute ago, and you failed.

Enough, I said, of these civilities. It will be better that I should ask you a question: Is the physician, taken in that strict sense of which you are speaking, a healer of the sick or a maker of money? And remember that I am now speaking of the true physician.

A healer of the sick, he replied.

And the pilot--that is to say, the true pilot--is he a captain of sailors or a mere sailor?

A captain of sailors.

The circumstance that he sails in the ship is not to be taken into account; neither is he to be called a sailor; the name pilot by which he is distinguished has nothing to do with sailing, but is significant of his skill and of his authority over the sailors.

Very true, he said.

Now, I said, every art has an interest?

Certainly.

For which the art has to consider and provide?

Yes, that is the aim of art.

And the interest of any art is the perfection of it--this and nothing else?

What do you mean?

I mean what I may illustrate negatively by the example of the body. Suppose you were to ask me whether the body is self-sufficing or has wants, I should reply: Certainly the body has wants; for the body may be ill and require to be cured, and has therefore interests to which the art of medicine ministers; and this is the origin and intention of medicine, as you will acknowledge. Am I not right?

Quite right, he replied.

But is the art of medicine or any other art faulty or deficient in any quality in the same way that the eye may be deficient in sight or the ear fail of hearing, and therefore requires another art to provide for the interests of seeing and hearing--has art in itself, I say, any similar liability to fault or defect, and does every art require another supplementary art to provide for its interests, and that another and another without end? Or have the arts to look only after their own interests? Or have they no need either of themselves or of another?--having no faults or defects, they have no need to correct them, either by the exercise of their own art or of any other; they have only to consider the interest of their subject-matter. For every art remains pure and faultless while remaining true--that is to say, while perfect and unimpaired. Take the words in your precise sense, and tell me whether I am not right."

Yes, clearly.

Then medicine does not consider the interest of medicine, but the interest of the body?

True, he said.

Nor does the art of horsemanship consider the interests of the art of horsemanship, but the interests of the horse; neither do any other arts care for themselves, for they have no needs; they care only for that which is the subject of their art?

True, he said.

But surely, Thrasymachus, the arts are the superiors and rulers of their own subjects?

To this he assented with a good deal of reluctance.

Then, I said, no science or art considers or enjoins the interest of the stronger or superior, but only the interest of the subject and weaker?

He made an attempt to contest this proposition also, but finally acquiesced.

Then, I continued, no physician, in so far as he is a physician, considers his own good in what he prescribes, but the good of his patient; for the true physician is also a ruler having the human body as a subject, and is not a mere money-maker; that has been admitted?

Yes.

And the pilot likewise, in the strict sense of the term, is a ruler of sailors and not a mere sailor?

That has been admitted.

And such a pilot and ruler will provide and prescribe for the interest of the sailor who is under him, and not for his own or the ruler's interest?

He gave a reluctant 'Yes.'

Then, I said, Thrasymachus, there is no one in any rule who, in so far as he is a ruler, considers or enjoins what is for his own interest, but always what is for the interest of his subject or suitable to his art; to that he looks, and that alone he considers in everything which he says and does.

When we had got to this point in the argument, and every one saw that the definition of justice had been completely upset, Thrasymachus, instead of replying to me, said: Tell me, Socrates, have you got a nurse?

Why do you ask such a question, I said, when you ought rather to be answering?

Because she leaves you to snivel, and never wipes your nose: she has not even taught you to know the shepherd from the sheep.

What makes you say that? I replied.

Because you fancy that the shepherd or neatherd fattens of tends the sheep or oxen with a view to their own good and not to the good of himself or his master; and you further imagine that the rulers of states, if they are true rulers, never think of their subjects as sheep, and that they are not studying their own advantage day and night. Oh, no; and so entirely astray are you in your ideas about the just and unjust as not even to know that justice and the just are in reality another's good; that is to say, the interest of the ruler and stronger, and the loss of the subject and servant; and injustice the opposite; for the unjust is lord over the truly simple and just: he is the stronger, and his subjects do what is for his interest, and minister to his happiness, which is very far from being their own. Consider further, most foolish Socrates, that the just is always a loser in comparison with the unjust. First of all, in private contracts: wherever the unjust is the partner of the just you will find that, when the partnership is dissolved, the unjust man has always more and the just less. Secondly, in their dealings with the State: when there is an income tax, the just man will pay more and the unjust less on the same amount of income; and when there is anything to be received the one gains nothing and the other much. Observe also what happens when they take an office; there is the just man neglecting his affairs and perhaps suffering other losses, and getting nothing out of the public, because he is just; moreover he is hated by his friends and acquaintance for refusing to serve them in unlawful ways. But all this is reversed in the case of the unjust man. I am speaking, as before, of injustice on a large scale in which the advantage of the unjust is more apparent; and my meaning will be most clearly seen if we turn to that highest form of injustice in which the criminal is the happiest of men, and the sufferers or those who refuse to do injustice are the most miserable--that is to say tyranny, which by fraud and force takes away the property of others, not little by little but wholesale; comprehending in one, things sacred as well as profane, private and public; for which acts of wrong, if he were detected perpetrating any one of them singly, he would be punished and incur great disgrace--they who do such wrong in particular cases are called robbers of temples, and man-stealers and burglars and swindlers and thieves. But when a man besides taking away the money of the citizens has made slaves of them, then, instead of these names of reproach, he is termed happy and blessed, not only by the citizens but by all who hear of his having achieved the consummation of injustice. For mankind censure injustice, fearing that they may be the victims of it and not because they shrink from committing it. And thus, as I have shown, Socrates, injustice, when on a sufficient scale, has more strength and freedom and mastery than justice; and, as I said at first, justice is the interest of the stronger, whereas injustice is a man's own profit and interest.

Thrasymachus, when he had thus spoken, having, like a bathman, deluged our ears with his words, had a mind to go away. But the company would not let him; they insisted that he should remain and defend his position; and I myself added my own humble request that he would not leave us. Thrasymachus, I said to him, excellent man, how suggestive are your remarks! And are you going to run away before you have fairly taught or learned whether they are true or not? Is the attempt to determine the way of man's life so small a matter in your eyes--to determine how life may be passed by each one of us to the greatest advantage?

And do I differ from you, he said, as to the importance of the enquiry?

You appear rather, I replied, to have no care or thought about us, Thrasymachus--whether we live better or worse from not knowing what you say you know, is to you a matter of indifference. Prithee, friend, do not keep your knowledge to yourself; we are a large party; and any benefit which you confer upon us will be amply rewarded. For my own part I openly declare that I am not convinced, and that I do not believe injustice to be more gainful than justice, even if uncontrolled and allowed to have free play. For, granting that there may be an unjust man who is able to commit injustice either by fraud or force, still this does not convince me of the superior advantage of injustice, and there may be others who are in the same predicament with myself. Perhaps we may be wrong; if so, you in your wisdom should convince us that we are mistaken in preferring justice to injustice.

And how am I to convince you, he said, if you are not already convinced by what I have just said; what more can I do for you? Would you have me put the proof bodily into your souls?

Heaven forbid! I said; I would only ask you to be consistent; or, if you change, change openly and let there be no deception. For I must remark, Thrasymachus, if you will recall what was previously said, that although you began by defining the true physician in an exact sense, you did not observe a like exactness when speaking of the shepherd; you thought that the shepherd as a shepherd tends the sheep not with a view to their own good, but like a mere diner or banqueter with a view to the pleasures of the table; or, again, as a trader for sale in the market, and not as a shepherd. Yet surely the art of the shepherd is concerned only with the good of his subjects; he has only to provide the best for them, since the perfection of the art is already ensured whenever all the requirements of it are satisfied. And that was what I was saying just now about the ruler. I conceived that the art of the ruler, considered as ruler, whether in a state or in private life, could only regard the good of his flock or subjects; whereas you seem to think that the rulers in states, that is to say, the true rulers, like being in authority.

Think! Nay, I am sure of it.

Then why in the case of lesser offices do men never take them willingly without payment, unless under the idea that they govern for the advantage not of themselves but of others? Let me ask you a question: Are not the several arts different, by reason of their each having a separate function? And, my dear illustrious friend, do say what you think, that we may make a little progress.

Yes, that is the difference, he replied.

And each art gives us a particular good and not merely a general one--medicine, for example, gives us health; navigation, safety at sea, and so on?

Yes, he said.

And the art of payment has the special function of giving pay: but we do not confuse this with other arts, any more than the art of the pilot is to be confused with the art of medicine, because the health of the pilot may be improved by a sea voyage. You would not be inclined to say, would you, that navigation is the art of medicine, at least if we are to adopt your exact use of language?

Certainly not.

Or because a man is in good health when he receives pay you would not say that the art of payment is medicine?

I should say not.

Nor would you say that medicine is the art of receiving pay because a man takes fees when he is engaged in healing?

Certainly not.

And we have admitted, I said, that the good of each art is specially confined to the art?

Yes.

Then, if there be any good which all artists have in common, that is to be attributed to something of which they all have the common use?

True, he replied.

And when the artist is benefited by receiving pay the advantage is gained by an additional use of the art of pay, which is not the art professed by him?

He gave a reluctant assent to this.

Then the pay is not derived by the several artists from their respective arts. But the truth is, that while the art of medicine gives health, and the art of the builder builds a house, another art attends them which is the art of pay. The various arts may be doing their own business and benefiting that over which they preside, but would the artist receive any benefit from his art unless he were paid as well?

I suppose not.

But does he therefore confer no benefit when he works for nothing?

Certainly, he confers a benefit.

Then now, Thrasymachus, there is no longer any doubt that neither arts nor governments provide for their own interests; but, as we were before saying, they rule and provide for the interests of their subjects who are the weaker and not the stronger--to their good they attend and not to the good of the superior.

And this is the reason, my dear Thrasymachus, why, as I was just now saying, no one is willing to govern; because no one likes to take in hand the reformation of evils which are not his concern without remuneration. For, in the execution of his work, and in giving his orders to another, the true artist does not regard his own interest, but always that of his subjects; and therefore in order that rulers may be willing to rule, they must be paid in one of three modes of payment: money, or honour, or a penalty for refusing.

Socrates - Glaucon

What do you mean, Socrates? said Glaucon. The first two modes of payment are intelligible enough, but what the penalty is I do not understand, or how a penalty can be a payment.

You mean that you do not understand the nature of this payment which to the best men is the great inducement to rule? Of course you know that ambition and avarice are held to be, as indeed they are, a disgrace?

Very true.

And for this reason, I said, money and honour have no attraction for them; good men do not wish to be openly demanding payment for governing and so to get the name of hirelings, nor by secretly helping themselves out of the public revenues to get the name of thieves. And not being ambitious they do not care about honour. Wherefore necessity must be laid upon them, and they must be induced to serve from the fear of punishment. And this, as I imagine, is the reason why the forwardness to take office, instead of waiting to be compelled, has been deemed dishonourable. Now the worst part of the punishment is that he who refuses to rule is liable to be ruled by one who is worse than himself. And the fear of this, as I conceive, induces the good to take office, not because they would, but because they cannot help--not under the idea that they are going to have any benefit or enjoyment themselves, but as a necessity, and because they are not able to commit the task of ruling to any one who is better than themselves, or indeed as good. For there is reason to think that if a city were composed entirely of good men, then to avoid office would be as much an object of contention as to obtain office is at present; then we should have plain proof that the true ruler is not meant by nature to regard his own interest, but that of his subjects; and every one who knew this would choose rather to receive a benefit from another than to have the trouble of conferring one. So far am I from agreeing with Thrasymachus that justice is the interest of the stronger. This latter question need not be further discussed at present; but when Thrasymachus says that the life of the unjust is more advantageous than that of the just, his new statement appears to me to be of a far more serious character. Which of us has spoken truly? And which sort of life, Glaucon, do you prefer?

I for my part deem the life of the just to be the more advantageous, he answered.

Did you hear all the advantages of the unjust which Thrasymachus was rehearsing?

Yes, I heard him, he replied, but he has not convinced me.

Then shall we try to find some way of convincing him, if we can, that he is saying what is not true?

Most certainly, he replied.

If, I said, he makes a set speech and we make another recounting all the advantages of being just, and he answers and we rejoin, there must be a numbering and measuring of the goods which are claimed on either side, and in the end we shall want judges to decide; but if we proceed in our enquiry as we lately did, by making admissions to one another, we shall unite the offices of judge and advocate in our own persons.

Very good, he said.

And which method do I understand you to prefer? I said.

That which you propose.

Well, then, Thrasymachus, I said, suppose you begin at the beginning and answer me. You say that perfect injustice is more gainful than perfect justice?

Socrates - Glaucon - Thrasymachus

Yes, that is what I say, and I have given you my reasons.

And what is your view about them? Would you call one of them virtue and the other vice?

Certainly.

I suppose that you would call justice virtue and injustice vice?

What a charming notion! So likely too, seeing that I affirm injustice to be profitable and justice not.

What else then would you say?

The opposite, he replied.

And would you call justice vice?

No, I would rather say sublime simplicity.

Then would you call injustice malignity?

No; I would rather say discretion.

And do the unjust appear to you to be wise and good?

Yes, he said; at any rate those of them who are able to be perfectly unjust, and who have the power of subduing states and nations; but perhaps you imagine me to be talking of cutpurses.

Even this profession if undetected has advantages, though they are not to be compared with those of which I was just now speaking.

I do not think that I misapprehend your meaning, Thrasymachus, I replied; but still I cannot hear without amazement that you class injustice with wisdom and virtue, and justice with the opposite.

Certainly I do so class them.

Now, I said, you are on more substantial and almost unanswerable ground; for if the injustice which you were maintaining to be profitable had been admitted by you as by others to be vice and deformity, an answer might have been given to you on received principles; but now I perceive that you will call injustice honourable and strong, and to the unjust you will attribute all the qualities which were attributed by us before to the just, seeing that you do not hesitate to rank injustice with wisdom and virtue.

You have guessed most infallibly, he replied.

Then I certainly ought not to shrink from going through with the argument so long as I have reason to think that you, Thrasymachus, are speaking your real mind; for I do believe that you are now in earnest and are not amusing yourself at our expense.

I may be in earnest or not, but what is that to you?--to refute the argument is your business.

Very true, I said; that is what I have to do: But will you be so good as answer yet one more question? Does the just man try to gain any advantage over the just?

Far otherwise; if he did would not be the simple, amusing creature which he is.

And would he try to go beyond just action?

He would not.

And how would he regard the attempt to gain an advantage over the unjust; would that be considered by him as just or unjust?

He would think it just, and would try to gain the advantage; but he would not be able.

Whether he would or would not be able, I said, is not to the point. My question is only whether the just man, while refusing to have more than another just man, would wish and claim to have more than the unjust?

Yes, he would.

And what of the unjust--does he claim to have more than the just man and to do more than is just.

Of course, he said, for he claims to have more than all men.

And the unjust man will strive and struggle to obtain more than the unjust man or action, in order that he may have more than all?

True.

We may put the matter thus, I said--the just does not desire more than his like but more than his unlike, whereas the unjust desires more than both his like and his unlike?

Nothing, he said, can be better than that statement.

And the unjust is good and wise, and the just is neither?

Good again, he said.

And is not the unjust like the wise and good and the just unlike them?

Of course, he said, he who is of a certain nature, is like those who are of a certain nature; he who is not, not.

Each of them, I said, is such as his like is?

Certainly, he replied.

Very good, Thrasymachus, I said; and now to take the case of the arts: you would admit that one man is a musician and another not a musician?

Yes.

And which is wise and which is foolish?

Clearly the musician is wise, and he who is not a musician is foolish.

And he is good in as far as he is wise, and bad in as far as he is foolish?

Yes.

And you would say the same sort of thing of the physician?

Yes.

And do you think, my excellent friend, that a musician when he adjusts the lyre would desire or claim to exceed or go beyond a musician in the tightening and loosening the strings?

I do not think that he would.

But he would claim to exceed the non-musician?

Of course.

And what would you say of the physician? In prescribing meats and drinks would he wish to go beyond another physician or beyond the practice of medicine?

He would not.

But he would wish to go beyond the non-physician?

Yes.

And about knowledge and ignorance in general; see whether you think that any man who has knowledge ever would wish to have the choice of saying or doing more than another man who has knowledge. Would he not rather say or do the same as his like in the same case?

That, I suppose, can hardly be denied.

And what of the ignorant? would he not desire to have more than either the knowing or the ignorant?

I dare say.

And the knowing is wise?

Yes.

And the wise is good?

True.

Then the wise and good will not desire to gain more than his like, but more than his unlike and opposite?

I suppose so.

Whereas the bad and ignorant will desire to

gain more than both?

Yes.

But did we not say, Thrasymachus, that the unjust goes beyond both his like and unlike? Were not these your words? They were.

They were.

And you also said that the lust will not go beyond his like but his unlike?

Yes.

Then the just is like the wise and good, and the unjust like the evil and ignorant?

That is the inference.

And each of them is such as his like is?

That was admitted.

Then the just has turned out to be wise and good and the unjust evil and ignorant.

Thrasymachus made all these admissions, not fluently, as I repeat them, but with extreme reluctance; it was a hot summer's day, and the perspiration poured from him in torrents; and then I saw what I had never seen before, Thrasymachus blushing. As we were now agreed that justice was virtue and wisdom, and injustice vice and ignorance, I proceeded to another point:

Well, I said, Thrasymachus, that matter is now settled; but were we not also saying that injustice had strength; do you remember?

Yes, I remember, he said, but do not suppose that I approve of what you are saying or have no answer; if however I were to answer, you would be quite certain to accuse me of haranguing; therefore either permit me to have my say out, or if you would rather ask, do so, and I will answer 'Very good,' as they say to story-telling old women, and will nod 'Yes' and 'No.'

Certainly not, I said, if contrary to your real opinion.

Yes, he said, I will, to please you, since you will not let me speak. What else would you have?

Nothing in the world, I said; and if you are so disposed I will ask and you shall answer.

Proceed.

Then I will repeat the question which I asked before, in order that our examination of the relative nature of justice and injustice may be carried on regularly. A statement was made that injustice is stronger and more powerful than justice, but now justice, having been identified with wisdom and virtue, is easily shown to be stronger than injustice, if injustice is ignorance; this can no longer be questioned by any one. But I want to view the matter, Thrasymachus, in a different way: You would not deny that a state may be unjust and may be unjustly attempting to enslave other states, or may have already enslaved them, and may be holding many of them in subjection?

True, he replied; and I will add the best and perfectly unjust state will be most likely to do so.

I know, I said, that such was your position; but what I would further consider is, whether this power which is possessed by the superior state can exist or be exercised without justice.

If you are right in you view, and justice is wisdom, then only with justice; but if I am right, then without justice.

I am delighted, Thrasymachus, to see you not only nodding assent and dissent, but making answers which are quite excellent.

That is out of civility to you, he replied.

You are very kind, I said; and would you have the goodness also to inform me, whether you think that a state, or an army, or a band of robbers and thieves, or any other gang of evil-doers could act at all if they injured one another?

No indeed, he said, they could not.

But if they abstained from injuring one another, then they might act together better?

Yes.

And this is because injustice creates divisions and hatreds and fighting, and justice imparts harmony and friendship; is not that true, Thrasymachus?

I agree, he said, because I do not wish to quarrel with you.

How good of you, I said; but I should like to know also whether injustice, having this tendency to arouse hatred, wherever existing, among slaves or among freemen, will not make them hate one another and set them at variance and render them incapable of common action?

Certainly.

And even if injustice be found in two only, will they not quarrel and fight, and become enemies to one another and to the just.

They will.

And suppose injustice abiding in a single person, would your wisdom say that she loses or that she retains her natural power?

Let us assume that she retains her power.

Yet is not the power which injustice exercises of such a nature that wherever she takes up her abode, whether in a city, in an army, in a family, or in any other body, that body is, to begin with, rendered incapable of united action by reason of sedition and distraction; and does it not become its own enemy and at variance with all that opposes it, and with the just? Is not this the case?

Yes, certainly.

And is not injustice equally fatal when existing in a single person; in the first place rendering him incapable of action because he is not at unity with himself, and in the second place making him an enemy to himself and the just? Is not that true, Thrasymachus?

Yes.

And O my friend, I said, surely the gods are just?

Granted that they are.

But if so, the unjust will be the enemy of the gods, and the just will be their friend?

Feast away in triumph, and take your fill of the argument; I will not oppose you, lest I should displease the company.

Well then, proceed with your answers, and let me have the remainder of my repast. For we have already shown that the just are clearly wiser and better and abler than the unjust, and that the unjust are incapable of common action; nay ing at more, that to speak as we did of men who are evil acting at any time vigorously together, is not strictly true, for if they had been perfectly evil, they would have laid hands upon one another; but it is evident that there must have been some remnant of justice in them, which enabled them to combine; if there had not been they would have injured one another as well as their victims; they were but half--villains in their enterprises; for had they been whole villains, and utterly unjust, they would have been utterly incapable of action. That, as I believe, is the truth of the matter, and not what you said at first. But whether the just have a better and happier life than the unjust is a further question which we also proposed to consider. I think that they have, and for the reasons which to have given; but still I should like to examine further, for no light matter is at stake, nothing less than the rule of human life.

Proceed.

I will proceed by asking a question: Would you not say that a horse has some end?

I should.

And the end or use of a horse or of anything would be that which could not be accomplished, or not so well accomplished, by any other thing?

I do not understand, he said.

Let me explain: Can you see, except with the eye?

Certainly not.

Or hear, except with the ear?

No.

These then may be truly said to be the ends of these organs?

They may.

But you can cut off a vine-branch with a dagger or with a chisel, and in many other ways?

Of course.

And yet not so well as with a pruning-hook made for the purpose?

True.

May we not say that this is the end of a pruning-hook?

We may.

Then now I think you will have no difficulty in understanding my meaning when I asked the question whether the end of anything would be that which could not be accomplished, or not so well accomplished, by any other thing?

I understand your meaning, he said, and assent.

And that to which an end is appointed has also an excellence? Need I ask again whether the eye has an end?

It has.

And has not the eye an excellence?

Yes.

And the ear has an end and an excellence also?

True.

And the same is true of all other things; they have each of them an end and a special excellence?

That is so.

Well, and can the eyes fulfil their end if they

are wanting in their own proper excellence and have a defect instead?

How can they, he said, if they are blind and cannot see?

You mean to say, if they have lost their proper excellence, which is sight; but I have not arrived at that point yet. I would rather ask the question more generally, and only enquire whether the things which fulfil their ends fulfil them by their own proper excellence, and fall of fulfilling them by their own defect?

Certainly, he replied.

I might say the same of the ears; when deprived of their own proper excellence they cannot fulfil their end?

True.

And the same observation will apply to all other things?

I agree.

Well; and has not the soul an end which nothing else can fulfil? for example, to superintend and command and deliberate and the like. Are not these functions proper to the soul, and can they rightly be assigned to any other?

To no other.

And is not life to be reckoned among the ends of the soul?

Assuredly, he said.

And has not the soul an excellence also?

Yes.

And can she or can she not fulfil her own ends when deprived of that excellence?

She cannot.

Then an evil soul must necessarily be an evil ruler and superintendent, and the good soul a good ruler?

Yes, necessarily.

And we have admitted that justice is the excellence of the soul, and injustice the defect of the soul?

That has been admitted.

Then the just soul and the just man will live well, and the unjust man will live ill?

That is what your argument proves.

And he who lives well is blessed and happy, and he who lives ill the reverse of happy?

Certainly.

Then the just is happy, and the unjust miserable?

So be it.

But happiness and not misery is profitable.

Of course.

Then, my blessed Thrasymachus, injustice can never be more profitable than justice.

Let this, Socrates, he said, be your entertainment at the Bendidea.

For which I am indebted to you, I said, now that you have grown gentle towards me and have left off scolding. Nevertheless, I have not been well entertained; but that was my own fault and not yours. As an epicure snatches a taste of every dish which is successively brought to table, he not having allowed himself time to enjoy the one before, so have I gone from one subject to another without having discovered what I sought at first, the nature of justice. I left that enquiry and turned away to consider whether justice is virtue and wisdom or evil and folly; and when there arose a further question about the comparative advantages of justice and injustice, I could not refrain from passing on to that. And the result of the whole discussion has been that I know nothing at all. For I know not what justice is, and therefore I am not likely to know whether it is or is not a virtue, nor can I say whether the just man is happy or unhappy.

Plato
The *Republic*

Book II - The Individual, The State, and Education

Socrates - Glaucon

WITH these words I was thinking that I had made an end of the discussion; but the end, in truth, proved to be only a beginning. For Glaucon, who is always the most pugnacious of men, was dissatisfied at Thrasymachus' retirement; he wanted to have the battle out. So he said to me: Socrates, do you wish really to persuade us, or only to seem to have persuaded us, that to be just is always better than to be unjust?

I should wish really to persuade you, I replied, if I could.

Then you certainly have not succeeded. Let me ask you now:--How would you arrange goods--are there not some which we welcome for their own sakes, and independently of their consequences, as, for example, harmless pleasures and enjoyments, which delight us at the time, although nothing follows from them?

I agree in thinking that there is such a class, I replied.

Is there not also a second class of goods, such as knowledge, sight, health, which are desirable not only in themselves, but also for their results?

Certainly, I said.

And would you not recognize a third class, such as gymnastic, and the care of the sick, and the physician's art; also the various ways of money-making--these do us good but we regard them as disagreeable; and no one would choose them for their own sakes, but only for the sake of some reward or result which flows from them?

There is, I said, this third class also. But why do you ask?

Because I want to know in which of the three classes you would place justice?

In the highest class, I replied,--among those goods which he who would be happy desires both for their own sake and for the sake of their results.

Then the many are of another mind; they think that justice is to be reckoned in the troublesome class, among goods which are to be pursued for the sake of rewards and of reputation, but in themselves are disagreeable and rather to be avoided.

I know, I said, that this is their manner of thinking, and that this was the thesis which Thrasymachus was maintaining just now, when he censured justice and praised injustice. But I am too stupid to be convinced by him.

I wish, he said, that you would hear me as well as him, and then I shall see whether you and I agree. For Thrasymachus seems to me, like a snake, to have been charmed by your voice sooner than he ought to have been; but to my mind the nature of justice and injustice have not yet been made clear. Setting aside their rewards and results, I want to know what they are in themselves, and how they inwardly work in the soul. If you, please, then, I will revive the argument of Thrasymachus. And first I will speak of the nature and origin of justice according to the common view of them. Secondly, I will show that all men who practise justice do so against their will, of necessity, but not as a good. And thirdly, I will argue that there is reason in this view, for the life of the unjust is after all better far than the life of the just--if what they say is true, Socrates, since I myself am not of their opinion. But still I acknowledge that I am perplexed when I hear the voices of Thrasymachus and myriads of others dinning in my ears; and, on the other hand, I have never yet heard the superiority of justice to injustice maintained by any one in a satisfactory way. I want to hear justice praised in respect of itself; then I shall be satisfied, and you are the person from whom I think that I am most likely to hear this; and therefore I will praise the unjust life to the utmost of my power, and my manner of speaking will indicate the manner in which I desire to hear you too praising justice and censuring injustice. Will you say whether you approve of my proposal?

Indeed I do; nor can I imagine any theme about which a man of sense would oftener wish to converse.

I am delighted, he replied, to hear you say so, and shall begin by speaking, as I proposed, of the nature and origin of justice.

Glaucon

They say that to do injustice is, by nature, good; to suffer injustice, evil; but that the evil is greater than the good. And so when men have both done and suffered injustice and have had experience of both, not being able to avoid the one and obtain the other, they think that they had better agree among themselves to have neither; hence there arise laws and mutual covenants; and that which is ordained by law is termed by them lawful and just. This they affirm to be the origin and nature of justice;--it is a mean or compromise, between the best of all, which is to do injustice and not be punished, and the worst of all, which is to suffer injustice without the power of retaliation; and justice, being at a middle point between the two, is tolerated not as a good, but as the lesser evil, and honoured by reason of the inability of men to do injustice. For no man who is worthy to be called a man would ever submit to such an agreement if he were able to resist; he would be mad if he did. Such is the received account, Socrates, of the nature and origin of justice.

Now that those who practise justice do so involuntarily and because they have not the power to be unjust will best appear if we imagine something of this kind: having given both to the just and the unjust power to do what they will, let us watch and see whither desire will lead them; then we shall discover in the very act the just and unjust man to be proceeding along the same road, following their interest, which all natures deem to be their good, and are only diverted into the path of justice by the force of law. The liberty which we are supposing may be most completely given to them in the form of such a power as is said to have been possessed by Gyges the ancestor of Croesus the Lydian. According to the tradition, Gyges was a shepherd in the service of the king of Lydia; there was a great storm, and an earthquake made an opening in the earth at the place where he was feeding his flock. Amazed at the sight, he descended into the opening, where, among other marvels, he beheld a hollow brazen horse, having doors, at which he stooping and looking in saw a dead body of stature, as appeared to him, more than human, and having nothing on but a gold ring; this he took from the finger of the dead and reascended. Now the shepherds met together, according to custom, that they might send their monthly report about the flocks to the king; into their assembly he came having the ring on his finger, and as he was sitting among them he chanced to turn the collet of the ring inside his hand, when instantly he became invisible to the rest of the company and they began to speak of him as if he were no longer present. He was astonished at this, and again touching the ring he turned the collet outwards and reappeared; he made several trials of the ring, and always with the same result-when he turned the collet inwards he became invisible, when outwards he reappeared. Whereupon he contrived to be chosen one of the messengers who were sent to the court; where as soon as he arrived he seduced the queen, and with her help conspired against the king and slew him, and took the kingdom. Suppose now that there were two such magic rings, and the just put on one of them and the unjust the other; no man can be imagined to be of such an iron nature that he would stand fast in justice. No man would keep his hands off what was not his own when he could safely take what he liked out of the market, or go into houses and lie with any one at his pleasure, or kill or release from prison whom he would, and in all respects be like a God among men. Then the actions of the just would be as the actions of the unjust; they would both come at last to the same point. And this we may truly affirm to be a great proof that a man is just, not willingly or because he thinks that justice is any good to him individually, but of necessity, for wherever any one thinks that he can safely be unjust, there he is unjust. For all men believe in their hearts that injustice is far more profitable to the individual than justice, and he who argues as I have been supposing, will say that they are right. If you could imagine any one obtaining this power of becoming invisible, and never doing any wrong or touching what was another's, he would be thought by the lookers-on to be a most wretched idiot, although they would praise him to one another's faces, and keep up appearances with one another from a fear that they too might suffer injustice. Enough of this. . . .

Adeimantus

On what principle, then, shall we any longer choose justice rather than the worst injustice? when, if we only unite the latter with a deceitful regard to appearances, we shall fare to our mind both with gods and men, in life and after death, as the most numerous and the highest authorities tell us. Knowing all this, Socrates, how can a man who has any superiority of mind or person or rank or wealth, be willing to honour justice; or indeed to refrain from laughing when he hears justice praised? And even if there should be some one who is able to disprove the truth of my words, and who is satisfied that justice is best, still he is not angry with the unjust, but is very ready to forgive them, because he also knows that men are not just of their own free will; unless, peradventure, there be some one whom the divinity within him may have inspired with a hatred of injustice, or who has attained knowledge of the truth--but no other man. He only blames injustice who, owing to cowardice or age or some weakness, has not the power of being unjust. And this is proved by the fact that when he obtains the power, he immediately becomes unjust as far as he can be.

The cause of all this, Socrates, was indicated by us at the beginning of the argument, when my brother and I told you how astonished we were to find that of all the professing panegyrists of justice--beginning with the ancient heroes of whom any memorial has been preserved to us, and ending with the men of our own time--no one has ever blamed injustice or praised justice except with a view to the glories, honours, and benefits which flow from them. No one has ever adequately described either in verse or prose the true essential nature of either of them abiding in the soul, and invisible to any human or divine eye; or shown that of all the things of a man's soul which he has within him, justice is the greatest good, and injustice the greatest evil. Had this been the universal strain, had you sought to persuade us of this from our youth upwards, we should not have been on the watch to keep one another from doing wrong, but every one would have been his own watchman, because afraid, if he did wrong, of harbouring in himself the greatest of evils. I dare say that Thrasymachus and others would seriously hold the language which I have been merely repeating, and words even stronger than these about justice and injustice, grossly, as I conceive, perverting their true nature. But I speak in this vehement manner, as I must frankly confess to you, because I want to hear from you the opposite side; and I would ask you to show not only the superiority which justice has over injustice, but what effect they have on the possessor of them which makes the one to be a good and the other an evil to him. And please, as Glaucon requested of you, to exclude reputations; for unless you take away from each of them his true reputation and add on the false, we shall say that you do not praise justice, but the appearance of it; we shall think that you are only exhorting us to keep injustice dark, and that you really agree with Thrasymachus in thinking that justice is another's good and the interest of the stronger, and that injustice is a man's own profit and interest, though injurious to the weaker. Now as you have admitted that justice is one of that highest class of goods which are desired indeed for their results, but in a far greater degree for their own sakes--like sight or hearing or knowledge or health, or any other real and natural and not merely conventional good--I would ask you in your praise of justice to regard one point only: I mean the essential good and evil which justice and injustice work in the possessors of them. Let others praise justice and censure injustice, magnifying the rewards and honours of the one and abusing the other; that is a manner of arguing which, coming from them, I am ready to tolerate, but from you who have spent your whole life in the consideration of this question, unless I hear the contrary from your own lips, I expect something better. And therefore, I say, not only prove to us that justice is better than injustice, but show what they either of them do to the possessor of them, which makes the one to be a good and the other an evil, whether seen or unseen by gods and men.

Herodotus (484 BCE – 425 BCE) was an ancient Greek historian and is often credited with being the first true historian in that he was the first (known) to systematically gather information, test the accuracy of accounts, and present historical narratives in a systematic and compelling fashion. In this incredibly brief excerpt we get a report showcasing the differences between ancient Greek and Callatian cultural practices with regard to how to dispose of their dead. Noting the fierce disagreement between cultures, "custom" is proclaimed "king o'er all"—that is, cultural standards dictate what is right and wrong for communities.

Herodotus
The History of Herodotus

Book III, Chapter 38

. . . Many other wild outrages of this sort did Cambyses commit, both upon the Persians and the allies, while he still stayed at Memphis; among the rest he opened the ancient sepulchres, and examined the bodies that were buried in them. He likewise went into the temple of Vulcan, and made great sport of the image. For the image of Vulcan is very like the Pataeci of the Phoenicians, wherewith they ornament the prows of their ships of war. If persons have not seen these, I will explain in a different way- it is a figure resembling that of a pigmy. He went also into the temple of the Cabiri, which it is unlawful for any one to enter except the priests, and not only made sport of the images, but even burnt them. They are made like the statue of Vulcan, who is said to have been their father.

Thus it appears certain to me, by a great variety of proofs, that Cambyses was raving mad; he would not else have set himself to make a mock of holy rites and long-established usages. For if one were to offer men to choose out of all the customs in the world such as seemed to them the best, they would examine the whole number, and end by preferring their own; so convinced are they that their own usages far surpass those of all others. Unless, therefore, a man was mad, it is not likely that he would make sport of such matters. That people have this feeling about their laws may be seen by very many proofs: among others, by the following. Darius, after he had got the kingdom, called into his presence certain Greeks who were at hand, and asked- "What he should pay them to eat the bodies of their fathers when they died?" To which they answered, that there was no sum that would tempt them to do such a thing. He then sent for certain Indians, of the race called Callatians, men who eat their fathers, and asked them, while the Greeks stood by, and knew by the help of an interpreter all that was said - "What he should give them to burn the bodies of their fathers at their decease?" The Indians exclaimed aloud, and bade him forbear such language. Such is men's wont herein; and Pindar was right, in my judgment, when he said, "Law [custom] is the king o'er all." ...

Marcus Tullius Cicero (106 BCE - 43 BCE) was not merely a "fan" of Greek philosophy who shared his interests with others. He was a careful thinker and a skilled writer who translated Greek thought into the Roman (Latin) language not only in the literal sense of translation, but also to the extent that he coined new Latin vocabulary to help elucidate difficult philosophical concepts. He helped bring ancient Greek thought to the Romans, and then helped to bring both Greek and Roman philosophy to the rest of Europe, somewhat in the Middle Ages—but especially in the Renaissance. His oratory skill and political talents caught the eye of Julius Caesar, who (in 60 BCE) invited Cicero to be the 4th member of his "partnership" with Pompey and Marcus Licinius Crassus. Cicero declined the offer to join what would become the First Triumvirate due to his concern that it would undermine the Republic.). In February, 44 BCE, Caesar was appointed "dictator for life." Roughly a month later, he was assassinated on the Ides of March (March 15th). Cicero had not, himself, participated in the conspiracy or assassination. However, Marcus Junius Brutus allegedly called out Cicero's name, bloodstained dagger in hand, and asked him to restore the Republic, and Cicero's own endorsement of the assassination was unmistakable. In the political instability that followed the assassination, a power struggle broke out between the assassins (led by Brutus and Cassius) and "loyalists" to Caesar (led by Mark Antony and Octavian). Cicero was a political leader—and found himself in direct opposition to Mark Antony. Cicero was the spokesman for the Senate, and Antony was a consul and the unofficial executor of Caesar's will. Cicero tried to manipulate Octavian into opposing Antony, but ultimately failed. Cicero wrote and spoke publicly against Antony in a series of speeches called the "Phillipics"—actions and writing that ultimately cost him his life. In 43 BCE, Antony, Octavian, and Lepidus formed the Second Triumvirate. They issued proscriptions against Roman citizens, including Cicero (and his brother and nephew). Cicero was assassinated on December 7th, 43 BCE. Antony then displayed Cicero's severed head and hands (the ones that wrote the Phillipics) in the Roman Forum in a final act of humiliation. In this very brief selection from "The Republic" that follows, Cicero has the character Philus advocate against any sort of universal notion of justice/goodness, and argue, instead, for what we would today call cultural relativism.

Cicero
The Republic
Book 3: 8-18

...

Scipio and his friends having again assembled, Scipio spoke as follows: — In our last conversation I promised to prove that honesty is the best policy in all states and commonwealths whatsoever. But if I am to plead in favour of strict honesty and justice in all public affairs, no less than in private, I must request Philus, or some one else, to take up the advocacy of the other side; the truth will then become more manifest, from the collision of opposite arguments, as we see every day exemplified at the Bar.

Philus.

—In good truth you have allotted me a marvellous creditable cause. So you wish me to plead for vice, do you?

Lælius.

—Perhaps you are afraid, lest in reproducing the ordinary objections made to justice in politics, you should seem to express your own sentiments. But this caution is ridiculous in you, my Philus; you, who are so universally respected as an almost unique example of the ancient probity and good faith; you, who are so familiar with the legal habit of disputing on both sides of a question, because you think this is the best way of getting at the truth.

Philus.

—Very well; I obey you, and wilfully with my eyes open, I will undertake this dirty business. Since those who seek for gold do not flinch at the sight of the mud, we, who search for justice, which is far more precious than gold, must overcome all dainty scruples. I will therefore, make use of the antagonist arguments of a foreigner, and assume his character in using them. The pleas, therefore, now to be delivered by Philus are those once employed by the Greek Carneades, accustomed to express whatever served his turn. Let it be understood, therefore, that I by no means express my own sentiments, but those of Carneades, in order that you may refute this philosopher, who was wont to turn the best causes into joke, through the mere wantonness of wit.

When Philus had thus spoken, he took a general review of the leading arguments that Carneades had brought forward to prove that justice was neither eternal, immutable, nor universal. Having put these sophistical arguments into their most specious and plausible form, he thus continued his ingenious pleadings.

Aristotle has treated this question concerning justice, and filled four large volumes with it. As to Chrysippus, I expected nothing grand or magnificent in him, for, after his usual fashion, he examines everything rather by the signification of words, than the reality of things. But it was surely worthy of those heroes of philosophy to ennoble by their genius a virtue so eminently beneficent and liberal, which every where exalts the social interests above the selfish, and teaches to love others rather than ourselves. It was worthy of their genius, we say, to elevate this virtue to a divine throne, close to that of Wisdom. Certainly they wanted not the intention to accomplish this. What else could be the cause of their writing on the subject, or what could have been their design? Nor could they have wanted genius, in which they excelled all men. But the weakness of their cause was too great for their intention and their eloquence to make it popular. In fact, this justice on which we reason may be a civil right, but no natural one; for if it were natural and universal, then justice and injustice would be recognized similarly by all men, just as the elements of heat and cold, sweet and bitter.

Now if any one, carried in the chariot of winged serpents, of which the poet Pacuvius makes mention, could take his flight over all nations and cities, and accurately observe their proceedings, he would see that the sense of justice and right varies in different regions. In the first place he would behold among the unchangeable people of Egypt, which preserves in its archives the memory of so many ages and events, a bull adored as a deity, under the name of Apis, and a multitude of other monsters, and all kinds of animals admitted by the natives into the number of the gods.

The Persians, on the other hand, regard all these forms of idolatry as impious, and it is affirmed that the sole motive of Xerxes for commanding the conflagration of the Athenian temples, was the belief that it was a superstitious sacrilege to keep confined within narrow walls the gods, whose proper home was the entire universe. Afterwards Philip, in his hostile projects against the Persians, and Alexander, in his expedition, alleged this plea for war, that it was necessary to avenge the temples of Greece. And the Greeks thought proper never to rebuild these fanes, that this monument of the impiety of the Persians might always remain before the eyes of their posterity.

How many, such as the inhabitants of Taurica along the Euxine Sea—as the King of Egypt Busiris—as the Gauls and the Carthaginians—have thought it exceedingly pious and agreeable to the gods to sacrifice men. Besides these religious discrepancies, the rules of life are so contradictory that the Cretans and Ætolians regard robbery as honourable. And the Lacedæmonians say that their territory extends to all places which they can touch with a lance. The Athenians had a custom of swearing by a public proclamation, that all the lands which produced olives and corn were their own. The Gauls consider it a base employment to raise corn by agricultural labour, and go with arms in their hands, and mow down the harvests of neighbouring peoples. And our Romans, the most equitable of all nations, in order to raise the value of our vines and olives, do not permit the races beyond the Alps to cultivate either vineyards or oliveyards. In this respect, it is said, we act with prudence, but not with justice. You see then that wisdom and policy are not always the same as equity. Lycurgus, the inventor of a most admirable jurisprudence, and most wholesome laws, gave the lands of the rich to be cultivated by the common people, who were reduced to slavery.

If I were to describe the diverse kinds of laws, institutions, manners, and customs, not only as they vary in the numerous nations, but as they vary likewise in single cities, as Rome for example, I should prove that they have had a thousand revolutions. For instance, that eminent expositor of our laws who sits in the present company, I mean Malilius, if you were to consult him relative to the legacies and inheritances of women, he would tell you that the present law is quite different from that he was accustomed to plead in his youth, before the Voconian enactment came into force—an edict which was passed in favour of the interests of the men, but which is evidently full of injustice with regard to women. For why should a woman be disabled from inheriting property? Why can a vestal virgin become an heir, while her mother cannot? And why, admitting that it is necessary to set some limit to the wealth of women, should Crassus' daughter, if she be his only child, inherit thousands without offending the law, while my daughter can only receive a small share in a bequest?

If this justice were natural, innate, and universal, all men would admit the same law and right, and the same men would not enact different laws at different times. If a just man and a virtuous man is bound to obey the laws, I ask what laws do you mean? Do you intend all the laws indifferently? Virtue does not permit this inconstancy in moral obligation—such a variation is not compatible with natural conscience. The laws are, therefore, based not on our sense of justice, but on our fear of punishment. There is, therefore, no natural justice, and hence it follows that men cannot be just by nature. . . .

Chapter 3
Free Will

Comprehension questions you should be able to answer after reading this introduction:

1. *What is the difference between "political freedom" and "metaphysical" freedom? Which one is the focus of the free will debate?*
2. *Describe the "mechanistic/causal" perspective. Describe the "free/spontaneous" perspective. How does each relate to the free will debate?*
3. *What is a "reductionist materialist?"*
4. *What are the basic elements of "determinism?" How does it account for human behavior?*
5. *What is the one (important) difference between compatibilism and determinism?*
6. *Explain how compatibilists define "free will." What are "internal causes?" What are "external causes?"*
7. *Explain why there is no more "choice" ("ability to do otherwise") in compatibilism than there is in determinism.*
8. *Explain the agency theorist's criticism of the compatibilist definition of free will.*
9. *How do agency theorists define free will?*
10. *What is substance dualism? How would a dualistic understanding of human nature make "choice" possible?*
11. *What is Leibniz's Law of Identity?*
12. *What are some of the arguments in favor of substance dualism?*
13. *What is event causation? What is agent causation?*
14. *What are some possible criticisms of agency theory?*

Before delving into any theories or vocabulary, before "biasing" your views with "official" philosophical positions, take a few minutes to reflect, using your own thoughts and your own vocabulary: Are you *free*? Think carefully before replying, as the issue is more complicated than it might first appear. In fact, take several minutes to reflect on the following questions, and even to jot down some notes.

1. What are ways in which you appear to be free? Why would you, or anyone, believe themselves to be free, to be in control of their own lives?
2. What are ways in which you appear to be unfree? Why would you, or anyone, believe themselves to not be in control of their own lives?
3. Finally, why does any of this matter? Aside from simple intellectual curiosity, why would someone (like your philosophy instructor by virtue of addressing this material, or me—possibly that same instructor—by virtue of writing about it) think this issue worthy of discussion? What's at stake?

If you followed instructions, you've spent a

few minutes thinking about those questions, and have at least generated a mental list of answers and thoughts provoked by the exercise. If you did not follow instructions, take a few minutes a do so now. Seriously.

The reason why it's important to think through these questions yourself is because the responses we consider will make far more sense, and be much more meaningful to you, if you can see how they have connected with your own thoughts on these matters. Let's consider the first question: what are ways in which you appear to be free? Among numerous possibilities, you probably came up with reasons similar to the following (among others):

- You live in a "free country."
- You're able to make all kinds of choices, everyday, from trivial things like ordering off a restaurant menu, to pivotal decisions like whether or not to go to college.
- You have a powerful intuition of "spontaneity." That is, it seems like you can just "do something" without anything or anyone else having forced you to do it.
- You are confident that other people (and presumably yourself as well) are responsible for their actions, and you get angry or disappointed or pleased with people accordingly.

Why would you believe you are not free? You probably came up with reasons similar to the following:

- Your behavior is restricted by both laws and customs.
- Your choices are constrained by what's available to you, and, in some cases, such as when one has a serious disability, or is profoundly poor, what's available might be very little indeed.
- Your behavior might be influenced, or even fully determined, by circumstances rather than personal choices. The sort of person you are is probably very strongly influenced, maybe even established, by your life experiences—especially your childhood experiences.
- An all-knowing, all-powerful God might have "predestined" you to follow a certain path, and you, as a mere mortal, lack the ability to defy God.

Finally, why does any of this matter? You probably came up with reasons similar to the following:

- Self-concept: Your very sense of self will be impacted by whether or not you are in control of your life. Are you in control of your life, or are you simply playing out a script written by Nature, or perhaps God?
- Meaning: This is the so-called "existential" significance of freedom. If your life is not up to you in any significant way, you might wonder why it's worth living. Why bother to do anything, if it's not "you" who's responsible for whatever it is that you do?
- Responsibility: When we hold people responsible for their actions, we implicitly assume that their actions were, in some important way, of their own doing. In other words, I don't arrest you for murdering Ricky if I know that it was actually Samantha who did it. Similarly, if you are not free, if you are not in control of how your life turns out, it might not seem appropriate to think that you are responsible for your actions—even if it was clearly your own body that performed them. Without responsibility, there is no justification for praise or blame.
- Morality: Very much related to the issue of responsibility, when we make moral value judgments, and say that one should tell the truth, we are implying that one is capable of telling the truth, or telling a lie—but that telling the truth is what one *should* do. Clearly, if my life and my actions are not under my control, it makes little sense to tell me what I should or should not do. Without the ability to provide moral imperatives, what function does morality serve? The concern is that without freedom, there is no responsibility, and without responsibility,

there is no (meaningful) notion of morality.

If it wasn't obvious before, it should be obvious now: this topic is actually very important. The answers you come up with, and the position you ultimately take, has a tremendous impact on your sense of self, your view of personal responsibility, and your sense of morality itself. So, are you free? As with most philosophical questions, it depends on who you ask, and what is meant by "free."

Freedom

Before delving into any of the major philosophical theories, we should first distinguish between what we can call "political" freedom and "metaphysical" freedom. Believe it or not, grammar can help us articulate the difference.

Political Freedom	**Metaphysical Freedom**
Verb: May	Verb: Can
Focus: Permission	Focus: Ability

Political freedom refers to what we are *allowed* to do (without legal consequences) by our government (or, more generally, by whoever holds power over us). For example, in the United States, I am not free to kill my neighbor just because he's playing his radio too loud when I want to sleep. If I do, we call that murder, and I will be punished if I'm caught. I'm not permitted to kill people just because they annoy me. I'm not "free" to do so. In other countries, a person might not be free to criticize the government. They are not permitted to do so. If they do, they could get punished. In the United States, we *are* allowed to criticize the government. Political freedom varies depending on where you live. Some people have lots of political freedom, some people have very little. No one who lives in an organized community has *total* political freedom, since any community will impose some restrictions on behavior.

Political freedom is an interesting philosophical issue that gives rise to all sorts of important questions:

- How much freedom, if any, should persons enjoy?
- What sorts of restrictions on freedom are legitimate?
- When is it acceptable to limit freedom? If it's necessary to prevent a terrorist attack? If it's necessary to protect society from a "bad influence?"
- What sorts of actions are defensible in the name and pursuit of freedom? Protests? Armed revolution?

As interesting as political philosophy is, that is not our current focus. Our focus is on *metaphysical* freedom. The difference might appear subtle at first, but it's important. Consider our discussion of political freedom above. I am not free to commit murder (and neither are you). But, can't I do it anyway? Sure, I'll become a fugitive and likely suffer all kinds of negative consequences for my action, but (unfortunately) it's all too obvious that people *can* commit murder even though they are not *permitted* to do so.

When we ask if we have *free will*, we're not asking about what we *may* do, what we are *permitted* to do—we're asking about what is *possible* for us to do. For example, if it is legally permissible for me to be a famous, outgoing, beloved social superstar, but I've inherited genes from my father that cause me to be shy, uncomfortable in public, and predisposed to introspection and seclusion, then even though I may (i.e., am allowed to) be a socialite, I can't become one. This is the sort of concern that arose before: that our lives are not under our control, that who we are, who we become, and what we do, is decided *for* us rather than *by* us.

To take a more serious example, what if serial killers truly can't help themselves? In the Showtime series Dexter, the main character is a serial killer. Dexter is an unusual sort of serial killer. He was mentored by a caring foster father and trained how to channel his murderous impulses in such a way that he only targeted rapists and murderers. His killing is still thought to be bad, but at least he only goes after those who "deserve it." Dexter has (seemingly) irresistible homicidal urges. Why? The explanation in the story is that he witnessed his own mother get murdered (with a chain saw!) before his very eyes when he was just a few years old. He was then left, unattended, for several days, sitting in a pool of his mother's blood, until he was eventually found and adopted by a police officer. The implication is clear: Dexter's traumatic childhood experience of blood and murder *caused* him to develop deviant homicidal desires that he otherwise would not have acquired. Why is Dexter a serial killer? Because of his childhood experiences over which he had no control.

Admittedly, Dexter is a fictional character, but similar sorts of psychological profiles are generated for real-life serial killers, serial rapists, child molesters, etc. Suppose, just for a moment, that there is something legitimate about such reasoning, and that people like that didn't *choose* to become serial killers, or child rapists, but found themselves to be such persons as a result of their DNA, or childhood experiences? If such a person truly can't control himself, and has no choice but to be a serial killer, does it make any sense to say that he is "free," that he is in control of his own life?

This is the sort of freedom that is at stake in the free will discussion: the freedom to be able to make one's own choices, as opposed to living out a life that is merely the product of one's DNA, or childhood, or any number of other causal influences; the freedom to be the author of your own life story, as opposed to merely being a character in a story "written" by outside forces.

With this clarified notion of metaphysical freedom in mind, go back over your responses to the reflection questions asked above, and see if anything has changed. Thinking specifically of metaphysical freedom (as opposed to political freedom), give a brief answer to those same three questions. Do you now believe you have "free will?"

Don't think that the answer to that question will be easy or obvious. The challenge posed by this question is that it appears *both* that we are free, *and* that we are not. We view the world, and our own lives, through two different perspectives—both of which seem accurate.

"Mechanistic" Perspective v. Perspective of Freedom

The first perspective we employ is the "scientific" perspective, the "mechanistic" perspective. This is the "cause-and-effect" perspective we employ all day, every day, to understand the world and its operations. According to this perspective, events are governed by the laws of physics, and if we simply understand the laws of physics well enough, and understand the antecedent conditions leading to the event well enough, we can predict with tremendous accuracy what will happen. Given sufficient information, Nature rarely surprises us. Try a simple experiment: pick up a small (non-fragile) object, such as a pencil. What will happen if you hold it up in the air, and then let it go? Have you made your prediction? Now, let it go. Let me guess: your object fell to the ground. Amazing....

Nature is orderly, reliable, predictable. This mechanistic perspective is convincing, reliable, and reinforced for us every day of our lives. We are very confident that this perspective is accurate. Now, the problem: human beings are a part of Nature. We are (ultimately) built of the very same sorts of particles (e.g., protons, neutrons, quarks, etc.) as is everything else in the universe.[31] If this perspective tells us that all objects in the universe are governed by the laws of physics, and that events are ultimately predictable, given enough information, then, if we are also objects in the universe, it would seem that we are also governed by those same laws of physics, and our actions are (in principle) equally predictable.

According to this perspective, events are the result of cause and effect relationships, not "free will." If we wouldn't describe the actions of your "small object" (e.g., a pencil) from the experiment above in terms of it "choosing" to fall to the ground, but would instead describe its actions in terms of gravitational forces, why shouldn't we use similar explanations for our own behavior,

[31] Note: the agency theorist will disagree with this, in an important way, as we will see later in this chapter.

given that we are part of the same mechanistic universe?

If this were the only viewpoint, there would be no free will debate. But, we have a second perspective. This second perspective is a perspective of spontaneity and freedom. According to this perspective, I can and do make free, un-coerced choices all the time, and so do you. When I get up in the morning, go to my closet, and select which shirt to wear to work, it sure *feels* like it really was up to me, in a meaningful sense, which shirt I picked. It felt like I could have picked any one of several available shirts, but I *chose* a particular shirt. It didn't feel like a forced choice, or like I was compelled. It didn't feel like my DNA or childhood experiences caused me to pick a particular shirt. Presumably, your experience is much the same. Every day, it seems like you make free choices, like you freely choose one action rather than another.

This is the most powerful argument in favor of free will: our extraordinarily powerful and convincing intuition that we are in control of our actions (at least to a significant degree). According to this perspective, despite what we think we know about the laws of physics and how events are governed, we *appear* to be different from other things in the universe—we appear to be free to choose our actions even if other things in the universe are not.

What a dilemma! On the one hand, we are convinced that the mechanistic perspective is true—according to which we are *not* free, not in control of our lives. On the other hand, we are convinced that the spontaneous perspective is also true—according to which we *are* free, are in control of our lives. How do we reconcile this seemingly contradictory stance? As always, it depends on whom you ask....

Determinism

There are two broad types of determinist theories: theistic determinism, and materialist (causal) determinism.

Theistic determinism describes any theory that claims that all events that occur happen by virtue of God's design. According to this view, God has a plan for the universe and for history. God, being sovereign over all Creation, is in control. If your life turns out a certain way, it's because God willed that it be so. If taken seriously, one can see how theistic determinism (sometimes understood in terms of "destiny," "fate," or "predestination") can be seen as a threat to freedom.

If God has pre-ordained the course of your life, and you have no ability to do anything else, then wouldn't it seem like your life is not your own, that you're playing a role scripted by someone else? Granted, that someone else is God, and if your life has to be scripted by someone other than you, God's a pretty good choice—but isn't your freedom lost all the same?

Not surprisingly, theological perspectives that include predestination generate controversy with regard to personal responsibility, praise and blame, and punishment and reward. One famous example is the Calvinist notion of the "elect." The elect are those who have been predestined for salvation. Those who were not predestined for salvation will not be saved, and will go to hell. One's status (i.e., whether or not one is among the elect) is established long before one is born—and there is nothing one can do to change it. If you weren't born among the elect, you will never be among the elect. Not surprisingly, one of the most common criticisms of this aspect of Calvinist theology is that it's "unfair." Although Calvinists are certainly capable of defending their theological point of view, it seems as if a terribly important aspect of one's life (i.e., one's eternal destination) has already been established, and is outside of one's control.

As interesting as theistic approaches to determinism are, their details are best addressed within a theological context rather than a philosophical one. After all, the nuts and bolts of theistic determinism (including Calvinism) invariably come down to particular doctrinal issues within particular religious traditions. Accordingly, we will focus on "materialist" determinism.

If asked whether or not you have free will, the materialist determinist's (hereafter referred to as simply the determinist, or determinism) answer is a resounding "no." Regarding our two competing perspectives (mechanistic, and spontaneous), the determinist claims that only the mechanistic perspective is accurate. The spontaneous perspective is an illusion. Why?

Such determinists are almost invariably "*reductionist materialists.*" This means that they believe everything in the universe consists of matter (or energy), that everything is physical, and that all events are explainable solely in terms of physical processes. There is no room in the universe for non-physical things, such as minds, or souls, or spirits (or God, for that matter). Not surprisingly, such determinists are usually atheists, and will claim that our appeals to minds or souls are "folk psychological" appeals to events that would be better understood by referencing the brain instead. The "mind" is simply the brain. Our mental actions, including decision-making, are brain-events. The brain is a physical object, governed by physical laws. Therefore, the operations of the brain are just as causally determined as any other object in the universe. The formal version of this argument is as follows:

1. All physical events are entirely caused, and governed by the laws of nature.
2. Anything entirely caused, and governed by the laws of nature, is "determined."
3. Humans are purely physical things.
4. Therefore, human actions are entirely physical events.
5. Therefore, human actions are entirely caused, and governed by the laws of nature.
6. Therefore, human actions are determined.

To be "determined" in this sense is just to say that whatever it is that we do, whatever actions we take, are the products of cause and effect relationships governed by the immutable laws of physics. In the case of inanimate objects, such as comets, we recognize that their actions are not the product of anything like "choice," but are entirely determined by the past and the laws of physics. For example, if you tell an astronomer enough information about where a particular comet is right now, she can tell you where that comet will be five minutes from now, or even a hundred years from now. No one would suppose that the comet will occupy a particular portion of space because it "wants to," or because it "chooses to." Its location, its trajectory—everything about that comet and what it does—is simply a matter of the laws of physics.

We're generally fairly confident about making similar claims about non-human animals (most of them, at least). When we think about the behaviors of fish and lizards, horses and cats and dogs, and maybe even "higher" animals such as chimpanzees and gorillas, we tend to think that their behavior is governed by "instinct" as opposed to rational and intentional choice. As smart as I believe my cat to be, I imagine that much, if not all, of what she does is driven by fairly basic, hard-wired biological imperatives and drives. This is just to say that we don't hold animals to be responsible for their actions in the same sort of way that we hold humans responsible for their own. If my cat "misbehaves," I don't think she is willfully making bad "choices." At most, I think she has some behavioral patterns that need to be corrected, if possible—and I then proceed to try to condition her to behave differently.

What about humans? Well, if we're physical in the same sort of way as is everything else in the universe, then there's nothing "special" or significantly different about the human animal. We might be more sophisticated in our behavior, but we're animals all the same. Humans, too, behave as we do not by anything like "choice" but as a result of genetic programming, instinct, conditioning (experienced in childhood and throughout our lives), etc.—all of which occurs in accordance with, and as a result of, the laws of physics.

"But," you may wonder, "isn't it obvious that I have free will? If my own will, my own free choice, is not responsible for my actions, then what is?"

"Any number of things," says the determinist.

You have probably already heard of the so-called "nature v. nurture" debate. This debate focuses on whether our nature (i.e., our DNA and other important biological influences) or our nurture (i.e., our upbringing and social experiences) is more responsible for our character and behavior. Notice, by the way, that "choice" was not presented as an option in the debate! The "nature/nurture" debate, whether it intends to or nor, *already* gestures at "determinism" by implying that our behavior is the product of either our biological propensities, or our social condition, or both—neither of which is under our control, and neither of which is an expression of anything like "choice."

Let's start with "nature," and let's start simply. With non-human animals, we're usually pretty comfortable with claiming that most, if not all, of their behaviors are driven by instinct as opposed to something like rational choice. We recognize that non-human creatures, such as insects, fish, birds, and mammals all display useful behaviors that help them to survive, feed, reproduce, etc. We're probably comfortable believing that insects don't "choose" to make hives, or gather pollen, or sting large threatening creatures, but rather do such things "automatically." So, too, with birds building nests, or fish swimming in schools, or squirrels gathering and hiding food. We tend to assume that non-human animals don't run away when something surprising happens because they choose to, but instead because of an instinctive aversion to possible predators. From a purely physical perspective, a purely naturalistic perspective, aren't we just another (admittedly complicated) animal? *Homo sapiens*? Another primate? If all other animals are driven by instinct rather than rational choice, why wouldn't we draw the same conclusion about the human animal?

While scientists are a long way from proving that particular genes or gene sequences can or do determine all of our particular behaviors, it is widely believed that, at the very least, certain behavioral dispositions are linked to certain genes or gene sequences. If this is true, then whether you are shy or outgoing, friendly or aggressive, obedient or rebellious, is less a matter of how you "choose" to be than which genes you inherited from your biological parents. If there really are genes that determine certain kinds of behaviors, or simply certain kinds of personalities (which, themselves, then determine certain kinds of behaviors), then, since your genetic inheritance is in no way under your control, you would have reason to think that your behavior is *determined*.

From a purely physical perspective, we can delve deeper than DNA and consider the behavior of the sub-atomic particles of which your body is made. They bump into one another in accordance with the laws of physics, right? The effects of those collisions are likewise governed by the laws of physics. Imagine that your body is a pool table, and all the atoms of your body are pool balls (this is very abstract, I know, but bear with me). The pool balls only move if acted upon, right? One must be struck by another (or at least by *something*) before it will move. And, if we know enough about the impact, we can predict very well the outcome of the collision. In other words, we can predict which direction the struck ball will go, and with roughly what speed, and so on—and we can predict any other collisions that might result from the first. Well, can't we understand all the events and actions concerning your body, at the sub-atomic level, to be various collisions and interactions of sub-atomic particles, all of which are governed by the laws of physics? Wouldn't that imply that if we only knew enough about the circumstances just prior to, and during, the impact, we would be able to predict the outcome as well? And, if we can predict the outcome, aren't we predicting what your body is going to do? Finally, if I'm able to predict what your body is going to do, am I not predicting what *you* are going to do? If you are purely physical, as determinists believe, we have reason to think that our actions are, in principle, just as predictable as the movements of pool balls, because our own behavior is just as causally determined.

Even if we think that "nurture" is more responsible for our behavior than is "nature," we're not any better off in terms of personal choice and free will. Determinists claim that social experiences can also play a deterministic role in our actions. We respond very reliably to certain stimuli. Pain and pleasure are very predictable in how they influence what we do. Punishment and reward are simply applications of painful or pleasurable experiences for the sake of some desired behavior. This assumption governs our social institutions and family life, our personal relationships and our legal codes. We don't like to be assaulted, so we punish anyone who does so, and threaten punishment to everyone else. The threat of the painful experience of being punished for assaulting another causes most of us to play nicely with one another instead. When our children lie, or refuse to clean up their room, or speak to us disrespectfully, or anything else we might not want them to do, we punish them with a time out, or a spanking, or a stern talking-to, or by withholding a privilege such as playing video games. Our assumption is that such interventions will *cause* the child to behave differently in the future. We can "nurture" our children, as well as other adults, to behave in the ways we prefer.

The impact of social experience is especially obvious in the case of childhood experiences. Consider the following two hypothetical situations:

	Child A	**Child B**
Parents	Attentive, supportive, nurturing	Absent, critical, abusive
Home	Plenty of food, safety	Malnourishment, dangerous conditions
Education	Good schools, educational hobbies and activities	Inadequate schools, no extracurricular activities or stimulation
Other		Repeatedly molested and verbally and physically abused

Given these two hypothetical children and their imagined early childhood experiences, isn't it a reasonable assumption that their two lives are likely to turn out in very different ways? Doesn't it seem to make a difference whether or not one grows up with families dealing with addiction problems, or with poverty, or subject to abuse? Even the most zealous champions of free will must concede that such circumstances at least have an *influence* on personality and behavior. The determinist merely claims that the influence goes beyond mere inclination, and amounts to determination.

In summary, according to the theory of determinism, free will is an illusion. Choice is an illusion. Because we are composed of the same materials as everything else in the universe, we are governed by the same laws of physics as everything else in the universe. All events, without exception, are the products are cause and effect sequences—and human events are no different. Who we are, and what we do, is not "up to us" in any meaningful way, but is instead *determined* by forces outside of our control.

If the case for determinism is so compelling, why do so many people nevertheless believe in the existence of free will? One word explains it: ignorance.

Now, before you get upset, thinking that determinists are insulting you (or anyone else) who believes in free will, understand that "ignorance" is being used in its literal sense: lacking information.

Determinists will point out that humans have a long history of offering superstitious (and ultimately *false*) explanations for events during those periods of time when humans didn't truly understand the cause of those events. For example, some humans used to explain the existence of thunder by claiming that Thor, god of thunder (among other things) was banging an anvil with his hammer, *mjölnir*. Indeed, the legacy of this explanation still exists in the Swedish word for thunder: *tordön* (literally, "Thor's rumble," or "Thor's thunder"). However, I suspect very few people (if any) still think that Thor is the cause of thunder. Instead, we now understand that thunder is the sound caused by rapidly expanding waves of compressed air, which is itself caused by the heat of lightning increasing the pressure of the air along its path to many times the normal atmospheric pressure. "Magical" explanations such as the use of Thor to explain lightning is a mere placeholder until a real, scientific explanation is discovered.

Determinists think that using free will to explain human behavior is like using Thor to explain thunder: it is a superstitious non-explanation that is a mere placeholder until the actual, scientific explanation is realized.

Determinists are often sympathetic to this error. As Baron d'Holbach (our source for determinism in this chapter) puts it,

> *It is the great complication of motion in man, it is the variety of his action, it is the multiplicity of causes that move him, whether simultaneously or in continual succession, that persuades him he is a free agent: if all his motions were simple, if the causes that move him did not confound themselves with each other, if they were distinct, if his machine was less complicated, he would perceive that all his actions were necessary, because he would be enabled to recur instantly to the cause that made him act.*

In other words, given how complex a "machine" is a human being, it is very difficult for any of us to offer a precise and accurate causal explanation of every human action. Our inability to do so causes some people to infer that there is no causal explanation, and then appeal to "free will" to fill the explanatory void. But, understandable though this mistake might be, it is still a mistake according to determinists. On the assumption that we are built of the same fundamental particles as everything else in the universe, it would seem to follow that we are governed by the same laws of physics as everything else. If we acknowledge that cause and effect explains the operations of everything else in the universe, we should be consistent and recognize that cause and effect (and not "free will") explains everything that we do as well.

Compatibilism

If you think you understand determinism, this next theory should be pretty simple, as it's (basically) identical in every way but one. Take everything that you know about determinism, and "copy and paste" it into compatibilism—but leave out one thing: determinism's claim that we have no free will.

Compatibilists claim we *do* have free will. In fact, that's why the theory is called compatibilism: because it claims that determinism is *compatible* with free will. That's it. That's the only difference—though it's a big one.

Let's review what the two theories have in common. Most determinists believe that everything in the universe (including ourselves) is physical. So do most compatibilists. Accordingly, determinists believe that everything in the universe is subject to the laws of physics. So do compatibilists. Determinists believe that every event has a cause, and that the cause is the product of antecedent conditions as governed by the laws of physics. So do compatibilists. Determinists believe that everything that happens has been causally determined to happen and could not have turned out any other way. So do compatibilists. Determinists believe that human actions are determined, and that we lack an "ability to do otherwise." So do compatibilists. For this reason, determinists claim we have no free will. This is where the compatibilist stops agreeing.

There have been many famous compatibilists in the history of Western philosophy, including the ancient Stoics, David Hume (included in this chapter), and Thomas Hobbes. More recently, a 20th century compatibilist, Walter Stace, introduced some helpful vocabulary. While our reading selection at the end of the chapter comes from Hume, we will also (first) consider Stace's contribution to the compatibilist position.

To begin with, both Hume and Stace believe that the free will debate has arisen largely due to confusion. A sign that the free will problem is not a real problem is the fact that all of us, including self-professed determinists, live *as if* we have free will and treat other people *as if* they do as well. It's reasonable to assume that if a determinist is the victim of a crime, he or she will still get upset—*as if* the criminal is responsible for the crime, as opposed to being a mere puppet of causal determination. Ask a determinist what she'd like to drink with dinner, and watch her "choose"—*as if* it were "up to her" what she's going to pick. This all suggests that we have free will. However, if compatibilists agree with determinists that all events are causally determined, what does it mean to say that we have free will? Considering that this definition of free will amounts to the only and only significant difference between determinism and compatibilism, this definition is incredibly important.

"Common usage" will be the key to understanding how it's possible both that we have free will, *and* that determinism is true. Compatibilists like Stace believe that there are correct and incorrect definitions of terms, proper and improper uses of words. When a word is used improperly, all kinds of interesting (and ridiculous) conclusions can be produced.

1. Humans are five-legged primates.
2. There are no five-legged primates.
3. Therefore, there are no humans.

In terms of its logical structure (validity), this argument is flawless—and yet, I'm confident that not a single person reading that argument accepts the conclusion as true. What's the problem with the argument? Go for the obvious answer: humans are *not* five-legged primates! If humans were five-legged primates, then it would follow that there are no humans—but that's not the case. To challenge the conclusion of this argument, it's not necessary to prove that humans exist. All that's necessary is to point out that the definition of "human" being used is incorrect. "Incorrect according to who?" you might ask. Incorrect according to "*common usage*."

Although it's true that one can, in a certain sense, define a word however one pleases, that doesn't mean anyone else will take you seriously should you do so. Language, after all, is an essentially cooperative project. Words acquire and have their meaning in large part by how they are used within a community of people speaking the same language and using those same words. "Five-legged primate" doesn't correspond to the common usage of "human," so it's an incorrect definition. Stace believes that philosophers have created false problems by failing to comply with the common usage of certain terms. The solution to these problems will be to correct the definition so that it does conform to common usage.

How does this apply to the free will problem? Determinists have defined free actions as those that are *not* causally determined. Looking around the world, they find no actions that are not causally determined. As a result, they conclude that there are no free actions. Compatibilists claim that "not being causally determined" is an incorrect definition of free will. They will appeal to common usage to establish the correct definition of free will and, having done so, are confident that we will recognize both that determinism is true *and* that we have free will.

At the beginning of the chapter, you were asked to consider ways in which you are free, and also ways in which you are not. With those thoughts in mind, participate in this follow-up exercise.

1. Think of a time in your life when you thought that you were not free, or that your freedom had been reduced, or challenged. What were the circumstances?
2. Think of the sorts of situations in which we say that people are not free. What are the properties of those situations?
3. Think of the sorts of circumstances in which we do not think people are responsible for their actions. What are the properties of those circumstances?
4. Think of a time in your life when you thought that you *were* free. What were the

circumstances?

Understand that participating in this sort of exercise isn't "busy work." For Stace, it's an essential step in his argument. Remember, his definitional standard is common usage. How do you ("commonly") use the word "free?" If you're anything like Stace, your answers to questions 1-4 above will have a few things in common. Compatibilists believe that your examples and thoughts on freedom will probably look like the following:

Lack of freedom: being in jail, being held prisoner, not being allowed to engage in desirable activities—in essence, not being able to do what you want to do.

Freedom: no (or few) constraints on activities—in essence, being able to do what you want to do.

Responsible: when someone acts "on purpose," intentionally, from their own desires.

Not responsible: when someone acts unintentionally, "by accident," contrary to their own desires

Compatibilists would point out that there's nothing deeply philosophical, mysteriously metaphysical, or terribly complicated about this understanding of freedom and responsibility. When we are able to do what we *want* to do, we call that "freedom." When someone or something prevents us from doing what we want to do, or when someone or something forces us to do something we do not want to do, we call that not being free (or being oppressed, or forced, or coerced, etc.).

Let's look at a simple and timely example: are you free to stop reading this paragraph right now? Yes, or no? I would assume that almost anyone would say yes. After all, nothing is stopping you from stopping your reading, right? No one has immobilized your head, propped open your eyeballs, pointed them at the words you're reading, and prevented you from stopping, right? *Right*? (If your answer is "wrong," please call 911 as soon as possible) If you wanted to stop reading, you could, right?

In fairness, I can imagine someone might think "no," but what that person would mean by that is something like this: "It's possible for me to stop reading, but I 'must' keep reading or else I won't understand the material, I'll get behind in the work, and my grade will suffer." In other words, there are undesirable consequences for stopping. Those undesirable consequences inspire continued reading. Compatibilists wouldn't deny this, but they would point out that there's a big difference between someone physically preventing you from stopping your reading, and there being a good reason for you to continue. If you doubt that it's possible for you to stop, try this simple little experiment. STOP READING! For the next ten seconds, do something else. Go to the bathroom, get a drink, rest your eyes, whatever—but stop reading.

If you tried, I bet you were able to do it. This was just a long-winded way of demonstrating that you are reading right now because you *want* to.

I'm not naïve. I don't presume that you "want to" in the sense that you are eagerly soaking up every word and can't wait to get to the next page. But, at the very least, you want to read these words right now because doing so serves some other desire of yours (e.g., getting a good grade in a philosophy class, learning about compatibilism, etc.)—and for that reason you are still doing what you want to do. Clearly, if you wanted to do something else more, you would be doing that "something else" instead.

Putting all this together, a compatibilist would say that your reading right now is a "free action," because you are doing what you want to do. If someone snatches the book (or computer screen) away from you and won't give it back, you can no longer do what you want to do. You're no longer free to read.

In summary, we are free when we can do what we want to do, and we are unfree when we can't, or when we are forced to do something we don't want to do. We are free when there are no external constraints on our ability to act on our desires.

This is our first, crude, compatibilist definition of freedom—and one that conforms to "common usage," it would seem.

The compatibilist definition of freedom is more complicated, of course. Remember, determinists believe that all events are causally determined, and for that reason there is no free will. Compatibilists agree with everything about determinism except the claim about there being no free will. That means that compatibilists *also* believe that all events are causally determined. Whether an action is free, or unfree, it will be the result of a causally determined sequence. Rather than distinguish free actions from unfree actions by saying that some actions are caused, and some are not, compatibilists will distinguish them on the basis of *what kind* of cause is the immediate (antecedent, or "proximate") cause of the event in question. To understand how this works, go back to the example of reading this section.

Let's suppose that you want to continue reading, and you do, in fact, continue to read. That sounds like being "free," right? You're able to do what you want: to continue reading. Is there a *cause* of your continuing to read? Of course there is. You continue to read because you want to. Is there a cause for you wanting to read? Of course there is. Maybe it's because you want to understand the material. Is there a cause for that? Maybe you want to get a good grade. Is there a cause for you wanting to get a good grade? Perhaps the cause is that you want to someday have a good job. Is there a cause for you wanting a good job? Perhaps its cause is a desire for financial security. Is there a cause for that desire? Maybe you grew up in a home where money was tight, and you learned the importance of being financially secure. Was there a cause for the money being "tight" in your home, growing up? Of course there was. This sequence goes on and on, far into the past long before you were born—in principle, all the way back to the very beginning of the universe. On this analysis, then, free actions certainly have causes—indeed, *every* event has a cause.

What about unfree actions? What would have to happen if we were to say you were *not* free to continue reading? Maybe you're reading this section on a computer, and the computer crashes, making it impossible for you to continue reading right now. Is there a cause for you being not free to read? Certainly: the computer crashed. Is there a cause for that? Maybe there was a power failure. Is there a cause for that? Maybe there was a lightning strike on a power line someplace. Is there a cause for the lightning strike? There was an electrical discharge from clouds. Is there a cause for that? Of course—and again, this sequence will go back far into the past, in principle to the very beginning of the universe. Unfree actions also have causes.

If this is so, then the difference between free and unfree actions isn't the difference between one kind of action being caused, and the other kind of action being uncaused. Instead, the difference will be the *kind* of cause.

The cause of your freely continuing to read was your own desire to read. Stace calls this kind of cause an "internal" cause because it's literally *internal* with respect to your body. Your desire is a product of some event in your brain. Your brain is inside your skull—hence, an "internal" cause.

What about when you were not free to continue reading? The cause, in that case, was "external." The computer crashing was an outside force (meaning, outside your body—unless you have an odd way of storing your computer!) that prevented you from acting on your desire.

The most common sorts of internal causes will be psychological states of various kinds: desires, motivations, beliefs, etc. External causes will include any causes that are external to your body, such as a power failure, a locked door, a car that won't start, handcuffs, a bouncer who is literally throwing you out of a bar, etc. If we want to know if an action is free or unfree, we can consult the following steps:

1. Identify the action under investigation
- Example: falling off a bridge to one's watery death below
2. Identify the immediate/antecedent cause of the action
- Example 1a: the deceased wanted to die
- Example 1b: the deceased was knocked off balance by a gust of wind

3. Determine whether the immediate/antecedent cause was "internal" or "external"
   - Example 1a: internal cause (one's own suicidal desire)
   - Example 1b: external cause (gust of wind)
4. If the immediate cause is internal, the action was freely done. If the immediate cause was external, it was probably not freely done.
   - Example 1a: suicide (the deceased is responsible)
   - Example 1b: accidental death (not responsible)
5. Or, as a short cut that works most of the time, just ask yourself: did the person do "it" (whatever "it" is) because she *wanted* to? If yes, then the action was freely done, by definition. If no, then it was probably not freely done.

Notice how this evaluation produces results consistent with our common sense intuitions. If someone falls off a bridge because he wanted to die, we call that a suicide attempt. We recognize that the person did it on purpose, and, if the person survives, we'll probably try to convince them not to do that again. On the other hand, if the person falls off the bridge because of a gust of wind, we call that an accident. If the person survives, we probably wouldn't see any need for suicide counseling because we would recognize that they didn't go over the edge on purpose.

Given this understanding of freedom, we can now see why compatibilists believe we have free will: we act freely *all the time*. For most of us, our usual experience is that we do things because we want to. Even unpleasant things like going to the dentist are still things we "want" to do for the sake of avoiding future tooth pain. We exercise our free will countless times every single day. Every time you do something because you want to, that is a free act, according to compatibilism. Thankfully, few of us encounter serious or prolonged limitations of our freedom. Most of us don't get kidnapped, or get locked up in a cage, or are forced to do something against our will. When such things do happen, we say that we weren't free, and we tend to take those sorts of events very seriously!

Now it's time for the "tricky" part.

It's very important to always keep in mind that the *only* (significant) difference between determinism and compatibilism is that determinists say there is no free will, and compatibilists say that there is.

According to determinism, your actions are all the result of antecedent causes as governed by the laws of physics. In principle, we can know what will happen in the future if we only had enough information about the past, and a sufficient understanding of the laws of physics. With inanimate objects, this is easily illustrated. In fact, whether the writers intended to or not, this was illustrated in the 2006 Adam Sandler movie, "Click."

In "Click," Sandler's character (Michael Newman) acquires a fantastic "universal remote control" that allows him to manipulate reality as if it were a video or digital recording. He can fast forward, rewind, and "pause" reality (among other things). In one scene, he takes advantage of the pause feature to gain some vengeance on an older child who has been making fun of his own younger son. The two children are tossing a baseball back and forth. When his son throws it, and the older boy raises his glove to catch it, Michael pauses the flow of time. Somehow personally immune to the "pause," he walks over and pushes the older boy's glove down a few inches. He steps back to where he had been standing, presses pause again (so that time continues to "play"), and watches as the baseball strikes the boy in the face, as the glove is no longer in the way to catch it. The only way that this physical comedy makes any sense is by virtue of the fact that Michael was able to predict where the ball would be, thanks to his knowledge of where the ball had been, and his common-sense understanding of the laws of physics. Because the ball was governed entirely by causal forces, knowledge of the ball's past plus knowledge of the laws of physics at work on the ball at that instant provided an accurate prediction of the future.

Each one of us makes use of this common sense understanding and predictive ability every day. If you knock a glass off a counter, and your reflexes are quick enough to do something about it, you intuitively "calculate" where you need to put your hand in your attempt to catch the glass. As the glass falls towards the ground, you are very, very confident that in the next second or so that glass is going to move a little bit closer to the ground, along the same path it's following. You would never think that it might, instead, suddenly fly several feet straight out to one side or another. Because you can perceive where the glass is at one moment in time, and what it's doing, and because of your basic understanding of the laws of physics, you can predict with very reliable accuracy where that glass will be in the near future.

We can make this common sense understanding more sophisticated by adding some technical vocabulary. Imagine that it's possible to freeze time, like in that movie I mentioned. Imagine that that single frozen split second of time provides a picture of the entire universe at that precise moment—like a single frame of a film. Call this the "total world picture," or TWP. If the determinist worldview is accurate (and both determinists and compatibilists believe that it is), then *if* we had access to (and understanding of) the TWP at a particular instant in time (TWP_1), and we had an adequate understanding of the laws of physics, we would know just what the next instant in time (TWP_2) will look like (i.e., what will be happening at TWP_2). In other words, we would be able to predict the future. Of course, none of us has the ability to predict the future with perfect accuracy, but that's easy enough to explain: none of us has full knowledge of the TWP at any particular instant in time, nor (probably) a perfect understanding of the laws of physics.

Because the future is the inevitable product of the past and the laws of physics, the future is "fixed." Although you and I don't *know* what the future holds, that's a feature of our own (understandable) ignorance, not any indication that the future is somehow "open" or not determined. There is one (inevitable and unyielding) path that the future can take, and it was "determined" at the very moment the universe came into existence. There are no alternate paths, no forks in the road, no options. The future is "fixed"—and that includes your own future as well. It's worth repeating: everything claimed about the TWP and the predictability of future events is believed by *both* determinists and compatibilists.

Remember those free and unfree actions, as described by compatibilists? You're free if you stop reading because that's what you want to do. You're unfree when you stop reading because your computer crashes, despite your desire to continue. Recall that both free and unfree events have causes. In other words, both are part of the TWP, and both are the inevitable (and theoretically predictable) products of a prior TWP and the laws of physics.

At TWP_I, you stop reading because you wanted to stop. The immediate cause is internal, and it's a free action. At TWP_{I-1}, you formed the desire to stop reading because your eyes had become tired. If someone had access to the information in TWP_{I-1}, that person would have been able to predict your stopping reading at TWP_I. At TWP_{I-2}, your eyes became tired due to some biological cause (we don't have to know exactly what it is, for the sake of this discussion). If someone had known the contents of TWP_{I-2}, he would have been able to predict the formation of your desire to stop reading at TWP_{I-1}. At TWP_{I-3}, the cause of your eyes getting tired was itself caused by some other event. If someone had known the contents of TWP_{I-3}, he would have been able to predict your eyes getting tired. We could repeat this sequence a split second further into the past each time, until eventually (at who knows when, $TWP_{I-1\ million}$?) we would reach a TWP of a time before your birth. Theoretically, we could keep going backwards until we reached TWP_1—the very first split second of time after the Big Bang. That means that someone with knowledge of TWP_1 could predict TWP_2, TWP_3, TWP_4 (etc.), and could therefore ultimately predict TWP_I: the split second in which you stopped reading because you *wanted* to.

There is nothing else you could have done at TWP_I, given all those previous TWPs. It was causally necessitated that you stop reading, and your life (at that moment) could not have turned out any way. There is no possible way you could have done anything different (like, continue to read, for example). This very same analysis applies to actions coming from external causes as well. That computer crash is part of a TWP just like everything else, and we could run the same backwards analysis, or the same prediction sequence starting at the Big Bang, whether the cause of the event in question is external, or internal. In other words, whether the action was free, or unfree, it was causally necessitated and couldn't have turned out any other way.

It's absolutely critical to understand this point. Compatibilism is very easily misunderstood, and when (and if) it is misunderstood, it's always misunderstood in the same sort of way: by overestimating the difference between determinism and compatibilism, and by mistakenly believing that compatibilists believe that we have genuine "choice" as opposed to all our actions being the causally necessitated result of antecedent events/causes.

There is no "choice" in compatibilism. Unfortunately, some compatibilists misleadingly claim otherwise. They will say that one could have chosen otherwise if one had desired otherwise. In other words, you could have done something else if you had wanted to do something else.

"Could I have chosen to continue reading, instead of stopping?" Absolutely! So long as you had wanted to continue reading, instead of stopping. Recall, however, that your desires are just as causally determined, just as much a necessary product of a previous TWP, as anything else. Your desires couldn't have been any different, unless your past had been different. Pretty clearly, you have no control over your past. It's not as if you can reach back through time and change your childhood experiences so that you have different desires in the present.

Normally, when we say that we have a "choice," it means that we have an "ability to do otherwise"—it means there are multiple options, and it really is possible for us to exercise any of them.

We simply do *not* have "choice," in that sense, according to compatibilism.

In fairness, the compatibilist will say that this doesn't matter. According to common usage, we are free when we are able to do what we want to do (i.e., when we act from internal causes). An ability to do otherwise, an ability that requires that we have the power to resist the causal necessity that governs everything in nature, is not what we "commonly" mean by freedom—or so the compatibilist claims. According to compatibilists, when we say we acted "freely" (as opposed to under coercion), we're not suggesting that we somehow exercised some magical ability to ignore the laws of physics and the causal necessity that governs all reality. Instead, all we're saying is that we did something because we wanted to, on purpose, intentionally, of our own will, etc. That is the "common usage" of "freedom" in the context of free actions. If someone wants to understand "freedom" as the ability to be immune to the laws of physics, then that person will have effectively defined free will out of existence (as compatibilists claim the determinists have done)—but why should the rest of us accept that needlessly "metaphysical" definition of free will? Isn't it the case that our usage of words like "free" and "unfree," "voluntary" and "involuntary" just indicate the much simpler, much more common-sense, and much more *real* experience of sometimes doing things because we want to, and other times being prevented from acting on our desires?

Because the only difference between determinism and compatibilism is the definition of freedom, your evaluation of compatibilism will depend almost exclusively on what you think of that definition. What do *you* mean by freedom? Are you free so long as you are able to do what you want to do—even if your actions, and the desires that produce them, couldn't have turned out any other way? If your answer is yes, you just might be a compatibilist. If, on the other hand, you think that freedom requires genuine "choice," a genuine "ability to do otherwise," then compatibilism isn't going to satisfy your standards of freedom.

Agency Theory

If you believe that you *do* have free will, but you disagree with the compatibilist interpretation of freedom, you might be an "agency theorist."

Indeed, I would guess that most people in the West are at least implicitly agency theorists (whether they realize it or not, and whether agency theory is *correct*, or not).

Most, but not all, agency theorists embrace a dualistic understanding of human nature. This means that, unlike (most) determinists and (most) compatibilists, agency theorists do not believe that human beings are purely physical. There is something about persons that can't be reduced to purely physical explanations, that goes beyond physiology and physics. There are many different names for this "something-that-can't-be-reduced-to-purely-physical-explanation:" "soul," "mind," "spirit," "self," or "will."

Depending on who you ask, those terms could all have different meanings, but, for our purposes, each could capture that "something" that agency theorists have in mind.

Whatever "it" is, it is *non-physical.* Call it mental, or spiritual, or simply non-physical—in any case, it does not share the same properties as physical things, and is not subject to physical laws in the same manner as are bodies.

This exception is of profound importance. Because the mind (or whatever you prefer to call it) is not physical, it is not subject to the laws of physics. Because it is not subject to the laws of physics, it is not bound by causal determinism. Therefore, there is something about us—perhaps that which is most fundamental to us—that is outside the scope of determinism. This exception creates the space for a powerful version of free will.

Substance Dualism

Why should anyone believe in this dualistic understanding of human nature? Although the idea that humans are non-physical souls (or minds) inhabiting physical bodies is a popular point of view, especially amongst people of faith, it is nevertheless an admittedly mysterious idea, and one that seemingly defies our experience of the world in terms of purely physical objects governed by the laws of nature.

The greatest challenge for, and criticism of, agency theorist accounts of free will is their reliance upon this dualistic understanding of human nature. We will therefore spend a small amount of time considering why anyone might accept this view, before returning to the particular issue of free will.

Anecdotally, and conventionally, for most people, their use of language betrays a dualistic understanding of human nature. Most of us to do not identify ourselves with our bodies, either with particular parts nor even our body as a whole. We speak of our bodies (and their parts) as objects, as possessions. "*My* stomach hurts." "I *lost* a tooth." "*My* hair is too long." "You *have* a nice body."[32]

The two basic possible understandings of human nature we will consider in this section are the *reductionist materialist* understanding of human nature, and the *substance dualist* understanding of human nature.

According to *substance dualism*, the brain is a physical object with physical properties, but the mind (or soul) is a *mental substance with mental properties.* If we take a sensation, such as pain, that pain sensation will be understood both as a physical event, in terms of certain electro-chemical properties and events in the physical brain, as well as a mental event—the conscious awareness of pain—for the non-physical mind. If this view of human nature is accurate, then several interesting things might follow:

- Although the mind (somehow) interacts with the body, it is not identical to the body.
- The mind "transcends" the body and its experiences, and is identical to none of them in particular. Therefore, the same mind can persist through time and experience (and bodily change), thereby preserving personal identity.
- Because the mind is not the body, it is

[32] In fairness, we shouldn't always read too much into the conventions of language. After all, we also still speak of the sun setting and rising, as though the sun were moving around the Earth, rather than the other way around. It's possible that language just hasn't caught up to a scientifically accurate understanding of human nature just yet.

possible for the mind to continue to exist after the death/destruction of the body (i.e., an "afterlife" is possible).

On the reductionist materialist interpretation of human nature, in contrast, "mental things" (e.g., thoughts, desires, etc.) are nothing other than physical things (e.g., particular sequences of neurons activating in the brain), and "mental events" (e.g., believing, desiring, etc.) are also merely brain events.

If there are any exceptions to this pattern (i.e., that every "mental" event is merely a brain event); if some claim ("X") is true with respect to some mental state, but is not true with respect to a brain state, then it would establish that *not all* mental activity is reducible to brain activity, and this would be an argument *in favor* of substance dualism.

This reasoning relies upon a principle known as Leibniz's Law of Identity, and will be a central feature of the argument for substance dualism. *According to Lebiniz's Law of Identity, two things are the same if, and only if, they have all the same properties at the same time.*

If you prefer a fancier formulation, "*x* is identical to *y*, if, and only if, for any property *p* attributable to *x* at time *t*, *p* is also attributable to *y* at time *t*."

For example, if Darth Vader is identical to Anakin Skywalker, then any property attributable to one (e.g., being the father of Luke and Leia) must also be attributable to the other. If *every* property attributable to one, is also attributable to the other, without exception, then they are identical. If, however, there are any properties attributable to one, but not the other (e.g., "being the smuggler who was frozen in carbonite"), then they are not identical. That is a fancy way of proving that Anakin Skywalker and Darth Vader are the same person, but Darth Vader and Han Solo are not the same person. While the properties of Star Wars characters are not particularly relevant to our topic, Leibniz's Law of Identity is.

The reductionist materialist claims that minds and brains are identical, that there is no distinct, non-physical mind or soul because we are all (and only) bodies. On a purely reductionist materialist understanding of human nature (i.e., the understanding employed by most determinists and compatibilists), "I" (along with everything else in the universe) am fully describable using the language of physics and chemistry. I am an object (a body) that is extended in a particular portion of space, with a certain shape, mass, size, etc. "I" am my body (in general), but probably especially my brain (and possibly my central nervous system).

If we apply Leibniz's Law of Identity, then, if minds are really just brains, then any property true of "minds" must also be true of brains (or at least of bodies, more generally). If, however, there are any properties that are true of minds but are *not* true of brains/bodies, then minds and brains are *not* identical—and the substance dualist can then argue that while bodies are physical, minds are non-physical.

Substance dualists usually offer several examples of mind-properties that are not also brain-properties (or vice versa). The first three examples we will consider come from Descartes (whom you might have studied in an earlier chapter).

Descartes – Meditation 2

...

4. But I do not yet know with sufficient clearness what I am, though assured that I am; and hence, in the next place, I must take care, lest perchance I inconsiderately substitute some other object in room of what is properly myself, and thus wander from truth, even in that knowledge (cognition) which I hold to be of all others the most certain and evident. For this reason, I will now consider anew what I formerly believed myself to be, before I entered on the present train of thought; and of my previous opinion I will retrench all that can in the least be invalidated by the grounds of doubt I have adduced, in order that there may at length remain nothing but what is certain and indubitable.

5. What then did I formerly think I was? Undoubtedly I judged that I was a man. But what is a man? Shall I say a rational animal? Assuredly not; for it would be necessary forthwith to inquire into what is meant by animal, and what by

rational, and thus, from a single question, I should insensibly glide into others, and these more difficult than the first; nor do I now possess enough of leisure to warrant me in wasting my time amid subtleties of this sort. I prefer here to attend to the thoughts that sprung up of themselves in my mind, and were inspired by my own nature alone, when I applied myself to the consideration of what I was. In the first place, then, I thought that I possessed a countenance, hands, arms, and all the fabric of members that appears in a corpse, and which I called by the name of body. It further occurred to me that I was nourished, that I walked, perceived, and thought, and all those actions I referred to the soul; but what the soul itself was I either did not stay to consider, or, if I did, I imagined that it was something extremely rare and subtile, like wind, or flame, or ether, spread through my grosser parts. As regarded the body, I did not even doubt of its nature, but thought I distinctly knew it, and if I had wished to describe it according to the notions I then entertained, I should have explained myself in this manner: By body I understand all that can be terminated by a certain figure; that can be comprised in a certain place, and so fill a certain space as therefrom to exclude every other body; that can be perceived either by touch, sight, hearing, taste, or smell; that can be moved in different ways, not indeed of itself, but by something foreign to it by which it is touched [and from which it receives the impression]; for the power of self-motion, as likewise that of perceiving and thinking, I held as by no means pertaining to the nature of body; on the contrary, I was somewhat astonished to find such faculties existing in some bodies.

6. But [as to myself, what can I now say that I am], since I suppose there exists an extremely powerful, and, if I may so speak, malignant being, whose whole endeavors are directed toward deceiving me? Can I affirm that I possess any one of all those attributes of which I have lately spoken as belonging to the nature of body? After attentively considering them in my own mind, I find none of them that can properly be said to belong to myself. To recount them were idle and tedious. Let us pass, then, to the attributes of the soul. The first mentioned were the powers of nutrition and walking; but, if it be true that I have no body, it is true likewise that I am capable neither of walking nor of being nourished. Perception is another attribute of the soul; but perception too is impossible without the body; besides, I have frequently, during sleep, believed that I perceived objects which I afterward observed I did not in reality perceive. Thinking is another attribute of the soul; and here I discover what properly belongs to myself. This alone is inseparable from me. I am--I exist: this is certain; but how often? As often as I think; for perhaps it would even happen, if I should wholly cease to think, that I should at the same time altogether cease to be. I now admit nothing that is not necessarily true. I am therefore, precisely speaking, only a thinking thing, that is, a mind (mens sive animus), understanding, or reason, terms whose signification was before unknown to me. I am, however, a real thing, and really existent; but what thing? The answer was, a thinking thing.

7. The question now arises, am I aught besides? I will stimulate my imagination with a view to discover whether I am not still something more than a thinking being. Now it is plain I am not the assemblage of members called the human body; I am not a thin and penetrating air diffused through all these members, or wind, or flame, or vapor, or breath, or any of all the things I can imagine; for I supposed that all these were not, and, without changing the supposition, I find that I still feel assured of my existence. But it is true, perhaps, that those very things which I suppose to be non-existent, because they are unknown to me, are not in truth different from myself whom I know. This is a point I cannot determine, and do not now enter into any dispute regarding it. I can only judge of things that are known to me: I am conscious that I exist, and I who know that I exist inquire into what I am. It is, however, perfectly certain that the knowledge of my existence, thus precisely taken, is not dependent on things, the existence of which is as yet unknown to me: and consequently it is not dependent on any of the things I can feign in imagination. Moreover, the phrase itself, I frame an image (efffingo), reminds me of my error; for I should in truth frame one if I

were to imagine myself to be anything, since to imagine is nothing more than to contemplate the figure or image of a corporeal thing; but I already know that I exist, and that it is possible at the same time that all those images, and in general all that relates to the nature of body, are merely dreams [or chimeras]. From this I discover that it is not more reasonable to say, I will excite my imagination that I may know more distinctly what I am, than to express myself as follows: I am now awake, and perceive something real; but because my perception is not sufficiently clear, I will of express purpose go to sleep that my dreams may represent to me the object of my perception with more truth and clearness. And, therefore, I know that nothing of all that I can embrace in imagination belongs to the knowledge which I have of myself, and that there is need to recall with the utmost care the mind from this mode of thinking, that it may be able to know its own nature with perfect distinctness.

8. But what, then, am I? A thinking thing, it has been said. But what is a thinking thing? It is a thing that doubts, understands, [conceives], affirms, denies, wills, refuses; that imagines also, and perceives.

1. Minds (unlike bodies) are "knowable."

If you read our earlier chapter on epistemology, you probably recall that Descartes attempted to prove the possibility of knowledge by means of his famous "*cogito ergo sum*." "I think, therefore I exist," is something that he can *know* to be true, any time he thinks that thought.

Descartes then proceeds to analyze just *what* he is, this "self" that he knows to exist whenever it thinks. He does some conceptual analysis of himself, as that thing that exists whenever it exists. "But what then am I? A thing that thinks. What is that? A thing that doubts, understands, affirms, denies, wills, refuses, and which also imagines and senses." This "thing" he identifies as a mind. His essence, as a mind, is to think. To say that thinking is his essence is to say that if thinking were removed from his mind, as a property, it would cease to be a mind. As Descartes puts it:

> *[S]eeing that I could pretend that I had no body and that there was no world nor any place where I was, but that I could not pretend, on that account, that I did not exist; and that, on the contrary, from the very fact that I thought about doubting the truth of other things, it followed very evidently and very certainly that I existed....From this I knew that I was a substance the whole essence or nature of which was merely to think, and which, in order to exist, needed no place and depended on no material things. Thus this 'I,' that is, the soul through which I am what I am, is entirely distinct from the body...*

In summary, Descartes knows that at least one mind exists (namely, himself!). Therefore, he knows minds exist. Bodies, on the other hand, are not *known* to exist. So-called physical objects might just be figments of his imagination, hallucinations, dreams, or even the deception of an "evil demon." Descartes can't even be certain that his own body exists. Perhaps he is a disembodied soul that is only imagining that he has a physical body? Maybe the entire physical world, and even object within it, is simply an illusion, a projection of Descartes' own mind? These are all far-fetched possibilities, to be sure—but the point remains that they are *possible*. The existence of bodies can be doubted, but the existence of minds can't be doubted. Descartes knows minds exist, but he doesn't know bodies exist.

Recall Leibniz's Law of Identity: two things are the same if, and only if, they have all the same properties at the same time. One property of minds is "indubitability" (not capable of being doubted), but bodies lack this property—instead, one of their properties is the opposite: "dubitability." Some of the properties of bodies (including brains) don't seem to apply to minds, and vice versa. According to Leibniz's law, therefore, minds and bodies/brains are not identical.

2. Minds and bodies have different essential properties.

This second example is very much related to our first. Descartes has analyzed himself as a mind, whose essence is to think. Bodies, in contrast, have a different essence. "Thinking" is certainly not essential to bodies, but "extension" (being extended in space) *is*. "I enumerate the [extended] thing's various parts. I ascribe to these parts certain sizes, shapes, positions, and movements from place to place; to these movements I ascribe various durations." Bodies, unlike minds, are describable in terms of properties that are quantifiable, and are therefore capable of being objects of scientific study.

Again, recall Leibniz's Law of Identity: two things are the same if, and only if, they have all the same properties at the same time. One property of minds (indeed, the *essential* property of minds) is thinking—but thinking is *not* an essential property of bodies, or even one of the properties of bodies at all (in most cases, to be sure, such as is the case with all inanimate, non-sentient bodies in the universe). Similarly, extension is a property of bodies (including brains)—indeed, it's the essential property of bodies—but being extended is *not* a property of minds. How much space does your mind fill? What part of space? What is the particular shape of your mind? Some of the properties of bodies (including brains) don't seem to apply to minds, and vice versa. According to Leibniz's law, therefore, minds and bodies/brains are not identical.

3. The mind (unlike bodies) is indivisible.

Our final example from Descartes is an extension of his analysis of the essential properties of bodies and minds. The essential property of bodies is extension. By definition, anything extended in space is capable of division. A candy bar is extended in space, and we can easily imagine the candy bar being split in half. Perhaps disturbingly, we can also imagine our own (extended) body being split in half! Such is the nature of bodies....But, the same can't be said of minds.

> *there is a great difference between a mind and a body, because the body, by its very nature, is something divisible, whereas the mind is plainly indivisible... insofar as I am only a thing that thinks, I cannot distinguish any parts in me....Although the whole mind seems to be united to the whole body, nevertheless, were a foot or an arm or any other bodily part amputated, I know that nothing would be taken away from the mind...*

It makes perfect sense to imagine the top half of my body, but it makes no sense to imagine the top half of my mind. We can speak of the left side of your brain, but not the left side of your mind. As Descartes says, "we cannot conceive of half a soul, as we can in the case of any body, however small." Because bodies are extended, they can be divided, and we can understand them in terms of parts. But, because minds are not extended, they are indivisible, and lack parts. Having different properties, minds and bodies/brains are not identical, according to Leibniz's Law.

The remaining arguments pertaining to Leibniz's Law are not necessarily associated with Descartes, but work in the same basic fashion.

4. Mental properties (and not physical properties) offer "private access."

I have "private access" to my own mental life, but I have to infer the existence and qualities of your mental life. I am aware of my own thoughts, but I have to "read" your body-language, tone of voice, and behavior to infer what you're thinking—unless you just tell me, of course. If I desire a glass of wine, I immediately and automatically *know* this, just by virtue of my awareness of my own thoughts and desires. You, on the other hand, can't tell that I desire a glass of wine unless I do something like ask for one, reach for one, stare at someone else's glass of wine, etc. But, notice that all the information you would use in that process is "public," available to you (or anyone else), or ever to me. If I had short-term memory problems, and you recorded my behavior on your cell phone, and then showed me that footage a few minutes later, I could infer, same as you, that I wanted a glass of wine.

To summarize, bodies are "public," as are physical states, in general. Mental states, on the other hand, are "private" (to the mind in question). Because minds and bodies have different properties ("private" v. "public"), they are not identical.

5. Some mental states (and not brain states) are "intentional."

Some of our mental states are "intentional." Another way of saying this is that they are "propositional attitudes." *Propositional attitudes are mental attitudes towards certain "states of affairs."* This might sound complicated, but is actually fairly simple. Propositional attitudes are characterized by their "about-ness." What they are "about" is a "state of affairs." For example:

- "I hope *that* my friends' marriage can be repaired."
- "I believe *that* there is a midterm exam on free will."
- "I desire *that* my favorite TV show be renewed for another season."
- "I fear *that* it will not be renewed."

As you can see, propositional attitudes include beliefs, fears, desires, etc., and such propositional attitudes are characterized by their "about-ness." Dualists claim that brain states, unlike mental states, cannot be intentional in this way. If a brain state is, for example, simply a sequence of neurons firing, how could that sequence of firing neurons be *about* anything? If a reductionist materialist wants to reduce mental states to brain states, then that would mean that my desire *for* a glass of wine is just some sequence of neural activity in my brain—but how could that sequence, even if we identify it as a desire, be, specifically, a desire for *wine*? Some mental states (e.g., propositional attitudes) are intentional. If brain states are not intentional, then mental states and brain states have different properties, and are therefore not identical.

6. Some mental states (but not brain states) have a "truth-value"

The last argument drawing upon Leibniz's Law concerns the fact that some mental states have "truth-values." As you might recall from our chapter on epistemology, claims have truth-values—which is just to say that a claim is either true or false, even if we're not sure which. My belief that it is still over 90 degrees outside, at the time of this writing is either true, or it is false.[33]

Some of my mental events (e.g., beliefs) have propositional content, and that content has a truth-value. Contrast this to brain states. Given that brain states are purely physical events, they have no propositional content at all. An electrical discharge in my brain has no truth-value. A sequence of neurons firing can't be true, or false—only claims (expressed via our beliefs and other assertions) have a truth-value. Since some mental states have properties (having a truth-value) that bodily states do not, minds and bodies have different properties, and are therefore not identical.

We've considered several arguments for substance dualism on the basis of Leibniz's Law, but will now consider a few more that rely on powerful intuitions, instead.

7. Our intuitive self-awareness implies dualism.

When I (or you, presumably) introspect, what I experience is that I *am* a "self" that *has* a body. I (as a "self") *have* experiences over time, but I am not identical with any of them, and my experience is that I am the *same* "self" that is having these experiences.

Bluntly, either we have this intuitive experience of being a self, distinct from our bodies, and distinct from particular experiences, because that experience is accurate and true, or else our experience is an illusion. However, that intuitive experience is very compelling and persuasive, so any evidence contradicting it would have to be

---

[33] Sad, but true: despite it being 7:37 PM, in Long Beach, it is still over 90 degrees outside!

even more compelling and persuasive. In the absence of such evidence, we have reason to believe that we are not identical to our bodies.

8. Our intuition of personal identity implies dualism.

My body changes over time. It grows and shrinks, and my cells are all replaced every few years. If I were identical to my body, and nothing other than my body/brain, it's difficult to see how identity would be preserved over time. How am I the same person when my body is not the same, over time? And yet, we have a powerful intuitive sense that we *are* the same person over time, that we are an enduring "self" that persists throughout our life history. "I" am the same "I" who *has* memories of past events, *has* experiences of the present moment, anticipates the future, etc.

A purely reductionist materialist account of the self doesn't seem capable of preserving personal identity, and so this intuition of being the same self over time would be an illusion. However, that intuitive experience is very compelling and persuasive, so any evidence contradicting it would have to be even more compelling and persuasive. In the absence of such evidence, we have reason to think that we are not identical to our bodies.

9. Our intuitions of genuine choice, spontaneity, responsibility, legitimate praise/blame, legitimate punishment / reward, and legitimate moral obligation all imply dualism.

Finally, with the possible exception of sociopaths, each one of us has a powerful set of intuitions concerning personal responsibility. We hold others responsible for their actions, as though they had a choice. When someone does something "bad," we get angry, or disappointed. This only makes sense, is only fair, if the person could have acted otherwise. Similarly, when we, ourselves, do something we think we shouldn't have, we feel guilty—but this only makes sense if we had a choice. Praise and blame each only make sense on the presupposition of choice, and personal responsibility. It makes no more sense to praise someone for doing something he could not help but do than it makes sense to praise me for having been born. In both cases, no choice was involved. The fact that we punish people for wrongdoing seems to presuppose personal responsibility. Otherwise, how is it fair to condemn people for actions they had no choice but to do? Finally, even the very notion of "right" and "wrong," good" and "bad" presupposes choice. A basic principle of ethics is that "ought implies can." That is, it only makes sense to say that someone ought to do something, if it is possible for that person to actually do it. Unless I have genuine choices in my life, it makes no sense to speak of what I "ought" to do.

All of these experiences of very powerful intuitions require that genuine choice is possible. But, on a purely reductionist materialist account of human nature, we have good reason to think that our behavior is causally determined—in which case, no choice is possible. So, either those intuitions concerning personal responsibility are all illusions, or else the reductionist materialist account of human nature is mistaken. If purely physical things are necessarily causally determined, but our intuitive experience suggests we are not causally determined, this might imply that we are not purely physical, and that we are not identical to our bodies.

Having now considered reasons why the dualist understanding of human nature might be true, let's return to the agency theorist interpretation of free will. Clearly, agency theorists reject the worldview shared by both determinists and compatibilists, as well as their specific views on freedom. What does "freedom" mean for an agency theorist?

Unlike compatibilists, who believe that to be free is to act from internal causes, agency theorists believe that freedom requires an ability to do otherwise. To put it differently, freedom requires genuine choice, genuine options.

According to this standard, I am free right now only if it truly is within my power to "do otherwise" than continue typing. That means it must truly be "up to me" in a meaningful sort of way, whether or not I continue typing. If I am compelled to continue by causal forces beyond my control, by my DNA, or childhood experiences—if stopping writing right now is not truly a live option for me, then I am not free. What's more, given the option of continuing to type or stopping, the deciding factor between those two choices must not be something about me, but me, myself. In other words, if my DNA causes me to continue, or if what I had for breakfast causes me to continue, then the act was not mine in any meaningful sort of way. But, if *I* (i.e., my "self," my mind, my soul, my will) am the deciding factor, then the act is truly *mine*.

Although the actual ways in which things like DNA, childhood experiences, daily events, and various other causal factors influence behavior is admittedly unclear according to agency theory, the idea is (roughly) that such things can *influence*, but they do not *cause*. A famous way of expressing this relationship is that it involves "inclination without necessitation."

Agency theorists are willing to acknowledge, of course, that how we are raised probably does exert a lot of influence over who we are, and how we behave. So, too, with our DNA, and our daily experiences. The difference between an agency theorist and a determinist (or compatibilist) is that the agency theorist believes that it is almost always possible, no matter how difficult, for us to override the influences of our childhood, or DNA, etc., and, by a sheer act of will, do something else, of our own choosing, instead. Only if we have this sort of freedom, this ability to choose our own path, are we truly free.

According to both determinism and compatibilism, the future is "fixed" because it is simply the product of the past pas governed by the laws of physics. This is why it is possible to predict the future, if only one had sufficient information.

With those two theories, it *appears* that we have choices, and decision-making points, but the "choices" have already been made, as they are predetermined by the prevailing causal factors. Not so with agency theory.

According to agency theory, the future is *not* fixed. Completely accurate prediction is not even possible *in principle*, let alone in practice, because the future has not been decided yet (at least not the future as it pertains to human actions).

It is impossible for me to know, with certainty, what you will do tomorrow, even if I know everything there is to know about you, because you have the power to surprise me, and do whatever you choose to do, even if this act is in defiance of powerful causal influences at work in your life. This is nothing less than the power to create the future. Indeed, each one of us is perpetually engaged in the cooperative project of creating the future by virtue of all the countless choices we make each and every day. Although the past is out of our control, the future is of our own making.

If this sounds like inspiring and awesome creative power, then your perception is correct. Indeed, this point of view gives to human beings so much power, and such special status in the universe, that some regard it as wishful thinking. The critic will find it implausible that human beings should be so different from everything else in the universe that we, somehow, have the power to defy causal determinism and the laws of physics, and create the future from our own free choices.

On the other hand, some find this image of humanity to be consistent with our own experience. After all, when we try to explain our actions, we can certainly talk about the physical aspects of our behavior, the muscles and tendons and neurons firing and so on—but what about the mysterious act that begins each action in the first place, what we might call "deciding" or "choosing" or "willing" to do something? For agency theorists, that component of human behavior is indispensable for providing a full account of human action, and that component does not admit of a purely physical description.

How are we to understand this special class of actions, those brought about not by causal determinism but by free choice? Some agency theorists distinguish two kinds of causes: event causes, and agent causes.

Event causation is the cause and effect relationship that governs all purely physical interactions. This causal relationship is something with which we are most familiar. One event causes another event, which causes another event, etc. The event of a pool cue striking a cue ball causes the event of the cue ball moving across the table at a certain trajectory, which causes the event of the cue ball striking the eight ball, which causes the event of the eight ball falling into the corner pocket. Determinists and compatibilists would say that event causation is the only causation that ever occurs.

Agent causation occurs when an event is caused not by another event, but by an "agent" (another term used to indicate that "something extra" otherwise referred to as soul, will, mind, etc.,). This "agent" is not an event, but a substance, and a non-physical substance at that. Therefore, we are dealing with a different sort of causal process altogether.

The critic will object that we have no good reason to believe that this "agent causation" exists, whereas event causation is well understood, and experienced continuously in our lives. The agency theorist will often claim, in response, that agent causation is actually *better* understood. Indeed, we understand event causation because we first experience agent causation. This can be explained by means of a story.

As very young children, we discover that have the ability to produce change in our environment. We can move objects around, we can summon large creatures that tend to our needs when we cry, etc. We understand this ability to produce change as causal power. Don't take this story too seriously. No one is suggesting that this is a conscious realization, as if, as a baby, I said to myself "hey, I can exert causal power and produce change in the world!" Instead, we should understand this as an intuitive awareness.

Continuing the story, we also discover that other things in our environment can exert causal power as well. I have the power to bring about change in the world by knocking the "sippy cup" from the high-chair to the floor, but so does my teddy bear. He, too, can knock the cup to the ground—and that large creature called "mommy" has the power to place the cup back on the table. The world is filled with things capable of bringing about change. Of course, my causal power and the teddy bear's causal power appear to be different. Teddy bear is passive. He never appears to act, only react. He can knock the cup over, but only after I have thrown him into the cup.

I, on the other hand, seem to have the power to bring about change without something first moving me. I appear to be active, and not merely passive. My causal power appears to be of a different kind, of a greater kind, than that of my teddy bear. This greater kind of causal power, the kind we come to understand first, is what agency theorists call agent causation. The other kind of causal power, the lesser kind employed by inanimate objects and other purely physical things, is what agency theorists call event causation. It is because we first recognize (agent) causal power in ourselves that we can recognize (event) causal power in the rest of nature.[34]

To be sure, agency theory is vulnerable to some criticisms and concerns, just like the other two theories. How exactly does agent causation work? If the "agent" (mind, soul, etc.) is non-physical, how does it interact with the (physical) body? What laws, or forces, are needed to explain causal interactions between minds and bodies, and why should we believe that such forces exist, aside from their necessity in explaining agent causation?

Another possible criticism concerns the curious vulnerability of the "mind" to *brain* injuries or conditions. If the mind is immaterial, and distinct from the brain, why would tumors, concussions, Alzheimer's disease, or even mere alcohol be able to impact our mental functioning? It seems, critics would argue, that such experiences are evidence that the "mind" just *is* the brain.

---

[34] In fairness, the determinist would claim that that story is profoundly misleading. It's simply not true (says the determinist) that, unlike my teddy bear, I was not first acted upon before acting. My actions, just the same as my teddy bear's, require some antecedent cause. The difference is that, in the case of the teddy bear knocking the cup over, the antecedent cause is obvious, whereas in the case of my own behavior, it's not easy to pinpoint the precise cause of my behavior (genetic influence? Childhood experience?).

In response, the noted dualist William Lane Craig says: "A dualist-interactionist does not take the soul to operate independently of the brain like a ghost in a machine. Rather, as the Nobel Prize-winning neurologist Sir John Eccles emphasizes, the soul uses the brain as an instrument to think, just as a musician uses a piano as an instrument to make music. If his piano is out of tune or damaged, then the pianist's ability to produce music will be impaired or even nullified. In the same way, says Eccles, if the soul's instrument of thought, the brain, is damaged or adversely affected, then the soul's ability to think will be impaired or nullified."[35]

Given these challenges, why would anyone embrace agency theory? The short answer is that some believe that this theory, despite its problems and limitations, is the one that most closely conforms to our intuitions and experience. The fact is that even if we don't really exercise genuine choice, it often seems as if we do. Even if the future is fixed, it often seems as if there are many paths our lives might take.

It certainly *seems* as if we often can, and do, make choices that involve genuine options.

Whenever we have a conflict between our intuitions (e.g., the intuition of spontaneous choice) and the claims of a theory (e.g., the claims of determinism), we have to decide which is mistaken: the theory, or our intuition.

Agency theorists fall on the side of favoring intuition, in this regard.

Exercises for Wisdom and Growth

1. How would your understanding of the world, and your expectations of treatment of yourself and others, change, depending on which of the above theories is true? If determinism is true? Compatibilism? Agency Theory?
2. Having now studied what determinists, compatibilists, and agency theorists mean by "freedom," what do *you* mean when you say that you are "free?" Do you agree with any of these theories? Why, or why not?
3. The philosopher Immanuel Kant claimed that we must act "on the presupposition" of freedom. That is, we can't help but act *as if* we have free will, whether we actually do, or not. Do you agree with that? Explain why, or why not.
4. How much do you think that your DNA, and your childhood experiences, have "caused" you to be the person you are today? Considering that, do you believe you "chose" to be "yourself," or has it been "chosen for you?" To what extent does that matter to you?

[35]http://www.reasonablefaith.org/questions-about-body-soul-interaction#ixzz3du1u0hiO

Paul-Henri Thiery, Baron d'Holbach (8 December 1723 – 21 January 1789) was a famous philosopher and patron of the French Enlightenment. His salon in Paris attracted several famous (regular) conversationalists, including Jean-Jacques Rousseau, Adam Smith, Denis Diderot, Benjamin Franklin, and David Hume. His most famous work is his "System of Nature", from which the following selection is excerpted. In this atheistic and materialist interpretation of Nature, d'Holbach argues that we are purely physical beings and thereby bound by the same deterministic laws of nature that govern all other bodies. Free will is an illusion and "choice" is simply an illusion masking the event of the more powerful cause amongst several necessarily bringing about its effect. "Deliberation" is merely a state of temporary equilibrium when our brains are suspended between roughly equal causal forces. Ignorance of such causal forces, understandably due to the complexity of our "machinery" and place in the causal web, produces belief in free will. Note also how he models good philosophy by virtue of his anticipation of, and attempt to refute, criticisms likely to arise against his own view.

Paul Henri Thiery, Baron d'Holbach

The System of Nature

Chapter XI, Of the System of Man's free agency.

THOSE who have pretended that the *soul* is distinguished from the body, is immaterial, draws its ideas from its own peculiar source, acts by its own energies without the aid of any exterior object; by a consequence of their own system, have enfranchised it from those physical laws, according to which all beings of which we have a knowledge are obliged to act. They have believed that the soul is mistress of its own conduct, is able to regulate its own peculiar operations; has the faculty to determine its will by its own natural energy; in a word, they have pretended man is a *free agent.*

It has been already sufficiently proved, that the soul is nothing more than the body, considered relatively to some of its functions, more concealed than others: it has been shown, that this soul, even when it shall be supposed immaterial, is continually modified conjointly with the body; is submitted to all its motion; that without this it would remain inert and dead: that, consequently, it is subjected to the influence of those material, to the operation those physical causes, which give impulse to the body; of which the mode of existence, whether habitual or transitory, depends upon the material elements by which it is surrounded; that form its texture; that constitute its temperament; that enter into it by the means of the aliments; that penetrate it by their subtility; the faculties which are called intellectual, and those qualities which are styled moral, have been explained in a manner purely physical; entirely natural: in the last place, it has been demonstrated, that all the ideas, all the systems, all the affections, all the opinions, whether true or false, which man forms to himself, are to be attributed to his physical powers; are to be ascribed to his material senses. Thus man is a being purely physical; in whatever manner he is considered, he is connected to universal Nature: submitted to the necessary, to the immutable laws that she imposes on all the beings she contains, according to their peculiar essences; conformable to the respective properties with which, without consulting them, she endows each particular species. Man's life is a line that Nature commands him to describe upon the surface of the earth: without his ever being able to swerve from it even for an instant. He is born without his own consent; his organizations does in no wise depend upon himself; his ideas come to him involuntarily; his habits are in the power of those who cause him to contract them; he is unceasingly modified by causes, whether visible or concealed, over which he has no controul; give the hue to his way of thinking, and determine his manner of acting. He is good or bad--happy or miserable--wise or foolish--reasonable or irrational, without his will going for anything in these various states. Nevertheless, in despite of the shackles by which he is bound, it is pretended he is a free agent, or that independent of the causes by which he is moved, he determines his own will; regulates his own condition.

However slender the foundation of this opinion, of which every thing ought to point out to him the error; it is current at this day for an incontestible truth, and believed enlightened; it is the basis of religion, which has been incapable of imagining how man could either merit reward or deserve punishment if he was not a free agent. Society has been believed interested in this system, because an idea has gone abroad, that if all the actions of man were to be contemplated as necessary, the right of punishing those who injure their associates would no longer exist. At length human vanity accommodated itself to an hypothesis which, unquestionable, appears to distinguish man from all other physical beings, by assigning to him the special privilege of a total independence of all other causes; but of which a very little reflection would have shown him the absurdity or even the impossibility.

As a part, subordinate to the great whole, man is obliged to experience its influence. To be a free agent it were needful that each individual was of greater strength than the entire of Nature; or, that he was out of this Nature: who, always in action herself, obliges all the beings she embraces, to act, and to concur to her general motion; or, as it has been said elsewhere, to conserve her active existence, by the motion that all beings produce in consequence of their particular energies, which result from their being submitted to fixed, eternal, and immutable laws. In order that man might be a free agent, it were needful that all beings should lose their essences; it is equally necessary that he himself should no longer enjoy physical sensibility; that he should neither know good nor evil; pleasure nor pain; but if this was the case, from that moment he would no longer be in a state to conserve himself, or render his existence happy; all beings would become indifferent to him; he would no longer have any choice; he would cease to know what he ought to love; what it was right he should fear; he would not have any acquaintance with that which he should seek after; or with that which it is requisite he should avoid. In short, man would be an unnatural being; totally incapable of acting in the manner we behold. It is the actual essence of man to tend to his well-being; to be desirous to conserve his existence; if all the motion of his machine springs as a necessary consequence from this primitive impulse; if pain warns him of that which he ought to avoid; if pleasure announces to him that which he should desire; if it is in his essence to love that which either excites delight, or, that from which he expects agreeable sensations; to hate that which makes him either fear contrary impressions; or, that which afflicts him with uneasiness; it must necessarily be, that he will be attracted by that which he deems advantageous; that his will shall he determined by those objects which he judges useful; that he will he repelled by those beings which he believes prejudicial, either to his habitual, or to his transitory mode of existence; by that which he considers disadvantageous. It is only by the aid of experience, that man acquires the faculty of understanding what he ought to love; of knowing what he ought to fear. Are his organs sound? his experience will he true: are they unsound? it will be false: in the first instance he will have reason, prudence, foresight; he will frequently foresee very remote effects; he will know, that what he sometimes contemplates as a good, may possibly become an evil, by its necessary or probable consequences: that what must be to him a transient evil, may by its result procure him a solid and durable good. It is thus experience enables him to foresee that the amputation of a limb will cause him painful sensation, he consequently is obliged to fear this operation, and he endeavours to avoid the pain; but if experience has also shown him, that the transitory pain this amputation will cause him may be the means of saving his life; the preservation, of his existence being of necessity dear to him, he is obliged to submit himself to the momentary pain with a view to procuring a permanent good, by which it will be overbalanced.

The will, as we have elsewhere said, is a modification of the brain, by which it is disposed to action or prepared to give play to the organs. This will is necessarily determined by the qualities, good or bad, agreeable or painful, of the object or the motive that acts upon his senses; or of which the idea remains with him, and is resuscitated by his memory. In consequence, he acts necessarily; his action is the result of the impulse he receives either from the motive, from the object, or from the idea, which has modified his brain, or disposed his will. When he does not act according to this impulse, it is because there comes some new cause, some new motive, some new idea, which modifies his brain in a different manner, gives him a new impulse, determines his will in another way; by which the action of the former impulse is suspended: thus, the sight of an agreeable object, or its idea, determines his will to set him in action to procure it; but if a new object or a new idea more powerfully attracts him, it gives a new direction to his will, annihilates the effect of the former, and prevents the action by which it was to be procured. This is the mode in which reflection, experience, reason, necessarily arrests or suspends the action of man's will; without this, he would, of necessity, have followed the anterior impulse which carried him towards a then desirable object. In all this he always acts according to necessary laws, from which he has no means of emancipating himself.

If, when tormented with violent thirst, he figures to himself an idea, or really perceives a fountain, whose limpid streams might cool his feverish habit, is he sufficient master of himself to desire or not to desire the object competent to satisfy so lively a want? It will no doubt be conceded, that it is impossible he should not be desirous to satisfy it; but it will be said,--If at this moment it is announced to him, the water he so ardently desires is poisoned, he will, notwithstanding his vehement thirst, abstain from drinking it; and it has, therefore, been falsely concluded that he is a free agent. The fact, however, is, that the motive in either case is exactly the same: his own conservation. The same necessity that determined him to drink, before he knew the water was deleterious, upon this new discovery, equally determines him not to drink; the desire of conserving himself, either annihilates or suspends the former impulse; the second motive becomes stronger than the preceding; that is, the fear of death, or the desire of preserving himself, necessarily prevails over the painful sensation caused by his eagerness to drink. But, (it will be said) if the thirst is very parching, an inconsiderate man, without regarding the danger, will risque swallowing the water. Nothing is gained by this remark: in this case, the anterior impulse only regains the ascendency; he is persuaded, that life may possibly be longer preserved, or that he shall derive a greater good by drinking the poisoned water, than by enduring the torment, which, to his mind, threatens instant dissolution: thus, the first becomes the strongest, and necessarily urges him on to action. Nevertheless, in either case, whether he partakes of the water, or whether he does not, the two actions will be equally necessary; they will be the effect of that motive which finds itself most puissant; which consequently acts in a most coercive manner upon his will.

This example will serve to explain the whole phaenomena of the human will. This will, or rather the brain, finds itself in the same situation as a bowl, which although it has received an impulse that drives it forward in a straight line, is deranged in its course, whenever a force, superior to the first, obliges it to change its direction. The man who drinks the poisoned water, appears a madman; but the actions of fools are as necessary as those of the most prudent individuals. The motives that determine the voluptuary, that actuate the debauchee to risk their health, are as powerful, their actions are as necessary, as those which decide the wise man to manage his. But, it will be insisted, the debauchee may be prevailed on to change his conduct; this does not imply that he is a free agent; but, that motives may be found sufficiently powerful to annihilate the effect of those that previously acted upon him; then these new motives determine his will to the new mode of conduct he may adopt, as necessarily as the former did to the old mode.

Man is said to *deliberate* when the action of

the will is suspended; this happens when two opposite motives act alternately upon him. To deliberate, is to hate and to love in succession; it is to be alternately attracted and repelled; it is to be moved sometimes by one motive, sometimes by another. Man only deliberates when he does not distinctly understand the quality of the objects from which he receives impulse, or when experience has not sufficiently apprised him of the effects, more or less remote, which his actions will produce. He would take the air, but the weather is uncertain; he deliberates in consequence; he weighs the various motives that urge his will to go out or to stay at home; he is at length determined by that motive which is most probable; this removes his indecision, which necessarily settles his will either to remain within or to go abroad: this motive is always either the immediate or ultimate advantage he finds or thinks he finds in the action to which he is persuaded.

Man's will frequently fluctuates between two objects, of which either the presence or the ideas move him alternately: he waits until he has contemplated the objects or the ideas they have left in his brain; which solicit him to different actions; he then compares these objects or ideas: but even in the time of deliberation, during the comparison, pending these alternatives of love and hatred, which succeed each other sometimes with the utmost rapidity, he is not a free agent for a single instant; the good or the evil which he believes he finds successively in the objects, are the necessary motives of these momentary wills; of the rapid motion of desire or fear that he experiences as long as his uncertainty continues. From this it will be obvious, that deliberation is necessary; that uncertainty is necessary; that whatever part he takes, in consequence of this deliberation, it will always necessarily be that which he has judged, whether well or ill, is most probable to turn to his advantage.

When the soul is assailed by two motives that act alternately upon it, or modify it successively, it deliberates; the brain is in a sort of equilibrium, accompanied with perpetual oscillations, sometimes towards one object, sometimes towards the other, until the most forcible carries the point, and thereby extricates it, from this state of suspense, in which consists the indecision of his will. But when the brain is simultaneously assailed by causes equally strong, that move it in opposite directions; agreeable to the general law of all bodies, when they are struck equally by contrary powers, it stops, it is in *nisu*; it is neither capable to will nor to act; it waits until one of the two causes has obtained sufficient force to overpower the other, to determine its will, to attract it in such a manner that it may prevail over the efforts of the other cause.

This mechanism, so simple, so natural, suffices to demonstrate, why uncertainty is painful; why suspense is always a violent state for man. The brain, an organ so delicate, so mobile, experiences such rapid modifications, that it is fatigued; or when it is urged in contrary directions, by causes equally powerful, it suffers a kind of compression, that prevents the activity which is suitable to the preservation of the whole, which is necessary to procure what is advantageous to its existence. This mechanism will also explain the irregularity, the indecision, the inconstancy of man; and account for that conduct, which frequently appears an inexplicable mystery, which indeed it is, under the received systems. In consulting experience, it will be found that the soul is submitted to precisely the same physical laws as the material body. If the will of each individual, during a given time, was only moved by a single cause or passion, nothing would be more easy than to foresee his actions; but his heart is frequently assailed by contrary powers, by adverse motives, which either act on him simultaneously or in succession; then his brain, attracted in opposite directions, is either fatigued, or else tormented by a state of compression, which deprives it of activity. Sometimes it is in a state of incommodious inaction; sometimes it is the sport of the alternate shocks it undergoes. Such, no doubt, is the state in which man finds himself, when a lively passion solicits him to the commission of crime, whilst fear points out to him the danger by which it is attended: such, also, is the condition of him whom remorse, by the continued labour of his distracted soul, prevents from enjoying the objects he has criminally obtained.

If the powers or causes, whether exterior or interior, acting on the mind of man, tend towards opposite points, his soul, is well as all other bodies, will take a mean direction between the two; in consequence of the violence with which his soul is urged, his condition becomes sometimes so painful that his existence is troublesome: he has no longer a tendency to his own peculiar conservation; he seeks after death, as a sanctuary against himself--as the only remedy to his despair: it is thus we behold men, miserable and discontented, voluntarily destroy themselves, whenever life becomes insupportable. Man is competent to cherish his existence, no longer than life holds out charms to him; when he is wrought upon by painful sensations, or drawn by contrary impulsions, his natural tendency is deranged, he is under the necessity to follow a new route; this conducts him to his end, which it even displays to him as the most desirable good. In this manner may be explained, the conduct of those melancholy beings, whose vicious temperaments, whose tortured consciences, whose chagrin, whose ennui, sometimes determine them to renounce life.

The various powers, frequently very complicated, that act either successively or simultaneously upon the brain of man, which modify him so diversely in the different periods of his existence, are the true causes of that obscurity in morals, of that difficulty which is found, when it is desired to unravel the concealed springs of his enigmatical conduct. The heart of man is a labyrinth, only because it very rarely happens that we possess the necessary gift of judging it; from whence it will appear, that his circumstances, his indecision, his conduct, whether ridiculous, or unexpected, are the necessary consequences of the changes operated in him; are nothing but the effect of motives that successively determine his will; which are dependent on the frequent variations experienced by his machine. According to these variations, the same motives have not, always, the same influence over his will, the same objects no longer enjoy the faculty of pleasing him; his temperament has changed, either for the moment, or for ever. It follows as a consequence, that his taste, his desires, his passions, will change; there can be no kind of uniformity in his conduct, nor any certitude in the effects to be expected.

Choice by no means proves the free-agency of man; he only deliberates when he does not yet know which to choose of the many objects that move him, he is then in an embarrassment, which does not terminate, until his will as decided by the greater advantage he believes be shall find in the object he chooses, or the action he undertakes. From whence it may he seen that choice is necessary, because he would not determine for an object, or for an action, if he did not believe that he should find in it some direct advantage. That man should have free-agency, it were needful that he should he able to will or choose without motive; or, that he could prevent motives coercing his will. Action always being the effect of his will once determined, as his will cannot be determined but by a motive, which is not in his own power, it follows that he is never the master of the determination of his own peculiar will; that consequently he never acts as a free agent. It has been believed that man was a free agent, because he had a will with the power of choosing; but attention has not been paid to the fact, that even his will is moved by causes independent of himself, is owing to that which is inherent in his own organization, or which belongs to the nature of the beings acting on him. Indeed, man passes a great portion of his life without even willing. His will attends the motive by which it is determined. If he was to render an exact account of every thing he does in the course of each day, from rising in the morning to lying down at night, he would find, that not one of his actions have been in the least voluntary; that they have been mechanical, habitual, determined by causes he was not able to foresee, to which he was either obliged to, yield, or with which he was allured to acquiesce; he would discover, that all the motives of his labours, of his amusements, of his discourses, of his thoughts, have been necessary; that they have evidently either seduced him or drawn him along. Is he the master of willing, not to withdraw his hand from the fire when he fears it will be burnt? Or has he the power to take away from fire the property which makes him fear it? Is he the master of not choosing a dish of meat which he knows to be agreeable, or analogous to his palate; of not preferring it to that which he knows to be disagreeable or dangerous? It is always according to his sensations, to his own peculiar experience, or to his suppositions, that he judges of things either well or ill; but whatever way be his judgment, it depends necessarily on his mode of feeling, whether habitual or accidental, and the qualities he finds in the causes that move him, which exist in despite of himself.

All the causes which by his will is actuated, must act upon him in a manner sufficiently marked, to give him some sensation, some perception, some idea, whether complete or incomplete, true or false; as soon as his will is determined, he must have felt, either strongly or feebly; if this was not the case he would have determined without motive: thus, to speak correctly, there are no causes which are truly indifferent to the will: however faint the impulse he receives, whether on the part of the objects themselves, or on the part of their images or ideas, as soon as his will acts, the impulse has been competent to determine him. In consequence of a slight, of a feeble impulse, the will is weak, it is this weakness of the will that is called *indifference.* His brain with difficulty perceives the sensation, it has received; it consequently acts with less vigour, either to obtain or remove the object or the idea that has modified it. If the impulse is powerful, the will is strong, it makes him act vigorously, to obtain or to remove the object which appears to him either very agreeable or very incommodious.

It has been believed man was a free agent, because it has been imagined that his soul could at will recall ideas, which sometimes suffice to check his most unruly desires. Thus, the idea of a remote evil frequently prevents him from enjoying a present and actual good: thus, remembrance, which is an almost insensible, a slight modification of his brain, annihilates, at each instant, the real objects that act upon his will. But he is not master of recalling to himself his ideas at pleasure; their association is independent of him; they are arranged in his brain, in despite of him, without his own knowledge, where they have made an impression more or less profound; his memory itself depends upon his organization;. its fidelity depends upon the habitual or momentary state in which he finds himself; when his will is vigorously determined to some object or idea that excites a very lively passion in him, those objects or ideas that would be able to arrest his action no longer present themselves to his mind; in those moments his eyes are shut to the dangers that menace him, of which the idea ought to make him forbear; he marches forward headlong towards the object by whose image he is hurried on; reflection cannot operate upon him in any way; he sees nothing but the object of his desires; the salutary ideas which might be able to arrest his progress disappear, or else display themselves either too faintly or too late to prevent his acting. Such is the case with all those who, blinded by some strong passion, are not in a condition to recall to themselves those motives, of which the idea alone, in cooler moments, would be sufficient to deter them from proceeding; the disorder in which they are, prevents their judging soundly; render them incapable of foreseeing the consequence of their actions; precludes them from applying to their experience; from making use of their reason; natural operations, which suppose a justness in the manner of associating their ideas; but to which their brain is then not more competent, in consequence of the momentary delirium it suffers, than their hand is to write whilst they are taking violent exercise.

Man's mode of thinking is necessarily determined by his manner of being; it must, therefore, depend on his natural organization, and the modification his system receives independently of his will. From this we are obliged to conclude, that his thoughts, his reflections, his manner of viewing things, of feeling, of judging, of combining ideas, is neither voluntary nor free. In a word, that his soul is neither mistress of the motion excited in it, nor of representing to itself, when wanted, those images or ideas that are capable of counterbalancing the impulse it receives. This is the reason why man, when in a passion, ceases to reason; at that moment reason is as impossible to be heard, as it is during an extacy, or in a fit of drunkenness. The wicked are never more than men who are either drunk or mad: if they reason, it is not until tranquillity is re-established in their machine; then, and not till then, the tardy ideas that present themselves to their mind, enable them to see the consequence of their actions, and give birth to ideas, that bring on them that trouble, which is designated *shame, regret, remorse*.

The errors of philosophers on the free-agency of man, have arisen from their regarding his will as the *primum mobile*, the original motive of his actions; for want of recurring back, they have not perceived the multiplied, the complicated causes, which, independently of him, give motion to the will itself, or which dispose and modify his brain, whilst he himself is purely passive in the motion he receives. Is he the master of desiring or not desiring an object that appears desirable to him? Without doubt it will be answered, No: but he is the master of resisting his desire, if he reflects on the consequences. But, I ask, is he capable of reflecting on these consequences when his soul is hurried along by a very lively passion, which entirely depends upon his natural organization, and the causes by which he is modified? Is it in his power to add to these consequences all the weight necessary to counterbalance his desire? Is he the master of preventing the qualities which render an object desirable from residing in it? I shall be told, he ought to have learned to resist his passions; to contract a habit of putting a curb on his desires. I agree to it without any difficulty: but in reply, I again ask, Is his nature susceptible of this modification? Does his boiling blood, his unruly imagination, the igneous fluid that circulates in his veins, permit him to make, enable him to apply true experience in the moment when it is wanted? And, even when his temperament has capacitated him, has his education, the examples set before him, the ideas with which he has been inspired in early life, been suitable to make him contract this habit of repressing his desires? Have not all these things rather contributed to induce him to seek with avidity, to make him actually desire those objects which you say he ought to resist....

In short, the actions of man are never free; they are always the necessary consequence of his temperament, of the received ideas, of the notions, either true or false, which he has formed to himself of happiness: of his opinions, strengthened by example, forfeited by education, consolidated by daily experience. So many crimes are witnessed on the earth, only because every thing conspires to render man vicious, to make him criminal; very frequently. the superstitions he has adopted, his government, his education, the examples set before him, irresistibly drive him on to evil: under these circumstances morality preaches virtue to him in vain. In those societies where vice is esteemed, where crime is crowned, where venality is constantly recompenced, where the most dreadful disorders are punished, only in those who are too weak to enjoy the privilege of committing them with impunity; the practice of virtue is considered nothing more than a painful sacrifice of fancied happiness. Such societies chastise, in the lower orders, those excesses which they respect in the higher ranks; and frequently have the injustice to condemn those in penalty of death, whom public prejudices, maintained by constant example, have rendered criminal.

Man, then, is not a free agent in any one instant of his life; he is necessarily guided in each step by those advantages, whether real or fictitious, that he attaches to the objects by which his passions are roused: these passions themselves are necessary in a being who, unceasingly tends towards his own happiness; their energy is necessary, since that depends on his temperament; his temperament is necessary, because it depends on the physical elements which enter into his composition; the modification of this temperament is necessary, as it is the infallible result, the inevitable consequence of the impulse he receives from the incessant action of moral and physical beings.

In despite of these proofs of the want of free-agency in man, so clear to unprejudiced minds, it will, perhaps, be insisted upon with no small feeling of triumph, that if it be proposed to any one to move or not to move his hand, an action in the number of those called *indifferent*, he evidently appears to be the master of choosing; from which it is concluded, evidence has been offered of his free-agency. The reply is, this example is perfectly simple; man in performing some action which he is resolved on doing, does not by any means prove his free-agency: the very desire of displaying this quality, excited by the dispute, becomes a necessary motive which decides his will either for the one or the other of these actions: what deludes him in this instance, or that which persuades him he is a free agent at this moment, is, that he does not discern the true motive which sets him in action; which is neither more nor less than the desire of convincing his opponent: if in the heat of the dispute he insists and asks, "Am I not the master of throwing myself out of the window?" I shall answer him, no; that whilst he preserves his reason, there is not even a probability that the desire of proving his free-agency, will become a motive sufficiently powerful, to make him sacrifice his life to the attempt; if, notwithstanding this, to prove he is a free agent, he should actually precipitate himself from the window, it would not be a sufficient warrantry to conclude he acted freely, but rather that it was the violence of his temperament which spurred him on to this folly. Madness is a state that depends upon the heat of the blood, not upon the will. A fanatic or a hero, braves death as necessarily as a more phlegmatic man or a coward flies from it. There is, in point of fact, no difference between the man who is cast out of the window by another, and the man who throws himself out of it, except that the impulse in the first instance comes immediately from without, whilst that which determines the fall in the second case, springs from within his own peculiar machine, having its more remote cause also exterior. When Mutius Scaevola held his hand in the fire, he was as much acting under the influence of necessity, caused by interior motives, that urged him to this strange action, as if his arm had been held by strong men; pride, despair, the desire of braving his enemy, a wish to astonish him, an anxiety to intimidate him, &c. were the invisible chains that held his hand bound to the fire. The love of glory, enthusiasm for their country, in like manner, caused Codrus and Decius to devote themselves for their fellow citizens. The Indian Calanus and the philosopher Peregrinus were equally obliged to burn themselves, by the desire of exciting the astonishment of the Grecian assembly.

It is said that free-agency is the absence of those obstacles competent to oppose themselves to the actions of man, or to the exercise of his faculties: it is pretended that he is a free agent, whenever, making use of these faculties, he produces the effect he has proposed to himself. In reply to this reasoning, it is sufficient to consider that it in no wise depends upon himself to place or remove the obstacles that either determine or resist him; the motive that causes his action is no more in his own power than the obstacle that impedes him, whether this obstacle or motive be within his own machine or exterior of his person: he is not master of the thought presented to his mind which determines his will; this thought is excited by some cause independent of himself.

To be undeceived on the system of his free-agency, man has simply to recur to the motive by which his will is determined, he will always find this motive is out of his own control. It is said, that in consequence of an idea to which the mind gives birth, man acts freely if he encounters no obstacle. But the question is, what gives birth to this idea in his brain? has he the power either to prevent it from presenting itself, or from renewing itself in his brain? Does not this idea depend either upon objects that strike him exteriorly and in despite of himself, or upon causes that without his knowledge act within himself and modify his brain? Can he prevent his eyes, cast without design upon any object whatever, from giving him an idea of this object, from moving his brain? He is not more master of the obstacles; they are the necessary effects of either interior or exterior causes, which always act according to their given properties. A man insults a coward, who is necessarily irritated against his insulter, but his will cannot vanquish the obstacle that cowardice places to the object of his desire, which is, to resent the insult; because his natural conformation, which does not depend upon himself, prevents his having courage. In this case the coward is insulted in despite of himself, and against his will is obliged patiently to brook the insult he has received.

The partizans of the system of free-agency appear ever to have confounded constraint with necessity. Man believes he acts as a free agent, every time he does not see any thing that places obstacles to his actions; he does not perceive that the motive which causes him to will is always necessary, is ever independent of himself. A prisoner loaded with chains is compelled to remain in prison, but he is not a free agent, he is not able to resist the desire to emancipate himself; his chains prevent him from acting, but they do not prevent him from willing; he would save himself if they would loose his fetters, but he would not save himself as a free agent, fear or the idea of punishment would be sufficient motives for his action.

Man may therefore cease to be restrained, without, for that reason, becoming a free agent: in whatever manner he acts, he will act necessarily; according to motives by which he shall be determined. He may be compared to a heavy body, that finds itself arrested in its descent by any obstacle whatever: take away this obstacle, it will gravitate or continue to fall; but who shall say this dense body is free to fall or not? Is not its descent the necessary effect of its own specific gravity? The virtuous Socrates submitted to the laws of his country, although they were unjust; notwithstanding the doors of his gaol were left open to him he would not save himself; but in this he did not act as a free agent; the invisible chains of opinion, the secret love of decorum, the inward respect for the laws, even when they were iniquitous, the fear of tarnishing his glory, kept him in his prison: they were motives sufficiently powerful, with this enthusiast for virtue, to induce him to wait death with tranquillity; it was not in his power to save himself, because he could find no potential motive to bring him to depart, even for an instant, from those principles to which his mind was accustomed.

Man, says he, frequently acts against his inclination, from whence he has falsely concluded he is a free agent; when he appears to act contrary to his inclination, he is determined to it by some motive sufficiently efficacious to vanquish this inclination. A sick man, with a view to his cure, arrives at conquering his repugnance to the most disgusting remedies: the fear of pain, the dread of death, then become necessary and intelligent motives; consequently, this sick man cannot be said, with truth, by any means, to act freely.

When it is said, that man is not a free agent, it is not pretended to compare him to a body moved by a simple impulsive cause: he contains within himself causes inherent to his existence; he is moved by an interior organ, which has its own peculiar laws; which is itself necessarily determined, in consequence of ideas formed from perceptions, resulting from sensations, which it receives from exterior objects. As the mechanism of these sensations, of these perceptions, and the manner they engrave ideas on the brain of man, are not known to him, because he is unable to unravel all these motions; because he cannot perceive the chain of operations in his soul, or the motive-principle that acts within him, he supposes himself a free agent; which, literally translated, signifies that he moves himself by himself; that he determines himself without cause; when he rather ought to say, he is ignorant how or for why he acts in the manner he does. It is true the soul enjoys an activity peculiar to itself, but it is equally certain that this activity would never be displayed if some motive or some cause did not put it in a condition to exercise itself, at least it will not be pretended that the soul is able either to love or to hate without being moved, without knowing the objects, without having some idea of their qualities. Gunpowder has unquestionably a particular activity, but this activity will never display itself, unless fire be applied to it; this, however, immediately sets in motion.

It is the great complication of motion in man, it is the variety of his action, it is the multiplicity of causes that move him, whether simultaneously or in continual succession, that persuades him he is a free agent: if all his motions were simple, if the causes that move him did not confound themselves with each other, if they were distinct, if his machine was less complicated, he would perceive that all his actions were necessary, because he would be enabled to recur instantly to the cause that made him act. A man who should be always obliged to go towards the west would always go on that side, but he would feel extremely well, that in so going he was not a free agent: if he had another sense, as his actions or his motion augmented by a sixth would be still more varied, much more complicated, he would believe himself still more a free agent than he does with his five senses.

It is, then, for want of recurring to the causes that move him, for want of being able to analyse, from not being competent to decompose the complicated motion of his machine, that man believes himself a free agent; it is only upon his own ignorance that he founds the profound yet deceitful notion he has of his free-agency, that he builds those opinions which he brings forward as a striking proof of his pretended freedom of action. If, for a short time, each man was willing to examine his own peculiar actions, to search out their true motives, to discover their concatenation, he would remain convinced that the sentiment he has of his natural free-agency is a chimera that must speedily be destroyed by experience.

Nevertheless, it must be acknowledged that the multiplicity, the diversity of the causes which continually act upon man, frequently without even his knowledge, render it impossible, or at least extremely difficult, for him to recur to the true principles of his own peculiar actions, much less the actions of others; they frequently depend upon causes so fugitive, so remote from their effects, and which, superficially examined, appear to have so little analogy, so slender a relation with them, that it requires singular sagacity to bring them into light. This is what renders the study of the moral man a task of such difficulty; this is the reason why his heart is an abyss, of which it is frequently impossible for him to fathom the depth. . . .

Every thing becomes an impulse to the will; a single word frequently suffices to modify a man for the whole course of his life, to decide for ever his propensities; an infant who has burned his finger by having approached it too near the flame of a lighted taper, is warned from thence, that he ought to abstain from indulging a similar temptation; a man, once punished and despised for having committed a dishonest action, is not often tempted to continue so unfavourable a course. Under whatever point of man is considered, he never acts but after the impulse given to his will, whether it be by the will of others, or by more perceptible physical causes. The particular organization decides the nature of the impulse; souls act upon souls that are analogous; inflamed, fiery imaginations, act with facility upon strong passions; upon imaginations easy to be inflamed, the surprising progress of enthusiasm; the hereditary propagation of superstition; the transmission of religious errors from race to race, the excessive ardour with which man seizes on the marvellous, are effects as necessary as those which result from the action and re-action of bodies.

In despite of the gratuitous ideas which man has formed to himself on his pretended free-agency; in defiance of the illusions of this suppose intimate sense, which, contrary to his experience, persuades him that he is master of his will,--all his institutions are really founded upon necessity: on this, as on a variety of other occasions, practice throws aside speculation. Indeed, if it was not believed that certain motives embraced the power requisite to determine the will of man, to arrest the progress of his passions, to direct them towards an end, to modify him; of what use would be the faculty of speech? What benefit could arise from education itself? What does education achieve, save give the first impulse to the human will, make man contract habits, oblige him to persist in them, furnish him with motives, whether true or false, to act after a given manner? When the father either menaces his son with punishment, or promises him a reward, is he not convinced these things will act upon his will? What does legislation attempt, except it be to present to the citizens of a state those motives which are supposed necessary to determine them to perform some actions that are considered worthy; to abstain from committing others that are looked upon as unworthy? What is the object of morals, if it be not to show man that his interest exacts he should suppress the momentary ebullition of his passions, with a view to promote a more certain happiness, a more lasting well-being, than can possibly result from the gratification of his transitory desires? Does not the religion of all countries suppose the human race, together with the entire of Nature, submitted to the irresistible will of a necessary being, who regulates their condition after the eternal laws of immutable wisdom? Is not God the absolute master of their destiny? Is it not this divine being who chooses and rejects? The anathemas fulminated by religion, the promises it holds forth, are they not founded upon the idea of the effects they will necessarily produce upon mankind? Is not man brought into existence without his own knowledge? Is he not obliged to play a part against his will? Does not either his happiness or his misery depend on the part he plays? . . .

Education, then, is only necessity shown to children: *legislation* is necessity shown to the members of the body politic: morals is the necessity of the relations subsisting between men, shown to reasonable beings: in short, man grants necessity in every thing for which he believes he has certain, unerring experience: that of which he does not comprehend the necessary connection of causes with their effects he styles *probability*: he would not act as he does, if he was not convinced, or, at least, if he did not presume he was, that certain effects will necessarily follow his actions. The *moralist* preaches reason, because he believes it necessary to man: the *philosopher* writes, because he believes truth must, sooner or later, prevail over falsehood: *tyrants* and *fanatical priests* necessarily hate truth, despise reason, because they believe them prejudicial to their interests: the *sovereign*, who strives to terrify crime by the severity of his laws, but who nevertheless, from motives of state policy sometimes renders it useful and even necessary to his purposes, presumes the motives he employs will be sufficient to keep his subjects within bounds. All reckon equally upon the power or upon the necessity of the motives they make use of; each individual flatters himself, either with or without reason, that these motives will have an influence on the conduct of mankind. The education of man is commonly so defective, so inefficacious, so little calculated to promote the end he has in view, because it is regulated by prejudice: even when this education is good, it is but too often speedily counteracted, by almost every thing that takes place in society. Legislation and politics are very frequently iniquitous, and serve no better purpose than to kindle passions in the bosom of man, which once set afloat, they are no longer competent to restrain. The great art of the moralist should be, to point out to man, to convince those who are entrusted with the sacred office of regulating his will, that their interests are identified; that their reciprocal happiness depends upon the harmony of their passions; that the safety, the power, the duration of empires, necessarily depend on the good sense diffused among the individual members; on the truth of the notions inculcated in the mind of the citizens, on the moral goodness that is sown in their hearts, on the virtues that are cultivated in their breasts; religion should not be admissible, unless it truly fortified, unless it really strengthened these motives. But in the miserable state into which error has plunged a considerable portion of the human species, man, for the most part, is seduced to be wicked: he injures his fellow-creature as a matter of conscience, because the strongest motives are held out to him to be persecuting; because his institutions invite him to the commission of evil, under the lure of promoting his own immediate happiness. In most countries superstition renders him a useless being, makes him an abject slave, causes him to tremble under its terrors, or else turns him into a furious fanatic, who is at once cruel, intolerant, and inhuman: in a great number of states arbitrary power crushes him, obliges him to become a cringing sycophant, renders him completely vicious: in those despotic states the law rarely visits crime with punishment, except in those who are too feeble to oppose its course? or when it has become incapable of restraining the violent excesses to which a bad government gives birth. In short, rational education is neglected; a prudent culture of the human mind is despised; it depends, but too frequently, upon bigotted, superstitious priests, who are interested in deceiving man, and who are sometimes impostors; or else upon parents or masters without understanding, who are devoid of morals, who impress on the ductile mind of their scholars those vices with which they are themselves tormented; who transmit to them the false opinions, which they believe they have an interest in making them adopt....

From all that has been advanced in this chapter, it results, that in no one moment of his existence man is a free agent: he is not the architect of his own conformation; this he holds from Nature, he has no controul over his own ideas, or over the modification of his brain; these are due to causes, that, in despite of him, very frequently without his own knowledge, unceasingly act upon him; he is not the master of not loving that which he finds amiable; of not coveting that which appears to him desirable; he is not capable of refusing to deliberate, when he is uncertain of the effects certain objects will produce upon him; he cannot avoid choosing that which he believes will be most advantageous to him: in the moment when his will is determined by his choice, he is not competent to act otherwise than he does: in what instance, then, is he the master of his own actions? In what moment is he a free agent?...

If he understood the play of his organs, if he was able to recall to himself all the impulsions they have received, all the modifications they have undergone, all the effects they have produced, he would perceive, that all his actions are submitted to that fatality which regulates his own particular system, as it does the entire system of the universe: no one effect in him, any more than in Nature, produce itself by chance; this, as has been before proved, is a word void of sense. All that passes in him, all that is done by him, as well as all that happens in Nature, or that is attributed to her, is derived from necessary laws, which produce necessary effects; from whence necessarily flow others.

Fatality is the eternal, the immutable, the necessary order established in Nature, or the indispensible connection of causes that act with the effects they operate. Conforming to this order, heavy bodies fall, light bodies rise; that which is analogous in matter, reciprocally attracts; that which is heterogeneous, mutually repels; man congregates himself in society, modifies each his fellow, becomes either virtuous or wicked; either contributes to his mutual happiness, or reciprocates his misery; either loves his neighbour, or hates his companion necessarily; according to the manner in which the one acts upon the other. From whence it may be seen, that the same necessity which regulates the physical, also regulates the moral world: in which every thing is in consequence submitted to fatality. Man, in running over, frequently without his own knowledge, often in despite of himself, the route which Nature has marked out for him, resembles a swimmer who is obliged to follow the current that carries him along; he believes himself a free agent, because he sometimes consents, sometimes does not consent, to glide with the stream; which, notwithstanding, always hurries him forward; he believes himself the master of his condition, because he is obliged to use his arms under the fear of sinking.

The false ideas he has formed to himself upon free-agency, are in general thus founded: there are certain events which he judges *necessary*; either because he sees they are effects that are constantly, are invariably linked to certain causes, which nothing seems to prevent; or because he believes he has discovered the chain of causes and effects that is put in play to produce those events: whilst he contemplates as *contingent*, other events, of whose causes he is ignorant; the concatenation of which he does not perceive; with whose mode of acting he is unacquainted: but in Nature, where every thing is connected by one common bond, there exists no effect without a cause. In the moral as well as in the physical world, every thing that happens is a necessary consequence of causes, either visible or concealed; which are, of necessity, obliged to act after their peculiar essences. *In man, free-agency is nothing more than necessity contained within himself.*

David Hume (7 May 1711 – 25 August 1776), like Descartes, is one of the most important and influential philosophers of the Western tradition. Considered a prominent figure of the Scottish Enlightenment, he was also an occasional attendee of d'Holbach's salon in Paris (see previous essay). Hume was not, however, a determinist, like d'Holbach. Instead, he was a compatibilist. In section 8 of his "Enquiry Concerning Human Understanding", he claims that the free will debate is the result of confusion concerning definitions. Humanity has always affirmed both "liberty" (free will) and "necessity" (determinism). He points out the extensive evidence for and confidence in causal necessity, and offers the same explanation as d'Holbach did for why people are reluctant to apply this necessity to human action: complexity. He then offers his characteristically "compatibilist" definition of free will as an absence of external restraint. He is confident that liberty, so understood, is compatible with necessity.

David Hume
An Enquiry Concerning Human Understanding

Section VIII, Of Liberty and Necessity

Part I

IT might reasonably be expected in questions which have been canvassed and disputed with great eagerness, since the first origin of science, and philosophy, that the meaning of all the terms, at least, should have been agreed upon among the disputants; and our enquiries, in the course of two thousand years, been able to pass from words to the true and real subject of the controversy. For how easy may it seem to give exact definitions of the terms employed in reasoning, and make these definitions, not the mere sound of words, the object of future scrutiny and examination? But if we consider the matter more narrowly, we shall be apt to draw a quite opposite conclusion. From this circumstance alone, that a controversy has been long kept on foot, and remains still undecided, we may presume that there is some ambiguity in the expression, and that the disputants affix different ideas to the terms employed in the controversy. For as the faculties of the mind are supposed to be naturally alike in every individual; otherwise nothing could be more fruitless than to reason or dispute together; it were impossible, if men affix the same ideas to their terms, that they could so long form different opinions of the same subject; especially when they communicate their views, and each party turn themselves on all sides, in search of arguments which may give them the victory over their antagonists. It is true, if men attempt the discussion of questions which lie entirely beyond the reach of human capacity, such as those concerning the origin of worlds, or the economy of the intellectual system or region of spirits, they may long beat the air in their fruitless contests, and never arrive at any determinate conclusion. But if the question regard any subject of common life and experience, nothing, one would think, could preserve the dispute so long undecided but some ambiguous expressions, which keep the antagonists still at a distance, and hinder them from grappling with each other.

This has been the case in the long disputed question concerning liberty and necessity; and to so remarkable a degree that, if I be not much mistaken, we shall find, that all mankind, both learned and ignorant, have always been of the same opinion with regard to this subject, and that a few intelligible definitions would immediately have put an end to the whole controversy. I own that this dispute has been so much canvassed on all hands, and has led philosophers into such a labyrinth of obscure sophistry, that it is no wonder, if a sensible reader indulge his ease so far as to turn a deaf ear to the proposal of such a question, from which he can expect neither instruction or entertainment. But the state of the argument here proposed may, perhaps, serve to renew his attention; as it has more novelty, promises at least some decision of the controversy, and will not much disturb his ease by any intricate or obscure reasoning.

I hope, therefore, to make it appear that all men have ever agreed in the doctrine both of necessity and of liberty, according to any reasonable sense, which can be put on these terms; and that the whole controversy, has hitherto turned merely upon words. We shall begin with examining the doctrine of necessity.

It is universally allowed that matter, in all its operations, is actuated by a necessary force, and that every natural effect is so precisely determined by the energy of its cause that no other effect, in such particular circumstances, could possibly have resulted from it. The degree and direction of every motion is, by the laws of nature, prescribed with such exactness that a living creature may as soon arise from the shock of two bodies as motion in any other degree or direction than what is actually produced by it. Would we, therefore, form a just and precise idea of necessity, we must consider whence that idea arises when we apply it to the operation of bodies.

It seems evident that, if all the scenes of nature were continually shifted in such a manner that no two events bore any resemblance to each other, but every object was entirely new, without any similitude to whatever had been seen before, we should never, in that case, have attained the least idea of necessity, or of a connexion among these objects. We might say, upon such a supposition, that one object or event has followed another; not that one was produced by the other. The relation of cause and effect must be utterly unknown to mankind. Inference and reasoning concerning the operations of nature would, from that moment, be at an end; and the memory and senses remain the only canals, by which the knowledge of any real existence could possibly have access to the mind. Our idea, therefore, of necessity and causation arises entirely from the uniformity observable in the operations of nature, where similar objects are constantly conjoined together, and the mind is determined by custom to infer the one from the appearance of the other. These two circumstances form the whole of that necessity, which we ascribe to matter. Beyond the constant conjunction of similar objects, and the consequent inference from one to the other, we have no notion of any necessity or connexion.

If it appear, therefore, that all mankind have ever allowed, without any doubt or hesitation, that these two circumstances take place in the voluntary actions of men, and in the operations of mind; it must follow, that all mankind have ever agreed in the doctrine of necessity, and that they have hitherto disputed, merely for not understanding each other.

As to the first circumstance, the constant and regular conjunction of similar events, we may possibly satisfy ourselves by the following considerations: It is universally acknowledged that there is a great uniformity among the actions of men, in all nations and ages, and that human nature remains still the same, in its principles and operations. The same motives always produce the same actions: the same events follow from the same causes. Ambition, avarice, self-love, vanity, friendship, generosity, public spirit: these passions, mixed in various degrees, and distributed through society, have been, from the beginning of the world, and still are, the source of all the actions and enterprises, which have ever been observed among mankind. Would you know the sentiments, inclinations, and course of life of the Greeks and Romans? Study well the temper and actions of the French and English: You cannot be much mistaken in transferring to the former most of the observations which you have made with regard to the latter. Mankind are so much the same, in all times and places, that history informs us of nothing new or strange in this particular. Its chief use is only to discover the constant and universal principles of human nature, by showing men in all varieties of circumstances and situations, and furnishing us with materials from which we may form our observations and become acquainted with the regular springs of human action and behaviour. These records of wars, intrigues, factions, and revolutions, are so many collections of experiments, by which the politician or moral philosopher fixes the principles of his science, in the same manner as the physician or natural philosopher becomes acquainted with the nature of plants, minerals, and other external objects, by the experiments which he forms concerning them. Nor are the earth, water, and other elements, examined by Aristotle, and Hippocrates, more like to those which at present lie under our observation than the men described by Polybius and Tacitus are to those who now govern the world.

Should a traveller, returning from a far country, bring us an account of men, wholly different from any with whom we were ever acquainted; men, who were entirely divested of avarice, ambition, or revenge; who knew no pleasure but friendship, generosity, and public spirit; we should immediately, from these circumstances, detect the falsehood, and prove him a liar, with the same certainty as if he had stuffed his narration with stories of centaurs and dragons, miracles and prodigies. And if we would explode any forgery in history, we cannot make use of a more convincing argument, than to prove, that the actions ascribed to any person are directly contrary to the course of nature, and that no human motives, in such circumstances, could ever induce him to such a conduct. The veracity of Quintus Curtius is as much to be suspected, when he describes the supernatural courage of Alexander, by which he was hurried on singly to attack multitudes, as when he describes his supernatural force and activity, by which he was able to resist them. So readily and universally do we acknowledge a uniformity in human motives and actions as well as in the operations of body.

Hence likewise the benefit of that experience, acquired by long life and a variety of business and company, in order to instruct us in the principles of human nature, and regulate our future conduct, as well as speculation. By means of this guide, we mount up to the knowledge of men's inclinations and motives, from their actions, expressions, and even gestures; and again descend to the interpretation of their actions from our knowledge of their motives and inclinations. The general observations treasured up by a course of experience, give us the clue of human nature, and teach us to unravel all its intricacies. Pretexts and appearances no longer deceive us. Public declarations pass for the specious colouring of a cause. And though virtue and honour be allowed their proper weight and authority, that perfect disinterestedness, so often pretended to, is never expected in multitudes and parties; seldom in their leaders; and scarcely even in individuals of any rank or station. But were there no uniformity in human actions, and were every experiment which we could form of this kind irregular and anomalous, it were impossible to collect any general observations concerning mankind; and no experience, however accurately digested by reflection, would ever serve to any purpose. Why is the aged husbandman more skilful in his calling than the young beginner but because there is a certain uniformity in the operation of the sun, rain, and earth towards the production of vegetables; and experience teaches the old practitioner the rules by which this operation is governed and directed.

We must not, however, expect that this uniformity of human actions should be carried to such a length as that all men, in the same circumstances, will always act precisely in the same manner, without making any allowance for the diversity of characters, prejudices, and opinions. Such a uniformity in every particular, is found in no part of nature. On the contrary, from observing the variety of conduct in different men, we are enabled to form a greater variety of maxims, which still suppose a degree of uniformity and regularity.

Are the manners of men different in different ages and countries? We learn thence the great force of custom and education, which mould the human mind from its infancy and form it into a fixed and established character. Is the behaviour and conduct of the one sex very unlike that of the other? Is it thence we become acquainted with the different characters which nature has impressed upon the sexes, and which she preserves with constancy and regularity? Are the actions of the same person much diversified in the different periods of his life, from infancy to old age? This affords room for many general observations concerning the gradual change of our sentiments and inclinations, and the different maxims which prevail in the different ages of human creatures. Even the characters, which are peculiar to each individual, have a uniformity in their influence;

otherwise our acquaintance with the persons and our observation of their conduct could never teach us their dispositions, or serve to direct our behaviour with regard to them.

I grant it possible to find some actions, which seem to have no regular connexion with any known motives, and are exceptions to all the measures of conduct which have ever been established for the government of men. But if we would willingly know what judgment should be formed of such irregular and extraordinary actions, we may consider the sentiments commonly entertained with regard to those irregular events which appear in the course of nature, and the operations of external objects. All causes are not conjoined to their usual effects with like uniformity. An artificer, who handles only dead matter, may be disappointed of his aim, as well as the politician, who directs the conduct of sensible and intelligent agents.

The vulgar, who take things according to their first appearance, attribute the uncertainty of events to such an uncertainty in the causes as makes the latter often fail of their usual influence; though they meet with no impediment in their operation. But philosophers, observing that, almost in every part of nature, there is contained a vast variety of springs and principles, which are hid, by reason of their minuteness or remoteness, find, that it is at least possible the contrariety of events may not proceed from any contingency in the cause, but from the secret operation of contrary causes. This possibility is converted into certainty by farther observation, when they remark that, upon an exact scrutiny, a contrariety of effects always betrays a contrariety of causes, and proceeds from their mutual opposition. A peasant can give no better reason for the stopping of any clock or watch than to say that it does not commonly go right: But an artist easily perceives that the same force in the spring or pendulum has always the same influence on the wheels; but fails of its usual effects, perhaps by reason of a grain of dust, which puts a stop to the whole movement. From the observation of several parallel instances, philosophers form a maxim that the connexion between all causes and effects is equally necessary, and that its seeming uncertainty in some instances proceeds from the secret opposition of contrary causes.

Thus, for instance, in the human body, when the usual symptoms of health or sickness disappoint our expectation; when medicines operate not with their wonted powers; when irregular events follow from any particular cause; the philosopher and physician are not surprised at the matter, nor are ever tempted to deny, in general, the necessity and uniformity of those principles by which the animal economy is conducted. They know that a human body is a mighty complicated machine: That many secret powers lurk in it, which are altogether beyond our comprehension: That to us it must often appear very uncertain in its operations: And that therefore the irregular events, which outwardly discover themselves, can be no proof that the laws of nature are not observed with the greatest regularity in its internal operations and government.

The philosopher, if he be consistent, must apply the same reasoning to the actions and volitions of intelligent agents. The most irregular and unexpected resolutions of men may frequently be accounted for by those who know every particular circumstance of their character and situation. A person of an obliging disposition gives a peevish answer: But he has the toothache, or has not dined. A stupid fellow discovers an uncommon alacrity in his carriage: But he has met with a sudden piece of good fortune. Or even when an action, as sometimes happens, cannot be particularly accounted for, either by the person himself or by others; we know, in general, that the characters of men are, to a certain degree, inconstant and irregular. This is, in a manner, the constant character of human nature; though it be applicable, in a more particular manner, to some persons who have no fixed rule for their conduct, but proceed in a continued course of caprice and inconstancy. The internal principles and motives may operate in a uniform manner, notwithstanding these seeming irregularities; in the same manner as the winds, rain, cloud, and other variations of the weather are supposed to be governed by steady principles; though not easily discoverable by human sagacity and enquiry.

Thus it appears, not only that the conjunction between motives and voluntary actions is as regular and uniform as that between the cause and effect in any part of nature; but also that this regular conjunction has been universally acknowledged among mankind, and has never been the subject of dispute, either in philosophy or common life. Now, as it is from past experience that we draw all inferences concerning the future, and as we conclude that objects will always be conjoined together which we find to have always been conjoined; it may seem superfluous to prove that this experienced uniformity in human actions is a source whence we draw inferences concerning them. But in order to throw the argument into a greater variety of lights we shall also insist, though briefly, on this latter topic.

The mutual dependence of men is so great in all societies that scarce any human action is entirely complete in itself, or is performed without some reference to the actions of others, which are requisite to make it answer fully the intention of the agent. The poorest artificer, who labours alone, expects at least the protection of the magistrate, to ensure him the enjoyment of the fruits of his labour. He also expects that, when he carries his goods to market, and offers them at a reasonable price, he shall find purchasers, and shall be able, by the money he acquires, to engage others to supply him with those commodities which are requisite for his subsistence. In proportion as men extend their dealings, and render their intercourse with others more complicated, they always comprehend, in their schemes of life, a greater variety of voluntary actions, which they expect, from the proper motives, to co-operate with their own. In all these conclusions they take their measures from past experience, in the same manner as in their reasonings concerning external objects; and firmly believe that men, as well as all the elements, are to continue, in their operations, the same that they have ever found them. A manufacturer reckons upon the labour of his servants for the execution of any work as much as upon the tools which he employs, and would be equally surprised were his expectations disappointed. In short, this experimental inference and reasoning concerning the actions of others enters so much into human life that no man, while awake, is ever a moment without employing it. Have we not reason, therefore, to affirm that all mankind have always agreed in the doctrine of necessity according to the foregoing definition and explication of it?

Nor have philosophers even entertained a different opinion from the people in this particular. For, not to mention that almost every action of their life supposes that opinion, there are even few of the speculative parts of learning to which it is not essential. What would become of history, had we not a dependence on the veracity of the historian according to the experience which we have had of mankind? How could politics be a science, if laws and forms of government had not a uniform influence upon society? Where would be the foundation of morals, if particular characters had no certain or determinate power to produce particular sentiments, and if these sentiments had no constant operation on actions? And with what pretence could we employ our criticism upon any poet or polite author, if we could not pronounce the conduct and sentiments of his actors either natural or unnatural to such characters, and in such circumstances? It seems almost impossible, therefore, to engage either in science or action of any kind without acknowledging the doctrine of necessity, and this inference from motive to voluntary actions, from characters to conduct.

And indeed, when we consider how aptly natural and moral evidence link together, and form only one chain of argument, we shall make no scruple to allow that they are of the same nature, and derived from the same principles. A prisoner who has neither money nor interest, discovers the impossibility of his escape, as well when he considers the obstinacy of the gaoler, as the walls and bars with which he is surrounded; and, in all attempts for his freedom, chooses rather to work upon the stone and iron of the one, than upon the inflexible nature of the other. The same prisoner, when conducted to the scaffold, foresees his death as certainly from the constancy and fidelity of his guards, as from the operation of the axe or wheel. His mind runs along a certain train of ideas: the refusal of the soldiers to consent to his escape; the action of the executioner; the separation of the head and body; bleeding, convulsive motions, and death. Here is a connected chain of natural causes and voluntary actions; but the mind feels no difference between them in passing from one link to another: Nor is it less certain of the future event than if it were connected with the objects present to the memory or senses, by a train of causes, cemented together by what we are pleased to call a physical necessity. The same experienced union has the same effect on the mind, whether the united objects be motives, volition, and actions; or figure and motion. We may change the name of things; but their nature and their operation on the understanding never change.

Were a man, whom I know to be honest and opulent, and with whom I live in intimate friendship, to come into my house, where I am surrounded with my servants, I rest assured that he is not to stab me before he leaves it in order to rob me of my silver standish; and I no more suspect this event than the falling of the house itself, which is new, and solidly built and founded.--But he may have been seized with a sudden and unknown frenzy.--So may a sudden earthquake arise, and shake and tumble my house about my ears. I shall therefore change the suppositions. I shall say that I know with certainty that he is not to put his hand into the fire and hold it there till it be consumed: and this event, I think I can foretell with the same assurance, as that, if he throw himself out at the window, and meet with no obstruction, he will not remain a moment suspended in the air. No suspicion of an unknown frenzy can give the least possibility to the former event, which is so contrary to all the known principles of human nature. A man who at noon leaves his purse full of gold on the pavement at Charing-Cross, may as well expect that it will fly away like a feather, as that he will find it untouched an hour after. Above one half of human reasonings contain inferences of a similar nature, attended with more or less degrees of certainty proportioned to our experience of the usual conduct of mankind in such particular situations.

I have frequently considered, what could possibly be the reason why all mankind, though they have ever, without hesitation, acknowledged the doctrine of necessity in their whole practice and reasoning, have yet discovered such a reluctance to acknowledge it in words, and have rather shown a propensity, in all ages, to profess the contrary opinion. The matter, I think, may be accounted for after the following manner. If we examine the operations of body, and the production of effects from their causes, we shall find that all our faculties can never carry us farther in our knowledge of this relation than barely to observe that particular objects are constantly conjoined together, and that the mind is carried, by a customary transition, from the appearance of one to the belief of the other. But though this conclusion concerning human ignorance be the result of the strictest scrutiny of this subject, men still entertain a strong propensity to believe that they penetrate farther into the powers of nature, and perceive something like a necessary connexion between the cause and the effect. When again they turn their reflections towards the operations of their own minds, and feel no such connexion of the motive and the action; they are thence apt to suppose, that there is a difference between the effects which result from material force, and those which arise from thought and intelligence. But being once convinced that we know nothing farther of causation of any kind than merely the constant conjunction of objects, and the consequent inference of the mind from one to another, and finding that these two circumstances are universally allowed to have place in voluntary actions; we may be more easily led to own the same necessity common to all causes. And though this reasoning may contradict the systems of many philosophers, in ascribing necessity to the determinations of the will, we shall find, upon reflection, that they dissent from it in words only, not in their real sentiment. Necessity, according to the sense in which it is here taken, has never yet been rejected, nor can ever, I think, be rejected by any philosopher. It may only, perhaps, be pretended that the mind can perceive, in the operations of matter, some farther connexion between the cause and effect; and connexion that has not place in voluntary actions of intelligent beings. Now whether it be so or not, can only appear upon examination; and it is incumbent on these philosophers to make good their assertion, by defining or describing that necessity, and pointing it out to us in the operations of material causes.

It would seem, indeed, that men begin at the wrong end of this question concerning liberty and necessity, when they enter upon it by examining the faculties of the soul, the influence of the understanding, and the operations of the will. Let them first discuss a more simple question, namely, the operations of body and of brute unintelligent matter; and try whether they can there form any idea of causation and necessity, except that of a constant conjunction of objects, and subsequent inference of the mind from one to another. If these circumstances form, in reality, the whole of that necessity, which we conceive in matter, and if these circumstances be also universally acknowledged to take place in the operations of the mind, the dispute is at an end; at least, must be owned to be thenceforth merely verbal. But as long as we will rashly suppose, that we have some farther idea of necessity and causation in the operations of external objects; at the same time, that we can find nothing farther in the voluntary actions of the mind; there is no possibility of bringing the question to any determinate issue, while we proceed upon so erroneous a supposition. The only method of undeceiving us is to mount up higher; to examine the narrow extent of science when applied to material causes; and to convince ourselves that all we know of them is the constant conjunction and inference above mentioned. We may, perhaps, find that it is with difficulty we are induced to fix such narrow limits to human understanding: but we can afterwards find no difficulty when we come to apply this doctrine to the actions of the will. For as it is evident that these have a regular conjunction with motives and circumstances and characters, and as we always draw inferences from one to the other, we must be obliged to acknowledge in words that necessity, which we have already avowed, in every deliberation of our lives, and in every step of our conduct and behaviour.[36]

---

[36]The prevalence of the doctrine of liberty may be accounted for, from another cause, viz. a false sensation of seeming experience which we have, or may have, of liberty or indifference, in many of our actions. The necessity of any action, whether of matter or of mind, is not, properly speaking, a quality in the agent, but in any thinking or intelligent being, who may consider the action; and it consists chiefly in the determination of his thoughts to infer the existence of that action from some preceding objects; as liberty, when opposed to necessity, is nothing but the want of that determination, and a certain looseness or indifference, which we feel, in passing, or not passing, from the idea of one object to that of any succeeding one. Now we may observe, that, though, in reflecting on human actions, we seldom feel such a looseness, or indifference, but are commonly able to infer them with considerable certainty from their motives, and from the dispositions of the agent; yet it frequently happens, that, in performing the actions themselves, we are sensible of something like it: And as all resembling objects are readily taken for each other, this has been employed as a demonstrative and even intuitive proof of human liberty. We feel, that our actions are subject to our will, on most occasions; and imagine we feel, that the will itself is subject to nothing, because, when by a denial of it we are provoked to try, we feel, that it moves easily every way, and produces an image of itself (or a Velleity, as it is called in the schools) even on that side, on which it did not settle. This image, or faint motion, we persuade ourselves, could, at that time, have been compleated into the thing itself; because, should that be denied, we find, upon a second trial, that, at present, it can. We consider not, that the fantastical desire of shewing liberty, is here the motive of our actions. And it seems certain, that, however we may imagine we feel a liberty within ourselves, a spectator can commonly infer our actions from our motives and character; and even where he cannot, he concludes in general, that he might, were he perfectly acquainted with every circumstance of our situation and temper, and the most secret springs of our complexion and disposition. Now this is the very essence of

But to proceed in this reconciling project with regard to the question of liberty and necessity; the most contentious question of metaphysics, the most contentious science; it will not require many words to prove, that all mankind have ever agreed in the doctrine of liberty as well as in that of necessity, and that the whole dispute, in this respect also, has been hitherto merely verbal. For what is meant by liberty, when applied to voluntary actions? We cannot surely mean that actions have so little connexion with motives, inclinations, and circumstances, that one does not follow with a certain degree of uniformity from the other, and that one affords no inference by which we can conclude the existence of the other. For these are plain and acknowledged matters of fact. By liberty, then, we can only mean a power of acting or not acting, according to the determinations of the will; this is, if we choose to remain at rest, we may; if we choose to move, we also may. Now this hypothetical liberty is universally allowed to belong to every one who is not a prisoner and in chains. Here, then, is no subject of dispute.

Whatever definition we may give of liberty, we should be careful to observe two requisite circumstances; First, that it be consistent with plain matter of fact; secondly, that it be consistent with itself. If we observe these circumstances, and render our definition intelligible, I am persuaded that all mankind will be found of one opinion with regard to it.

It is universally allowed that nothing exists without a cause of its existence, and that chance, when strictly examined, is a mere negative word, and means not any real power which has anywhere a being in nature. But it is pretended that some causes are necessary, some not necessary. Here then is the advantage of definitions. Let any one define a cause, without comprehending, as a part of the definition, a necessary connexion with its effect; and let him show distinctly the origin of the idea, expressed by the definition; and I shall readily give up the whole controversy. But if the foregoing explication of the matter be received, this must be absolutely impracticable. Had not objects a regular conjunction with each other, we should never have entertained any notion of cause and effect; and this regular conjunction produces that inference of the understanding, which is the only connexion, that we can have any comprehension of. Whoever attempts a definition of cause, exclusive of these circumstances, will be obliged either to employ unintelligible terms or such as are synonymous to the term which he endeavours to define.[37] And if the definition above mentioned be admitted; liberty, when opposed to necessity, not to constraint, is the same thing with chance; which is universally allowed to have no existence.

Part II

THERE is no method of reasoning more common, and yet none more blameable, than, in philosophical disputes, to endeavour the refutation of any hypothesis, by a pretence of its dangerous consequences to religion and morality. When any opinion leads to absurdities, it is certainly false; but it is not certain that an opinion is false, because it is of dangerous consequence. Such topics, therefore, ought entirely to be forborne; as serving nothing to the discovery of truth, but only to make the person of an antagonist odious. This I observe in general, without pretending to draw any advantage from it. I frankly submit to an examination of this kind, and shall venture to affirm that the doctrines, both of necessity and of liberty, as above explained, are not only consistent with morality, but are absolutely essential to its support.

---

necessity, according to the foregoing doctrine.

[37]Thus, if a cause be defined, that which produces any thing, it is easy to observe, that producing is synonymous to causing. In like manner, if a cause be defined, that by which any thing exists, this is liable to the same objection. For what is meant by these words, by which? Had it been said, that a cause is that after which any thing constantly exists; we should have understood the terms. For this is, indeed, all we know of the matter. And this constantly forms the very essence of necessity, nor have we any other idea of it.

Necessity may be defined two ways, conformably to the two definitions of cause, of which it makes an essential part. It consists either in the constant conjunction of like objects, or in the inference of the understanding from one object to another. Now necessity, in both these senses, (which, indeed, are at bottom the same) has universally, though tacitly, in the schools, in the pulpit, and in common life, been allowed to belong to the will of man; and no one has ever pretended to deny that we can draw inferences concerning human actions, and that those inferences are founded on the experienced union of like actions, with like motives, inclinations, and circumstances. The only particular in which any one can differ, is, that either, perhaps, he will refuse to give the name of necessity to this property of human actions: but as long as the meaning is understood, I hope the word can do no harm: or that he will maintain it possible to discover something farther in the operations of matter. But this, it must be acknowledged, can be of no consequence to morality or religion, whatever it may be to natural philosophy or metaphysics. We may here be mistaken in asserting that there is no idea of any other necessity or connexion in the actions of body: But surely we ascribe nothing to the actions of the mind, but what everyone does, and must readily allow of. We change no circumstance in the received orthodox system with regard to the will, but only in that with regard to material objects and causes. Nothing, therefore, can be more innocent, at least, than this doctrine.

All laws being founded on rewards and punishments, it is supposed as a fundamental principle, that these motives have a regular and uniform influence on the mind, and both produce the good and prevent the evil actions. We may give to this influence what name we please; but, as it is usually conjoined with the action, it must be esteemed a cause, and be looked upon as an instance of that necessity, which we would here establish.

The only proper object of hatred or vengeance is a person or creature, endowed with thought and consciousness; and when any criminal or injurious actions excite that passion, it is only by their relation to the person, or connexion with him. Actions are, by their very nature, temporary and perishing; and where they proceed not from some cause in the character and disposition of the person who performed them, they can neither redound to his honour, if good; nor infamy, if evil. The actions themselves may be blameable; they may be contrary to all the rules of morality and religion: but the person is not answerable for them; and as they proceeded from nothing in him that is durable and constant, and leave nothing of that nature behind them, it is impossible he can, upon their account, become the object of punishment or vengeance. According to the principle, therefore, which denies necessity, and consequently causes, a man is as pure and untainted, after having committed the most horrid crime, as at the first moment of his birth, nor is his character anywise concerned in his actions, since they are not derived from it, and the wickedness of the one can never be used as a proof of the depravity of the other.

Men are not blamed for such actions as they perform ignorantly and casually, whatever may be the consequences. Why? but because the principles of these actions are only momentary, and terminate in them alone. Men are less blamed for such actions as they perform hastily and unpremeditatedly than for such as proceed from deliberation. For what reason? but because a hasty temper, though a constant cause or principle in the mind, operates only by intervals, and infects not the whole character. Again, repentance wipes off every crime, if attended with a reformation of life and manners. How is this to be accounted for? but by asserting that actions render a person criminal merely as they are proofs of criminal principles in the mind; and when, by an alteration of these principles, they cease to be just proofs, they likewise cease to be criminal. But, except upon the doctrine of necessity, they never were just proofs, and consequently never were criminal.

It will be equally easy to prove, and from the same arguments, that liberty, according to that definition above mentioned, in which all men agree, is also essential to morality, and that no human actions, where it is wanting, are susceptible of any moral qualities, or can be the objects either of approbation or dislike. For as actions are objects of our moral sentiment, so far only as they are indications of the internal character, passions, and affections; it is impossible that they can give rise either to praise or blame, where they proceed not from these principles, but are derived altogether from external violence.

I pretend not to have obviated or removed all objections to this theory, with regard to necessity and liberty. I can foresee other objections, derived from topics which have not here been treated of. It may be said, for instance, that, if voluntary actions be subjected to the same laws of necessity with the operations of matter, there is a continued chain of necessary causes, pre-ordained and pre-determined, reaching from the original cause of all to every single volition of every human creature. No contingency anywhere in the universe; no indifference; no liberty. While we act, we are, at the same time, acted upon. The ultimate Author of all our volitions is the Creator of the world, who first bestowed motion on this immense machine, and placed all beings in that particular position, whence every subsequent event, by an inevitable necessity, must result. Human actions, therefore, either can have no moral turpitude at all, as proceeding from so good a cause; or if they have any turpitude, they must involve our Creator in the same guilt, while he is acknowledged to be their ultimate cause and author. For as a man, who fired a mine, is answerable for all the consequences whether the train he employed be long or short; so wherever a continued chain of necessary causes is fixed, that Being, either finite or infinite, who produces the first, is likewise the author of all the rest, and must both bear the blame and acquire the praise which belong to them. Our clear and unalterable ideas of morality establish this rule, upon unquestionable reasons, when we examine the consequences of any human action; and these reasons must still have greater force when applied to the volitions and intentions of a Being infinitely wise and powerful. Ignorance or impotence may be pleaded for so limited a creature as man; but those imperfections have no place in our Creator. He foresaw, he ordained, he intended all those actions of men, which we so rashly pronounce criminal. And we must therefore conclude, either that they are not criminal, or that the Deity, not man, is accountable for them. But as either of these positions is absurd and impious, it follows, that the doctrine from which they are deduced cannot possibly be true, as being liable to all the same objections. An absurd consequence, if necessary, proves the original doctrine to be absurd; in the same manner as criminal actions render criminal the original cause, if the connexion between them be necessary and inevitable.

This objection consists of two parts, which we shall examine separately; First, that, if human actions can be traced up, by a necessary chain, to the Deity, they can never be criminal; on account of the infinite perfection of that Being from whom they are derived, and who can intend nothing but what is altogether good and laudable. Or, Secondly, if they be criminal, we must retract the attribute of perfection, which we ascribe to the Deity, and must acknowledge him to be the ultimate author of guilt and moral turpitude in all his creatures.

The answer to the first objection seems obvious and convincing. There are many philosophers who, after an exact scrutiny of all the phenomena of nature, conclude, that the WHOLE, considered as one system, is, in every period of its existence, ordered with perfect benevolence; and that the utmost possible happiness will, in the end, result to all created beings, without any mixture of positive or absolute ill or misery. Every physical ill, say they, makes an essential part of this benevolent system, and could not possibly be removed, even by the Deity himself, considered as a wise agent, without giving entrance to greater ill, or excluding greater good, which will result from it. From this theory, some philosophers, and the ancient Stoics among the rest, derived a topic of consolation under all afflictions, while they taught their pupils that those ills under which they laboured were, in reality, goods to the universe; and that to an enlarged view, which could comprehend the whole system of nature, every event became an object of joy and exultation. But though this topic be specious and sublime, it was soon found in practice weak and ineffectual. You would surely more irritate than appease a man lying under the racking pains of the gout by preaching up to him the rectitude of those general laws, which produced the malignant humours in his body, and led them through the proper canals, to the sinews and nerves, where they now excite such acute torments. These enlarged views may, for a moment, please the imagination of a speculative man, who is placed in ease and security; but neither can they dwell with constancy on his mind, even though undisturbed by the emotions of pain or passion; much less can they maintain their ground when attacked by such powerful antagonists. The affections take a narrower and more natural survey of their object; and by an economy, more suitable to the infirmity of human minds, regard alone the beings around us, and are actuated by such events as appear good or ill to the private system.

The case is the same with moral as with physical ill. It cannot reasonably be supposed, that those remote considerations, which are found of so little efficacy with regard to one, will have a more powerful influence with regard to the other. The mind of man is so formed by nature that, upon the appearance of certain characters, dispositions, and actions, it immediately feels the sentiment of approbation or blame; nor are there any emotions more essential to its frame and constitution. The characters which engage our approbation are chiefly such as contribute to the peace and security of human society; as the characters which excite blame are chiefly such as tend to public detriment and disturbance: whence it may reasonably be presumed, that the moral sentiments arise, either mediately or immediately, from a reflection of these opposite interests. What though philosophical meditations establish a different opinion or conjecture; that everything is right with regard to the WHOLE, and that the qualities, which disturb society, are, in the main, as beneficial, and are as suitable to the primary intention of nature as those which more directly promote its happiness and welfare? Are such remote and uncertain speculations able to counterbalance the sentiments which arise from the natural and immediate view of the objects? A man who is robbed of a considerable sum; does he find his vexation for the loss anywise diminished by these sublime reflections? Why then should his moral resentment against the crime be supposed incompatible with them? Or why should not the acknowledgment of a real distinction between vice and virtue be reconcileable to all speculative systems of philosophy, as well as that of a real distinction between personal beauty and deformity? Both these distinctions are founded in the natural sentiments of the human mind: And these sentiments are not to be controuled or altered by any philosophical theory or speculation whatsoever.

The second objection admits not of so easy and satisfactory an answer; nor is it possible to explain distinctly, how the Deity can be the mediate cause of all the actions of men, without being the author of sin and moral turpitude. These are mysteries, which mere natural and unassisted reason is very unfit to handle; and whatever system she embraces, she must find herself involved in inextricable difficulties, and even contradictions, at every step which she takes with regard to such subjects. To reconcile the indifference and contingency of human actions with prescience; or to defend absolute decrees, and yet free the Deity from being the author of sin, has been found hitherto to exceed all the power of philosophy. Happy, if she be thence sensible of her temerity, when she pries into these sublime mysteries; and leaving a scene so full of obscurities and perplexities, return, with suitable modesty, to her true and proper province, the examination of common life; where she will find difficulties enough to employ her enquiries, without launching into so boundless an ocean of doubt, uncertainty, and contradiction!

The final selection for this chapter comes from a contemporary of Hume, and another figure of the Scottish Enlightenment. The Reverend Thomas Reid (7 May 1710 – 7 October 1796) advocated "common sense" philosophy, and, in this excerpt, argues against the compatibilist interpretation of free will, claiming, instead, that determinism and free will are incompatible. Genuine liberty and personal responsibility requires genuine choice, an ability to do otherwise. He insists that only if the agent herself is the cause of the determination of her will is she free and accountable with regard to that action. He then distinguishes "active" from "passive" causal power, with active power associated with the "self-caused" acts of free agents. Finally, he proposes that motives and other causal forces influence our choices, but do not necessitate them.

Thomas Reid: *Essays on the active powers of the human mind; An inquiry into the human mind on the principles of common sense; and An essay on quantity.*

Essay IV. Of the Liberty of Moral Agents.

Chapter I. The Notions of Moral Liberty and Necessity Stated.

I. Moral liberty. BY the liberty of a moral agent, I under stand, a power over the determinations of one's own will.

If, in any action, he had power to will what he did, or not to will it, in that action he is free. But if, in every voluntary action, the determination of his will be the necessary consequence of something involuntary in the state of his mind, or of something in his external circumstances, he is not free; he has not what I call the liberty of a moral agent, but is subject to necessity.

This liberty supposes the agent to have understanding and will; for the determinations of the will are the sole object about which this power is employed; and there can be no will without, at least, such a degree of understanding as gives the conception of that which we will.

[The liberty of a moral agent implies, not only a conception of what he wills, but some degree of practical judgment or reason.]

For if he has not the judgment to discern one determination to be preferable to another, either in itself, or for some purpose which he intends, what can be the use of a power to determine? His determinations must be made perfectly in the dark, without reason, motive, or end. They can neither be right nor wrong, wise nor foolish. Whatever the consequences may be, they cannot be imputed to the agent, who had not the capacity of foreseeing them, or of perceiving any reason for acting otherwise than he did.

We may perhaps be able to conceive a being endowed with power over the determinations of his will, without any light in his mind to direct that power to some end. But such power would be given in vain. No exercise of it could be either blamed or approved. As nature gives no power in vain, I see no ground to ascribe a power over the determinations of the will to any being who has no judgment to apply it to the direction of his conduct, no discernment of what he ought or ought not to do.

For that reason, in this Essay, I speak only of the liberty of moral agents, who are capable of acting well or ill, wisely or foolishly, and this, for distinction's sake, I shall call moral liberty.

II. The voluntary actions of brutes determined by the present predominant passion. What kind, or what degree of liberty belongs to brute animals, or to our own species, before any use of reason, I do not know. We acknowledge that they have not the power of self-government. [Such of their actions as may be called voluntary, seem to be invariably determined by the passion or appetite, or affection or habit, which is strongest at the time.]

This seems to be the law of their constitution, to which they yield, as the inanimate creation does, without any conception of the law, or any intention of obedience.

But of civil or moral government, which are addressed to the rational powers, and require a conception of the law and an intentional obedience, they are, in the judgment of all mankind, incapable. Nor do I see what end could be served by giving them a power over the determinations of their own will, unless to make them intractable by discipline, which we see they are not.

III. [The effect of moral liberty is, That it is in the power of the agent to do well or ill.] This power, like every other gift of God, may be abused. The right use of this gift of God is to do well and wisely, as far as his best judgment can direct him, and thereby merit esteem and approbation. The abuse of it is to act contrary to what he knows or suspects to be his duty and his wisdom, and thereby justly merit disapprobation and blame.

IV. [By necessity, I understand the want of that moral liberty which I have above defined.]

If there can be a better and a worse in actions on the system of necessity, let us suppose a man necessarily determined in all cases to will and to do what is best to be done, he would surely be innocent and inculpable. But, as far as I am able to judge, he would not be entitled to the esteem and moral approbation of those who knew and believed this necessity. What was, by an ancient author, said of Cato, might indeed be said of him.

He was good because he could not be otherwise. But this saying, if understood literally and strictly, is not the praise of Cato, but of his constitution, which was no more the work of Cato, than his existence.

On the other hand, if a man be necessarily determined to do ill, this case seems to me to move pity, but not disapprobation. He was ill, because he could not be otherwise. Who can blame him? Necessity has no law.

If he knows that he acted under this necessity, has he not just ground to exculpate himself? The blame, if there be any, is not in him, but in his constitution. If he be charged by his Maker with doing wrong, may he not expostulate with him, and say, Why hast thou made me thus? I may be sacrificed at thy pleasure for the common good, like a man that has the plague, but not for ill desert; for thou knowest that what I am charged with is thy work, and not mine.

V. [Such are my notions of moral liberty and necessity, and of the consequences inseparably connected with both the one and the other.]

This moral liberty a man may have, though it do not extend to all his actions, or even to all his voluntary actions. He does many things by instinct, many things by the force of habit with out any thought at all, and consequently without will. In the first part of life, he has not the power of self-government any more than the brutes. That power over the determinations of his own will, which belongs to him in ripe years, is limited, as all his powers are; and it is perhaps beyond the reach of his understanding to define its limits with precision. We can only say, in general, that it extends to every action for which he is accountable.

This power is given by his Maker, and at his pleasure, whose gift it is: it may be enlarged or diminished, continued or with drawn. No power in the creature can be independent of the Creator. His hook is in its nose; he can give it line as far as he sees fit, and when he pleases, can restrain it, or turn it whithersoever he will. Let this be always understood, when we ascribe liberty to man, or to any created being.

VI. [Supposing it therefore to be true, That man is a free agent, it may be true, at the same time, that his liberty may be impaired or lost, (1) by disorder of body or mind, as in melancholy, or in madness; it may be impaired or lost (2) by vicious habits; it may, in particular cases, (3) be restrained by Divine interposition.]

We call a man a free agent in the same way as we call him a reasonable agent. In many things he is not guided by reason, but by principles similar to those of the brutes. His reason is weak at best.

It is liable to be impaired or lost, by his own fault, or by other means. In like manner, he may be a free agent, though his freedom of action may have many similar limitations.

The liberty I have described has been represented by some philosophers as inconceivable, and as involving an absurdity.

"Liberty, they say, consists only in a power to act as we will; and it is impossible to conceive in any being a greater liberty than this. Hence it follows, that liberty does not extend to the determinations of the will, but only to the actions consequent to its determination, and depending upon the will. To say that we have power to will such an action, is to say, that we may will it, if we will. This supposes the will to be determined by a prior will; and, for the same reason, that will must be deter mined by a will prior to it, and so on in an infinite series of wills, which is absurd. To act freely, therefore, can mean nothing more than to act voluntarily; and this is all the liberty that can be conceived in man, or in any being."

This reasoning, first, I think, advanced by Hobbes, has been very generally adopted by the defenders of necessity. It is grounded upon a definition of liberty totally different from that which I have given, and therefore does not apply to moral liberty, as above defined.

VII. Three additional meanings of the word liberty. [But it is said that this is the only liberty that is possible, that is conceivable, that does not involve an absurdity.]

It is strange, indeed ! if the word liberty has no meaning but this one. I shall mention three, all very common. The objection applies to one of them, but to neither of the other two.

[Liberty is sometimes opposed to external force or confinement of the body. Sometimes it is opposed to obligation by law, or by lawful authority. Sometimes it is opposed to necessity.]

1 . It is opposed to confinement of the body by superior force. So we say a prisoner is set at liberty when his fetters are knocked off, and he is discharged from confinement. This is the liberty defined in the objection; and I grant that this liberty extends not to the will, neither does the confinement, because the will cannot be confined by external force.

2. Liberty is opposed to obligation by law, or lawful authority. This liberty is a right to act one way or another, in things which the law has neither commanded nor forbidden; and this liberty is meant when we speak of a man's natural liberty, his civil liberty, his Christian liberty. It is evident that this liberty, as well as the obligation opposed to it, extends to the will: for it is the will to obey that makes obedience; the will to transgress that makes a transgression of the law. Without will there can be neither obedience nor transgression. Law supposes a power to obey or to transgress; it does not take away this power, but proposes the motives of duty and of interest, leaving the power to yield to them, or to take the consequence of transgression.

3. Liberty is opposed to necessity, and in this sense it extends to the determinations of the will only, and not to what is consequent to the will.

In every voluntary action, the determination of the will is the first part of the action, upon which alone the moral estimation of it depends. It has been made a question among philosophers, Whether, in every instance, this determination be the necessary consequence of the constitution of the person, and the circum stances in which he is placed; or whether he had not power in many cases, to determine this way or that?

This has, by some, been called the philosophical notion of liberty and necessity; but it is by no means peculiar to philosophers. The lowest of the vulgar have, in all ages, been prone to have recourse to this necessity, to exculpate themselves or their friends in what they do wrong, though, in the general tenor of their conduct, they act upon the contrary principle.

VIII. Whether this notion of moral liberty be conceivable or not, every man must judge for himself. To me there appears no difficulty in conceiving it. I consider the determination of the will as an effect. This effect must have a cause which had power to produce it; and the cause must be either the person himself, whose will it is, or some other being. The first is as easily conceived as the last. If the person was the cause of that determination of his own will, he was free in that action, and it is justly imputed to him, whether it be good or bad. But, if another being was the cause of this determination, either by producing it immediately, or by means and instruments under his direction, then the determination is the act and deed of that being, and is solely imputable to him.

But it is said, "That nothing is in our power but what depends upon the will, and therefore the will itself cannot be in our power." I answer, That this is a fallacy arising from taking a common saying in a sense which it never was intended to convey, and in a sense contrary to what it necessarily implies.

In common life, when men'speak of what is, or is not, in a man's power, they attend only to the external and visible effects, which only can be perceived, and which only can affect them. Of these, it is true, that nothing is in a man's power, but what depends upon his will, and this is all that is meant by this common saying.

But this is so far from excluding his will from being in his power, that it necessarily implies it. For to say that what depends upon the will is in a man's power, but the will is not in his power, is to say that the end is in his power, but the means necessary to that end are not in his power, which is a contradiction.

[In many propositions which we express universally, there is an exception necessarily implied, and therefore always under stood. Thus when we say, that all things depend upon God, God himself is necessarily excepted. In like manner, when we say, that all that is in our power depends upon the will, the will itself is necessarily excepted: [for if the will be not, nothing else can be in our power.] Every effect must be in the power of its cause. The determination of the will is an effect, and there fore must be in the power of its cause, whether that cause be the agent himself, or some other being.

From what has been said in this chapter, I hope the notion of moral liberty will be distinctly understood, and that it appears that this notion is neither inconceivable, nor involves any absurdity or contradiction.

Chapter II. Of the Words Cause and Effect, Action, and Active Power

I. The use of ambiguous terms has impeded our reasonings about moral liberty. THE writings upon liberty and necessity have been much darkened, by the ambiguity of the words used in reasoning upon that subject. The words cause and effect, action and active power, liberty and necessity, are related to each other. The meaning of one determines the meaning of the rest. When we attempt to define them, we can only do it by synonymous words which need definition as much. There is a strict sense in which those words must be used, if we speak and reason clearly about moral liberty; but to keep to this strict sense is difficult, be cause in all languages they have, by custom, got a great latitude of signification.

As we cannot reason about moral liberty, without using those ambiguous words, it is proper to point out, as distinctly as possible, their proper and original meaning, in which they ought to be understood in treating of this subject, and to show from what causes they have become so ambiguous in all languages, as to darken and embarrass our reasonings upon it.

[Every thing that begins to exist, must have a cause of its existence, which had power to give it existence.] [And every thing that undergoes any change, must have some cause of that change.]

That neither existence, nor any mode of existence, can begin without an efficient cause, is a principle that appears very early in the mind of man; and it is so universal, and so firmly rooted in human nature, that the most determined scepticism cannot eradicate it.

It is upon this principle that we ground the rational belief of a Deity. But that is not the only use to which we apply it. Every man's conduct is governed by it every day, and almost every hour of his life. And if it were possible for any man to root out this principle from his mind, he must give up every thing that is called common prudence, and be fit only to be confined as insane.

From this principle it follows, that every thing which under goes any change, must either be the efficient cause of that change in itself, or it must be changed by some other being.

In the first case it is said to have active power, and to act in producing that change. In the second case it is merely passive, or is acted upon, and the active power is in that being only which produces the change.

II. Active power. The name of a cause and of an agent, is properly given to that being only, which, by its active power, produces some change in itself, or in some other being. The change, whether it be of thought, of will, or of motion, is the effect. Active power, therefore, is a quality in the cause, which enables it to produce the effect. And the exertion of that active power in producing the effect, is called action, agency, efficiency. [In order to the production of any effect, there must be in the cause not only power, but the exertion of that power: for power that is not exerted produces no effect.]

All that is necessary to the production of any effect, is power, is an efficient cause to produce the effect, and the exertion of that power: for it is a contradiction to say, that the cause has power to produce the effect, and exerts that power, and yet the effect is not produced. The effect cannot be in his power, un less all the means necessary to its production be in his power.

It is no less a contradiction to say, that a cause has power to produce a certain effect, but that he cannot exert that power: for power which cannot be exerted is no power, and is a contra diction in terms.

To prevent mistake, it is proper to observe, that a being may have a power at one time which it has not at another. It may commonly have a power, which, at a particular time, it has not. Thus, a man may commonly have power to walk or to run; but he has not this power when asleep, or when he is confined by superior force. In common language, he may be said to have a power which he cannot then exert. But this popular expression means only that he commonly has this power, and will have it when the cause is removed which at present deprives him of it: for when we speak strictly and philosophically, it is a contradiction to say that he has this power, at that moment when he is deprived of it.

[These, I think, are necessary consequences from the principle first mentioned, that every change which happens in nature must have an efficient cause which had power to produce it.]

III. [Another principle, which appears very early in the mind of man, is, That we are efficient causes in our deliberate and voluntary actions.]

Of the Words Cause and Effect, etc.

We are conscious of making an exertion, sometimes with difficulty, in order to produce certain effects. An exertion made deliberately and voluntarily, in order to produce an effect, implies a conviction that the effect is in our power. No man can deliberately attempt what he does not believe to be in his power. The language of all mankind, and their ordinary conduct in life, demonstrate, that they have a conviction of some active power in themselves to produce certain motions in their own and in other bodies, and to regulate and direct their own thoughts. This conviction we have so early in life, that we have no remembrance when, or in what way, we acquired it.

That such a conviction is at first the necessary result of our constitution, and that it can never be entirely obliterated, is, I think, acknowledged by one of the most zealous defenders of necessity. Such are the influences to which all mankind, without distinction, are exposed, that they necessarily refer actions (I mean refer them ultimately) first of all to themselves and others; and it is a long time before they begin to consider themselves and others as instruments in the hand of a superior agent. Consequently, the associations which refer actions to themselves, get so confirmed, that they are never entirely obliterated; and therefore the common language, and the common feelings of mankind, will be adapted to the first, the limited and imperfect, or rather erroneous, view of things."

It is very probable that the very conception or idea of active power, and of efficient causes, is derived from our voluntary exertions in producing effects; and that, if we were not conscious of such exertions, we should have no conception at all of a cause, or of active power, and consequently no conviction of the necessity of a cause of every change which we observe in nature.

IV. [It is certain that we can conceive no kind of active power but what is similar or analogous to that which we attribute to our selves; that is, a power which is exerted by will and with under standing. Our notion, even of Almighty power, is derived from the notion of human power, by removing from the former those imperfections and limitations to which the latter is subjected.]

It may be difficult to explain the origin of our conceptions and belief concerning efficient causes and active power. [The common theory, that all our ideas are ideas of sensation or reflection, and that all our belief is a perception of the agreement or the disagreement of those ideas, appears to be repugnant, both to the idea of an efficient cause, and to the belief of its necessity.]

An attachment to that theory has led some philosophers to deny that we have any conception of an efficient cause, or of active power, because efficiency and active power are not ideas, either of sensation or reflection. They maintain, therefore, that a cause is only something prior to the effect, and constantly con joined with it. This is Mr. Hume's notion of a cause, and seems to be adopted by Dr. Priestley, who says, "That a cause cannot be defined to be any thing, but such previous circumstances as are constantly followed by a certain effect, the constancy of the result making us conclude, that there must be a sufficient reason, in the nature of the things, why it should be produced in those circumstances."

But theory ought to stoop to fact, and not fact to theory. Every man who understands the language knows, that neither priority, nor constant conjunction, nor both taken together, imply efficiency. Every man, free from prejudice, must assent to what Cicero has said: "Itaque non sic causa intelligi debet, ut quod cuique antecedat, id et causa sit, sed quod cuique efficienter antecedit." "That which precedes any thing is not to be considered as its cause, but that which precedes it efficiently"

[The very dispute, whether we have the conception of an efficient cause, shows that we have. For though men may dispute about things which have no existence, they cannot dispute about things of which they have no conception.]

V. Recapitulation. What has been said in this chapter is intended to show, That the conception of causes, of action and of active power, in the strict and proper sense of these words, is found in the minds of all men very early, even in the dawn of their rational life. It is therefore probable, that, in all languages, the words by which these conceptions were expressed were at first distinct and unambiguous; yet it is certain, that, among the most enlightened nations, these words are applied to so many things of different natures, and used in so vague a manner, that it is very difficult to reason about them distinctly.

This phenomenon, at first view, seems very unaccountable. But a little reflection may satisfy us, that it is a natural consequence of the slow and gradual progress of human knowledge.

And since the ambiguity of these words has so great influence upon our reasoning about moral liberty, and furnishes the strongest objections against it, it is not foreign to our subject to show whence it arises. [When we know the causes that have produced this ambiguity, we shall be less in danger of being misled by it, and the proper and strict meaning of the words will more evidently appear.]...

VIII....

To say that man is a free agent, is no more than to say that, in some instances, he is truly an agent and a cause, and is not merely acted upon as a passive instrument. On the contrary, to say that he acts from necessity, is to say that he does not act at all, that he is no agent, and that, for any thing we know, there is only one agent in the universe, who does every thing that is done, whether it be good or ill....

Chapter IV. Of the Influence of Motives

I. THE modern advocates for the doctrine of necessity lay the stress of their cause upon the influence of motives.

" Every deliberate action," they say, " must have a motive. When there is no motive on the other side, this motive must determine the agent:

when there are contrary motives, the strongest must prevail: we reason from men's motives to their actions, as we do from other causes to their effects: if man be a free agent, and be not governed by motives, all his actions must be mere caprice, rewards and punishments can have no effect, and such a being must be absolutely ungovernable."

In order therefore to understand distinctly, in what sense we ascribe moral liberty to man, it is necessary to understand what influence we allow to motives. To prevent misunderstanding, which has been very common upon this point, I offer the following observations:

Esssay IV. Chapter IV.

I. I grant that all rational beings are influenced, and ought to be influenced by motives. But the influence of motives is of a very different nature from that of efficient causes. They are neither causes nor agents. They suppose an efficient cause, and can do nothing without it. We cannot, without absurdity, suppose a motive, either to act, or to be acted upon; it is equally incapable of action and of passion; because it is not a thing that exists, but a thing that is conceived; it is what the schoolmen called an ens rationis. Motives, therefore, may influence to action, but they do not act. They may be compared to advice, or exhortation, which leaves a man still at liberty. For in vain is advice given when there is not a power either to do, or to for bear, what it recommends. In like manner, motives suppose liberty in the agent, otherwise they have no influence at all.

It is a law of nature, with respect to matter, that every motion and change of motion is proportional to the force impressed, and in the direction of that force. The scheme of necessity supposes a similar law to obtain in all the actions of intelligent beings; which, with little alteration, may be expressed thus: every action, or change of action, in an intelligent being, is proportional to the force of motives impressed, and in the direction of that force.

The law of nature respecting matter is grounded upon this principle that matter is an inert, inactive substance, which does not act, but is acted upon; and the law of necessity must be grounded upon the supposition, that an intelligent being is an inert, inactive substance, which does not act, but is acted upon.

II. [2. Rational beings, in proportion as they are wise and good, will act according to the best motives; and every rational being, who does otherwise, abuses his liberty.] The most perfect being, in every thing where there is a right and a wrong, a better and a worse, always infallibly acts according to the best motives. This indeed is little else than an identical proposition; for it is a contradiction to say, that a perfect being does what is wrong or unreasonable. But to say, that he does not act freely, because he always does what is best, is to say, that the proper use of liberty destroys liberty, and that liberty consists only in its abuse.

The moral perfection of the Deity consists, not in having no power to do ill, otherwise, as Dr. Clarke justly observes, there would be no ground to thank him for his goodness to us any more than for his eternity or immensity; but his moral perfection consists in this, that, when he has power to do every thing, a power which cannot be resisted, he exerts that power only in doing what is wisest and best. To be subject to necessity is to have no power at all; for power and necessity are opposites. We grant, therefore, that motives have influence, similar to that of advice or persuasion; but this influence is perfectly consistent with liberty, and indeed supposes liberty.

III. [3. Whether every deliberate action must have a motive, depends on the meaning we put upon the word deliberate.] If, by a deliberate action, we mean an action wherein motives are weighed, which seems to be the original meaning of the word, surely there must be motives, and contrary motives, otherwise they could not be weighed. But if a deliberate action means only, as it commonly does, an action done by a cool and calm determination of the mind, with forethought and will, I believe there are innumerable such actions done without a motive.

This must be appealed to every man's consciousness. I do many trifling actions every day, in which, upon the most careful reflection, I am conscious of no motive; and to say that I may be influenced by a motive of which I am not conscious, is, in the first place, an arbitrary supposition without any evidence, and then, it is to say, that I may be convinced by an argument which never entered into my thought.

Cases frequently occur, in which an end that is of some importance may be answered equally well by any one of several different means. In such cases, a man who intends the end finds not the least difficulty in taking one of these means, though he be firmly persuaded, that it has no title to be preferred to any of the others.

To say that this is a case that cannot happen, is to contradict the experience of mankind; for surely a man who has occasion to lay out a shilling, or a guinea, may have two hundred that are of equal value, both to the giver and to the receiver, any one of which will answer his purpose equally well. To say, that, if such a case should happen, the man could not execute his purpose, is still more ridiculous, though it have the authority of some of the schoolmen, who determined, that the ass, between two equal bundles of hay, would stand still till it died of hunger.

IV. [If a man could not act without a motive, he would have no power at all; for motives are not in our power; and he that has not power over a necessary mean, has not power over the end.]

That an action done without any motive can neither have merit nor demerit, is much insisted on by the writers for necessity, and triumphantly, as if it were the very hinge of the controversy. I grant it to be a self-evident proposition, and I know no author that ever denied it.

How insignificant soever, in moral estimation, the actions may be which are done without any motive, they are of moment in the question concerning moral liberty. For, if there ever was any action of this kind, motives are not the sole causes of human actions. And if we have the power of acting without a motive, that power, joined to a weaker motive, may counterbalance a stronger.

V. [4. It can never be proved, that when there is a motive on one side only, that motive must determine the action.]

According to the laws of reasoning, the proof is incumbent on those who hold the affirmative; and I have never seen a shadow of argument which does not take for granted the thing in question, to wit, that motives are the sole causes of actions.

Is there no such thing as wilfulness, caprice, or obstinacy among mankind? If there be not, it is wonderful that they should have names in all languages. If there be such things, a single motive, or even many motives, may be resisted.

VI. Motives of the same kind may be compared. [5. When it is said, that of contrary motives the strongest always prevails, this can neither be affirmed nor denied with understanding, until we know distinctly what is meant by the strongest motive.]

I do not find, that those who have advanced this as a self- evident axiom, have ever attempted to explain what they mean by the strongest motive, or have given any rule by which we may judge which of two motives is the strongest.

How shall we know whether the strongest motive always prevails, if we know not which is strongest? There must be some test by which their strength is to be tried, some balance in which they may be weighed, otherwise, to say that the strongest motive always prevails, is to speak without any meaning. We must therefore search for this test or balance, since they who have laid so much stress upon this axiom, have left us wholly in the dark as to its meaning. I grant, that when the contrary motives are of the same kind, and differ only in quantity, it may be easy to say which is the strongest. Thus a bribe of a thousand pounds is a stronger motive than a bribe of a hundred pounds. But when the motives are of different kinds, as money and fame, duty and worldly interest, health and strength, riches and honour, by what rule shall we judge which is the strongest motive?

Either we measure the strength of motives, merely by their prevalence, or by some other standard distinct from their prevalence.

If we measure their strength merely by their prevalence, and by the strongest motive mean only the motive that prevails, it will be true indeed that the strongest motive prevails; but the proposition will be identical, and mean no more than that the strongest motive is the strongest motive. From this surely no conclusion can be drawn.

[If it should be said, that by the strength of a motive is not meant its prevalence, but the cause of its prevalence; that we measure the cause by the effect, and from the superiority of the effect conclude the superiority of the cause, as we conclude that to be the heaviest weight which bears down the scale: I answer, that, according to this explication of the axiom, it takes for granted that motives are the causes, and the sole causes of actions.]

Nothing is left to the agent, but to be acted upon by the motives, as the balance is by the weights. The axiom supposes, that the agent does not act, but is acted upon; and, from this supposition, it is concluded that he does not act. This is to reason in a circle, or rather it is not reasoning but begging the question.

Contrary motives may very properly be compared to advocates pleading the opposite sides of a cause at the bar. It would be very weak reasoning to say, that such an advocate is the most powerful pleader, because sentence was given on his side. The sentence is in the power of the judge, not of the advocate. It is equally weak reasoning, in proof of necessity, to say, such a motive prevailed, therefore it is the strongest; since the defenders of liberty maintain that the determination was made by the man, and not by the motive.

VII. [We are therefore brought to this issue, that unless some measure of the strength of motives can be found distinct from their prevalence, it cannot be determined, whether the strongest motive always prevails or not. If such a measure can be found and applied, we may be able to judge of the truth of this maxim, but not otherwise.]

Every thing that can be called a motive is addressed either to the animal or to the rational part of our nature. Motives of the former kind are common to us with the brutes; those of the latter are peculiar to rational beings. We shall beg leave, for distinction's sake, to call the former, animal motives, and the latter, rational.

Hunger is a motive in a dog to eat; so is it in a man. According to the strength of the appetite, it gives a stronger or a weaker impulse to eat. And the same thing may be said of every other appetite and passion. Such animal motives give an impulse to the agent, to which he yields with ease; and, if the impulse be strong, it cannot be resisted without an effort which requires a greater or a less degree of self-command. Such motives are not addressed to the rational powers. Their influence is immediately upon the will. We feel their influence, and judge of their strength, by the conscious effort which is necessary to resist them.

VIII. Animal test of the strength of motives. When a man is acted upon by contrary motives of this kind, he finds it easy to yield to the strongest. They are like two forces pushing him in contrary directions. To yield to the strongest, he needs only to be passive. By exerting his own force, he may resist; but this requires an effort of which he is conscious. [The strength of motives of this kind is perceived, not by our judgment, but by our feeling; and that is the strongest of contrary motives to which he can yield with ease, or which it requires an effort of self-command to resist; and this we may call the animal test of the strength of motives.]

If it be asked, whether, in motives of this kind, the strongest always prevails? I answer, That in brute-animals I believe it does. They do not appear to have any self-command; an appetite or passion in them is overcome only by a stronger contrary one. On this account, they are not accountable for their actions, nor can they be the subjects of law.

But in men who are able to exercise their rational powers, and have any degree of self-command, the strongest animal motive does not always prevail. The flesh does not always prevail against the spirit, though too often it does. And if men were necessarily determined by the strongest animal motive, they could no more be accountable, or capable of being governed by law, than brutes are.

IX. Rational motives defined. Let us next consider rational motives, to which the name of motive is more commonly and more properly given. Their influence is upon the judgment, by convincing us that such an action ought to be done, that it is our duty, or conducive to our real good, or to some end which we have determined to pursue.

They do not give a blind impulse to the will as animal motives do. They convince, but they do not impel, unless, as may often happen, they excite some passion of hope, or fear, or desire. Such passions may be excited by conviction, and may operate in its aid as other animal motives do. But there may be conviction without passion; and [the conviction of what we ought to do, in order to some end which we have judged fit to be pursued, is what I call a rational motive.]

Brutes, I think, cannot be influenced by such motives. They have not the conception of ought and ought not. Children acquire these conceptions as their rational powers advance; and they are found in all of ripe age, who have the human faculties.

X. Rational test of the strength of motives. [If there be any competition between rational motives, it is evident that the strongest, in the eye of reason, is that which it is most our duty and our real happiness to follow.] Our duty and our real happiness are ends which are inseparable; and they are the ends which every man, endowed with reason, is conscious he ought to pursue in preference to all others. [This we may call the rational test of the strength of motives. A motive which is the strongest, according to the animal test, may be, and very often is, the weakest according to the rational.]

[The grand and the important competition of contrary motives is between the animal, on the one hand, and the rational oil the other. This is the conflict between the flesh and the spirit, upon the event of which the character of men depends.]

If it be asked, which of these is the strongest motive? The answer is, That the first is commonly strongest, when they are tried by the animal test. If they were not so, human life would be no state of trial. It would not be a warfare, nor would virtue require any effort or self-command. No man would have any temptation to do wrong. But when we try the contrary motives by the rational test, it is evident that the rational motive is always the strongest.

And now, I think, it appears that the strongest motive, according to either of the tests I have mentioned, does not always prevail.

[In every wise and virtuous action, the motive that prevails is the strongest, according to the rational test, but commonly the weakest according to the animal. In every foolish, and in every vicious action, the motive that prevails is commonly the strongest according to the animal test, but always the weakest according to the rational.]

XI. [6. It is true, that we reason from men's motives to their actions, and in many cases with great probability, but never with absolute certainty. And to infer from this, that men are necessarily determined by motives, is very weak reasoning.]

For, let us suppose, for a moment, that men have moral liberty, I would ask, what use may they be expected to make of this liberty? It may surely be expected that, of the Various actions within the sphere of their power, they will choose what pleases them most for the present, or what appears to be most for their real, though distant good. When there is a competition between these motives, the foolish will prefer present gratification; the wise, the greater and more distant good.

Now, is not this the very way in which we see men act? Is it not from the presumption that they act in this way, that we reason from their motives to their actions? Surely it is. Is it not weak reasoning, therefore, to argue, that men have not liberty, because they act in that very way in which they would act if they had liberty? It would surely be more like reasoning, to draw the contrary conclusion from the same premises.

XII. [7. Nor is it better reasoning to conclude, that if men are not necessarily determined by motives, all their actions must be capricious.]

To resist the strongest animal motives when duty requires, is so far from being capricious, that it is, in the highest degree, wise and virtuous. And we hope this is often done by good men.

To act against rational motives, must always be foolish, vicious, or capricious. And it cannot be denied that there are too many such actions done.

But is it reasonable to conclude, that because liberty may be abused by the foolish and the vicious, therefore it can never be put to its proper use, which is to act wisely and virtuously?

XIII. [8. It is equally unreasonable to conclude, that if men are not necessarily determined by motives, rewards and punishments would have no effect. With wise men they will have their due effect; but not always with the foolish and the vicious.]

Let us consider what effect rewards and punishments do really, and in fact, produce, and what may be inferred from that effect, upon each of the opposite systems of liberty and of necessity.

I take it for granted that, in fact, the best and wisest laws, both human and divine, are often transgressed, notwithstanding the rewards and punishments that are annexed to them. If any man should deny this fact, I know not how to reason with him. From this fact, it may be inferred with certainty, upon the supposition of necessity, that, in every instance of transgression, the motive of reward or punishment was not of sufficient strength to produce obedience to the law. This implies a fault in the lawgiver; but there can be no fault in the transgressor who acts mechanically by the force of motives. We might as well impute a fault to the balance, when it does not raise a weight of two pounds by the force of one pound.

XIV. The supposition of necessity precludes rewards and punishments liberty gives efficacy to both. [Upon the supposition of necessity, there can be neither reward nor punishment, in the proper sense, as those words imply good and ill desert.] Reward and punishment are only tools employed to produce a mechanical effect. When the effect is not produced, the tool must be unfit or wrong applied.

Upon the supposition of liberty, rewards and punishments will have a proper effect upon the wise and the good; but not so upon the foolish and the vicious, when opposed by their animal passions or bad habits; and this is just what we see to be the fact. Upon this supposition, the transgression of the law implies no defect in the law, no fault in the lawgiver; the fault is solely in the transgressor. And it is upon this supposition only that there can be either reward or punishment, in the proper sense of the words, because it is only on this supposition that there can be good or ill desert.

Chapter 4
Personal Identity: Metaphysics

Comprehension questions you should be able to answer after reading this introduction:

1. *What is meant by the "persistence of personal identity?"*
2. *Explain the "body criterion" for personal identity.*
3. *Explain the "Theseus' ship" criticism of the bodily criterion. How does this apply to the human body?*
4. *Explain the "brain criterion" for personal identity?*
5. *Explain the "split-brain" criticism of the brain criterion.*
6. *Explain the "psychological-state" criterion for personal identity as found in Locke. What role does memory play for this criterion?*
7. *What is the difference between a "man" and a "person," according to Locke? What establishes the identity of each?*
8. *What is the difference between semantic/factual memories and episodic/personal memories? Which are used to establish personal identity?*
9. *How does Locke account for "ruptures" of consciousness in his theory of identity?*
10. *What is Reid's "transitivity" objection to Locke's theory?*
11. *Explain Reid's "simple" view of identity? What is the "self," and what makes it the same self over time?*
12. *Explain Hume's "bundle view" of personal identity.*
13. *According to Locke, what causes the mistaken belief in a single, continuous self?*

Personal identity covers a range of philosophical issues, from Ancient to Contemporary. We can get a sense of what some of the identity issues are by considering a few questions that might, at first glance, seem embarrassingly simple, but which, after only a moment's consideration, are revealed to be complicated and philosophically rich.

Who are you? What defines you, as a person? What makes you the person you are (as opposed to someone else)? Is it race or ethnicity? Gender? Sexual orientation? Socioeconomic class? Ability/disability? Your worldviews? Your preferences and aversions? Hobbies? Relationships? Personal history? Self-concept (which might or might not be accurate—your self-concept might be that you're fair and unbiased when, in fact, you harbor a variety of prejudicial beliefs)?

What is the *evidence for* personal identity? This is distinct from what *constitutes* personal identity. For example, first-person experiential memories might be *good evidence* that I am the same person I was 10 minutes ago without it being the case that memory is what *made me* the same person. By analogy, a DNA test might be evidence that you committed a crime, even though the crime was really committed by your (evil) identical twin.

What is the "person" in personal identity? Is

the "self" a biological organism? A brain? An immaterial soul? A bundle of perceptions? A social construct? A work of "art?"

Do "you" (however defined) *persist* through time? In what sense is it true and accurate when you point to a photo of a five-year-old child and say that the child is "you?"

We can organize these clusters of questions into two basic, broader questions:

1. What (if anything) allows the same identity to persist over time?
2. What (if anything) constitutes personal identity in the first place?

The second question concerns what makes "me," *me* (or "you," *you*). What establishes the "self" or "I" that might (or might not) persist over time? Am I determined in some sort of important way by a particular kind of "essence?" Am I the product of my genes and/or upbringing? Am "I" a creative project that must be fashioned by my own free choices over the course of my life? Am "I" a social construct forged by the dominant social forces of my time and community? Whatever the "I" is, what is its nature? Is it purely physical? Biological? An immaterial soul? An irreducible center of conscious awareness? We will consider those issues in our next chapter, after having considered the first question of persistence in the remainder of this chapter.

Persistence of Personal Identity

This first question concerns whether and how the self (however it might be conceived) can "survive" over time. Am I the same person who once resided in my mother's womb, as a fetus? Am I the same person who grew up in Clovis, California? Am I the same person I was when I was in college? Will I be the same person I am now, 40 years in the future (should I live so long), when I have retired? Are you the same person who read the previous paragraph of this chapter, however long ago?

The initial tension is probably obvious. Identity implies sameness, while change indicates a lack of sameness. The basic issue, then, is whether something can change and yet remain the same thing, in some meaningful sense, and, if so, how.

Change is a general threat to the persistence of personal identity, but not all change is equally "threatening. If someone claims that "you've changed," or they say something like, "I don't even know you anymore," that person is probably not making a sincere and literal assertion that one person used to exist, but no longer does, and another person has taken his or her place! Instead, those are usually just dramatic ways of expressing that a person's appearance, values, or behavior have changed—while implicitly assuming that the same person is the one whose appearance/values/behavior have changed. Indeed, claiming that "you" have changed makes no sense if taken to be a serious denial of personal identity. The "you" would be inapplicable to the person you're speaking to, since he or she is a new person, and the "you" refers to the old (no longer existing) person who has been replaced.

You might be wondering why any of this even matters. For one, it seems to matter with regard to personal responsibility and punishment. In 2015, 94-year old Oskar Groening was sentenced to four years in prison for crimes he committed more than half a century ago—specifically, 300,000 counts of accessory to murder for the role he played as "Bookkeeper of Auschwitz." Another man, Gerhard Sommer, was initially charged with 342 cases of murder for his actions as a 22-year-old soldier in the 16th SS Panzer Division, in which he allegedly helped massacre more than 500 civilians in Tuscany, including 119 children, in 1944. He was spared a trial only because he was declared unfit due to severe dementia.[38]

Beyond such headline-worthy examples of these, it certainly seems to matter, even in "non-Nazi" cases, whether the same "self" persists through time. If you are reading this chapter, it is likely (though not certain) that you are a college

38 http://time.com/3958690/5-most-wanted-nazis/

student. It is also likely that one of the reasons you are a college student is because you believe that acquiring a college degree will benefit you in the future. What if the "you" who is working hard and taking college classes won't be around in the future to enjoy the benefits of that hard work? What if "future-you," in some meaningful sense, is someone *else*? Would you have the same motivation to work hard and study if "you" won't be around to reap the benefits? Or, imagine the absurdity of working all month to earn a paycheck that "future-you" (who is meaningfully different and not *you*) will collect and spend instead.

These are not mere philosophical abstractions. From 2003 to 2005, the case of Terry Schiavo (a Florida woman who had been brain-dead but maintained on life-support machines for over a decade) took center stage in American politics, as Florida politicians, the U.S. Congress, and even the President of the United States, took stances in the fight over whether or not feeding tubes should be withdrawn from her. Eventually, no less than the U.S. Supreme Court finally ruled in favor of Michael Schiavo (her husband), allowing the feeding tubes to be withdrawn (against the wishes of her parents, and numerous pro-life politicians).

2016 Republican Presidential candidate Jeb Bush, who had been Governor of Florida at the time, proudly affirmed his efforts to keep her alive (siding with her parents and against her husband) over a decade later, during his Presidential campaign. "It broke my heart that we weren't successful at sustaining this person's life, so she could be loved by her mom and dad. But the courts decided otherwise, and I was respectful of that."[39]

By the time of Terry's death, her brain weighed just over a pound—less than half the size of a normal adult brain. The autopsy report declared that the brain had "no remaining discernible neurons."[40] She was blind, and incapable of any sensation—even pain. Her parents and some politicians were fighting to keep "Terry" alive, but was a person still in existence at all? [41] If so, in what way was that "person" still "Terry?"

Clearly, whether or not persons "persist" over time matters, and that we do persist is presupposed in countless acts and by countless assumptions we make every day. Most of us are very confident that we remain the same person (barring very unusual circumstances) over time. What remains to be seen, however, is whether we have any *good*, philosophically substantiated *reasons* to think that our confidence is warranted. What we need is to establish a criterion for personal identity, and then see if that criterion is satisfied in the case of persons such as you and me.

Criteria for personal identity, in general, can be defined as the necessary and sufficient conditions that determine whether "temporally distinct person stages" (e.g., Ted on 12-5-15 and Ted on 12-4-15) are stages of one (same) continuous person. We will now consider the most prominent criteria for personal identity, starting with the body criterion.

Body criterion

The body criterion for personal identity is, at first glance, both obvious and compelling. If we think of most attributions of identity, when we want to know whether something is the same, particular instance of that "something," we have a fairly simple notion in mind—though one that is not necessarily easy to articulate!

If I'm looking for my car in a parking lot, I know what I'm looking for. What makes my car *my* car is the fact that I own it, but what makes a *particular car* my car is that it happens to be that

[39] http://www.politico.com/story/2015/04/jeb-bush-terri-schiavo-case-117075#ixzz3tCl86vBd

[40] http://www.politico.com/magazine/story/2015/01/jeb-bush-terri-schiavo-114730?o=4

[41] Some changes might not be from one person into another person, but from a person (however defined) into a non-person. For example, Terry Schiavo's injuries arguably caused the person who was Terry Schiavo to cease to exist (although her body continued to live), as opposed to replacing Terry Schiavo with some other person.

specific instance of a 2009 Camry Hybrid that I happen to own. I own a 2009 Camry Hybrid, but that certainly doesn't mean I can walk up to just any such Camry and consider it mine! Only a very *specific* Camry is mine.

Most of the time, it's pretty easy to figure out which car is mine in a parking lot. If I have remembered where I parked, I can usually just spot my car in the midst of lots of other (different) cars and right away know that it is mine. On one occasion, though, it wasn't so easy. I was outside a local AAA office, where I had just renewed my license plates. I walked over to my car, bent down, and placed the new sticker on my license plate. I then was shocked to realize I had placed the sticker on the wrong car! Amazingly enough, another car of the exact same color, make, and model, was parked next to my own—and I had just placed the new sticker on someone else's car. I quickly and surreptitiously removed the sticker and placed it on my license plate, hoping no one would see me and think I was stealing someone else's sticker!

How I made the mistake is fairly easy to understand. Another car looked very similar to my own, and I wasn't paying close enough attention to what I was doing. How did I know I had put the sticker on the wrong car? Well, for one, the license plate number was wrong! My car has a unique sequence of letters and numbers to identify it, much like each human body has a unique fingerprint (and everyone except for identical twins has unique DNA). Even if someone had made a duplicate license plate and placed it on another car, there are other indicators. My car has a thin scratch in the paint along its right side. My car has a campus parking sticker hanging from the rear view mirror. My car has some napkins stored in the glove compartment, as well as an insurance card that has my name on it.

Even if, inexplicably, someone made the effort to mimic every single one of these elements of my car in another car, there would still, in principle, be a way to differentiate my car from other, seemingly identical cars: my car has had a continuous physical existence over time. That is just to say that it has only ever occupied one particular part of space at a given moment, and that it would be possible to trace the movement of that car from one part of space, to another part of space (e.g., from my driveway to a AAA parking lot), over time, via all those interconnecting parts of space (i.e., the route between my house and the AAA lot). This is very easy to imagine if we suppose that a GPS tracking device were planted in my car. The other Camry, the look-alike, for all its physical resemblance, is a different car because its own physical history is different from that of my car. It has occupied different parts of space, at different times—including being parked in a different parking spot in the AAA lot.

Under normal circumstances, it is not difficult to establish a criterion according to which one physical object (e.g., my Camry) has a distinct identity from another physical object (e.g., its look-alike at the AAA lot): they have distinct physical *bodies* that have remained more or less intact, and have moved, uninterrupted, through space, over time. So far, so good.

While it might be easy, though, to establish the identity of my car against another person's car, there still remains the question of how my car *remains the same car* over time, even when compared only against itself. Despite its initial "obviousness," the body criterion for physical artifacts has actually long been regarded as problematic. Ancient philosophers, as reported by Plutarch, took varying positions as whether a ship (an example very similar to that of my car) retained the same identity after going through successive changes.

> *The ship wherein Theseus and the youth of Athens returned had thirty oars, and was preserved by the Athenians down even to the time of Demetrius Phalereus, for they took away the old planks as they decayed, putting in new and stronger timber in their place, insomuch that this ship became a standing example among the philosophers, for the logical question of things that grow; one side holding that the ship remained the same, and the other contending that it was*

not the same.[42]

Imagine a slightly different version of the same ship thought experiment. Suppose that one piece of the original ship ("Theseus") is replaced each day, for however many days are needed to have replaced every single part. As each part is removed, it is carefully collected and transported to a warehouse. The replacement parts going into the original ship are each made of plastic (regardless of whether the original part was wood, metal, etc.), and painted blue.

At the end of this process, the "original" ship is now composed entirely of blue plastic. All the old pieces that have been sent to the warehouse are meticulously reassembled. There are now two ships: A and B.

A is the blue plastic ship, that started out as "Theseus," but changed, one piece at a time, into what it is now.

B started out as a pile of pieces from "Theseus," collected one a time, before being reassembled in a warehouse.

Which one is "Theseus?" A, or B? Or neither? Or both?

The adaptation of the Theseus example to my car should be easy. In truth, my car has undergone continuous change over time. I have replaced tires numerous times, as well as brakes and various fluids. The floor mats have been replaced, as have the original hubcaps. The paint has become scratched and faded compared to its condition a few years ago. I still have confidence that it's the "same car" that I bought those years ago, but when should I start to lose that confidence? After how many replaced items? How many cosmetic changes? What if I replace every single piece of the car, one piece at a time, and someone else takes all the original parts and reassembles them? Which one of those Camrys is the "same car," and which is the new one?

Philosophically, while we might find persistence issues for any kind of object to be interesting, practically speaking, it is cases of (human) personal identity that matter to us. When we apply the body criterion to personal identity, we could argue that the body criterion is the only standard of personal identity we employ *outside* of philosophical contexts.

If someone points to a man and asks "is that Ted?" you don't normally consider anything other than whether or not the male body you're seeing is the one that corresponds to Ted's body, in much the same sort of way that there is normally nothing complicated about answering whether a certain car being indicated is my car. Only in "weird" circumstances would any confusion, uncertainty, or questions arise.

If, for example, you learned that I have a twin brother, you might not be certain whether or not the person you're seeing is "me," or my twin brother. Or, if you learn that I had significant cosmetic surgery to my face, or had gained or lost a lot of weight, there might be some ambiguity as to whether the person you're seeing is me. Most of the time, though, we don't agonize over such concerns, and identifying someone as themselves is a fairly straightforward exercise of bodily recognition. That doesn't mean, however, that there aren't legitimate challenges to a strict application of the body criterion.

Clearly, *change* makes the body criterion much more complicated than it might have seemed, as we saw in the "Theseus" example. A similar issue that immediately arises when attempting to apply the body criterion to personal identity is that the human body is constantly changing. Our skin cells are replaced every month, and every cell in our skeleton is replaced every seven years.[43] Our bodies change in ways

[42] http://classics.mit.edu/Plutarch/theseus.html

[43] http://stemcell.stanford.edu/research/ Note: the commonly held belief that "*every* cell in the body is replaced every seven years," while much repeated, appears to be an overstatement. Some neurons in the cerebral cortex do not appear to regenerate when they die, and are therefore not replaced. The cerebral cortex is a vitally important part of the brain in that it is responsible for our cognitive abilities, such as reasoning and language use, as well as being a storehouse for memories. (http://m.pnas.org/content/103/33/12219.full)

analogous to the change in Theseus' ship, or my car. Do any of those changes represent challenges to establishing the persistence of personal identity?

One response is to say "no," that the body criterion does not require some obsessive demand for absolute material sameness of an object over time. Persistence of physical artifacts (like ships, tables, cars, houses, etc.) does not require retention of literally (and only) the same matter over time, since such things can be repaired or modified while retaining their "sameness," for all practical purposes. The bodily criterion for personal identity never demands numerically/materially identical bodies to persist over time, as it would be an immediate non-starter, since that is an *impossible* demand for *any* physical object, including the human body.

Instead, the bodily criterion claims that person P_1 at time T_1 is the same as person P_2 at time T_2 so long as their bodies are identical, or that any replacements or modifications have been the result of a series of "gradual" changes. This can be taken to illustrate that physical artifacts do not maintain strict, absolute identity over time. For physical artifacts, a "loose" sort of identity is claimed instead—one that is admittedly somewhat arbitrary and that admits of degrees—and that same "looseness" could apply to our own personal identity over time as well.

Another response to the problem of change for the bodily criterion is to recognize that not all body parts seem equally essential when it comes to satisfying the criterion. If I lose a big toe to frostbite, for example, I don't think anyone would seriously question whether or not I am the same person I was before the amputation. But, what if my *brain* is transplanted into another person's skull? The brain seems especially important for persistent personal identity—so much so that, for some, it establishes an alternative criterion.

Brain criterion

There's no doubt that the brain seems to be especially important with regard to personal identity. The aforementioned case of Terry Schiavo can be seen as an example of this. It certainly seems plausible that it was the severity of her brain damage that allowed any serious questions as to whether she was still "Terry." Although her body, overall, bore a resemblance to Terry Schiavo, the fact that her brain was so severely damaged caused many, including her husband, to conclude that "Terry" was no longer there.

Perhaps a more plausible variant of the bodily criterion, then, is to just use the brain to establish identity. You are the same person throughout the span of your life on the very reasonable assumption that "you" (in terms of your consciousness, memories, behaviors, dispositions, personality traits, etc.) have been the manifestation of and have been borne by the same brain over that lifetime. Should damage of the brain be sufficient to destroy memory, or drastically alter personality traits, we might well raise some sincere identity questions—certainly much more than we would should the change be the loss of a limb, or the loss of hair, or the addition of a scar!

Although the brain criterion seems like a possible improvement over the bodily criterion, and better able to weather the challenge of basic bodily change, the brain criterion is vulnerable to certain criticisms as well.

Imagine that it is medically possible to do brain transplants. Imagine also that John suffers a devastating injury to his body, though his brain remains intact and healthy. Imagine that Mark suffers a devastating and irreversible brain injury, though the rest of his body remains otherwise healthy and intact. Now imagine that Mark's "dead" brain is removed from his body, and John's healthy brain is placed into the now empty skull, with all the appropriate nerves and blood vessels connected.

Who is it that will awaken from that surgery?

Is it Mark, even though his brain (and presumably all of Mark's memories and personality) have been replaced by John's?

Is it John, even though he's now interacting with the world through what at least used to be Mark's body?

Is it someone else entirely? "Johnson," perhaps? What reasons would you give, in any of those cases?

Intuitively, it seems that there would be little reason to think the person is still Mark, given that none of Mark's personality, memories, feelings, goals, dreams, etc. remain. But, in that case, what seems to make Mark himself (rather than John) *are those things* (i.e., memories, personality traits, etc.), rather than his general physical form. If you agree, you might assume that you subscribe to the brain criterion, given that the brain seems essential for those things—but don't be too hasty. The thought-experiment gets more strange!

The brain is made up of two hemispheres (left and right). Each controls the opposite side of the body, and each is associated with different cognitive functions. For example, the left hemisphere is generally associated with math and language skills, while the right hemisphere is associated with musical skill and pattern recognition—though these associations are not absolute or permanent. When one hemisphere is damaged (by a stroke, for example), the other hemisphere can acquire its functions (though gradually).

The hemispheres are connected to each other by a bundle of fibres called the corpus callosum. In some extreme cases of epilepsy, the corpus callosum is severed (to provide relief from extreme seizures), separating the two hemispheres. Fascinating results have been recorded.

> *Long-term observations showed that each disconnected hemisphere possesses not only a separate sensory-motor interface with the environment, its own perceptual, mnestic, cognitive and linguistic repertoires, but also a distinct personality, as well as characteristic preferences and dislikes.... Thus, the two hemispheres have similar, but not identical, concepts of self, past and future, family, social culture and history . . . . After some testing experience with the patients, examiners spontaneously refer to the two hemispheres as if they were distinct people, e.g., "the LH was upset at the RH responses today". While such references may be regarded as shorthand for patterns of behavior with specific lateralized stimuli and responses, they nonetheless express a strong phenomenological sense of two coexisting streams of consciousness. Both hemispheres can probably be simultaneously and independently conscious; both can simultaneously possess conflicting wills so that the split-brain can exhibit two distinct, and possibly incompatible, loci of moral responsibility....*[44]

These interesting findings from "split-brain" cases produce what is known as the "fission problem" for the brain criterion. Assume each hemisphere (L & R) is capable of maintaining memory, personality traits, retention of worldview, etc. It is a current medical fact that human beings can survive with one of their brain hemispheres destroyed and/or removed. A 2013 study of children who had undergone "hemispherectomy" as a treatment for very severe epilepsy found that 83% of the patients were able to walk independently, 70% had satisfactory speaking skills, nearly 60% could mainstream in schools with assistance, and 5 of 24 adults who had the surgery were maintaining employment.[45]

For the purposes of our thought-experiment, imagine the results are even *more* impressive. Knowing that a human can survive (mostly intact, in real life—and fully intact, for the purposes of

---

44 http://www.its.caltech.edu/~jbogen/text/ref130.htm

45 http://www.today.com/health/taking-out-half-kids-brain-can-be-best-option-stop-6C10983490

our thought-experiment) with only one brain hemisphere, imagine that the corpus callosum of "Juana's" brain is severed. Now consider each of the following scenarios with regard to those hemispheres.

- Scenario 1: Left hemisphere is intact; right hemisphere is destroyed as medical waste.
- Scenario 2: Right hemisphere is intact; left hemisphere is destroyed as medical waste.
- Scenario 3: Left hemisphere is intact and transplanted into recently emptied skull of another human ("Shawna"), with all appropriate nerves and blood vessels connected; right hemisphere is destroyed as medical waste.
- Scenario 4: Right hemisphere is intact and transplanted into recently emptied skull of another human ("Lana"), with all appropriate nerves and blood vessels connected; left hemisphere is destroyed as medical waste.
- Scenario 5: Right hemisphere is intact and transplanted into recently emptied skull of another human ("Lana"), with all appropriate nerves and blood vessels connected; left hemisphere is intact and transplanted into recently emptied skull of another human ("Shawna"), with all appropriate nerves and blood vessels connected.

In which of those scenarios, did Juana survive? "Where" is Juana? Since Juana can survive (as Juana) with only one hemisphere, she seems to have persisted in both scenarios 1 and 2. Those same hemispheres that sustained personal identity in scenarios 1 or 2 are equally present and viable in scenarios 3 and 4—they're just located in another human body. So far, Juana has survived in scenarios 1, 2, 3, and 4. What about scenario 5? Well, if she survived in scenario 3, as well as in scenario 4, it seems like she would also have survived in scenario 5, since 5 is just the combination of both 3 and 4.

In scenario 5, rather than waste a perfectly good hemisphere (each of which constitutes "Juana"), both were placed in donor bodies. By that reasoning, "Juana" is now in the skulls of *both* "Lana" *and* "Shawna"—but this is logically impossible, and incoherent! The *same* person can't be *two distinct* people at the *same* time, and in the same respect—not without explicit logical contradiction, at least. If Juana is *both* Lana and Shawna after the operation, and Lana is scared but Shawna isn't, then Juana is simultaneously both scared and not-scared. If Lana is asleep and Shawna is awake, then Juana is simultaneously both awake and asleep. That's literally nonsense.

These sorts of thought-experiments, bizarre though they might seem, might provide insight into some deeper intuitions about personal identity. Some would argue that the confusion that results from them is because it isn't really the brain (as a particular hunk of living matter) that establishes identity, but rather it is what the brain *does*.

The reason why the brain is more intuitively associated with personal identity than is the big toe, or either arm or leg, or arguably any other part of the body, is that the brain seems to be the organ that stores memories, is vulnerable with respect to personality (in ways that other parts of the body are not), and is connected with beliefs and values—at least by virtue of our reasoning abilities that allow us to form and accept beliefs, and deliberate over values in the first place.

What makes split-brain scenarios so thought-provoking is that those capacities and memories seem to be located in multiple places at the same time. It's not so much that I identity more with one hemisphere of my brain than another, or even both hemispheres taken together, as that I identify with those memories, beliefs, values, and personality traits. When all of those things can be located in two different skulls, it's puzzling to know which one is "me." Perhaps that puzzlement indicates that what *really* matters for personal identity are those traits, memories, etc., regardless of how they are stored and facilitated?

Psychological state criterion

The psychological state criterion (sometimes,

specifically, the memory criterion) acknowledges the special significance placed on certain psychological states in our attribution of personal identity. Memories, character traits, goals, desires, aversions, and values all factor prominently into our considerations of personal identity.

Certainly, though we might say that someone is "different" after losing an arm in an accident, we don't usually mean that they are literally a different person. We probably just mean that they have different capabilities now (e.g., not being able to hold things in the arm they no longer have), and perhaps that their demeanor is changed (e.g., depressed after the loss of a limb).

The brain seems to be a special case of a body part—certainly much more important to identity than an arm. If a person's brain is severely damaged or altered, we might actually assert that he or she is a different person—and mean it in a serious sort of way. What do we mean, though, in such a case? *Probably* that the person's personality is different, that they have lost their memories of their past life and relationships, that they no longer care about the same things they used to, etc. It seems, then, that what *really* matters for personal identity is not a particular hunk of flesh (even the brain), but rather certain psychological traits and capacities. This was the view of our first famous philosopher of this chapter: John Locke.

Locke

Locke's famous discussion of personal identity occurs in his *Essay Concerning Human Understanding*, in a chapter entitled "Of Identity and Diversity" (part of which is included at the end of this chapter). Locke's account has been profoundly influential, and much of the literature on personal identity since Locke has been either an attempt to refute him, or to defend/supplement him.

There is an interesting historical context for Locke's writing worth mentioning, since some of his text might otherwise seem confusing. Locke was motivated to offer an account of personal identity that would be consistent with the Christian doctrines of human immortality, final judgment, and the resurrection of the dead. Given a Christian worldview, these are not mere "thought experiments" but rather "facts" that any account of personal identity must be able to accommodate.

The "simple" view of identity, according to which persons are immaterial souls that survive not only bodily change but bodily death, is (and was) an obvious way to account for identity while accommodating those Christian doctrines.[46] Locke, though, tries to offer an account of identity that is indifferent as to whether the soul is immaterial, or a material substance to which God has "superadded" certain cognitive powers.[47] If successful, his account of persistent identity will "work" whether materialism (i.e., the worldview according to which only physical things exist) or substance dualism (the worldview according to which both physical and non-physical things exist, and in which persons are immaterial souls inhabiting physical bodies) prevails.

One advantage of his account (or so he thought) is that it allows us to make sense of some of our intuitive attachments that are puzzling on a substance dualist account of identity. For example, the concern that we have for ourselves is different from the concern we have for others. This is not to say that we don't care about others, but a key difference, of course, is that however empathetic we might be, we don't literally feel another person's pain or fear, nor suffer another person's punishment (or enjoy their rewards, for that matter). I might feel sorry for another person who is sentenced to prison, but if I am the one sentenced, I also have to serve the sentence!

If we take personal identity to consist in a singular immaterial soul existing through time, as the "simple" view will claim, then, if reincarnation is real, "my" soul might have animated countless other human bodies before my own. Perhaps my soul once animated the body of Adolf Hitler?

[46] Indeed, this is one of the alternative views we will consider later in this chapter.

[47] Locke, *Essay* IV, iii.6.

The problem, of course, is that I don't think of myself as Hitler! I have no memories of Hitler's life, nor do I share his beliefs and values. For Locke, to discover that some immaterial substance (i.e., a soul) was shared between my life and Hitler's no more connects me to Hitler, as a person, than would the discovery that our bodies shared some of the same atoms. Even if we could somehow prove beyond any doubt that my soul used to animate Hitler's body, it would be profoundly unfair to put *me* on trial for *his* crimes against humanity! It would be just as silly to do so if we discovered that we shared some atoms in common. Even if we shared the same soul, we would not, on Locke's view, be the same *person*.

An important distinction, for Locke, is that between "man" and "person." By properly defining each of those terms (often confused and used interchangeably), we can get to the foundation of what we really think constitutes personal identity.

A "man," for Locke, is the human animal (as animal), and is *not* identical to a "person." Indeed, he thinks someone can be the same "man" without being the same "person."

For Locke, "Man" is the sound that signals the idea we have of a particular instance of the human animal—but this is not identical to our idea of "person."

Anyone who has ever viewed a dead body (at a funeral, for example) has probably shared the following experience with me. At every funeral I have attended that included a viewing, whenever I looked upon the body, I had a distinct impression that what I was viewing was *not* the person I had once known. Bodies in caskets, in my experience, look like wax figures. The lack of life, animation, vitality . . . all those lacking elements cause me to acknowledge (using Locke's terminology) that the body I am viewing is the "man" I once knew (as opposed to a different human), but not the "person" I once knew. Similarly, if the body were still alive, but in a coma, we might draw the same conclusion—as indeed I did when I visited a friend, as a teenager, who had been in a terrible car accident and was comatose. The body I was viewing (though still alive) was the "man" I had gone to school with, but didn't seem in any meaningful way to be the "person" I had known.

The identity of a "man" is established in the same way as the identity of other animals: "participation of the same continued life, by constantly fleeting particles of matter, in succession vitally united to the same organized body."[48] A "man" endures over time, even though it consists, at different times, of a variety of different basic substances (e.g., atoms). By analogy, Locke thinks that a person can endure, over time, despite being borne by a variety of different substances (material, as in a changing body, or immaterial, as in a soul that has lapses of consciousness, or even gets reincarnated, and certainly (according to Christian doctrine) gets resurrected at the final judgment).

> *The question being what makes the same person; and not whether it be the same identical substance, which always thinks in the same person, which, in this case, matters not at all: different substances, by the same consciousness (where they do partake in it) being united into one person, as well as different bodies by the same life are united into one animal, whose identity is preserved in that change of substances by the unity of one continued life. For, it being the same consciousness that makes a man be himself to himself, personal identity depends on that only, whether it be annexed solely to one individual substance, or can be continued in a succession of several substances. For as far as any intelligent being can repeat the idea of any past action with the same consciousness it had of it at first, and with the same consciousness it has of any present action; so far it is the same personal self. For it is by the consciousness it has of its present thoughts and actions, that it is self to itself now, and so will be the same self, as far as the same consciousness can extend to*

[48] *Essay* II, xxvii.6.

> *actions past or to come. and would be by distance of time, or change of substance, no more two persons, than a man be two men by wearing other clothes to-day than he did yesterday, with a long or a short sleep between: the same consciousness uniting those distant actions into the same person, whatever substances contributed to their production.*[49]

With regard to the resurrection of the dead, if identity is found in material "sameness," then the resurrection is a confusing doctrine. Certainly, our bodies undergo change with regard to the particular atoms that comprise them under normal circumstances. There are also bizarre issues that arise if we consider an example like cannibalism. Voltaire (humorously) entertained this scenario.

> *A soldier from Brittany goes into Canada; there, by a very common chance, he finds himself short of food, and is forced to eat an Iroquois whom he killed the day before. The Iroquois had fed on Jesuits for two or three months; a great part of his body had become Jesuit. Here, then, the body of a soldier is composed of Iroquois, of Jesuits, and of all that he had eaten before. How is each to take again precisely what belongs to him? And which part belongs to each?*[50]

If identity is based on material sameness, the Iroquois is part Jesuit, and the Soldier is part Iroquois and part Jesuit. At the resurrection, who gets which atoms?[51]

The better approach, for Locke, is to establish relevant personal identity by appealing neither to material sameness, nor even to continuity of biological life. For the same reason, he will reject identity based on the sameness of an immaterial substance. If having different atoms over time, or sharing atoms with other bodies across time, makes no difference to personal identity, then why would the fact that the substance in question is immaterial (rather than material) suddenly make a difference? If we acknowledge the possibility that the same soul might reside in multiple bodies throughout history (e.g., reincarnation), then we have the same basic problems as arise with the sharing of atoms. In neither case is persistent identity established. He will appeal, instead, to an identity established by *psychological criteria*.

> *Whether the same immaterial substance remaining, there may be two distinct persons; which question seems to me to be built on this,- Whether the same immaterial being, being conscious of the action of its past duration, may be wholly stripped of all the consciousness of its past existence, and lose it beyond the power of ever retrieving it again: and so as it were beginning a new account from a new period, have a consciousness that cannot reach beyond this new state. All those who hold pre-existence are evidently of this mind; since they allow the soul to have no remaining consciousness of what it did in that pre-existent state, either wholly separate from body, or informing any other body; and if they should not, it is plain experience would be against them. So that personal identity, reaching no further than consciousness reaches, a pre-existent spirit not having continued so many ages in a state of silence, must needs make different persons. Suppose a Christian Platonist or a Pythagorean should, upon God's having ended all his works of*

[49] Locke, An Essay Concerning Human Understanding, Book 2, Chapter XXVII.10.

[50] Voltaire, "The Soul, Identity and Immortality" in Edwards, Paul (Ed). Immortality. Prometheus. 1997 pp. 141-147.

[51] Perhaps interestingly, St. Augustine offered an answer to this dilemma centuries prior. In the case of cannibalism, the flesh in question would "be restored to the man in whom it became human flesh" (*City of God*, Bk. XXII, Ch. 20). Basically, whoever had the flesh first (presumably the person who was eaten) will get it back. . . .

creation the seventh day, think his soul hath existed ever since; and should imagine it has revolved in several human bodies; as I once met with one, who was persuaded his had been the soul of Socrates (how reasonably I will not dispute; this I know, that in the post he filled, which was no inconsiderable one, he passed for a very rational man, and the press has shown that he wanted not parts or learning;)- would any one say, that he, being not conscious of any of Socrates's actions or thoughts, could be the same person with Socrates? Let any one reflect upon himself, and conclude that he has in himself an immaterial spirit, which is that which thinks in him, and, in the constant change of his body keeps him the same: and is that which he calls himself: let him also suppose it to be the same soul that was in Nestor or Thersites, at the siege of Troy, (for souls being, as far as we know anything of them, in their nature indifferent to any parcel of matter, the supposition has no apparent absurdity in it), which it may have been, as well as it is now the soul of any other man: but he now having no consciousness of any of the actions either of Nestor or Thersites, does or can he conceive himself the same person with either of them? Can he be concerned in either of their actions? attribute them to himself, or think them his own, more than the actions of any other men that ever existed? So that this consciousness, not reaching to any of the actions of either of those men, he is no more one self with either of them than if the soul or immaterial spirit that now informs him had been created, and began to exist, when it began to inform his present body; though it were never so true, that the same spirit that informed Nestor's or Thersites' body were numerically the same that now informs his. For this would no more make him the same person with Nestor, than if some of the particles of matter that were once a part of Nestor were now a part of this man; the same immaterial substance, without the same consciousness, no more making the same person, by being united to any body, than the same particle of matter, without consciousness, united to any body, makes the same person. But let him once find himself conscious of any of the actions of Nestor, he then finds himself the same person with Nestor.[52]

In the imagined case of reincarnation, if there is no psychological connection to those past lives (e.g., memories), then we simply do not have the same sort of "backward looking" attitudes towards the events of those lives like we do with our current life that we actually remember. If someone could somehow *prove* that my soul animated Hitler's body, but I had no memory of that life, I would not have the same feelings, attitudes, or connection to Hitler's life as I do to my own, that I remember reasonably well. For Locke, this is an indicator that sameness of an immaterial soul, no more than sameness of a material body, does not constitute personal identity. Instead, what matters to us, ultimately, are memories.

What makes a person a *person* in the first place is consciousness, and what makes a person the *same person* over time is identity of consciousness, for Locke.

This being premised, to find wherein personal identity consists, we must consider what person stands for;- which, I think, is a thinking intelligent being, that has reason and reflection, and can consider itself as itself, the same thinking thing, in different times and places; which it does only by that consciousness which is inseparable from thinking, and, as it seems to me, essential to it:. . . For, since consciousness always accompanies thinking, and it is that which makes every one to be what he calls self, and thereby

[52] Locke, *Essay*, Book 2, XXVII.13.

> *distinguishes himself from all other thinking things, in this alone consists personal identity, i.e. the sameness of a rational being: and as far as this consciousness can be extended backwards to any past action or thought, so far reaches the identity of that person; it is the same self now it was then; and it is by the same self with this present one that now reflects on it, that that action was done.*[53]

Consciousness, in this sense, should be understood as being "witness to one's own acts," or "knowledge of oneself," or "knowledge of one's own acts and thoughts." To be conscious of oneself, then, is to be a witness to one's own thoughts or actions. *Sameness* of consciousness, then, means shared knowledge between your current self and past selves—and this implies *memories*, of course. Consciousness, in general, is not the same thing as memory, but identity of consciousness (shared consciousness) will certainly be understood in terms of memory.

For Locke, memory is crucial to establishing identity, but we need to be clear what kinds of memory we're talking about. I remember, for example, that Sacramento is the capital of the State of California, and that 8 x 8 = 64, but those aren't the sorts of memories that establish personal identity. I have also memorized all of the U.S. Presidents, in order, but if I should someday no longer be able to remember those Presidents, I don't think that 'Ted" will have ceased to exist!

To properly understand the role of memory for Locke, we need to distinguish what are sometimes called semantic (or factual) memories, from what are sometimes called episodic (or personal) memories.

Semantic/factual memories contain a "that" clause, which is just to that say that such memories are described as remembering *that* X. For example, I remember *that* 2 x 2 = 4.[54] Episodic/personal memories, in contrast are described in terms of S remembering F-ing.[55] For example, I remember *texting* Portia this morning.

Episodic memories also have, as a necessary condition, what is called the "previous awareness condition," according to which one has an episodic memory of an event only if one was an agent or witness to the event. For example, I was the agent texting Portia, in my episodic memory of that event.

Episodic memories are the memories that matter, for Locke. These are experiential (episodic/personal) memories—and, of course, such memories are implicitly "first-person." It would be very strange if *I* had a memory of *your* experience, from your point of view!

To summarize Locke's position up to this point: a "man" is a biological being—a particular human animal. The identity of a man is established in the same way as every other animal: "participation of the same continued life, by constantly fleeting particles of matter, in

[53] Locke, *Essay*, Book 2, XXVII.9.

[54] In contrast, Reid considers semantic/factual memories as not being memories at all, in the "proper" sense of the term. Instead of memories, such things are better classified as belief or knowledge. For example, "remembering that" 2 x 2 = 4 is really just knowing that 2 x 2 = 4. Reid prefers not to use "memory" for both semantic/factual and episodic/personal "memories" as this can confuse the terminology. For example, I "remember" that my family visited Catalina when I was a young child, though I have no episodic memory of the trip. Reid would say that it's more accurate to claim that I know that the trip happened, and that I went to Catalina as a child, but not that I remember it. "Remembering that" I went to Catalina, in that case, is more like "remembering that" 2 x 2 = 4 than like remembering that I had a protein shake for breakfast this morning. The key difference is that I actually remember drinking ("F-ing") the shake (episodically), unlike Catalina, where I have no memory of going ("F-ing").

[55] Given what "F-ing" usually means in everyday language, this terminology might be unfortunate, or else amusing, but it's the standard way it is expressed in the philosophical literature…

succession vitally united to the same organized body."[56] A "person," however, is not the same thing as a "man." A "person" is a thinking thing, typified by consciousness, and established by continuity of memory. What makes a person the *same* person over time is that continuity of memory—something which could be established whether the memories are housed in a purely physical substance or an immaterial soul.

> *The question being what makes the same person; and not whether it be the same identical substance, which always thinks in the same person, which, in this case, matters not at all: different substances, by the same consciousness (where they do partake in it) being united into one person, as well as different bodies by the same life are united into one animal, whose identity is preserved in that change of substances by the unity of one continued life. For, it being the same consciousness that makes a man be himself to himself, personal identity depends on that only, whether it be annexed solely to one individual substance, or can be continued in a succession of several substances. For as far as any intelligent being can repeat the idea of any past action with the same consciousness it had of it at first, and with the same consciousness it has of any present action; so far it is the same personal self. For it is by the consciousness it has of its present thoughts and actions, that it is self to itself now, and so will be the same self, as far as the same consciousness can extend to actions past or to come. and would be by distance of time, or change of substance, no more two persons, than a man be two men by wearing other clothes to-day than he did yesterday, with a long or a short sleep between: the same consciousness uniting those distant actions into the same person, whatever substances contributed to their production.*[57]

On the surface, this "memory criterion" for personal identity seems fairly straightforward and intuitively plausible. I am the same person I was an hour ago because I remember waiting in line at the Post Office an hour ago (as of the time of writing this sentence). I am the same person I was yesterday because I remember what I did yesterday. I am the same person I was in 1994 because I remember graduating from High School in that year. So far, so good. A problem immediately arises, though, when we realize just how many moments of time, presumably from our own past, that we *don't* remember. Locke himself raises this same concern.

> *Consciousness makes personal identity. But it is further inquired, whether it be the same identical substance. This few would think they had reason to doubt of, if these perceptions, with their consciousness, always remained present in the mind, whereby the same thinking thing would be always consciously present, and, as would be thought, evidently the same to itself. But that which seems to make the difficulty is this, that this consciousness being interrupted always by forgetfulness, there being no moment of our lives wherein we have the whole train of all our past actions before our eyes in one view, but even the best memories losing the sight of one part whilst they are viewing another; and we sometimes, and that the greatest part of our lives, not reflecting on our past selves, being intent on our present thoughts, and in sound sleep having no thoughts at all, or at least none with that consciousness which remarks our waking thoughts,- I say, in all these cases, our consciousness being interrupted, and we losing the sight of our past selves, doubts are raised whether we are the same thinking thing, i.e. the same*

[56] *Essay* II, xxvii.6.

[57] *Essay*, Book 2, XXVII.10.

> *substance or no.*[58]

The issue with which we are now dealing is "ruptures" in consciousness and memory. No matter how good your memory, it should go without saying that there are periods of your life that you do not currently remember. You probably don't remember much of your early childhood. You almost certainly remember nothing of being born—let alone your time as a fetus in the womb! At the very least, you don't remember several hours' of each day because you are asleep and unconscious during those hours. According to Locke, these concerns,

> *Which, however reasonable or unreasonable, concerns not personal identity at all. The question being what makes the same person; and not whether it be the same identical substance, which always thinks in the same person, which, in this case, matters not at all: different substances, by the same consciousness (where they do partake in it) being united into one person, as well as different bodies by the same life are united into one animal, whose identity is preserved in that change of substances by the unity of one continued life. For, it being the same consciousness that makes a man be himself to himself, personal identity depends on that only, whether it be annexed solely to one individual substance, or can be continued in a succession of several substances. For as far as any intelligent being can repeat the idea of any past action with the same consciousness it had of it at first, and with the same consciousness it has of any present action; so far it is the same personal self. For it is by the consciousness it has of its present thoughts and actions, that it is self to itself now, and so will be the same self, as far as the same consciousness can extend to actions past or to come. and would be by distance of time, or change of substance, no more two persons, than a man be two men by wearing other clothes to-day than he did yesterday, with a long or a short sleep between: the same consciousness uniting those distant actions into the same person, whatever substances contributed to their production.*[59]

With regard to "ruptures" of consciousness resulting from sleep, Locke seems to think they are of no importance. The fact that there seems to be an experience of consciousness, followed by a "rupture," then followed by another experience of consciousness united by common memories allows us to be confident that it is the person, in each case, in the same sort of way that we could be so confident if the rupture were much longer, and the result of reincarnation. In Locke's view, gaps of hundreds or even thousands of years (if possible) present no challenge to personal identity, so long as there are shared memories. A gap of just a few years, by comparison, is even easier to accommodate!

Of course, the "ruptures" or "gaps" mentioned were not only those resulting from loss of consciousness, such as in sleep. There was also the issue that there are certain parts of each of our lives that we just can't remember anymore. Recall Locke's phrasing: "For as far as any intelligent being can repeat the idea of any past action with the same consciousness it had of it at first, and with the same consciousness it has of any present action; so far it is the same personal self."

There are a couple of interpretation of that memory criterion, depending on how we wish to interpret the word "can." One interpretation of "can" requires something like immediate access to memories. In this stringent sense, I "can" remember my 10th birthday only in the event that I can, at this very moment, call to mind an experiential memory of that occasion. By that standard, my 10th birthday represents a "rupture," because I can't recall it in that manner. If this is our interpretation of "can," then our lives are riddled with countless ruptures, and Locke's memory

[58] Ibid.

[59] Ibid.

criterion seems to fail to be effective upon even a surface examination. For that reason, a looser interpretation of "can" is recommended by Locke's supporters.

I have lots of memories that I can't access at this very moment, but that I *could* access with a bit of help. We all experience something like this when, as a result of a conversation and some prompting, we suddenly recall something that we couldn't remember before. I can't remember my 10th birthday, but if my mother were to show me some photographs of that day, and have a conversation with me about it, I suspect that the memories would resurface. Perhaps in extreme cases something like hypnosis could be used to trigger forgotten memories. The point is that if we allow "can" to mean something like a "capability," we will eliminate many, if not most, of those "ruptures" resulting from poor memory.

There might be some periods of our life that we literally *can't* recall, no matter how much prompting we receive, no matter how many conversations, no matter how many photos we're offered. In such extreme cases, Locke claims that there really is a legitimate rupture in personal identity.

> *Suppose I wholly lose the memory of some parts of my life, beyond a possibility of retrieving them, so that perhaps I shall never be conscious of them again; yet am I not the same person that did those actions, had those thoughts that I once was conscious of, though I have now forgot them? To which I answer, that we must here take notice what the word I is applied to; which, in this case, is the man only. And the same man being presumed to be the same person, I is easily here supposed to stand also for the same person. But if it be possible for the same man to have distinct incommunicable consciousness at different times, it is past doubt the same man would at different times make different persons; . . .*[60]

I don't know that there's any amount of hypnosis or viewing of ultrasounds (assuming one is available) that would allow you to remember the time you spent as a fetus in your mother's womb. I suspect the brain isn't even capable of forming enduring first-person experiential memories at that stage of development. Indeed, it's questionable whether a "person" exists at all, at that stage of life—let alone one who could endure in terms of a continuity of consciousness. In that case, Locke would say that while you (today) and you (as a fetus) are the same "man," in that you are the same biological organism united by continuous life, you are not the same "person." Similarly, if I were to experience a serious brain injury such that certain memories were literally destroyed, and it was literally impossible for me to recall anything of my life prior to my accident, then, in a serious (and tragic!) sort of way, I really would be a different person after the accident than I was before—even though I would be the same "man."

The psychological state criterion is arguably the most popular of the criteria in philosophical circles, though it, too, is subject to criticism—especially when memory in considered central. Reid provides an example of such a criticism when he points out a "transitivity problem" for memory as a criterion of personal identity.

> *Suppose a brave officer to have been flogged when a boy at school for robbing an orchard, to have taken a standard from the enemy in his first campaign, and to have been made a general in advanced life; suppose, also, which must be admitted to be possible, that, when he took the standard, he was conscious of his having been flogged at school, and that, when made a general, he was conscious of his taking the standard, but had absolutely lost the consciousness of his flogging.*
>
> *These things being supposed, it follows,*

[60] *Essay*, Book 2, XXVII.20

from Mr. Locke's doctrine, that he who was flogged at school is the same person who took the standard, and that he who took the standard is the same person who was made a general. Whence it follows, if there be any truth in logic, that the general is the same person with him who was flogged at school. But the general's consciousness does not reach so far back as his flogging; therefore, according to Mr. Locke's doctrine, he is not the person who was flogged. Therefore the general is, and at the same time is not, the same person with him who was flogged at school.[61]

Consider the following adaptation of Reid's example: Ted (Y) who enrolled at Claremont McKenna College in 1994 remembers Ted (X) who moved to California in 1984. Ted (Z) who wrote a chapter on personal identity in 2015 remembers enrolling at CMC, but not moving to California. Using continuity of memory as our standard, X and Y are the same; Y and Z are the same; but X and Z are *not* the same. The problem with this is that identity is transitive, though memory continuity seems not to be. An illustration of transitivity might help.

- Ted is shorter than Ken
- Cole is shorter than Ted
- Therefore, Cole is shorter than Ken

If that seemed "logical" to you, you're right! If Ted is shorter than Ken, and Cole is shorter than Ted, then it must be the case that Cole is shorter than Ken as well. But, in our "problem case" of personal identity, something different seems to happen.

- X = 1984 Ted
- Y = 1994 Ted
- Z = 2015 Ted
- X is Y = 1984 Ted is the same person as 1994 Ted
- Y is Z = 1994 Ted is the same person as 2015 Ted
- X is not Z = 1984 Ted is not the same person as 2015 Ted

So, even though 1984 Ted is the same as 1994 Ted, and 1994 Ted is the same as 2015 Ted, somehow 1984 Ted is not the same as 2015 Ted. If you're confused, you should be, according to this criticism.

Also, if memory establishes personal identity, then any lapse of memory is a rupture of identity. To be honest, although I retain some memories of my childhood (specific events, family vacations, traumatic incidents, etc.), most of my childhood is lost to the fog of forgetfulness. I don't recall *anything*, for example, about my 10th birthday. Does that mean that I was a different person on that birthday? Does this criterion mean that for countless segments of "your" life (that you don't remember), including all the time you have been asleep in your life, "you" were someone else!

In fairness to Locke, some small modifications to his criterion are possible and they might help with this issue. We already considered one such modification in the Locke section above, in which we consider that someone "can" recall an event loosely, in terms of it not being impossible (i.e., it is at least possible the person could remember the event, given some prompting).

Contemporary supporters of Locke could also "soften" his requirements by claiming that persistent personal identity doesn't require a literally unbroken chain of vivid first-person experiential memories. A strict application of the memory requirement would mean that, at best, and on a typical day, I am "Ted" from approximately 5 AM until 9:30 PM, then not-Ted from 9:30 PM until 5 AM the next day. Also, since I don't remember eating lunch last Wednesday (though I'm confident that I did), my identity was "ruptured" last Wednesday—and countless other times as well, no doubt.

Instead of such a stringent requirement, we

[61] Thomas Reid, *Essays on the Intellectual Powers of Man. Essay* Three: Of Memory. Chapter 4: Of Identity. 1785.

might employ a revised memory criterion that requires only "psychological continuity." Going back to our previous example, this revised requirement establishes persistent identity between 1984 Ted, 1994 Ted, and 2015 Ted so long as there exists an overlapping chain of *some* direct memories. So long as 2015 Ted has *some* memories of 2014, 2013, 2012, etc., stretching back to 1984, then psychological continuity between 1984 Ted and 2015 has been established—and this should be enough for persistent identity (according to this revised standard). I don't have to recall every minute of every day for the last 30 years in order to be considered the same person (fundamentally) as I was back in 1984. So long as some memories pertaining to each of the intervening years exist, the connection exists. If, for some reason, I literally had no memories at all of the span of time between 1996 and 1998, then something strange has happened, and we might legitimately claim that an identity rupture took place. That doesn't necessarily mean that 2015 Ted is not the same as 1994 Ted, but at the very least it seems like "Ted" was interrupted from 1996 to 1998, and perhaps "rebooted" after that lapse.

Another possible revision shifts away from Locke's exclusive emphasis on memory, and includes other kinds of psychological connections as well. Maintaining a connected body of beliefs (i.e., a "worldview") over time, for example, or maintaining a consistent set of basic desires, intentions, and values over time, as another example, in addition to memory, could serve to establish psychological continuity.

Certainly such things are subject to change over time, just as our bodies are. We're all continually adding beliefs to our worldview (or revising them), and our goals, values, and desires change as we mature and acquire new life experiences. When I was a child, I "intended" to be a zoo-keeper, then a lawyer, then a doctor, then a businessman, then a foreign service employee, then a lawyer again, and then eventually a philosophy professor. For nearly 15 years of my life, I was a dedicated vegetarian, but am not currently a vegetarian anymore. My political values have shifted over time, sometimes to the "right," and sometimes to the "left."

Much as the body criterion can be challenged by the problem of bodily change (and possibly overcome such challenges), so too can the psychological continuity criterion be challenged by memory lapses, or changes in psychological connections. Defenders of the psychological continuity criterion believe that memory lapses and (gradual) changes to psychological features can be reasonably accommodated, but critics (such as Reid) will argue that such challenges are too daunting, and signal that a different criterion is needed.

Reid

To accommodate concerns about bodily change, half-brains, memory lapses, and changing psychological traits, some philosophers have proposed using none of those things as the criterion for personal identity. "I" am neither my body, nor my brain, nor my memories, nor my personality traits or values (etc.). Instead, I am something that *has* or displays all of those things. Changes or ruptures in those things no more threatens my persistent identity than does changing a pair of shoes on my feet. All of those things might be *evidence* of who am I, and that I am the same person, but none of those things is a worthy candidate for what *makes* me the same person, over time.

This alternative interpretation of personal identity is sometimes called "absolute," or "strict," or "simple," or even "common sense" identity. Indeed, Reid says of this view: "The conviction which every man has of his identity, as far back as his memory reaches, needs no aid of philosophy to strengthen it; and no philosophy can weaken it, without first producing some degree of insanity."[62]

[62] Thomas Reid, *Essays* on the Intellectual Powers of Man. *Essay* Three: Of Memory. Chapter 4: Of Identity. 1785.

This view, or something like it, is espoused by Plato and Descartes (among others)—though, for our purposes, we will focus on the account offered by Reid.

Reid thinks that the self is a simple, immaterial substance with various active powers. He also thinks that (strict) identity only applies to substances without parts and with uninterrupted existence. In effect, only "personal identity" is *real* identity. All other uses of "identity" are convenient uses of speech.

Reid disagrees with Locke with regard to the importance of memory, and thinks that memory is not necessary for identity since we all are, in fact, agents or witnesses to events that we can't (episodically) remember. Reid's example is that he knows who "suckled" him, though he doesn't remember it.

Memory, in addition to not being necessary for identity, is also not sufficient for identity, since it isn't the recollection of an episodic memory that *makes* you the same person who witnessed the event.

> *To say that my remembering that I did such a thing, or, as some choose to express it, my being conscious that I did it, makes me to have done it, appears to me as great an absurdity as it would be to say, that my belief that the world was created made it to be created.*[63]

Reid and Locke both agree that memory and consciousness are fleeting and non-continuous, but personal identity is supposed to be continuous and uninterrupted. From Reid's perspective, using memory as our criterion reduces identity to diversity—destroying the very identity it was trying to establish. Instead, Reid thinks identity is to be located in *that which* remembers and thinks. Memory doesn't create identity, though it does provide evidence for it.

> *It is very true, that my remembrance that I did such a thing is the evidence I have that I am the identical person who did it. . . .*[64]

For Reid, if S remembers at time Ti (episodically) an event at time T_1, then S must have existed at time T_1. Episodic memory is logically sufficient for establishing personal identity at the time in question. This evidence is "immediate." It's not that I recall F-ing at time T_1 and then infer from that that it was I who F'd at time T_1. The inference is already contained in the episodic memory itself.

The "I" of identity is a single, unified "thing" at any given time. This "I" may experience multiple sensations at once, or in succession, but is identical to none of those sensations. Rather, it is that which *has* the sensations in the first place, and that which unites them into experiences of a single person.

> *My personal identity, therefore, implies the continued existence of that indivisible thing which I call myself. Whatever this self may be, it is something which thinks, and deliberates, and resolves, and acts, and suffers. I am not thought, I am not action, I am not feeling; I am something that thinks, and acts, and suffers. My thoughts, and actions, and feelings, change every moment: they have no continued, but a successive, existence; but that self, or I, to which they belong, is permanent, and has the same relation to all the succeeding thoughts, actions, and feelings which I call mine.*[65]

This "I" is often (though not necessarily) understood in terms of substance dualism, where the "I" is an immaterial soul or ego.[66] Reid thinks that a person has no parts, and is therefore a

---

[63] Ibid.

[64] Ibid.

[65] Ibid.

[66] For a defense of substance dualism in general, and the view that bodies and minds are distinct substances, see the Reid section of the Free Will Chapter of this book—particularly the section dealing with Leibniz's Law of Identity.

metaphysically simple substance.

> *A part of a person is a manifest absurdity. When a man loses his estate, his health, his strength, he is still the same person, and has lost nothing of his personality. If he has a leg or an arm cut off, he is the same person he was before. The amputated member is no part of his person, otherwise it would have a right to a part of his estate, and be liable for a part of his engagements. It would be entitled to a share of his merit and demerit, which is manifestly absurd. A person is something indivisible, and is what Leibniz calls a monad.*[67]

Don't be intimidated or confused by the reference to "monads." A monad, as coined by Leibniz, is an indivisible, immaterial substance that was offered as an alternative to the atomism popular in Leibniz's time. A possibly helpful (if not still mysterious) way of thinking about "monads" is to replace them with the popular notion of "souls." Souls, assuming they exist, are regarded as immaterial, as opposed to physical. As immaterial, they have no physical properties (e.g., mass, weight, color, size, etc.). As indivisible, they have no parts. It sounds strange to speak of the soul as having a "right side" or a "left side," or to speak of "half" of a soul. Reid similar calls it "absurd" to speak of part of a person. Persons *are* souls, and are no more divisible than are souls. What makes a person the same person over time is the continuous existence of that same soul, which is the bearer of our various psychological states (including memories). Neither changes to the body nor changes to memories are threats to enduring personal identity, since the same soul persists throughout any such change.

Both Locke and Reid agree that there is an enduring self, although they disagree as to its nature and how it persists. As an alternative to each of the preceding views on personal identity, we have the "bundle" view, most commonly associated with David Hume, according to which there is no enduring self at all! Personal identity is an illusion perpetrated by the imagination.

Hume

Hume discusses personal identity in two places: Section VI, Part IV, Book I of *The Treatise of Human Nature*," and in an appendix published in another edition of that same book a year later.[68]

For Hume, persistent personal identity is an illusion, a fiction created by the imagination. It is not merely the identity of persons that fail to persist over time, for Hume, but the identity of all things, since our experience of change is inconsistent with our notion of identity: the idea of an object which "remains invariable and uninterrupted thro' a suppos'd variation of time."[69] Identity implies duration, but duration implies change, and that means that genuine (strict) persistent identity is a contradiction in terms!

Our notion of identity, whether in objects or in persons, is produced (as a mistake!) by the same psychological mechanism.

> *The identity, which we ascribe to the mind of man, is only a fictitious one, and of a like kind with that which we ascribe to vegetables and animal bodies. It cannot, therefore, have a different origin, but must proceed from a like operation of the imagination upon like objects.*[70]

According to Hume, we actually experience distinct (discrete) perceptions, but an act of the imagination blends them into a "single" continuous object. By way of analogy, when we watch an animated show, what we are "really" seeing is a series individual drawings. The first 13

---

[67] Reid.

[68] In the appendix, Hume declares himself dissatisfied with the account he previously offered, but confesses that he doesn't know how to make it better.

[69] David Hume, *A Treatise of Human Nature* (1739), Book I, Part IV, Section VI.

[70] Ibid.

seasons of the Simpsons were made with hand-drawn animated cells (before switching to computer animation). For every *second* of the cartoon, 24 images are presented. They are presented to us so rapidly, though, that we don't experience them as 24 distinct pictures, but as one continuous image.

> *In order to justify to ourselves this absurdity, we often feign some new and unintelligible principle, that connects the objects together, and prevents their interruption or variation. Thus we feign the continu'd existence of the perceptions of our senses, to remove the interruption: and run into the notion of a soul, and self, and substance, to disguise the variation. But we may farther observe, that where we do not give rise to such a fiction, our propension to confound identity with relation is so great, that we are apt to imagine something unknown and mysterious, connecting the parts, beside their relation; and this I take to be the case with regard to the identity we ascribe to plants and vegetables. And even when this does not take place, we still feel a propensity to confound these ideas, tho' we are not able fully to satisfy ourselves in that particular, nor find anything invariable and uninterrupted to justify our notion of identity.*[71]

This misunderstood act of the imagination is also the source of our (mistaken) belief in an enduring substance like a "soul."

> *Thus the controversy concerning identity is not merely a dispute of words. For when we attribute identity, in an improper sense, to variable or interrupted objects, our mistake is not confin'd to the expression, but is commonly attended with a fiction, either of something invariable and uninterrupted, or of something mysterious and inexplicable, or at least with a propensity to such fictions.*[72]

And:

> *That action of the imagination, by which we consider the uninterrupted and invariable object, and that by which we reflect on the succession of related objects, are almost the same to the feeling, nor is there much more effort of thought requir'd in the latter case than in the former. The relation facilitates the transition of the mind from one object to another, and renders its passage as smooth as if it contemplated one continu'd object. This resemblance is the cause of the confusion and mistake, and makes us substitute the notion of identity, instead of that of related objects. However at one instant we may consider the related succession as variable or interrupted, we are sure the next to ascribe to it a perfect identity, and regard it as enviable and uninterrupted.*[73]

We might understand Hume's view as claiming that what we mistakenly regard as a continuous, enduring self is more like a Simpson's episode: a rapidly experienced series of distinct perceptions that get blended together by the imagination in such a way that we think there is a single thing that has existed throughout the whole sequence.

On a related note: for Hume there are "impressions" and "ideas." He argued that *legitimate* ideas are those that arise from impressions (e.g., a sense impression). With regard to personal identity, Hume observes that we have no impression of a "self." Hume claims he never has any perception corresponding to that notion, never has any perception of a single thing that he identifies as the "self."

---

[71] Ibid.

[72] Ibid.

[73] Ibid.

For my part, when I enter most intimately into what I call myself, I always stumble on some particular perception or other, of heat or cold, light or shade, love or hatred, pain or pleasure. I never can catch myself at any time without a perception, and never can observe anything but the perception. When my perceptions are remov'd for any time, as by sound sleep; so long am I insensible of myself, and may truly be said not to exist. And were all my perceptions remov'd by death, and cou'd I neither think, nor feel, nor see, nor love, nor hate after the dissolution of my body, I shou'd be entirely annihilated, nor do I conceive what is farther requisite to make me a perfect non-entity. If anyone, upon serious and unprejudic'd reflection thinks he has a different notion of himself, I must confess I can reason no longer with him. All I can allow him is, that he may be in the right as well as I, and that we are essentially different in this particular. He may, perhaps, perceive something simple and continu'd, which he calls himself; tho' I am certain there is no such principle in me.

But setting aside some metaphysicians of this kind, I may venture to affirm of the rest of mankind, that they are nothing but a bundle or collection of different perceptions, which succeed each other with an inconceivable rapidity, and are in a perpetual flux and movement. Our eyes cannot turn in their sockets without varying our perceptions. Our thought is still more variable than our sight; and all our other senses and faculties contribute to this change; nor is there any single power of the soul, which remains unalterably the same, perhaps for one moment. The mind is a kind of theatre, where several perceptions successively make their appearance; pass, re-pass, glide away, and mingle in an infinite variety of postures and situations. There is properly no simplicity in it at one time, nor identity in different; whatever natural propension we may have to imagine that simplicity and identity. The comparison of the theatre must not mislead us. They are the successive perceptions only, that constitute the mind; nor have we the most distant notion of the place, where these scenes are represented, or of the materials, of which it is compos'd.[74]

From where, then, could the idea of a "self" arise? Only as an idea formed by the imagination—which means that our idea of the self is not "legitimate." The "self" is not a distinct, single enduring substance—nor anything at all, for that matter! Instead, "we" are merely bundles of impressions, a varying succession of perceptions "which succeed each other with an inconceivable rapidity, and are in a perpetual flux and movement." He compares the mind to a theatre, suggesting that our various perceptions are like actors appearing and disappearing from the stage—though he is quick to caution us against reading too much into the theatre analogy. We are not to think that the "self" might be the theatre itself, or the stage, or a patron viewing the show. "They are the successive perceptions only, that constitute the mind; nor have we the most distant notion of the place, where these scenes are represented, or of the materials, of which it is compos'd." So, the mind is like a theatre, but very much unlike a theatre!

A possible problem with Hume's view is that it's by no means obvious that Hume should know what a perception of the self would be, or feel like. It's possible that he perceives the "self" all the time, but just doesn't recognize it. Moreover, it seems problematic to expect to "see" the self at all, given that the self is the very thing doing the seeing! Except with the help of mirrors or photos, I never see my own eyeballs—but that's because they are the very organs doing the seeing! Even in a world without reflective surfaces, it would seem

---

[74] Ibid.

odd to deny the existence of eyeballs just because we can never see them directly.

Another possible problem with Hume's view concerns how it is that these perceptions get "bundled" in the way they apparently do. Presumably, if you and I are in the same perceptual situation, our perceptions will be similar to each other's (e.g., if we're both in a theatre watching the same movie, we're both going to be seeing similar things, such as whatever is being projected on to the screen). Why do I not regard some of *your* perceptions as "mine" (and vice versa)? We presume that we have separate minds, with separate "bundles" of experiences, but what accounts for the distinct "bundling" if there is no enduring self that can gather a group of perceptions into a single "bundle?" According to Hume's account, the mind surveys a bundle of impressions and then mistakenly imagines the existence of a single, unified, enduring self—but if that is a mistake, *what is making the mistake*, if not the self? Indeed, when Hume says (of himself) "I never catch myself," he seems to be presupposing the self in the very mention of the "I" that never catches itself!

Summary

We have now considered a variety of interpretations regarding the persistence of personal identity. Hume proposes that such identity is an illusion, while other philosophers disagreed as to the best way to establish identity. We considered both the body and brain criteria, but focused on the psychological state/memory criterion popularized by Locke, and the "simple" view offered by Reid. Which of those interpretations, if any, is best, is left for you to decide.

Whether or not the same self persists over time is only one portion of the cluster of issues concerning personal identity, though. Other issues concern how the self is formed, and who (or what) is responsible for that formation. The next chapter will focus on those questions under two broad headings: social-construction and self-fashioning.

John Locke (1632-1704) was a profound influential philosopher, in general. In 1689, Locked published An Essay Concerning Human Understanding, from which the following is an excerpt. In this section, he establishes the various criteria for identity of various substances, ultimately arguing that continued consciousness, as established by memory, is what establishes the identity of a person over time.

John Locke
An Essay Concerning Human Understanding

Book 2
Chapter XXVII
Of Identity and Diversity

1. Wherein identity consists. Another occasion the mind often takes of comparing, is the very being of things, when, considering anything as existing at any determined time and place, we compare it with itself existing at another time, and thereon form the ideas of identity and diversity. When we see anything to be in any place in any instant of time, we are sure (be it what it will) that it is that very thing, and not another which at that same time exists in another place, how like and undistinguishable soever it may be in all other respects: and in this consists identity, when the ideas it is attributed to vary not at all from what they were that moment wherein we consider their former existence, and to which we compare the present. For we never finding, nor conceiving it possible, that two things of the same kind should exist in the same place at the same time, we rightly conclude, that, whatever exists anywhere at any time, excludes all of the same kind, and is there itself alone. When therefore we demand whether anything be the same or no, it refers always to something that existed such a time in such a place, which it was certain, at that instant, was the same with itself, and no other. From whence it follows, that one thing cannot have two beginnings of existence, nor two things one beginning; it being impossible for two things of the same kind to be or exist in the same instant, in the very same place; or one and the same thing in different places. That, therefore, that had one beginning, is the same thing; and that which had a different beginning in time and place from that, is not the same, but diverse. That which has made the difficulty about this relation has been the little care and attention used in having precise notions of the things to which it is attributed.

2. Identity of substances. We have the ideas but of three sorts of substances: 1. God. 2. Finite intelligences. 3. Bodies.

First, God is without beginning, eternal, unalterable, and everywhere, and therefore concerning his identity there can be no doubt.

Secondly, Finite spirits having had each its determinate time and place of beginning to exist, the relation to that time and place will always determine to each of them its identity, as long as it exists.

Thirdly, The same will hold of every particle of matter, to which no addition or subtraction of matter being made, it is the same. For, though these three sorts of substances, as we term them, do not exclude one another out of the same place, yet we cannot conceive but that they must necessarily each of them exclude any of the same kind out of the same place: or else the notions and names of identity and diversity would be in vain, and there could be no such distinctions of substances, or anything else one from another. For example: could two bodies be in the same place at the same time; then those two parcels of matter must be one and the same, take them great or little; nay, all bodies must be one and the same. For, by the same reason that two particles of matter may be in one place, all bodies may be in one place: which, when it can be supposed, takes away the distinction of identity and diversity of one and more, and renders it ridiculous. But it being a contradiction that two or more should be one, identity and diversity are relations and ways of comparing well founded, and of use to the understanding.

Identity of modes and relations. All other things being but modes or relations ultimately terminated in substances, the identity and diversity of each particular existence of them too will be by the same way determined: only as to things whose existence is in succession, such as are the actions of finite beings, v.g. motion and thought, both which consist in a continued train of succession, concerning their diversity there can be no question: because each perishing the moment it begins, they cannot exist in different times, or in different places, as permanent beings can at different times exist in distant places; and therefore no motion or thought, considered as at different times, can be the same, each part thereof having a different beginning of existence.

3. Principium Individuationis. From what has been said, it is easy to discover what is so much inquired after, the principium individuationis; and that, it is plain, is existence itself; which determines a being of any sort to a particular time and place, incommunicable to two beings of the same kind. This, though it seems easier to conceive in simple substances or modes; yet, when reflected on, is not more difficult in compound ones, if care be taken to what it is applied: v.g. let us suppose an atom, i.e. a continued body under one immutable superficies, existing in a determined time and place; it is evident, that, considered in any instant of its existence, it is in that instant the same with itself. For, being at that instant what it is, and nothing else, it is the same, and so must continue as long as its existence is continued; for so long it will be the same, and no other. In like manner, if two or more atoms be joined together into the same mass, every one of those atoms will be the same, by the foregoing rule: and whilst they exist united together, the mass, consisting of the same atoms, must be the same mass, or the same body, let the parts be ever so differently jumbled. But if one of these atoms be taken away, or one new one added, it is no longer the same mass or the same body. In the state of living creatures, their identity depends not on a mass of the same particles, but on something else. For in them the variation of great parcels of matter alters not the identity: an oak growing from a plant to a great tree, and then lopped, is still the same oak; and a colt grown up to a horse, sometimes fat, sometimes lean, is all the while the same horse: though, in both these cases, there may be a manifest change of the parts; so that truly they are not either of them the same masses of matter, though they be truly one of them the same oak, and the other the same horse. The reason whereof is, that, in these two cases- a mass of matter and a living body- identity is not applied to the same thing.

4. Identity of vegetables. We must therefore consider wherein an oak differs from a mass of matter, and that seems to me to be in this, that the one is only the cohesion of particles of matter any how united, the other such a disposition of them as constitutes the parts of an oak; and such an organization of those parts as is fit to receive and distribute nourishment, so as to continue and frame the wood, bark, and leaves, &c., of an oak, in which consists the vegetable life. That being then one plant which has such an organization of parts in one coherent body, partaking of one common life, it continues to be the same plant as long as it partakes of the same life, though that life be communicated to new particles of matter vitally united to the living plant, in a like continued organization conformable to that sort of plants.

For this organization, being at any one instant in any one collection of matter, is in that particular concrete distinguished from all other, and is that individual life, which existing constantly from that moment both forwards and backwards, in the same continuity of insensibly succeeding parts united to the living body of the plant, it has that identity which makes the same plant, and all the parts of it, parts of the same plant, during all the time that they exist united in that continued organization, which is fit to convey that common life to all the parts so united.

5. Identity of animals. The case is not so much different in brutes but that any one may hence see what makes an animal and continues it the same. Something we have like this in machines, and may serve to illustrate it. For example, what is a watch? It is plain it is nothing but a fit organization or construction of parts to a certain end, which, when a sufficient force is added to it, it is capable to attain. If we would suppose this machine one continued body, all whose organized parts were repaired, increased, or diminished by a constant addition or separation of insensible parts, with one common life, we should have something very much like the body of an animal; with this difference, That, in an animal the fitness of the organization, and the motion wherein life consists, begin together, the motion coming from within; but in machines the force coming sensibly from without, is often away when the organ is in order, and well fitted to receive it.

6. The identity of man. This also shows wherein the identity of the same man consists; viz. in nothing but a participation of the same continued life, by constantly fleeting particles of matter, in succession vitally united to the same organized body. He that shall place the identity of man in anything else, but, like that of other animals, in one fitly organized body, taken in any one instant, and from thence continued, under one organization of life, in several successively fleeting particles of matter united to it, will find it hard to make an embryo, one of years, mad and sober, the same man, by any supposition, that will not make it possible for Seth, Ismael, Socrates, Pilate, St. Austin, and Caesar Borgia, to be the same man. For if the identity of soul alone makes the same man; and there be nothing in the nature of matter why the same individual spirit may not be united to different bodies, it will be possible that those men, living in distant ages, and of different tempers, may have been the same man: which way of speaking must be from a very strange use of the word man, applied to an idea out of which body and shape are excluded. And that way of speaking would agree yet worse with the notions of those philosophers who allow of transmigration, and are of opinion that the souls of men may, for their miscarriages, be detruded into the bodies of beasts, as fit habitations, with organs suited to the satisfaction of their brutal inclinations. But yet I think nobody, could he be sure that the soul of Heliogabalus were in one of his hogs, would yet say that hog were a man or Heliogabalus.

7. Idea of identity suited to the idea it is applied to. It is not therefore unity of substance that comprehends all sorts of identity, or will determine it in every case; but to conceive and judge of it aright, we must consider what idea the word it is applied to stands for: it being one thing to be the same substance, another the same man, and a third the same person, if person, man, and substance, are three names standing for three different ideas;- for such as is the idea belonging to that name, such must be the identity; which, if it had been a little more carefully attended to, would possibly have prevented a great deal of that confusion which often occurs about this matter, with no small seeming difficulties, especially concerning personal identity, which therefore we shall in the next place a little consider.

8. Same man. An animal is a living organized body; and consequently the same animal, as we have observed, is the same continued life communicated to different particles of matter, as they happen successively to be united to that organized living body. And whatever is talked of other definitions, ingenious observation puts it past doubt, that the idea in our minds, of which the

sound man in our mouths is the sign, is nothing else but of an animal of such a certain form. Since I think I may be confident, that, whoever should see a creature of his own shape or make, though it had no more reason all its life than a cat or a parrot, would call him still a man; or whoever should hear a cat or a parrot discourse, reason, and philosophize, would call or think it nothing but a cat or a parrot; and say, the one was a dull irrational man, and the other a very intelligent rational parrot. A relation we have in an author of great note, is sufficient to countenance the supposition of a rational parrot.

His words are: "I had a mind to know, from Prince Maurice's own mouth, the account of a common, but much credited story, that I had heard so often from many others, of an old parrot he had in Brazil, during his government there, that spoke, and asked, and answered common questions, like a reasonable creature: so that those of his train there generally concluded it to be witchery or possession; and one of his chaplains, who lived long afterwards in Holland, would never from that time endure a parrot, but said they all had a devil in them. I had heard many particulars of this story, and as severed by people hard to be discredited, which made me ask Prince Maurice what there was of it. He said, with his usual plainness and dryness in talk, there was something true, but a great deal false of what had been reported. I desired to know of him what there was of the first. He told me short and coldly, that he had heard of such an old parrot when he had been at Brazil; and though he believed nothing of it, and it was a good way off, yet he had so much curiosity as to send for it: that it was a very great and a very old one; and when it came first into the room where the prince was, with a great many Dutchmen about him, it said presently, What a company of white men are here! They asked it, what it thought that man was, pointing to the prince. It answered, Some General or other. When they brought it close to him, he asked it, D'ou venez-vous? It answered, De Marinnan. The Prince, A qui estes-vous? The Parrot, A un Portugais. The Prince, Que fais-tu la? Parrot, Je garde les poulles. The Prince laughed, and said, Vous gardez les poulles? The Parrot answered, Oui, moi; et je scai bien faire; and made the chuck four or five times that people use to make to chickens when they call them. I set down the words of this worthy dialogue in French, just as Prince Maurice said them to me. I asked him in what language the parrot spoke, and he said in Brazilian. I asked whether he understood Brazilian; he said No, but he had taken care to have two interpreters by him, the one a Dutchman that spoke Brazilian, and the other a Brazilian that spoke Dutch; that he asked them separately and privately, and both of them agreed in telling him just the same thing that the parrot had said. I could not but tell this odd story, because it is so much out of the way, and from the first hand, and what may pass for a good one; for I dare say this Prince at least believed himself in all he told me, having ever passed for a very honest and pious man: I leave it to naturalists to reason, and to other men to believe, as they please upon it; however, it is not, perhaps, amiss to relieve or enliven a busy scene sometimes with such digressions, whether to the purpose or no."

I have taken care that the reader should have the story at large in the author's own words, because he seems to me not to have thought it incredible; for it cannot be imagined that so able a man as he, who had sufficiency enough to warrant all the testimonies he gives of himself, should take so much pains, in a place where it had nothing to do, to pin so close, not only on a man whom he mentions as his friend, but on a Prince in whom he acknowledges very great honesty and piety, a story which, if he himself thought incredible, he could not but also think ridiculous. The Prince, it is plain, who vouches this story, and our author, who relates it from him, both of them call this talker a parrot: and I ask any one else who thinks such a story fit to be told, whether, if this parrot, and all of its kind, had always talked, as we have a prince's word for it this one did,- whether, I say, they would not have passed for a race of rational animals; but yet, whether, for all that, they would have been allowed to be men, and not parrots? For I presume it is not the idea of a thinking or rational being alone that makes the idea of a man in most people's sense: but of a body, so and so shaped, joined to it: and if that be the idea of a man, the same successive body not shifted all at once, must, as well as the same immaterial spirit, go to the making of the same man.

9. Personal identity. This being premised, to find wherein personal identity consists, we must consider what person stands for;- which, I think, is a thinking intelligent being, that has reason and reflection, and can consider itself as itself, the same thinking thing, in different times and places; which it does only by that consciousness which is inseparable from thinking, and, as it seems to me, essential to it: it being impossible for any one to perceive without perceiving that he does perceive. When we see, hear, smell, taste, feel, meditate, or will anything, we know that we do so. Thus it is always as to our present sensations and perceptions: and by this every one is to himself that which he calls self:- it not being considered, in this case, whether the same self be continued in the same or divers substances. For, since consciousness always accompanies thinking, and it is that which makes every one to be what he calls self, and thereby distinguishes himself from all other thinking things, in this alone consists personal identity, i.e. the sameness of a rational being: and as far as this consciousness can be extended backwards to any past action or thought, so far reaches the identity of that person; it is the same self now it was then; and it is by the same self with this present one that now reflects on it, that that action was done.

10. Consciousness makes personal identity. But it is further inquired, whether it be the same identical substance. This few would think they had reason to doubt of, if these perceptions, with their consciousness, always remained present in the mind, whereby the same thinking thing would be always consciously present, and, as would be thought, evidently the same to itself. But that which seems to make the difficulty is this, that this consciousness being interrupted always by forgetfulness, there being no moment of our lives wherein we have the whole train of all our past actions before our eyes in one view, but even the best memories losing the sight of one part whilst they are viewing another; and we sometimes, and that the greatest part of our lives, not reflecting on our past selves, being intent on our present thoughts, and in sound sleep having no thoughts at all, or at least none with that consciousness which remarks our waking thoughts,- I say, in all these cases, our consciousness being interrupted, and we losing the sight of our past selves, doubts are raised whether we are the same thinking thing, i.e. the same substance or no. Which, however reasonable or unreasonable, concerns not personal identity at all. The question being what makes the same person; and not whether it be the same identical substance, which always thinks in the same person, which, in this case, matters not at all: different substances, by the same consciousness (where they do partake in it) being united into one person, as well as different bodies by the same life are united into one animal, whose identity is preserved in that change of substances by the unity of one continued life. For, it being the same consciousness that makes a man be himself to himself, personal identity depends on that only, whether it be annexed solely to one individual substance, or can be continued in a succession of several substances. For as far as any intelligent being can repeat the idea of any past action with the same consciousness it had of it at first, and with the same consciousness it has of any present action; so far it is the same personal self. For it is by the consciousness it has of its present thoughts and actions, that it is self to itself now, and so will be the same self, as far as the same consciousness can extend to actions past or to come. and would be by distance of time, or change of substance, no more two persons, than a man be two men by wearing other clothes to-day than he did yesterday, with a long or a short sleep between: the same consciousness uniting those distant actions into the same person, whatever substances contributed to their production.

11. Personal identity in change of substance. That this is so, we have some kind of evidence in

our very bodies, all whose particles, whilst vitally united to this same thinking conscious self, so that we feel when they are touched, and are affected by, and conscious of good or harm that happens to them, as a part of ourselves; i.e. of our thinking conscious self. Thus, the limbs of his body are to every one a part of Himself; he sympathizes and is concerned for them. Cut off a hand, and thereby separate it from that consciousness he had of its heat, cold, and other affections, and it is then no longer a part of that which is himself, any more than the remotest part of matter. Thus, we see the substance whereof personal self consisted at one time may be varied at another, without the change of personal identity; there being no question about the same person, though the limbs which but now were a part of it, be cut off.

12. Personality in change of substance. But the question is, Whether if the same substance which thinks be changed, it can be the same person; or, remaining the same, it can be different persons?

And to this I answer: First, This can be no question at all to those who place thought in a purely material animal constitution, void of an immaterial substance. For, whether their supposition be true or no, it is plain they conceive personal identity preserved in something else than identity of substance; as animal identity is preserved in identity of life, and not of substance. And therefore those who place thinking in an immaterial substance only, before they can come to deal with these men, must show why personal identity cannot be preserved in the change of immaterial substances, or variety of particular immaterial substances, as well as animal identity is preserved in the change of material substances, or variety of particular bodies: unless they will say, it is one immaterial spirit that makes the same life in brutes, as it is one immaterial spirit that makes the same person in men; which the Cartesians at least will not admit, for fear of making brutes thinking things too.

13. Whether in change of thinking substances there can be one person. But next, as to the first part of the question, Whether, if the same thinking substance (supposing immaterial substances only to think) be changed, it can be the same person? I answer, that cannot be resolved but by those who know what kind of substances they are that do think; and whether the consciousness of past actions can be transferred from one thinking substance to another. I grant were the same consciousness the same individual action it could not: but it being a present representation of a past action, why it may not be possible, that that may be represented to the mind to have been which really never was, will remain to be shown. And therefore how far the consciousness of past actions is annexed to any individual agent, so that another cannot possibly have it, will be hard for us to determine, till we know what kind of action it is that cannot be done without a reflex act of perception accompanying it, and how performed by thinking substances, who cannot think without being conscious of it. But that which we call the same consciousness, not being the same individual act, why one intellectual substance may not have represented to it, as done by itself, what it never did, and was perhaps done by some other agent- why, I say, such a representation may not possibly be without reality of matter of fact, as well as several representations in dreams are, which yet whilst dreaming we take for true- will be difficult to conclude from the nature of things. And that it never is so, will by us, till we have clearer views of the nature of thinking substances, be best resolved into the goodness of God; who, as far as the happiness or misery of any of his sensible creatures is concerned in it, will not, by a fatal error of theirs, transfer from one to another that consciousness which draws reward or punishment with it. How far this may be an argument against those who would place thinking in a system of fleeting animal spirits, I leave to be considered. But yet, to return to the question before us, it must be allowed, that, if the same consciousness (which, as has been shown, is quite a different thing from the same numerical figure or motion in body) can be transferred from one thinking substance to another, it will be possible that two thinking substances may make but one

person. For the same consciousness being preserved, whether in the same or different substances, the personal identity is preserved.

14. Whether, the same immaterial substance remaining, there can be two persons. As to the second part of the question, Whether the same immaterial substance remaining, there may be two distinct persons; which question seems to me to be built on this,- Whether the same immaterial being, being conscious of the action of its past duration, may be wholly stripped of all the consciousness of its past existence, and lose it beyond the power of ever retrieving it again: and so as it were beginning a new account from a new period, have a consciousness that cannot reach beyond this new state. All those who hold pre-existence are evidently of this mind; since they allow the soul to have no remaining consciousness of what it did in that pre-existent state, either wholly separate from body, or informing any other body; and if they should not, it is plain experience would be against them. So that personal identity, reaching no further than consciousness reaches, a pre-existent spirit not having continued so many ages in a state of silence, must needs make different persons. Suppose a Christian Platonist or a Pythagorean should, upon God's having ended all his works of creation the seventh day, think his soul hath existed ever since; and should imagine it has revolved in several human bodies; as I once met with one, who was persuaded his had been the soul of Socrates (how reasonably I will not dispute; this I know, that in the post he filled, which was no inconsiderable one, he passed for a very rational man, and the press has shown that he wanted not parts or learning;)- would any one say, that he, being not conscious of any of Socrates's actions or thoughts, could be the same person with Socrates? Let any one reflect upon himself, and conclude that he has in himself an immaterial spirit, which is that which thinks in him, and, in the constant change of his body keeps him the same: and is that which he calls himself: let him also suppose it to be the same soul that was in Nestor or Thersites, at the siege of Troy, (for souls being, as far as we know anything of them, in their nature indifferent to any parcel of matter, the supposition has no apparent absurdity in it), which it may have been, as well as it is now the soul of any other man: but he now having no consciousness of any of the actions either of Nestor or Thersites, does or can he conceive himself the same person with either of them? Can he be concerned in either of their actions? attribute them to himself, or think them his own, more than the actions of any other men that ever existed? So that this consciousness, not reaching to any of the actions of either of those men, he is no more one self with either of them than if the soul or immaterial spirit that now informs him had been created, and began to exist, when it began to inform his present body; though it were never so true, that the same spirit that informed Nestor's or Thersites' body were numerically the same that now informs his. For this would no more make him the same person with Nestor, than if some of the particles of matter that were once a part of Nestor were now a part of this man; the same immaterial substance, without the same consciousness, no more making the same person, by being united to any body, than the same particle of matter, without consciousness, united to any body, makes the same person. But let him once find himself conscious of any of the actions of Nestor, he then finds himself the same person with Nestor.

15. The body, as well as the soul, goes to the making of a man. And thus may we be able, without any difficulty, to conceive the same person at the resurrection, though in a body not exactly in make or parts the same which he had here,- the same consciousness going along with the soul that inhabits it. But yet the soul alone, in the change of bodies, would scarce to any one but to him that makes the soul the man, be enough to make the same man. For should the soul of a prince, carrying with it the consciousness of the prince's past life, enter and inform the body of a cobbler, as soon as deserted by his own soul, every one sees he would be the same person with the prince, accountable only for the prince's actions: but who would say it was the same man? The body

too goes to the making the man, and would, I guess, to everybody determine the man in this case, wherein the soul, with all its princely thoughts about it, would not make another man: but he would be the same cobbler to every one besides himself. I know that, in the ordinary way of speaking, the same person, and the same man, stand for one and the same thing. And indeed every one will always have a liberty to speak as he pleases, and to apply what articulate sounds to what ideas he thinks fit, and change them as often as he pleases. But yet, when we will inquire what makes the same spirit, man, or person, we must fix the ideas of spirit, man, or person in our minds; and having resolved with ourselves what we mean by them, it will not be hard to determine, in either of them, or the like, when it is the same, and when not.

16. Consciousness alone unites actions into the same person. But though the same immaterial substance or soul does not alone, wherever it be, and in whatsoever state, make the same man; yet it is plain, consciousness, as far as ever it can be extended- should it be to ages past- unites existences and actions very remote in time into the same person, as well as it does the existences and actions of the immediately preceding moment: so that whatever has the consciousness of present and past actions, is the same person to whom they both belong. Had I the same consciousness that I saw the ark and Noah's flood, as that I saw an overflowing of the Thames last winter, or as that I write now, I could no more doubt that I who write this now, that saw' the Thames overflowed last winter, and that viewed the flood at the general deluge, was the same self,- place that self in what substance you please- than that I who write this am the same myself now whilst I write (whether I consist of all the same substance, material or immaterial, or no) that I was yesterday. For as to this point of being the same self, it matters not whether this present self be made up of the same or other substances- I being as much concerned, and as justly accountable for any action that was done a thousand years since, appropriated to me now by this self-consciousness, as I am for what I did the last moment.

17. Self depends on consciousness, not on substance. Self is that conscious thinking thing,- whatever substance made up of, (whether spiritual or material, simple or compounded, it matters not)- which is sensible or conscious of pleasure and pain, capable of happiness or misery, and so is concerned for itself, as far as that consciousness extends. Thus every one finds that, whilst comprehended under that consciousness, the little finger is as much a part of himself as what is most so. Upon separation of this little finger, should this consciousness go along with the little finger, and leave the rest of the body, it is evident the little finger would be the person, the same person; and self then would have nothing to do with the rest of the body. As in this case it is the consciousness that goes along with the substance, when one part is separate from another, which makes the same person, and constitutes this inseparable self: so it is in reference to substances remote in time. That with which the consciousness of this present thinking thing can join itself, makes the same person, and is one self with it, and with nothing else; and so attributes to itself, and owns all the actions of that thing, as its own, as far as that consciousness reaches, and no further; as every one who reflects will perceive.

18. Persons, not substances, the objects of reward and punishment. In this personal identity is founded all the right and justice of reward and punishment; happiness and misery being that for which every one is concerned for himself, and not mattering what becomes of any substance, not joined to, or affected with that consciousness. For, as it is evident in the instance I gave but now, if the consciousness went along with the little finger when it was cut off, that would be the same self which was concerned for the whole body yesterday, as making part of itself, whose actions then it cannot but admit as its own now. Though, if the same body should still live, and immediately from the separation of the little finger have its own peculiar consciousness, whereof the little finger

knew nothing, it would not at all be concerned for it, as a part of itself, or could own any of its actions, or have any of them imputed to him.

19. Which shows wherein personal identity consists. This may show us wherein personal identity consists: not in the identity of substance, but, as I have said, in the identity of consciousness, wherein if Socrates and the present mayor of Queinborough agree, they are the same person: if the same Socrates waking and sleeping do not partake of the same consciousness, Socrates waking and sleeping is not the same person. And to punish Socrates waking for what sleeping Socrates thought, and waking Socrates was never conscious of, would be no more of right, than to punish one twin for what his brother-twin did, whereof he knew nothing, because their outsides were so like, that they could not be distinguished; for such twins have been seen.

20. Absolute oblivion separates what is thus forgotten from the person, but not from the man. But yet possibly it will still be objected,- Suppose I wholly lose the memory of some parts of my life, beyond a possibility of retrieving them, so that perhaps I shall never be conscious of them again; yet am I not the same person that did those actions, had those thoughts that I once was conscious of, though I have now forgot them? To which I answer, that we must here take notice what the word I is applied to; which, in this case, is the man only. And the same man being presumed to be the same person, I is easily here supposed to stand also for the same person. But if it be possible for the same man to have distinct incommunicable consciousness at different times, it is past doubt the same man would at different times make different persons; which, we see, is the sense of mankind in the solemnest declaration of their opinions, human laws not punishing the mad man for the sober man's actions, nor the sober man for what the mad man did,- thereby making them two persons: which is somewhat explained by our way of speaking in English when we say such an one is "not himself," or is "beside himself"; in which phrases it is insinuated, as if those who now, or at least first used them, thought that self was changed; the selfsame person was no longer in that man.

21. Difference between identity of man and of person. But yet it is hard to conceive that Socrates, the same individual man, should be two persons. To help us a little in this, we must consider what is meant by Socrates, or the same individual man.

First, it must be either the same individual, immaterial, thinking substance; in short, the same numerical soul, and nothing else.

Secondly, or the same animal, without any regard to an immaterial soul.

Thirdly, or the same immaterial spirit united to the same animal.

Now, take which of these suppositions you please, it is impossible to make personal identity to consist in anything but consciousness; or reach any further than that does.

For, by the first of them, it must be allowed possible that a man born of different women, and in distant times, may be the same man. A way of speaking which, whoever admits, must allow it possible for the same man to be two distinct persons, as any two that have lived in different ages without the knowledge of one another's thoughts.

By the second and third, Socrates, in this life and after it, cannot be the same man any way, but by the same consciousness; and so making human identity to consist in the same thing wherein we place personal identity, there will be no difficulty to allow the same man to be the same person. But then they who place human identity in consciousness only, and not in something else, must consider how they will make the infant Socrates the same man with Socrates after the resurrection. But whatsoever to some men makes a man, and consequently the same individual man, wherein perhaps few are agreed, personal identity can by us be placed in nothing but consciousness, (which is that alone which makes what we call self,) without involving us in great absurdities.

22. But is not a man drunk and sober the same person? why else is he punished for the fact he commits when drunk, though he be never afterwards conscious of it? Just as much the same person as a man that walks, and does other things in his sleep, is the same person, and is answerable for any mischief he shall do in it. Human laws punish both, with a justice suitable to their way of knowledge;- because, in these cases, they cannot distinguish certainly what is real, what counterfeit: and so the ignorance in drunkenness or sleep is not admitted as a plea. For, though punishment be annexed to personality, and personality to consciousness, and the drunkard perhaps be not conscious of what he did, yet human judicatures justly punish him; because the fact is proved against him, but want of consciousness cannot be proved for him. But in the Great Day, wherein the secrets of all hearts shall be laid open, it may be reasonable to think, no one shall be made to answer for what he knows nothing of, but shall receive his doom, his conscience accusing or excusing him.

23. Consciousness alone unites remote existences into one person. Nothing but consciousness can unite remote existences into the same person: the identity of substance will not do it; for whatever substance there is, however framed, without consciousness there is no person: and a carcass may be a person, as well as any sort of substance be so, without consciousness.

Could we suppose two distinct incommunicable consciousnesses acting the same body, the one constantly by day, the other by night; and, on the other side, the same consciousness, acting by intervals, two distinct bodies: I ask, in the first case, whether the day and the night- man would not be two as distinct persons as Socrates and Plato? And whether, in the second case, there would not be one person in two distinct bodies, as much as one man is the same in two distinct clothings? Nor is it at all material to say, that this same, and this distinct consciousness, in the cases above mentioned, is owing to the same and distinct immaterial substances, bringing it with them to those bodies; which, whether true or no, alters not the case: since it is evident the personal identity would equally be determined by the consciousness, whether that consciousness were annexed to some individual immaterial substance or no. For, granting that the thinking substance in man must be necessarily supposed immaterial, it is evident that immaterial thinking thing may sometimes part with its past consciousness, and be restored to it again: as appears in the forgetfulness men often have of their past actions; and the mind many times recovers the memory of a past consciousness, which it had lost for twenty years together. Make these intervals of memory and forgetfulness to take their turns regularly by day and night, and you have two persons with the same immaterial spirit, as much as in the former instance two persons with the same body. So that self is not determined by identity or diversity of substance, which it cannot be sure of, but only by identity of consciousness.

24. Not the substance with which the consciousness may be united. Indeed it may conceive the substance whereof it is now made up to have existed formerly, united in the same conscious being: but, consciousness removed, that substance is no more itself, or makes no more a part of it, than any other substance; as is evident in the instance we have already given of a limb cut off, of whose heat, or cold, or other affections, having no longer any consciousness, it is no more of a man's self than any other matter of the universe. In like manner it will be in reference to any immaterial substance, which is void of that consciousness whereby I am myself to myself: if there be any part of its existence which I cannot upon recollection join with that present consciousness whereby I am now myself, it is, in that part of its existence, no more myself than any other immaterial being. For, whatsoever any substance has thought or done, which I cannot

recollect, and by my consciousness make my own thought and action, it will no more belong to me, whether a part of me thought or did it, than if it had been thought or done by any other immaterial being anywhere existing.

25. Consciousness unites substances, material or spiritual, with the same personality. I agree, the more probable opinion is, that this consciousness is annexed to, and the affection of, one individual immaterial substance.

But let men, according to their diverse hypotheses, resolve of that as they please. This every intelligent being, sensible of happiness or misery, must grant- that there is something that is himself, that he is concerned for, and would have happy; that this self has existed in a continued duration more than one instant, and therefore it is possible may exist, as it has done, months and years to come, without any certain bounds to be set to its duration; and may be the same self, by the same consciousness continued on for the future. And thus, by this consciousness he finds himself to be the same self which did such and such an action some years since, by which he comes to be happy or miserable now. In all which account of self, the same numerical substance is not considered as making the same self, but the same continued consciousness, in which several substances may have been united, and again separated from it, which, whilst they continued in a vital union with that wherein this consciousness then resided, made a part of that same self. Thus any part of our bodies, vitally united to that which is conscious in us, makes a part of ourselves: but upon separation from the vital union by which that consciousness is communicated, that which a moment since was part of ourselves, is now no more so than a part of another man's self is a part of me: and it is not impossible but in a little time may become a real part of another person. And so we have the same numerical substance become a part of two different persons; and the same person preserved under the change of various substances. Could we suppose any spirit wholly stripped of all its memory or consciousness of past actions, as we find our minds always are of a great part of ours, and sometimes of them all; the union or separation of such a spiritual substance would make no variation of personal identity, any more than that of any particle of matter does. Any substance vitally united to the present thinking being is a part of that very same self which now is; anything united to it by a consciousness of former actions, makes also a part of the same self, which is the same both then and now.

26. "Person" a forensic term. Person, as I take it, is the name for this self. Wherever a man finds what he calls himself, there, I think, another may say is the same person. It is a forensic term, appropriating actions and their merit; and so belongs only to intelligent agents, capable of a law, and happiness, and misery. This personality extends itself beyond present existence to what is past, only by consciousness,- whereby it becomes concerned and accountable; owns and imputes to itself past actions, just upon the same ground and for the same reason as it does the present. All which is founded in a concern for happiness, the unavoidable concomitant of consciousness; that which is conscious of pleasure and pain, desiring that that self that is conscious should be happy. And therefore whatever past actions it cannot reconcile or appropriate to that present self by consciousness, it can be no more concerned in than if they had never been done: and to receive pleasure or pain, i.e. reward or punishment, on the account of any such action, is all one as to be made happy or miserable in its first being, without any demerit at all. For, supposing a man punished now for what he had done in another life, whereof he could be made to have no consciousness at all, what difference is there between that punishment and being created miserable? And therefore, conformable to this, the apostle tells us, that, at the great day, when every one shall "receive according to his doings, the secrets of all hearts shall be laid open." The sentence shall be justified by the consciousness all persons shall have, that they themselves, in what bodies soever they appear, or what substances soever that consciousness adheres to, are the same that committed those

actions, and deserve that punishment for them.

27. Suppositions that look strange are pardonable in our ignorance. I am apt enough to think I have, in treating of this subject, made some suppositions that will look strange to some readers, and possibly they are so in themselves. But yet, I think they are such as are pardonable, in this ignorance we are in of the nature of that thinking thing that is in us, and which we look on as ourselves. Did we know what it was, or how it was tied to a certain system of fleeting animal spirits; or whether it could or could not perform its operations of thinking and memory out of a body organized as ours is; and whether it has pleased God that no one such spirit shall ever be united to any but one such body, upon the right constitution of whose organs its memory should depend; we might see the absurdity of some of those suppositions I have made. But taking, as we ordinarily now do (in the dark concerning these matters), the soul of a man for an immaterial substance, independent from matter, and indifferent alike to it all; there can, from the nature of things, be no absurdity at all to suppose that the same soul may at different times be united to different bodies, and with them make up for that time one man: as well as we suppose a part of a sheep's body yesterday should be a part of a man's body to-morrow, and in that union make a vital part of Meliboeus himself, as well as it did of his ram.

28. The difficulty from ill use of names. To conclude: Whatever substance begins to exist, it must, during its existence, necessarily be the same: whatever compositions of substances begin to exist, during the union of those substances, the concrete must be the same: whatsoever mode begins to exist, during its existence it is the same: and so if the composition be of distinct substances and different modes, the same rule holds. Whereby it will appear, that the difficulty or obscurity that has been about this matter rather rises from the names ill-used, than from any obscurity in things themselves. For whatever makes the specific idea to which the name is applied, if that idea be steadily kept to, the distinction of anything into the same and divers will easily be conceived, and there can arise no doubt about it.

29. Continuance of that which we have made to he our complex idea of man makes the same man. For, supposing a rational spirit be the idea of a man, it is easy to know what is the same man, viz. the same spirit- whether separate or in a body- will be the same man. Supposing a rational spirit vitally united to a body of a certain conformation of parts to make a man; whilst that rational spirit, with that vital conformation of parts, though continued in a fleeting successive body, remains, it will be the same man. But if to any one the idea of a man be but the vital union of parts in a certain shape; as long as that vital union and shape remain in a concrete, no otherwise the same but by a continued succession of fleeting particles, it will be the same man. For, whatever be the composition whereof the complex idea is made, whenever existence makes it one particular thing under any denomination the same existence continued preserves it the same individual under the same denomination.

The Reverend Thomas Reid (7 May 1710 – 7 October 1796) advocated "common sense" philosophy, and, in this excerpt, argues for the so-called "simple" view of identity: the self is a simple, immaterial substance. Persons are souls, and what makes a person the same person over time is the continuous existence of that same soul, which is the bearer of our various psychological states (including memories).

Thomas Reid
Essays on the Intellectual Powers of Man
Essay Three: Of Memory (1785)

Chapter 4 – Of Identity

The conviction which every man has of his identity, as far back as his memory reaches, needs no aid of philosophy to strengthen it; and no philosophy can weaken it, without first producing some degree of insanity.

The philosopher, however, may very properly consider this conviction as a phenomenon of human nature worthy of his attention. If he can discover its cause, an addition is made to his stock of knowledge; if not, it must be held as a part of our original constitution, or an effect of that constitution produced din a manner unknown to us.

We may observe, first of all, that this conviction is indispensably necessary to all exercise of reason. The operations of reason, whether in action or in speculation, are made up of successive parts. The antecedent are the foundation of the consequent, and, without the conviction that the antecedent have been seen or done by me, I could have no reason to proceed to the consequent, in any speculation, or in any active project whatever.

There can be no memory of what is past without the conviction that we existed at the time remembered. There may be good arguments to convince me that I existed before the earliest thing I can remember; but to suppose that my memory reaches a moment farther back than my belief and conviction of my existence, is a contradiction.

The moment a man loses this conviction, as if he had drunk the water of Lethe, past things are done away; and, in his own belief, he then begins to exist. Whatever was thought, or said, or done, or suffered before that period, may belong to some other person; but he can never impute it to himself, or take any subsequent step that supposes it to be his doing.

From this it is evident that we must have the conviction of our own continued existence and identity, as soon as we are capable of thinking or doing anything, on account of what we have thought, or done, or suffered before; that is, as soon as we are reasonable creatures.

That we may form as distinct a notion as we are able of this phenomenon of the human mind, it is proper to consider what is meant by identity in general, what by our own personal identity, and how we are led into that invincible belief and conviction which every man has of his own personal identity, as far as his memory reaches.

Identity in general I take to be a relation between a thing which is known to exist at one time, and a thing which is known to have existed at another time. If you ask whether they are one and the same, or two different things, every man of common sense understands the meaning of your question perfectly. Whence we may infer with certainty, that every man of common sense has a clear and distinct notion of identity.

If you ask a definition of identity, I confess I can give none; it is too simple a notion to admit of logical definition: I can say it is a relation, but I cannot find words to express the specific difference between this and other relations, though I am in no danger of confounding it with any other. I can say that diversity is a contrary relation, and that similitude and dissimilitude are another couple of contrary relations, which every man easily distinguishes in his conception from identity and diversity.

I see evidently that identity supposes an uninterrupted continuance of existence. That which has ceased to exist cannot be the same with that which afterwards begins to exist; for this would be to suppose a being to exist after it ceased to exist, and to have had existence before it was produced, which are manifest contradictions. Continued uninterrupted existence is therefore necessarily implied in identity.

Hence we may infer, that identity cannot, in its proper sense, be applied to our pains, our pleasures, our thought, or any operation of our minds. The pain felt this day is not the same individual pain which I felt yesterday, though they may be similar in kind and degree, and have the same cause. The same may be said of every feeling, and of every operation of mind. They are all successive in their nature, like time itself, no two moments of which can be the same moment.

It is otherwise with the parts of absolute space. They always are, and were, and will be the same. So far, I think, we proceed upon clear ground in fixing the notion of identity in general.

It is perhaps more difficult to ascertain with precision the meaning of personality; but it is not necessary in the present subject: it is sufficient for our purpose to observe, that all mankind place their personality in something that cannot be divided or consist of parts. A part of a person is a manifest absurdity. When a man loses his estate, his health, his strength, he is still the same person, and has lost nothing of his personality. If he has a leg or an arm cut off, he is the same person he was before. The amputated member is no part of his person, otherwise it would have a right to a part of his estate, and be liable for a part of his engagements. It would be entitled to a share of his merit and demerit, which is manifestly absurd. A person is something indivisible, and is what Leibniz calls a monad.

My personal identity, therefore, implies the continued existence of that indivisible thing which I call myself. Whatever this self may be, it is something which thinks, and deliberates, and resolves, and acts, and suffers. I am not thought, I am not action, I am not feeling; I am something that thinks, and acts, and suffers. My thoughts, and actions, and feelings, change every moment: they have no continued, but a successive, existence; but that self, or I, to which they belong, is permanent, and has the same relation to all the succeeding thoughts, actions, and feelings which I call mine.

Such are the notions that I have of my personal identity. But perhaps it may be said, this may all be fancy without reality. How do you know-what evidence have you-that there is such a permanent self which has a claim to all the thoughts, actions, and feelings which you call yours?

To this I answer, that the proper evidence I have of all this is remembrance, I remember that twenty years ago I conversed with such a person; I remember several things that passed in that conversation: my memory testifies, not only that this was done, but that it was done by me who now remember it. If it was done by me, I must have existed at that time, and continued to exist from that time to the present: if the identical person whom I call myself had not a part in that conversation, my memory is fallacious; it gives a distinct and positive testimony of what is not true. Every man in his senses believes what he distinctly remembers, and everything he remembers convinces him that he existed at the time remembered.

Although memory gives the most irresistible evidence of my being the identical person that did such a thing, at such a time, I may have other good evidence of things which befell me, and which I do not remember: I know who bare me, and suckled me, but I do not remember these events.

It may here be observed (though the observation would have been unnecessary, if some great philosophers had not contradicted it), that it is not my remembering any action of mine that makes me to be the person who did it. This remembrance makes me to know assuredly that I did it; but I might have done it, though I did not remember it. That relation to me, which is expressed by saying that I did it, would be the same, though I had not the least remembrance of it. To say that my remembering that I did such a thing, or, as some choose to express it, my being conscious that I did it, makes me to have done it, appears to me as great an absurdity as it would be to say, that my belief that the world was created made it to be created.

When we pass judgment on the identity of other persons than ourselves, we proceed upon other grounds, and determine from a variety of circumstances, which sometimes produce the firmest assurance, and sometimes leave room for doubt. The identity of persons has often furnished matter of serious litigation before tribunals of justice. But no man of a sound mind ever doubted of his own identity, as far as he distinctly remembered. The identity of a person is a perfect identity: wherever it is real, it admits of no degrees; and it is impossible that a person should be in part the same, and in part different; because a person is a monad, and is not divisible into parts. The evidence of identity in other persons than ourselves does indeed admit of all degrees, from what we account certainty, to the least degree of probability. But still it is true, that the same person is perfectly the same, and cannot be so in part, or in some degree only. For this cause, I have first considered personal identity, as that which is perfect in its kind, and the natural measure of that which is imperfect.

We probably at first derive our notion of identity from that natural conviction which every man has from the dawn of reason of his own identity and continued existence. The operations of our minds are all successive, and have no continued existence. But the thinking being has a continued existence, and we have an invincible belief, that it remains the same when all its thoughts and operations change.

Our judgments of the identity of objects of sense seem to be formed much upon the same grounds as our judgments of the identity of other persons than ourselves. Wherever we observe great similarity, we are apt to presume identity, if no reason appears to the contrary. Two objects ever so like, when they are perceived at the same time, cannot be the same; but if they are presented to our senses at different times, we are apt to think them the same, merely from their similarity.

Whether this be a natural prejudice, or from whatever cause it proceeds, it certainly appears in children from infancy; and when we grow up, it is confirmed in most instances by experience: for we rarely find two individuals of the same species that are not distinguishable by obvious differences.

A man challenges a thief whom he finds in possession of his horse or his watch, only on similarity. When the watchmaker swears that he sold this watch to such a person, his testimony is grounded on similarity. The testimony of witnesses to the identity of a person is commonly grounded on no other evidence.

Thus it appears, that the evidence we have of our own identity, as far back as we remember, is totally of a different kind from the evidence we have of the identity of other persons, or of objects of sense. The first is grounded on memory, and gives undoubted certainly. The last is grounded on similarity, and on other circumstances, which in many cases are not so decisive as to leave no room for doubt.

It may likewise be observed, that the identity of objects of sense is never perfect. All bodies, as they consist of innumerable parts that may be disjoined from them by a great variety of causes, are subject to continual changes of their substance, increasing, diminishing, changing insensibly. When such alterations are gradual, because language could not afford a different name for every different state of such a changeable being, it retains the same name, and is considered as the same thing. Thus we say of an old regiment, that it did such a thing a century ago, though there now is not a man alive who then belonged to it. We say a tree is the same in the seed-bed and in the forest. A ship of war, which has successively changed her anchors, her tackle, her sails, her masts, her planks, and her timbers, while she keeps the same name, is the same.

The identity, therefore, which we ascribe to bodies, whether natural or artificial, is not perfect identity; it is rather something which, for the convenience of speech, we call identity. It admits of a great change of the subject, providing the change be gradual; sometimes, even of a total change. And the changes which is common language are made consistent with identity differ from those that are thought to destroy it, not in kind, but in number and degree. It has no fixed nature when applied to bodies; and questions about the identity of a body are very often questions about words. But identity, when applied to persons, has no ambiguity, and admits not of degrees, or of more and less. It is the foundation of all rights and obligations, and of all accountableness; and the notion of it is fixed and precise.

CHAPTER 6
OF MR. LOCKE'S ACCOUNT OF OUR PERRSONAL IDENTITY

In a long chapter upon Identity and Diversity, Mr. Locke has made many ingenious and just observations, and some which I think cannot be defended. I shall only take notice of the account he gives of our own personal identity. His doctrine upon this subject has been censured by Bishop Butler, in a short *Essay* subjoined to his Analogy, with whose sentiments I perfectly agree.

Identity, as was observed (Chap. 4 of this *Essay*), supposes the continued existence of the being of which it is affirmed, and therefore can be applied only to things which have a continued existence. While any being continues to exist, it is the same being; but two beings which have a different beginning or a different ending of their existence cannot possibly by the same. To this, I think, Mr. Locke agrees.

He observes, very justly, that, to know what is meant by the same person, we must consider what the word person stands for; and he defines a person to be an intelligent being, endowed with reason and with consciousness, which last he thinks inseparable from thought.

From this definition of a person, it must necessarily follow, that, while the intelligent being continues to exist and to be intelligent, it must be the same person. To say that the intelligent being is the person, and yet that the person ceases to exist while the intelligent being continues, or that the person continues while the intelligent being ceases to exist, is to my apprehension a manifest contradiction.

One would think that the definition of a person should perfectly ascertain the nature of personal identity, or wherein it consists, though it might still be a question how we come to know and be assured of our personal identity. Mr. Locke tells us, however, "that personal identity, that is, the sameness of a rational being, consists in consciousness alone, and, as far as this consciousness can be extended backwards to any past action or thought, so far reaches the identity of that person. So that whatever has the consciousness of present and past actions is the same person to whom they belong."

This doctrine has some strange consequences, which the author was aware of. Such as, that if the same consciousness can be transferred from one intelligent being to another, which he thinks we cannot show to be impossible, then two or twenty intelligent beings may be the same person. And if the intelligent being may lose the consciousness of the actions done by him, which surely is possible, then he is not the person that did those actions; so that one intelligent being may be two or twenty different persons, if he shall so often lose the consciousness of this former actions. There is another consequence of this doctrine, which follows no less necessarily, though Mr. Locke probably did not see it. It is, that a man may be, and at the same time not be, the person that did a particular action.

Suppose a brave officer to have been flogged when a boy at school for robbing an orchard, to have taken a standard from the enemy in his first campaign, and to have been made a general in advanced life; suppose, also, which must be admitted to be possible, that, when he took the standard, he was conscious of his having been flogged at school, and that, when made a general, he was conscious of his taking the standard, but had absolutely lost the consciousness of his flogging.

These things being supposed, it follows, from Mr. Locke's doctrine, that he who was flogged at school is the same person who took the standard, and that he who took the standard is the same person who was made a general. Whence it follows, if there be any truth in logic, that the general is the same person with him who was flogged at school. But the general's consciousness does not reach so far back as his flogging; therefore, according to Mr. Locke's doctrine, he is not the person who was flogged. Therefore the general is, and at the same time is not, the same person with him who was flogged at school.

Leaving the consequences of this doctrine to those who have leisure to trace them, we may observe, with regard to the doctrine itself, First, that Mr. Locke attributes to consciousness the conviction we have of our past actions, as if a man may now be conscious of what he did twenty years ago. It is impossible to understand the meaning of this, unless by consciousness he meant memory, the only faculty by which we have an immediate knowledge of our past actions.

Sometimes, in popular discourse, a man says he is conscious that he did such a thing, meaning that he distinctly remembers that he did it. It is unnecessary, in common discourse, to fix accurately the limits between consciousness and memory. This was formerly shown to be the case with regard to sense and memory: and therefore distinct remembrance is sometimes called sense, sometimes consciousness, without any inconvenience. But this ought to be avoided in philosophy, otherwise we confound the different powers of the mind, and ascribe to one what really belongs to another. If a man can be conscious of what he did twenty years or twenty minutes ago, there is no use for memory, nor ought we to allow that there is any such faculty. The faculties of consciousness and memory are chiefly distinguished by this, that the first is an immediate knowledge of the present, the second an immediate knowledge of the past. When, therefore, Mr. Locke's notion of personal identity is properly expressed, it is, that personal identity consists in distinct remembrance: for, even in the popular sense, to say that I am conscious of a part action means nothing else than that I distinctly remember that I did it.

Secondly, it may be observed, that, in this doctrine, not only is consciousness confounded with memory, but, which is still more strange, personal identity is confounded with the evidence which we have or our personal identity. It is very true, that my remembrance that I did such a thing is the evidence I have that I am the identical person who did it. And this, I am apt to think, Mr. Locke meant. But to say that my remembrance that I did such a thing, or my consciousness, makes me the person who did it, is, in my apprehension, an absurdity too gross to be entertained by any man who attends to the meaning of it; for it is to attribute to memory or consciousness a strange magical power of producing its object, though that object must have existed before the memory or consciousness which produced it.

Consciousness is the testimony of one faculty; memory is the testimony of another faculty; and to say that the testimony is the cause of the thing testified, this surely is absurd, if anything be, and could not have been said by Mr. Locke, if he had not confounded the testimony with the thing testified.

When a horse that was stolen is found and claimed by the owner, the only evidence he can have, or that a judge or witnesses can have, that this is the very identical horse which was his property, is similitude. But would it not be ridiculous from this to infer that the identity of a horse consists in similitude only? The only evidence I have that I am the identical person who did such actions is, that I remember distinctly I did them; or, as Mr. Locke expresses it, I am conscious I did them. To infer from this, that personal identity consists in consciousness, is an argument which, if it had any force, would prove the identity of a stolen horse to consist solely in similitude.

Thirdly, is it not strange that the sameness or identity of a person should consist in a thing which is continually changing, and is not any two minutes the same? Our consciousness, our memory, and every operation of the mind, are still flowing like the water of a river, or like time itself. The consciousness I have this moment can no more be the same consciousness I had last moment, than this moment can be the last moment.

Identity can only be affirmed of things which have a continued existence. Consciousness, and every kind of thought, are transient and momentary, and have no continued existence; and, therefore, if personal identity consisted in consciousness, it would certainly follow, that no man is the same person any two moments of his life; and as the right and justice of reward and punishment are founded on personal identity, no man could be responsible for his actions.

But though I take this to be the unavoidable consequence of Mr. Locke's doctrine concerning personal identity, and though some persons may have liked the doctrine the better on this account, I am far from imputing any a doctrine which he believed to draw this consequence after it.

Fourthly, there are many expressions used by Mr. Locke, in speaking of personal identity, which to me are altogether unintelligible, unless we suppose that he confounded that sameness or identity which we ascribed to an individual with the identity which, in common discourse, is often ascribed to many individuals of the same species.

When we say that pain and pleasure, consciousness and memory, are the same in all men, this sameness can only mean similarity, or sameness of kind. That the pain of one man can be the same individual pain with that of another man is no less impossible, than that one man should be another man: the pain felt by me yesterday can no more be the pain I feel to-day, than yesterday can be this day; and the same thing may be said of every passion and of every operation of the mind. The same kind or species of operation may be in different men, or in the same man at different times; but it is impossible that the same individual operation should be in different men, or in the same man at different times.

When Mr. Locke, therefore, speaks of "the same consciousness being continued through a succession of different substances;" when he speaks of "repeating the idea of a past action, with the same consciousness we had of it at the first," and of "the same consciousness extending to actions past and to come"; these expressions are to me unintelligible, unless he means not the same individual consciousness, but a consciousness that is similar, or of the same kind.

If our personal identity consists in consciousness, as this consciousness cannot be the same individually any two moments, but only of the same kind, it would follow, that we are not for any two moments the same individual persons, but the same kind of persons.

As our consciousness sometimes ceases to exist, as in sound sleep, our personal identity must cease with it. Mr. Locke allows, that the same thing cannot have two beginnings of existence, so that our identity would be irrecoverably gone every time we ceased to think, if it was but for a moment

.

David Hume (7 May 1711 – 25 August 1776) is one of the most important and influential philosophers of the Western tradition. Considered a prominent figure of the Scottish Enlightenment, his writings cover an impressive range of topics. The excerpt below is from his Treatise on Human Nature. In this section, he argues against the existence of a single, unified, discrete "self," claiming, instead, that the "self" is merely a "bundle" of impressions.

David Hume
A Treatise of Human Nature (1739)

Book I: Of the understanding
Part IV: Of the sceptical and other systems of philosophy
Section VI: Of Personal Identity

[Paragraph numbering was not included in the original text and has been added for ease of reference.]

1. There are some philosophers, who imagine we are every moment intimately conscious of what we call our SELF; that we feel its existence and its continuance in existence; and are certain, beyond the evidence of a demonstration, both of its perfect identity and simplicity. The strongest sensation, the most violent passion, say they, instead of distracting us from this view, only fix it the more intensely, and make us consider their influence on *self* either by their pain or pleasure. To attempt a farther proof of this were to weaken its evidence; since no proof can be deriv'd from any fact, of which we are so intimately conscious; nor is there any thing, of which we can be certain, if we doubt of this.

2. Unluckily all these positive assertions are contrary to that very experience, which is pleaded for them, nor have we any idea of *self*, after the manner it is here explain'd. For from what impression cou'd this idea be deriv'd? This question 'tis impossible to answer without a manifest contradiction and absurdity; and yet 'tis a question, which must necessarily be answer'd, if we wou'd have the idea of self pass for clear and intelligible. It must be some one impression, that gives rise to every real idea. But self or person is not any one impression, but that to which our several impressions and ideas are suppos'd to have a reference. If any impression gives rise to the idea of self, that impression must continue invariably the same, thro' the whole course of our lives; since self is suppos'd to exist after that manner. But there is no impression constant and invariable. Pain and pleasure, grief and joy, passions and sensations succeed each other, and never all exist at the same time. It cannot, therefore, be from any of these impressions, or from any other, that the idea of self is deriv'd; and consequently there is no such idea.

3. But farther, what must become of all our particular perceptions upon this hypothesis? All these are different, and distinguishable, and separable from each other, and may be separately consider'd, and may exist separately, and have no need of any thing to support their existence. After what manner, therefore, do they belong to self; and how are they connected with it? For my part, when I enter most intimately into what I call *myself*, I always stumble on some particular perception or other, of heat or cold, light or shade,

love or hatred, pain or pleasure. I never can catch *myself* at any time without a perception, and never can observe any thing but the perception. When my perceptions are remov'd for any time, as by sound sleep; so long am I insensible of *myself*, and may truly be said not to exist. And were all my perceptions remov'd by death, and cou'd I neither think, nor feel, nor see, nor love, nor hate after the dissolution of my body, I shou'd be entirely annihilated, nor do I conceive what is farther requisite to make me a perfect non-entity. If any one, upon serious and unprejudic'd reflection thinks he has a different notion of *himself*, I must confess I can reason no longer with him. All I can allow him is, that he may be in the right as well as I, and that we are essentially different in this particular. He may, perhaps, perceive something simple and continu'd, which he calls *himself*; tho' I am certain there is no such principle in me.

4. But setting aside some metaphysicians of this kind, I may venture to affirm of the rest of mankind, that they are nothing but a bundle or collection of different perceptions, which succeed each other with an inconceivable rapidity, and are in a perpetual flux and movement. Our eyes cannot turn in their sockets without varying our perceptions. Our thought is still more variable than our sight; and all our other senses and faculties contribute to this change; nor is there any single power of the soul, which remains unalterably the same, perhaps for one moment. The mind is a kind of theatre, where several perceptions successively make their appearance; pass, re-pass, glide away, and mingle in an infinite variety of postures and situations. There is properly no *simplicity* in it at one time, nor *identity* in different; whatever natural propension we may have to imagine that simplicity and identity. The comparison of the theatre must not mislead us. They are the successive perceptions only, that constitute the mind; nor have we the most distant notion of the place, where these scenes are represented, or of the materials, of which it is compos'd.

5. What then gives us so great a propension to ascribe an identity to these successive perceptions, and to suppose ourselves possest of an invariable and uninterrupted existence thro' the whole course of our lives? In order to answer this question, we must distinguish betwixt personal identity, as it regards our thought or imagination, and as it regards our passions or the concern we take in ourselves. The first is our present subject; and to explain it perfectly we must take the matter pretty deep, and account for that identity, which we attribute to plants and animals; there being a great analogy betwixt it, and the identity of a self or person.

6. We have a distinct idea of an object, that remains invariable and uninterrupted thro' a suppos'd variation of time; and this idea we call that of *identity* or *sameness*. We have also a distinct idea of several different objects existing in succession, and connected together by a close relation; and this to an accurate view affords as perfect a notion of *diversity*, as if there was no manner of relation among the objects. But tho' these two ideas of identity, and a succession of related objects be in themselves perfectly distinct, and even contrary, yet 'tis certain, that in our common way of thinking they are generally confounded with each other. That action of the imagination, by which we consider the uninterrupted and invariable object, and that by which we reflect on the succession of related objects, are almost the same to the feeling, nor is there much more effort of thought requir'd in the latter case than in the former. The relation facilitates the transition of the mind from one object to another, and renders its passage as smooth as if it contemplated one continu'd object. This resemblance is the cause of the confusion and mistake, and makes us substitute the notion of identity, instead of that of related objects. However at one instant we may consider the related succession as variable or interrupted, we are sure the next to ascribe to it a perfect identity, and regard it as enviable and uninterrupted. Our propensity to this mistake is so great from the resemblance above-mention'd, that we fall into it before we are aware; and tho' we incessantly correct ourselves by reflection, and return to a more accurate method of thinking, yet we cannot long sustain our philosophy, or take off this biass

from the imagination. Our last resource is to yield to it, and boldly assert that these different related objects are in effect the same, however interrupted and variable. In order to justify to ourselves this absurdity, we often feign some new and unintelligible principle, that connects the objects together, and prevents their interruption or variation. Thus we feign the continu'd existence of the perceptions of our senses, to remove the interruption: and run into the notion of a *soul*, and *self*, and *substance*, to disguise the variation. But we may farther observe, that where we do not give rise to such a fiction, our propension to confound identity with relation is so great, that we are apt to imagine something unknown and mysterious, connecting the parts, beside their relation; and this I take to be the case with regard to the identity we ascribe to plants and vegetables. And even when this does not take place, we still feel a propensity to confound these ideas, tho' we are not able fully to satisfy ourselves in that particular, nor find any thing invariable and uninterrupted to justify our notion of identity.

7. Thus the controversy concerning identity is not merely a dispute of words. For when we attribute identity, in an improper sense, to variable or interrupted objects, our mistake is not confin'd to the expression, but is commonly attended with a fiction, either of something invariable and uninterrupted, or of something mysterious and inexplicable, or at least with a propensity to such fictions. What will suffice to prove this hypothesis to the satisfaction of every fair enquirer, is to shew from daily experience and observation, that the objects, which are variable or interrupted, and yet are suppos'd to continue the same, are such only as consist of a succession of parts, connected together by resemblance, contiguity, or causation. For as such a succession answers evidently to our notion of diversity, it can only be by mistake we ascribe to it an identity; and as the relation of parts, which leads us into this mistake, is really nothing but a quality, which produces an association of ideas, and an easy transition of the imagination from one to another, it can only be from the resemblance, which this act of the mind bears to that, by which we contemplate one continu'd object, that the error arises. Our chief business, then, must be to prove, that all objects, to which we ascribe identity, without observing their invariableness and uninterruptedness, are such as consist of a succession of related objects.

8. In order to this, suppose any mass of matter, of which the parts are contiguous and connected, to be plac'd before us; 'tis plain we must attribute a perfect identity to this mass, provided all the parts continue uninterruptedly and invariably the same, whatever motion or change of place we may observe either in the whole or in any of the parts. But supposing some very *small* or *inconsiderable* part to be added to the mass, or subtracted from it; tho' this absolutely destroys the identity of the whole, strictly speaking; yet as we seldom think so accurately, we scruple not to pronounce a mass of matter the same, where we find so trivial an alteration. The passage of the thought from the object before the change to the object after it, is so smooth and easy, that we scarce perceive the transition, and are apt to imagine, that 'tis nothing but a continu'd survey of the same object.

9. There is a very remarkable circumstance, that attends this experiment; which is, that tho' the change of any considerable part in a mass of matter destroys the identity of the whole, let we must measure the greatness of the part, not absolutely, but by its *proportion* to the whole. The addition or diminution of a mountain wou'd not be sufficient to produce a diversity in a planet: tho' the change of a very few inches wou'd be able to destroy the identity of some bodies. 'Twill be impossible to account for this, but by reflecting that objects operate upon the mind, and break or interrupt the continuity of its actions not according to their real greatness, but according to their proportion to each other: And therefore, since this interruption makes an object cease to appear the same, it must be the uninterrupted progress o the thought, which constitutes the imperfect identity.

10. This may be confirm'd by another phenomenon. A change in any considerable part of a body destroys its identity; but 'tis remarkable, that where the change is produc'd *gradually* and

insensibly we are less apt to ascribe to it the same effect. The reason can plainly be no other, than that the mind, in following the successive changes of the body, feels an easy passage from the surveying its condition in one moment to the viewing of it in another, and at no particular time perceives any interruption in its actions. From which continu'd perception, it ascribes a continu'd existence and identity to the object.

11. But whatever precaution we may use in introducing the changes gradually, and making them proportionable to the whole, 'tis certain, that where the changes are at last observ'd to become considerable, we make a scruple of ascribing identity to such different objects. There is, however, another artifice, by which we may induce the imagination to advance a step farther; and that is, by producing a reference of the parts to each other, and a combination to some *common end* or purpose. A ship, of which a considerable part has been chang'd by frequent reparations, is still considered as the same; nor does the difference of the materials hinder us from ascribing an identity to it. The common end, in which the parts conspire, is the same under all their variations, and affords an easy transition of the imagination from one situation of the body to another.

12. But this is still more remarkable, when we add a *sympathy* of parts to their *common end*, and suppose that they bear to each other, the reciprocal relation of cause and effect in all their actions and operations. This is the case with all animals and vegetables; where not only the several parts have a reference to some general purpose, but also a mutual dependence on, and connexion with each other. The effect of so strong a relation is, that tho' every one must allow, that in a very few years both vegetables and animals endure a *total* change, yet we still attribute identity to them, while their form, size, and substance are entirely alter'd. An oak, that grows from a small plant to a large tree, is still the same oak; tho' there be not one particle of matter, or figure of its parts the same. An infant becomes a man, and is sometimes fat, sometimes lean, without any change in his identity.

13. We may also consider the two following phaenomena, which are remarkable in their kind. The first is, that tho' we commonly be able to distinguish pretty exactly betwixt numerical and specific identity, yet it sometimes happens, that we confound them, and in our thinking and reasoning employ the one for the other. Thus a man, who hears a noise, that is frequently interrupted and renew'd, says, it is still the same noise; tho' 'tis evident the sounds have only a specific identity or resemblance, and there is nothing numerically the same, but the cause, which produc'd them. In like manner it may be said without breach of the propriety of language, that such a church, which was formerly of brick, fell to ruin, and that the parish rebuilt the same church of free-stone, and according to modern architecture. Here neither the form nor materials are the same, nor is there any thing common to the two objects, but their relation to the inhabitants of the parish; and yet this alone is sufficient to make us denominate them the same. But we must observe, that in these cases the first object is in a manner annihilated before the second comes into existence; by which means, we are never presented in any one point of time with the idea of difference and multiplicity: and for that reason are less scrupulous in calling them the same.

14. Secondly, We may remark, that tho' in a succession of related objects, it be in a manner requisite, that the change of parts be not sudden nor entire, in order to preserve the identity, yet where the objects are in their nature changeable and inconstant, we admit of a more sudden transition, than wou'd otherwise be consistent with that relation. Thus as the nature of a river consists in the motion and change of parts; tho' in less than four and twenty hours these be totally alter'd; this hinders not the river from continuing the same during several ages. What is natural and essential to any thing is, in a manner, expected; and what is expected makes less impression, and appears of less moment, than what is unusual and extraordinary. A considerable change of the former kind seems really less to the imagination, than the most trivial alteration of the latter; and by breaking less the continuity of the thought, has

less influence in destroying the identity.

15. We now proceed to explain the nature of *personal identity*, which has become so great a question in philosophy, especially of late years in *England*, where all the abstruser sciences are study'd with a peculiar ardour and application. And here 'tis evident, the same method of reasoning must be continu'd. which has so successfully explain'd the identity of plants, and animals, and ships, and houses, and of all the compounded and changeable productions either of art or nature. The identity, which we ascribe to the mind of man, is only a fictitious one, and of a like kind with that which we ascribe to vegetables and animal bodies. It cannot, therefore, have a different origin, but must proceed from a like operation of the imagination upon like objects.

16. But lest this argument shou'd not convince the reader; tho' in my opinion perfectly decisive; let him weigh the following reasoning, which is still closer and more immediate. 'Tis evident, that the identity, which we attribute to the human mind, however perfect we may imagine it to be, is not able to run the several different perceptions into one, and make them lose their characters of distinction and difference, which are essential to them. 'Tis still true, that every distinct perception, which enters into the composition of the mind, is a distinct existence, and is different, and distinguishable, and separable from every other perception, either contemporary or successive. But, as, notwithstanding this distinction and separability, we suppose the whole train of perceptions to be united by identity, a question naturally arises concerning this relation of identity; whether it be something that really binds our several perceptions together, or only associates their ideas in the imagination. That is, in other words, whether in pronouncing concerning the identity of a person, we observe some real bond among his perceptions, or only feel one among the ideas we form of them. This question we might easily decide, if we wou'd recollect what has been already prov'd at large, that the understanding never observes any real connexion among objects, and that even the union of cause and effect, when strictly examin'd, resolves itself into a customary association of ideas. For from thence it evidently follows, that identity is nothing really belonging to these different perceptions, and uniting them together; but is merely a quality, which we attribute to them, because of the union of their ideas in the imagination, when we reflect upon them. Now the only qualities, which can give ideas an union in the imagination, are these three relations above-mention'd. These are the uniting principles in the ideal world, and without them every distinct object is separable by the mind, and may be separately considered, and appears not to have any more connexion with any other object, than if disjoin'd by the greatest difference and remoteness. 'Tis, therefore, on some of these three relations of resemblance, contiguity and causation, that identity depends; and as the very essence of these relations consists in their producing an easy transition of ideas; it follows, that our notions of personal identity, proceed entirely from the smooth and uninterrupted progress of the thought along a train of connected ideas, according to the principles above-explain'd.

17. The only question, therefore, which remains, is, by what relations this uninterrupted progress of our thought is produc'd, when we consider the successive existence of a mind or thinking person. And here 'tis evident we must confine ourselves to resemblance and causation, and must drop contiguity, which has little or no influence in the present case.

18. To begin with *resemblance*; suppose we cou'd see clearly into the breast of another, and observe that succession of perceptions, which constitutes his mind or thinking principle, and suppose that he always preserves the memory of a considerable part of past perceptions; 'tis evident that nothing cou'd more contribute to the bestowing a relation on this succession amidst all its variations. For what is the memory but a faculty, by which we raise up the images of past perceptions? And as an image necessarily resembles its object, must not the frequent placing of these resembling perceptions in the chain of thought, convey the imagination more easily from one link to another, and make the whole seem like

the continuance of one object? In this particular, then, the memory not only discovers the identity, but also contributes to its production, by producing the relation of resemblance among the perceptions. The case is the same whether we consider ourselves or others.

19. As to *causation*; we may observe, that the true idea of the human mind, is to consider it as a system of different perceptions or different existences, which are link'd together by the relation of cause and effect, and mutually produce, destroy, influence, and modify each other. Our impressions give rise to their correspondent ideas; and these ideas in their turn produce other impressions. One thought chaces another, and draws after it a third, by which it is expell'd in its turn. In this respect, I cannot compare the soul more properly to any thing than to a republic or commonwealth, in which the several members are united by the reciprocal ties of government and subordination, and give rise to other persons, who propagate the same republic in the incessant changes of its parts. And as the same individual republic may not only change its members, but also its laws and constitutions; in like manner the same person may vary his character and disposition, as well as his impressions and ideas, without losing his identity. Whatever changes he endures, his several parts are still connected by the relation of causation. And in this view our identity with regard to the passions serves to corroborate that with regard to the imagination, by the making our distant perceptions influence each other, and by giving us a present concern for our past or future pains or pleasures.

20. As a memory alone acquaints us with the continuance and extent of this succession of perceptions, 'tis to be considered, upon that account chiefly, as the source of personal identity. Had we no memory, we never shou'd have any notion of causation, nor consequently of that chain of causes and effects, which constitute our self or person. But having once acquir'd this notion of causation from the memory, we can extend the same chain of causes, and consequently the identity of our persons beyond our memory, and can comprehend times, and circumstances, and actions, which we have entirely forgot, but suppose in general to have existed. For how few of our past actions are there, of which we have any memory? Who can tell me, for instance, what were his thoughts and actions on the 1st of *January* 1715, the 11th of *March* 1719, and the 3rd of *August* 1733? Or will he affirm, because he has entirely forgot the incidents of these days, that the present self is not the same person with the self of that time; and by that means overturn all the most established notions of personal identity? In this view, therefore, memory does not so much *produce* as *discover* personal identity, by shewing us the relation of cause and effect among our different perceptions. 'Twill be incumbent on those, who affirm that memory produces entirely our personal identity, to give a reason why we can thus extend our identity beyond our memory.

21. The whole of this doctrine leads us to a conclusion, which is of great importance in the present affair, *viz.* that all the nice and subtile questions concerning personal identity can never possibly be decided, and are to be regarded rather as grammatical than as philosophical difficulties. Identity depends on the relations of ideas; and these relations produce identity, by means of that easy transition they occasion. But as the relations, and the easiness of the transition may diminish by insensible degrees, we have no just standard, by which we can decide any dispute concerning the time, when they acquire or lose a title to the name of identity. All the disputes concerning the identity of connected objects are merely verbal, except so far as the relation of parts gives rise to some fiction or imaginary principle of union, as we have already observed.

22. What I have said concerning the first origin and uncertainty of our notion of identity, as apply'd to the human mind, may be extended with little or no variation to that of *simplicity*. An object, whose different co-existent parts are bound together by a close relation, operates upon the imagination after much the same manner as one perfectly simple and indivisible and requires not a much greater stretch of thought in order to its conception. From this similarity of operation we attribute a simplicity to it, and feign a principle of

union as the support of this simplicity, and the center of all the different parts and qualities of the object.

Thus we have finish'd our examination of the several systems of philosophy, both of the intellectual and natural world; and in our miscellaneous way of reasoning have been led into several topics; which will either illustrate and confirm some preceding part of this discourse, or prepare the way for our following opinions. 'Tis now time to return to a more close examination of our subject, and to proceed in the accurate anatomy of human nature, having fully explain'd the nature of our judgment and understandings.

Chapter 5
Personal Identity: "Politics"

Comprehension questions you should be able to answer after reading this introduction:

1. *What is meant by "identity politics?"*
2. *Explain how Supreme Court decisions such as Dred Scott, Ozawa, and Thind can be used as evidence for the social-construction of race.*
3. *What is the difference between "racialism" and "racism?" What do they have in common?*
4. *What is the "popular account" of race?*
5. *What is the difference between a "race" and a "racialized group," as described by Blum?*
6. *How do identity-politics movements attempt to combat/address racism? In what ways might these same movements by "racialist," though not racist?*

Social Construction of the Self: "Identity Politics"

Both social-construction of the self and self-fashioning (which we will address at the end of this chapter), interestingly enough, can be approached under the larger tent of "identity politics." Identity politics refers to a variety of political issues and arguments focusing on the various interests and perspectives people have by virtue of their identity, or aspects of their identity. The most common examples of this concern racial or ethnic identity, sexual orientation, gender identity, socioeconomic class, religious identity, and disability—though countless other examples are possible.[75]

"Identity" was the Dictionary.com "word of the year" for 2015.[76] This selection was inspired by Caitlyn Jenner provoking discussion of gender identity, of Rachel Dolezal provoking discussion of racial identity, Miley Cyrus declaring herself "pansexual," and the "Black Lives Matter" movement, among others—all of which pertain to identity politics, as opposed to our previously considered issue of enduring personal identity over time.[77]

To see just how pervasive and automatic is our focus on such matters, consider how you would describe yourself to someone else. In fact, imagine that I'm asking about you right now, and come up with your "I am. . ." response.

---

75 Someone might "self-identify," in an existentially meaningful way, for example, as a vegetarian, or a Civil War reenactor, or a Dr. Who fan, or a "Belieber," etc.

76 http://www.cnn.com/2015/12/08/living/word-of-the-year-dictionary-com-feat/index.html

77 As you will see as the remainder of the chapter unfolds, my examples and discussions will focus mostly on African-Americans. Please don't read any special significance into that selection. The cultural and media prominence of the Black Lives Matter movement in 2015 and 2016, and the related social unrest stemming from cases of alleged police brutality or unnecessary force against black men in places like Ferguson, contribute to this choice. I hope it needn't be said that similar sorts of issues and analyses apply to Latinos, Asian-Americans, etc.

I am :

How did you answer? It's unlikely that you described yourself as a "monad" (Reid), or a "thing which thinks" (Locke), or a "bundle of impressions" (Hume)!

Although you might have been abstract enough to describe yourself as a "person" or "human," you *probably* described yourself, instead, in terms of your age (generation), race or ethnicity, sexual orientation, relationship status, profession, socioeconomic status, political affiliation, ideology, disability, gender, and possibly some reference to your pets or hobbies! Whether they should or should not, clearly such things are considered to be part (and perhaps constitutive) of who we are, as persons.[78]

For all of these possible "anchors" or "foundations" for identity (i.e., race, gender, sexual orientation, etc.), not merely entire chapters, but entire books could be (and have been) written. We can't possibly hope to be so ambitious, and so will focus on just one such foundation: race/ethnicity.

If someone were to ask you your race, the answer probably comes to your mind instantly. "White" (or Caucasian). "Black" (or perhaps African-American). Latino. Chicano. Hispanic. Asian. Chinese. Indian. Native American. Mixed...

We think and speak as though these terms are fixed and clear, when that is, in fact, far from the case. We will begin by considering some important vocabulary, both as they are commonly used, as well as in more philosophically "precise" terms. We will also consider a variety of perspectives, for the sake of balance.

Let us begin, then, with the "everyday" meanings of race and ethnicity. In common usage, these are often muddled, or treated as though interchangeable. Indeed, we can try to dodge our own confusion as to the exact meaning of those terms by the use of the combined term "race/ethnicity!"

Although interpretations vary, for our purposes we will say that "race," as the term is *commonly* used, refers to a biological type of human being (e.g., the "white race," the "black race," etc.). whereas ethnicity refers to learned cultural behaviors that are often *associated* with a certain ancestry and physical appearance.

Race has been presumed to be biologically transmitted, whereas ethnicity is thought to be culturally transmitted. In use, both "Irish" and "Scottish" people might be considered members of the "white race," though of different ancestry and cultural heritage. Similarly, in common usage, anyone with a Spanish surname and descended from a Spanish-speaking people might be considered ethnically Hispanic, including Spaniards—though Spaniards would not be "Latinos," since they don't come from "Latin America." To further complicate matters, there is also the consideration of nationality, since

---

78 In this regard, *I* am a middle-aged, white, male, Christian, married (heterosexual) man, who is highly educated (Ph.D.) and falls in the upper-middle socioeconomic class. That is not intended as boasting, but as a confession: I am very much aware that every one of those features places me in a position of relative privilege. Although I will devote a good portion of this chapter discussing race, racial identity, and politics, I am very much aware that I have never personally experienced what it is like to be a member of a marginalized group, and I undoubtedly have numerous "blind spots" as a result. Although I think I have good reasons for the positions I advance in this chapter, in no way do I deny the potential validity and persuasiveness of other perspectives, informed by other sorts of experiences.

Hispanic/Latino people from Mexico are distinct from those hailing from El Salvador.

Rather than trying to parse the nuances of various ethnic distinctions, I would like to address a more foundational (and possibly more controversial) issue: the nature of race itself. Although the view I'm about to present has become increasingly accepted, especially among biologists, anthropologists, and sociologists, it might nevertheless come as a surprise to some of you: "race," as a biological concept, is a *fiction*—a "*social construct*" created and perpetuated in cultures but not existing in nature. The evidence for this "socially constructed" interpretation of race is both ample, and, I think, compelling. Let's begin with some history.

Race?

The history of the meaning of "race" reveals just how mercurial the concept has been. In ancient Greece and Rome, race referred to group membership in terms of one's ancestral place and culture. The Greeks, for example, were a "race." The Greeks recognized physical differences amongst people (e.g., the darker skin of Africans, the lighter skin of Northern Europeans, etc.), but did not presume superiority or inferiority on such bases (though they did regard their own *culture* (Greece) as superior!).

In the Middle Ages, race referred more to one's "lineage," as in personal family ancestry, or a people of common origin and history. For example, there was the Anglo-Saxon "race" (i.e., "Germanic" people who came to inhabit what is now England and Wales), the Norman "race" (i.e., the descendants of Viking raiders who populated the region of Normandy in what is now France), and the Teutons (i.e., descendants of "Germanic" tribes).

When European powers turned to conquest, colonization, and slavery, racial thinking began to develop as a rationale for these actions—though race was *still* not a biological concept. As of the 17th century, race referred more to a culture or civilization in a particular area. The French, for example, would have been considered a "race."

The 18th century saw race in terms of religious and cultural divisions. Throughout these centuries, for example, Native Americans and Africans were regarded first as "heathens" (and therefore "inferior"—but because they weren't Christians, not because of their biology). Then, they became "savages" (and therefore "inferior," but because they were "uncivilized," not because of their biology).

With the spread of slavery, neither religion nor culture was sufficient to justify differential treatment, since both could be overcome by conversion or education. An educated, Christian African would no longer be a "heathen" or a "savage." What could justify his continued enslavement? To remain viable, differential treatment (including enslavement) had to be founded on something permanent and unchangeable.

The focus on Africans for the slave population was practical, rather than rooted in racial ideology (at least initially). Of the various groups of people who had been used for cheap (or slave) labor in the "New World," Africans proved most suitable. Poor Europeans were insufficient in number, and could easily blend in with the population of free persons if they escaped slavery. Native Americans could escape and seek refuge with other (free) tribes, and were vulnerable to European diseases anyway. Africans, in contrast, were easily identifiable thanks to their skin color, stood out amongst European settlers, were accustomed to the heat prevalent in the Southern American colonies and Caribbean (unlike European workers, for example), had no local groups to which they could escape (unlike Native Americans), and were generally unfamiliar with the territory.

Africans would need to be classified as a distinct (and "inferior") race to justify their enslavement, and to allow the pretense of consistency when the United States of America emerged from the Declaration of Independence and the Constitutional Convention. The highest legal authority in the United States shamefully sealed the status of "Blacks" in the *Dred Scott v. Sandford* of 1857.

. . . It is difficult at this day to realize the state of public opinion in relation to that unfortunate race which prevailed in the civilized and enlightened portions of the world at the time of the Declaration of Independence and when the Constitution of the United States was framed and adopted. But the public history of every European nation displays it in a manner too plain to be mistaken.

They had for more than a century before been regarded as beings of an inferior order, and altogether unfit to associate with the white race either in social or political relations, and so far inferior that they had no rights which the white man was bound to respect, and that the negro might justly and lawfully be reduced to slavery for his benefit. He was bought and sold, and treated as an ordinary article of merchandise and traffic whenever a profit could be made by it. This opinion was at that time fixed and universal in the civilized portion of the white race. It was regarded as an axiom in morals as well as in politics which no one thought of disputing or supposed to be open to dispute, and men in every grade and position in society daily and habitually acted upon it in their private pursuits, as well as in matters of public concern, without doubting for a moment the correctness of this opinion.[79]

Note that while the ruling ostensibly applies only to slaves and their descendants, the rationale for the ruling refers to the "unfortunate race" (i.e., "Blacks") who are "so far inferior that they had no rights which the white man was bound to respect."

The Dred Scott case not only established that escaped slaves had no rights of citizens, but that the very "race" of people of whom those slaves belong are inherently inferior and without any rights at all! This was not the last time the Supreme Court validated unmistakably racist ideas, nor even the last time the Supreme Court helped to define race itself, as we shall see a little later in this section.

By the late 18th and early 19th centuries, race had emerged as a biological concept, alongside the development of modern biological science and classification methods. Linnaeus (1701-1778) was the founder of modern taxonomy, and applied his thinking to humans as well as other animals. He identified four distinct kinds of humans, and believed them to have been created distinctly/differently by God: Asiaticus, Europaeus, Africanus, and Americanus. These four groups were "natural kinds" by which all actual humans could be sorted and understood.

Despite the obvious ability to interbreed with members of the other "kinds," Linnaeus thought of these kinds as "species-like"—implying natural, permanent, and important differences between them. His typological descriptions of each included not only physical traits, but mental and personality traits as well. According to his stereotypes, Asiaticus is ruled by emotion and ritual, whereas Europaeus is ruled by laws and intelligence; Americanus is ruled by custom and superstition, whereas Africanus is ruled by caprice and whim. Conveniently enough, it was his *own* "kind" that was governed by reason and law, whereas all other "races" were naturally governed by mere opinion and whatever passing fancy caught their attention.

An alternative to Linnaeus developed even in his own time. Louis Leclerc developed a classification system that didn't claim inherent (and inherited) natural differences, but instead focused on different cultural conditions. "Those marks which distinguish men who inhabit different regions of the Earth are not original, but purely superficial."[80]

[79] *Dred Scott v. Sandford*. Full text available here: http://teachingamericanhistory.org/library/document/dred-scott-v-sandford/

[80] Audrey Smedly, Race in North America: Origin and Evolution of a Worldview. 2nd ed. 1993. p.165.

Linnaeus' approach prevailed, though, and its legacy included a biological basis for race, assuming significant and immutable differences, as well as the confusion of cultural factors for innate (biological) factors to account for differences in communities.

By the mid-19th century, race was firmly accepted in terms of biological groupings of human beings (e.g., "Negroid," "Caucasoid," "Mongoloid") who shared inherited physical, mental, and moral traits that are different from those of other races.

It can't be overlooked that race, as a biological concept, was developed by American scientists during the periods of both slavery and segregation, and was instrumental in the justification of both practices. Racial classification made a big difference in one's legal status in the United States. In 1790, Congress' first act was to restrict naturalized citizenship to "free white persons" only. Blacks were included in 1870 (after the Civil War, of course), but East Asians and Filipinos had to wait until 1952! Considerations of the naturalness and immutability of race found also their way into interpretations of law, as the Supreme Court once again offered its "enlightened" opinions on the issue.

Takao Ozawa was born in Japan in 1875, but moved to California in 1894, where he attended UC Berkeley. He moved to what was then the "territory" of Hawaii, and applied for naturalization in 1914. The U.S. District Attorney of Hawaii opposed his application on the grounds that Ozawa was of the Japanese race, and therefore not a white person. Ozawa fought this judgment for eight years, with his case ultimately reaching the Supreme Court. Among several arguments he offered, one was literal: his skin color was "white."

Although he was of Japanese ancestry, his skin color was literally the same pinkish color as that of "white" people. Therefore, he was a white person. The Court rejected his logic.

> *Manifestly, the test [of race] afforded by the mere color of the skin of each individual is impracticable as that differs greatly among persons of the same race, even among Anglo-Saxons, ranging by imperceptible gradations from the fair blond to the swarthy brunette, the latter being darker than many of the lighter hued persons of the brown or yellow races.*[81]

Here, the Court accepts and asserts that skin color does *not* reliably correlate with racial identity. However, rather than rejecting racial classification in biological terms, the "experts," anthropologists, and scientists of the time resorted to continually shifting standards to maintain their racial groupings. So would the Court.

Rejecting Ozawa's claim based on skin color, the Court ruled that "the words 'white person' are synonymous with the words 'a person of the Caucasian race.'" However, just three months later, the Court rejected its very own equivalence of "white" and "Caucasian" in *United States v. Thind.*

Bhagat Singh Thind came to the United States from India on July 4th, 1913. Importantly, anthropologists of that era had classified Asian Indians as "Caucasians" rather than "Mongolians." Thind seized on this and applied for naturalization on the grounds that he was Caucasian, and therefore a "white person."

The Ninth Circuit Court of Appeals asked, "Is a high caste Hindu of full Indian blood, born at Amrit Sar, Punjab, India, a white person?" Note already the conflation of religion (Hindu) with "race," the assumption that "race" is something carried by blood, and even that something like place of birth is somehow relevant to whether someone is "white."

The Court accepted that Thind was Caucasian. "It may be true that the blond Scandinavian and the brown Hindu have a common ancestor in the dim reaches of antiquity, but the average man knows perfectly well that there are unmistakable and profound differences between them today."

---

81 Ozawa v. United States.

The Court then argued that the word "Caucasian" is "at best a conventional term." "What we now hold is that the words 'free white persons' are words of common speech, to be interpreted in accordance with the understanding of the common man, synonymous with the word 'Caucasian' only as that word is popularly understood."

In *Ozawa*, the Court rejected literal "whiteness" in the sense of pinkish skin, in favor of a "scientific" classification, in order to exclude a person of Japanese ancestry from being considered "white." In *Thind*, just three months later, the *same Court* abandoned "science" altogether, appealing to the "understanding of the common man" to exclude someone from India from being considered "white."

The mental gymnastics performed by the Justices to preserve racial preferences is breathtaking, but we can't ignore the fact that these decisions had profound life-impacting results. Neither East Asians nor Asian Indians, nor, indeed, anyone who wasn't "white"—as understood by the "common man"—could be or could become citizens. Not only did this ostracize and limit the rights of such persons, these decisions even *stripped away* the citizenship of at least 65 Asian Indians to whom it had previously been granted. One such person was Vaisho Das Bagai.

Vaisho had renounced his British citizenship to become an American. With his American citizenship stripped away, he became a citizen of no country at all. Because he was not a citizen (any longer), he was no longer allowed to own property in California, and was forced to sell his home and general store. The U.S. Government even refused to grant him a passport to visit his family in India. He committed suicide in 1928, and sent one of his suicide notes to the San Francisco Examiner:

> *I came to America thinking, dreaming and hoping to make this land my home. Sold my properties and brought more than twenty-five thousand dollars (gold) to this country, established myself and tried my very best to give my children the best American education.*
>
> *In year 1921 the Federal court at San Francisco accepted me as a naturalized citizen of the United States and issued to my name the final certificate, giving therein the name and description of my wife and three sons. In last 12 or 13 years we all made ourselves as much Americanized as possible.*
>
> *But they now come to me and say, I am no longer an American citizen. They will not permit me to buy my home and, lo, they even shall not issue me a passport to go back to India. Now what am I? What have I made of myself and my children?*
>
> *We cannot exercise our rights, we cannot leave this country. Humility and insults, who is responsible for all this? Myself and American government.*
>
> *I do not choose to live the life of an interned person; yes, I am in a free country and can move about where and when I wish inside the country. Is life worth living in a gilded cage? Obstacles this way, blockades that way, and the bridges burnt behind.*[82]

Although both the effect of, and very probably the intent behind, the Court decisions was racist, that racism was predicated on deeply held (and arguably *false*) premises. Those premises, however, were (and are) *widely believed*.

The "popular account" of race, for the last 150 years or so, is that races are real, naturally occurring, and more stable/real/natural than contingent human groupings such as nationality or religion. Many would agree, for example, that "France" is a contingent historical artifact that

---

82 http://www.aiisf.org/stories-by-author/876-bridges-burnt-behind-the-story-of-vaishno-das-bagai

didn't always exist, didn't have to exist, and could cease to exist (e.g., if Hitler had won the Second World War).

So too with religion. Scientology hasn't always existed, and very few people (if any) still worship the ancient Egyptian pantheon (e.g., Isis and Osiris). Races, on the other hand, are generally regarded as older, inevitable, immutable, and more "natural."

The racial assumptions that emerged from the 18th and 19th centuries included profound (and damaging) ideas:

- All humans fall into one, and only one, distinct, natural, fixed race.[83]
- These races are presumed to differ (essentially) in significant physical, mental, and moral qualities.
- Every member of a race is thought to possess their races "essence," and this essence is transmitted to one's children.
- There are physical indicators that allegedly correlate with race membership, and that provide mental "shortcuts." For example, dark skin and curly hair indicates that someone is "Black," which also means (according to *racist stereotypes*) that that person is lazy.
- A natural hierarchy is thought to exist based on the "natural superiority" of some races over others. Although the precise number of races and their relative placement varies, in the United States it has always been the assumption that "whites" were at the top and "blacks" were at the bottom.

The belief that there are distinct, natural races, and that each race has its own particular "essence" that is transmitted by biological means, is known as "racialism."[84] This is not to be confused with racism! Racism certainly includes racialist beliefs, but *adds* to them notions of superiority/inferiority, negative stereotypes, and moral judgments. In other words, racism is value-laden, whereas racialism is value-neutral.

- **Racialism**: beliefs and actions presupposing the existence of biologically-transmitted racial "essences."[85]
- **Racism**: negative value judgments and actions based on racialist assumptions.[86]

[83] The racism inherent to racial essentialism (originally, at least) is evident in the "one drop rule." Historically, in the United States, one was "white" if they had no "black" ancestry anywhere in the family lineage. Even "one drop" of "black" meant that you were not "white." The assumptions lurking behind the "one-drop" rule are hardly ancient history, by the way. In March of 2016, a 6-year old girl was taken from her ("white") foster parents in Santa Clarita, California, after having lived with them for four years. Her biological parents had lost custody of her after a child abuse investigation. Her mother also had substance abuse issues, and her father had a criminal record. She was removed from foster care, though, because she is "1.5% Choctaw," and a 1978 federal law was invoked (The Indian Child Welfare Act, designed to prevent large numbers of native American children to be adopted away from their tribal heritage and placed in non-Native American households). Although this child had never actually been exposed to any Native American culture, the mere "fact" that she was 1.5% Choctaw meant she was "Native American" under federal law, and therefore subject to the Indian Child Welfare Act. http://m.nydailynews.com/news/national/girl-6-foster-family-native-american-law-article-1.2572704

[84] Note: this term is used by different people in different ways. I offer a specific definition of this term in this section, and it is that specific definition that is presupposed for the remainder of this chapter.

[85] This is not to be confused with ethnicism or ethnocentrism, both of which concern ethnicity, which refers to *learned cultural behaviors and norms*, as distinct from biologically-transmitted traits.

[86] There is also what is known as "institutional

Arguably, most Americans are "racialists," whether they realize it or not, and whether or not they are additionally *racists*. This is so despite the clear evidence for the social construction of race (as seen by our survey of history and Supreme Court rulings above), and despite the lack of evidence for *biologically-based* races or racial essentialism.

To put it plainly, there is no genetic basis for racial classification. There are no general racial characteristics that are shared by all members of the same "race," nor any genes shared by all such members. 85.4% of genetic differences between humans occur *within* a population ("race"), with roughly 85% of all human genetic variation found in a random sample of two people from the *same* tribal/ethnic group, from the same region. Genetic differences between people of different "races" are only marginally greater than that of two people from the same "race." Even the study of diseases that are more prevalent in certain "races" (e.g., sickle cell anemia in "Blacks") is based on *social definitions of race*. Nor is there any "race" found in or transmitted by blood. Although we might say that someone has "Native American blood" in them, there are only four major blood types (A, B, AB, and O), that can be additionally "positive" or "negative"—but none of these correspond to racial membership.

It's worth noting that only some patterns of physical features have acquired any racial significance. We don't regard height (e.g., "over seven feet tall," or "under five feet tall") as a signifier of racial membership, nor do we regard being a "redhead" as indicative of one's race. Not even skin color reliably picks out a particular group of people (e.g., some Australian Aborigines are darker in complexion than many African-Americans, but are not regarded as "black"—at least not by Americans). Simply put, which physical differences or similarities "count" has been historically arbitrary. Again and again, the pattern was the same: "races" were first defined based on socio-cultural conventions, and then physical means of classification were selected based on their usefulness in discriminating between the already-created socially constructed groups.

Finally, if race were truly and merely a matter of physical features, there could be no distinction between "looking white" (for example) and actually *being* white. To "appear white" just would mean that one *is* white, if personal appearance were all that mattered. And yet, for centuries there has been a meaningful notion of "passing" in the United States. . . .

Although it might seem like I'm belaboring the point, establishing the lack of a genetic basis for race is *important* because, without genetic carriers, racial traits can't be biologically *inherited*.

Children might model behavior exhibited by their parents, but this doesn't entail anything resembling genetic destiny. "Lazy" parents might inspire laziness in *any* child, including an adopted child from another "race." Moreover, such learned behaviors could include a fondness for cloth napkins as much as "laziness"—neither of which is biological nor essentialist.

Although races seemingly don't exist as biological entities, there are certainly what Lawrence Blum calls "*racialized groups*."[87] Blum describes "*racialization*" as the:

> *treating of groups as if there were inherent and immutable differences between them; as if certain somatic characteristics marked the presence of significant*

---

racism," which, in general, is racism expressed and practiced by social and political institutions, as distinct from racism by individuals. Institutional racism can be conscious and intentional, such as segregation laws, or unconscious and racist in its effects, rather than intentions, such as disparate minimum prison sentences for crack and powder cocaine. Institutional racism can be both a product and a source of embedded racist cultural practices within our social structure. This then creates barriers and privileges based on race through socio-political institutions.

[87] Lawrence Blum, I'm not a Racist, But. . . The Moral Quandary of Race. 2002.

characteristics of mind, emotion, and character; and as if some were of greater worth than others.[88]

Racialized groups can shift over time. The "Irish" used to be a "race," but are now an "ethnicity." To say that races are "social constructions," that there are not "races" in the sense of biological kinds but that instead there are "racialized" groups, is *not* to deny "race" any kind of existence at all! Nations are "social constructions," as is the State of California, but both are "real." Neither the USA nor California, however, have existed or will exist "naturally" and immutably throughout time. Nor is it the case that someone born in California necessarily and immutably inherits any particular physical, intellectual, social, or moral traits as a result of the particular State in which they are born!

Analogously, "races," as biological groupings, don't exist as natural artifacts—but racialized groups are real, treated as real, and *experienced* as real by their members. Members of racialized groups are often treated in similar ways, and thus often share similar experiences (e.g., being followed in stores, being asked if they speak English, being asked "where are you from?", etc.). This shared experience can contribute to someone adopting a group identity, and this self-identification can further contribute to the members' "racialization."

Finally, it's important to note that racialized thinking (racialism) can result not just in negative racist stereotyping (or worse), but also more well-meaning agendas such as using race to create diversity at colleges and universities. This leads us to the notion of "identity politics."

Identity Politics

Identity politics in the United States involves stigmatized groups transforming their sense of self by rejecting and/or rewriting negative "scripts" that have been offered by the dominant group within the larger community. Whether on the basis of race, gender, sexual orientation, disability, or religious affiliation, the basic idea is that some groups of people have been marginalized on those bases, and have been told a story about themselves that is negative. Identity politics seek to transform that group membership from a "negative" into a "positive" through political activism, "consciousness-raising," reframing, and other activities.

The implicit assumption behind identity politics is that people can internalize oppressive messages from the dominant group. As examples, some black people value lighter skin, or describe some women as having "good" hair (i.e., straight hair), etc. In addition, women inherit the norms of "female" (as defined and transmitted by males!), LGBT persons inherit an identity in contrast to heteronormativity, etc. Identity politics seeks to correct and reframe those messages.

In 2015, student protests ignited across numerous American college and university campuses, including Ithaca College, Smith College, the University of Missouri, Yale, Harvard, Princeton, and my own alma mater, Claremont McKenna College (among others). Students were generally protesting campus conditions for students of color, citing a lack of diversity and cultural sensitivity, and an abundance of "micro-aggressions."

At Claremont McKenna College, Dean of Students Mary Spellman was compelled to resign after protests, and a hunger strike by a student. "Students of Color" issued a letter of their complaints and demands to CMC President Chodosh on April 9th, 2015. It included the creation of a Diversity Chair in the Dean of Students Office, funding for multicultural clubs, a resource center for students of color, greater diversity in faculty and staff, a mentoring program for first year students of color, mandatory and periodic racial sensitivity trainings for all professors, and improved mental health services to cater to the "unique and diverse needs of students of color," among other things.[89]

---

[88] Blum, 147

[89] The full letter is available here:

The Black Student Union at Oberlin College also issued a list of demands to their College President. In their own words: "these are not polite requests, but concrete and unmalleable demands. Failure to meet them will result in a full and forceful response from the community you fail to support."

The demands included: a 4% increase in Black student enrollment per year (reaching a 40% increase by 2022[90]), an increase in specifically Black female instrumentalists in the Jazz department; more Black administrators in the Offices of Financial Aid, Student Health, Student Accounts, the President, Disabilities, the Dean, and Residential Education; that "all Black prospective students be interviewed by admissions officers that are trained in race consciousness practices for undergraduate admissions;" financial aid workshops for Black students by Black financial aid officers; a change in graduation requirements to include an "Intro to the Black Experience" (or similar) course; the recruiting of Black faculty in all of the following departments: politics, philosophy, economics, theater, dance sociology, neuroscience, chemistry, biology, history, classics, physics, creative writing, psychology, athletics, art, anthropology, computer science, cinema studies, comparative American studies, geology, environmental studies, math, religion, rhetoric and composition, and gender sexuality and feminist studies; an increase in the number of black psychologists in the Counseling Center; the creation of designated safe spaces for "Africana identifying students" in several buildings including the library and science center; the immediate promotion to tenure or tenure track for 17 specifically-named faculty; that a Black woman be hired as the head of the Jazz vocal department; that the Black student leaders (who developed these demands, presumably) be provided an $8.20/hour stipend for the organizing efforts; and that eight specifically-named administrators and professors be fired immediately—among numerous other demands.[91]

My point is *not* to invalidate or question any of the particular example demands, nor to question the lived experiences of the students who made them. Indeed, there are many legitimate, well-documented disparities and additional obstacles experienced by ethnic minorities in Academia, the workplace, and American society, in general. Minority students, for example, have higher attrition rates in college than do their white peers. This is *not* because of absurd biologically-essentialist reasons, but because of a variety of other reasons, including the fact that attrition rates are *lower* at "highly selective" institutions, where minority students are still underrepresented; and because there is a correlation between completion rates and the time spent pursuing a degree. Minority students are more likely to be part-time students (because of work or family responsibilities), to have to take remedial classes (because of a higher chance of coming from "underperforming" high schools), and to start off in community college (for a variety of reasons, including socio-economic reasons)—all of which correlate to longer times for degree completion, and therefore higher attrition rates.[92] Given these lower college completion rates for minority students, it's both understandable and appropriate that impacted students would be motivated to advocate for support systems that could help to bridge that gap, including staff and faculty that are sensitive to their needs and

https://docs.google.com/document/d/19BRi1esJ4rlzBLHAQEBHSl7e0wrEiUtLsF5eRdl90No/edit?pref=2&pli=1

90 This was not a demand that 40% of the students be black, of course, but rather that the black student population be 40% larger than its current number.

91 The full documentation of their demands is available here: https://www.scribd.com/doc/293326897/Oberlin-College-Black-Student-Union-Institutional-Demands

92 http://fivethirtyeight.com/features/race-gap-narrows-in-college-enrollment-but-not-in-graduation/

particular experiences and backgrounds.

To the extent that these students have grown up in a culture, and sub-cultures, in which their experience has been "racialized," it is likely that their racialist assumptions are inherited and absorbed as part of their basic worldview, as opposed to some sort of contingent belief that could easily be cast aside in the face of a counter-argument. If their life experience, including experiences of racism and marginalization, has *taught* them that they are irreversibly "other," then it should come as no surprise that their self-advocacy relies on that same premise, however much they are trying to "flip the script." I want to stress once again that my point is *not* to diminish (let alone deny) the significance or tenacity of their experiences, but rather, in the role of a philosopher, to challenge the racialist (and sometimes plainly *racist*) premises that drive their oppressive experiences, as well as the racialist (as *distinct* from racist) premises that drive (some of) their own responses.

As an example, CMC student activists declare that students of color have "unique" mental health needs. Both CMC and Oberlin activists demand more "diverse" faculty—with Oberlin students demanding specifically black, and, in some cases, specifically black female faculty (as well as black administrators in various offices, and black financial aid counselors).

What assumptions might be being made here? Perhaps that *any* black person hired has the same "essence" as the black students, and will therefore be sensitive to the unique needs and concerns that *only* black students have (which, again, implies racial essentialism). Of course, such an assumption is patently *false*. What if Oberlin College hired black faculty and administrators for every single position demanded by those students—but hired black candidates who *disagreed* with the students' general position and demands? Clearly, not every black person (academic or otherwise) believes and values exactly the same things! There is a big political difference, for example, between Doctor Cornel West[93] and Doctor Ben Carson.[94] Would Ben Carson be a satisfying hire for the neuroscience program at Oberlin, or is he the "wrong kind" of black person?

Ironically enough, Ben Carson himself raised such issues in the context of his 2016 Presidential bid. Referring to President Obama, he said "He's an 'African' American. He was, you know, raised white. Many of his formative years were spent in Indonesia. So, for him to, you know, claim that, you know, he identifies with the experience of black Americans, I think, is a bit of a stretch... Like most Americans, I was proud that we broke the color barrier when he was elected, but I also recognize that his experience and my experience are night-and-day different. He didn't grow up like I grew up by any stretch of the imagination, not even close." In reference to his own experiences, he said that most of the racism he experiences comes from "progressives." "I think the way that I'm treated, you know, by the left is racism. Because they assume because you're black, you have to think a certain way. And if you don't think that way, you're 'Uncle Tom,' you're worthy of every horrible epithet they can come up with; whereas, if I weren't black, then I would just be a Republican."[95]

This gets us to the "normalizing" aspect of racialism. The very notion that there is a "wrong kind" of black person suggests a core of not merely traits, but also beliefs and values that every member of that "race" *should* emulate. A variety of terms, usually meant to be derogatory, are used to express this very notion: "Oreo." "Banana." "Coconut." In each case, the suggestion is the same: although the person is "black" (or "yellow"/Asian, or "brown"/Latino) on the "outside," that person is "white" on the "inside."

By this line of thinking, racial group members are *supposed* to believe and value certain things, and behave and comport themselves in various

[93] http://www.cornelwest.com/

[94] https://www.bencarson.com/

[95] http://www.cnn.com/2016/02/23/politics/ben-carson-barack-obama-raised-white/index.html

ways, by virtue of their group membership. Others are *supposed* to recognize (and respect) those things about that group. In some cases, this appears just to be another instance of racial stereotyping.

Many years ago, all of the professors on my campus took part in "diversity training"—one of the more common demands of student activists. The point of this training was to help us all to be conscious of racist stereotyping, to avoid it, and to be sensitive and respectful to students (and faculty) of color—all of which are worthwhile goals. A close paraphrase of the advice that the "expert diversity trainer" provided is as follows.

> *"We must avoid racist stereotypes, and we must be sensitive to different cultures and their values and practices. For example, African-Americans are more loud, demonstrative, and participatory in conversations. . ."*

As the expert continued her presentation, many of my peers looked around at each other uncomfortably. It seemed that the presenter was invoking *racialist* stereotypes in the very attempt to dispel *racist* stereotypes—with the only difference being that she was presenting these generalizations about different races without any tone of negativity—which is what made them racialist, as opposed to racist.

Nevertheless, she was suggesting that we see every student we encounter first through the lens of what we presume their race to be, then to recall a handful of generalizations about that race, and then finally to tailor our treatment of that student on the basis of those generalizations. "Angela is black, so she is accustomed to animated conversations and expects to be interrupted while speaking, much as I should expect her to interrupt me. Maria, on the other hand, is Latina, and is therefore probably very family-oriented. I should keep in mind that she might have less time to do homework since she probably has to help around the house. Chan, though, is probably Chinese, so he will likely be very studious and respectful, even if very quiet in class—so I shouldn't expect him to participate much. . . . "

Although undoubtedly well-intentioned, it's difficult not to sense that something eerily similar is lurking behind both this kind of diversity training as well as overtly racist beliefs. That eerie similarity is racialism—the idea that there are distinct biological "kinds" corresponding to our categories of race, and that these "kinds" reliably indicate not only physical, but also intellectual and moral, traits.

When seen in such lights, we see the paradox of racial identity politics: it can invoke the very (essentialist) constructs that were/are oppressive in the first place, and is prone to the same racialism (racial essentialism) that informs racism. That is, different groups of people (i.e., different "races") have certain qualities by virtue of their racial "essence." This kind of essentialist thinking suggests that there is a single axis of identity that is discrete and separable, and that should be prioritized.

In fairness, someone might object that while biologically-based racial essentialism is false, what is being invoked is not race, but culture. Rather than claiming that there is some sort of black "gene" or "essence" transmitted biologically, there is a black *culture* that is transmitted via the usual means of enculturation/socialization (e.g., the influence of parents, peers, mass media, pop-culture, and other sources of cultural competency). In this way, concerns about "race" being unscientific are moot, since socialization is understood via the social "sciences" (such as sociology) rather than biology or genetics. Using this approach, our "race" vocabulary should properly shift to speaking solely in terms of ethnicity. If so, someone would be "black" in the same sort of way that someone would be "Irish."

Thinking in terms of ethnicity makes racial identity a matter of culture, rather than biology. "Culture," generally, refers to shared, socially constructed aspects of the social environment, including laws, language, educational systems and other social institutions, marriage (and other relationship institutions and norms), as well as all the unspoken "rules" and norms that establish the "ethos" ("character") of the community.

At first glance, this shift is a clear improvement. Racism, after all, seems to presuppose a biologically based racial essence (racialism). Only if certain persons are *inherently* "inferior" by virtue of their inalienable racial membership could it make sense to discriminate on the basis of race. But, if races are replaced with culturally-transmitted ethnicities, no one is "inherently" anything! Certain behaviors and traits might be acquired via socialization, but this is neither genetic destiny nor unalterable. If "those people" have a "poor work ethic," or have "too many children outside of marriage," this is a product of culture, not biology—and cultures can be changed, or escaped.

The now-controversial comedian Bill Cosby sparked both enthusiastic agreement and equally enthusiastic outrage when he gave the now-famous "pound cake" speech in 2004 to commemorate the 50th anniversary of *the Brown v. Board of Education* Supreme Court decision. A partial transcript follows, juxtaposed with responses from Dr. Michael Eric Dyson:[96]

> *Cosby: "Just forget telling your child to join the Peace Corps. It's right around the corner. (laughter) It's standing on the corner. It can't speak English. It doesn't want to learn English. I can't even talk the way these people talk."*

> *Dyson: "Cosby's poisonous view of young folks who speak a language he can barely parse [Ebonics] simmers with hostility and resentment." And "Fat Albert and the Cosby Kids, Cosby's lauded '70s television cartoon series, won greater acceptance for a new cast of black identities and vernacular language styles. Cosby has made money and gained further influence from using forms of black English he now violently detests."*

> *Cosby: "People with their hat on backwards, pants down around the crack. Isn't that a sign of something, or are you waiting for Jesus to pull his pants up (laughter and clapping)."*

> *Dyson: "Baggy clothes express identity among black youth, and not just beginning with hip-hop culture. Moreover, young black entrepreneurs like Sean 'P. Diddy' Combs and Russell Simmons have made millions from their clothing lines."*

> *Cosby: "Those people are not Africans, they don't know a damned thing about Africa. With names like Shaniqua, Shaligua, Mohammed and all that crap and all of them are in jail."*

> *Dyson: "Names like Shaniqua and Taliqua are meaningful cultural expressions of self-determination. I think that it does have something to do with African roots of black identity, and perhaps with Cosby's ignorance and discomfort with those roots. Cosby's ornery, ill-informed diatribe against black-naming is a snapshot of his assault on poor black identity." And "Given the vicious way blacks have been targeted for incarceration, Cosby's comments about poor blacks who end up in jail are dangerously naïve and empirically wrong."*

> *Cosby: "The city and all these people have to pick up the tab on them [poor African Americans] because they don't want to accept that they have to study to get an education."*

> *Dyson: "If the rigidly segregated education system continues to fail poor blacks by*

96 http://www.michaelericdyson.com/cosby/points.html Please note that the portions of Cosby's speech include references to audience applause. The full transcript of Cosby's speech may be accessed here: http://www.rci.rutgers.edu/~schochet/101/Cosby_Speech.htm

failing to prepare their children for the world of work, then admonitions to 'stay in school' may ring hollow. In suburban neighborhoods, there are $60-million schools with state-of-the-art technology, while inner city schools desperately fight for funding for their students."

Cosby: "I'm talking about these people who cry when their son is standing there in an orange suit. Where were you when he was two? (clapping) Where were you when he was twelve? (clapping) Where were you when he was eighteen, and how come you don't know he had a pistol? (clapping)"

Dyson: "And then there are the problems of the working poor: folk who rise up early every day and often work more than forty hours a week, and yet barely, if ever, make it above the poverty level. We must acknowledge the plight of both poor black (single) mothers and poor black fathers, and the lack of social support they confront. Hence, it is incredibly difficult to spend as much time with children as poor black parents might like, especially since they will be demonized if they fail to provide for their children's basic needs."

Cosby: "All this child knows is 'gimme, gimme, gimme.' These people want to buy the friendship of a child and the child couldn't care less and these people are not parenting. They're buying things for the kid. $500 sneakers, for what? And they won't spend $250 on Hooked on Phonics. (clapping)"

Dyson: "And yet, some of the engaged critique he [Cosby] seeks to make of black folk—of their materialism, their consumptive desires, their personal choices their moral aspirations, their social conscience—is broadcast with much more imagination and insight in certain quarters of hip-hop culture. (Think of Kanye West's track, "All Falls Down," which displays a self-critical approach to the link between consumption and the effort to ward off racial degradation.)"

Cosby: "I don't know who these people [poor African Americans] are."

Dyson: "The poor folk Cosby has hit the hardest are most vulnerable to the decisions of the powerful groups of which he has demanded the least: public policy makers, the business and social elite and political activists. Poor black folk cannot gain asylum from the potentially negative effects of Cosby's words on public policy makers and politicians who decide to put into play measures that support Cosby's narrow beliefs."

Cosby: "They're [poor African Americans] just hanging out in the same place, five or six generations sitting in the projects when you're just supposed to stay there long enough to get a job and move out."

Dyson: "Cosby completely ignores shifts in the economy that give value to some work while other work, in the words of William Julius Wilson 'disappears.' In our high-tech, high-skilled economy where low-skilled work is being scaled back, phased out, exported, or severely under-compensated, all the right behavior in the world won't create better jobs with more pay."

Cosby: "God is tired of you."

Dyson: "No matter how you judge Cosby's comments, you can't help but believe that a great deal of his consternation with the poor stems from his desire to remove the shame he feels in their presence and about their activity in the world. There's nothing like a formerly poor black multimillionaire bashing poor blacks to lend credence to the ancient assaults they've endured from the dominant culture."

Cosby: "You can't land a plane with 'why you ain't.' You can't be a doctor with that kind of crap coming out of your mouth. Where did these people get the idea that they're moving ahead on this."

Dyson: "Cosby's overemphasis on personal responsibility, not structural features, wrongly locates the source of poor black suffering—and by implication its remedy—in the lives of the poor."

While in recent years, Bill Cosby has been a controversial person mainly due to the increased and increasingly detailed coverage of his numerous sexual assault allegations, but he has long-been controversial for his statements critical of the black community, and certain aspects of black culture.[97]

Critics of Cosby accuse him of elitism and for failing to grasp the impact of institutional racism and other social forces on the well-documented problems faced by the black community: unemployment, poverty, teen pregnancy, incarceration, addiction, etc.

Supporters of Cosby agree with his emphasis on personal responsibility as the solution to a host of self-created (or at least self-perpetuated) problems.

Whichever interpretation (if either) you think most plausible, note that *neither* interpretation is relying, in any obvious way, upon any notion of "race" as a biological concept at all. Cosby isn't concerned that young black men are somehow genetically predisposed to violence (or any other similarly absurd notion). He's concerned about the *socializing* influence of "gangsta rap." "What do record producers think when they churn out that gangsta rap with antisocial, women-hating messages?, Do they think that black male youth won't act out what they have repeated since they were old enough to listen?"[98]

Nor is Dyson appealing to anything remotely biological in his own comments. He points to the socializing influence of institutionalized racism, and social determinants of health, prosperity, upward mobility, etc.

Whether one is "conservative" or "progressive," perhaps the obvious solution to the conceptual clumsiness of "race" is to think of "race" as a reference to ethnicity and/or culture, instead. If one does so on the assumption that, in so doing, racism—or even its more well-intentioned relative, racialism—will fade away, then I think one is probably mistaken.

Replace racism with ethnocentrism. "The 'white race' might not be superior, but 'white culture'" *is*, says the racist-with-a-new-title. "Black men aren't biologically prone to criminal behavior, but black culture *socializes* them into criminality nevertheless," says the ethnocentrist (who sounds a heck of a lot like a racist. . . .).

Even the normalizing aspect of racialism discussed above finds a new form with ethnicity. Ethnic minorities who "act white" aren't failing to live up to their biologically inherited racial essence—they're just failing to honor and express their *culture*. The question immediately arises, of course, as to *who* gets to *define* that culture, and its acceptable expressions, and why it's imperative for someone who *looks like* they're a member of that ethnicity or culture to emulate its norms.

To put it bluntly, what is "black culture?" The hip-hop lifestyle celebrated by "Young Money" artists like Lil Wayne and Drake? Does that speak to the experience of black men and women who

---

[97] For the benefit of any reader who struggles to take Cosby seriously due to the deeply troubling sexual assault allegations against Bill Cosby, please consider that Cosby's views are expressed in the 2007 book *Come On People: On the Path from Victims to Victors*, co-authored by Dr. Alvin Poussaint. If it will help, imagine the views come from Dr. Poussaint alone, and evaluate them solely based on content rather than source.

[98] http://www.nbcnews.com/id/21279731/print/1/displaymode/1098/

grew up in View Park-Windsor Hills?[99] Should the son of two medical doctors who grew up living next door to the actress Loretta Divine (an actual View Park resident), in a 5,000 square foot home, feel obliged to get a gold "grill?" Should the son of a single-mother growing up on public assistance in a small apartment in Inglewood do so? Or, should he emulate the lifestyle and values of the wealthy medical doctor instead? Which of these rather distinct lifestyles is a proper representative of "the" black culture? And who gets to make this determination? What counts as a "culture?" Are all cultures equally good? Should all cultures be respected, or are some worthy of revision or even removal?[100] Shifting our talk from race as a biological concept, to race as a cultural concept (i.e., ethnicity), solves some problems, but generates some of its own. . . .

Most of the issues and arguments raised in the context of race or ethnicity apply to other axes of identity as well: gender, sexual orientation, socio-economic status, religion, etc. In each case, some property or group membership is being identified as somehow "essential" with regard to *who you are*. In the case of race, this seems potentially problematic given the social construction of race, and the racist history of the construction and use of racial categories.

The "persistence" issue we addressed in the previous chapter considers on what basis we remain the same self over time. Now, though, we're considering who or what does (or should) *define* that enduring self. Assuming "you" are the same "you" today as you were five years ago, *who* are "you?"

As we've just seen, identity politics (in general) relies upon particular traits (e.g., race, gender, sexual orientation, etc.) as the foundation for identity, and often tries to reclaim and redescribe racial and cultural identities (etc.) against a historical background in which some of those identities were marginalized. Not everyone agrees with this approach, however—favoring, instead, a more "radical" project of self-creation, often invoking a narrative metaphor for oneself and one's life, and proposing that we should take on the task of writing the story of that self and that life as *individuals*.

Self-Fashioning[101]

Appeals for self-creation, or self-fashioning, have a long and impressive pedigree running from the "medical" models of the Ancient Greeks and Romans through the "aesthetic" models of Friedrich Nietzsche, Michel Foucault, and Richard Rorty (among others). These ideas have made their way into both pop-philosophy and pop-psychology. An "Amazon" search (in the psychology category alone) for "self-creation" yields 2,375 books. A similar search for "authenticity" in the much smaller philosophy category still yields 260 books.

The potential appeal here is probably obvious: rather than allowing yourself to be defined by others, defined in terms of your socioeconomic circumstances, or ethnicity, or religion, or sexuality, or any other aspect of you that is not necessarily *you*, you are encouraged to define *yourself*, to create yourself, to fashion yourself as the person you desire to be.

To be fair, this is undoubtedly easier for some to accomplish, than others. As a white male, I am rarely identified by others as primarily "white" or

---

[99] This is an unincorporated part of Los Angeles County nicknamed "Black Beverly Hills." The population is 84.8% African-American, with an average income of $90,000—tens of thousands of dollars above the county average for white families, and more than double the median income of L.A. County black families. http://www.latimes.com/local/la-me-adv-view-park-20150719-story.html#page=1

[100] We consider basic issues of culture, as well as cultural relativism, in the ethics chapter of this book.

[101] Some of the following section is adapted from my paper entitled "The Private and Public Appeal of Self-Fashioning," originally published in Issue 31 of the *Journal of Nietzsche Studies* (2006). That material is used here with the kind permission of Penn State University Press.

"male"—at least not usually in any way that is detectable or distressing to me. A feature of both white privilege and male privilege is that I am more free to define myself by my deeds, interests, hobbies, idiosyncrasies, etc., than is a woman (who will be *seen* as "female") or a member of an ethnic minority (who will be *seen* as "black," for example), regardless of how they might define themselves. This is patently unfair, of course, and makes the project of self-creation as described in this section a more difficult process for such persons, whatever merits the project has. . . .

The notion of "self-fashioning" is probably as old as Western philosophy itself. Since at least Pythagoras, there has been something "self-serving" and transformation about philosophy. Philosophical wisdom was valued not just for the sake of pondering all kinds of interesting things, but because it was believed that it contributed to, and was, indeed, necessary for, the personal transformation that was itself needed for personal flourishing.

Most of the ancient philosophical schools had some particular vision of human nature, and offered a variety of philosophical exercises meant to allow the student to transform himself (or herself) in the image of that vision. Whether it be increasingly abstract thinking meant to bring us closer to the Platonic "Form" of "Man," or an Aristotelian pursuit of the "Golden Mean" meant to help us to fulfill our purest human potential, or whether it be a Stoic recognition of the things under our control for the sake of making progress towards becoming a "Sage," the theme of a human being "in progress" was a familiar one for ancient philosophers.

It must be noted that, for these ancient philosophical schools, there was no notion of "originality" implied or expected of one's "self-fashioning." Indeed, to try to come up with your own unique model of flourishing would have been to deny some fundamental assumptions of (most of) these schools—namely, that there is *a* way reality is and, therefore, *a* human nature that is proper to us.

In general, ancient philosophers were all in pursuit of "the good life," but because they had different worldviews, their vision of what constitutes that good life varied, and therefore too did their visions of how best to achieve it. In each case, though, there was a generally agreed upon model, or target. As examples: aligning your will with that of Nature, for the Stoics; or restraining our desires to only those that are both natural and necessary, for the Epicureans. The goal of self-fashioning was to identity those parts of you that are contrary to that ideal, and transform yourself so that you better approximate that ideal, bit by bit.

> *If you do not see your own beauty yet, do as the sculptor does with a statue which must become beautiful: he pares away this part, scratches that other part, makes one place smooth, and cleans another, until he causes a beautiful face to appear in the statue. In the same way, you too must pare away what is superfluous, straighten what is crooked, purify all that is dark, in order to make it gleam. And never cease sculpting your own statue, until the divine light of virtue shines within you.*[102]

Millennia later, as the core assumption that there is *a* "human nature" became increasingly challenged, alternative models of self-fashioning emerged—models that emphasized "originality" rather than "conformity" to existing (and possibly suspect) ideals. One of the more notorious proponents of this proto-existentialist appeal for authenticity and self-creation was Friedrich Nietzsche.

Rejecting both "Platonism" and Christianity alike, Nietzsche believed that because not all people are fundamentally the same, it is absurd to suppose that the same values (or models for life) are appropriate for all people. There are no absolute moral rules or standards, no single blueprint for humanity to which we should all aspire.

---

[102] Plotinus, *Enneads*, I 6(1), 9, 7ff.

This is not to say that Nietzsche was some sort of amoral anarchist, let alone some sort of immoral sociopath. It is not "morality" that he wants to challenge so much as the belief that moralities have an unconditioned, universal validity. Although there is no one set of behaviors valid for all persons, there are moralities that are *conditionally* valid. They are validated on the basis of their ability to "enhance life," given a certain person's own particular constitution—and we do not all have equally "robust" constitutions, according to Nietzsche.

In contrast to "herd morality" and mediocrity, Nietzsche encourages the capable few, the elite, to overcome and master themselves, to achieve their potential and to become the "justification" for mankind. Such a genuinely original and creative person "transvalues" traditional morals, and adopts her own "good" and "evil."

For Nietzsche, the "good" or noble person is someone whose "will to power" is channeled creatively, someone who looks at herself as an artwork in progress, who takes control of herself and masters herself. This artistic metaphor is pervasive in Nietzsche's writings.

> *it is only as an aesthetic phenomenon that existence and the world are eternally justified.*[103]

> *To 'give style' to one's character--a great and rare art! It is practiced by those who survey all the strengths and weaknesses of their nature and fit them into an artistic plan until every one of them appears as art and reason and even weaknesses delight the eye.*[104]

Nietzsche's "heroes" and role-models tended to be artists, rather than warrior or politicians. In references to the writer, Goethe, he says:

> *He did not retire from life but put himself in the midst of it; he was not fainthearted but took as much as possible upon himself, over himself, into himself. What he wanted was totality; . . . he disciplined himself to wholeness, he created himself.*[105]

What makes great persons *great* is their power to channel and transform their own inner drive (their "will to power').

> *Once you suffered passions and called them evil. But now you have only your virtues left: they grew out of your passions.... Once you had wild dogs in your cellar, but in the end they turned into birds and lovely singers.*[106]

The lovely and poetic imagery Nietzsche uses here portrays someone transforming their inner drive and passions, something they once regarded as "evil," into something beautiful: "birds and lovely singers."

For yourself, using this model, you might ask: "how can I take what is inside me: my desires and dreams and ambitions; how can I take the life that I find myself in, and the 'self' that I have been told I am—and turn all those things into something 'beautiful?'"

For Nietzsche, part of what it is to be "good" (according to his own taste, of course!) is to not take life for granted, to not simply go along with the "herd," and to make of yourself a work of art. For those up to the challenge, *authenticity* should be one's goal—not that he believes very many are capable of this achievement! Most of us allow ourselves to be defined by others, and unthinkingly play out that assigned role.

In our previous section, we briefly considered identity politics. It should be clear where identity politics and a Nietzschean strain of "authenticity" collide. We might imagine him scoffing at anyone letting themselves be defined as "Black," "White," "Latino," or "Gay" or "Straight"—or any other "herd" label, laughing at anyone who would passively act out the role assigned to them, as

[103] Nietzsche, *The Birth of Tragedy*, section 5.
[104] Nietzsche, *The Gay Science*, section 290.
[105] Nietzsche, *Twilight of the Idols*, section 49.
[106] Nietzsche, Thus Spake Zarathustra, I:5.

opposed to creating an authentic self of one's own.

Authenticity comes in two general stages, for those up to the task. The first is when we liberate ourselves from conditioning, rationalizations, illusions, and masks. This is a "negative" stage where one "hammers" one's "idols." It is important to note, though, that hammers are used for both destruction *and* construction; they destroy, but they also build.

After having broken our "tablets" of value, we freely assimilate values and norms consistent with our own nature in the second stage. This is the "positive" stage where we rebuild ourselves, and in which Nietzsche encourages those who can, the few, the "free spirits," to "become who we are."

> *Be your self! All you are now doing, thinking, desiring is not you yourself.... We are responsible to ourselves for our own existence; consequently, we want to be the true helmsman of this existence and refuse to allow our existence to resemble a mindless act of chance. One has to take a somewhat bold and dangerous line with this existence: especially as, whatever happens, we are bound to lose it.... There exists in the world a single path along which no one can go except you: whither does it lead? Do not ask, go along it.*[107]

The greatest and rarest of such "free spirits" could be considered the *Übermensch*. This "Superman" ("Overman" is a more accurate translation—and one that doesn't conjure up images of spandex and capes!) would be the pinnacle of self-mastery, strong, confident, free—even a replacement for "God" (since Nietzsche believed that "God is dead.").

Despite the fact that the overwhelming number of his admirers think that Nietzsche is writing to "them," in reality, he was writing to a tiny, terribly select few—an elite group into which most of us just would not qualify. Want to find out if *you* qualify?

Respond to the following statements using the following scale:
1 = Strongly Disagree/Very non-Descriptive
2 = Disagree/non-Descriptive
3 = Agree/Descriptive
4 = Strongly Agree/Very Descriptive

1) I feel guilty about what I've done in the past or what sort of person I am.
2) I feel angry about the wrongs I've suffered in the past.
3) I would make a lot of changes if I had my life to live over again.
4) I often have strong desires to do things I don't really want to do, and so I must resist my desires.
5) I don't have many highs or lows. Sometimes it seems like nothing matters much.
6) There is so much world suffering that it would be better if the world had never existed.
7) I need favorable feedback from others in order to feel good about myself.
8) One of the best things about doing nice things for others is the gratitude. Absent that gratitude, I wish I could take it back.

[After answering the questions, and adding up your score, consult this footnote to check your result. [108]]

[107] Nietzsche, "Schopenhauer as Educator," in *Untimely Meditations*. section 1.

[108] A score of 8 on the self-assessment above indicates *Übermenschlichkeit* (or, more likely, self-delusion!).

The "Overman" is also someone mentally strong enough to affirm the "Eternal Recurrence" of the same.

> *The greatest weight.-- What, if some day or night a demon were to steal after you into your loneliest loneliness and say to you: "This life as you now live it and have lived it, you will have to live once more and innumerable times more; and there will be nothing new in it, but every pain and every joy and every thought and sigh and everything unutterably small or great in your life will have to return to you, all in the same succession and sequence - even this spider and this moonlight between the trees, and even this moment and I myself. The eternal hourglass of existence is turned upside down again and again, and you with it, speck of dust!"*
>
> *Would you not throw yourself down and gnash your teeth and curse the demon who spoke thus?... Or how well disposed would you have to become to yourself and to life to crave nothing more fervently than this ultimate eternal confirmation and seal?*[109]

The idea of the eternal recurrence is actually an ancient idea, finding a home in Stoic cosmology, for example. Nietzsche's version, however, is best interpreted as an "existential imperative" rather than a cosmological hypothesis.

The question is simply this: given a chance, would you do everything in your life, all over again, exactly the same—all the pains, frustrations, and losses, as well as the triumphs and happy moments—and would you will to do so forever. Finally, could you will that this be so, and be *joyful* in the willing? To do so is to truly "embrace Fate"—what Nietzsche called "*Amor Fati.*" The ability to do so is also, he thought, a profoundly *rare* thing, and anyone capable of doing so has truly executed a beautiful work-of-art self.

The life-as-art metaphor is often (rightfully) associated with Nietzsche, but so too is a "life-as-narrative" metaphor—replacing the imagery of the visual arts with that of writing. This "life-as-narrative" approach is one to which Richard Rorty seemed sympathetic. He advocates the creation of one's *own* "final vocabulary." That is, the "set of words which [we] employ to justify [our] actions, [our] beliefs, and [our] lives.... They are the words in which we tell, sometimes prospectively and sometimes retrospectively, the story of our lives."[110] According to Rorty, Nietzsche hoped that once we realized Plato's "true world" was a fiction, we would seek comfort at our deaths by being the sort of animal who, "by describing himself in his own terms, had created himself."[111] To understand why this is thought of as inventing a new language of self-description it is useful to quote Rorty at length.

> *The process of coming to know oneself, confronting one's contingency, tracking one's causes home, is identical with the process of inventing a new language—that is, of thinking up some new metaphors. For any literal description of one's individuality, which is to say any use of an inherited language-game for this purpose, will necessarily fail. . . . To fail as a poet—and thus, for Nietzsche, to fail as a human being—is to accept somebody else's description of oneself, to execute a previously prepared program, to write, at most, elegant variations on previously written poems.*[112]

New metaphors are needed for this

[109] *The Gay Science*, section 341.
[110] Richard Rorty, *Contingency, Irony, and Solidarity* (Cambridge University Press, 1989), 73.
[111] Ibid., 27.
[112] Ibid., 27-28.

redescription or else, by relying on inherited vocabulary, we simply describe ourselves in such a way that we are copies, or at best slightly altered copies, of other persons. Presumably, labels referring to race, ethnicity, generation, socioeconomic class, sexual orientation, and the like, would be examples of inheriting "copied" vocabularies.

If an original self-redescription must be (literally) literary, then most of us are left with little hope in our project of self-creation. Trite love poems and banal diary entries will prove insufficient to the task of self-fashioning, and the great mass of humanity will be at the mercy of others' descriptions. Rorty avoids this narrow (and possibly elitist) approach by having a more generous understanding of writer, character, and text.

One need not *literally* create a text wherein one can explore redescription. Instead, *everything we do* can be seen as a symbolic and artistic gesture. The intellectual or artist might be especially talented, and *their* self-descriptions will undoubtedly prove to be more famous and more influential, but their efforts need not be considered unique. The intellectual is a special case of human, "just somebody who does with marks and noises what other people do with their spouses and children, their fellow workers, the tools of their trade, the cash accounts of their businesses, the possessions they accumulate in their homes, the music they listen to, the sports they play or watch, or the trees they pass on their way to work."[113] Or, as Nietzsche acknowledges, "everything bears witness to what we are, our friendships and enemies, our glance and the clasp of our hand, our memory and that which we do not remember, our books and our handwriting."[114] Few of us will create a literary text, but *all of us* will contribute to our life-as-text, and so create our self-as-character.

Rorty's hope is that continual redescription will *make* the best possible self.[115] The layperson's chance for greatness lies in inventing a new language of self-description either by literally redescribing herself in novel ways, or by *symbolically* redescribing herself through novel activity, through actions that in some way deviate from rote conformity, that offer up a new and unexpected description of herself, that contribute to an original narrative of her life. "The perfect life will be one which closes in the assurance that the last of his final vocabularies, at least, really was wholly *his*."[116]

While everyone fashions himself or herself and continually describes and redescribes himself or herself, nothing about self-fashioning entails that such self-description will be *original*. *If* one describes oneself via an entirely inherited "final vocabulary," then to the extent that this vocabulary informs one's actions (i.e., one's self-fashioning), the self that is fashioned and described is cast in the mold of another (or countless others). Those who can overcome convention, on the other hand, can become an original, authentic self and are "free spirits."

> *He is called a free spirit who thinks differently from what, on the basis of his origin, environment, his class and profession, or on the basis of the dominant views of his age, would have been expected of him. . . . he has liberated himself from tradition.*[117]

Richard Shusterman would counter that not only is it unlikely that these valuable efforts will result in strictly "original" life-narratives, but that there is no need for them to be "original."

> *Even if the ethical goal of narrative self-creation be modeled on the creation of an aesthetic work of art, it still does not follow that such creation must be radically novel and altogether unique. For neither do artworks require such radical and*

[113]Ibid., 36-37.
[114] "Schopenhauer as Educator," section 1.
[115]Rorty, 80.
[116]Ibid., 97.
[117] Nietzsche, Human, all too Human. A Book for Free Spirits. I, 225.

idiosyncratic originality in order to be aesthetically satisfying, as we can see most clearly in classical and medieval art. To think that true artistic creation precludes established types and variations on familiar formulas is to confuse art with the artistic ideology of romantic individualism and the modernist avant-garde, a historically parochial confusion to which Rorty falls victim. One can style oneself aesthetically, create one's life as a work of art, by adopting and adapting familiar roles and life-styles, adjusting these generic forms to one's individual contingent circumstances.... There was no need to invent an entirely new formula; there was nothing inartistic about elegant variations on the familiar."[118]

Though there is much less consensus on appropriate life-styles today, "this merely provides us with more materials and models for artistic self-fashioning."[119] This is just to say that we shouldn't take the "life-as-narrative" metaphor too far and conclude that only truly original (let alone popular) narratives have value and are worth pursuing. This emphasis on originality in art is a relatively recent focus, historically, and certainly not the only approach to artistry available to us. Indeed, as mentioned, ancient philosophers would often employ artistic metaphors, but with the assumption that a blue print for human flourishing, based on our "Nature," was already available to us, and the best efforts at self-fashioning were those that most closely emulated that single ideal vision.

To create a beautiful version of "you," there is no need to create a "you" somehow completely different and in contrast to others' visions. Indeed, ironically, there is something conformist about our collective pursuit of and obsession with originality these days! Shusterman claims there is no reason why being like others is incompatible with being oneself—unless autonomy is conflated with radical individualism. He goes on to claim that the "Rortian compulsion to create oneself in a novel fashion can itself be seen as a form of non-autonomy, a bondage to the new and individualistic."[120]

Aside from the possible aesthetic appeal, is there any good reason to adopt this vocabulary of "self-fashioning," and "lives-as-narratives?" Perhaps Rorty chooses to do so because thinking of others, like us, as self-creative can reduce the difference between "us" and "them." While only a few "poems" become famous and celebrated, if every human life *is* a poem, at least we've all got that in common! Accepting such a view might make it more difficult for us to view others as fundamentally unlike ourselves.

Seeing others as in the process of writing their own life-as-poem helps us to see others as being immersed in their own projects just as we are. Perhaps such a perspective will expand the community of people-like-us, making it more difficult for us to rationalize cruelty and oppression.

To put it plainly, if we each recognize that other people—even those that seem very "other" than ourselves (e.g., on the basis of religion, race, socioeconomic status, sexuality, etc.)—are each and all involved in the process of writing their own idiosyncratic life-narratives by virtue of the actual living of their lives, if we see each life as a poem-in-progress, then perhaps we can find some point of commonality in our shared struggles as poets?

I might not understand your "poem," nor even like it very much, on the basis of my own taste, but perhaps I can at least recognize the effort you're making, and see in you the same sort of creative struggle that I see in myself, and hope that others will see in me as well. I might not personally understand the experiences of students protesting for more ethnically diverse faculty and students at college campuses, but if I can recognize their fundamentally creative efforts at crafting their life

[118]Richard Shusterman, *Prgamatist Aesthetics. Living Beauty, Rethinking Art.* 2nd edition (New York: Rowman & Littlefield Publishers, Inc., 2000), 253-254.

[119]Ibid.

[120]Ibid.

narrative as being similar to mine, then perhaps I can be more empathetic to their cause, even if the language of our respective life poems is different? Seeing every human life as a "poem" might serve to reinforce respecting the autonomy and dignity of persons.

Conclusion

The last two chapters have covered quite a lot of material, and from a variety of different directions. The central, unifying theme, however, has been one of personal identity.

We started with the intertwining questions of what constitutes "identity" in the first place, and what (if anything) allows that identity to persist over time. How, if at all, do "you" remain the same person throughout your life? To that end, we considered a variety of traditional criteria: body, brain, psychological state/memory, and the "simple" (substance dualist) criterion.

We then shifted from metaphysics to politics in our consideration of identity politics. We focused on race, though we could just as well have considered religion, socioeconomic status, gender, sexuality, or any number of other possible axes of identity. In that section, we explored how identity can be established and defined (at times, problematically) by external forces, and with potentially serious political consequences.

Finally, we shifted from politics to existential considerations. What if our identity is our own to define, and even to create? In that section, we considered some of the issues and complications arising from this notion of self-creation.

I hope it's obvious, by now, that there are numerous philosophical aspects of personal identity, and that these produce significant practical impact on our lives, ranging from determinations of personal responsibility, criminal liability, political activism, and self-concept. I will close this chapter by quoting from an atypical philosophical source: a contemporary rock band called Switchfoot.

This is your life, are you who you want to be?
This is your life, are you who you want to be?
This is your life, is it everything you dreamed that it would be?
When the world was younger and you had everything to lose[121]

[121] This is the chorus from their song, "This is Your Life."

Chapter 6
Political Philosophy

Comprehension questions you should be able to answer after reading this introduction:

1. *What is the "State of Nature," according to Hobbes? What are its features? What is it like?*
2. *What does it mean to say that Hobbes is a "nominalist" with regard to concepts like "justice" and "(moral) goodness?"*
3. *What does Hobbes mean by a "law of nature?" What are the first three laws of nature, according to Hobbes?*
4. *What is a "social contract?" What is the purpose of forming a social contract? Why does Hobbes think the State of Nature would inspire us to want to form a social contract?*
5. *What is a "sovereign," and why does Hobbes think we need one?*
6. *Why does Hobbes think the power of the sovereign must be absolute?*
7. *Why does Hobbes think that it is impossible for the sovereign to act unjustly?*
8. *What is Rawls' "Original Position" (OP)?*
9. *What is the "veil of ignorance" (VOI)? Explain what is meant by "ignorance," in this context. Of what are participants "ignorant?" What is the purpose of this ignorance?*
10. *What are Rawls' Two Principles of Justice? (POJ)*
11. *What are the "basic liberties" described in the 1st POJ?*
12. *What are the "primary goods" in the 2nd POJ? What two conditions must be met to justify an unequal distribution of primary goods? How could an unequal distribution of primary goods be to everyone's advantage?*
13. *Who are the "least advantaged?" Why should we focus on them, when considering applications of the two Principles of Justice?*
14. *What does Rawls mean by each of the following? Reasonable pluralism, well-ordered society, overlapping consensus, comprehensive moral doctrine, public reason, stability.*
15. *What does it mean to be constrained by "public reason" in the context of political debates and activism?*
16. *According to Rawls, when it is acceptable to "resist" our institutions and laws?*

Although this will be a painfully brief treatment of the subject matter, don't let the brevity mislead you; political philosophy is a terribly important sub-field of philosophy, and is one of the more obviously practical uses of philosophy. Political philosophy is just what it sounds like: philosophy applied to political issues.

Entire books can be (and have been) written about each of the many topics within political philosophy. Such an investigation lies far beyond our scope, however. We will embark upon the much more modest project of a brief investigation of one answer to one question: "what justifies the State?" We will then conclude with a follow-up investigation of the proper distribution of rights and resources, once the State is established, and how to address the "problem" of reasonable pluralism.

Questions that arise in political philosophy include (but are not limited to) the following:

- What justifies the State?
- What sorts of governmental systems are legitimate?
- When, if ever, and to what extent, is civil disobedience morally acceptable?
- What rights, if any, do citizens have?
- What is the legitimate extent of the State's power to limit individual freedom?
- What makes a law just or unjust?
- How should the resources of the State be distributed amongst its citizens?
- What principles should govern relations between States?
- When, if ever, is war justifiable?

What Justifies the State?

Another way of phrasing this question is to ask why we should submit ourselves to government authority. Before proceeding, answer the following questions:

1. What is the purpose of government?
2. Why does (or should) government exist?
3. What do you "get" from living under the authority of your government?
4. What do you "lose," from living under the authority of your government?

There are many possible responses to those questions, and the way one answers them indicates the sort of political philosophy one (usually) embraces. For example, conservatives tend to claim that the purpose of the State is for the protection of life, liberty, and property against domestic and foreign threats. Liberals usually add that the purpose of government is also to provide certain goods to its citizens. But why should we live under a government at all?

Consider for a moment just what government does to you: it limits your freedom! How, you might ask? Simple: your freedom is restricted by all the laws and regulations enforced by the government. The government restricts your behavior in a great many ways. It forbids some behaviors, and requires others. Moreover, it takes your money through taxation and uses that money for all kinds of purposes—some of which you might not approve. Additionally, in the United States, men over the age of 18 (with a few exceptions) are required to register for the draft, and may be *forced* to enlist in the military in times of conflict. Refuse, and you may go to jail instead.

Still, despite all the complaining that most of us do, at one time or another, about our government, it is very hard to find anyone who seriously advocates that we should have no government at all. Why? Because, despite the inconvenience of our behavior being restricted, despite the annoyance of taxes, and despite the aggravation of corrupt or incompetent politicians, the alternative to government is far, far worse. This alternative is referred to as the "State of Nature."

Hobbes

The State of Nature (hereafter referred to as the SON), is a notion often attributed to Thomas Hobbes. Hobbes was born in Westport England, on April 5th, 1588. He was brilliant, even as a child—learning Latin, Greek, French, and Italian, in addition to his own native English. He translated Euripides' "Medea" from Greek to Latin at the age of fourteen, and then entered Oxford University at the age of fifteen. After receiving his bachelor's degree five years later in 1608, he was invited to join the Cavendish household (headed by William Cavendish, the Earl of Devonshire) as a tutor. He remained connected to the family for decades, often living with them, and remaining a bachelor his entire life.

In addition to his work with the Cavendish family, he also served as a tutor to King Charles II of France, and acted as secretary for Sir Francis

Bacon from 1618-1622. Between 1634 and 1637 he met Galileo Galilei, Rene Descartes, and Pierre Gassendi. Hobbes contributed some criticisms of Descartes' work, to which Descartes offered replies. It is said that their relationship was cool, if not outright acrimonious.[122]

The political context in which we must understand Hobbes' life and thought is one of change and anxiety. The Tudor dynasty ended with Queen Elizabeth's death in 1603. Her cousin James became the first "Stuart" ruler, and embraced the notion of the "divine right" of kings. Accordingly, he tried to rule without the approval of parliament. When James died in 1625, his son Charles I soon found himself at war with both France and Spain. To fund these wars, Charles imposed taxes without parliamentary consent. Hobbes, acting as secretary to the Earl of Devonshire, helped collect these taxes. Eventually, the Civil War of 1642-1646 broke out in protest of these taxes (as well as some religious issues). The King lost the civil war, was executed, and the monarchy was abolished. The Republic of Oliver Cromwell was established, and Hobbes (fearing persecution due to the essay he had written in support of the Royalist position) fled from England to France, where he stayed until 1651.

Hobbes eventually returned to England and "made peace" with the Commonwealth by agreeing to take an oath of Loyalty (the "Engagement Oath"). He immediately generated controversy, though, with the publication of his *Leviathan* in that same year.

Amazingly, Hobbes works managed to anger just about every faction in England. He angered Parliament because, even though he technically endorsed the idea that government is made legitimate by the consent of the governed, he also claimed that this consent entails absolute monarchy. He angered the Royalists because, even though he advocated for absolute monarchy, he denied the divine right of kings. He angered the Church by his materialist worldview, and undeniably heretical (if not outright atheistic) claims about God, miracles, revelation, and the Bible.[123]

Nevertheless, Hobbes managed to die an old man, at the age of 91, on December 3rd, 1679. His reputation as an alleged atheist followed him even after his death. *Leviathan* was publicly burned at Oxford on June 21st, 1683, and all of his works were placed on the Vatican's Index of Prohibited Books (joining Machiavelli's!) in 1703.

Overall, Hobbes experienced a country that was always insecure, always at the brink of civil war and calamity. Peace and security were constantly in jeopardy, he thought, because of the greater demand from the growing middle class, and even farmers, for liberty and political participation. The cultural trend was to regard the authority of the Bible (and the Church), and even one's own conscience, as being above that of the king and his agents—or at least comparable. The result of all this "liberty" was instability, and the promise of strife and misery.

Method

Like other scholars of his time, Hobbes saw no distinction between philosophy and science, and

---

122 Descartes wrote the following about Hobbes in a letter to Marsenne (1641): "Having now had time to read the last piece by Englishman [Hobbes], I find complete confirmation of the opinion of him that I expressed to you two weeks ago. I think it would be best for me to have nothing more to do with him, and thus to refrain from answering him. If his temperament is what I think it is, it will be hard for us to exchange views without becoming enemies. It's better for us both to leave things where they are. Please don't tell him any more than you have to of what you know of my unpublished views, because I'm pretty sure that this is someone who is looking to acquire a reputation at my expense, and by sharp practice."

123 For example, not only does he claim that humans are entirely material, but he also insisted that God must be a material (corporeal) being as well, describing God as a "corporeal spirit." As a result of all this, his book was debated by a committee in the House of Commons in 1666 as a possible item of criminal heresy!

he drew political implications from the discoveries of science, rejecting the claims and insights of classical political philosophy as unscientific. Such views were not based on deductive reasoning, but merely their own experience. "In these westerne parts of the world, we are made to receive our opinions concerning the Institution, and Rights of Common-wealths, from Aristotle, Cicero, and other men, Greeks and Romanes, that living under Popular States, derived those Rights, not from the Principles of Nature, but transcribed them into their books, out of the Practice of their own Common-wealths."[124]

Unlike nearly the entire tradition before him, who believed that the State is natural, and that existing States would conform (more, or less, or not at all) to that natural ideal, Hobbes flatly denies any pre-existing "ideal." Hobbes was convinced that political philosophy should be just as scientifically-based as geometry, astronomy, and "natural philosophy." "The science of making and maintaining commonwealths has definite and infallible rules, as does arithmetic and geometry."[125] To that end, Hobbes embraced a radical "nominalism," framing both geometry and political science as disciplines which start from arbitrary/conventional definitions, which then deduce conclusions on the basis of those definitions.[126]

He also rejected any "teleological" accounts of human nature or politics, denying any natural "ends" to which we incline and towards which we should act. Instead, he interprets politics mathematically, and mechanically, in terms of causes and effects. "A final cause has no place but in such things as have sense and will; and this also I shall prove hereafter to be an efficient cause." In the introduction to *Leviathan*, he proposes: "For what is the heart but a spring; and the nerves, but so many strings, and the joints, but so many wheels, giving the motion to the whole body, such as was intended by the artificer?"

The State of Nature

Although Hobbes rejected both teleological views of human nature, as well as natural law approaches, in general, this certainly didn't mean that he rejected the idea that humans had a "nature"—he just interpreted this nature in purely mechanical fashion. Like any machine, the human machine requires a source of "animation." The "passions" are that source. While the objects of our passion may vary, the same general passions (e.g., desire, fear, hope) drive all human behavior, in a mechanically-necessary (causally determined) fashion. Pleasure, for example, is "nothing really but motion about the heart, as conception is nothing but motion in the head."

These passions will play a critical role in his understanding of the motivational foundations of civil society: "The Passions that encline men to Peace, are Feare of Death; Desire of such things as are necessary to commodious living; and a Hope by their Industry to obtain them."[127]

Humans are equally driven by passions, but are equal in other important respects as well. Hobbes claimed that we are all (roughly) equal both physically and mentally. "Nature hath made men so equall, in the faculties of body, and mind; as that though there bee found one man sometimes manifestly stronger in body, or of quicker mind then another; yet when all is reckoned together, the difference between man, and man, is not so considerable, as that one man can thereupon claim to himselfe any benefit, to which another may not pretend, as well as he. For as to the strength of body, the weakest has strength enough to kill the strongest, either by secret machination, or by confederacy with others, that are in the same danger with himselfe."[128]

---

124 Leviathan, XXI.

125 Ibid., XX.

126 For example, we stipulate what a triangle is (e.g., a 3-side plane figure), and then deduce more information by building on that definition (e.g., that the interior angles of a triangle add up to 180 degrees).

127 *Leviathan*, XIII.

128 Ibid., XIII.

This is an admittedly ominous sort of equality. In effect, it is an equality of vulnerability, of fear, and of danger. Even though some people are physically stronger than others, even the strongest among us is still flesh and bone, equally mortal, and can be overcome by physically weaker foes through cleverness or strength of numbers. Therefore, this basic "equality" will be, for Hobbes, a source of tension and conflict. Conflict is the "natural" state for humanity—in the absence of political society.

This absence of political society is a key assumption driving this notion of the "State of Nature." The State of Nature is a state of anarchy. It may be conceived as either a pre-political environment, or the condition that obtains when a government loses control over its populace. "It may peradventure be thought, there was never such a time, nor condition of warre as this; and I believe it was never generally so, over all the world: but there are many places, where they live so now. For the savage people in many places of America, except the government of small Families, the concord whereof dependeth on naturall lust, have no government at all; and live at this day in that brutish manner, as I said before. Howsoever, it may be perceived what manner of life there would be, where there were no common Power to feare; by the manner of life, which men that have formerly lived under a peacefull government, use to degenerate into, in a civill Warre."[129]

The State of Nature, then, is the hypothetical state of existence we would experience in the absence of any governing authority. It is a state of literal anarchy, of basic (physical and intellectual) equality, and a state of absolute freedom. There are literally no restrictions on behavior, beyond what is physically impossible for us to achieve. No laws, no rules—not even notions of right or wrong, justice or injustice. In the State of Nature, every person has a right to anything deemed necessary for self-preservation.

> *To this warre of every man against every man, this also is consequent; that nothing can be Unjust. The notions of Right and Wrong, Justice and Injustice have there no place. Where there is no common Power, there is no Law: where no Law, no Injustice. Force, and Fraud, are in warre the two Cardinall vertues. Justice, and Injustice are none of the Faculties neither of the Body, nor Mind. If they were, they might be in a man that were alone in the world, as well as his Senses, and Passions. They are Qualities, that relate to men in Society, not in Solitude. It is consequent also to the same condition, that there be no Propriety, no Dominion, no Mine and Thine distinct; but onely that to be every mans that he can get; and for so long, as he can keep it.*[130]

Similarly, in the next section of *Leviathan*:

> *And because the condition of Man, (as hath been declared in the precedent Chapter) is a condition of Warre of every one against every one; in which case every one is governed by his own Reason; and there is nothing he can make use of, that may not be a help unto him, in preserving his life against his enemyes; It followeth, that in such a condition, every man has a Right to every thing; even to one anothers body. And therefore, as long as this naturall Right of every man to every thing endureth, there can be no security to any man, (how strong or wise soever he be,) of living out the time, which Nature ordinarily alloweth men to live.*[131]

As a "nominalist," Hobbes denies the independent reality of such concepts as "justice." "A name or appellation therefore is the voice of man, arbitrarily imposed, for a mark to bring to his mind some conception concerning the thing on which it is imposed."[132] In the State of Nature, as mentioned, "the notions of right and wrong,

[129] Ibid., XIII.
[130] Ibid., XIII.
[131] Ibid., XIV.
[132] Elements of Law, 5.2-3

justice and injustice, have there no place." Those terms acquire meaning only within the State, as specified by the sovereign. Indeed, justice is merely a name used to classify an idea. Good and evil are mere words, "ever used with relation to the person that useth them: there being nothing simply and absolutely so; nor any common rule of good and evil, to be taken from the nature of the objects themselves." What is "just" (as we will see) is determined by the will of the sovereign (whatever the sovereign *names* "just"), and is expressed in the laws of his State.

Even the difference between monarchy and tyranny is subjective. Those who dislike monarchy call it tyranny, those who dislike aristocracy call it oligarchy, and those who dislike polity (democracy) call it mob-rule or anarchy. "There be other names of Government, in the Histories, and books of Policy; as Tyranny, and Oligarchy: But they are not the names of other Formes of Government, but of the same Formes misliked. For they that are discontented under Monarchy, call it Tyranny; and they that are displeased with Aristocracy, called it Oligarchy: so also, they which find themselves grieved under a Democracy, call it Anarchy, (which signifies want of Government;) and yet I think no man believes, that want of Government, is any new kind of Government: nor by the same reason ought they to believe, that the Government is of one kind, when they like it, and another, when they mislike it, or are oppressed by the Governours."[133]

Hobbes rejects any meaningful distinction between types of government, and also, importantly, rejects the classical idea of man as a naturally political animal –"which axiom, though received by most, is most certainly false."[134]

It is neither from our nature, nor in fulfillment of our nature, that we form political communities. It is self-interest alone that brings us into community with others. For Hobbes, humans are all equally driven by passions, egoistically motivated, lacking any innate notion of right or wrong, and fundamentally anti-social. Humans are power-seekers, and subject to a "perpetual and restless desire of power after power, that ceases only in death."[135] All other goods (e.g., wealth, knowledge, reputation, etc.) are valued because they facilitate acquiring power. Even happiness itself is conceived as a "continual satisfaction of desire, from one object to another." [136] Reason, then, is no longer the instrument by which we determine what is morally right and wrong. It is, instead, the practical instrument by which we determine which specific course of action will best satisfy our passions.

The combination of our being driven by our amoral passions, and the anarchy of the environment in the State of Nature, diminishes any hope of cooperation, and promotes conflict. This is why the State of Nature was described as "a war of every man against every man."[137] Our primary, driving motivations are competition, "diffidence" (fear, suspicion), and "glory."[138] Without external constraints on our behavior, our passions will drive us to "invade" one another for personal gain. Under these perilous conditions, "war" is more advantageous than "peace." Even those who are satisfied with their lot in life are fools to pursue peace in the State of Nature, as they "would not be able, long time, by standing only on their defense, to subsist."[139] Recalling our presupposed basic physical and intellectual equality, Hobbes envisions conflict and insecurity.

> *From this equality of ability, ariseth equality of hope in the attaining of our Ends. And therefore if any two men desire the same thing, which neverthelesse they cannot both enjoy, they become enemies; and in the way to their End, (which is principally their owne conservation, and sometimes their delectation only,) endeavour to destroy, or subdue one an*

133 Leviathan, XIX.

134 Hobbes, *De Cive*, 1.2

135 Leviathan, XI.

136 Ibid., XI.

137 Ibid., XII.

138 Ibid., XIII.

139 Ibid., XIII. Note the similarity to Machiavelli with regard to the safety of "peaceful" States!

> *other. And from hence it comes to passe, that where an Invader hath no more to feare, than an other mans single power; if one plant, sow, build, or possesse a convenient Seat, others may probably be expected to come prepared with forces united, to dispossesse, and deprive him, not only of the fruit of his labour, but also of his life, or liberty. And the Invader again is in the like danger of another.*[140]

If you are continually fearful for your safety, think about how that will impact your behavior. The fruits of civilization, such as education, invention, science, technology, art, and recreation, all require that a certain basic level of security has been achieved. If you are fearful that you might die if you leave your home, you're unlikely to go to school, or take a piano lesson, or play some basketball. If the fruits of your labors aren't secured by property laws and police protection, you'll be unlikely to try to amass much wealth, because anything you can't keep with you at all times is so likely to be stolen as to not be worth the effort it will take to obtain it in the first place.

Imagine that we're in the State of Nature, and I spend the day gathering nuts and berries. You hide in the bushes, watching. At the end of the day, I return home to my shelter that I spent several days building, to enjoy my dinner of nuts and berries. You sneak up behind me, hit me over the head with a branch you collected, and steal my nuts, berries, and shelter. What, exactly, was the point of my investing all that effort in building a shelter, and gathering food? Instead, it would make much more sense for me to live a bare, subsistence kind of life—never bothering to acquire more than I can use at that very moment, and always looking over my shoulder in case you (or anyone else) is plotting against me.

Such a world will have no industries or universities, no artistic achievements or great accomplishments of humanity. In order to enjoy any of those things, we need to feel safe. In order to feel safe, we need to be protected. Since no one is so powerful as to be able to protect himself against anyone and everyone (in whatever number), we can't manage this alone. Hobbes' mechanistic account of human motivation and behavior leaves no room for moral "choice." To change behavior, the conditions promoting those behaviors must be changed—and that means leaving the State of Nature.

The very same self-interested passions that drive us to war in the State of Nature drive us to civil society. Humans are machines moved by means of two basic drives: desire for power, and fear of death. The desire for power produces our problems in the state of nature. The fear of death inspires the social contract. "The Passions that encline men to Peace, are Feare of Death; Desire of such things as are necessary to commodious living; and a Hope by their Industry to obtain them. And Reason suggesteth convenient Articles of Peace, upon which men may be drawn to agreement."[141]

In addition to these basic drives, Hobbes proposes that there are "Laws of Nature"—though he means something very different by this term, than did those who came before him. By "law of nature" he means some sort of prudential rule, dictated and determined by reason, which promotes self-preservation. "A LAW OF NATURE, (Lex Naturalis,) is a Precept, or generall Rule, found out by Reason, by which a man is forbidden to do, that, which is destructive of his life, or taketh away the means of preserving the same; and to omit, that, by which he thinketh it may be best preserved."[142]

Specifically, reason prescribes "That every man, ought to endeavour Peace, as farre as he has hope of obtaining it; and when he cannot obtain it, that he may seek, and use, all helps, and advantages of Warre."[143] Following from this precept is the first "Law of Nature," to seek peace. "The first, and Fundamentall Law of Nature; which is, 'To seek Peace, and follow it.'"

The second Law of Nature follows from the

140 Ibid., XIII.

141 Ibid., XIII.

142 Ibid., XIV.

143 Ibid., XIV.

first. "From this Fundamentall Law of Nature, by which men are commanded to endeavour Peace, is derived this second Law; 'That a man be willing, when others are so too, as farre-forth, as for Peace, and defence of himselfe he shall think it necessary, to lay down this right to all things; and be contented with so much liberty against other men, as he would allow other men against himselfe.'"[144] This mutual transfer of rights (to "everything") is a social contract.

The Social Contract

Contract approaches weren't entirely new—not even in Hobbes' time. Glaucon, in the *Republic*, offered one well before Hobbes, and both presuppose the same basic motivation: egoism. All such approaches make politics a matter of *nomos* (convention) rather than *physis* (nature). It is conceivable that humans not be in community with each other. Indeed, this hypothetical scenario is precisely what we imagine when we consider the State of Nature.

As parties to the contract, in exchange for the promise of peace and security, we agree amongst ourselves to limit our behavior so long as others will, too. In other words, I will agree not to kill you, so long as you agree not to kill me. I'll agree not to steal your stuff, so long as you agree to the same.

The only right never surrendered in this way is our basic right of self-defense. The whole point if surrendering rights in the SON is for the sake of self-preservation. "Whensoever a man Transferreth his Right, or Renounceth it; it is either in consideration of some Right reciprocally transferred to himselfe; or for some other good he hopeth for thereby. For it is a voluntary act: and of the voluntary acts of every man, the object is some Good To Himselfe. And therefore there be some Rights, which no man can be understood by any words, or other signes, to have abandoned, or transferred. As first a man cannot lay down the right of resisting them, that assault him by force, to take away his life; because he cannot be understood to ayme thereby, at any Good to himselfe."[145] To surrender the right to self-preservation for the sake of self-preservation, makes no sense, of course.

With regard to all of the freedom we surrender, and all the promises we make, the third law of nature is that we *honor* whatever contracts we make. "From that law of Nature, by which we are obliged to transferre to another, such Rights, as being retained, hinder the peace of Mankind, there followeth a Third; which is this, That Men Performe Their Covenants Made: without which, Covenants are in vain, and but Empty words; and the Right of all men to all things remaining, wee are still in the condition of Warre."[146]

Self-interest drives us into the social contract, but doesn't guarantee that we'll honor it. For some, short-term advantage will blind them to long-term self-interest, and such foolish contract-breakers risk forcing us all back into the State of Nature. A coercive power (the "Sovereign") is needed to enforce the social contract, since "covenants without the sword are but words."[147]

This is but the natural conclusion that reason leads us to, according to Hobbes. It is our fear of death that gets is to accept rules in the first place. Only fear of death (as punishment) can get us to obey those rules. If we want the peace promised by the rules, we must implicitly will the rules (and their enforcement) as well. The sovereign must apply enough fear of punishment to overpower any other passion for criminal gain.

[144] Ibid., XIV.
[145] Ibid., XIV.
[146] Ibid., XV.
[147] Ibid., XVII.

The Sovereign

The social contract tradition denies the "divine right" of kings, and claims that the State (and sovereign) derive their authority from the consent of the governed. Obviously, not every State is formed by the explicit forging of a contract. Some people are conquered and subjected to a sovereign. For Hobbes, that doesn't matter. When we form a contract, it is driven by fear of one another. When we submit to a conqueror, we are driven by fear of the conqueror. Either way, the cause is the same, as is the motivation. So long as we "submit," there is at least implicit "consent."[148]

While not divine ordained, the sovereign is, nevertheless, absolute, "or else there is no sovereignty at all."[149] Rights transferred to the sovereign are henceforth non-transferable, and unlimited in application. The sovereign's purpose is to preserve the State and enforce the social contract, and may do "whatever he shall think necessary to be done" for that purpose.[150]

Sovereignty can't be divided. For Hobbes, there is value in limited power, no security in "checks and balances." Given human nature, the power of the sovereign must be greater than that of any other person, or collection of them. "If there be no power erected, or not great enough for our security, every man will rely, and may lawfully rely, on his own strength and art for caution against all other men."[151] As power-seekers, all individuals and factions will seek to acquire more power, if granted any at all—thereby chipping away at the strength and effectiveness of the sovereign. For the same reason, he denies independent authority for the church, and would make the sovereign the head of both church and State.

This emphasis on undivided sovereignty is driven by a fear of civil war, which he regarded as more dangerous than even foreign enemies. This fear of factions and emphasis on unity was nothing new. It goes all the back to and through the writings of Cicero, Aristotle, and Plato, as well. In Antiquity, unity was sought and promoted by means of crafting the best kind of State, and instilling virtue in the rulers and citizens. For Hobbes, this is all misguided both in the sense of being ineffective (factionalism is better prevented by concentrating all power in one place!), and in the sense of having misunderstood the true nature of "justice."

The sovereign must be absolute. All authority rests with, and ends with, the sovereign. The liberty of the subject is understood as just whatever is not forbidden by law.

Law is simply "the word of him that by right hath command over others," so the law is simply whatever the sovereign decrees. Nor is there any such thing as an unjust law. "Since therefore it belongs to kings to discern good and evil, wicked are those, though usual, sayings, that he only is King who does righteously, and that kings must not be obeyed unless they command us just things." Instead, "Legitimate kings therefore make the things they command just, by commanding them, and which they forbid, unjust, by forbidding them. But private men, while they assume to themselves the knowledge of good and evil, desire to be even as kings; which cannot be with the

148 Ibid., XX.
149 Ibid., XX.
150 Ibid., XVIII.
151 Ibid., XVII.

safety of the commonweal."[152] To say that a law is "unjust" can only mean that the sovereign has replaced an old law with a new one.

Given the "absoluteness" of his power, there is no right to rebel against the sovereign, of course. The only time subjects are released from their obligation of obedience to the sovereign is if the sovereign is literally incapable of fulfilling his enforcement function, either because he has been overthrown (or slain), or because he has abdicated his authority.

Thus far we have considered only the unlimited authority of the sovereign, but this authority does come with some obligation on the sovereign's part. The obligations of the ruler are ostensibly simple: "all the duties of the ruler are contained in this one sentence, 'the safety of the people is the supreme law.'"[153] We may derive from this basic obligation four particular themes:

1. Defense of the subjects against foreign threats.
2. Keeping internal peace and security.
3. "Enriching" the public "as much as consistent with public security."
4. Granting "harmless liberties"—harmless because they don't undermine peace or security.

These "harmless liberties" reveal the nature of subjects under their absolute sovereign. The subjects have surrendered all political power and rights to the sovereign, and have ceased to be "political." What remains is economic activity: producing, selling, and buying. This might be an early anticipation of the citizen (or subject) as "consumer."

The Sovereign's primary responsibility is to enforce the "social contract" we've created, and he (or she) does so by punishment, and the threat of punishment. We can still choose to break the contract, but if we do, and we get caught, we're going to be punished. Presumably, the threat of that punishment is enough to inspire most of us to obey the contract most of the time. As a result, we enjoy peace, safety, and security (in theory). As a result of that, we can feel more confident in our possessions and work to acquire more wealth and more things, we can bother to pursue education, we can bother with science and technology and art, and we can bother to pursue and enjoy hobbies and recreational activities. Society flourishes, and our own life satisfaction increases.

Such is Hobbes' "social contract" theorist's answer to what justifies the State, to why we form and submit ourselves to government. Simple self-interest urges us to do so. The alternative (the SON) is so bad, that no one in her right mind would prefer it to living within a State.

Not surprisingly, there's much more to the social contract approach than that! For example, you could easily imagine someone saying that the SON doesn't look so bad, if one's government happens to be a brutal, genocidal dictatorship. As bad as the SON is, it's not so bad that we would gratefully accept just any form of government in its place. After answering why we should have government, we must then try to figure out what kind.

In the remainder of this chapter, we will consider one brief attempt to justify a particular kind of government, and to justify a particular vision of rights and privileges for persons under that government. The political philosophy of John Rawls is a 20th century version of the social contract approach—sometimes called an "enlightened social contract."

John Rawls

Rawls was born on Febuary 21st, 1921. Before he died in 2002, he taught at both Harvard and Oxford. He is undeniably a candidate for the most famous and important American philosopher of the 20th century. He was presented with a National Humanities Medal by President Bill Clinton in 1999, in recognition of how Rawls's work "helped a whole generation of learned Americans revive

152 *De Cive*, 12.1

153 Ibid., 13.2

their faith in democracy itself."[154]

His most famous work is *A Theory of Justice*, first published in 1979. This book revolutionized contemporary ethical and political thought, and is now regarded as "one of the primary texts in political philosophy," according to Cambridge Dictionary of Philosophy.

At the heart of Rawls' philosophy is a 20th century version of the social contract approach—sometimes called an "enlightened" social contract. We will consider his approach to the social contract tradition first with regard to such fundamental issues as forms of government, basic rights and privileges, and distribution of resources and opportunities. We will then turn to the issue that occupied Rawls at the end of his career and life: the "problem" of pluralism.

The Original Position

As mentioned, Rawls is part of the same social contract tradition that we have studied in previous chapters; a tradition that includes such theorists as Hobbes and Locke. In each case, they had their own particular vision of State of Nature—and Rawls is no different, in that regard.

Central to understanding Rawls' interpretation of the social contract tradition is his idea of the "original position." The "original position" (hereafter referred to as the OP) is another hypothetical situation, another thought-experiment analogous to that of the State of Nature itself. *The OP is the hypothetical meeting that Rawls imagines taking place when people collectively decide to leave the State of Nature and create a government under which to live.*

So, imagine a meeting of all the people who will be living in that new society. They have gathered together in order to decide upon the most fundamental political questions, such as what kind of government they will have, what sorts of laws, what sorts of rights (if any), how to distribute the resources of their society, and so on. What sort of decision-making procedure could participants employ, in the OP, in order to produce a government and laws that will be just and fair, that will be agreeable to everyone in the society?

To promote fairness, Rawls imagines that participants in the OP must first pass through a "veil of ignorance" (hereafter: VOI). Imagine that everyone must pass under a curtain before entering the meeting hall, and, when they do, this curtain temporarily suppresses all kinds of memories and information—it induces a selective "ignorance." Obviously, this is an imaginary process, but Rawls thinks it gives us insight into the requirements of justice. The image below should look somewhat familiar, as a simpler version of it was used in our previous explanation of Hobbes. There, the idea was that we emerge from the State of Nature to create a social contract, and then appoint a sovereign to enforce that contract. In the expanded version applicable to Rawls, we emerge from the State of Nature into the OP, where we will decide on the social contract and sovereign—but a key feature of the OP is that we are behind the VOI.

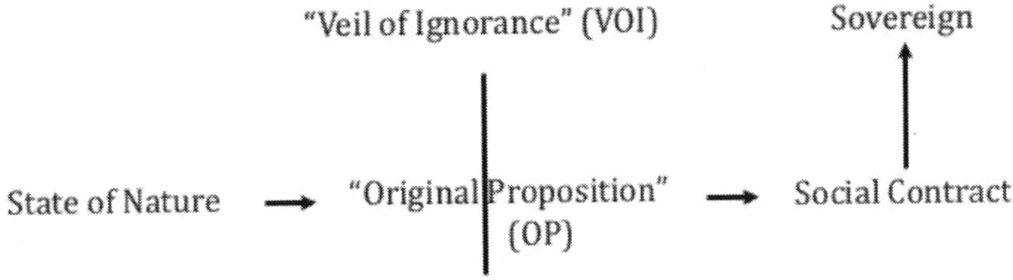

154 "The National Medal Of The Arts And The National Humanities Medal". Clinton4.nara.gov. 1999-09-29.

Behind the veil, participants are "ignorant" as concerns a variety of pieces of demographic information. These include:

- Race and ethnicity
- Gender
- Age
- Physical and mental ability or disability
- Sexual orientation
- Religious affiliation
- Socioeconomic status
- Generation (e.g., "baby boomer," "Gen X")
- Vision of the good life (i.e., personal values)

In other words, the participants become ignorant of anything and everything that tells them who they are within their society. Once behind the VOI, a participant will not know his/her gender, or race, or age; s/he will not know if s/he is a genius or someone with a mental disability, an Olympic class athlete or someone with profound physical disabilities, a devout Christian or a Muslim or an atheist, a billionaire or a homeless person. Participants do not know to what generation they belong (meaning, a generation that has already lived and died, or living now, or one not yet born), or even what they find valuable in life.

Participants are not ignorant of everything, of course. To begin with, they have *concepts* of all of those things (e.g., race, gender, religion, etc.)—they just don't know how those concepts apply to themselves, or other participants.

In addition, in order to make important political decisions, they must have other kinds of basic knowledge intact. In order to decide what sort of government to create, what sorts of tax systems to enact, etc., participants must have a rudimentary understanding of the following:

- Basic economics
- Basic political theory
- Basic science
- Basic social sciences (including psychology and sociology, and that different persons have different worldviews and values)

Note the repetition of the word "basic." No one is suggesting that participants all have a Ph.D. in economics, or are professional psychologists. Instead, they are assumed to have the basic everyday understanding of the world and how it works that you and I already possess. They understand that there are different kinds of political systems (e.g., democracy, monarchy, theocracy, etc.) and have basic understanding of how they work. They have a basic understanding of economics (e.g., supply and demand). They have a basic understanding of human psychology (e.g., motivation, behavioral tendencies, etc.).

This sort of knowledge will allow them to decide between different forms of government, and will allow them to agree upon certain approaches to social and economic policy. The value of what they *do* know is obvious, but what's the value of what they do *not* know (i.e., all that demographic information suppressed by the VOI)? If you haven't figured it out already, you'll probably be stunned by how obvious the answer is.

As Rawls puts it: *The purpose of the veil of ignorance is to ensure that principles of justice are chosen such that "no one is advantaged or disadvantaged in the choice of principles by the outcome of natural chance or the contingency of social circumstances."* Put another way, if you don't know who you are, you can't use that information when making your decisions. In one word, *the purpose of the VOI is fairness.*

As an example, consider the very basic question of what sort of government ("sovereign") to create/appoint. A participant in the OP suggests a dictatorship, in which one person wields all power, and everyone else has to submit to that one person's power. Keeping in mind that you don't know who you are when you step out from behind the VOI, would you agree to a dictatorship? Of course not! It's likely that the only way you would agree to a dictatorship is if you knew you were going to be the dictator. But, behind the VOI, you don't know who you are. Maybe you're the dictator, but it's much more likely that you're not.

So, what system would you agree to, then?

Probably some form of democracy, since, in a democracy, (almost) everyone (in theory) has a right to participate in the political process. With a democratic political system, it doesn't matter who you are behind the VOI. If you agree to a democracy, you will have a presumably equal right to participate in basic political decision-making no matter who you happen to be.

To continue with the same example, having agreed upon "democracy," you now turn to the question of who will vote. Suppose that someone proposes that only property-owning white males will be allowed to vote. Would you agree to that behind the VOI? Of course not! You don't know whether or not you own property (socioeconomic status), whether or not you're white (race/ethnicity), or whether or not you're male (gender). Suppose you agree to this, then step out from behind the VOI to discover you're an African-American woman. Now you can't vote. Pretty foolish of you, right? If you don't know your own race or ethnicity, you're not going to agree to any law or policy that privileges one race over another. So too with gender. So too with religion. Would you agree to form a State in which everyone must be Christian, if you had to make this decision behind the VOI? No way. For all you know, you're Muslim, or Hindu, or an atheist. For the very same reason, you would never agree to a social contract in which everyone was bound by Sharia law, nor one in which the exercise of religion (in general) was banned. None of those outcomes would be *fair*.

As previously stated, the primary purpose of the VOI is to ensure fairness. How do we ensure fairness? Recall that Rawls' theory is situated within the Social Contract tradition.

> *Here we face a difficulty for any political conception of justice that uses the idea of a contract, whether social or otherwise. The difficulty is this: we must find some point of view, removed from and not distorted by the particular features and circumstances of the all-encompassing background framework, from which a fair agreement between free and equal persons can be reached. The original position, with the feature I have called 'the veil of ignorance,' is this point of view.*[155]

The participants in the OP are not presumed to be idealists, seeking to create a utopia for all. Much more modestly, they are merely presumed to be self-interested. I want the best social contract for myself. You want the best one for yourself. And so on. How can we take that basic self-interest, and turn it towards fairness? By preventing participants from using certain (presumably politically irrelevant) pieces of information, such as race or gender, in making their decisions.

Perhaps controversially, or perhaps in a display of common-sense, Rawls thinks that the contingencies of birth are morally arbitrary. No one "deserves" to be born into a rich or poor family, into one ethnic group or another, into one sex or gender or sexual orientation, more or less naturally intelligent or physically gifted, etc. These are unearned accidents of birth. Since none of us "deserves" them, none of us is entitled to any benefit we might receive (or penalty we might suffer) due to the contingency of our birth. Bluntly: things like race, gender, sexual orientation, religious affiliation, socioeconomic status (etc.) shouldn't *matter* in the context of constructing a just and fair social contract, and the just and fair political, legal, and economic institutions that will govern it, or the just and fair laws that should flow from those institutions. Since those things shouldn't matter, we shouldn't take them into consideration—and the VOI attempts to enforce that.

In theory, *the only principles, laws, and policies you would agree to behind the VOI are those that you would agree to no matter who you are in society*. If you would agree to them, no matter whom you are, that's a pretty good indicator that

155 John Rawls, "Justice as Fairness: Political not Metaphysical," Philosophy and Public Affairs, 14(3), 1985, p. 235.

they're fair. In essence, if I don't know who I will be once I step out from behind the VOI, the contract that's best for "me" will turn out to be the contract that is best for anyone and everyone.

Test Your Understanding

For each of the following examples, evaluate whether or not you would agree to them from behind the VOI (and be able to explain why):

- Racially segregated schools
- Laws prohibiting the issuing of State marriage licenses for same-sex couples
- Laws requiring members of the clergy to perform same-sex marriage ceremonies, regardless of their theological views on homosexuality
- Laws requiring wheelchair access into buildings
- Laws protecting people against housing discrimination on the basis of mental illness
- Requiring prayers in public schools

Using this basic approach, we could test every single policy proposal, law, and political decision by the standard of "would I agree to this behind the VOI?" However, Rawls offers us a shortcut. Rawls believed that the basic outcome of the OP and decisions made behind the VOI could be summarized by two basic principles of justice:

1. "each person is to have an equal right to the most extensive scheme of equal basic liberties compatible with a similar scheme of liberties for others."
2. "social and economic inequalities are to be arranged so that they are both (a) reasonably expected to be to everyone's advantage and (b) attached to positions and offices open to all."

The first principle of justice (hereafter referred to as a POJ) deals with basic rights and liberties and applies to the design of the political constitution of the society. The second POJ deals with the just distribution of what Rawls calls "primary goods" (including wealth), and therefore to the economic institutions and policies of the society.

Basic Liberties

Rawls claims that participants behind the VOI would agree to equal access to, and an equal share of, certain **basic liberties**. If you are a United States citizen, or live in the U.S., or have merely heard of the U.S., you are probably familiar with the sorts of liberties he has in mind:

1. political liberty (the right to vote and hold public office)
2. freedom of speech and assembly
3. liberty of conscience and thought
4. freedom of the person (e.g., freedom from psychological oppression, physical assault, dismemberment, etc.)
5. the right to hold personal property
6. freedom from arbitrary arrest and seizure

Certainly the idea that we have the right of free speech and the free exercise of religion is neither original nor unique to Rawls. One of the impressive things about Rawls' philosophy, though, is that he gives us a way to explain *why* we think we all do (or should) have such liberties, and why we think (for the most part), that everyone should have them equally. Moreover, his justification for such a right does not depend upon any particular religious, worldview—unlike Locke, perhaps. Recall that, for Locke, our rights, even in the State of Nature, come by virtue of our being equally created by God. What if you are an atheist, and don't believe that anyone is created by God, equally or otherwise, because God doesn't exist? If, on the other hand, we derive our rights based on what we would (theoretically) agree to beind the VOI, then we have a justification for that right whether your worldview is religious, or naturalistic.

Let's start with the equal right to participate in the political process (i.e., democratic self-governance). Why do we think it just that we have such a right, and that is unjust if it is denied us? Think about what you would agree to behind the VOI. Not knowing who you are, it would be foolish of you to deny political participation to anyone on the basis of such things as race, gender, income, etc., because you might unwittingly disenfranchise yourself in the process.

So, what *would* you agree to? Who should be allowed to participate? *Everyone*—or, at least almost everyone, with few and defensible exceptions.[156] In that way, no matter who you are when you step out from behind the VOI, you have a right to self-governance. How much of a right? An equal right. In that way, no matter who you are, you have no less (nor any more) of a right than anyone else. Not only would it be foolish of you to agree to a contract where some people have rights, and others don't (while not knowing into which group you fall!), it would also be foolish of you to agree to a contract in which some people have a greater share of a right than do others (again, while not knowing into which group you fall).

As one more example, let's consider certain civil liberties pertaining to criminal trials. Some people express frustration with the fact that it costs more to execute a condemned criminal in the U.S. than to imprison him for the rest of his life.[157] How is this possible? How could a few seconds of electricity, or a single bullet, or a dose of poison, be more expensive than room and board for life? Many of you already know the answer: because of the lengthy and expensive appeals process.

It's not as if a criminal is sentenced to death and is then dragged out behind the courthouse and shot. Instead, most condemned criminals spend decades filing appeals to their conviction, and the State must pay for its own attorneys and associated fees every single time—and often must pay for the condemned person's lawyer as well. By the time a couple decades go by, the cost adds up.

"I have the solution!" you exclaim. "Eliminate all those costly appeals! If a judge or jury finds the guy guilty, and sentences him to death, drag him out of the room and shoot him. Problem solved."

And yet, we have all those appeals and "safety nets" in place to protect convicted criminals. Why would we (or should we) have all those protections in place? Go behind the VOI, and you'll find your answer. Not knowing who you are, you don't know if you're someone who has been, or ever will be, involved in the criminal justice system. It's a possibility though. Not knowing your income level, you don't know if you'll be able to

---

156 Note: Some of you might be thinking that the fact that one must be 18 years old, or older, to vote in the U.S. signifies a violation of Rawls' procedure. After all, you don't know how old you are behind the VOI. However, no matter who you are behind the VOI, you probably recognize that children aren't terribly well equipped (mentally, and in terms of maturity) to vote. You are aware of basic human nature behind the VOI, after all. Moreover, all one needs do in order to overcome this age discrimination is survive to the age of 18. Unlike denying the vote on the basis of race or gender, which is nothing one can "out grow," a minimum age requirement is a temporary distinction, and could survive the scrutiny of the VOI.

157 For example, according to the Death Penalty Information Center, if the Governor of the State of California "commuted the sentences of those remaining on death row to life without parole, it would result in an immediate savings of $170 million per year, with a savings of $5 billion over the next 20 years." (http://www.deathpenaltyinfo.org/costs-death-penalty)

afford an attorney—but you better believe you'd want one! So, behind the VOI, you would agree that everyone should have access to a lawyer, even if they can't afford to pay for one personally.

You'd want other protections in place, too. You'd want for *the State* to have to *prove* that you're guilty, instead of you having to prove that you're innocent. You'd want the State to have to present evidence against you, in public, as opposed to being able to arrest, try, and convict you on evidence unseen (or maybe even on no evidence at all).

What about all those expensive appeals? You'd want those too. A dirty, ugly, fact is that innocent people have been, and continue to be, convicted of crimes they did not commit. Set aside conspiracy theories and crooked cops, sometimes people just plain make a mistake, and point to the wrong guy in a police lineup, or think they remember seeing someone who they didn't really see. It happens. It happens in death penalty cases as well.

In the year 2000, Illinois Governor George Ryan (a death penalty *supporter*) put an indefinite hold on executions in his state after 13 death row inmates' convictions were overturned. Also in 2000, the most comprehensive study (at that time) of death penalty cases in the U.S. found that 2/3 of all capital sentences that were reviewed were overturned when appealed due to either errors or inappropriate conduct during the trial. Examples of problems included incompetent defense teams, evidence suppressed by police and prosecutors, misinformed jurors, and biased judges.

DNA evidence alone has resulted in the post-conviction exoneration of 329 people (so far)—and 20 of them had been sentenced to death.[158] People awaiting execution on death row have been found innocent, and released, before it was too late. It's reasonable to believe that, sometimes, it was already too late — and an innocent person was put to death.[159] Imagine that you are that innocent person, wrongfully convicted and facing execution. Wouldn't you want a right to an appeal, every reasonable chance to prove that a mistake was made, before it's too late? That's why, behind the VOI, recognizing that someday we might be the person needing those protections, we would agree to them—despite the inconvenience, annoyance, and expense, when we're not the ones having to worry about it.

We could conduct this same exercise with each of the basic liberties. Put yourself behind the VOI, and ask yourself what you would agree to, and you'll be able to figure out why each of those basic liberties makes the list and, just as importantly, why the first POJ requires that each of us has an equal share of those liberties.

Primary Goods

We now turn to the second POJ. As a reminder, according to the second POJ, "social and economic inequalities are to be arranged so that they are both (a) reasonably expected to be to everyone's advantage and (b) attached to positions and offices open to all."

The second POJ, then, concerns the just distribution of "primary goods." *"Primary good" is simply a term used to signify those things which nearly all of us want, all things considered, and that we typically would rather have more of, than less.* Primary goods are those things which are useful in the pursuit of a wide range of visions of the good life. Examples of primary goods include:

- the basic right and liberties addresses in the 1st POJ
- freedom to move and choose from among a wide variety of occupations
- income and wealth
- access to educational resources
- access to health care
- the social bases of self-respect that give citizens a sense of dignity and self-worth

It's hard to find someone who doesn't want

158 http://www.innocenceproject.org/know/

159 http://www.sfgate.com/crime/article/Judge-says-California-executed-man-who-6300005.php?cmpid=fb-desktop

income, and the opportunity to earn it; who doesn't want access to health care or education, and so on. A harch fact concerning some of these primary goods, though, is that they are finite. There is not an infinite amount of wealth, or educational access, or health care to go around. A simple illustration is available if you have ever had to sit in the waiting area of an emergency room waiting for medical attention for yourself or a loved one. Many patients with only a few doctors results in a long wait. Because some primary goods are limited, it's inevitable that we come up with some method of distributing them—this is an issue with which every society must contend, and that must be addressed by any social contract.

There are many possible methods of distribution. One person could get everything. Or a few people get most, and the rest fight for the scraps. Or, (as of 2013), the wealthiest 160,000 families could own as much wealth as the poorest 145 *million* families combined.[160] Or, everyone gets an equal share—or any number of distributions in-between. Which, distribution, though, is *fair* (given Rawls' approach)? Put yourself behind the VOI, and find out.

What would you agree to behind the VOI? We might assume that a participant's default choice of distribution will be "equal" — everyone has an exactly equal share of each primary good. That would mean that we all have an equal educational opportunity, equal access to health care, an equal standard of living, and so on. Why would we agree to that? Because no matter who I am once I step out from behind the VOI, I'm no worse off than anyone else. No one else has better health care, or a better standard of living, etc. However, while this might be our default distribution, Rawls claims that we don't have to stick with the default.

There is a way in which some inequality is permissible and just. *An unequal distribution of primary goods is acceptable if and only if everyone is better off by virtue of that unequal distribution than they would have been had the distribution be equal.* How is that possible? Consider the following two bar graphs.

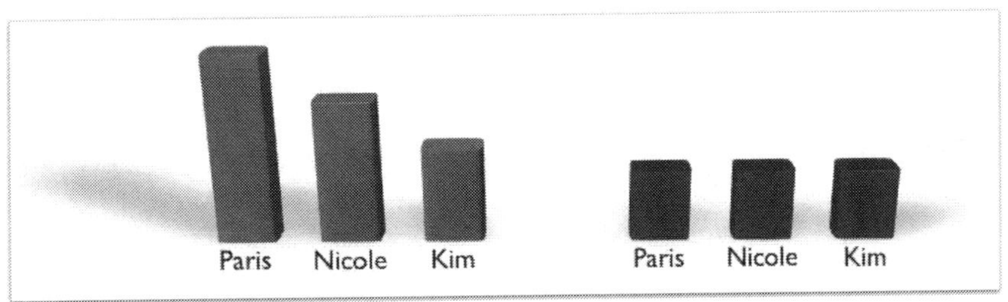

These two graphs represent the distribution of primary goods in two hypothetical communities ("left," and "right"). These are very simple communities, as each contains only three people: Paris, Nicole, and Kim. Obviously, this is a grossly oversimplified picture, with only three people in each community, but that's all we need to illustrate the point. In the left-side community, there is an *un*equal distribution of primary goods. Paris has more of those goods (e.g., wealth, income, access to education, etc.) than Nicole and Kim, and Nicole has more than Kim. In the right-side community, there is a perfectly even distribution instead. Paris, Nicole, and Kim each have an exactly equal share of those goods.

Although our default distribution that we would agree to behind the VOI would be

160 http://fortune.com/2014/10/31/inequality-wealth-income-us/

the kind we see in the right-side community (i.e., a perfectly equal distribution), Rawls acknowledges that unequal distributions would be agreeable so long as they are "reasonably expected to be to everyone's advantage" and "attached to positions and offices open to all."

To be attached to positions and offices open to all simply means that it must be possible, in principle, for anyone to enjoy the greater share of the distribution. There must be genuine equality of opportunity (though not a guaranteed equality of outcome).

> *...fair equality of opportunity is said to require not merely that public offices and social positions be open in the formal sense, but that all should have a fair chance to attain them. To specify the idea of fair chance we say: supposing that there is a distribution of native endowments, those who have the same level of talent and ability and the same willingness to use these gifts should have the same prospects of success regardless of their social class of origin, the class into which they are born and develop until the age of reason. In all parts of society there are to be roughly the same prospects of culture and achievement for those similarly motivated and endowed.*[161]

If it's possible for some people to become wealthier than others, that possibility must be open to everyone (in theory). Laws or customs that allowed only people of a particular race, or religion, or gender, for example, to attain great wealth, or to attend the best schools, would not satisfy this requirement, and would be considered unjust.

As to the first requirement, that the unequal distribution be to everyone's advantage, we can see how this is possible by comparing the two graphs. Notice that although the distribution is unequal in the left-side community, and some people are better off than others, every member of left-side is better off than she would be in right-side. Paris has a greater amount of primary goods in left-side than she does is right-side. So do Nicole and Kim. This is important. Behind the VOI, I don't know who I am in society (e.g., Paris, Nicole, or Kim). If I had to choose between left-side and right-side, why would I pick left-side? Because no matter whom I am in left-side, I'm better off. Even if I'm the worst off, comparatively (Kim), I still have more in left-side than I do in right-side. It makes sense, then, for me to pick left-side, no matter who I might turn out to be.

Some of you might be thinking to yourself that this is an unfair comparison, that each person is comparatively better off in left-side than in right-side because there are more primary goods to distribute in left-side. This is true. If you take the total combined area of each bar in left-side, and compare it to the total combined area of each bar in right-side, left-side does produce a much greater overall area, representing a greater amount of primary goods to distribute. This isn't necessarily cause for suspicion, though — it's the product of a basic promise of capitalism.

A key assumption behind capitalism — especially the *laissez-faire* variety — is that by allowing people to pursue wealth and luxury, the economy is stimulated and grows larger than it would be under a more egalitarian system.[162]

If I knew that no matter how hard I

---

[161] John Rawls, *Justice as Fairness: A Restatement*. Erin Kelly, ed. (Cambridge: Harvard University Press 2001, pp. 43-44.

[162] An argument advanced in a previous chapter, by Adam Smith, of course.

worked, and no matter how much I risked, I would never be any (materially) better off than my neighbor, I (allegedly) wouldn't have the incentive to work so hard or take those risks — but that hard work and risk-taking is precisely what produces economic growth and improves society. Billionaires are far wealthier than the average citizen, but they don't just swim around in a tank of money; they *use* it. That use of money creates jobs, and the wealth "trickles down" to others, ultimately making everyone better off than they otherwise would have been — or so the argument goes. This sort of reasoning explains how the unequal distribution in left-side makes everyone better off compared to the equal distribution found in right-side. By allowing Paris to be so much more fabulously wealthy than Kim, it makes Kim better off too (i.e., better off than she would have been in a perfectly equal distribution).

Rawls was profoundly critical of *actual* U.S. economic policy, and thought that our own systems of distribution did not actually satisfy this requirement, but he was open to the possibility, in principle, that unequal distributions could be justified. We need to be careful that these unequal distributions really are to everyone's advantage, though, and one way to do this is by focusing on the "least advantaged," and how they are impacted by the proposed unequal distribution. Who are these least advantaged?

> *...persons whose family and class origins are more disadvantaged than others, whose natural endowments (as realized) permit them to fare less well, and whose fortune and luck in the course of life turn out to be less happy, all within the normal range . . . and with the relevant measures based on social primary goods.*[163]

Candidates for the "least advantaged" include (but are not limited to) the homeless, the sick, the injured, victims of natural disasters, people with physical or mental disabilities, and people belonging to groups that have traditionally been discriminated against (e.g., on the basis of race, gender, religion, etc.).

"Least advantaged" is not necessarily a permanent classification. If I get hurt at work, that can place me among the "least advantaged" for a time, but if I heal and can return to work and normal life, my relative disadvantage goes away.

If a group of people is discriminated against, its members may be amongst the least advantaged, but *if* circumstances *truly* change and there is no longer any stigma or harm attached to that group membership, people belonging to that group will no longer count as "least advantaged" (for that reason).

Remember, too, that we're talking about a *relative* disadvantage. If I'm blind, it's going to be more difficult for me to succeed in life than if I had use of my eyes—not impossible, but more difficult. If I'm a woman in a society that is somewhat gender biased, it will be more difficult for me to succeed—not impossible, just more difficult.

In an ideal (Rawlsian) world, everyone has an equal chance at a good life. In the real world, we face obstacles that shouldn't be there: discrimination, for example, or even just plain bad luck. Unequal distributions of primary goods are justifiable only if they are to everyone's advantage, and a good way to see if everyone is better off is to check with the least advantaged. If they're better off, it's a good bet that everyone else is too.

It's important to remember that society is not obliged to arrange its practices and institutions so as to guarantee a perfectly equal distribution of goods. Instead, the

163 John Rawls, *A Theory of Justice*, revised edition. Harvard University Press, 1999. p.83.

arrangements must be such that at least those actions and policies that result in an unequal distribution of goods bring about a state of affairs in which the least-advantaged are better off than they would have been in the absence of the action or policy.

Pluralism

Having established the basic foundation for Rawls' approach to the social contract tradition in terms of the original position, veil of ignorance, and two principles of justice, we will now turn to the political issue that occupied him in the latter stages of his life and career, and which might seem especially relevant to the current U.S. political climate: the "problem" of reasonable pluralism. We will first explore the concept of reasonable pluralism itself, consider Rawls' "solution" for it, and then consider how President Barack Obama employed a Rawlsian political philosophy in his own approach to public policy.

Pluralism, in general, merely refers to the fact that a variety of different worldviews exist. Some worldviews are religious (e.g., Christianity, Islam, Hindiusm, etc.), and some are purely naturalistic (e.g., atheism, humanism, etc.). Even within these broad categories of religious and naturalistic, there are widely differing worldviews. Anglican Christianity is quite different from Wahabist Islam, for example. Religious and moral values range across a wide spectrum, and these values influence our political beliefs and values as well.

There is a difference, though, between mere pluralism and *reasonable* pluralism. Mere pluralism simply recognizes the plurality of views. Reasonable pluralism refers to the idea that no one worldview has an obvious monopoly on rationality. That is just to say that smart, sincere, reasonable people can be Christian, Muslim, atheists, Buddhists, etc. Such persons can be pro-life, or pro-choice; vegetarian, or omnivores; for or against the death penalty. It is simply not the case that one worldview is "obviously" true, and anyone subscribing to any other is "crazy."

Is the existence of reasonable pluralism in Western democratic societies also the *problem* of reasonable pluralism? Can a "well-ordered society" achieve the "overlapping consensus" of reasonable "comprehensive moral doctrines" needed to achieve "stability?" Before addressing that question, it's important to identify some key vocabulary.

- *Well-ordered society*: a society in which everyone accepts, and knows that everyone else accepts, the basic principles of justice, in which the main social and political institutions of that society satisfy those principles of justice, and in which the citizens regard their basic institutions as just and comply with their demands.

- Comprehensive moral doctrine: a "worldview," including views on morality, religion, etc.

- Overlapping consensus: when citizens support and obey laws and public policies for reasons internal to their own comprehensive moral doctrines, supporting the same law but for possibly different reasons.

- Stability: when citizens willingly obey their society's laws and policies, even in cases of sincere disagreement.

Rawls gives serious consideration to the problem of reasonable pluralism in his book entitled *Political Liberalism*, where one of his foci is to answer the question of how it is possible for a just and stable society of free and equal citizens to exist and endure when its citizens "remain profoundly divided by reasonable religious, philosophical, and moral doctrines."[164]

Stability is an important issue because laws and policies are *coercive*. Citizens tend to accept coercion when they recognize that the coercion is legitimate, but resist when they think it is not. Laws forbidding murder and laws forbidding African-Americans from eating at lunch counters were, are, and should be received very differently, and afforded very different levels of respect. Acts of civil disobedience for the sake of pedophilia and acts of civil disobedience for the sake of ending segregation are (and should be) regarded with very different degrees of acceptance and respect.

Rawls' goal is to "uncover the conditions of the possibility of a reasonable public basis of justification on fundamental political questions' given the fact of 'reasonable pluralism' in a democratic culture."[165] To this end, he develops a political conception of justice that does not rely on any particular comprehensive moral doctrine for its foundation and that could, in theory, be endorsed by adherents of many different (and even competing) comprehensive moral doctrines. This political conception of justice is intended to be consistent and harmonious with various, competing, comprehensive doctrines so as to achieve the above-mentioned "overlapping consensus." His account of justice as "fairness," involving the ideas of the original position, veil of ignorance (etc.) described earlier in this chapter is an example of just such a political conception of justice. In theory, people from a wide range of worldviews could agree upon the procedures and principles provided by his theory (or so he hoped, at least), resulting in an overlapping consensus and a stable society.

It is important to note that Rawls is asking about stability with respect to a *well-ordered* society. If a society is well-ordered, then it is a society "in which everyone accepts, and knows that everyone else accepts, the very same principles of justice"[166] As well, the main social and political institutions of that society are believed, with good reason, to satisfy those principles. Finally, the citizens regard the society's basic institutions as just, have a normally effective sense of justice themselves, and so generally comply with their society's basic institutions.

In other words, if you live in a "well-ordered society," everyone in your society has a basic, shared sense of justice and what it requires, your government and laws are themselves just, and, as such, inspire you (and others) to obey those (just) laws and respect those (just) institutions.

The possible "problem" is that some *reasonable* comprehensive doctrines could be so at odds, in certain places, with the principles of justice and the just society that results from them, that an overlapping consensus would not be achieved, and stability would not be achieved either.

Why would pluralism represent a threat to the stability of such a society? Generally, because pluralism entails different (and sometimes competing) views of the demands of morality and what constitutes a good and right way to live—and therefore what sorts of laws and public policies might be necessary and appropriate.

The most obvious possible tensions arise from religiously-based moral doctrines, in which an adherent might believe it morally imperative that one abstain from certain behaviors (or perform others), but such is not the belief of other fellow citizens. For example, the consumption of alcohol is

164 John Rawls, *Political Liberalism*, p. xxxix.

165 Ibid.,p. xxi.

166 Ibid., p. 35.

forbidden by Islam on the basis of scripture—but the appeal to the Qur'an will hardly be persuasive to anyone who isn't a Muslim, and who has no other reason to believe drinking alcohol is morally wrong.[167] Unless the Muslim seeking to ban alcohol by means of public policy can somehow demonstrate that the "principles of justice" require the prohibition of alcohol consumption, it is entirely possible (indeed *likely*) that other citizens, who subscribe to other, reasonable, comprehensive moral doctrines (i.e., nearly any other major worldview than Islam), will disagree with and resist the proposed ban on alcohol—and be *reasonable* in so doing.

It's worth taking a moment, here, to make an important point: the *truth* of Islam (or any other comprehensive moral doctrine) is *not* what is up for debate here. Islam might offer a true account of what is right and wrong, or it might not. That is beside the point.

What is at issue here is what is reasonable to do or require within a political context. If everyone within a society was Muslim, and shared the same core values, then it is unlikely that there would be much disagreement as regards alcohol—nor would any ban on alcohol consumption likely be controversial or seem unreasonable. But, in a great many communities (including the United States), it is simply not the case that "everyone" is *anything*: not Muslim, not Christian, not Buddhist, not atheist. Instead, we are a mix of (mostly) reasonable and, at times, competing comprehensive moral doctrines.

To put it bluntly, if I am a Christian I would probably find it unreasonable to be denied some wine at dinner (let alone at communion!) just because my Muslim neighbor's God (in whom I don't believe) forbids it, just as if I were an atheist, I might find it unreasonable for my Christian neighbor to make homosexual activity illegal because his God (in whom I don't believe) thinks it an "abomination."[168]

Given the existence of reasonable pluralism, is it even possible to achieve the overlapping consensus of reasonable comprehensive moral doctrines needed for stability? Even if citizens have deep disagreements on certain issues because of their different worldviews, can there be enough "buy-in" to achieve a stable, well-ordered society?

To explore this issue of stability in the face of pluralism, we will consider the political hot-button of abortion—considering what (little) Rawls had to say about abortion, and how the moral and political issues surrounding abortion present a "stability" issue.

First, and for the record, what did Rawls say about abortion, himself? We will consider two representative quotations from Rawls (with underlining added for emphasis):

1. Regarding the troubled question of abortion: consider the question in terms of these three important political values: the due respect for human life, the ordered reproduction of political society over time, including the family in some form, and finally the equality of women as equal citizens.. . . any reasonable balance of these three values will give a woman a duly qualified right to decide whether or not to end her pregnancy during the

---

[167] "you who believe! Intoxicants, gambling, al-ansāb, and al-azlām (arrows for seeking luck or decision) are an abomination of Shayṭān's (Satan's) handiwork. So avoid that in order that you may be successful."
—Qur'an, Surah 5 (al-Ma'idah), ayah 90

[168] Not all Christians believe this, of course. . .
.

first trimester.... [A]t this early stage of pregnancy the political value of the equality of women is overriding, and this right is required to give it substance and force. (*Political Liberalism*)

2. In particular, when hotly disputed questions, such as that of abortion, arise which may lead to a stand-off between different political conceptions, citizens must vote on the question according to their complete ordering of political values. Indeed, this is a normal case: unanimity of views is not to be expected. Reasonable political conceptions of justice do not always lead to the same conclusion; nor do citizens holding the same conception always agree on particular issues. Yet the outcome of the vote, as I said before, is to be seen as legitimate provided all government officials, supported by other reasonable citizens, of a reasonably just constitutional regime sincerely vote in accordance with the idea of public reason. This doesn't mean the outcome is true or correct, but that it is reasonable and legitimate law, binding on citizens by the majority principle.

   Some may, of course, reject a legitimate decision, as Roman Catholics may reject a decision to grant a right to abortion. They may present an argument in public reason for denying it and fail to win a majority. But they need not themselves exercise the right to abortion. They can recognize the right as belonging to legitimate law enacted in accordance with legitimate political institutions and public reason, and therefore not resist it with force. Forceful resistance is unreasonable: it would mean attempting to impose by force their own comprehensive doctrine that a majority of other citizens who follow public reason, not unreasonably, do not accept. Certainly Catholics may, in line with public reason, continue to argue against the right to abortion. Reasoning is not closed once and for all in public reason any more than it is closed in any form of reasoning. Moreover, that the Catholic Church's nonpublic reason requires its members to follow its doctrine is perfectly consistent with their also honoring public reason.

   I do not discuss the question of abortion in itself since my concern is not with that question but rather to stress that political liberalism does not hold that the ideal of public reason should always lead to a general agreement of views, nor is it a fault that it does not. Citizens learn and profit from debate and argument, and when their arguments follow public reason, they instruct society's political culture and deepen their understanding of one another even when agreement cannot be reached. (*Public Reason Revisited*)

In brief, Rawls appears to believe that women have a right to make their own reproductive choices, at least within the first trimester of pregnancy—but far more important than his personal view on abortion, and far more relevant for our purposes in this chapter, is what he says about those who disagree.

> *...unanimity of views is not to be expected. Reasonable political conceptions of justice do not always lead to the same conclusion; nor do citizens holding the same conception always agree on particular issues. Yet the outcome of the vote, as I said before, is to be seen as legitimate provided all government officials, supported by other reasonable citizens, of a reasonably just constitutional regime sincerely vote in accordance with the idea of public reason. This doesn't mean the outcome is true or correct, but that it is reasonable and legitimate law, binding on citizens by the majority principle.*

It is inevitable that citizens will disagree with each other on various laws and policy issues—even important, high-stakes issues like abortion, war, the death penalty, environmental policy, etc. Nevertheless, the policy outcome might still be the result of fair and legitimate political processes (e.g., a majority vote subject to just Constitutional constraints), in which case the law or policy is reasonable and legitimate—even if not "true."[169] The hypothetical Catholics who disagree are certainly free to abstain from abortion themselves, and to continue to vote against abortion access, and preach against it at the pulpit or over the dinner table—but what they may not do is use *force* to impose their will on their fellow citizens.

> *Forceful resistance is unreasonable: it would mean attempting to impose by force their own comprehensive doctrine that a majority of other citizens who follow public reason, not unreasonably, do not accept.*

In fairness, though, just how much force will an appeal to "reasonableness" have? If one believes that "abortion is murder," and one's "just" society not only permits the murder of unborn babies but perhaps even subsidizes and otherwise supports it by means of health care policies, one is likely to be dismayed at the unwillingness of one's public institutions to do the "right" thing. What does this admittedly hard case tell us about pluralism and Rawls' ability to address it?

Whether or not such a scenario indicates a stability problem depends upon whether or not the pro-life activists in question are "reasonable." Rawls defines a person as reasonable when, among equals, "*they are ready to propose principles and standards as fair terms of cooperation and to abide by them willingly, given the assurance that others will likewise do so. Those norms they view as reasonable for everyone to accept and therefore as justifiable to them; and they are ready to discuss the fair terms that others propose.*"[170]

Unreasonable persons, on the other hand, "*plan to engage in cooperative schemes but are unwilling to honor, or even to propose, except as a necessary public pretense, any general principles or standards for specifying fair terms of cooperation. They are ready to violate such terms as suits their interests when circumstances allow.*"

To put this in very simple, non-political

---

[169] This is just to say that it could, in fact, be *true* that there is a God who forbids abortion, and therefore laws that allow abortion are "false"—but those laws might nevertheless have been the result of just, fair, and reasonable political processes.

[170] Pritchard, Michael S. and Robison, Wade L (1999) "Justice and the Treatment of Animals: A Critique of Rawls," in Richardson, Henry S. and Weithman, Paul J. (ed.) *The Philosophy of Rawls: A Collection of Essays*, New York: Garland Publishing, Inc. p. 49.

terms: imagine that you and a friend both want to play a new video game, and are trying to decide who gets to go first. You agree to flip a coin and the winner of the coin toss will get to play first, and then after one hour the other person gets to play. Your friend then reveals to you the following: "Just so you know, if I win the coin toss, everything will go as planned. But, if I lose, I'm just going to beat you up, and play first anyway—oh, and you won't get a turn at all, let alone the first one." Your friend doesn't sound very reasonable! What's the point of even doing the coin toss at all, if your friend isn't going to abide by the outcome anyway? Similarly, what's the point of an election if one side intends to assassinate the opposing candidate and impose a military coup if they should happen to lose? Democracy is great, so long as "we" win—but if we lose, to hell with voting? For Rawls, "reasonable" people intend to abide by the rules, even if they "lose." "Unreasonable" people are willing to cheat and ignore the rules if they should "lose."

Returning to the example of abortion, certain sorts of responses from our activist in question would be indicative of unreasonableness. Obvious examples would be things like bombing abortion clinics, murdering abortion providers, violent overthrow of the government or an election result, etc. Far less dramatic than any of those things is an unwillingness to honor "public reason."

Public Reason

The idea of public reason limits political discussion and deliberation primarily (and at the least) done by judges and justices, government officials (especially legislators and executives), and political candidates and their campaign spokespersons. *Ideally*, it applies to ordinary citizens as well whenever they personally deliberate upon, endorse or reject, and ultimately vote on a given policy.

> *A democratic government should justify its policies solely in terms of values that every reasonable citizen can endorse, at least when matters of basic justice are at stake. And, since the policies of a democratic government are ultimately the policies of the people, ordinary citizens should, in voting or in public advocacy, also support only those positions on matters of basic justice that can be justified in this way.*[171]

Or, as Rawls states in "The Idea of Public Reason Revisited":

> *Our exercise of political power is proper only when we sincerely believe that the reasons we offer for our political actions—were we to state them as government officials—are sufficient, and we also think that other citizens might reasonably accept those reasons.*[172]

The central claim of **public reason** is that, when dealing with the scope of basic liberty and other matters of basic justice, citizens should take only those positions that are defendable from some liberal political conception of justice, independently of any wider comprehensive moral doctrine.

According to Rawls, if a policy addresses "fundamental issues," it must be supported

---

171 Peter de Marneffe, 'Rawls' Idea of Public Reason,' Pacific Philosophical Quarterly, 1994, 75 (3/4), p. 233.

172 Rawls, "The Idea of Public Reason Revisited," in: Freeman, Samuel (ed.) *John Rawls: Collected Papers*, Cambridge: Harvard University Press, p. 578.

by the political values of public reason. "Since the exercise of political power must be legitimate, the ideal of citizenship imposes a moral, not a legal, duty—the duty of civility—to be able to explain to one another on those fundamental questions how the principles and policies they advocate and vote for can be supported by the political values of public reason."[173]

In other words, while it is (of course) not illegal (in the United States) to invoke religious reasons for opposition to abortion, and, if you do, you certainly do not violate any legal obligations of citizenship, it is, nevertheless, a "duty of civility" to offer reasons that are not unique to any particular worldview (e.g., Christian), but that instead draw on "public reason."

The point of invoking public reasons is a recognition that we have a duty to justify our policy decisions to one another by appealing to public values and public standards, principles of reasoning and pieces of evidence that all citizens could reasonably endorse and that do not rely on controversial theories, metaphysical assumptions, or controversial evidence.

To use an admittedly extreme example, imagine a small but wealthy organization of citizens lobbies to end (and ban) all vaccination of children, and their reason for this is that they have received telepathic communications from an alien mothership warning that only unvaccinated children will be allowed to "beam up" when the ship comes to claim us and take us to our new home in another galaxy. Needless to say, very few of us will be persuaded by appeals to telepathic messages from aliens. Similarly, if People for the Ethical Treatment of Animals (PETA) lobbied to ban all animal experimentation and meat consumption because their members all claim to have been animals in one of their many past lives, they would find no allies among the majority of citizens who do not believe in reincarnation. Perhaps wisely, PETA focuses on the far less controversial claim that animals experience pain—something that we can all acknowledge, and something which (could) appeal to any and all of us.

The moral/civil "demands" of public reason do not apply to everything and every context. Rawls claims that, at minimum, public reasons should be invoked when deep, fundamental issues of justice are at stake, such as "constitutional essentials" and matters of basic justice. When political decisions concern things like who gets to vote (or whether to impose voter-ID laws), which religions are to be tolerated (or whether to provide public financial support to private church charities), who can own property, who should be assured equality of opportunity—basically, anything involving the basic liberties described earlier in this chapter—then public reasons should be provided so that, in theory, people from across a wide variety of comprehensive moral doctrines could understand, and agree to, the reasons provided for one's policy stance.

Even when dealing with constitutional essentials and basic liberties, the demand of public reason is merely that public reasons be provided, not that non-public reasons be excluded. Citizens may offer nonpublic reasons as support for their views so long as the public reasons are themselves sufficient to render their answer to a political question "reasonable." A sufficient reason is one that is "good enough, standing on its own, to justify the position taken in public political debate."[174]

Reasonable comprehensive doctrines,

[173] John Rawls, *Political Liberalism*, p. 217.

[174] Peter de Marneffe, "Rawls' Idea of Public Reason," *Pacific Philosophical Quarterly*, 1994, p. 230, note 12.

> *religious or non-religious, may be introduced in public political discourse at any time, provided that in due course proper political reasons—and not reasons given solely by comprehensive doctrines—are presented that are sufficient to support whatever the comprehensive doctrines introduced are said to support. This injunction to present proper political reasons I refer to as the proviso, and it specifies public political culture as distinct from the background culture.*[175]

Thus, groups are not entirely prevented from appealing to the values from their comprehensive doctrines when promoting policies concerning fundamental issues, but they are obliged to use such values as *supplements* to their already sufficient argument that has been made under the restrictions set by the idea of public reason. A policy issue that isn't so "fundamental" (i.e., doesn't pertain to basic justice or constitutional essentials, such as how much public funding to provide for State parks) need not be justified by public reason at all, but Rawls says that it is nevertheless "usually highly desirable to settle political questions by invoking the values of public reason."[176] That is, while it is not required that non-essential issues be justified by public reason, it's a good and desirable thing if they are.

Why would citizens, individually or collectively, agree to abide by the limits of public reason? Rawls thinks that this is because they might recognize that it is the reasonable and morally civil thing to do. This is so because "except by endorsing a reasonable constitutional democracy, there is no other way fairly to ensure the liberty of its adherents consistent with the equal liberties of other reasonable free and equal citizens."[177]

That is, a reasonable comprehensive moral doctrine will recognize that *reasonable* political judgments cannot be overridden according to the dictates of a particular comprehensive doctrine without trampling on the rights of other free, equal, and reasonable citizens.

Those who wish to override their fellow citizens when the reasonable judgments of the majority are at odds with the values of their own doctrine are *un*reasonable because they refuse to honor the reasonable judgments arrived at by their fellow citizens through legitimate majoritarian political procedures. What could this be other than an attempt to *coerce* others into accepting one's own beliefs? In the case of our hypothetical pro-life activist, *she* believes that abortion is murder. Clearly, not everyone else does!

What might our pro-lifer do in such a situation? One option would be to attempt to coerce others into compliance through acts of sabotage, intimidation, or civil disobedience. As an extreme example, Dr. George Tiller was shot and killed by Scott Roeder in 2009. Dr. Tiller was one of only a few doctors willing to perform late-term abortions, and Roeder publicly confessed to the killing, offering the following as his justification: "preborn children's lives were in imminent danger."[178]

However, according to Rawls, "Forceful resistance is unreasonable: it would mean

---

175 Rawls, "The Idea of Public Reason Revisited," in: Freeman, Samuel (ed.) *John Rawls: Collected Papers*, Cambridge: Harvard University Press, p. 591.

176 Rawls, Political Liberalism, p. 215.

177 Rawls, "The Idea of Public Reason Revisited," in: Freeman, Samuel (ed.) *John Rawls: Collected Papers*, Cambridge: Harvard University Press., p. 590.

178 AP: Man admits killing Kansas abortion doctor". *MSNBC*. Associated Press. November 9, 2009. Retrieved January 21, 2010.

attempting to impose by force their own comprehensive doctrine that a majority of other citizens who follow public reason, not unreasonably, do not accept."[179] If our pro-lifer is "reasonable," she must honor the policies and laws of her society—though she is free to use *legitimate* means to alter policies. For example, she might support Operation Rescue financially, educate herself on the merits of the pro-life position, sponsor and participate in "speak-outs" and consciousness-raising events, wear and distribute pro-life t-shirts and caps, lobby her elected representatives, and otherwise attempt to persuade her fellow citizens that abortion is wrong.

A Christian pro-lifer who adheres to the constraints of public reason will recognize that not all her fellow citizens share her theological worldview—nor even do all her fellow *Christian* citizens share her political stance on abortion. Recognizing that other (reasonable) citizens subscribe to other (reasonable) worldviews, she will not base her public opposition to abortion solely on a reference to a Bible verse—a reference that many of her fellow citizens (e.g., atheists, Hindus, Buddhists, etc.) will not accept as authoritative.[180] Instead, she will attempt to offer reasons to oppose abortion that could, in theory, be agreeable regardless of one's particular worldview.

Given that most of us, for example, agree that someone taking our own life (in most cases) would be a bad thing, perhaps the pro-lifer could offer an argument demonstrating the basic similarity between a fetus and an adult with respect to the default value of life itself, and propose that just as (generally speaking) it would be wrong to deprive an adult of his or her life without proper justification, so too is it wrong (in general) to deprive a fetus of its life (without proper justification).[181]

This strategy does not require that the pro-lifer accept that other worldviews are equally true, nor that she abandon her own faith and convictions. It merely acknowledges that, in the public political sphere, it is "reasonable" to advocate for or against policy positions without relying solely on potentially controversial (and not universally recognized) values and beliefs.

Depending on what sorts of expectations she has, and on what sorts of activities in which she's willing to engage, our pro-lifer is either reasonable or unreasonable. If *unreasonable*, then, surprisingly enough, there is no "stability" problem. This is so because of the way Rawls defines the stability issue to begin with.

Recall that our focus is on a well-ordered society. Rawls claims a well-ordered democratic society can be well-ordered by a political conception of justice so long as two conditions are met. The first is that citizens from *reasonable* comprehensive doctrines (at least) belong to the overlapping consensus. That is, they generally endorse that conception of justice. The second condition is that "unreasonable comprehensive doctrines do not gain enough currency to undermine society's essential justice."[182]

The overlapping consensus is built from *reasonable* comprehensive doctrines. If our

[179] Rawls, "The Idea of Public Reason Revisited," in: Freeman, Samuel (ed.) *John Rawls: Collected Papers*, Cambridge: Harvard University Press, p. 606.

[180] For example, Job 31:15: "Did not he that made me in the womb make him? and did not one fashion us in the womb?"

[181] Please don't assume that this is my advocacy against abortion access, nor that this is the best (let alone only) way to formulate such a strategy. This example is just that: an example.

[182] John Rawls, *Political Liberalism* , p. 39.

pro-lifer's comprehensive moral doctrine is unreasonable in the ways described above, then she is not part of the overlapping consensus in the first place. Accordingly, she is not a threat to *stability*—though she might well be a threat to the well-orderedness of the society if her comprehensive moral doctrine is both unreasonable and gains sufficient "currency."

To step away from our pro-lifer for a moment, consider the example of ISIS (or ISIL). The particular Salafist version of Islam espoused by this organization is an example of a comprehensive moral doctrine. Using Rawls' vocabulary, it is also undeniably an "unreasonable" comprehensive moral doctrine because, among other things, it opposes democracy!

Adherents to this worldview believe that their views are "the truth," that all opposing views are heretical or blasphemous, and that even voting itself is morally wrong. Clearly, sincere members of ISIS would not abide by the outcome of a fair election that doesn't go their way, if they are opposed to elections in the first place! Anywhere where ISIS has gained "sufficient currency" (e.g., ISIS-controlled portions of Syria or Iraq) are simply not "well-ordered" societies governed by a liberal political conception of justice. The stability concern does not arise here because there is no well-ordered society to be stable, or unstable, in the first place.

The United States, however, is not ISIS-controlled Syria or Iraq, and a case could be made that U.S. society is well-ordered.[183] Here, though, the same as "there," well-orderedness can be threatened by "unreasonable" groups who grow too large or too influential—and this is precisely the worry behind the possible problem of pluralism. Though the analogy with ISIS might be uncomfortable and overly provocative, it's not difficult to see how the analogy can be made.

Why should we assume that a sincere pro-lifer would be persuaded by the appeal to reasonableness? Why assume that she would acknowledge that it is unreasonable to expect others to comply with the demands of *her* comprehensive moral doctrine (forcibly, if necessary) given the reality of reasonable pluralism? If our pro-lifer believes her doctrine to be *true*, what force does an appeal to "reasonableness" have on her? Michael Huemer, using the example of a religious fundamentalist, argues that appeals to reasonableness will be effective only insofar as the dissident values reasonableness more than his "truth."

> *If a view which entails that I should do act A is true, whereas another view which entails that I should not do A is, while false, more 'reasonable' than the first, then what must I do? Ex hypothesi, I should do act A—that is, act in accordance with the first view.*[184]

His general point is that any value (such as "reasonableness") brought to bear on a comprehensive doctrine will be *evaluated from the viewpoint of that doctrine*. We might imagine our pro-lifer scoffing at appeals to reasonableness, if reasonableness demands that she tolerate the "murder" of unborn children. Indeed, the aforementioned Roeder posted a comment on the Operation Rescue website, claiming that Dr. "Tiller is the concentration camp 'Mengele' of our day and needs to be stopped before he and those who protect him bring judgment upon our nation."[185]

---

183 A claim subject to debate, of course. . . .

184 Michael Huemer, "Rawls' Problem of Stability," *Social Theory and Practice*, 22(3), p. 383.

185 "Shooter In Kansas Physician Killing Held Extreme Beliefs". Anti-Defamation League.

Needless to say, urging someone like Roeder to be "reasonable" might be unpersuasive, much as urging members of ISIS to be "reasonable" might be. This is *not* to suggest that people opposed to abortion are "just like members of ISIS!" This is only to point out that appeals to "reasonableness" will only be persuasive to the extent that one values reasonableness, and it's not difficult to imagine any number of comprehensive moral doctrines in which "reasonableness" is less important that "truth," or "God's will."

Be that as it may, Rawls claims that the zeal to embody the whole truth in politics is incompatible with an idea of public reason belonging to democratic citizenship. In other words, if a citizen believes that policy should conform to the dictates of her comprehensive doctrine *regardless* of what the majority of her fellow citizens (reasonably) believe because the "truth" of her doctrine trumps the demand for "reasonableness" in political deliberation, this citizen is herself unreasonable. "When there is a plurality of reasonable doctrines, it is unreasonable or worse to want to use the sanctions of state power to correct, or to punish, those who disagree with us."[186] Such persons certainly exist, maybe even in a hypothetical well-ordered society, but in such a society, as unreasonable, they are not part of the overlapping consensus of reasonable comprehensive moral doctrines anyway.

Does this mean that it could *never* be reasonable, from a Rawlsian perspective, for a pro-lifer (or adherents to any other comprehensive moral doctrine) to insist that her values be enforced? That it is never justifiable to "act up" in defense of one's values? As it turns out, resistance is, sometimes, justifiable.

Under the principle of fairness, a person is required to "do his part as defined by the rules of an institution" given two conditions:

1. The institution is itself just (i.e., satisfies the principles of justice).
2. The person has voluntarily accepted the benefits provided by the institution

That is, someone who benefits from a just institution is obligated to fulfill her obligations as defined by the institution. On the other hand, "it is not possible to be bound to unjust institutions, or at least to institutions which exceed the limits of tolerable injustice."[187]

We are morally bound to *just* institutions, but *not* to those that are intolerably unjust. A society with an inadequate political conception of justice, or one in which the public institutions are not themselves just (or permit gross injustice to occur) is not one with respect to which one must necessarily be tolerant. As examples, Rawls appeals to both the abolitionist and civil rights movements.

Both slavery and racial discrimination violate the principles of justice. That such things were not only permitted, but even legislated and enforced by the political institutions of the country at the time, is indicative that our public institutions, at least with respect to those issues, were *unjust*. Both abolitionists and leaders of the civil rights movement extensively appealed to their comprehensive moral doctrines (typically, religiously-based) to provide arguments against those practices—though they certainly also appealed to the *public* (shared) values of freedom and equality. Rawls supposes that such activists "could have seen their actions as the best way to

June 2, 2009. Archived from the original on June 8, 2009. Retrieved June 3, 2009.

186 Rawls, Political Liberalism, p. 138.

187 Rawls, A Theory of Justice. Revised Edition, p. 96.

bring about a well-ordered and just society in which the ideal of public reason could eventually be honored. . . . Given those historical conditions, it was not unreasonable of them to act as they did for the sake of the ideal of public reason itself."[188]

Exactly *when* civil disobedience, inspired by our comprehensive moral doctrines, is justified is a complicated question, and beyond the scope of this chapter. With certain issues, and in certain scenarios, however, justice might not only allow, but *depend upon*, an activist doing more than simply attempting to persuade others, through the use of public reasons, to change the problematic policies. By definition, such a society is not a well-ordered society, and so our focus will have shifted from stability issues to the justice of civil disobedience, but this is nevertheless one scenario in which more aggressive measures might be appropriate.

Summary

John Rawls offers an interpretation of the social contract tradition that attempts to not only establish the bases for a just and fair constitution and political institutions, but also define the basic principles of justice that will determine the legitimacy of our laws and policies, and establish our basic liberties. This conception of justice as fairness is an example of a political conception of justice that is not dependent upon any particular comprehensive moral doctrine, but is intended to be consistent with a wide variety of them. In this way, Rawls offers an example of how an overlapping consensus of reasonable comprehensive moral doctrines can be achieved.

By justifying our policy positions within the limits of public reason, we promote and preserve the legitimacy of those policies such that, even when we "lose," we still respect the legitimacy of that outcome, and will honor the results, despite our disagreement. In this way, the well-ordered society becomes and remains stable, despite the existence of a reasonable plurality of worldviews.

This is all as it *should* be, of course, according to Rawls. Whether the United States is well-ordered to begin with, and whether the appeal of "reasonableness" remains persuasive to a sufficient number of citizens, is another matter....

Appendix: President Barack Obama and John Rawls

In this appendix, I would like to offer a concrete example of where political philosophy has concrete policy implications. Far from being a "merely theoretical" exercise, political theories can, and do, influence politicians and policies alike.

There is reason to believe that President Obama is familiar with the work of John Rawls. For one, his Columbia college roommate says so:

> *Mr. Boerner recalls Mr. Obama wrapping himself in a green sleeping bag (seen in this photo Mr. Boerner took) to keep warm when they studied at home. They listened to reggae. Bob Marley. Peter Tosh. Talked philosophy. Theories of justice and John Rawls. Mr. Boerner recalled Mr. Obama joking that he would rather be spending his time pondering Lou Rawls, the singer.*[189]

[188] John Rawls, *Political Liberalism*, pp. 250-251.

[189] http://cityroom.blogs.nytimes.com/2009/01/20/recollections-of-obamas-ex-roommate/comment-page-2/

Far more compelling than an appeal to his roommate's memory, though, is a comparison of some excerpts of one of President Obama's speeches with statements written by Rawls himself.[190]

Both Rawls and Obama are concerned with the "problem" of reasonable pluralism.

> *"How it is possible for a just and stable society of free and equal citizens to exist and endure when its citizens 'remain profoundly divided by reasonable religious, philosophical, and moral doctrines?'" (Rawls)*

> *"I answered with what has come to be the typically liberal response in such debates - namely, I said that we live in a pluralistic society, that I can't impose my own religious views on another, . . ." (Obama*

Both see the value of, and need for, and "overlapping consensus" of comprehensive moral doctrines.

> *Overlapping consensus: wide-spread agreement on core issues involving various (and even competing) comprehensive moral doctrines—necessary for a stable, well-ordered society. (paraphrase of Rawls)*

> *"Moreover, if we progressives shed some of these biases, we might recognize some overlapping values that both religious and secular people share when it comes to the moral and material direction of our country." (Obama—emphasis added)*

Both recognize the importance of being able to articulate one's policy positions by appealing to shared values, and reasons that could, in principle, be endorsed by a wide variety of people—even though who do not agree with one's own comprehensive moral doctrine.

> *(Rawls)*
> *"Our exercise of political power is proper only when we sincerely believe that the reasons we offer for our political actions—were we to state them as government officials—are sufficient, and we also think that other citizens might reasonably accept those reasons."*

> *(Obama, with emphasis added)*
> *"Whatever we once were, we are no longer just a Christian nation; we are also a Jewish nation, a Muslim nation, a Buddhist nation, a Hindu nation, and a nation of nonbelievers.*

> *And even if we did have only Christians in our midst, if we expelled every non-Christian from the United States of America, whose Christianity would we teach in the schools? Would we go with James Dobson's, or Al Sharpton's? Which passages of Scripture should guide our public policy? . . .*

> *This brings me to my second point. Democracy demands that the religiously motivated translate their concerns into universal, rather than religion-specific, values. It requires*

[190]The full transcript of this speech is available here: http://www.nytimes.com/2006/06/28/us/politics/2006obamaspeech.html?_r=0

that their proposals be subject to argument, and amenable to reason. I may be opposed to abortion for religious reasons, but if I seek to pass a law banning the practice, I cannot simply point to the teachings of my church or evoke God's will. I have to explain why abortion violates some principle that is accessible to people of all faiths, including those with no faith at all.

Now this is going to be difficult for some who believe in the inerrancy of the Bible, as many evangelicals do. But in a pluralistic democracy, we have no choice. Politics depends on our ability to persuade each other of common aims based on a common reality. It involves the compromise, the art of what's possible. At some fundamental level, religion does not allow for compromise. It's the art of the impossible. If God has spoken, then followers are expected to live up to God's edicts, regardless of the consequences. To base one's life on such uncompromising commitments may be sublime, but to base our policy making on such commitments would be a dangerous thing. And if you doubt that, let me give you an example.

We all know the story of Abraham and Isaac. Abraham is ordered by God to offer up his only son, and without argument, he takes Isaac to the mountaintop, binds him to an altar, and raises his knife, prepared to act as God has commanded.

Of course, in the end God sends down an angel to intercede at the very last minute, and Abraham passes God's test of devotion.

But it's fair to say that if any of us leaving this church saw Abraham on a roof of a building raising his knife, we would, at the very least, call the police and expect the Department of Children and Family Services to take Isaac away from Abraham. We would do so because we do not hear what Abraham hears, do not see what Abraham sees, true as those experiences may be. So the best we can do is act in accordance with those things that we all see, and that we all hear, be it common laws or basic reason."

While Rawls thinks that we have a moral and civil duty to one another to advocate for our policy positions by appealing to reasons subject to the limits of public reason, he also recognizes that non-public reasons may be invoked as well, as a supplement.

(Rawls)
"Reasonable comprehensive doctrines, religious or non-religious, may be introduced in public political discourse at any time, provided that in due course proper political reasons—and not reasons given solely by comprehensive doctrines—are presented that are sufficient to support whatever the comprehensive doctrines introduced are said to support."

(Obama, with emphasis added)

"But what I am suggesting is this secularists are wrong when they ask believers to leave their religion at the door before entering into the public square. Frederick Douglas, Abraham Lincoln, Williams Jennings Bryant, Dorothy Day, Martin Luther King -

> *indeed, the majority of great reformers in American history - were not only motivated by faith, but repeatedly used religious language to argue for their cause. So to say that men and women should not inject their "personal morality" into public policy debates is a practical absurdity."*

Perhaps more forcefully than Rawls, President Obama recognizes the importance and value of one's comprehensive moral doctrine. However, he also clearly recognizes the importance of being able to "translate" those values into shared, overlapping values.

> *"Democracy demands that the religiously motivated translate their concerns into universal, rather than religion-specific, values. It requires that their proposals be subject to argument, and amenable to reason. I may be opposed to abortion for religious reasons, but if I seek to pass a law banning the practice, I cannot simply point to the teachings of my church or evoke God's will. I have to explain why abortion violates some principle that is accessible to people of all faiths, including those with no faith at all." (Obama)*

None of the preceding is meant to suggest that President Obama was exclusively, or even primarily, "Rawlsian" in his political theory or practice. It is, however, a clear example of where theory meets practice, and when a political philosopher can influence the decisions and strategies of actual political leaders. However theoretical political philosophy might be, we should always remember that the *point* of these theories is to ultimately find application in the actual political institutions, policies, and lives of real people.

Thomas Hobbes (5 April 1588 – 4 December 1679) was a prominent philosopher, political theorist, and historian (among his other talents). His ideas were very influential for other social contract theorists, and political philosophers in general. Though he supported absolute monarchy, his ideas contributed to those developed by the writers of the U.S. Constitution and the Declaration of Independence. In this selection from "Leviathan," Hobbes describes the hypothetical "state of nature." Among the more important features of the state of nature are our basic physical and mental equality, and the lack of any sort of governing authority. This equality, coupled with anarchy, results in unacceptably high insecurity and misery. The antidote to this is a social contract that will provide order and rules of conduct, and the "sovereign" (government) who will enforce that contract.

Thomas Hobbes

Leviathan[191]

...

CHAPTER XIII. OF THE NATURALL CONDITION OF MANKIND, AS CONCERNING THEIR FELICITY, AND MISERY

Nature hath made men so equall, in the faculties of body, and mind; as that though there bee found one man sometimes manifestly stronger in body, or of quicker mind then another; yet when all is reckoned together, the difference between man, and man, is not so considerable, as that one man can thereupon claim to himselfe any benefit, to which another may not pretend, as well as he. For as to the strength of body, the weakest has strength enough to kill the strongest, either by secret machination, or by confederacy with others, that are in the same danger with himselfe.

And as to the faculties of the mind, (setting aside the arts grounded upon words, and especially that skill of proceeding upon generall, and infallible rules, called Science; which very few have, and but in few things; as being not a native faculty, born with us; nor attained, (as Prudence,) while we look after somewhat els,) I find yet a greater equality amongst men, than that of strength. For Prudence, is but Experience; which equall time, equally bestowes on all men, in those things they equally apply themselves unto. That which may perhaps make such equality incredible, is but a vain conceipt of ones owne wisdome, which almost all men think they have in a greater degree, than the Vulgar; that is, than all men but themselves, and a few others, whom by Fame, or for concurring with themselves, they approve. For such is the nature of men, that howsoever they may acknowledge many others to be more witty, or more eloquent, or more learned; Yet they will hardly believe there be many so wise as themselves: For they see their own wit at hand, and other mens at a distance. But this proveth rather that men are in that point equall, than unequall. For there is not ordinarily a greater signe of the equall distribution of any thing, than that every man is contented with his share.

---

191 http://www.gutenberg.org/files/3207/3207-h/3207-h.htm

From Equality Proceeds Diffidence

From this equality of ability, ariseth equality of hope in the attaining of our Ends. And therefore if any two men desire the same thing, which neverthelesse they cannot both enjoy, they become enemies; and in the way to their End, (which is principally their owne conservation, and sometimes their delectation only,) endeavour to destroy, or subdue one an other. And from hence it comes to passe, that where an Invader hath no more to feare, than an other mans single power; if one plant, sow, build, or possesse a convenient Seat, others may probably be expected to come prepared with forces united, to dispossesse, and deprive him, not only of the fruit of his labour, but also of his life, or liberty. And the Invader again is in the like danger of another.

From Diffidence Warre

And from this diffidence of one another, there is no way for any man to secure himselfe, so reasonable, as Anticipation; that is, by force, or wiles, to master the persons of all men he can, so long, till he see no other power great enough to endanger him: And this is no more than his own conservation requireth, and is generally allowed. Also because there be some, that taking pleasure in contemplating their own power in the acts of conquest, which they pursue farther than their security requires; if others, that otherwise would be glad to be at ease within modest bounds, should not by invasion increase their power, they would not be able, long time, by standing only on their defence, to subsist. And by consequence, such augmentation of dominion over men, being necessary to a mans conservation, it ought to be allowed him.

Againe, men have no pleasure, (but on the contrary a great deale of griefe) in keeping company, where there is no power able to over-awe them all. For every man looketh that his companion should value him, at the same rate he sets upon himselfe: And upon all signes of contempt, or undervaluing, naturally endeavours, as far as he dares (which amongst them that have no common power, to keep them in quiet, is far enough to make them destroy each other,) to extort a greater value from his contemners, by dommage; and from others, by the example.

So that in the nature of man, we find three principall causes of quarrel. First, Competition; Secondly, Diffidence; Thirdly, Glory.

The first, maketh men invade for Gain; the second, for Safety; and the third, for Reputation. The first use Violence, to make themselves Masters of other mens persons, wives, children, and cattell; the second, to defend them; the third, for trifles, as a word, a smile, a different opinion, and any other signe of undervalue, either direct in their Persons, or by reflexion in their Kindred, their Friends, their Nation, their Profession, or their Name.

Out Of Civil States,

There Is Alwayes Warre Of Every One Against Every One Hereby it is manifest, that during the time men live without a common Power to keep them all in awe, they are in that condition which is called Warre; and such a warre, as is of every man, against every man. For WARRE, consisteth not in Battell onely, or the act of fighting; but in a tract of time, wherein the Will to contend by Battell is sufficiently known: and therefore the notion of Time, is to be considered in the nature of Warre; as it is in the nature of Weather. For as the nature of Foule weather, lyeth not in a showre or two of rain; but in an inclination thereto of many dayes together: So the nature of War, consisteth not in actuall fighting; but in the known disposition thereto, during all the time there is no assurance to the contrary. All other time is PEACE.

The Incommodites Of Such A War

Whatsoever therefore is consequent to a time of Warre, where every man is Enemy to every man; the same is consequent to the time, wherein men live without other security, than what their own strength, and their own invention shall furnish them withall. In such condition, there is no place for Industry; because the fruit thereof is uncertain; and consequently no Culture of the Earth; no Navigation, nor use of the commodities that may be imported by Sea; no commodious Building; no Instruments of moving, and removing such things as require much force; no Knowledge of the face of the Earth; no account of Time; no Arts; no Letters; no Society; and which is worst of all, continuall feare, and danger of violent death; And the life of man, solitary, poore, nasty, brutish, and short.

It may seem strange to some man, that has not well weighed these things; that Nature should thus dissociate, and render men apt to invade, and destroy one another: and he may therefore, not trusting to this Inference, made from the Passions, desire perhaps to have the same confirmed by Experience.

Let him therefore consider with himselfe, when taking a journey, he armes himselfe, and seeks to go well accompanied; when going to sleep, he locks his dores; when even in his house he locks his chests; and this when he knows there bee Lawes, and publike Officers, armed, to revenge all injuries shall bee done him; what opinion he has of his fellow subjects, when he rides armed; of his fellow Citizens, when he locks his dores; and of his children, and servants, when he locks his chests. Does he not there as much accuse mankind by his actions, as I do by my words? But neither of us accuse mans nature in it. The Desires, and other Passions of man, are in themselves no Sin. No more are the Actions, that proceed from those Passions, till they know a Law that forbids them; which till Lawes be made they cannot know: nor can any Law be made, till they have agreed upon the Person that shall make it.

It may peradventure be thought, there was never such a time, nor condition of warre as this; and I believe it was never generally so, over all the world: but there are many places, where they live so now. For the savage people in many places of America, except the government of small Families, the concord whereof dependeth on naturall lust, have no government at all; and live at this day in that brutish manner, as I said before. Howsoever, it may be perceived what manner of life there would be, where there were no common Power to feare; by the manner of life, which men that have formerly lived under a peacefull government, use to degenerate into, in a civill Warre.

But though there had never been any time, wherein particular men were in a condition of warre one against another; yet in all times, Kings, and persons of Soveraigne authority, because of their Independency, are in continuall jealousies, and in the state and posture of Gladiators; having their weapons pointing, and their eyes fixed on one another; that is, their Forts, Garrisons, and Guns upon the Frontiers of their Kingdomes; and continuall Spyes upon their neighbours; which is a posture of War. But because they uphold thereby, the Industry of their Subjects; there does not follow from it, that misery, which accompanies the Liberty of particular men.

In Such A Warre, Nothing Is Unjust

To this warre of every man against every man, this also is consequent; that nothing can be Unjust. The notions of Right and Wrong, Justice and Injustice have there no place. Where there is no common Power, there is no Law: where no Law, no Injustice. Force, and Fraud, are in warre the two Cardinall vertues. Justice, and Injustice are none of the Faculties neither of the Body, nor Mind. If they were, they might be in a man that were alone in the world, as well as his Senses, and Passions. They are Qualities, that relate to men in Society, not in Solitude. It is consequent also to the same condition, that there be no Propriety, no Dominion, no Mine and Thine distinct; but onely that to be every mans that he can get; and for so long, as he can keep it. And thus much for the ill condition, which man by meer Nature is actually placed in; though with a possibility to come out of it, consisting partly in the Passions, partly in his Reason.

The Passions That Incline Men To Peace

The Passions that encline men to Peace, are Feare of Death; Desire of such things as are necessary to commodious living; and a Hope by their Industry to obtain them. And Reason suggesteth convenient Articles of Peace, upon which men may be drawn to agreement. These Articles, are they, which otherwise are called the Lawes of Nature: whereof I shall speak more particularly, in the two following Chapters.

CHAPTER XIV. OF THE FIRST AND SECOND NATURALL LAWES, AND OF CONTRACTS

Right Of Nature What

The RIGHT OF NATURE, which Writers commonly call Jus Naturale, is the Liberty each man hath, to use his own power, as he will himselfe, for the preservation of his own Nature; that is to say, of his own Life; and consequently, of doing any thing, which in his own Judgement, and Reason, hee shall conceive to be the aptest means thereunto.

Liberty What

By LIBERTY, is understood, according to the proper signification of the word, the absence of externall Impediments: which Impediments, may oft take away part of a mans power to do what hee would; but cannot hinder him from using the power left him, according as his judgement, and reason shall dictate to him.

A Law Of Nature What

A LAW OF NATURE, (Lex Naturalis,) is a Precept, or generall Rule, found out by Reason, by which a man is forbidden to do, that, which is destructive of his life, or taketh away the means of preserving the same; and to omit, that, by which he thinketh it may be best preserved. For though they that speak of this subject, use to confound Jus, and Lex, Right and Law; yet they ought to be distinguished; because RIGHT, consisteth in liberty to do, or to forbeare; Whereas LAW, determineth, and bindeth to one of them: so that Law, and Right, differ as much, as Obligation, and Liberty; which in one and the same matter are inconsistent.

Naturally Every Man Has Right To Everything

And because the condition of Man, (as hath been declared in the precedent Chapter) is a condition of Warre of every one against every one; in which case every one is governed by his own Reason; and there is nothing he can make use of, that may not be a help unto him, in preserving his life against his enemyes; It followeth, that in such a condition, every man has a Right to every thing; even to one anothers body. And therefore, as long as this naturall Right of every man to every thing endureth, there can be no security to any man, (how strong or wise soever he be,) of living out the time, which Nature ordinarily alloweth men to live.

The Fundamental Law Of Nature

And consequently it is a precept, or generall rule of Reason, "That every man, ought to endeavour Peace, as farre as he has hope of obtaining it; and when he cannot obtain it, that he may seek, and use, all helps, and advantages of Warre." The first branch, of which Rule, containeth the first, and Fundamentall Law of Nature; which is, "To seek Peace, and follow it." The Second, the summe of the Right of Nature; which is, "By all means we can, to defend our selves."

The Second Law Of Nature

From this Fundamentall Law of Nature, by which men are commanded to endeavour Peace, is derived this second Law; "That a man be willing, when others are so too, as farre-forth, as for Peace, and defence of himselfe he shall think it necessary, to lay down this right to all things; and be contented with so much liberty against other men, as he would allow other men against himselfe." For as long as every man holdeth this Right, of doing any thing he liketh; so long are all men in the condition of Warre. But if other men will not lay down their Right, as well as he; then there is no Reason for any one, to devest himselfe of his: For that were to expose himselfe to Prey, (which no man is bound to) rather than to dispose himselfe to Peace. This is that Law of the Gospell; "Whatsoever you require that others should do to you, that do ye to them." And that Law of all men, "Quod tibi feiri non vis, alteri ne feceris."

. . .

Covenants Extorted By Feare Are Valide

Covenants entred into by fear, in the condition of meer Nature, are obligatory. For example, if I Covenant to pay a ransome, or service for my life, to an enemy; I am bound by it. For it is a Contract, wherein one receiveth the benefit of life; the other is to receive mony, or service for it; and consequently, where no other Law (as in the condition, of meer Nature) forbiddeth the performance, the Covenant is valid. Therefore Prisoners of warre, if trusted with the payment of their Ransome, are obliged to pay it; And if a weaker Prince, make a disadvantageous peace with a stronger, for feare; he is bound to keep it; unlesse (as hath been sayd before) there ariseth some new, and just cause of feare, to renew the war. And even in Common-wealths, if I be forced to redeem my selfe from a Theefe by promising him mony, I am bound to pay it, till the Civill Law discharge me. For whatsoever I may lawfully do without Obligation, the same I may lawfully Covenant to do through feare: and what I lawfully Covenant, I cannot lawfully break.

The Former Covenant To One, Makes Voyd The Later To Another

A former Covenant, makes voyd a later. For a man that hath passed away his Right to one man to day, hath it not to passe to morrow to another: and therefore the later promise passeth no Right, but is null.

A Mans Covenant Not To Defend Himselfe, Is Voyd

A Covenant not to defend my selfe from force, by force, is alwayes voyd. For (as I have shewed before) no man can transferre, or lay down his Right to save himselfe from Death,

Wounds, and Imprisonment, (the avoyding whereof is the onely End of laying down any Right,) and therefore the promise of not resisting force, in no Covenant transferreth any right; nor is obliging. For though a man may Covenant thus, "Unlesse I do so, or so, kill me;" he cannot Covenant thus "Unless I do so, or so, I will not resist you, when you come to kill me." For man by nature chooseth the lesser evill, which is danger of death in resisting; rather than the greater, which is certain and present death in not resisting. And this is granted to be true by all men, in that they lead Criminals to Execution, and Prison, with armed men, notwithstanding that such Criminals have consented to the Law, by which they are condemned.

. . .

CHAPTER XV. OF OTHER LAWES OF NATURE

The Third Law Of Nature, Justice

From that law of Nature, by which we are obliged to transferre to another, such Rights, as being retained, hinder the peace of Mankind, there followeth a Third; which is this, That Men Performe Their Covenants Made: without which, Covenants are in vain, and but Empty words; and the Right of all men to all things remaining, wee are still in the condition of Warre.

Justice And Injustice What

And in this law of Nature, consisteth the Fountain and Originall of JUSTICE. For where no Covenant hath preceded, there hath no Right been transferred, and every man has right to every thing; and consequently, no action can be Unjust. But when a Covenant is made, then to break it is Unjust: And the definition of INJUSTICE, is no other than The Not Performance Of Covenant. And whatsoever is not Unjust, is Just.

Justice And Propriety Begin With The Constitution of Common-wealth But because Covenants of mutuall trust, where there is a feare of not performance on either part, (as hath been said in the former Chapter,) are invalid; though the Originall of Justice be the making of Covenants; yet Injustice actually there can be none, till the cause of such feare be taken away; which while men are in the naturall condition of Warre, cannot be done. Therefore before the names of Just, and Unjust can have place, there must be some coercive Power, to compell men equally to the performance of their Covenants, by the terrour of some punishment, greater than the benefit they expect by the breach of their Covenant; and to make good that Propriety, which by mutuall Contract men acquire, in recompence of the universall Right they abandon: and such power there is none before the erection of a Common-wealth. And this is also to be gathered out of the ordinary definition of Justice in the Schooles: For they say, that "Justice is the constant Will of giving to every man his own." And therefore where there is no Own, that is, no Propriety, there is no Injustice; and where there is no coerceive Power erected, that is, where there is no Common-wealth, there is no Propriety; all men having Right to all things: Therefore where there is no Common-wealth, there nothing is Unjust. So that the nature of Justice, consisteth in keeping of valid Covenants: but the Validity of Covenants begins not but with the Constitution of a Civill Power, sufficient to compell men to keep them: And then it is also that Propriety begins.

Justice Not Contrary To Reason

The Foole hath sayd in his heart, there is no such thing as Justice; and sometimes also with his tongue; seriously alleaging, that every mans conservation, and contentment, being committed to his own care, there could be no reason, why every man might not do what he thought conduced thereunto; and therefore also to make, or not make; keep, or not keep Covenants, was not against Reason, when it conduced to ones benefit. He does not therein deny, that there be Covenants; and that they are sometimes broken, sometimes kept; and that such breach of them may be called Injustice, and the observance of them Justice: but he questioneth, whether Injustice, taking away the feare of God, (for the same Foole hath said in his heart there is no God,) may not sometimes stand with that Reason, which dictateth to every man his own good; and particularly then, when it conduceth to such a benefit, as shall put a man in a condition, to neglect not onely the dispraise, and revilings, but also the power of other men. The Kingdome of God is gotten by violence; but what if it could be gotten by unjust violence? were it against Reason so to get it, when it is impossible to receive hurt by it? and if it be not against Reason, it is not against Justice; or else Justice is not to be approved for good. From such reasoning as this, Succesfull wickednesse hath obtained the Name of Vertue; and some that in all other things have disallowed the violation of Faith; yet have allowed it, when it is for the getting of a Kingdome. And the Heathen that believed, that Saturn was deposed by his son Jupiter, believed neverthelesse the same Jupiter to be the avenger of Injustice: Somewhat like to a piece of Law in Cokes Commentaries on Litleton; where he sayes, If the right Heire of the Crown be attainted of Treason; yet the Crown shall descend to him, and Eo Instante the Atteynder be voyd; From which instances a man will be very prone to inferre; that when the Heire apparent of a Kingdome, shall kill him that is in possession, though his father; you may call it Injustice, or by what other name you will; yet it can never be against Reason, seeing all the voluntary actions of men tend to the benefit of themselves; and those actions are most Reasonable, that conduce most to their ends. This specious reasoning is nevertheless false.

For the question is not of promises mutuall, where there is no security of performance on either side; as when there is no Civill Power erected over the parties promising; for such promises are no Covenants: But either where one of the parties has performed already; or where there is a Power to make him performe; there is the question whether it be against reason, that is, against the benefit of the other to performe, or not. And I say it is not against reason. For the manifestation whereof, we are to consider; First, that when a man doth a thing, which notwithstanding any thing can be foreseen, and reckoned on, tendeth to his own destruction, howsoever some accident which he could not expect, arriving may turne it to his benefit; yet such events do not make it reasonably or wisely done. Secondly, that in a condition of Warre, wherein every man to every man, for want of a common Power to keep them all in awe, is an Enemy, there is no man can hope by his own strength, or wit, to defend himselfe from destruction, without the help of Confederates; where every one expects the same defence by the Confederation, that any one else does: and therefore he which declares he thinks it reason to deceive those that help him, can in reason expect no other means of safety, than what can be had from his own single Power. He therefore that breaketh his Covenant, and consequently declareth that he thinks he may with reason do so, cannot be received into any Society, that unite themselves for Peace and defence, but by the errour of them that receive him; nor when he is received, be retayned in it, without seeing the danger of their errour; which errours a man cannot reasonably reckon upon as the means of his security; and therefore if he be left, or cast out of Society, he perisheth; and if he live in Society, it is by the errours of other men, which he could not foresee, nor reckon upon; and consequently against the reason of his preservation; and so, as all men that contribute not to his destruction, forbear him onely out of ignorance of what is good for themselves.

As for the Instance of gaining the secure and perpetuall felicity of Heaven, by any way; it is frivolous: there being but one way imaginable; and that is not breaking, but keeping of Covenant.

And for the other Instance of attaining Soveraignty by Rebellion; it is manifest, that though the event follow, yet because it cannot reasonably be expected, but rather the contrary; and because by gaining it so, others are taught to gain the same in like manner, the attempt thereof is against reason. Justice therefore, that is to say, Keeping of Covenant, is a Rule of Reason, by which we are forbidden to do any thing destructive to our life; and consequently a Law of Nature.

There be some that proceed further; and will not have the Law of Nature, to be those Rules which conduce to the preservation of mans life on earth; but to the attaining of an eternall felicity after death; to which they think the breach of Covenant may conduce; and consequently be just and reasonable; (such are they that think it a work of merit to kill, or depose, or rebell against, the Soveraigne Power constituted over them by their own consent.) But because there is no naturall knowledge of mans estate after death; much lesse of the reward that is then to be given to breach of Faith; but onely a beliefe grounded upon other mens saying, that they know it supernaturally, or that they know those, that knew them, that knew others, that knew it supernaturally; Breach of Faith cannot be called a Precept of Reason, or Nature.

. . .

Nothing Done To A Man, By His Own Consent Can Be Injury

Whatsoever is done to a man, conformable to his own Will signified to the doer, is no Injury to him. For if he that doeth it, hath not passed away his originall right to do what he please, by some Antecedent Covenant, there is no breach of Covenant; and therefore no Injury done him. And if he have; then his Will to have it done being signified, is a release of that Covenant; and so again there is no Injury done him.

. . .

The Science Of These Lawes, Is The True Morall Philosophy

And the Science of them, is the true and onely Moral Philosophy. For Morall Philosophy is nothing else but the Science of what is Good, and Evill, in the conversation, and Society of mankind. Good, and Evill, are names that signifie our Appetites, and Aversions; which in different tempers, customes, and doctrines of men, are different: And divers men, differ not onely in their Judgement, on the senses of what is pleasant, and unpleasant to the tast, smell, hearing, touch, and sight; but also of what is conformable, or disagreeable to Reason, in the actions of common life. Nay, the same man, in divers times, differs from himselfe; and one time praiseth, that is, calleth Good, what another time he dispraiseth, and calleth Evil: From whence arise Disputes, Controversies, and at last War.

And therefore so long as man is in the condition of meer Nature, (which is a condition of War,) as private Appetite is the measure of Good, and Evill: and consequently all men agree on this, that Peace is Good, and therefore also the way, or means of Peace, which (as I have shewed before) are Justice, Gratitude, Modesty, Equity, Mercy, & the rest of the Laws of Nature, are good; that is to say, Morall Vertues; and their contrarie Vices, Evill. Now the science of Vertue and Vice, is Morall Philosophie; and therfore the true Doctrine of the Lawes of Nature, is the true Morall Philosophie. But the Writers of Morall Philosophie, though they acknowledge the same Vertues and Vices; Yet not seeing wherein consisted their Goodnesse; nor that they come to be praised, as the meanes of peaceable, sociable, and comfortable living; place them in a mediocrity of passions: as if not the Cause, but the Degree of daring, made Fortitude; or not the Cause, but the Quantity of a gift, made Liberality.

These dictates of Reason, men use to call by the name of Lawes; but improperly: for they are but Conclusions, or Theoremes concerning what conduceth to the conservation and defence of themselves; whereas Law, properly is the word of him, that by right hath command over others. But yet if we consider the same Theoremes, as delivered in the word of God, that by right commandeth all things; then are they properly called Lawes.

...

PART II. OF COMMON-WEALTH

CHAPTER XVII. OF THE CAUSES, GENERATION, AND DEFINITION OF A COMMON WEALTH

The End Of Common-wealth, Particular Security

The finall Cause, End, or Designe of men, (who naturally love Liberty, and Dominion over others,) in the introduction of that restraint upon themselves, (in which wee see them live in Common-wealths,) is the foresight of their own preservation, and of a more contented life thereby; that is to say, of getting themselves out from that miserable condition of Warre, which is necessarily consequent (as hath been shewn) to the naturall Passions of men, when there is no visible Power to keep them in awe, and tye them by feare of punishment to the performance of their Covenants, and observation of these Lawes of Nature set down in the fourteenth and fifteenth Chapters.

Which Is Not To Be Had From The Law Of Nature:

For the Lawes of Nature (as Justice, Equity, Modesty, Mercy, and (in summe) Doing To Others, As Wee Would Be Done To,) if themselves, without the terrour of some Power, to cause them to be observed, are contrary to our naturall Passions, that carry us to Partiality, Pride, Revenge, and the like. And Covenants, without the Sword, are but Words, and of no strength to secure a man at all. Therefore notwithstanding the Lawes of Nature, (which every one hath then kept, when he has the will to keep them, when he can do it safely,) if there be no Power erected, or not great enough for our security; every man will and may lawfully rely on his own strength and art, for caution against all other men. And in all places, where men have lived by small Families, to robbe and spoyle one another, has been a Trade, and so farre from being reputed against the Law of Nature, that the greater spoyles they gained, the greater was their honour; and men observed no other Lawes therein, but the Lawes of Honour; that is, to abstain from cruelty, leaving to men their lives, and instruments of husbandry. And as small Familyes did then; so now do Cities and Kingdomes which are but greater Families (for their own security) enlarge their Dominions, upon all pretences of danger, and fear of Invasion, or assistance that may be given to Invaders, endeavour as much as they can, to subdue, or weaken their neighbours, by open force, and secret arts, for want of other Caution, justly; and are rememdbred for it in after ages with honour.

Nor From The Conjunction Of A Few Men Or Familyes

Nor is it the joyning together of a small number of men, that gives them this security; because in small numbers, small additions on the one side or the other, make the advantage of strength so great, as is sufficient to carry the Victory; and therefore gives encouragement to an Invasion. The Multitude sufficient to confide in for our Security, is not determined by any certain number, but by comparison with the Enemy we feare; and is then sufficient, when the odds of the Enemy is not of so visible and conspicuous moment, to determine the event of warre, as to move him to attempt.

Nor From A Great Multitude, Unlesse Directed By One Judgement

And be there never so great a Multitude; yet if their actions be directed according to their particular judgements, and particular appetites, they can expect thereby no defence, nor protection, neither against a Common enemy, nor against the injuries of one another. For being distracted in opinions concerning the best use and application of their strength, they do not help, but hinder one another; and reduce their strength by mutuall opposition to nothing: whereby they are easily, not onely subdued by a very few that agree together; but also when there is no common enemy, they make warre upon each other, for their particular interests. For if we could suppose a great Multitude of men to consent in the observation of Justice, and other Lawes of Nature, without a common Power to keep them all in awe; we might as well suppose all Man-kind to do the same; and then there neither would be nor need to be any Civill Government, or Common-wealth at all; because there would be Peace without subjection.

And That Continually

Nor is it enough for the security, which men desire should last all the time of their life, that they be governed, and directed by one judgement, for a limited time; as in one Battell, or one Warre. For though they obtain a Victory by their unanimous endeavour against a forraign enemy; yet afterwards, when either they have no common enemy, or he that by one part is held for an enemy, is by another part held for a friend, they must needs by the difference of their interests dissolve, and fall again into a Warre amongst themselves.

...

The Generation Of A Common-wealth

The only way to erect such a Common Power, as may be able to defend them from the invasion of Forraigners, and the injuries of one another, and thereby to secure them in such sort, as that by their owne industrie, and by the fruites of the Earth, they may nourish themselves and live contentedly; is, to conferre all their power and strength upon one Man, or upon one Assembly of men, that may reduce all their Wills, by plurality of voices, unto one Will: which is as much as to say, to appoint one man, or Assembly of men, to beare their Person; and every one to owne, and acknowledge himselfe to be Author of whatsoever he that so beareth their Person, shall Act, or cause to be Acted, in those things which concerne the Common Peace and Safetie; and therein to submit their Wills, every one to his Will, and their Judgements, to his Judgment. This is more than Consent, or Concord; it is a reall Unitie of them all, in one and the same Person, made by Covenant of every man with every man, in such manner, as if every man should say to every man, "I Authorise and give up my Right of Governing my selfe, to this Man, or to this Assembly of men, on this condition, that thou give up thy Right to him, and Authorise all his Actions in like manner." This done, the Multitude so united in one Person, is called a COMMON-WEALTH, in latine CIVITAS. This is the Generation of that great LEVIATHAN, or rather (to speake more reverently) of that Mortall God, to which wee owe under the Immortall God, our peace and defence. For by this Authoritie, given him by every particular man in the Common-Wealth, he hath the use of so much Power and Strength conferred on him, that by terror thereof, he is inabled to forme the wills of them all, to Peace at home, and mutuall ayd against their enemies abroad.

The Definition Of A Common-wealth

And in him consisteth the Essence of the Common-wealth; which (to define it,) is "One Person, of whose Acts a great Multitude, by mutuall Covenants one with another, have made themselves every one the Author, to the end he may use the strength and means of them all, as he shall think expedient, for their Peace and Common Defence."

Soveraigne, And Subject, What

And he that carryeth this Person, as called SOVERAIGNE, and said to have Soveraigne Power; and every one besides, his SUBJECT.

The attaining to this Soveraigne Power, is by two wayes. One, by Naturall force; as when a man maketh his children, to submit themselves, and their children to his government, as being able to destroy them if they refuse, or by Warre subdueth his enemies to his will, giving them their lives on that condition. The other, is when men agree amongst themselves, to submit to some Man, or Assembly of men, voluntarily, on confidence to be protected by him against all others. This later, may be called a Politicall Common-wealth, or Common-wealth by Institution; and the former, a Common-wealth by Acquisition. And first, I shall speak of a Common-wealth by Institution.

CHAPTER XVIII. OF THE RIGHTS OF SOVERAIGNES BY INSTITUTION

The Act Of Instituting A Common-wealth, What

A Common-wealth is said to be Instituted, when a Multitude of men do Agree, and Covenant, Every One With Every One, that to whatsoever Man, or Assembly Of Men, shall be given by the major part, the Right to Present the Person of them all, (that is to say, to be their Representative;) every one, as well he that Voted For It, as he that Voted Against It, shall Authorise all the Actions and Judgements, of that Man, or Assembly of men, in the same manner, as if they were his own, to the end, to live peaceably amongst themselves, and be protected against other men.

The Consequences To Such Institution, Are

I. The Subjects Cannot Change The Forme Of Government

From this Institution of a Common-wealth are derived all the Rights, and Facultyes of him, or them, on whom the Soveraigne Power is conferred by the consent of the People assembled.

First, because they Covenant, it is to be understood, they are not obliged by former Covenant to any thing repugnant hereunto. And Consequently they that have already Instituted a Common-wealth, being thereby bound by Covenant, to own the Actions, and Judgements of one, cannot lawfully make a new Covenant, amongst themselves, to be obedient to any other, in any thing whatsoever, without his permission. And therefore, they that are subjects to a Monarch, cannot without his leave cast off Monarchy, and return to the confusion of a disunited Multitude; nor transferre their Person from him that beareth it, to another Man, or other Assembly of men: for they are bound, every man to every man, to Own, and be reputed Author of all, that he that already is their Soveraigne, shall do, and judge fit to be done: so that any one man dissenting, all the rest should break their Covenant made to that man, which is injustice: and they have also every man given the Soveraignty to him that beareth their Person; and therefore if they depose him, they take from him that which is his own, and so again it is injustice. Besides, if he that attempteth to depose his Soveraign, be killed, or punished by him for such attempt, he is author of his own punishment, as being by the Institution, Author of all his Soveraign shall do: And because it is injustice for a man to do any thing, for which he may be punished by his own authority, he is also upon that title, unjust. And whereas some men have pretended for their disobedience to their Soveraign, a new Covenant, made, not with men, but with God; this also is unjust: for there is no Covenant with God, but by mediation of some body that representeth Gods Person; which none doth but Gods Lieutenant, who hath the Soveraignty under God. But this pretence of Covenant with God, is so evident a lye, even in the pretenders own consciences, that it is not onely an act of an unjust, but also of a vile, and unmanly disposition.

2. Soveraigne Power Cannot Be Forfeited

Secondly, Because the Right of bearing the Person of them all, is given to him they make Soveraigne, by Covenant onely of one to another, and not of him to any of them; there can happen no breach of Covenant on the part of the Soveraigne; and consequently none of his Subjects, by any pretence of forfeiture, can be freed from his Subjection. That he which is made Soveraigne maketh no Covenant with his Subjects beforehand, is manifest; because either he must make it with the whole multitude, as one party to the Covenant; or he must make a severall Covenant with every man. With the whole, as one party, it is impossible; because as yet they are not one Person: and if he make so many severall Covenants as there be men, those Covenants after he hath the Soveraignty are voyd, because what act soever can be pretended by any one of them for breach thereof, is the act both of himselfe, and of all the rest, because done in the Person, and by the Right of every one of them in particular. Besides, if any one, or more of them, pretend a breach of the Covenant made by the Soveraigne at his Institution; and others, or one other of his Subjects, or himselfe alone, pretend there was no such breach, there is in this case, no Judge to decide the controversie: it returns therefore to the Sword again; and every man recovereth the right of Protecting himselfe by his own strength, contrary to the designe they had in the Institution. It is therefore in vain to grant Soveraignty by way of precedent Covenant. The opinion that any Monarch receiveth his Power by Covenant, that is to say on Condition, proceedeth from want of understanding this easie truth, that Covenants being but words, and breath, have no force to oblige, contain, constrain, or protect any man, but what it has from the publique Sword; that is, from the untyed hands of that Man, or Assembly of men that hath the Soveraignty, and whose actions are avouched by them all, and performed by the strength of them all, in him united. But when an Assembly of men is made Soveraigne; then no man imagineth any such Covenant to have past in the Institution; for no man is so dull as to say, for example, the People of Rome, made a Covenant with the Romans, to hold the Soveraignty on such or such conditions; which not performed, the Romans might lawfully depose the Roman People. That men see not the reason to be alike in a Monarchy, and in a Popular Government, proceedeth from the ambition of some, that are kinder to the government of an Assembly, whereof they may hope to participate, than of Monarchy, which they despair to enjoy.

3. No Man Can Without Injustice Protest Against The

Institution Of The Soveraigne Declared By The Major Part. Thirdly, because the major part hath by consenting voices declared a Soveraigne; he that dissented must now consent with the rest; that is, be contented to avow all the actions he shall do, or else justly be destroyed by the rest. For if he voluntarily entered into the Congregation of them that were assembled, he sufficiently declared thereby his will (and therefore tacitely covenanted) to stand to what the major part should ordayne: and therefore if he refuse to stand thereto, or make Protestation against any of their Decrees, he does contrary to his Covenant, and therfore unjustly. And whether he be of the Congregation, or not; and whether his consent be asked, or not, he must either submit to their decrees, or be left in the condition of warre he was in before; wherein he might without injustice be destroyed by any man whatsoever.

4. The Soveraigns Actions Cannot Be Justly Accused By The Subject

Fourthly, because every Subject is by this Institution Author of all the Actions, and Judgements of the Soveraigne Instituted; it followes, that whatsoever he doth, it can be no injury to any of his Subjects; nor ought he to be by any of them accused of Injustice. For he that doth any thing by authority from another, doth therein no injury to him by whose authority he acteth: But by this Institution of a Common-wealth, every particular man is Author of all the Soveraigne doth; and consequently he that complaineth of injury from his Soveraigne, complaineth of that whereof he himselfe is Author; and therefore ought not to accuse any man but himselfe; no nor himselfe of injury; because to do injury to ones selfe, is impossible. It is true that they that have Soveraigne power, may commit Iniquity; but not Injustice, or Injury in the proper signification.

5. What Soever The Soveraigne Doth, Is Unpunishable By The Subject

Fiftly, and consequently to that which was sayd last, no man that hath Soveraigne power can justly be put to death, or otherwise in any manner by his Subjects punished. For seeing every Subject is author of the actions of his Soveraigne; he punisheth another, for the actions committed by himselfe.

6. The Soveraigne Is Judge Of What Is Necessary For The Peace

And Defence Of His Subjects

And because the End of this Institution, is the Peace and Defence of them all; and whosoever has right to the End, has right to the Means; it belongeth of Right, to whatsoever Man, or Assembly that hath the Soveraignty, to be Judge both of the meanes of Peace and Defence; and also of the hindrances, and disturbances of the same; and to do whatsoever he shall think necessary to be done, both beforehand, for the preserving of Peace and Security, by prevention of discord at home and Hostility from abroad; and, when Peace and Security are lost, for the recovery of the same. And therefore,

And Judge Of What Doctrines Are Fit To Be Taught Them

Sixtly, it is annexed to the Soveraignty, to be Judge of what Opinions and Doctrines are averse, and what conducing to Peace; and consequently, on what occasions, how farre, and what, men are to be trusted withall, in speaking to Multitudes of people; and who shall examine the Doctrines of all bookes before they be published. For the Actions of men proceed from their Opinions; and in the wel governing of Opinions, consisteth the well governing of mens Actions, in order to their Peace, and Concord. And though in matter of Doctrine, nothing ought to be regarded but the Truth; yet this is not repugnant to regulating of the same by Peace. For Doctrine Repugnant to Peace, can no more be True, than Peace and Concord can be against the Law of Nature. It is true, that in a Common-wealth, where by the negligence, or unskilfullnesse of Governours, and Teachers, false Doctrines are by time generally received; the contrary Truths may be generally offensive; Yet the most sudden, and rough busling in of a new Truth, that can be, does never breake the Peace, but onely somtimes awake the Warre. For those men that are so remissely governed, that they dare take up Armes, to defend, or introduce an Opinion, are still in Warre; and their condition not Peace, but only a Cessation of Armes for feare of one another; and they live as it were, in the procincts of battaile continually. It belongeth therefore to him that hath the Soveraign Power, to be Judge, or constitute all Judges of Opinions and Doctrines, as a thing necessary to Peace, thereby to prevent Discord and Civill Warre.

7. The Right Of Making Rules, Whereby The Subject May Every Man Know What Is So His Owne, As No Other Subject Can Without Injustice Take It From Him

Seventhly, is annexed to the Soveraigntie, the whole power of prescribing the Rules, whereby every man may know, what Goods he may enjoy and what Actions he may doe, without being molested by any of his fellow Subjects: And this is it men Call Propriety. For before constitution of Soveraign Power (as hath already been shewn) all men had right to all things; which necessarily causeth Warre: and therefore this Proprietie, being necessary to Peace, and depending on Soveraign Power, is the Act of the Power, in order to the publique peace. These Rules of Propriety (or Meum and Tuum) and of Good, Evill, Lawfull and Unlawfull in the actions of subjects, are the Civill Lawes, that is to say, the lawes of each Commonwealth in particular; though the name of Civill Law be now restrained to the antient Civill Lawes of the City of Rome; which being the head of a great part of the World, her Lawes at that time were in these parts the Civill Law.

8. To Him Also Belongeth The Right Of All Judicature And Decision Of Controversies:

Eightly, is annexed to the Soveraigntie, the Right of Judicature; that is to say, of hearing and deciding all Controversies, which may arise concerning Law, either Civill, or naturall, or concerning Fact. For without the decision of Controversies, there is no protection of one Subject, against the injuries of another; the Lawes concerning Meum and Tuum are in vaine; and to every man remaineth, from the naturall and necessary appetite of his own conservation, the right of protecting himselfe by his private strength, which is the condition of Warre; and contrary to the end for which every Common-wealth is instituted.

9. And Of Making War, And Peace, As He Shall Think Best:

Ninthly, is annexed to the Soveraignty, the Right of making Warre, and Peace with other Nations, and Common-wealths; that is to say, of Judging when it is for the publique good, and how great forces are to be assembled, armed, and payd for that end; and to levy mony upon the Subjects, to defray the expenses thereof. For the Power by which the people are to be defended, consisteth in their Armies; and the strength of an Army, in the union of their strength under one Command; which Command the Soveraign Instituted, therefore hath; because the command of the Militia, without other Institution, maketh him that hath it Soveraign. And therefore whosoever is made Generall of an Army, he that hath the Soveraign Power is alwayes Generallissimo.

10. And Of Choosing All Counsellours, And Ministers, Both Of Peace, And Warre:

Tenthly, is annexed to the Soveraignty, the choosing of all Councellours, Ministers, Magistrates, and Officers, both in peace, and War. For seeing the Soveraign is charged with the End, which is the common Peace and Defence; he is understood to have Power to use such Means, as he shall think most fit for his discharge.

11. And Of Rewarding, And Punishing, And That (Where No Former Law hath Determined The Measure Of It) Arbitrary:

Eleventhly, to the Soveraign is committed the Power of Rewarding with riches, or honour; and of Punishing with corporall, or pecuniary punishment, or with ignominy every Subject according to the Lawe he hath formerly made; or if there be no Law made, according as he shall judge most to conduce to the encouraging of men to serve the Common-wealth, or deterring of them from doing dis-service to the same.

12. And Of Honour And Order

Lastly, considering what values men are naturally apt to set upon themselves; what respect they look for from others; and how little they value other men; from whence continually arise amongst them, Emulation, Quarrells, Factions, and at last Warre, to the destroying of one another, and diminution of their strength against a Common Enemy; It is necessary that there be Lawes of Honour, and a publique rate of the worth of such men as have deserved, or are able to deserve well of the Common-wealth; and that there be force in the hands of some or other, to put those

Lawes in execution. But it hath already been shown, that not onely the whole Militia, or forces of the Common-wealth; but also the Judicature of all Controversies, is annexed to the Soveraignty. To the Soveraign therefore it belongeth also to give titles of Honour; and to appoint what Order of place, and dignity, each man shall hold; and what signes of respect, in publique or private meetings, they shall give to one another.

These Rights Are Indivisible

These are the Rights, which make the Essence of Soveraignty; and which are the markes, whereby a man may discern in what Man, or Assembly of men, the Soveraign Power is placed, and resideth. For these are incommunicable, and inseparable. The Power to coyn Mony; to dispose of the estate and persons of Infant heires; to have praeemption in Markets; and all other Statute Praerogatives, may be transferred by the Soveraign; and yet the Power to protect his Subject be retained. But if he transferre the Militia, he retains the Judicature in vain, for want of execution of the Lawes; Or if he grant away the Power of raising Mony; the Militia is in vain: or if he give away the government of doctrines, men will be frighted into rebellion with the feare of Spirits. And so if we consider any one of the said Rights, we shall presently see, that the holding of all the rest, will produce no effect, in the conservation of Peace and Justice, the end for which all Common-wealths are Instituted. And this division is it, whereof it is said, "A kingdome divided in it selfe cannot stand:" For unlesse this division precede, division into opposite Armies can never happen. If there had not first been an opinion received of the greatest part of England, that these Powers were divided between the King, and the Lords, and the House of Commons, the people had never been divided, and fallen into this Civill Warre; first between those that disagreed in Politiques; and after between the Dissenters about the liberty of Religion; which have so instructed men in this point of Soveraign Right, that there be few now (in England,) that do not see, that these Rights are inseparable, and will be so generally acknowledged, at the next return of Peace; and so continue, till their miseries are forgotten; and no longer, except the vulgar be better taught than they have hetherto been.

And Can By No Grant Passe Away Without Direct Renouncing Of The Soveraign Power

And because they are essentiall and inseparable Rights, it follows necessarily, that in whatsoever, words any of them seem to be granted away, yet if the Soveraign Power it selfe be not in direct termes renounced, and the name of Soveraign no more given by the Grantees to him that Grants them, the Grant is voyd: for when he has granted all he can, if we grant back the Soveraignty, all is restored, as inseparably annexed thereunto.

The Power And Honour Of Subjects Vanisheth In The Presence Of The Power Soveraign

This great Authority being indivisible, and inseparably annexed to the Soveraignty, there is little ground for the opinion of them, that say of Soveraign Kings, though they be Singulis Majores, of greater Power than every one of their Subjects, yet they be Universis Minores, of lesse power than them all together. For if by All Together, they mean not the collective body as one person, then All Together, and Every One, signifie the same; and the speech is absurd. But if by All Together, they understand them as one Person (which person the Soveraign bears,) then the power of all together, is the same with the Soveraigns power; and so again the speech is absurd; which absurdity they see well enough, when the Soveraignty is in an Assembly of the people; but in a Monarch they see it not; and yet the power of Soveraignty is the same in whomsoever it be placed.

And as the Power, so also the Honour of the Soveraign, ought to be greater, than that of any, or all the Subjects. For in the Soveraignty is the fountain of Honour. The dignities of Lord, Earle, Duke, and Prince are his Creatures. As in the presence of the Master, the Servants are equall, and without any honour at all; So are the Subjects, in the presence of the Soveraign. And though they shine some more, some lesse, when they are out of his sight; yet in his presence, they shine no more than the Starres in presence of the Sun.

Soveraigne Power Not Hurtfull As The Want Of It, And The Hurt Proceeds For The Greatest Part From Not Submitting Readily, To A Lesse

But a man may here object, that the Condition of Subjects is very miserable; as being obnoxious to the lusts, and other irregular passions of him, or them that have so unlimited a Power in their hands. And commonly they that live under a Monarch, think it the fault of Monarchy; and they that live under the government of Democracy, or other Soveraign Assembly, attribute all the inconvenience to that forme of Common-wealth; whereas the Power in all formes, if they be perfect enough to protect them, is the same; not considering that the estate of Man can never be without some incommodity or other; and that the greatest, that in any forme of Government can possibly happen to the people in generall, is scarce sensible, in respect of the miseries, and horrible calamities, that accompany a Civill Warre; or that dissolute condition of masterlesse men, without subjection to Lawes, and a coercive Power to tye their hands from rapine, and revenge: nor considering that the greatest pressure of Soveraign Governours, proceedeth not from any delight, or profit they can expect in the dammage, or weakening of their subjects, in whose vigor, consisteth their own selves, that unwillingly contributing to their own defence, make it necessary for their Governours to draw from them what they can in time of Peace, that they may have means on any emergent occasion, or sudden need, to resist, or take advantage on their Enemies. For all men are by nature provided of notable multiplying glasses, (that is their Passions and Self-love,) through which, every little payment appeareth a great grievance; but are destitute of those prospective glasses, (namely Morall and Civill Science,) to see a farre off the miseries that hang over them, and cannot without such payments be avoyded.

Chapter 7
Philosophy of Religion I – "Proving" God Exists

Comprehension questions you should be able to answer after reading this introduction:

1. *What is the difference between philosophy of religion and theology (or religious studies)?*
2. *What is the "GCB?"*
3. *What does existence "in re" mean? Existence "in intellectu?"*
4. *Why does Anselm think the GCB must exist both "in tellectu" and "in re?"*
5. *What is Gaunilo's "greatest conceivable lost island" objection to the ontological argument?*
6. *What is a predicate, and how does this relate to Kant's criticism of the ontological argument?*
7. *What is Aquinas' argument from motion ("1st Way")?*
8. *What is Aquinas' argument from causation ("2nd Way")?*
9. *What is the "matching strategy?"*
10. *What is the Kalam Cosmological Argument (KCA)?*
11. *Why does Craig think an "actual infinite" can only exist "in intellectu," but not "in re," and why is this important for the KCA?*
12. *What are the features of the "First Cause" that Craig believes can be revealed by philosophical conceptual analysis?*
13. *What are some possible examples of "design" in the universe?*
14. *What is Paley's "watch argument?" How is it supposed to work? What is it supposed to demonstrate?*
15. *What is the fine-tuning version of the design argument (DA) (in general)? What is Ross' version? What is the "privileged planet" version (Gonzalez & Richards)?*
16. *What is the "weak analogy" criticism of the DA?*
17. *How can evolution be seen as a threat to the DA?*
18. *What is the "multi-verse" criticism of the DA?*
19. *What is the "part to whole reasoning" criticism of the DA?*
20. *What is the "limited conclusion" criticism of the DA? How does Paley respond to it?*

The philosophy of religion is a prominent and thriving aspect of philosophy in general. It tends to be popular because religion is popular (even for those hostile to it). As one might expect, philosophy of religion is simply an examination of religious issues using the tools of philosophy. As such, a great many topics fall into its domain. A very incomplete list might include the following:

- Arguments for or against the existence of God
- Examining the relationship between omniscience and human free will
- Examining the relationship between Providence or predestination and free will
- Examining the problem of evil
- Examining whether the alleged properties of God are internally consistent
- Examining the epistemological properties of faith

The list can go on and on, but this is sufficient to get a crude idea of what we talk about when doing philosophy of religion. You might have noticed something conspicuous in the list: it was all very "generic." That is, there were no obvious references to particular religious traditions. No mention of Jesus, or Moses, or Allah, for example. There's a reason for that. Although there are always exceptions, and although the lines are often blurred, and although not everyone always plays by these rules, there is a difference between philosophy and theology.

Theology, in general, is an examination of religious issues from within the perspective of a particular religious tradition. This is why we have Christian theology, Jewish theology, Muslim theology, etc. We even have further divisions within the same religion: Protestant theology, Catholic theology, etc. Some of you might have noticed that I've not mentioned Buddhism, Hinduism, or any other non-Western religious tradition. There's a reason for that. I'm a Western philosopher, and my expertise is in the Western philosophical tradition. The concept of God that is usually addressed in Western philosophy is drawn from the great religions of the West: Christianity, Judaism, and Islam. This is not to say that there is no such thing as philosophy of Buddhism. It is to say that such a focus is an uncommon specialty in the West—though quite common in the East! In other words, don't read too much into the selectivity of the traditions we're addressing. It's simply a culturally-contingent outcome.

As mentioned, theology usually works from within a particular religious tradition. Though this is certainly not a requirement, it is often the case that theologians are themselves a member of that same religious tradition. A great many Christian theologians are priests or pastors, or at least consider themselves Christians. A great many Jewish theologians are rabbis, or are, at the very least, Jewish. And so on. What's more, theology can take for granted what philosophy must put to the question. What do I mean by that?

Christian theologians don't tend to spend very much time trying to convince their readers that God exists, or that the Christian experience of God is the correct one. It's taken as a "given." They're preaching to the choir, in that respect. There are always exceptions, but for the most part, theologians take for granted the most basic assumptions of their religion and use those foundational assumptions to explore more focused and subtle aspects of the religion. Philosophers of religion, on the other hand, will often focus on those very foundational issues, trying, for example, to prove the existence of God. Consider the different ways a theologian and a philosopher might explore prophecy.

Theologian (Christian)	Philosopher of Religion
What is the best interpretation of the Book of Revelation?	To what extent is belief in prophetic claims epistemically warranted?
Who is the Church and what will happen to it during the "end times"?	Is prophecy compatible with personal freedom and responsibility?

Don't get hung up on trying to discern the precise differences between theology and philosophy. That's not the point, and it's bound to be a frustrating exercise. The point in mentioning this contrast is mainly to provide for appropriate expectations of what's to come. Most people taking introductory level philosophy classes are not exactly experts in philosophy (if they were, I'm puzzled as to why they would be taking an introductory philosophy class!), and misunderstandings of what philosophy is, and is not, abound.

Students enrolling in a philosophy of religion course, or upon noting that there will be a unit on philosophy of religion in a general introductory course, will often misinterpret what that means, and will anticipate something akin to a Bible study class. This misunderstanding is exacerbated by at least two additional factors. First, in popular book stores (e.g., Barnes & Noble), the philosophy section is often next to (or mixed in with) the religious studies section, or even the "new age" section. Plato's *Republic* sits next to a book on the use of healing crystals, and Nietzche's *Beyond Good and Evil* sits next to a concordance to the Bible. Second, at least at the community college level, there is usually no distinct religious studies department, and religious studies courses are actually labeled "philosophy courses." At my own college, for example, we used to offer an introduction to world religions course. It was, in essence, an introduction to the concept of religion, a general overview of the historical development of religions, and a basic survey of the major religious traditions of the world. The course was part history, part anthropology, part literature, and part comparative religion. If any philosophy was done in the course, it was incidental to the actual goal and methods of the course. Yet, this course was named *Philosophy* 150.

Again, let's not dwell overmuch on this issue. For our purposes, understand that philosophy and theology are two distinct (equally legitimate and impressive) disciplines, each with their own methods and foci. Understand, too, that because we are approaching religious issues from the perspective of philosophy, the sorts of questions we will ask, and answers we will seek, will tend to be abstracted away from the more specific historical and doctrinal elements of any particular (Western) religious tradition.

One can spend an entire semester exploring only philosophy of religion and still have managed only to scratch the surface. Indeed, one can acquire a Ph.D. with this focus, and even spend an entire career dedicated to its exploration, and still have much more work to do. We're going to cover far, far less than that. In this chapter, we will consider the three primary arguments for God's existence in the Western philosophical tradition.

Arguments for the Existence of God

There are many different types of arguments for God's existence. At its most basic level, an argument for God's existence is simply an attempt to prove God's existence, or at least to justify belief in the existence of God. Some arguments rely explicitly on overtly "religious" pieces of evidence—the argument from the occurrence of miracles, for example. Such arguments, though interesting, are not usually addressed by philosophers of religion (though they might be terrific material for theologians). There is a simple explanation for this: it doesn't do us much good to assume the very thing we are trying to prove.

If our question concerns whether there is a God, and if we are trying to explore this question in a way that will be satisfying to believers and skeptics alike, appealing to miracles will be controversial, to say the least. Since miracles are usually understood to be the supernatural suspension or overriding of the laws of nature, the existence of the supernatural is presupposed in a key premise of the argument. If I'm an atheist, and don't believe in the supernatural, I'm not going to believe in miracles either. The argument will go nowhere for me. Imagine the following conversation:

Theist: "Hey, Mr. Atheist! You should believe that God exists!"

Atheist: "Why?"

Theist: "Because of miracles. I've seen hundreds of people being miraculously healed by ministers on TV, and the Bible is filled with accounts of miracles. How can we explain the occurrence of those miracles if there isn't a God?"

Atheist: "What miracles? What you call 'biblical accounts of miracles,' I call myths and fairy tales. What you can 'miraculous healings on TV,' I call fraud, preying on people's hopes and fears for money, and the placebo effect."

Not very effective, is it? This is not to disparage miracles, or their possibility—it's simply to point out that if one is not already predisposed to accept accounts of the supernatural, appealing to miracles will not accomplish much. What most philosophers of religion will try to do, then, is appeal to premises that are much less controversial, and much more acceptable to skeptics. There are three dominant types of arguments for God's existence in the Western tradition: the ontological, cosmological, and design arguments.

The Ontological Argument

The Ontological argument for God's existence attempts to establish the existence of God by arguing that existence is part of God's essential "being" (ontology). That is, the very concept of God entails God's necessary existence. There have been several attempts to employ the ontological argument throughout the history of Western philosophy, involving such notables as Descartes and Alvin Plantinga (more recently), but the most famous version was advanced by St. Anselm. The following is an excerpt from Anselm's *Proslogion*:

> *Therefore, Lord, you who give knowledge of the faith, give me as much knowledge as you know to be fitting for me, because you are as we believe and that which we believe. And indeed we believe you are something greater than which cannot be thought. Or is there no such kind of thing, for "the fool said in his heart, 'there is no God'" (Ps. 13:1, 52:1)? But certainly that same fool, having heard what I just said, "something greater than which cannot be thought," understands what he heard, and what he understands is in his thought, even if he does not think it exists. For it is one thing for something to exist in a person's thought and quite another for the person to think that thing exists. For when a painter thinks ahead to what he will paint, he has that picture in his thought, but he does not yet think it exists, because he has not done it yet. Once he has painted it he has it in his thought and thinks it exists because he has done it. Thus even the fool is compelled to grant that something greater than which cannot be thought exists in thought, because he understands what he hears, and whatever is understood exists in thought. And certainly that greater than which cannot be understood cannot exist only in thought, for if it exists*

only in thought it could also be thought of as existing in reality as well, which is greater. If, therefore, that than which greater cannot be thought exists in thought alone, then that than which greater cannot be thought turns out to be that than which something greater actually can be thought, but that is obviously impossible. Therefore something than which greater cannot be thought undoubtedly exists both in thought and in reality.

Or, as a formal paraphrase:

1. By definition, God is a being "greater than which cannot be thought" (the greatest conceivable being, or GCB).
2. Something that exists both in reality (*in re*) and in imagination (*in intellectu*) is greater than something that exists solely in one's imagination.
3. God exists *in intellectu*.
4. If God did exist both *in re* and *in intellectu*, then God would not be a being "greater than which cannot be thought" (the GCB).
5. Therefore, God must exist in reality.

Before delving into the effectiveness of the OA, it's necessary to unpack some of its key components. The central assumption of the OA is that existence is a "great-making" property. What is a "great-making" property? There are any number of ways to answer that question, but I think the contemporary philosopher of religion, Steven Davis, says it best when he describes a great-making property in terms of "power, ability, freedom of action." In this very specific context, "greatness" refers to things like the ability to produce effects, to bring about change, to successfully exercise one's will, etc. I'm going to refer to this collection of terms as "power," from now on. If we accept this understanding of "great-making," then some properties would be considered great-making, and others wouldn't. Having a beard probably doesn't equate with having greater power, so "bearded" doesn't seem to be a great-making property (in this sense)—but being sentient (as opposed to being an inanimate object, for example) would seem to enhance a thing's "power." My cat has greater ability to exert her will than does my office chair, and I have greater such ability than both of them. Therefore, sentience is a great-making property, and "higher" forms of sentience (e.g., intentionality, rationality, etc.) would be greater still.

With this understanding of "great-making" in mind, two questions need to addressed:

1. Is greatness (so defined) a comparative property that allows for a maximum (i.e., "the greatest")?
2. Is existence a great-making property?

Is greatness comparative, and such that it allows for a maximum? Well, if we're understanding greatness in terms of "power," then the answer is readily available. Certainly power is comparative, as we recognize that some things are more (or less) powerful than others. Is there a maximal case of power? Omnipotence (being "all-powerful") would be the obvious maximal case of power. So, unless you think that omnipotence (i.e., being capable of bringing about any logically possible state of affairs) is an incoherent concept, the answer to our first question appears to be "yes."

What about our second question? Is existence a great-making property? Anselm clearly believes it is, and this is implied in the second premise of his argument. To see why existence might be regarded as a great-making property, we need to understand his particular vocabulary. Anselm points out that things can exist in two different ways: "*in intellectu*," and "*in re*." To exist "*in intellectu*" is to exist "in the mind," as a mental object. To exist "*in re*" is to exist "out there," in "reality"—not merely "in the mind." Unicorns exist in my mind. I have a concept of a unicorn. I can think about unicorns and conjure up mental pictures of unicorns. Therefore, unicorns exist "*in intellectu*." I don't believe that they exist "*in re*," however. In other words, I don't think there are any actual horses with pretty horns coming out of their foreheads, running around in the world, munching on grass and looking majestic. My cat also exists *"in intellectu."* I have a mental concept of my cat. I can think about her, conjure up a mental image of her, etc. An important difference between my cat and a unicorn, though, is that my cat also exists *"in re."* That is, she doesn't exist only in my mind, but she's "out there" in the world as well—in fact, I'm looking at her right now. It's possible that there are things that exist *"in re"* but not *"in intellectu."* Perhaps there exists a chemical element not yet discovered or even imagined by us. Such a compound would exist "out there in the world" even though we have no concept of it just yet. To summarize, then: some things exist *"in intellectu"* only, some things might exist *"in re"* only, and some things exist both *"in intellectu"* and *"in re."*

Having distinguished these two forms of existence, Anselm claims that a thing that exists both *"in intellectu"* and *"in re"* is greater than something that exists *"in intellectu"* only. This might not be an obvious point, but I think it can be demonstrated without too much work if we keep in mind the concept of greatness we've been assuming. If we understand greatness in terms of "power," then there's a certain, obvious sense in which things that exist both *"in re"* as well as *"in intellectu"* have greater power. My cat has more power than the unicorn that exists only in my mind. My cat can exert her will and produce change in the world (e.g., eat bugs, shred curtains, warm up a bed, befoul a litter box, etc.). The unicorn in my mind can't do *anything* unless my mind makes it—which really indicates that it's my mind that has the power, and not the mental unicorn. Something that exists *"in re"* and not only *"in intellectu,"* therefore, has more "power" than something that exists only *"in intellectu."* Therefore, something that exists *"in re"* is *greater* than that which exists only *"in intellectu."*

Let us now turn from cats and unicorns, to the God that is the focus of the OA. Most atheists would grant that "God" exists *"in intellectu,"* at least.[192] Clearly, lots of people have an idea of "God" in their heads—but that's the problem, according to atheists: "God" exists *only* in their heads! "God" is no more "real" than unicorns or the tooth-fairy. Just as the tooth-fairy exists *"in intellectu,"* but not *"in re,"* so too does "God" (like other mythical creatures) exist *"in intellectu,"* but not *"in re."*

Anselm thinks that chain of reasoning is self-contradictory, and the following arguments attempts to demonstrate this.

1. The GCB exists *"in intellectu"* but not *"in re."*
2. Existence is greater *"in re"* than existence *"in intellectu"* alone.
3. The GCB's existence *"in re"* is conceivable.
4. If the GCB did not exist *"in re,"* then the GCB would be greater than the GCB is.
5. It is conceivable that there is a being greater than the GCB.
6. It is false that the GCB exists *"in intellectu"* but not *"in re."*
7. Therefore, the GCB exists *"in re."*

This argument is an example of argument by contradiction, or a (formal) *"reductio ad absurdum"* argument. We start with the assumption that the GCB exists *only* in the mind. This assumption is then shown to generate a contradiction (occurring in line 5 above). This allows us to negate our starting assumption, thereby establishing that the GCB exists in "reality" as well as in the mind.

To reinforce this point, remember that Anselm thinks that a God that exists *"in re"* is greater than a God which exists only *"in intellectu."* This is probably obvious. A God that actually exists in the world has more power than an imaginary one existing only in our minds! But remember: God is defined as the greatest conceivable being (GCB), or, as Anselm words it, "something greater

[192] I say most, instead of all, because some atheists think that "God" is an incoherent concept, and therefore doesn't even exist in the mind. This is not the view of most atheists or agnostics, however.

than which cannot be thought." A God which exists only "*in intellectu*" (the "God" that atheists have in mind (literally)), is not as great as one that exists "*in re*" as well. Therefore, that "God" is *not* the GCB, since a greater being than "God" *can* be conceived: namely, the one that exists "*in re*" as well. God, understood as the GCB, *must* exist "*in re*" as well as "*in intellectu*"—the very concept of God as the GCB entails it. But, if God exists "*in re*" as well as "*in intellectu*," then God exists "out there," in the world, and not just in some people's heads. In other words, God exists.

Criticism of the OA

If this argument seems "fishy" to you, you're in good company. As famous as this argument is, its criticism is equally (if not more) famous. Criticism began in Anselm's own time, and one of the more famous critiques came from Gaunilo, who, in effect, offered a *reductio ad absurdum* objection to the OA.[193]

> *For example: it is said that somewhere in the ocean is an island, which, because of the difficulty, or rather the impossibility, of discovering what does not exist, is called the lost island. And they say that this island has an inestimable wealth of all manner of riches and delicacies in greater abundance than is told of the Islands of the Blest; and that having no owner or inhabitant, it is more excellent than all other countries, which are inhabited by mankind, in the abundance with which it is stored.*
>
> *Now if some one should tell me that there is such an island, I should easily understand his words, in which there is no difficulty. But suppose that he went on to say, as if by a logical inference: "You can no longer doubt that this island which is more excellent than all lands exists somewhere, since you have no doubt that it is in your understanding. And since it is more excellent not to be in the understanding alone, but to exist both in the understanding and in reality, for this reason it must exist. For if it does not exist, any land which really exists will be more excellent than it; and so the island already understood by you to be more excellent will not be more excellent."*
>
> *If a man should try to prove to me by such reasoning that this island truly exists, and that its existence should no longer be doubted, either I should believe that he was jesting, or I know not which I ought to regard as the greater fool: myself, supposing that I should allow this proof; or him, if he should suppose that he had established with any certainty the existence of this island. For he ought to show first that the hypothetical excellence of this island exists as a real and indubitable fact, and in no wise as any unreal object, or one whose existence is uncertain, in my understanding.*[194]

Gaunilo's criticism is sometimes called the "lost island" criticism, or the "greatest conceivable island" objection. His point is that if we allow the sort of reasoning employed in the OA, we can prove the existence of *anything*. Since we shouldn't be able to prove the existence of just anything, there must be something wrong with the OA.

Gaunilo invites us to imagine the "greatest conceivable island." He proposes (in parody of the OA) that an island which exists "*in re*" is greater than one that exists "*in intellectu*" only. Therefore, such an island must actually exist out in the ocean somewhere, otherwise it wouldn't be the greatest conceivable island. You're supposed to think that

[193] Gaunilo, it's worth pointing out, was a Christian monk. He is a perfect illustration that it is possible to agree with someone's conclusion, but find fault with their argument. As a monk, it's safe to assume that he agreed with St. Anselm that God exists. However, he didn't think that the OA *proved* it.

[194] Gaunilo, "In Behalf of the Fool," section 6.

there's something absurd about proving the existence of a hypothetical island in that fashion, so, therefore, there must also be something absurd about proving the existence of God with the OA.

Has Gaunilo succeeded? Supporters of Anselm think not—and neither did Anselm himself, though, to be honest, he doesn't really directly address the island argument except to repeat himself. Supporters of Anselm, though, have tackled the island objection head on, and their reply is based on the meaning of "greatness" that we had to establish earlier on. What does "greatness" mean with regard to an island? Well, according to Gaunilo, it means something like having an "inestimable wealth of all manner of riches and delicacies." Apparently, being uninhabited also makes an island great—at least according to his example. One problem with the island objection, thus far, is that "greatness" is clearly referring to different things in Gaunilo's example than in the OA. Greatness in the OA refers to "power," but obviously islands aren't the sorts of things that have "power," in the same sort of way. Moreover, the qualities Gaunilo has in mind don't seem to allow a maximum. What would be the "maximum" with regard to "riches and delicacies?" Presumably, we're dealing with things like mineral deposits, fruit trees, etc. What's the "maximum" ("greatest") with regard to fruit? An infinite amount of fruit? But, how could an infinite amount of fruit grow on an island which, by definition, must be a finite body bounded by water? The problem with Gaunilo's example seems to be that the "greatest conceivable island" doesn't seem to even exist, in any clear sort of way, "*in intellectu*"—and, since the notions of "greatness" being employed are different, Gaunilo and Anselm are basically talking past one another.

Does this mean that Gaunilo's style of objection is worthless, then? No. A variant of his objection claims that the OA could just as easily prove the existence of the "greatest conceivable evil being" as it could prove the existence of God. After all, the OA (at best) proves the existence of an omnipotent being. Nothing about the OA, by itself, demands that this being be the God that is described by Anselm's Christian faith.

That's correct.

Assuming that the OA works perfectly, it does seem "only" to establish the existence of an omnipotent being. By itself, it does not prove the existence of an omnipotent being who also spoke to Moses by means of a burning bush, or who became incarnate in the person of Jesus of Nazareth, etc. Like all the other major (philosophical) TAs, the "God" that is proved (best-case scenario) is a generic "God of the philosophers" who might, or might not, be the same God that is described in the various Western theistic traditions. If someone wanted to prove that *their* God exists, they would have to appeal to more than just the TAs we're going to consider in this book. But, that being granted, let's be fair: even if the OA *only* proves the existence of an omnipotent being, that's still a pretty big deal! But does the OA do even that?

Although criticism of the argument began with Anselm's contemporary, Gaunilo, it was made legendary by Immaeul Kant. For those interested, Immanuel Kant (1724 –1804) was an 18th-century German philosopher.[195] He is generally regarded as a terribly influential philosopher, certainly among the most important in the Western tradition.

If you ask philosophy majors, "what was Kant's criticism of the ontological argument?" many of them will be able to provide the answer: "existence isn't a predicate!" Fewer than many will actually be able to give a decent explanation of what that means.

A predicate is a fancy grammatical term that (roughly) means the same thing as "property" or "quality." A thing (e.g., an apple) will have various properties (e.g., being edible, being red, being a certain size, having a certain mass, etc.). Those properties are also its "predicates." The ontological argument asks us to compare two possible gods: one that exists in reality as well as in the mind, and one that exists only in the mind. The suggestion is that there is a qualitative

[195] Like Gaunilo, Kant believed that God exists as well—he just didn't think the OA could prove it.

difference in the properties (predicates) of these two gods.

God$_1$	**God$_2$**
Omniscient	Omniscient
Omnipotent	Omnipotent
Eternal	Eternal
Perfectly good	Perfectly good
Exists	Does not exist

If we compare these two "gods," it appears that one has the property of existence, and the other does not. Since Anselm claimed that existence was a "great making" property, the god that exists is greater than the god that does not, and, since God is the greatest conceivable being, it must be the case that God$_1$ (and not God$_2$) is God. Lo and behold, that just happens to be the one with existence as a property. Therefore, God exists.

Kant's complaint (as mentioned above) is that we can't treat existence as property/predicate like that.

> *"Being" is obviously not a real predicate; that is, it is not a concept of something which could be added to the concept of a thing. It is merely the positing of a thing, or of certain determinations, as existing in themselves. Logically, it is merely the copula of a judgment. The proposition "God is omnipotent" contains two concepts, each of which has its object -- God and omnipotence. The small word "is" adds no new predicate, but only serves to posit the predicate in its relation to the subject. If, now, we take the subject (God) with all its predicates (among which is omnipotence), and say "God is," or "There is a God," we attach no new predicate to the concept of God, but only posit it as an object that stands in relation to my concept. The content of both must be one and the same; nothing can have been added to the concept, which expresses merely what is possible, by my thinkings its object (through the expression "it is") as given absolutely. Otherwise stated, the real contains no more than the merely possible. A hundred real thalers does not contain the least coin more than a hundred possible thalers. For as the latter signify the concept and the former the object and the positing of the concept, should the former contain more than the latter, my concept would not, in that case, express the whole object, and would not therefore be an adequate concept of it. My financial position, however, is affected very differently by a hundred real thalers than it is by the mere concept of them (that is, of the possibility). For the object, as it actually exists, is not analytically contained in my concept, but is added to my concept (which is a determination of my state) synthetically; and yet the conceived hundred thalers are not themselves in the least increased through thus acquiring existence outside my concept.*
>
> *By whatever and by however many predicates we may think a thing -- even if we completely determine it -- we do not make the least addition to the thing when we further declare that this thing is. Otherwise it would not be exactly the same thing that exists, but something more than we had thought in the concept: and we could not, therefore, say that the object of my concept exists. If we think in a thing every feature of reality except one, the missing reality is not added by my saying that this defective thing exists."*[196]

According to Kant, existence doesn't "add" to the qualitative description of a thing in the way that redness does, or fragility does. Or, the way the complaint is usually expressed, "existence is not a 'real' predicate." A predicate (understood grammatically) is something that modifies a subject. Linguistically, any word whatsoever can

196 Kant's "Critique of Pure Reason," section A599/B627.

be a "logical predicate"—which is just to say that the word can occupy the predicate slot in a sentence. Consider the following examples:

1. The horse is *fast*.
2. The horse is a *horse*.
3. The horse is a *fish*.
4. The horse is *flurbin*.

In each case, the underlined word (horse) is the subject, and the italicized word is the predicate. The first example actually makes sense and the predicate adds something meaningful to the subject. We now know that the horse is fast. The second example is coherent, but not terribly interesting. Nothing has been "added" to the subject. The third example is just plain weird. Self-contradictory, in fact. Given the concept of "horse," it can't be a fish. The last example is nonsense. "Flurbin" is a meaningless word I just made up. Needless to say, it doesn't "add" anything to its subject either.

The point of all of this is that while any word can stand, in a sentence, as a predicate, not every predicate is what Kant is calling a "real" predicate. A "real" predicate "adds" something to its subject. "Fast" is a real predicate for "horse," since it adds something to "horse." Existence, according to Kant, is not a "real" predicate.

According to this criticism, when someone says that God exists, they are not saying that there is a thing (God) and that God possesses the property of existence. If existence worked as a property like that, it would mean that atheists are claiming that there is a God who lacks the property of existence—but this is to both affirm God's existence ("there is a God. . . .") and *deny it* ("who lacks the property of existence") *at the same time*. Aside from being silly, this also violates a fundamental law of logic, the law of non-contradiction—and one doesn't want to do that.

So, if existence isn't a property/predicate, what *do* we mean when we say that something exists? To say that something exists is to say that it is exemplified, or instantiated, in the world. Existence doesn't tell us about the subject (e.g., an apple, or God), it tells us about the world—namely, that the world contains whatever that subject is. Try to follow this: when I say that an apple exists but that Santa Claus does not, I'm not describing the properties/predicates of apples or Santa, I'm describing the properties/predicates of this world, namely, that *this world* has the property of including apples, but lacks the property of including Santa Claus.

If you're not convinced, yet, that existence is not a ("real") predicate of things, ask yourself, what does "existence" add to my qualitative description of a subject? Once I've described an apple's color, mass, size, and so on, what "more" is added if I toss "existence" onto the pile? The concept of the apple is the same (in terms of its color, size, mass, etc.) whether it exists or not—but the *world* is different based on whether or not the apple exists. To claim the apple exists says something about this world—that it contains something matching up to the qualitative description of the apple, but it doesn't tell us anything interesting about the apple itself.

Why is this so important? Remember, the ontological argument was driven by the comparison between the God that exists in reality, and the god that does not. The God with the property of existence is greater than the one which lacks that property. But, if Kant is right (and most philosophers and theologians believe he was), that kind of comparison is impossible, because existence can't be placed on the list of properties. After removing existence as a property/predicate, do the same comparison we tried before.

God$_1$	**God$_2$**
Omniscient	Omniscient
Omnipotent	Omnipotent
Eternal	Eternal
Perfectly good	Perfectly good

Which one is greater now? Obviously, the concepts are identical. We can compare the *world* in which there is a God with a *world* in which there is none, but we can't compare the *God* who exists with one who does not. Without that comparison, the ontological argument goes nowhere.

So, is the OA "dead?" Not necessarily. You might have noticed a few paragraphs ago when I said that *most* philosophers seem to think that Kant was right about existence not being a "real" predicate. Some argue that, in some contexts, existence *does* operate as a "real" predicate.

> *But what about those linguistic contexts in which the existence of the thing being discussed is not necessarily presupposed? To say that the thing exists may well, in those cases, expand our concept of it. I am quite sure that my concept of the Loch Ness Monster would change if someone were to convince me that the creature exists, that there really is (let's say) a reproducing colony of plesiosaurs in the loch left over from the Cretaceous period. Here 'exists' is a real predicate.*[197]

Even using Kant's own example of a hundred thalers, Davis points out that existence "adds" something to the concept in question: a hundred imaginary thalers have no purchasing power, whereas a hundred real thalers do. In fairness to Kant, he seems to recognize this ("My financial position, however, is affected very differently by a hundred real thalers than it is by the mere concept of them. . .") but nevertheless doesn't grant that existence operates as a real predicate. Davis simply disagrees, at least in certain contexts. If the subject is the Loch Ness Monster, Davis claims that "existence" does seem to "add" to our concept of Nessie.[198] If the subject is God, would "existence" add to our concept of God as well, or would it only add to our concept of the world?

The Cosmological Argument

Why is there something, rather than nothing? What accounts for the existence of the universe? What is the original source of all motion and change in the universe?

The cosmological argument (CA) offers "God" as an answer to those profound questions. Made famous by St. Thomas Aquinas, and more recently by William Lane Craig, this argument attempts to establish the existence of God as an explanation for the existence of this universe, or for the motion or "effects" we see in the universe.

There are several versions of this argument. We will first consider the version of the CA offered by Aquinas, and then consider the more contemporary version offered by Craig: the "Kalam Cosmological Argument (KCA)."

Aquinas

First, note that the CA, unlike the OA, is an "*a posteriori*" argument. That is, it is based on and draws from experience. "Experience of what?" you might ask. Several different things, according to Aquinas. In the famous passage from his *Summa Theologica*, usually referred to as "the Five Ways," Aquinas offers three different variations of the CA. The "first way" concerns motion, the "second way" concerns causation, and the "third way" concerns contingency and necessity.

> *I answer that, The existence of God can be proved in five ways.*
>
> *The first and more manifest way is the argument from motion. It is certain, and evident to our senses, that in the world some things are in motion. Now whatever is in motion is put in motion by another, for nothing can be in motion except it is in potentiality to that towards which it is in motion; whereas a thing moves inasmuch as it is in act. For motion is nothing else than the reduction of something from potentiality to actuality. But nothing can*

---

197 Steven Davis, "God, Reason, and Theistic Proofs," p. 34.

198 I imagine Kant might agree that a concept has indeed changed, but not in the way Davis claims. Our concept of the *world* would be changed in that it now includes "God" as a (rather significant) feature. This is just to reiterate his assertion that to say that a thing exists doesn't "add" to our concept of the thing, but only means that the thing is "instantiated" in the world.

be reduced from potentiality to actuality, except by something in a state of actuality. Thus that which is actually hot, as fire, makes wood, which is potentially hot, to be actually hot, and thereby moves and changes it. Now it is not possible that the same thing should be at once in actuality and potentiality in the same respect, but only in different respects. For what is actually hot cannot simultaneously be potentially hot; but it is simultaneously potentially cold. It is therefore impossible that in the same respect and in the same way a thing should be both mover and moved, i.e. that it should move itself. Therefore, whatever is in motion must be put in motion by another. If that by which it is put in motion be itself put in motion, then this also must needs be put in motion by another, and that by another again. But this cannot go on to infinity, because then there would be no first mover, and, consequently, no other mover; seeing that subsequent movers move only inasmuch as they are put in motion by the first mover; as the staff moves only because it is put in motion by the hand. Therefore it is necessary to arrive at a first mover, put in motion by no other; and this everyone understands to be God.

The "first way," as mentioned, concerns motion. The intuition behind this version of the CA is fairly obvious, and can be presented formally as follows:

1. Everything that is in motion is moved by something else. ("Now whatever is in motion is put in motion by another")
2. Infinite regress is impossible. ("But this cannot go on to infinity, because then there would be no first mover, and, consequently, no other mover")
3. Therefore, there must be a first mover. ("Therefore it is necessary to arrive at a first mover, put in motion by no other")
4. ("and this everyone understands to be God")

I place the 4th premise in parentheses to indicate its special status in the argument. What you will discover about nearly every TA is that their conclusions don't (and typically can't) specify a specific "God" as understood from within a specific religious tradition. Instead, they will mention a "GCB" (as in the OA), or a "prime mover," "first cause," or "necessary being" (as in the CA), etc. Aquinas is no different in this respect, initially. The conclusion of the CA as described in the first way is simply that there must be a "first mover." As a point of clarification, he offers that "this everyone understands to be God." In other words, the first mover "proved" by the CA is identical to the God that is described by Aquinas' own faith tradition.

This "*matching strategy*" is quite common, and you will encounter it often. Anselm argued for the GCB, but he, of course, believed that the GCB was identical to his God. Paley argues that the universe is probably the product of intelligent design, but he, of course, believes the "designer" to be his God. Craig will argue that there must an objective, transcendent source of moral values, but he, of course, believes that source to be his God.

Note that the "match" has not been proven by these arguments, even if the arguments are thought to be persuasive arguments—but nor is that what they are trying to accomplish. Remember my point earlier about TAs serving best to establish warrant for beliefs. If, for example, someone believes in a God who created the universe and set it in motion, the CA does not prove the existence of that God, but the theist would likely (and understandably) consider a philosophical proof of a "first cause" to provide evidence for her belief in her God that she believes responsible for the very same thing.

Let us return to the first way. Again, the intuition is simple: everything that we observe in motion has been set into motion by something else. Either there is a "prime mover" that began this motion, or else we have an infinite regress of movers. But, on the assumption that such an infinite regress is impossible, there must be a "prime mover" instead—and some people (like Aquinas) identify this prime mover to be God. But why should we assume an infinite regress is impossible? Why couldn't motion just go on "forever," including forever backwards in time, such that no "first mover" is posited? The alleged impossibility of an infinite regress is critically important to every version of the CA of which I am aware. Accordingly, the reasons why some think such an infinite regress is impossible is important enough to deserve its own section later in this chapter.

You will see, for example, the appeal to the impossibility of an infinite regress in Aquinas' second way.

> *The second way is from the nature of the efficient cause. In the world of sense we find there is an order of efficient causes. There is no case known (neither is it, indeed, possible) in which a thing is found to be the efficient cause of itself; for so it would be prior to itself, which is impossible. Now in efficient causes it is not possible to go on to infinity, because in all efficient causes following in order, the first is the cause of the intermediate cause, and the intermediate is the cause of the ultimate cause, whether the intermediate cause be several, or only one. Now to take away the cause is to take away the effect. Therefore, if there be no first cause among efficient causes, there will be no ultimate, nor any intermediate cause. But if in efficient causes it is possible to go on to infinity, there will be no first efficient cause, neither will there be an ultimate effect, nor any intermediate efficient causes; all of which is plainly false. Therefore it is necessary to admit a first efficient cause, to which everyone gives the name of God.*

1. Every effect has a cause. ("In the world of sense we find there is an order of efficient causes")
2. An effect cannot be self-caused ("There is no case known (neither is it, indeed, possible) in which a thing is found to be the efficient cause of itself")
3. An infinite regress of causes is impossible. ("Now in efficient causes it is not possible to go on to infinity")
4. Therefore, there must be a first cause. ("Therefore it is necessary to admit a first efficient cause")
5. ("to which everyone gives the name of God.")

Once again, note the matching strategy. This second version of the CA does not, strictly speaking, prove "God's" existence, even in the best of cases. At most, it proves the existence of a "first cause"—and Aquinas identifies this first cause as being God.

Also note the similarity with the first way. Aquinas is appealing to "efficient causes" rather than "motion," but the structure and strategy are basically the same. An "efficient cause" is an Aristotelian term—a philosopher to whom Aquinas owes much.[199] Aristotle actually describes four kinds of causes.

1. Material cause
2. Efficient cause
3. Formal cause
4. Final cause

A thing's Material cause is its matter, the raw materials of which it is made. Using the example of a statue, its Material cause is marble (or whatever kind of stone the sculptor used). An Efficient cause is a thing's origin—the process responsible for it being what it is. In the case of the statue, its Efficient cause is the sculptor and her tools. The Formal cause is a thing's essence, the governing idea giving it its structure and form. For the statue, its Formal cause is the vision of the completed

[199] Indeed, Aquinas so respected Aristotle that when he references him, he calls him simply "The Philosopher."

sculpture entertained by the sculptor. Finally, we have the Final cause. The Final cause is the end or purpose ("telos") that the thing is to fulfill. With the statue, perhaps its Final cause is to depict the likeness of Aristotle.

Aquinas' second way focuses on the concept of an efficient cause. That is good news, for us, since when most of us (today) think about or speak of causes, we usually mean an efficient cause. My typing on a keyboard is the efficient cause of words appearing on the screen. My neighbor pressing a button is the efficient cause of my doorbell ringing, and so on. The basic idea behind the "second way" version of the CA is that every effect has an efficient cause. Things don't "just happen" from no cause whatsoever. Aquinas claims that for any effect, the cause of that effect must either be itself, or something else. However, an effect can't be "self-caused" (i.e., the cause of itself) "for so it would be prior to itself, which is impossible." Think of it this way: imagine that you asked me what caused my doorbell to ring, and I answered "itself." You would probably be puzzled by this answer. "Itself? What could Professor Preston mean? Does he mean that there is something faulty with the wiring, so that the doorbell sometimes rings without someone touching the button?" That would make sense, but then my answer would have been misleading. In that case, something like an electrical surge would have been the cause of the ringing. My claim (bizarre as it was) was that the ringing sound of the doorbell itself (the effect) was the cause of the ringing. The ringing caused the ringing. If you think that sounds silly, Aquinas would agree. What sense does it make to claim that the effect caused *itself*? Given that our *usual* experience of causation involves a temporal relationship in which the cause is (temporally) prior to the effect, to say that the effect caused itself would require the effect to have existed before it existed!

Not surprisingly, then, Aquinas rules out "self-causation" to account for the experience of efficient causation we all share. On the assumption that an infinite regress of causes is impossible (again: important enough to get its own section later), that leaves only a "first cause" to account for causation in general. Aquinas believes this "first cause" to be God.

Craig

The KCA is a variant of the CA, called the "Kalam" CA because it developed in the "Kalam" ("discursive") tradition of Islamic philosophy (notably by Al-Kindi and Al-Ghazali). The KCA owes its present popularity to the American philosopher of religion William Lane Craig. His version of the KCA is quite simple in its formulation.

1. Everything that begins to exist has a cause.
2. The universe began to exist.
3. Therefore, the universe must have a cause.

The first premise is thought to be relatively uncontroversial. In our experience, everything that begins to exist has a cause. Objects don't spring forth from "nothing." Causality runs through every event that we've ever experienced. What's more, if it were possible for things to come to exist from (literally) *nothing*, why don't we observe such magical events occurring? The fact is that we don't. Quite the contrary. It's theoretically possible, of course, that there might be some things that begin to exist without any cause whatsoever, but we have no experience of that, and the burden of proof is presumably on those that would wish to deny premise one, rather than on those who assert it.

The second premise asserts that the universe began to exist. It's possible that the universe is, instead, eternal, and has always existed—but you won't find many astronomers today willing to make that claim. The dominant "big bang" model of the universe claims that the universe (including both space and time) came into existence roughly 14 billion years ago.[200] If we assume the big bang

[200] Some astrophysicists propose that the big bang is part of an eternal cycle in which the universe

model is accurate (as Craig does), it does indeed indicate that the universe began to exist several billion years ago.

Must we rely on assumption only, though? Craig believes a variety of evidence exists to support the second premise of the KCA, both scientific and philosophical. We will begin with some of his philosophical evidence.

If the universe never began to exist, and is, instead, "eternal," then history is an infinite series of events stretching into the past. Craig thinks that such an infinite series is impossible to attain "*in re*," though we might have a perfectly decent abstract concept of such infinitude "*in intellectu*." The argument that attempts to show that an actually existing ("*in re*") infinite number of things (such as historical events stretching back infinitely into the past) cannot exist is as follows:

1. The universe can be understood as either a finite series, or an infinite series.
2. If finite, then there is a "beginning."
3. If infinite, then the series of all past events is infinite, and there is no "beginning" to the series.
4. A beginning-less series of events in time entails an actually infinite number of things.
5. But, an actually infinite series of events can't exist.
6. Therefore, a beginning-less series of events in time cannot exist.
7. Therefore, the universe began to exist.

Premise 1 seems to be a statement of the logical possibilities: the universe consists of either a finite series of events, or an infinite series. Premise 2 acknowledges that if the series is finite, it necessarily has a beginning simply by virtue of our concept of "finite." If, however, the series is infinite, then there is no beginning (premise 3). Premise 4 claims that an infinite series entails an actually infinite number of things (e.g., moments in time, events, movements of particles, etc.). Here, it would be useful to distinguish "actual infinites" from "potential infinites." Since we're using these terms in the context of Craig's argument, we'll use the terms as he understands them.

> *An actual infinite is a collection of definite and discrete members whose number is greater than any natural number 0, 1, 2, 3 . . . This sort of infinity is used in set theory to designate sets that have an infinite number of members, such as {0, l, 2, 3 . . .}. The symbol for this kind of infinity is the Hebrew letter aleph: ℵ. The number of members in the set of natural numbers is ℵ0. By contrast, a potential infinite is a collection that is increasing toward infinity as a limit but never gets there. The symbol for this kind of infinity is the lemniscate: ∞. Such a collection is really indefinite, not infinite. For example, any finite distance can be subdivided into potentially infinitely many parts. You can just keep on dividing parts in half forever, but you will never arrive at an actual "infinitieth" division or come up with an actually infinite number of parts."*[201]

Premise 5 claims that an actually infinite series of events can't exist—and the rest of the argument follows from that, to the conclusion that the universe began to exist. This premise is the key to the KCA, and is the premise most likely to be challenged. As such, it requires justification. Why can't an "actual infinite" exist?

Technically, an actual infinite *can* exist (according to Craig), but (returning to our previous vocabulary), only "*in intellectu*." That is, the concept of an actual infinite can be a

---

expands from a singularity, then eventually contracts, then has another big bang, then another contraction, and so on for all eternity. This "oscillating" model does not claim that the universe began to exist, but it's also not a generally accepted model of our universe. Indeed, there are many arguments against this model.

[201] William Lane Craig, *Reasonable Faith*, pp. 116-117.

meaningful and productive item in a particular "universe of discourse" (e.g,. set theory), but that doesn't mean that actual infinites exist "*in re*" as well. We can have conversations, and populate our "universe of discourse" with all sorts of things that make sense within the context of that conversation. I could, for example, have a conversation with a friend about Darth Vader. Within the context of Star Wars, Darth Vader is Luke's Skywalker's father, and he was also a Sith Lord. Those words have meaning, and anyone familiar enough with the Star Wars "universe of discourse" can understand the conversation, participate in it, draw conclusions, make inferences, etc. None of that means there really is some guy named Darth Vader out there somewhere in space who can manipulate the dark side of the Force! Analogously, mathematicians can have meaningful conversations in which actual infinites are a useful part of a coherent conversation—but that doesn't mean that actual infinites exist "out there" ("*in re*"). To imagine they could (or do) is to invite absurdities, as Craig observes.

First, consider a simple demonstration involving sets. In an infinite set, a part of the set can be equal to the whole set. For example, the set of all whole numbers is infinite. The set of all even numbers is also infinite. Even though even numbers are a subset of whole numbers (seemingly equal to ½ of the set of whole numbers), even numbers can, nevertheless, be placed in a 1-to-1 correlation with whole numbers and are therefore equal in number. That's sort of dizzying, when you think about it. In fairness, if all we're doing is playing around with "math," then, dizzying though the exercise might be, we might think we can get away with it. After all, we're only manipulating abstract (mathematical) objects. But, what happens when we try to import actual infinitude into the real (physical) world?

Craig famously uses the example of "Hilbert's Hotel"[202] to demonstrate that absurd consequences result when we try to imagine actual infinites existing "*in re*." What follows is a rough paraphrase of Craig's argument.

When we imagine a hotel with a finite number of rooms (i.e., any and every hotel of which we have any experience), we have a perfectly decent understanding of the consequences of there being no vacancies. If all the rooms are already occupied, there are no more rooms available. No one else can check in—at least not until someone else checks out. The math is simple, and easy to visualize. Suppose there are twenty rooms, each with only one occupant. That means there are twenty guests. Suppose one guest checks out. There are now nineteen guests, and one empty room. Suppose three more guests check out. There are now sixteen guests, and four empty rooms. Suppose four guests check in. There are now twenty guests (again), and no empty rooms. Easy, and obvious.

Now imagine a hotel with an infinite number of rooms. Keep in mind that this must be a physically-existing hotel; an actual "brick and mortar" building, occupying space, with features otherwise consistent with hotels. It will not do to imagine some sort of "mental" hotel, or a "non-spatial" hotel, since the very issue at stake is whether or not an actual infinite (in this case, a hotel with an actually infinite number of rooms) is possible "*in re*." This hotel, as stated, has an infinite number of rooms. Each room is occupied by a single guest, indicating that each of the infinitely many rooms is occupied, and that there are no vacancies due to presence of the infinite number of guests already staying at the hotel.

Now imagine someone enters the lobby, hoping to stay at the hotel. The manager, eager to please, shifts the guest in room #1 into room #2, the guest in room #2 into room #3, and so on out to infinity. There is now an open room (#1), and the new guest checks in. Even though every room was already occupied, a room was made vacant without anyone needing to check out or double-up—and the number of guests remains exactly the same (infinitely many).

Now imagine an infinite number of guests arrive in town for a convention on the absurdities of actual infinites, and they all wish to check in.

[202] Named after the German mathematician David Hilbert.

The manager, eager to please, shifts the guest in room #1 into room #2, the guest in room #2 into room #4, the guest in room #3 into room #6, the guest in room #4 into room #8 (etc.—with each guest being placed into the room equal to twice the number of her original room number). As a result, every odd-numbered room is now vacant. There are an infinite number of odd-numbered rooms, which is just perfect for that infinite number of new guests! So, an infinite number of new guests have arrived and have been accommodated, even though every room was already occupied, no one had to check out, and the total number of guests remains the same (infinitely many) despite the addition of an infinite number of new guests.

If you're thinking to yourself "that doesn't make any sense," then you have grasped Craig's point. Actual infinitude, while perfectly at home and coherent within the context of a purely abstract, mathematical "universe of discourse," ceases to be coherent once transported into the physical world. If that is correct, then we have a philosophical demonstration that actual infinites cannot exist "*in re*." If an eternal universe entails an actual infinite, then the universe can't be eternal (i.e., it must have begun to exist).[203]

In addition to philosophical arguments (of which we reviewed just one) demonstrating that the universe began to exist, Craig also points to a variety of scientific evidence that also supports that premise. Allow me a blunt disclaimer: I am a philosopher, not a physicist or astrophysicist. It is undoubtedly true that an astrophysicist could (and, one would hope, *would*) explain the following scientific evidence in more detail and greater sophistication. It should go without saying that we will only be scratching the surface, rather than plumbing the depths, of these fascinating ideas—but, for our purposes, that will have to do.

We will briefly consider two different lines of scientific evidence in support of the claim that the universe began to exist. The first concerns the expansion of the universe. Before the 20th century, astronomers assumed the universe was stationary and eternal, but in 1917 Einstein's General Theory of Relativity suggested that the universe could not be eternal and stationary. Shortly thereafter, Alexander Friedman and Georges Lemaître predicted an expanding universe. In 1929, Edwin Hubble's observation of the "red shift" of light from distant galaxies confirmed the expansion predicted by Friedman and Lemaître, and demanded by Einstein's theory. In brief, it demonstrated that the universe was expanding over time, and, if we "ran time backwards," the universe would shrink back down into a singularity of infinite density at a finite point in the past (approximately 14 billion years ago). "Big Bang" cosmology had arrived. According to this model, all matter and energy, and even space and time themselves, came into existence from "nothing" by virtue of the Big Bang. The basic assumption of this Big Bang model (implied by the expansion of the universe) is that the universe came into existence at some point in the very distant past.

The second line of scientific evidence we will consider involves the 2nd law of thermodynamics. According to this 2nd law, within a closed system, processes will tend towards a state of equilibrium. Unless new energy is injected into the system, the system's processes will eventually run down and quit "processing. A practical application of this admittedly abstract principle is the fact that when you add hot water to a bath tub, the water disperses throughout the tub evenly, as opposed to some portions of the tub being hot, while others are cold. The application of this 2nd law to the universe is surprisingly similar to our bathtub example. On a purely naturalistic worldview, the universe is "everything." It is a closed system,

[203] It's worth noting, in connection to another version of the CA we examined earlier in this chapter, that the infinite series that the KCA is ruling out appears to be a linear series (i.e., one in which one event causes another event, which causes another event, which causes another event, etc.). Recall that the other CA ruled out an infinite hierarchical series. If both arguments "work," then both linear and hierarchical infinite series will have been established as impossible.

comprising all matter and energy, and everything that exists. As a closed system, the 2nd law will apply to the universe. Over time, it will "run down" and achieve a state of equilibrium. Astrophysicists refer to this as "heat death." Oddly enough, there are two versions of this heat death: cold, and hot.

A "hot" heat death would occur if the universe's own gravitational pull is greater than the expansion force of the universe. In that case, the universe would expand (for a time), and then contract back on itself, crushing all matter and energy into a single, massive black hole from which the universe could not reemerge. But, if the universe has existed "forever," this should have already happened, and the current universe could not exist. Obviously, this event hasn't happened!

A "cold" heat death would occur if the force of expansion is greater than the gravitational force of the universe. In that case, the universe continues to expand, with all objects in the universe receding further and further apart from each other. Over time, the distances between objects will become incomprehensively vast. As Craig relates the data, "at 10^{30} years the universe will consist of 90 percent dead stars, and 9 percent supermassive black holes formed by the collapse of galaxies, and 1 percent atomic matter, mainly hydrogen. Elementary particle physics suggests that thereafter protons will decay into electrons and positrons, so that space will be filled with a rarefied gas so thin that the distance between an electron and a positron will be about the size of the present galaxy. At 10^{100} years, some scientists believe that the black holes themselves will dissipate by a strange effect predicted by quantum mechanics. The mass and energy associated with a black hole so warp space that they are said to create a 'tunnel' or 'worm-hole' through which the mass and energy are ejected in another region of space. As the mass of a black hole decreases, its energy loss accelerates, so that it is eventually dissipated into radiation and elementary particles. Eventually all black holes will completely evaporate and all the matter in the ever-expanding universe will be reduced to a thin gas of elementary particles and radiation. Equilibrium will prevail throughout, and the entire universe will be in its final state, from which no change will occur."[204]

At this point, the same question arises as was posed of the "hot" version of heat death: if the universe has existed "forever," why hasn't this already occurred? With respect to either version of heat death, the universe, over time, is "doomed" to either collapse in on itself, or else expand forever to a state of changeless, cold darkness. If an infinite amount of time has already passed, it would seem that either fate would have already occurred—but clearly this is not the case, thus suggesting that time is not infinite in the past. In other words, the universe began to exist. According to the KCA, if the universe began to exist, it must have had a cause. . . .

Criticism of the CA

Like all TAs, the CA (including the KCA) has been subject to scrutiny and criticism. We will now consider some of the more common criticisms to have arisen over the centuries.

1. "What caused the First Cause (God)?"

All versions of the CA rely (among other things) on the assumption that "something" can't come from "nothing." The universe, therefore, must have come from "something." According to the KCA, because the universe began to exist, it must have a cause of its existence. It's understandable that a critic of the CA (or KCA) would wonder why the same demands shouldn't be placed on this First Cause (presumed to be God). Wouldn't it be the case that God would also need to have come from "something?" That God must have a cause of God's existence as well? Or, if not, then why can a theist accept God as a "brute fact" that doesn't require a cause, while the naturalist can't do the same for the universe itself?

In response to that criticism, defenders of the CA usually point out that God (in the Western traditions) is thought to be a necessary being.

---

204 Craig, *Reasonable Faith*, 143.

Necessary beings (by definition) are eternal, they never came into existence, nor will ever go out of existence. Questions of the form "what caused X?" can only apply to contingent beings, not necessary beings.

Is this a case of special pleading? Not necessarily. This exemption from needing a causal explanation would apply to *any* necessary being, not just God. If someone could demonstrate that a necessary being is a logical impossibility, or an incoherent concept, then, of course, the argument falls apart. But, if one accepts the possibility of a necessary being, and if the CA proves the existence of at least one necessary being, then that necessary being does not require a cause of its existence, because *there could be no such cause.*

The same sort of reasoning is going to apply to the KCA. Recall that the KCA claims that whatever *begins to exist* has a cause. It makes no such claim about things that never began to exist. The cause of the universe is thought to be eternal, and therefore never began to exist—therefore, it doesn't have a cause of its own existence. Certainly, *if* the universe was eternal, and therefore never began to exist, it would not have a cause either—but the universe being eternal is contrary to both the philosophical arguments above as well as the Big Bang cosmology that dominates astrophysics.

2. All versions of the CA fail to prove God's existence.

This criticism is obviously true, up to a point. None of the versions of the CA (including the KCA) have "God" in their conclusion. Aquinas explicitly appeals to the "matching strategy" in his versions of the CA: "and this everyone understands to be God." To be sure, if the CA works, it proves the existence of a "first cause," or "prime mover unmoved," or "NB," and these philosophical concepts might or might not be the God described in the Western theistic traditions. Additional argument will need to be offered to provide some possible insight into the nature of that cause. Indeed, Craig believes that philosophical conceptual analysis reveals several intriguing features of this cause of the universe.

- Non-spatial (because it's the cause of space itself)
- Non-temporal (because it's the cause of time itself)
- Unchanging (because it's non-temporal, and time is, among other things, a measure of change)
- Non-physical/immaterial (because it's unchanging, and physical things are subject to change)
- Uncaused/beginningless (because it's the First Cause)
- One/singular (if we apply Ockham's razor, and resist "multiplying causes without necessity")
- Unimaginably powerful, even if not omnipotent (since it created the entire universe from "nothing," without any material cause)
- Personal (because, according to Craig, only persons/minds, and abstract objects, such as numbers, are timeless and material, and of the two, only persons can cause events to occur)

Craig's conceptual analysis is bold, and powerful (if successful). If his argument is correct, we have a philosophical reason to conclude that the universe had a cause of its existence. If his conceptual analysis is correct, we can deduce several fascinating features of this First Cause—all of which serve the "matching strategy," and imply that God is that First Cause.

The Design Argument

The Design Argument (DA) is ancient. Although what was being "proved" was, of course, not the same thing as with contemporary versions, we find examples of the DA from both Plato and Aristotle.

> *from the order of the motion of the stars, and of all things under the dominion of the*

mind that ordered the universe (Plato, Laws, 12.966E, emphasis added).

When thus they would suddenly gain sight of the earth, seas, and the sky; when they should come to know the grandeur of the clouds and the might of the winds; when they should behold the sun and should learn its grandeur and beauty as well as its power to cause the day by shedding light over the sky; and again, when the night had darkened the lands and they should behold the whole of the sky spangled and adorned with stars; and when they should see the changing lights of the moon as it waxes and wanes, and the risings and settings of all these celestial bodies, their courses fixed and changeless throughout all eternity–when they should behold all these things, most certainly they would have judged both that there exist gods and that all these marvelous works are the handiwork of the gods. (Aristotle, Fragment, "On Philosophy," emphasis added)

We also find an implicit DA in the Psalms (19:1) of the Old Testament:

The heavens declare the glory of God;
the skies proclaim the work of his hands.
Day after day they pour forth speech;
night after night they reveal knowledge.
They have no speech, they use no words;
no sound is heard from them.
Yet their voice goes out into all the earth,
their words to the ends of the world. (emphasis added)

And, in the New Testament, we find the following:

For what can be known about God is plain to them, because God has shown it to them. Ever since the creation of the world his eternal power and divine nature, invisible though they are, have been understood and seen through the things he has made. (Romans 1:19-21, emphasis added).

We will examine the classic version of the design argument, and its more contemporary variation called the "fine-tuning" argument. Any version of the design argument will possess several key features.

1. The DA is based on experience, observation, and inference.

Some arguments for God's existence (e.g., the ontological argument) don't require any information gathering, or empirical evidence. Not so with the design argument. The design argument requires us to observe our world, note its features, and then seek the best explanation for those features. Based on our experience of what we observe about our world, we infer an explanation for what we've observed.

2. The DA is probabilistic (not certain).

Because the design argument is an inductive (inferential) argument, it does not establish its conclusion with certainty—nor does it even try to. Any honest version of a design argument will have very carefully (and relatively modestly) worded conclusions. You should never see a conclusion of a design argument that asserts that it is certain that God is responsible for the "design" of our universe. Instead, you should see conclusions similar to the following examples:

- It is likely (or very likely) that God exists.
- God is the best available explanation for the apparent design of our world.
- The most probable explanation of the "fine-tuning" of our universe is God.

As we'll see later on, even these conclusions are a little bit "ambitious," but we'll get to that soon enough.

3. The DA is an attempt to establish (the likelihood of) God's existence by "reason" rather than "faith."

This is a feature of all philosophical theistic arguments, really. In the case of the design argument, it attempts to show the likelihood of God's existence as the best available explanation for the apparent "design" in Nature. If the argument works the way it is supposed to, it doesn't require the skeptic to presuppose anything about the world, or supernatural events. Instead, it prods the skeptic into acknowledging that this world appears to have a certain order, structure, or apparent design to it, and the argument offers two general possible explanations for that: intentional design, or random and unguided natural development. Between the two, the design argument will claim that intentional design seems most plausible—and this indicates the existence of some sort of "designer."

What sort of "apparent design" are we talking about? What follows are several kinds of candidates for "apparent design." It is possible that you might think that only some, or even none, of these candidates are actual indicators of design, but understand that these are the sorts of things that people using the DA tend to have in mind.

First, consider our own solar system. The orbits of all the planets around the sun are mathematically precise, elliptical, and predictable. Astronomers can tell us with staggering accuracy exactly where each planet will be on any given day of the year. You and I need not lose any sleep tonight worrying that Mars is going to crash into the Earth. It's just not going to happen. The mathematical structure and geometric precision of our solar system resembles (to some) a machine. Our solar system appears to be *designed* to function as it does.

For another possible example, consider ecosystems. Critics, and even average citizens, will sometimes express surprise, or even contempt, when environmental activists cry alarm when seemingly insignificant creatures are threatened. For example, many environmentally-oriented organizations are growing increasingly concerned about the toxicity of the Earth's oceans (as a result of pollution of various kinds, including fertilizer, among other products). The focus of this big problem might be smaller than you'd expect: krill. Krill are tiny shrimp-like invertebrates that fill the oceans. They consume phytoplankton and zooplankton (microscopic organisms), and are themselves eaten by many other creatures, including some kinds of whales. The problem is that certain kinds of pollutants inhibit the growth of invertebrate exoskeletons, and this means that krill might (ultimately) die out. "Who cares about krill?" you might wonder. Well, considering the concept of an ecosystem, we might all have a reason to care about the fate of krill. The fate of the krill is tied to the fate of everything that eats it (fish, whales, etc.). The fate of those things is tied to the fate of those who eat (or use, or care about) *them* (i.e., humans). The fate of the krill is even tied to oxygen-production in our atmosphere. In brief, these tiny shrimp-like creatures are pretty important to us.

What does any of this have to do with "design?" Some describe ecosystems as vast, intricate, biological machines, with each species serving as a gear or cog in that machine. Remove one of those gears, and the machine breaks down (or at least has to "adjust"). Suppose Nature is like a giant biological machine. What do we know about machines? They're *designed.*

Some marvel at the structure and operations of the human body. We can only go into the briefest of detail, but our heart is a pump, our kidneys are filters, and the skeleton and muscular system make up a system of pulleys and levers capable of brute force as well as intricate fine motor skills. Engineers, inspired by the "machinery" of our own anatomy, replicate it with robotics. If you look at a robot "arm," it's easy to see the "shoulder," "elbow," "wrist," "fingers," etc. Perhaps there's something to the analogy. We know that robots have the features they do because they were designed that way by engineers. Perhaps we have the features we do because we were "designed" that way as well.

There is another, common, example of the machinery of Nature: the laws of physics themselves. Briefly, as far as we know, the laws of physics are uniform, constant, the same throughout the whole universe, and mathematically simple. Our universe is not chaotic, it's ordered. Our universe's operations are understandable, and predictable, and can be expressed in surprisingly simple mathematical terms. There is math at the foundation of Nature, math that we can discover, understand, and put to our use. This order, simplicity, intelligibility, and predictability inspire some to see "design" behind these fundamental laws.

Finally, the emergence of life itself is sometimes taken as evidence of design. What we know is that our universe is extraordinarily hostile to life. So far as we know, the Earth is the only place in the entire universe capable of supporting life (as we know it). Everywhere else, the universe is deadly. What are the odds that life could emerge in our universe? We'll address this more when we get to the "fine-tuning" argument, but, for now, the answer is that the odds are *really, really bad* that life could emerge by chance alone. If not by chance, then by what? "Design," perhaps?

William Paley

Paley's argument is simple (on its surface). Paley invites us to imagine a scenario in which we are taking a country hike. We notice a stone upon the path. No big deal, right? No explanation needed—it's just a stone! Suppose, instead, that we spotted a watch?

All of the sudden, explanation is needed. The kind of answer that was permissible for the stone isn't permissible for the watch. Although we can get away with speculating that the stone has always been there, and was formed from natural processes, if we were to suggest the same of the watch, we would look foolish. Why? Because there are important and obvious differences between watches and stones.

The watch has numerous features that indicate intentional design: geometric shapes, the interconnected (and moving) parts, the fact that there are *words* and *numbers* on the watch, etc. How are we confident that those are not the results of natural forces? Because, in our experience, Nature never (ever) produces, by itself, objects that look like that watch! When was the last time you saw a natural object (e.g., a rock, an orange, etc.) with numbers and letters on it (that hadn't been put there by a human)?

Simply put, in our experience, although Nature often produces stone, it never produces watches. Humans do. So, when we encounter a watch, we naturally and confidently infer that someone, at some time, must have created it. Its features are taken to be such compelling evidence of design that we can't help but come to that conclusion. Indeed, he argues that it is a natural, inevitable, and unavoidable inference that the watch must have been designed.

The application of the watch story to the design argument is simply this: Paley claims that Nature has features similar to those of a watch, and that we should, therefore, infer a similar conclusion as to its origin.

1. Human artifacts (like watches) are products of intelligent design.
2. Nature resembles human artifacts.
3. Therefore, Nature is also a product of intelligent design.

The first premise should be uncontroversial. We know, from experience, that human artifacts (like watches) are products of intelligent design. Watches, or cars, or computers, or iPhones have the features they do because humans *designed* them that way.

The second premise is the potentially controversial one. *How* does Nature resemble human artifacts? In all those ways mentioned previously in this chapter: the structure of the solar system, human anatomy, the laws of physics, ecosystems, etc. Or, we can simply default to Paley's most famous example:

> *WERE there no example in the world, of contrivance, except that of the eye, it would be alone sufficient to support the conclusion which we draw from it, as to the necessity of an intelligent Creator. It could never be got rid of; because it could not be accounted for by any other supposition, which did not contradict all the principles*

> *we possess of knowledge; the principles, according to which, things do, as often as they can be brought to the test of experience, turn out to be true or false. Its coats and humours, constructed, as the lenses of a telescope are constructed, for the refraction of rays of light to a point, which forms the proper action of the organ; the provision in its muscular tendons for turning its pupil to the object, similar to that which is given to the telescope by screws, and upon which power of direction in the eye, the exercise of its office as an optical instrument depends; the further provision for its defence, for its constant lubricity and moisture, which we see in its socket and its lids, in its gland for the secretion of the matter of tears, its outlet or communication with the nose for carrying off the liquid after the eye is washed with it; these provisions compose altogether an apparatus, a system of parts, a preparation of means, so manifest in their design, so exquisite in their contrivance, so successful in their issue, so precious, and so infinitely beneficial in their use, as, in my opinion, to bear down all doubt that can be raised upon the subject.*

Finally, how do we arrive at the conclusion from those premises? Here, there is some difference of opinion. Most interpreters of Paley tend to think that his argument parallels that of Hume's character "Cleanthes" (more on that later) and is therefore an argument by analogy. Other interpreters readily admit that Hume's version of the DA is analogical, but that Paley's version isn't, technically, an argument by analogy. Rather than claiming "similar effects" observed in watches and Nature, this interpretation claims that it is *identical* effects (i.e., ordered arrangements) observed in each.[205] For our purposes, the subtleties of these distinctions (i.e., analogy v. inference) needn't be resolved, and can be left to specialists in both Paley and Hume. I personally think that the argument is analogical, in effect, even if it was not intended (strictly speaking) to be an argument by analogy—so we will continue as though it were an argument by analogy.

We engage in analogical reasoning all the time. It's indispensable to us on a daily basis. As a very simple example, suppose you look out a window right now and see smoke on the horizon. Any wild guesses as to what the cause of that smoke is? Fire, right? Did you *know* that it was fire? Probably not, but you'd still be pretty confident that it was. In your experience, every time you see smoke, there's a fire that caused it (or at least something burning, even if there are no visible flames). When you see smoke again, you draw upon your previous experiences with smoke and infer that the new case of smoke has a similar cause as all the previous cases: fire.

	Effect	**Cause**
Yesterday	Smoke	fire
Today	Smoke	?

All it takes to conclude that fire is (probably) responsible for today's smoke is previous experience with fire and smoke, and basic reasoning skills. Now let's apply this reasoning to the design argument.

---

[205] Indeed, some interpretations of Paley don't even agree that his argument is inductive. A deductive version of his argument is as follows: (1) We know that intelligent agents are capable of producing effects marked by the three properties of (i) relation to an end, (ii) relation of the parts to one another, and (iii) possession of a common purpose. (2) No other cause has ever been observed to produce effects possessing these three properties. (3) Therefore, if there are systems in Nature possessing these same properties, then the only cause adequate to account for these natural effects is an intelligent agent.

	Effect	Cause
Watch	structure / function / purpose	design
Universe	structure / function / purpose	?

Paley is asking us to take a familiar object (a watch), and note the features that are evidence of design. Then, he invites us to notice similar features in the universe. If we know what causes those features in a watch (design), and we see those same kinds of features in the universe, we are led to infer that the cause is probably similar as well: design.

> *Is it possible to believe that the eye was formed without any regard to vision; that it was the animal itself which found out that, although formed with no such intention, it would serve to see with? . . . There cannot be design without a designer, contrivance without a contriver...The marks of design are too strong to be got over. Design must have had a designer. That designer must have been a person. That person must have been God.*

Where there's smoke, there's fire....

Before considering any criticisms of this kind of argument, let us review a contemporary variation of the design argument known as the "fine-tuning" argument. This argument is also based on observation and inference, but the fine-tuning argument is based on probability calculations (both formal and informal). One of the virtues of this variation is that it is scientific. That is, it attempts to make use of the very latest findings of physics, astrophysics, and astronomy (not to mention statistics and probability). This is interesting because it flies in the face of the stereotype that science and religion must, for some reason, be "enemies." Another virtue of the fine-tuning argument is that it is contemporary. There are many philosophers, theologians, and scientists working on (and against) the fine-tuning argument right now.

"Fine-tuning" Argument

Older versions of the DA (e.g., those offered by Aquinas and Paley) tend to be arguments by analogy, or rely on biological examples of design, or both.[206] As we will see later in this chapter, either tendency can be vulnerable to certain sorts of criticism. More contemporary versions of the DA known as "fine-tuning" arguments (FT), on the other hand, operate differently, and are therefore immune to most of the older criticisms usually leveled at the DA. They will invite new criticism of their own, of course, but before addressing criticism (new or old), let's see how the FT arguments work.

To begin with, I can't resist pointing out what Paley had to say, centuries ago, on this topic:

> *My opinion of Astronomy has always been, that it is not the best medium through which to prove the agency of an intelligent Creator; but that, this being proved, it shows, beyond all other sciences, the magnificence of his operations. The mind which is once convinced, it raises to sublimer views of the Deity than any other subject affords; but it is not so well adapted, as some other subjects are, to the purpose of argument. We are destitute of the means of examining the constitution of the heavenly bodies....After all; the real subject of admiration is, that we understand so much of astronomy as we do. That an animal confined to the surface of one of the planets; bearing a less*

[206] In what was perhaps an anticipation of these fine-tuning arguments, Paley's *Natural Theology* does include some non-biological examples, but his overwhelming focus (several hundred pages worth!) is biological examples of design.

> *proportion to it than the smallest microscopic insect does to the plant it lives upon; that this little, busy, inquisitive creature, by the use of senses which were given to it for its domestic necessities, and by means of the assistance of those senses which it has had the art to procure, should have been enabled to observe the whole system of worlds to which its own belongs; the changes of place of the immense globes which compose it; and with such accuracy, as to mark out beforehand, the situation in the heavens in which they will be found at any future point of time; and that these bodies, after sailing through regions of void and trackless space, should arrive at the place where they were expected, not within a minute, but within a few seconds of a minute, of the time prefixed and predicted: all this is wonderful, whether we refer our admiration to the constancy of the heavenly motions themselves, or to the perspicacity and precision with which they have been noticed by mankind.*

Paley clearly preferred biological examples, but this might have been largely due to the literal closeness and availability of biological specimens, in contrast to the limited observations of astronomical objects, available in his time. Astronomers today are much better equipped and much better informed.

As the name suggests, FT arguments appeal to apparent "fine-tuning" observed in Nature. There are several variants of FT arguments, each emphasizing different purposes for which the universe appears to be finely tuned. In terms of the tuning itself, however, there appears to be two kinds:

- Constants of Nature
- Arbitrary physical quantities

The "constants of Nature" refer to a variety of values exhibited by Nature, of which the following is a partial listing:

Speed of light *c*: 2.99792458·108 m/s
Fine structure constant: 1 / 137.0359895
Electron rest mass *me*: 9.1093897·10-31 kg
Proton rest mass *mp*: 1.6726231·10-27 kg
Neutron rest mass *mn*: 1.6749286·10-27 kg
Gravitational constant *G*: (6.673 +- 0.010)·10-11 m3/kg·s2
Acceleration due to gravity *g*: 9.80665 m/s2

These constants are *included* in natural laws, but are not *determined* by them. For example, the Law of Gravity is *F* = *G Ma* Mb / r2, where G = (6.673 +- 0.010)·10-11 m3/kg·s2. The gravitational force (F) between two objects is determined not only by their respective masses (Ma and Mb), and by the distance between them (r), but also by the value for G (above). This value for G is the *same* no matter what two bodies we're dealing with, and no matter the distance between them.

The claim offered by FT arguments is that these constants must be "finely tuned" for life to be possible. To provide a sense of scale, consider the following values.

- Number of seconds in the entire history of the universe: 10^{17} (1 followed by 17 zeroes)
- Number of subatomic particles in the known universe: 10^{80}
- If the weak force constant were altered by 1 part out of 10^{100}, no life would be possible
- If the cosmological constant were altered by 1 part out of 10^{120}, no life would be possible

The point, of course, is that these values seem to be calibrated with a precision that defies our comprehension—and this calibration begs for an explanation.

The other sort of fine-tuning involves various arbitrary physical quantities in the universe present as initial conditions of the universe, and on which the laws of nature operate. One of the more commonly cited such quantities is the amount of "entropy" present at the very beginning of the universe. Similar to the values cited for various constants of Nature, the amount of entropy needed for our universe to have existed as it does is also (and even more) staggering. The odds of the "low entropy" initial state of the universe (necessary for our universe to exist as it does) are 1 in $10^{10^{123}}$. Stephen Hawking has estimated that a decrease or increase of even 1 part in a hundred thousand million million (one second after the Big Bang) would have prevented the formation of galaxies. In other words, the odds of our universe existing as it does, where even *matter* is possible (let alone life!), is staggeringly poor by chance alone. Instead, proponents of FT arguments will claim, the universe appears to have been finely tuned for that outcome.

Note that I mentioned the conditions needed for matter (let alone life). This is an important distinction, actually. Oftentimes, the argument is presented using the language of "life as we know it." If the initial low entropy conditions had not been met, "life as we know it" would not have been possible. An immediate and common response is to propose that life "*other* than as we know it" would have possible instead, and we're then invited to imagine a colorful host of science fiction aliens, or (more abstractly) silicon-based life (as opposed to carbon-based), or sentient energy, etc. The FT argument (if successful) is more powerful than that, however.

> *By 'life' scientists mean the property of organisms to take in food, extract energy from it, grow, adapt to their environment, and reproduce. The point is that in order for the universe to permit life so-defined, whatever form organisms might take, the constants and quantities of the universe have to be incomprehensibly fine-tuned. In the absence of fine-tuning not even atomic matter or chemistry would exist, not to speak of planets where life might evolve.*[207]

Variations of FT arguments are abundant. Here is one offered by Hugh Ross[208]:

Hugh Ross

1. The combination of physical constants (and range for variables) we observe in our universe is the only one capable of supporting life.
2. Numerous other combinations were possible.
3. Fine-tuning of the constants so as to support life is not improbable if there was a designer.
4. Such fine-tuning is highly improbable under chance alone [approximately much less than 1 chance in one hundred billion, trillion, trillion, trillion exists that even one such planet (capable of producing/sustaining life) would occur anywhere in the universe].
5. Therefore, the best available explanation for the fine tuning is a designer.

Let us (quickly) review the argument, one line at a time. The first premise appeals to the conditions necessary for life, as we know it. There are dozens and dozens of such conditions, ranging from the common-sense examples to those that only scientists are likely to understand.

Take a common-sense example: our planet must reside within a limited band of distance from the sun in order for life, as we know it, to be possible. If our planet were outside of this "circumstellar habitable zone," we could not live. If the Earth were very much closer to the sun, the planet would be too hot for us to survive. Much further away, and it would be too cold. Instead, we live in what is sometimes jokingly referred to as the "Goldilocks Zone:" it is neither too hot, nor too cold; it is "just right."

As additional examples of the sorts of factors has in mind, consider this very brief list:

1. galaxy size

---

207 Craig, *Reasonable* Faith, 159.

208 Ross is a contemporary "apologist," seeking to defend belief in Christianity. It is noteworthy that he has a degree in physics, and a Ph.D. in astronomy. Thus, he approaches this issue as a believer *and* a scientist. For more on Ross and his work, review his website: www.reasons.org.

- if too large: infusion of gas and stars would disturb sun's orbit and ignite too many galactic eruptions
- if too small: insufficient infusion of gas to sustain star formation for long enough time

2. supernovae eruptions
   - if too close: life on the planet would be exterminated by radiation
   - if too far: not enough heavy element ashes would exist for the formation of rocky planets
   - if too infrequent: not enough heavy element ashes present for the formation of rocky planets
   - if too frequent: life on the planet would be exterminated
   - if too soon: heavy element ashes would be too dispersed for the formation of rocky planets at an early enough time in cosmic history
   - if too late: life on the planet would be exterminated by radiation
3. parent star distance from center of galaxy
   - if farther: quantity of heavy elements would be insufficient to make rocky planets; wrong abundances of silicon, sulfur, and magnesium relative to iron for appropriate planet core characteristics
   - if closer: galactic radiation would be too great; stellar density would disturb planetary orbits; wrong abundances of silicon, sulfur, and magnesium relative to iron for appropriate planet core characteristics
4. parent star color
   - if redder: photosynthetic response would be insufficient
   - if bluer: photosynthetic response would be insufficient
5. distance from parent star
   - if farther: planet would be too cool for a stable water cycle
   - if closer: planet would be too warm for a stable water cycle
6. thickness of crust
   - if thicker: too much oxygen would be transferred from the atmosphere to the crust
   - if thinner: volcanic and tectonic activity would be too great

The second premise points out the obvious: for every one of these conditions, the outcome *could* have been different. Returning to our previous example, the Earth could have been slightly closer to the sun, or further, or a lot closer, or a lot further, or any number of locations in between.

This premise serves to illustrate that there are a staggering number of possible universes we might have had. Remember, there is a wide range of what was possible for every single one of the approximately 100 conditions needed for life. Multiply all the possible outcomes for each one by the total number of conditions we're tracking and we end up with a *really, really big* number of possible universes.

The third premise encourages us to consider the possible explanations for the actual universe we have. The universe was either intentionally designed, or it wasn't. Logic and common sense combine with that statement of the obvious. *If* the universe were intentionally designed, there's nothing surprising about us having a universe capable of supporting life. In other words, *if* God exists, and *if* God created the universe, and *if* God wanted that universe to support life, it stands to reason we would have the kind of universe that we actually have (i.e., one in which life is possible!).

The fourth premise considers the *other* possibility, that the universe is *not* the product of intelligent/intentional design. If we can't appeal to intentional design, we must appeal to blind natural processes instead. That we have the universe we do, one capable of supporting life, is not anything planned, but is the product of really good luck. What are odds that we would be so lucky? According to Ross' math, there is less than one chance in a hundred billion, trillion, trillion, trillion that even one planet capable of supporting life would exist anywhere in the universe.

The conclusion? Given two possible explanations for the *fact* that we *do* live in a universe capable of supporting life, the best available explanation is intentional/intelligent design. Is it possible that we just got lucky? Sure, but it's very *improbable*. Ross' strategy is to cause us to marvel at how many things have to line up just right in order for life to exist, recognize how unlikely that is by chance alone, and conclude that intentional design is the best available explanation instead.

Another recent version of the fine-tuning argument is worth mentioning due to its unique contribution to the design argument. I call this the "privileged planet" argument, after the book and documentary of the same name. As you'll see, the argument is almost identical to Ross', with one notable exception.

"The Privileged Planet" (as developed by Guillermo Gonzalez and Jay Richards)

1. Background conditions of the universe must be "finely tuned" for intelligent life to exist in our universe.
2. Background conditions of the universe must be "finely tuned" for intelligent life to be able observe and study the universe.
3. Therefore, the odds against intelligent life existing and situated so as to study the universe are staggeringly small (by chance alone).
4. The odds are quite good, if the universe was *intentionally* "fine-tuned" for such a result.
5. Intelligent life exists, and in such a place that permits tremendous observation and study of the universe.
6. Therefore, the best available explanation for this fact is *intentional* "fine-tuning."

The unique contribution of Gonzalez and Richards may be found starting in the second premise. Beyond the conditions needed for life, they also focus on the conditions needed for scientific study of the universe itself. They point out that not only must conditions be "just right" for life to exist, but they must also be "just right" for us to be able to study the universe in the manner we have. In many cases, the conditions needed for life, and those needed for scientific discovery will be the same (obviously, if I can't survive our atmosphere, I can't study it either!), but in many cases, the conditions needed for study are "extra." Their simplest and most memorable example involves a total solar eclipse.

A total solar eclipse occurs when the Moon passes between the Earth and the Sun. What makes a *total* eclipse possible is that the Moon and Sun appear to be exactly the same size, and therefore the moon can completely block the sun for a brief period of time. They're not the same size, of course. The sun is about 400 times larger than the moon, but it's also 400 times further away. This gives them the same *apparent* size. This is far more important than most realize.

That we can experience a total eclipse does much more than present us with an opportunity to see something really pretty—it gives us an opportunity to study the chromosphere (the outer edge of the atmosphere) of the sun. The ratio of size and distance are critical here. If the moon were slightly larger, it would block too much of the sun; slightly smaller, and it would block too little. If it were slightly closer to the Earth, it would appear too large; slightly further away, and it would appear too small. Given the Earth, moon, and Sun being "just right" in terms of size and distance, just enough of the sun's light is blocked in order for scientists to study the sun's outer atmosphere. This allowed for the discovery of helium, and for an understanding of the composition of the sun. Since stars are simply other suns, this, in turn, opened up the field of astronomy and allowed scientists to learn about distant stars by comparing the properties of the light generated from those distant stars to that generated by our own. As a result, star types, age of stars, distances, and so on became available for study. What's more, a full solar eclipse allowed for a confirmation of Einstein's general theory of relativity. Notice that this goes beyond what's needed for life. Our moon could be slightly bigger or smaller, and we could still survive—but we couldn't make use of a total solar eclipse.

There are many more examples, but they go beyond the scope of our present project. Suffice it to say that Gonzalez and Richards will use these examples the same way that Ross did. Considering the conditions needed for a planet to permit both life and scientific discovery,[209] they will ask us to consider the two possible explanations for the fact that we *do* have the conditions sufficient for both: intentional design, or chance.

If the universe were intentionally designed, there would be nothing terribly surprising about the fact that our universe both supports life and is amenable to scientific study. If the universe were the product of lucky natural processes, though, the chances of our having a universe that not only meets the conditions needed for life but also for scientific study, are staggeringly bad: one in one thousandth of one trillionth, according to their *conservative* estimation.

Just like Ross, they encourage us to conclude that the best available explanation for the universe we have is intentional design. In fact, Jay Richards cleverly claims that the universe's features "suggest conspiracy rather than coincidence"

Whichever version of an FT argument we consider, they have basic features in common. While older versions of the DA generally operate by analogy, FT variants are presented as inferences to the best explanation. If various constants and arbitrary quantities had to have particular values (or obtain values within a very narrow range) for our universe to exist as it does, and be life-permitting, what is the best explanation of the fact that the universe does exhibit those values? In general, we can present the core argument driving any FT argument in the following way:

1. The fine-tuning of the universe is due to physical necessity, chance, or design.
7. It is not due to physical necessity or chance.[210]
8. Therefore, it is due to design.

As we have done with other arguments, we'll consider this one line at a time. The first premise claims that the apparent fine-tuning of the universe is due to one of the following: physical necessity, chance, or design. This premise is simply meant to exhaust the logical possibilities. Note that "fine-tuning" doesn't (and can't) mean "designed" without begging the question. So, fine-tuning, at this stage, just means that the features in question (i.e., the various constants and quantities) do, in fact, exhibit just the right values that they must exhibit in order for a life-possible universe to exist.

The second premise claims that this fine-tuning is not due to physical necessity or chance. With regard to physical necessity, this seems relatively uncontroversial. After all, why should we think that a life-prohibiting universe be physically impossible? Let alone logically impossible? Indeed, life-prohibiting universes seem far more *likely*—a point conceded by naturalists and theists alike. The far more plausible alternative to "design" is "chance." Admittedly, the odds of a universe like ours arising from unguided natural processes alone is breathtakingly poor—just consult any of the odds provided above! However, contemporary work involving multi-verse theories are summoned to provide support for precisely this alternative to

---

[209] A partial list includes the presence of liquid water, being located within the circumstellar habitable zone, having the right thickness of terrestrial crust, having a sufficient planetary magnetic field, having an oxygen-nitrogen atmosphere, having a large moon, orbiting a spectral type G2 dwarf main sequence star, being protected by gas giants, possessing a thin and transparent atmosphere, being located within a spiral galaxy, being located within the galactic habitable zone, having access to the visible light portion of the EM spectrum, having the right moon-planet-star relationship, etc.

[210] Where "chance" must mean to something like "unguided/unintentional natural processes."

design. We will get to that, and other objections, momentarily. For now, however, let us acknowledge that *if* physical necessity and chance have been eliminated as the best explanations for the fine-tuning we observe in the universe, the only remaining explanation is design. In that case, the universe *appears* finely-tuned because it *is* finely-tuned.

As we have seen thus far, the DA is actually a collection of a variety of different kinds of arguments united by their general attempt to establish "design" as the best explanation for various features we observe in the universe. Older versions of the DA generally operate by analogy. FT arguments don't. Some versions of the DA employ biological examples, while others don't. Criticisms of the DA may be organized around which type of DA they address. We will begin with a criticism applying only to analogical versions of the DA, then consider a criticism applying only to DAs using biological examples of design, and conclude with several criticisms that could apply to any DA we've considered.

Paley and Hume

Before delving into criticism, I wish to engage in an act of personal/professional confession that I hope serves as a cautionary tale.

Paley published his *Natural Theology* in 1802. Hume's *Dialogues Concerning Natural Religion* was published three years after Hume's own death, in 1779. In case it wasn't obvious, Hume's criticism of the DA was published 23 years before Paley published his DA, and was written even earlier than that.

For years, I conveyed what I myself had been taught, and had read in numerous anthologies, about this unusual temporal relationship: "Paley seems to have been unaware of Hume's work and, therefore, unfortunately, didn't respond to his criticisms." Their non-encounter was taken to be one of the more glaring and unfortunate cases in the history of philosophy of "two ships passing in the night." If only Paley had been more well-read, he would have known that Hume offered numerous, "devastating" criticisms of the DA, and Paley, perhaps, could have tried to defend himself from them. What a shame, what a waste.

What a myth.

After years of teaching this story myself, I discovered, after reading more of Paley, and more carefully, the abject and undeniable *falsity* of this common view of the intellectual relationship between Paley and Hume. Paley mentions Hume, and the *Dialogues*, by name, in chapter 26 of *Natural Theology*.

> *Mr. Hume, in his posthumous dialogues, asserts, indeed, of idleness, or aversion to labour (which he states to lie at the root of a considerable part of the evils which mankind suffer), that it is simple and merely bad.*

Not only was Paley obviously aware not only of Hume's existence, but also that of the specific work in which the DA is criticized, Paley also addressed those criticisms, either implicitly, or, at times, explicitly. Indeed, one of Paley's chapter titles refers specifically to one of Hume's criticisms (as we'll see later).

I mention all this partly out of penance for my role in unwittingly perpetuating a falsehood about Paley, but also as a cautionary tale: just because something is repeated, from teacher to student, from one generation to another, doesn't necessarily mean that it's *true*.

Having now explored several different versions of the DA, we will now turn to several criticisms.

Criticism of the Analogical DA: Weak Analogy (Hume)

This criticism applies to any analogical version of the DA—including Paley's, if his version is indeed analogical. Any argument by analogy will only be as strong as the analogy itself. In other words, if the two things being compared are very similar, the argument has the potential to be quite strong. If the two things being compared are not very similar, the argument is weakened. We even have an expression in English to capture this idea: "that's like comparing apples and oranges." We use this expression when we think that the things being compared just aren't sufficiently similar to make the desired point.

In reality, we engage in reasoning by analogy, or (more generally), inferential reasoning all the time. Many times, there is nothing faulty with this kind of reasoning at all. Indeed, without this kind of reasoning, much of what we reason about would be impossible. This kind of reasoning is problematic, however, when the analogy become strained.

For example, suppose that you are in my class and you see me clutch my chest, complain of shortness of breath and chest pains, and then collapse onto the floor. Despite the fact that few (if any) of you are medical doctors, I'm sure you all have an educated hypothesis concerning what's wrong with me: a heart attack. How do you know this? Because you've seen (or heard about) other people with the same symptoms, and in those cases, it was a heart attack. What does that have to do with me? I'm a different person, after all. Certainly, but I'm still a *person*. Different or not, I'm a human being just like all those other patients. Because human beings are all so biologically similar, it's reasonable for us to assume that our bodies operate and react in very similar ways. Since we all have the same kind of heart, it's reasonable for us to think that heart attacks will be experienced in very similar ways by any and all of us. If this kind of reasoning was faulty, medicine would be impossible. It is only because this kind of reasoning by analogy *does* work that we can accumulate theories of *human* health.

Continuing with the same example, suppose you come up with an amateur diagnosis of "heart attack." Suppose that there also happens to be a portable defibrillator in our classroom (don't ask why—just go with it).

Having seen enough television to know how this works, you leap into action, apply the shock paddles to my chest, shout "clear," and give me a good jolt. My heart starts beating again. Why would you think the paddles would help me in this situation? Because other human beings who were having heart attacks have been helped by the use of defibrillators—and I'm similar enough to other human beings for you to be confident it would work on me too.

Suppose that I return home, with a new appreciation for life, and having purchased my own portable defibrillator that I keep with me at all times (just in case). Upon returning home, I discover, to my horror, that my beloved cat Morgana is lying motionless, with her tiny paw clutching her chest. I freak out, then calm myself, and remember that wonderful defibrillator. I apply it to my cat's torso, and give her a good jolt. Any educated guesses as to how that's going to turn out? Probably nowhere near so well. Why? Because although my cat and I are both mammals, and both have hearts, we're not the same species, and not even close to the same size. The amount of voltage appropriate to shock me and that appropriate for a cat are likely to be pretty different. Because of some significant differences between myself and my cat, I should not be so confident that a medical intervention that worked on me will also work on my cat.

As a final example, suppose I then look out on my balcony and notice that one of my cactus plants appears to be dead. My defibrillator battery still has some charge, so I head outside and give my cactus a good jolt. Pretty foolish, right? Why? Perhaps because my cactus is a plant? Because it doesn't even have a heart? Because the differences between humans and cacti are so great that very little medical information about one can be applied to the other?

What does any of this have to do with the design argument? Hume claims that the design argument is a weak analogy, that the two things being compared (the universe, and human artifacts, such as watches) are nowhere near similar enough to be able to draw compelling conclusions as to a similar origin.

> *If we see a house, Cleanthes, we conclude, with the greatest certainty, that it had an architect or builder; because this is precisely that species of effect which we have experienced to proceed from that species of cause. But surely you will not affirm, that the universe bears such a resemblance to a house, that we can with*

> *the same certainty infer a similar cause, or that the analogy is here entire and perfect. The dissimilitude is so striking, that the utmost you can here pretend to is a guess, a conjecture, a presumption concerning a similar cause; and how that pretension will be received in the world, I leave you to consider...(Hume, Dialogues Concerning Natural Religion)*

Moreover, the analogy is being driven by a unique sample (this is the one and only universe of which we have any experience), and a limited exposure to that unique sample at that (see the "part to whole reasoning" criticism later in this chapter)! An interesting feature of this criticism is that its success or failure depends entirely upon whether you think the analogy is weak, or strong, and our sample inadequate or adequate. That is, if you agree with Hume and believe that comparing watches and universes involves a hopeless analogy, and that the information we have at our disposal is insufficient to drive the analogy anyway, then you will agree with him that analogical versions of the design argument are weak. If, on the other hand, you think that the universe does resemble a watch in certain interesting ways, and that we have sufficient information on which to base that analogy, then you will disagree with Hume's criticism from the very start.

Criticism of Biologically-based DAs: Evolution

Although I believe the legendary conflict between evolution and theism to be exaggerated (in other words, there are interpretations of evolution and interpretations of theism that are not mutually exclusive, or even terribly antagonistic), there is a genuine sense in which evolution can be seen as a serious stumbling block for the design argument. Indeed, Richard Dawkins has claimed that "there has probably never been a more devastating rout of popular belief by clever reasoning than Charles Darwin's destruction of the argument from design."[211] In simple terms, the theory of evolution is a challenge to the design argument because the theory of evolution denies that there is any "design" in nature at all.

Remember, the design argument relies upon observing "design-like" features in nature, and inferring that the best explanation for this is that those features really are the result of intentional design. *If* one could demonstrate that the "design-like" features aren't really products of design, but can instead be explained by appealing to purely naturalistic processes in which design is not present, the design argument would be ruined. This is precisely what the theory of evolution threatens to do.

First we must realize what the theory of evolution claims, and does not claim. This will be a scandalously brief treatment. Please bear in mind that I am a philosophy professor, not a professor of evolutionary biology, and that my Ph.D. is in philosophy, not evolutionary biology. If you're hoping for a nuanced and advanced exposition of evolutionary theory, you need to read someone else's book! But, for our purposes, we need only the basics.

"Evolution 101"

Evolution:	a change in the gene pool of a population over time.
Gene pool:	the set of all genes in a species or population.
Species:	all the individuals of a group that can exchange genes with one another
Gene:	hereditary unit that can be passed on (usually unaltered) for many generations.

Now that we have some core vocabulary in place, we can summarize the (general, basic) process of evolution:

Genes mutate.
Individuals are "selected," as a result of

[211] Richard Dawkins, *The God Delusion*, p.103.

competition.

Populations evolve.

Mutation is a random process that increases genetic variation within a population. Mutations can be beneficial, harmful, or neither with respect to the organism in question—but most mutations are either neutral or harmful. Only a very small percentage of mutations are somehow beneficial.

A simple way to think of mutation is as a copying error in which gene sequences are altered. When cells divide, they make copies of their DNA. Sometimes, the process is not executed perfectly, and the copy is not exactly the same. This deviance is a mutation. In movies and comic books, mutation occurs as the result of exposure to chemicals or radiation. Exposure to certain chemicals or radiation causes DNA to break down. Cells repair themselves, but sometimes the repairs are imperfect—resulting in a mutation. Although this is a "real thing," don't expect super-powered mutants to rampage through neighborhoods any time soon. Also, although environmental factors (such as radiation) might influence the rate of mutation, most evolutionary biologists believe that those factors don't influence the "direction" or mutation. In other words, living in an environment with high radiation levels might cause mutations to occur more often, but they won't cause mutations specifically pertaining to radiation, such as resistance to it. Mutation is capricious, and this is why it's called *random* genetic mutation. Whether or not a mutation occurs is independent of whether the mutation will actually be useful to the organism, let alone with respect to how, specifically, it might be useful.

The only sorts of mutations that matter on an evolutionary scale are those that will get passed on to offspring ("germ line mutations"). Such mutations can occur in several different ways. One way is when the mutation produces no perceivable effect on the phenotype (observable characteristics) of the organism at all. In such cases, a mutation might occur in a portion of DNA that has no function, for example. Or, such mutations can produce a *small* change in the phenotype, such as a change in coloration, or ear shape. Or, such mutations could produce a *significant* change in the phenotype, such as resistance to antibiotics in bacteria strains. These are all effects of mutation on the individual organism, and its offspring.

With regard to the population, random genetic mutation *increases* genetic variation within a gene pool, but natural selection *decreases* genetic variation by culling "unfit" variants from the pool.

Some types of organisms within a population produce more offspring than others. Given time, this greater frequency will increase the numbers of this more prolific type within a population, and the population will change (evolve) to resemble that type. Living things are in competition with each other for food and reproductive access. Some members of each species are better (even if only slightly) at surviving and reproducing. This could be for any number of reasons. Perhaps they are stronger, or faster, or more clever, or blend in with their surroundings, or store fat more easily, or are resistant to a certain disease, etc. Survival is "sexy." To put it bluntly: dead creatures aren't very good at reproducing.

Arguably the most cited example of this process at work involves the "peppered moths" of England. Two major variants of this moth species occur in that area, and they are genetically identical except that one variant (a variation of a single gene) produces more melanin, causing it to be much darker in color. As a result, some moths within the population are white with black speckles, and others are just black.

Historical records (such as records of moth specimen collections) reveal that the population has changed over time. Prior to the Industrial Revolution, and in rural areas far from industrial centers, the white speckled variants were more common, and the black variation quite rare. During and after the Industrial Revolution, when lots of coal was being burned, the population of moths shifted such that the black variant was much more prominent—up to 90%, in fact, although in rural areas the white speckled variation was still more numerous. What could account for these facts?

This species of moth spends much of its time perched on tree trunks. Before the Industrial Revolution, or in rural areas, such trees would grow lichen and the "speckled" moths would blend in very nicely against the trunks. This made them difficult to see, whereas the black variants were much more visible. As a result, the black ones got eaten more often, and therefore were less likely to reproduce. The population of moths favored the speckled variant. During the Industrial Revolution, however, urban areas were polluted by the soot of burning coal. This soot settled on tree trunks, killing the lichen and causing the trunks to appear black. In that context, the speckled moth is more visible, while the black variant blends in. The speckled moth got eaten more often, the black variant reproduced more successfully, and the population of moths changed over time to favor the black variant. As a footnote to this story, with the imposition of environmental regulations since the 1950's, the air has gotten cleaner, soot has been reduced, and the tree trunks grow lichen again. The result? Once again, the speckled variant is favored, and the black variant has diminished within the population of moths.

To summarize this example: as a result of random genetic mutation, some moths are darker in color than their white/speckled peers. Given a particular environmental context ("sooty trees"), this mutation was advantageous and was therefore "selected" via natural selection. Over time, the population of moths changed (evolved) to reflect this.

Please note that the claim is that it is *populations* that evolve, not individual organisms (though natural selection occurs at the level of the individual). Continuing with that example, it's not as though a particular moth is growing darker over the span of its life, and seeing its chance for survival increase incrementally all the while. Rather, some moths reflect the mutation, and others don't. It just so happens that the mutation, in that case, is beneficial, and therefore gets passed down to new generations of moths. The population of moths, over a long span of time and many generations, changes to reflect this advantageous trait. As another example, *humans* have evolved, and continue to evolve, but individual human beings do not. In other words "Ted Preston" (I, the author) does not "evolve," but rather the species to which I belong evolves. To illustrate this, consider the uncomfortable example of obesity.

I have weighed various amounts over the span of my life thus far, sometimes "thinner," sometimes "heavier." The general explanation for why I weigh more or less at various times of my life (excluding obvious factors like being a tiny child as opposed to being a grown adult!) probably doesn't require much more insight than daily caloric intake and physical activity variations. My behavior contributes to my personal weight increases and losses, but it's not as if "humanity" is somehow being genetically altered to be fatter or thinner along with me.

That being said, a case can be made that humans, in general (at least in populations where food is abundant) *are* growing "heavier." Much talk is generated about the "obesity epidemic" in America, for example. Some medical doctors and nutritionists think there is an evolutionary explanation for this general trend of obesity. The idea is (roughly) this: *long* ago our human ancestors had far less reliable access to food. Hunting and gathering was not always successful, and sometimes humans starved. In that kind of environment, the tendency to store and retain fat would be advantageous. Those fat reserves could be used in "lean" times to allow the human to survive a bit longer, when food is scarce. Some humans were born, as a result of random genetic mutations, with a gene (or sequence of genes) that caused them to store fat more readily than other humans. That was advantageous to them. They were more likely to survive than their skinny, fast metabolism neighbors. Because they were more likely to survive, they were more likely to reproduce, and they passed this "store fat" gene down to their children. Over time, this advantageous trait continued to be "selected for" and the population of humans changed, over a *long* span of time, such that the tendency to store fat became a common feature.

In those days, long ago, the tendency to store fat didn't entail that those early humans were all pleasantly plump, of course. There wasn't a surplus of food to make that possible, and there was plenty of physical activity with which to burn calories. Instead, it just meant that they didn't become "famine-skinny" so easily, and were more likely to survive. Needless to say, times and circumstances have changed. In America, for example, you find very few "hunter/gatherers." We have an abundance of high calorie (processed) foods at our disposal, and many of us lead sedentary lives. Exercise is no longer a necessity for most of us, but a hobby, or a luxury pursued (often) for the sake of vanity. We still have our ancestors' disposition to retain fat, but we don't have our ancestors' food or lifestyle. The result? Many of us "retain" fat far more readily, and in excess, of what we would prefer, or is healthy.

On the assumption that this evolutionary account of our expanding waistlines is accurate, it reveals an important feature of natural selection: what is advantageous (selected for) is contingent upon the environmental circumstances at the time. The ability to retain fat might have promoted survival thousands of years ago, but might prove to impede survival now that our diets and lifestyles have changed.[212] Similarly, having a really long neck might be advantageous when there are tall plants to eat, but should all those plants die out, and the only plants that remain are low-lying shrubs, that long neck is no longer advantageous.

It is a very common *mis*understanding to believe that evolution "aims" at particular outcomes, or that the "goal" of evolution is survival, or reproductive fitness. In truth, classic evolutionary theory claims no such thing. Consider the following interpretations of a giraffe's long neck:

> Design-minded theist: "The giraffe was designed to have a long neck. The reason it was designed that way was so that it could reach leaves on high branches."

> Misguided wanna-be evolutionist: "The giraffe evolved to have a long neck, over time, in order to reach those leaves on the high branches."

> Evolutionist who knows what she's talking about: "Long ago, some proto-giraffes were born pre-disposed to have slightly longer necks than their peers—perhaps as a result of a random genetic mutation. This enabled them to reach higher branches, which gave them an advantage over others of their species. As a result, they had better reproductive success, and passed along that advantageous trait (i.e., a longer neck) to their offspring. Over a tremendous span of time, this trend continued and produced giraffes as we now know them."

The differences between the two understandings of evolution are subtle, at first glance, but terribly important. The *mistaken* view ascribes purpose, goals, aims, objectives, etc., to evolution—as if the proto-giraffe wanted to have a longer neck, and somehow made its offspring have longer necks as a result of its desire. The accurate view is that no one and no thing was trying to have a longer neck, or was supposed to have a longer neck. That some proto-giraffes had slightly longer necks was the result of a random genetic mutation. That mutation just so happened to prove beneficial. As a result, it was passed along to new generations of proto-giraffes, until, eventually, the species we know as giraffes came into being. Nature wasn't trying to make a giraffe. Nature doesn't "try" to do anything, in that sense (according to evolutionary theory). It's not the case that the giraffe grew a long neck in *order* to reach the leaves; it grew a long neck, and, as a

212 Of course, strictly speaking, we need only to survive long enough to reproduce. So long as we delay our strokes and heart attacks long enough to have children, we've done the job our genes need us to do.

result, was *able* to reach the leaves—and that gave it a reproductive advantage over its shorter-neck cousins.

Once we grasp this basic but important aspect of evolutionary theory, its challenge to the design argument should be clear. The design argument involves taking notice of various features in nature, detecting "design" in those features, and inferring that where there is design, there is likely a designer (or designers).

For the strict evolutionist, what appears to be "design" to someone like Paley, is instead the result of natural selection in conjunction with random genetic mutation (and other factors serving to increase or decrease genetic diversity within a population). Instead of appealing to design, the evolutionist can appeal to natural selection. If there is no design, there is no need to posit a designer.

General Criticism: Who designed the "Designer?"

Some critics of the DA, including such notable persons as Hume, and Richard Dawkins (echoing Hume in Dawkins' *The God Delusion*), raise the following sort of objection: "the designer hypothesis immediately raises the larger problem of who designed the designer." The objection seems to be that the design hypothesis doesn't actually accomplish anything since it merely pushes our explanation back one step. We appeal to a designer to account for the universe, but now we need something to account for the designer.

I don't editorialize often, but this is one of those rare occasions when I will.

I have never understood why anyone has taken this to be a serious, credible objection. This is not to say that there are no serious, credible objections to the DA—indeed there are. This, however, is not one of them, in my opinion.

Explanations have "stopping points" based on what we're trying to explain. If I'm trying to explain why my car won't start, and I discover that the battery has no charge, I have an explanation for why my car won't start. It would be bizarre if someone then pointed out that because I don't know who made my battery, and under what circumstances it was made, I therefore have "accomplished nothing" with my explanation. If astronauts visit Mars and discover an ancient pyramid covered in what appears to be patterns of symbols, they would undoubtedly explain the existence of that pyramid by appealing to the historic presence of *some kind* of intelligent being or beings who constructed that pyramid. It would be absurd to deflate their discovery by pointing out that they don't know who those beings were, or what their ultimate origins are—and therefore the pyramid has no explanation. The explanatory process does not require an infinite regress of explanation, nor could it allow it. As William Lane Craig puts it, "in order to recognize an explanation as the best, you don't need to be able to explain the explanations. In fact, such a requirement would lead to an infinite regress of explanations, so that nothing could ever be explained and science would be destroyed."

While it is undoubtedly true that, even if the DA works, it has not provided an explanation for the existence of the "designer," nor particular features exhibited by the "designer," this is no serious objection to the DA itself. After all, it's not attempting to provide that information! *If* the DA provides the best explanation for the features of our universe, then it has "done its job" (in that context).

General Criticism: the Weak Anthropic Principle

This criticism is based upon the recognition that "chance" is an alternative to design as a means to account for the fine-tuning of the universe necessary for life (or other purposes). A weak appeal to chance, sometimes invoked by critics of FT arguments, is simply a recognition that of the obscenely many possible configurations of the universe, *any* particular configuration is equally improbable, such that there is nothing especially improbable about our current (life-permitting) configuration. In other words, the universe had to turn out *somehow*, and any particular "somehow" is going to be unlikely, by chance alone. Therefore, a life-permitting "somehow" requires no special explanation.

This criticism overlooks a key point motivating the FT arguments, however. Consider a different example that should illustrate the point. Imagine that a computer program (or smartphone "app") is going to randomly generate a number between 1 and 100. Unless the number is 100, however, the computer (or phone) will explode, causing you great bodily harm. The odds of any particular number (1-100) being generated is the same: 1 in 100. So, it's true that the odds of any of those numbers being generated are the same. It's equally likely that you'll get 100 as that you'll get 23. There's nothing more shocking about getting 100 than getting 23, in terms of the odds.

This sort of observation is sometimes combined with what is known as the "weak anthropic principle" (WAP) to produce a criticism of the FT argument. Roughly, the WAP claims that conditions that are observed in the universe must allow the observer to exist. In other words, in order for there to even be observations about a universe in the first place, it has to be the sort of universe where observers could exist to make the observations! We shouldn't be surprised to discover that this universe is one where life is possible. If it weren't, we wouldn't be here to make any observations anyway.

In another (rare) editorial moment, allow me to say that this criticism, by itself, is silly—and I think it's easily shown to be so. The WAP sort of criticism relies upon a fundamental misunderstanding of what's being observed and explained in FT arguments.

Let's consider a different example. Imagine you have been kidnapped by a serial killer obsessed with Las Vegas games of chance. You are tied up in a chair, while the serial killer shuffles a deck of cards. He tells you that he's going to randomly deal you five cards from the deck, and that he is going to kill you—unless four of your cards happen to be aces. You are justifiably terrified. After all, the odds of being randomly dealt four aces in a five card hand is 1 in 54,145! Let's face it, you're doomed. . . He deals the cards, and you are shocked and relieved beyond description to discover that four of those five cards are, in fact aces. The serial killer notices the look of surprise on your face and asks, "why are you so surprised? After all, the odds of any particular hand are going to be terribly poor. It's just as likely that you would get four aces as that you would get four kings, for example. Nothing so interesting about what just happened. Moreover, unless you got four aces, you wouldn't be here right now to wonder about it. So, there really is nothing to explain..."

Although you probably wouldn't want to argue overly much with the serial killer, it's obvious that he has missed the point. It might be true that any particular hand is terribly unlikely, or even equally unlikely as any other hand, but that's not relevant to our example. The deck was stacked against you (pardon the pun). If *any* hand other than four aces was generated, you would be killed. The odds of getting those four aces was 1 in 54,145, but the odds of getting anything else (thereby resulting in your murder) was 54,144 in 54,145. To put it mildly, those odds are nowhere near the same. It was vastly more likely that you would get a lethal hand than the solitary life-saving hand that you, in fact, got dealt. Or, to return to our exploding cell phone example from above, while it is true that the odds of getting any particular number (1-100) are identical: 1 in 100—the odds of getting 100 and *any other number than 100* are *not* identical: 1 in 100 v. 99 in 100.

Proponents of the FT argument will point out the universe has dealt us a life-saving hand. Virtually any other hand would have been lethal. It's true that any particularly configuration is equally likely, but the odds of a life-possible configuration are way worse than a life-impossible configuration. That a life-possible universe is the one that we find ourselves in is, therefore, pretty darned surprising! And, while it's certainly true that we couldn't comment on the universe's features at all if the universe wasn't life-permitting, that fact doesn't make our universe's features any more likely. In our serial killer example, if you had been dealt anything other than those four aces, you wouldn't be around to comment on your lucky hand—but that doesn't make the hand any less extraordinary. In fact, in that scenario, you would probably suspect that the deal hadn't been truly random. Maybe the serial killer is trying to torture you with near-death experiences? The odds of getting four aces by chance alone are so poor that, although it is *possible*, you would probably suspect "cheating" in the event that it did occur. This is precisely the point of FT arguments: although it is *possible* that our universe's features could be the result of unguided processes alone, the odds of that are so poor that "cheating" is the better explanation.

General Criticism: The Multi-verse

The previous criticism (the WAP), by itself, doesn't accomplish much. However, if it is combined with another idea, a much more promising criticism emerges.

The driving force of the FT argument is the vast improbability of a life-possible universe existing by unguided natural processes alone. Given such long odds, and the fact that such a universe exists anyway, the better explanation is design—or so the argument claims. But what if there was a way to improve the odds?

Imagine the "shell game" employed by street hustlers around the world. In the standard version of the shell game, players bet money that they can find an object (e.g., marble, rock, etc.) that has been hidden under one of three shells (or cups, etc.), which have themselves been shuffled around in an attempt to make it difficult to know under which shell the object will be found. Assuming the object actually is under one of the shells (and that the hustler didn't hide it with some legerdemain instead!), the odds of finding it just by a chance guess alone is one in three. What if the game offered some very generous rules, though? What if, after your first guess, you get to guess again (with no further shuffling)? Your odds have improved to one in two. What if, after your second unlucky guess, you're allowed a third (with no further shuffling)? Your odds are now one in one. In other words, given enough tries, you *will* find the object—and this would be true no matter how many shells there were. If the marble was hidden under one of a thousand shells, you would still eventually, inevitably, find that marble if you got to keep trying until you found it! Even that improbable hand of four aces will eventually be dealt, by chance alone, if you're allowed to play approximately 54,145 times.

According to multi-verse cosmology (sometimes called "many-worlds," or "world-ensemble"), such impressive probabilistic resources are available to us—or at least they might be. This is not a textbook in astrophysics, so we're not going to delve into multi-verse theory in any significant detail, but the basic idea behind it is that this universe is not *the* universe, but rather *a* universe—just one universe in a larger multi-verse containing infinitely many other universes.

Suppose, for the sake of argument, that this were true: that there exists a multi-verse comprised of infinitely many randomly ordered universes. How would this be a threat to the FT argument?

The FT argument claims that the odds of the universe having its features by chance alone are staggeringly poor. According to Hugh Ross' math, for example, the odds are less than one in a hundred billion, trillion, trillion, trillion. But, what if you got a hundred billion, trillion, trillion, trillion "tries?" What if you had an *infinite* number of "tries?" Given so many tries, you will have greatly increased your "probabilistic resources," and thereby have guaranteed the admittedly unlikely outcome, still by virtue of chance alone. In other words, if there exists an infinite number of randomly ordered universes, a life-possible universe *will* be generated, by chance alone, no matter how poor the odds of such a universe existing. And, when we recall that the WAP recognizes observable universes must have properties that permit observers to exist, we have an explanation for why we're in this universe rather than in one of those infinitely many other (life-impossible) universes.

The multi-verse is supposed to serve as an alternative to intelligent design with regard to explaining the admittedly very poor odds of the universe existing, with the properties it has, by "luck" alone. The basic idea is simple: given enough probabilistic resources, any outcome *will* occur no matter how unlikely it is, so long as it's a possible outcome. Returning to the poker example, the odds of getting four aces in a hand of five card stud poker is one in 54,145, but if you play long enough (an infinite number of hands, for example), you *will* get that hand by luck alone—but notice what we have to be assuming in order for that to be true: the deck gets shuffled each time.

Suppose you get dealt a hand, and you don't get four aces. "No problem," you think, "since I'm going to play 'forever,' I will eventually get those four aces anyway." The dealer takes back your five cards, and, rather than shuffling them back into the deck, simply places them right back on top of the deck in reverse order. You then get dealt your second hand. It should come as no surprise to you that you didn't get the four aces that time either. You got the exact same hand! You can play "forever," and you will never get those four aces *unless* the deck gets shuffled. Randomization is needed in order to provide the probabilistic resources necessary to get those four aces by luck alone.

With that in mind, reconsider the multi-verse as a means of providing the probabilistic resources necessary to generate a life possible universe by natural processes alone. In order for an infinite number of universes to provide a life-possible universe, the universes' features must be randomized. That is, the universes have to be "shuffled" each time they are formed. A multi-verse containing an infinite number of universes with the exact same properties does nothing to increase the odds of getting a life possible universe. Instead, you would just have an infinite number of "dead" universes. Each universe has to represent a new "shuffling," and a new "hand"—but why should we assume that the multi-verse randomizes universes? What mechanism could account for that? Why would it be necessary that the universes have randomly different features from each other? Why couldn't they all be the same, or at least similar?

Some critics of the multi-verse as an alternative to intelligent design claim that in order for universes to be randomized, the multiverse itself must be "fine-tuned" to make that happen. The fine-tuning of the multi-verse then needs an explanation. Is the multi-verse, then, a product of intelligent design (designed, it would seem, so as to randomly generate an infinite number of universes, in some of which life is possible)? Or, do we postulate a bigger multi-verse in which our own multi-verse is randomly generated, *ad infinitum*? In other words, the multi-verse just pushes back the need for a design explanation one step, but without eliminating it—or so the critic of the multi-verse explanation claims.

General Criticism: The Problem of "Part-to-Whole Reasoning" (Hume)

"Part to Whole Reasoning" (hereafter, PTWR) occurs whenever we draw a conclusion about a large "body" based off of information gathered from a smaller part of that body. Science works in this way, as does statistics and surveying. Very often, there is nothing problematic with this sort of reasoning at all.

For example, beaches are sometimes closed because of water contamination. Certainly, those responsible for testing didn't empty the whole ocean and bring it back to their lab for testing! Instead, they took a sample of the water (a part), tested it, and then drew conclusions about the whole. When the sample of water shows contamination, this is taken to be a sufficient indicator that the water around that entire beach is contaminated. Is this hasty reasoning? No, because we know enough about water to know that soluble substances diffuse throughout a body of water. If the water is polluted at a particular point (A) along a beach, it's probably polluted a few feet from (A) as well.

PTWR goes wrong when our sample (the part) is not a representative sample of the whole. If the sample is too small, for example, we can't draw conclusions (with confidence) concerning the whole. If the water along Long Beach has a lot of oil in it, we can't infer that the entire ocean has a lot of oil in it. The ocean is really big, and sampling the water along one beach city just isn't enough. Similarly, if you survey one person and ask her who she's going to vote for in the next Presidential election, it would be wildly irresponsible to pronounce the next President as a result of your survey. A sample of one (out of over 200 million eligible voters in the U.S.!) is just not big enough to warrant that conclusion.

Again, what does any of this have to do with the design argument? Remember the structure of the analogical DA:

1. Human artifacts (like watches) are products of intelligent design.
2. Nature resembles human artifacts.
3. Therefore, Nature is also a product of intelligent design.

Premise two claims that Nature resembles human artifacts. Not only would Hume claim that this suffers from a weak analogy, he also claims that the information upon which this claim is based is far too small a sample to justify the conclusion. Premise two makes claims about all of Nature, the whole universe. Obviously, no one has "sampled" the whole universe, so that claim is based on a smaller sample, and the assumption that the rest of the universe is fairly similar to what we have already experienced. Perhaps it is, but do we *know* that it is? Design enthusiasts might suggest that we've already justified a similar example: water testing. We don't have to sample the whole ocean to know the beach should be closed, just like we don't need to sample the whole universe to know that it resembles human artifacts. Water sampled just off the beach is sufficient, just like the universe as viewed from our "beach" (Earth) is sufficient.

Or is it? Here, Hume would say that there is a very big difference between water, and the universe: prior experience. The reason why we're confident in making claims about a large body of water based on a relatively small sample of water is because we know, *from experience*, that soluble substances diffuse throughout water. Try adding sugar to your coffee without that assumption! Whether we're dealing with water in a cup, or in a tub, or in a pool, or in the ocean, we have observed again and again the properties of water, and what happens when substances dissolve in it.

Perhaps our universe is similar to water in the sense that properties applicable to one portion of it will be applicable to all parts as well, but can we know this to be true? Our confidence in the case of water is based on previous experience with other bodies of water. How many universes have you experienced before this one? If we had somehow experienced several other previous universes, and if in each one of them the qualities of the universe were uniform, and found to be the same throughout the whole cosmos, then we would have reason to be confident that this universe is also uniform in that respect. But, considering that this universe is unique for us, the only one with which we have any experience, we can't draw upon our prior experience to justify that assumption. We can *assume* that the universe is similar throughout, and that the "order" we observe in our own cosmic neighborhood really is representative of the universe in general, but an assumption is not at all the same thing as a proof. If Hume is right, and we aren't entitled to our claims about the universe, as a whole, this is a serious problem for that kind of design argument, as it threatens to destroy its second premise. Maybe the universe resembles human artifacts in our own part of the universe, but perhaps the rest of it is very different, chaotic, and not at all like a watch. Hume is not saying that the universe, and its laws and operations are *not* uniform, but he is saying that he just doesn't know (with confidence), one way or another. If we don't know that much, we should be careful about making analogies involving assumptions about the universe....

Paley flatly disagrees, claiming that:

> *if other parts of nature were inaccessible to our inquiries, or even if other parts of nature presented nothing to our examination but disorder and confusion, the validity of this example would remain the same. If there were but one watch in the world, it would not be less certain that it had a maker. If we had never in our lives seen any but one single kind of hydraulic machine, yet if of that one kind we understood the mechanism and use, we*

should be as perfectly assured that it proceeded from the hand and thought and skill of a workman, as if we visited a museum of the arts, and saw collected there twenty different kinds of machines for drawing water, or a thousand different kinds for other purposes. Of this point each machine is a proof independently of all the rest. So it is with the evidences of a divine agency. The proof is not a conclusion which lies at the end of a chain of reasoning, of which chain each instance of contrivance is only a link, and of which, if one link fail, the whole falls; but it is an argument separately supplied by every separate example. An error in stating an example affects only that example. The argument is cumulative, in the fullest sense of that term. The eye proves it without the ear; the ear without the eye. The proof in each example is complete; for when the design of the part, and the conduciveness of its structure to that design is shown, the mind may set itself at rest; no future consideration can detract any thing from the force of the example.

According to Paley, even a single example (such as a human eyeball) is sufficient to detect design in Nature just as only a single watch would invite the same conclusion.

The PTWR criticism boils down to a question of reasoning, and to a related empirical issue. The "reasoning" issue is whether it's problematic to infer (or deduce, as the case might be) design from a single sample. If you side with Paley, you'll answer "no." If you side with Hume, then we must face the empirical issue: just how much of the universe have we "sampled," and how well do we understand that sample? It's reasonable to think that Paley was much more vulnerable to this criticism, a couple centuries ago, than contemporary astro-physicists such as Hugh Ross are today. With the help of satellites, the Hubble telescope, and radio telescopes, astronomers today are likely to claim that their "sample" of the universe is pretty impressive—perhaps impressive enough to make general claims about the properties of the universe throughout. For this reason, although the problem of PTWR could apply to any version of the DA (and is therefore included as a "general" criticism), it is arguable that more contemporary FT arguments are less vulnerable to it due to their broader and more comprehensive empirical basis.

General Criticism: The Problem of the "Limited Conclusion" (Hume)

When we reach this criticism, Hume is willing to be generous for the sake of argument. Just for the sake of argument, suppose that the design argument works perfectly. What has it "proven?" Each version of the design argument that we've considered can establish, at best, the likelihood of intentional/intelligent design. Notice that "intentional design" is consistent with every major (Western) religious tradition. Design implies "designer," but who is this designer? The God of Christianity? Islam? Judaism? The design argument works for all three. For that matter, why should we assume there is only one designer?

> *And what shadow of an argument, continued Philo, can you produce, from your hypothesis, to prove the unity of the Deity? A great number of men join in building a house or ship, in rearing a city, in framing a commonwealth; why may not several deities combine in contriving and framing a world? This is only so much greater similarity to human affairs. By sharing the work among several, we may so much further limit the attributes of each, and get rid of that extensive power and knowledge, which must be supposed in one deity, and which, according to you, can only serve to weaken the proof of his existence. And if such foolish, such vicious creatures as man, can yet often unite in framing and executing one plan, how much more those deities or demons, whom we may suppose several degrees more perfect! (Hume, Dialogues Concerning Natural Religion)*

If we consult our own experience, we discover that the bigger the project, and the more complicated it is, the more people it takes to design and build it. I might be able to build, on my own, a tool shed given enough time and some instructions, but I could never, ever build an entire skyscraper all by myself. The bigger the project, the more builders are required. What could be bigger than the universe? Yet, instead of supposing that many designers are needed, theists usually appeal to a single designer instead?

"Because of Ockham's razor," you might reply.

Ockham's razor refers to a principle of explanatory simplicity: "*entia non sunt multiplicanda praeter necessitatem.*" In case your Latin is a bit rusty, this translates into "entities must not be multiplied beyond necessity." The much more common way of expressing this principle is this: *all else being equal, the simpler the explanation, the better.*

Applied to the design argument, one might think that, all else being equal, an explanation requiring one designer is more simple than an explanation requiring several. So, according to Ockham's razor, we should prefer a monotheistic version of the design argument. Hume was prepared for this.

> *To multiply causes without necessity, is indeed contrary to true philosophy: but this principle applies not to the present case. Were one deity antecedently proved by your theory, who were possessed of every attribute requisite to the production of the universe; it would be needless, I own, (though not absurd,) to suppose any other deity existent. But while it is still a question, whether all these attributes are united in one subject, or dispersed among several independent beings, by what phenomena in nature can we pretend to decide the controversy?*

In other words, had we already established the existence of one designer capable of designing the whole universe, that one designer would indeed be a better explanation, all things considered—but the existence of that designer is the very thing in question, and can't be taken as an assumption at this stage. That means that several designers (polytheism) are as much a candidate as is monotheism.

Hume gets a bit playful with this criticism, and a bit irreverent.

> *In a word, Cleanthes, a man who follows your hypothesis is able perhaps to assert, or conjecture, that the universe, sometime, arose from something like design: but beyond that position he cannot ascertain one single circumstance; and is left afterwards to fix every point of his theology by the utmost license of fancy and hypothesis. This world, for aught he knows, is very faulty and imperfect, compared to a superior standard; and was only the first rude essay of some infant deity, who afterwards abandoned it, ashamed of his lame performance: it is the work only of some dependent, inferior deity; and is the object of derision to his superiors: it is the production of old age and dotage in some superannuated deity; and ever since his death, has run on at adventures, from the first impulse and active force which it received from him.*

For all we know, this is a lousy "rough draft" of a universe. Maybe the designer(s) are ashamed of it. Maybe the designer(s) hate us, or couldn't care less? Hume isn't saying any of these things are true, but he is saying they *could* be true, even if the design argument works just the way it's supposed to. In the best-case scenario, if the argument from design works, we can conclude that the universe is (probably) the product of intelligent design, but we can't determine the number of designers, or the properties of the designer(s), or the will of the designer(s), or any particular feature of any specific religious tradition.

This is why Hume grants (sarcastically) that (at best) the argument can conclude that "the universe, sometime, arose from something like design." But, what he gives in one sentence, he takes away just a few words later: "but beyond that position he cannot ascertain one single circumstance; and is left afterwards to fix every point of his theology by the utmost license of fancy and hypothesis."

Fancy and hypothesis? In other words, all of the particular elements of the major religious traditions of the West are feats of imagination. They're made up. No wonder he waited until he was dead to have his *Dialogues* published. In the 18th century, this would have been a very unpopular statement to make.

A major feature of the "Paley and Hume myth" to which I used to subscribe was that this criticism, in particular, was undeniably true. The conclusion of the DA is necessarily vague, and can't demonstrate the existence of any particular deity as described in any particular religious tradition.

Hume is at least partially right about this.

That's correct. Hume is right, in one very important (but limited) way. If someone uses the design argument, all by itself, and thinks she can produce a conclusion specific to a particular religious tradition, such a person is guilty of the very thing Hume is here criticizing.

1. Human artifacts (like watches) are products of intelligent design.
2. The universe resembles humanartifacts.
3. Therefore, Jesus is Lord.

Anyone who dares to present the design argument as above deserves Hume's criticism. The design argument can't produce that conclusion—it's simply not built to do so. However, even though Hume is right about the design argument not being capable of proving any particular religious tradition to be true, the design argument can still be seen as rather useful.

Suppose someone wants to convince an atheist friend that Jesus is, indeed, Lord. The design argument alone can't do it, but why accept the design argument all by itself? Suppose the design argument is effective in establishing its more modest conclusion: the universe is probably the product of intelligent (intentional) design. The atheist friend, if he or she has accepted the design argument, modest conclusion and all, has now accepted a *personal* explanation for the existence and properties of the universe. Atheism is now no longer an option. No particular religion has been established, but *something* "religious" is going to serve as the explanation for Nature. What's more, Paley argues that the DA, while not able to establish the specific truth of Christianity, is able to provide several features of the "designer" that facilitate the "matching strategy."

Chapter 24 of *Natural Theology* is dedicated to identifying features of the designer by means of conceptual analysis. Paley acknowledges the limitations of the DA, but claims:

"Nevertheless, if we be careful to imitate the documents of our religion, by confining our explanations to what concerns ourselves, and do not affect more precision in our ideas than the subject allows of, the several terms which are employed to denote the attributes of the Deity, may be made, even in natural religion, to bear a sense consistent with truth and reason, and not surpassing our comprehension.

These terms are; Omnipotence, omniscience, omnipresence, eternity, self-existence, necessary existence, spirituality."

To address each of those properties would be too much of a tangent, for the purposes of this one section of but one chapter of this book, so we'll consider just one, as it directly addresses Hume's claim that the DA is problematic because, in our experience, all "designers" are embodied—rather unlike the God of Christianity.

> *Contrivance, if established, appears to me to prove every thing which we wish to prove. Amongst other things, it proves the personality of the Deity, as distinguished from what is sometimes called nature, sometimes called a principle: which terms, in the mouths of those who use them philosophically, seem to be intended, to admit and to express an efficacy, but to exclude and to deny a personal agent. Now that which can contrive, which can design, must be a person. These capacities constitute personality, for they imply*

consciousness and thought. They require that which can perceive an end or purpose; as well as the power of providing means, and of directing them to their end. They require a centre in which perceptions unite, and from which volitions flow; which is mind. The acts of a mind prove the existence of a mind: and in whatever a mind resides, is a person. The seat of intellect is a person. We have no authority to limit the properties of mind to any particular corporeal form, or to any particular circumscription of space. These properties subsist, in created nature, under a great variety of sensible forms. Also every animated being has its sensorium, that is, a certain portion of space, within which perception and volition are exerted. This sphere may be enlarged to an indefinite extent; may comprehend the universe; and, being so imagined, may serve to furnish us with as good a notion, as we are capable of forming, of the immensity of the Divine Nature, i. e. of a Being, infinite, as well in essence as in power; yet nevertheless a person....of this however we are certain, that whatever the Deity be, neither the universe, nor any part of it which we see, can be He. The universe itself is merely a collective name: its parts are all which are real; or which are things. Now inert matter is out of the question: and organized substances include marks of contrivance. But whatever includes marks of contrivance, whatever, in its constitution, testifies design, necessarily carries us to something beyond itself, to some other being, to a designer prior to, and out of, itself. No animal, for instance, can have contrived its own limbs and senses; can have been the author to itself of the design with which they were constructed. That supposition involves all the absurdity of self-creation, i.e. of acting without existing. Nothing can be God, which is ordered by a wisdom and a will, which itself is void of; which is indebted for any of its properties to contrivance ab extra. The not having that in his nature which requires the exertion of another prior being (which property is sometimes called self-sufficiency, and sometimes self-comprehension), appertains to the Deity, as his essential distinction, and removes his nature from that of all things which we see. Which consideration contains the answer to a question that has sometimes been asked, namely, Why, since something or other must have existed from eternity, may not the present universe be that something? The contrivance perceived in it, proves that to be impossible. Nothing contrived, can, in a strict and proper sense, be eternal, forasmuch as the contriver must have existed before the contrivance.

Here, Paley argues that the DA establishes that the designer is a "person," because design implies consciousness and thought. Moreover, every *embodied* person is limited to "a certain portion of space, within which perception and volition are exerted," but the "volition" exhibited in the design of Nature is co-extensive with Nature itself, and not confined to any particular body. Nor can we identify the designer with the whole "body" (i.e., Nature) itself. "But whatever includes marks of contrivance, whatever, in its constitution, testifies design, necessarily carries us to something beyond itself, to some other being, to a designer prior to, and out of, itself." It is Nature that bears the marks of design, so something "beyond" Nature must be the source of that design. Since Nature exhausts the physical realm, the designer must be non-physical ("spiritual"), and a person.

How could we presume just one designer? "What shadow of an argument, continued Philo, can you produce, from your hypothesis, to prove the unity of the Deity?" In the chapter entitled "Of the Unity of the Deity," Paley addresses this specific question.[213]

> *Of the "Unity of the Deity," the proof is, the uniformity of plan observable in the universe. The universe itself is a system; each part either depending upon other parts, or being connected with other parts by some common law of motion, or by the presence of some common substance. One principle of gravitation causes a stone to drop towards the earth, and the moon to wheel round it. One law of attraction carries all the different planets about the sun....It may likewise be acknowledged, that no arguments which we are in possession of, exclude the ministry of subordinate agents. If such there be, they act under a presiding, a controlling will; because they act according to certain general restrictions, by certain common rules, and, as it should seem, upon a general plan: but still such agents, and different ranks, and classes, and degrees of them, may be employed.*

That Nature exhibits uniformity in its "design" (e.g., one law of gravitation throughout the whole known universe) is evidence, for Paley, of one source of design, as opposed to several. He admits that this does not rule out "intermediary agents" (a pantheon of divine agents? Angels? Devils?), but even in that case they appear to be under the direction of one, commanding will. Even if there are many members of a divine construction crew, there appears to be a single architect. . . .

Does the DA prove Christianity to be true, then? No. In that respect, at least, Hume is clearly right—but Paley concedes this fact, and readily acknowledges that revealed theology must take over where natural theology leaves off. The eager theist can now make use of other arguments to try to establish the truth of her own religion, specifically. The design argument can't succeed all by itself, but in the best of scenarios, it can open the door, or it could at least provide warrant (justification) for what the theist already believes.

Conclusion

All three arguments we considered have roots in ancient philosophy, as well as enjoying some contemporary adaptations. The DA and CA, in particular, have received contemporary "upgrades" and revision to keep pace with developing thought and emerging scientific understanding of the universe. While none of these arguments are likely to "prove" the existence of God, what they might accomplish is to increase justification of theistic belief, for those who find the arguments persuasive.

In our next chapter, we will turn to a very different kind of argument—one which claims that it is *unlikely* that God exists.

---

213 Still more evidence that Paley was well aware of Hume's criticism, and responsive to it.

St. Thomas Aquinas (1225 – 7 March 1274) was a Dominican priest and arguably the greatest theologian and philosopher the Catholic Church has ever produced. He is credited with incorporating Aristotle's philosophy into a Christian worldview (much as St. Augustine is credited with "Christianizing" Plato). This brief selection from his celebrated "Summa Theologica" includes his famous "five ways" (five arguments for God's existence). The first two arguments are variations of cosmological arguments, with one appealing to motion and the other to efficient causes. The third is a modal argument involving possibility and necessity. The fourth argument concerns "gradations" of qualities in things, and the implied ultimate source of qualities. Finally, he offers a teleological argument based on the seemingly "directed" features of Nature. Aside from the historical value of these arguments, they are important to consider in the context of contemporary philosophy of religion, as both cosmological and teleological arguments remain prominent, as are modal arguments to a lesser extent.

St. Thomas Aquinas
Summa Theologica
Treatise on The One God

Question 2: The Existence of God (Three Articles)

Whether God exists?

Objection 1: It seems that God does not exist; because if one of two contraries be infinite, the other would be altogether destroyed. But the word "God" means that He is infinite goodness. If, therefore, God existed, there would be no evil discoverable; but there is evil in the world. Therefore God does not exist.

Objection 2: Further, it is superfluous to suppose that what can be accounted for by a few principles has been produced by many. But it seems that everything we see in the world can be accounted for by other principles, supposing God did not exist. For all natural things can be reduced to one principle which is nature; and all voluntary things can be reduced to one principle which is human reason, or will. Therefore there is no need to suppose God's existence.

On the contrary, It is said in the person of God: "I am Who am."

I answer that, The existence of God can be proved in five ways.

The first and more manifest way is the argument from motion. It is certain, and evident to our senses, that in the world some things are in motion. Now whatever is in motion is put in motion by another, for nothing can be in motion except it is in potentiality to that towards which it is in motion; whereas a thing moves inasmuch as it is in act. For motion is nothing else than the reduction of something from potentiality to actuality. But nothing can be reduced from potentiality to actuality, except by something in a state of actuality. Thus that which is actually hot, as fire, makes wood, which is potentially hot, to be actually hot, and thereby moves and changes it. Now it is not possible that the same thing should be at once in actuality and potentiality in the same respect, but only in different respects. For what is actually hot cannot simultaneously be potentially hot; but it is simultaneously potentially cold. It is therefore impossible that in the same respect and in the same way a thing should be both mover and moved, i.e. that it should move itself. Therefore, whatever is in motion must be put in motion by another. If that by which it is put in motion be itself put in motion, then this also must needs be put in motion by another, and that by another again. But this cannot go on to infinity, because then there would be no first mover, and, consequently, no other mover; seeing that subsequent movers move only inasmuch as they are put in motion by the first mover; as the staff moves only because it is put in motion by the hand. Therefore it is necessary to arrive at a first mover, put in motion by no other; and this everyone understands to be God.

The second way is from the nature of the efficient cause. In the world of sense we find there is an order of efficient causes. There is no case known (neither is it, indeed, possible) in which a thing is found to be the efficient cause of itself; for so it would be prior to itself, which is impossible. Now in efficient causes it is not possible to go on to infinity, because in all efficient causes following in order, the first is the cause of the intermediate cause, and the intermediate is the cause of the ultimate cause, whether the intermediate cause be several, or only one. Now to take away the cause is to take away the effect. Therefore, if there be no first cause among efficient causes, there will be no ultimate, nor any intermediate cause. But if in efficient causes it is possible to go on to infinity, there will be no first efficient cause, neither will there be an ultimate effect, nor any intermediate efficient causes; all of which is plainly false. Therefore it is necessary to admit a first efficient cause, to which everyone gives the name of God.

The third way is taken from possibility and necessity, and runs thus. We find in nature things that are possible to be and not to be, since they are found to be generated, and to corrupt, and consequently, they are possible to be and not to be. But it is impossible for these always to exist, for that which is possible not to be at some time is not. Therefore, if everything is possible not to be, then at one time there could have been nothing in existence. Now if this were true, even now there would be nothing in existence, because that which does not exist only begins to exist by something already existing. Therefore, if at one time nothing was in existence, it would have been impossible for anything to have begun to exist; and thus even now nothing would be in existence---which is absurd. Therefore, not all beings are merely possible, but there must exist something the existence of which is necessary. But every necessary thing either has its necessity caused by another, or not. Now it is impossible to go on to infinity in necessary things which have their necessity caused by another, as has been already proved in regard to efficient causes. Therefore we cannot but postulate the existence of some being having of itself its own necessity, and not receiving it from another, but rather causing in others their necessity. This all men speak of as God.

The fourth way is taken from the gradation to be found in things. Among beings there are some more and some less good, true, noble and the like. But "more" and "less" are predicated of different things, according as they resemble in their different ways something which is the maximum, as a thing is said to be hotter according as it more nearly resembles that which is hottest; so that there is something which is truest, something best, something noblest and, consequently, something which is uttermost being; for those things that are greatest in truth are greatest in being, as it is written in Metaph. ii. Now the maximum in any genus is the cause of all in that genus; as fire, which is the maximum heat, is the cause of all hot things. Therefore there must also be something which is to all beings the cause of their being, goodness, and every other perfection; and this we call God.

The fifth way is taken from the governance of the world. We see that things which lack intelligence, such as natural bodies, act for an end, and this is evident from their acting always, or nearly always, in the same way, so as to obtain the best result. Hence it is plain that not fortuitously, but designedly, do they achieve their end. Now whatever lacks intelligence cannot move towards an end, unless it be directed by some being endowed with knowledge and intelligence; as the arrow is shot to its mark by the archer. Therefore some intelligent being exists by whom all natural things are directed to their end; and this being we call God.

Reply to Objection 1: As Augustine says (Enchiridion xi): "Since God is the highest good, He would not allow any evil to exist in His works, unless His omnipotence and goodness were such as to bring good even out of evil." This is part of the infinite goodness of God, that He should allow evil to exist, and out of it produce good.

Reply to Objection 2: Since nature works for a determinate end under the direction of a higher agent, whatever is done by nature must needs be traced back to God, as to its first cause. So also whatever is done voluntarily must also be traced back to some higher cause other than human reason or will, since these can change or fail; for all things that are changeable and capable of defect must be traced back to an immovable and self-necessary first principle, as was shown in the body of the Article.

William Paley (July 1743 – 25 May 1805) was an important philosopher and Christian apologist. This excerpt from his "Natural Theology" includes one of the most famous arguments for God's existence from the Western tradition. He begins with a thought experiment in which we find a watch. He concludes that we would confidently infer that the watch had a creator and was designed, based on its features, despite several possible objections to this reasoning that could be produced. The point of this thought experiment is clear when he delivers his analogy: Nature is like a watch. As such, conclusions we draw from watches (i.e., that they are designed), can be applied to Nature (i.e., that it is probably designed as well). While more contemporary design arguments focus on "fine-tuning," some analogical arguments still exist, and remind us of Paley's famous argument.

William Paley, D.D. Late Archdeacon of Carlisle *Natural Theology; Or, Evidences of the Existence and Attributes of the Deity. Collected from the Appearances of Nature.*

Chapter I. State of the Argument.

IN crossing a heath, suppose I pitched my foot against a *stone*, and were asked how the stone came to be there; I might possibly answer, that, for any thing I knew to the contrary, it had lain there for ever: nor would it perhaps be very easy to show the absurdity of this answer. But suppose I had found a *watch* upon the ground, and it should be inquired how the watch happened to be in that place; I should hardly think of the answer which I had before given, that, for any thing I knew, the watch might have always been there. Yet why should not this answer serve for the watch as well as for the stone? why is it not as admissible in the second case, as in the first? For this reason, and for no other, viz. that, when we come to inspect the watch, we perceive (what we could not discover in the stone) that its several parts are framed and put together for a purpose, *e. g.* that they are so formed and adjusted as to produce motion, and that motion so regulated as to point out the hour of the day; that, if the different parts had been differently shaped from what they are, of a different size from what they are, or placed after any other manner, or in any other order, than that in which they are placed, either no motion at all would have been carried on in the machine, or none which would have answered the use that is now served by it. To reckon up a few of the plainest of these parts, and of their offices, all tending to one result:-- We see a cylindrical box containing a coiled elastic spring, which, by its endeavour to relax itself, turns round the box. We next observe a flexible chain (artificially wrought for the sake of flexure), communicating the action of the spring from the box to the fusee. We then find a series of wheels, the teeth of which catch in, and apply to, each other, conducting the motion from the fusee to the balance, and from the balance to the pointer; and at the same time, by the size and shape of those wheels, so regulating that motion, as to terminate in causing an index, by an equable and measured progression, to pass over a given space in a given time. We take notice that the wheels are made of brass in order to keep them from rust; the springs of steel, no other metal being so elastic; that over the face of the watch there is placed a glass, a material employed in no other part of the work, but in the room of which, if there had been any other than a transparent substance, the hour could not be seen without opening the case. This mechanism being observed (it requires indeed an examination of the instrument, and perhaps some previous knowledge of the subject, to perceive and understand it; but being once, as we have said, observed and understood), the inference, we think, is inevitable, that the watch must have had a maker: that there must have existed, at some time, and at some place or other, an artificer or artificers who formed it for the purpose which we find it actually to answer; who comprehended its construction, and designed its use.

I. Nor would it, I apprehend, weaken the conclusion, that we had never seen a watch made; that we had never known an artist capable of making one; that we were altogether incapable of executing such a piece of workmanship ourselves, or of understanding in what manner it was performed; all this being no more than what is true of some exquisite remains of ancient art, of some lost arts, and, to the generality of mankind, of the more curious productions of modern manufacture. Does one man in a million know how oval frames are turned? Ignorance of this kind exalts our opinion of the unseen and unknown artist's skill, if he be unseen and unknown, but raises no doubt in our minds of the existence and agency of such an artist, at some former time, and in some place or other. Nor can I perceive that it varies at all the inference, whether the question arise concerning a human agent, or concerning an agent of a different species, or an agent possessing, in some respects, a different nature.

II. Neither, secondly, would it invalidate our conclusion, that the watch sometimes went wrong, or that it seldom went exactly right. The purpose of the machinery, the design, and the designer, might be evident, and in the case supposed would be evident, in whatever way we accounted for the irregularity of the movement, or whether we could account for it or not. It is not necessary that a machine be perfect, in order to show with what design it was made: still less necessary, where the only question is, whether it were made with any design at all.

III. Nor, thirdly, would it bring any uncertainty into the argument, if there were a few parts of the watch, concerning which we could not discover, or had not yet discovered, in what manner they conduced to the general effect; or even some parts, concerning which we could not ascertain, whether they conduced to that effect in any manner whatever. For, as to the first branch of the case; if by the loss, or disorder, or decay of the parts in question, the movement of the watch were found in fact to be stopped, or disturbed, or retarded, no doubt would remain in our minds as to the utility or intention of these parts, although we should be unable to investigate the manner according to which, or the connexion by which, the ultimate effect depended upon their action or assistance; and the more complex is the machine, the more likely is this obscurity to arise. Then, as to the second thing supposed, namely, that there were parts which might be spared, without prejudice to the movement of the watch, and that we had proved this by experiment,--these superfluous parts, even if we were completely assured that they were such, would not vacate the reasoning which we had instituted concerning other parts. The indication of contrivance remained, with respect to them, nearly as it was before.

IV. Nor, fourthly, would any man in his senses think the existence of the watch, with its various machinery, accounted for, by being told that it was one out of possible combinations of material forms; that whatever he had found in the place where he found the watch, must have contained some internal configuration or other; and that this configuration might be the structure now exhibited, viz. of the works of a watch, as well as a different structure.

V. Nor, fifthly, would it yield his inquiry more satisfaction to be answered, that there existed in things a principle of order, which had disposed the parts of the watch into their present form and situation. He never knew a watch made by the principle of order; nor can he even form to himself an idea of what is meant by a principle of order, distinct from the intelligence of the watch-maker.

VI. Sixthly, he would be surprised to hear that the mechanism of the watch was no proof of contrivance, only a motive to induce the mind to think so:

VII. And not less surprised to be informed, that the watch in his hand was nothing more than the result of the laws of *metallic* nature. It is a perversion of language to assign any law, as the efficient, operative cause of any thing. A law presupposes an agent; for it is only the mode, according to which an agent proceeds: it implies a power; for it is the order, according to which that power acts. Without this agent, without this power, which are both distinct from itself, the *law* does nothing; is nothing. The expression, "the law of metallic nature," may sound strange and harsh to a philosophic ear; but it seems quite as justifiable as some others which are more familiar to him, such as "the law of vegetable nature," "the law of animal nature," or indeed as "the law of nature" in general, when assigned as the cause of phænomena, in exclusion of agency and power; or when it is substituted into the place of these.

VIII. Neither, lastly, would our observer be driven out of his conclusion, or from his confidence in its truth, by being told that he knew nothing at all about the matter. He knows enough for his argument: he knows the utility of the end: he knows the subserviency and adaptation of the means to the end. These points being known, his ignorance of other points, his doubts concerning other points, affect not the certainty of his reasoning. The consciousness of knowing little, need not beget a distrust of that which he does know.

Chapter II. State of the Argument

SUPPOSE, in the next place, that the person who found the watch, should, after some time, discover that, in addition to all the properties which he had hitherto observed in it, it possessed the unexpected property of producing, in the course of its movement, another watch like itself (the thing is conceivable); that it contained within it a mechanism, a system of parts, a mould for instance, or a complex adjustment of lathes, files, and other tools, evidently and separately calculated for this purpose; let us inquire, what effect ought such a discovery to have upon his former conclusion.

I. The first effect would be to increase his admiration of the contrivance, and his conviction of the consummate skill of the contriver. Whether he regarded the object of the contrivance, the distinct apparatus, the intricate, yet in many parts intelligible mechanism, by which it was carried on, he would perceive, in this new observation, nothing but an additional reason for doing what he had already done,--for referring the construction of the watch to design, and to supreme art. If that construction *without* this property, or which is the same thing, before this property had been noticed, proved intention and art to have been employed about it; still more strong would the proof appear, when he came to the knowledge of this further property, the crown and perfection of all the rest.

II. He would reflect, that though the watch before him were, *in some sense*, the maker of the watch, which was fabricated in the course of its movements, yet it was in a very different sense from that, in which a carpenter, for instance, is the maker of a chair; the author of its contrivance, the cause of the relation of its parts to their use. With respect to these, the first watch was no cause at all to the second: in no such sense as this was it the author of the constitution and order, either of the parts which the new watch contained, or of the parts by the aid and instrumentality of which it was produced. We might possibly say, but with great latitude of expression, that a stream of water ground corn: but no latitude of expression would allow us to say, no stretch of conjecture could lead us to think, that the stream of water built the mill, though it were too ancient for us to know who the builder was. What the stream of water does in the affair, is neither more nor less than this; by the application of an unintelligent impulse to a mechanism previously arranged, arranged independently of it, and arranged by intelligence, an effect is produced, viz. the corn is ground. But the effect results from the arrangement. The force of the stream cannot be said to be the cause or author of the effect, still less of the arrangement. Understanding and plan in the formation of the mill were not the less necessary, for any share which the water has in grinding the corn: yet is this share the same, as that which the watch would have contributed to the production of the new watch, upon the supposition assumed in the last section. Therefore,

III. Though it be now no longer probable, that the individual watch, which our observer had found, was made immediately by the hand of an artificer, yet doth not this alteration in anywise affect the inference, that an artificer had been originally employed and concerned in the production. The argument from design remains as it was. Marks of design and contrivance are no more accounted for now, than they were before. In the same thing, we may ask for the cause of different properties. We may ask for the cause of the colour of a body, of its hardness, of its head; and these causes may be all different. We are now asking for the cause of that subserviency to a use, that relation to an end, which we have remarked in the watch before us. No answer is given to this question, by telling us that a preceding watch produced it. There cannot be design without a designer; contrivance without a contriver; order without choice; arrangement, without any thing capable of arranging; subserviency and relation to a purpose, without that which could intend a purpose; means suitable to an end, and executing their office, in accomplishing that end, without the end ever having been contemplated, or the means accommodated to it. Arrangement, disposition of parts, subserviency of means to an end, relation of instruments to a use, imply the presence of intelligence and mind. No one, therefore, can rationally believe, that the insensible, inanimate watch, from which the watch before us issued, was the proper cause of the mechanism we so much admire in it;--could be truly said to have constructed the instrument, disposed its parts, assigned their office, determined their order, action, and mutual dependency, combined their several motions into one result, and that also a result connected with the utilities of other beings. All these properties, therefore, are as much unaccounted for, as they were before.

IV. Nor is any thing gained by running the difficulty farther back, *i. e.* by supposing the watch before us to have been produced from another watch, that from a former, and so on indefinitely. Our going back ever so far, brings us no nearer to the least degree of satisfaction upon the subject. Contrivance is still unaccounted for. We still want a contriver. A designing mind is neither supplied by this supposition, nor dispensed with. If the difficulty were diminished the further we went back, by going back indefinitely we might exhaust it. And this is the only case to which this sort of reasoning applies. Where there is a tendency, or, as we increase the number of terms, a continual approach towards a limit, *there*, by supposing the number of terms to be what is called infinite, we may conceive the limit to be attained: but where there is no such tendency, or approach, nothing is effected by lengthening the series. There is no difference as to the point in question (whatever there may be as to many points), between one series and another; between a series which is finite, and a series which is infinite. A chain, composed of an infinite number of links, can no more support itself, than a chain composed of a finite number of links. And of this we are assured (though we never *can* have tried the experiment), because, by increasing the number of links, from ten for instance to a hundred, from a hundred to a thousand, &c. we make not the smallest approach, we observe not the smallest tendency, towards self-support. There is no difference in this respect (yet there may be a great difference in several respects) between a chain of a greater or less length, between one chain and another, between one that is finite and one that is infinite. This very much resembles the case before us. The machine which we are inspecting, demonstrates, by its construction, contrivance and design. Contrivance must have had a contriver; design, a designer; whether the machine immediately proceeded from another machine or not. That circumstance alters not the case. That other machine may, in like manner, have proceeded from a former machine: nor does that alter the case; contrivance must have had a contriver. That former one from one preceding it: no alteration still; a contriver is still necessary. No tendency is perceived, no approach towards a diminution of this necessity. It is the same with any and every succession of these machines; a succession of ten, of a hundred, of a thousand; with one series, as with another; a series which is finite, as with a series which is infinite. In whatever other respects they may differ, in this they do not. In all equally, contrivance and design are unaccounted for.

The question is not simply, How came the first watch into existence? which question, it may be pretended, is done away by supposing the series of watches thus produced from one another to have been infinite, and consequently to have had no-such *first*, for which it was necessary to provide a cause. This, perhaps, would have been nearly the state of the question, if no thing had been before us but an unorganized, unmechanized substance, without mark or indication of contrivance. It might be difficult to show that such substance could not have existed from eternity, either in succession (if it were possible, which I think it is not, for unorganized bodies to spring from one another), or by individual perpetuity. But that is not the question now. To suppose it to be so, is to suppose that it made no difference whether we had found a watch or a stone. As it is, the metaphysics of that question have no place; for, in the watch which we are examining, are seen contrivance, design; an end, a purpose; means for the end, adaptation to the purpose. And the question which irresistibly presses upon our thoughts, is, whence this contrivance and design? The thing required is the intending mind, the adapting hand, the intelligence by which that hand was directed. This question, this demand, is not shaken off, by increasing a number or succession of substances, destitute of these properties; nor the more, by increasing that number to infinity. If it be said, that, upon the supposition of one watch being produced from another in the course of that other's movements, and by means of the mechanism within it, we have a cause for the watch in my hand, viz. the watch from which it proceeded. I deny, that for the design, the contrivance, the suitableness of means to an end, the adaptation of instruments to a use (all which we discover in the watch), we have any cause whatever. It is in vain, therefore, to assign a series of such causes, or to allege that a series may be carried back to infinity; for I do not admit that we have yet any cause at all of the phænomena, still less any series of causes either finite or infinite. Here is contrivance, but no contriver; proofs of design, but no designer.

V. Our observer would further also reflect, that the maker of the watch before him, was, in truth and reality, the maker of every watch produced from it; there being no difference (except that the latter manifests a more exquisite skill) between the making of another watch with his own hands, by the mediation of files, lathes, chisels, &c. and the disposing, fixing, and inserting of these instruments, or of others equivalent to them, in the body of the watch already made in such a manner, as to form a new watch in the course of the movements which he had given to the old one. It is only working by one set of tools, instead of another.

The conclusion of which the *first* examination of the watch, of its works, construction, and movement, suggested, was, that it must have had, for the cause and author of that construction, an artificer, who understood its mechanism, and designed its use. This conclusion is invincible. A *second* examination presents us with a new discovery. The watch is found, in the course of its movement, to produce another watch, similar to itself; and not only so, but we perceive in it a system or organization, separately calculated for that purpose. What effect would this discovery have, or ought it to have, upon our former inference? What, as hath already been said, but to increase, beyond measure, our admiration of the skill, which had been employed in the formation of such a machine? Or shall it, instead of this, all at once turn us round to an opposite conclusion, viz. that no art or skill whatever has been concerned in the business, although all other evidences of art and skill remain as they were, and this last and supreme piece of art be now added to the rest? Can this be maintained without absurdity? Yet this is atheism.

Chapter III. Application of the Argument

THIS is atheism: for every indication of contrivance, every manifestation of design, which existed in the watch, exists in the works of nature; with the difference, on the side of nature, of being greater and more, and that in a degree which exceeds all computation. I mean that the contrivances of nature surpass the contrivances of art, in the complexity, subtility, and curiosity of the mechanism; and still more, if possible, do they go beyond them in number and variety; yet, in a multitude of cases, are not less evidently mechanical, not less evidently contrivances, not less evidently accommodated to their end, or suited to their office, than are the most perfect productions of human ingenuity.

I know no better method of introducing so large a subject, than that of comparing a single thing with a single thing; an eye, for example, with a telescope. As far as the examination of the instrument goes, there is precisely the same proof that the eye was made for vision, as there is that the telescope was made for assisting it. They are made upon the same principles; both being adjusted to the laws by which the transmission and refraction of rays of light are regulated. I speak not of the origin of the laws themselves; but such laws being fixed, the construction, in both cases, is adapted to them. For instance; these laws require, in order to produce the same effect, that the rays of light, in passing from water into the eye, should be refracted by a more convex surface, than when it passes out of air into the eye. Accordingly we find that the eye of a fish, in that part of it called the crystalline lens, is much rounder than the eye of terrestrial animals. What plainer manifestation of design can there be than this difference? What could a mathematical-instrument-maker have done more, to show his knowledge of his principle, his application of that knowledge, his suiting of his means to his end; I will not say to display the compass or excellence of his skill and art, for in these all comparison is indecorous, but to testify counsel, choice, consideration, purpose?...

Chapter VI. The Argument Cumulative.

WERE there no example in the world, of contrivance, except that of the *eye*, it would be alone sufficient to support the conclusion which we draw from it, as to the necessity of an intelligent Creator. It could never be got rid of; because it could not be accounted for by any other supposition, which did not contradict all the principles we possess of knowledge; the principles, according to which, things do, as often as they can be brought to the test of experience, turn out to be true or false. Its coats and humours, constructed, as the lenses of a telescope are constructed, for the refraction of rays of light to a point, which forms the proper action of the organ; the provision in its muscular tendons for turning its pupil to the object, similar to that which is given to the telescope by screws, and upon which power of direction in the eye, the exercise of its office as an optical instrument depends; the further provision for its defence, for its constant lubricity and moisture, which we see in its socket and its lids, in its gland for the secretion of the matter of tears, its outlet or communication with the nose for carrying off the liquid after the eye is washed with it; these provisions compose altogether an apparatus, a system of parts, a preparation of means, so manifest in their design, so exquisite in their contrivance, so successful in their issue, so precious, and so infinitely beneficial in their use, as, in my opinion, to bear down all doubt that can be raised upon the subject. And what I wish, under the title of the present chapter, to observe is, that if other parts of nature were inaccessible to our inquiries, or even if other parts of nature presented nothing to our examination but disorder and confusion, the validity of this example would remain the same. If there were but one watch in the world, it would not be less certain that it had a maker. If we had never in our lives seen any but one single kind of hydraulic machine, yet, if of that one kind we understood the mechanism and use, we should be as perfectly assured that it proceeded from the hand, and thought, and skill of a workman, as if we visited a museum of the arts, and saw collected there twenty different kinds of machines for drawing water, or a thousand different kinds for other purposes. Of this point, each machine is a proof, independently of all the rest. So it is with the evidences of a Divine agency. The proof is not a conclusion which lies at the end of a chain of reasoning, of which chain each instance of contrivance is only a link, and of which, if one link fail, the whole falls; but it is an argument separately supplied by every separate example. An error in stating an example, affects only that example. The argument is cumulative, in the fullest sense of that term. The eye proves it without the ear; the ear without the eye. The proof in each example is complete; for when the design of the part, and the conduciveness of its structure to that design is shown, the mind may set itself at rest; no future consideration can detract any thing from the force of the example....

Chapter XXIV. Of the Natural Attributes of the Deity

IT is an immense conclusion, that there is a GOD; a perceiving, intelligent, designing, Being; at the head of creation, and from whose will it proceeded. The *attributes* of such a Being, suppose his reality to be proved, must be adequate to the magnitude, extent, and multiplicity of his operations: which are not only vast beyond comparison with those performed by any other power, but, so far as respects our conceptions of them, infinite, because they are unlimited on all sides.

Yet the contemplation of a nature so exalted, however surely we arrive at the proof of its existence, overwhelms our faculties. The mind feels its powers sink under the subject. One consequence of which is, that from painful abstraction the thoughts seek relief in sensible images. Whence may be deduced the ancient, and almost universal propensity to idolatrous substitutions. They are the resources of a labouring imagination. False religions usually fall in with the natural propensity; true religions, or such as have derived themselves from the true, resist it.

It is one of the advantages of the revelations which we acknowledge, that, whilst they reject idolatry with its many pernicious accompaniments, they introduce the Deity to human apprehension, under an idea more personal, more determinate, more within its compass, than the theology of nature can do. And this they do by representing him exclusively under the relation in which he stands to ourselves; and, for the most part, under some precise character, resulting from that relation, or from the history of his providences. Which method suits the span of our intellects much better than the universality which enters into the idea of God, as deduced from the views of nature. When, therefore, these representations are well founded in point of authority (for all depends upon that), they afford a condescension to the state of our faculties, of which, they who have most reflected on the subject, will be the first to acknowledge the want and the value.

Nevertheless, if we be careful to imitate the documents of our religion, by confining our explanations to what concerns ourselves, and do not affect more precision in our ideas than the subject allows of, the several terms which are employed to denote the attributes of the Deity, may be made, even in natural religion, to bear a sense consistent with truth and reason, and not surpassing our comprehension.

These terms are; Omnipotence, omniscience, omnipresence, eternity, self-existence, necessary existence, spirituality.

"Omnipotence," "omniscience," "infinite" power, "infinite" knowledge, are *superlatives;* expressing our conception of these attributes in the strongest and most elevated terms which language supplies. We ascribe power to the Deity under the name of "omnipotence," the strict and correct conclusion being, that a power which could create such a world as this is, must be, beyond all comparison, greater than any which we experience in ourselves, than any which we observe in other visible agents; greater also than any which we can want, for our individual protection and preservation, in the Being upon whom we depend. It is a power, likewise, to which we are not authorized, by our observation or knowledge, to assign any limits of space or duration.

Very much of the same sort of remark is applicable to the term "omniscience," infinite knowledge, or infinite wisdom. In strictness of language, there is a difference between knowledge and wisdom; wisdom always supposing action, and action directed by it. With respect to the first, viz. *knowledge*, the Creator must know, intimately, the constitution and properties of the things which he created; which seems also to imply a foreknowledge of their action upon one another, and of their changes; at least, so far as the same result from trains of physical and necessary causes. His omniscience also, as far as respects things present, is deducible from his nature, as an intelligent being, joined with the extent, or rather the universality, of his operations. Where he acts, he is; and where he is, he perceives. The *wisdom* of the Deity, as testified in the works of creation, surpasses all idea we have of wisdom, drawn from the highest intellectual operations of the highest class of intelligent beings with whom we are acquainted; and, which is of the chief importance to us, whatever be its compass or extent, which it is evidently impossible that we should be able to determine, it must be adequate to the conduct of that order of things under which we live. And this is enough. It is of very inferior consequence, by what terms we express our notion, or rather our admiration, of this attribute. The terms, which the piety and the usage of language have rendered habitual to us, may be as proper as any other. We can trace this attribute much beyond what is necessary for any conclusion to which we have occasion to apply it. The degree of knowledge and power, requisite for the formation of created nature, cannot, with respect to us, be distinguished from infinite.

The Divine "omnipresence" stands, in natural theology, upon this foundation. In every part and place of the universe with which we are acquainted, we perceive the exertion of a power, which we believe, mediately or immediately, to proceed from the Deity. For instance; in what part or point of space, that has ever been explored, do we not discover attraction? In what regions do we not find light? In what accessible portion of our globe, do we not meet with gravity, magnetism, electricity; together with the properties also and powers of organized substances, of vegetable or of animated nature? Nay further, we may ask, What kingdom is there of nature, what corner of space, in which there is any thing that can be examined by us, where we do not fall upon contrivance and design? The only reflection perhaps which arises in our minds from this view of the world around us is, that the laws of nature every where prevail; that they are uniform and universal. But what do we mean by the laws of nature, or by any law? Effects are produced by power, not by laws. A law cannot execute itself. A law refers us to an agent. Now an agency so general, as that we cannot discover its absence, or assign the place in which some effect of its continued energy is not found, may, in popular language at least, and, perhaps, without much deviation from philosophical strictness, be called universal: and, with not quite the same, but with no inconsiderable propriety, the person, or Being, in whom that power resides, or from whom it is derived, may be taken to be *omnipresent*. He who upholds all things by his power, may be said to be every where present.

This is called a virtual presence. There is also what metaphysicians denominate an essential ubiquity; and which idea the language of Scripture seems to favour: but the former, I think, goes as far as natural theology carries us.

"Eternity" is a negative idea, clothed with a positive name. It supposes, in that to which it is applied, a present existence; and is the negation of a beginning or an end of that existence. As applied to the Deity, it has not been controverted by those who acknowledge a Deity at all. Most assuredly, there never was a time in which nothing existed, because that condition must have continued. The universal *blank* must have remained; nothing could rise up out of it; nothing could ever have existed since; nothing could exist now. In strictness, however, we have no concern with duration prior to that of the visible world. Upon this article therefore of theology, it is sufficient to know, that the contriver necessarily existed before the contrivance.

"Self-existence" is another negative idea, *viz.* the negation of a preceding cause, as of a progenitor, a maker, an author, a creator.

"Necessary existence" means demonstrable existence.

"Spirituality" expresses an idea, made up of a negative part, and of a positive part. The negative part consists in the exclusion of some of the known properties of matter, especially of solidity, of the *vis inertiæ*, and of gravitation. The positive part comprises perception, thought, will, power, *action*, by which last term is meant, the origination of motion; the quality, perhaps, in which resides the essential superiority of spirit over matter, "which cannot move, unless it be moved; and cannot but move, when impelled by another (*Note:* Bishop Wilkins's Principles of Natural Religion, p. 106.)." I apprehend that there can be no difficulty in applying to the Deity both parts of this idea.

Chapter XXV. The Unity of the Deity.

OF the "Unity of the Deity," the proof is, the *uniformity* of plan observable in the universe. The universe itself is a system; each part either depending upon other parts, or being connected with other parts by some common law of motion, or by the presence of some common substance. One principle of gravitation causes a stone to drop towards the earth, and the moon to wheel round it. One law of attraction carries all the different planets about the sun. This philosophers demonstrate. There are also other points of agreement amongst them, which may be considered as marks of the identity of their origin, and of their intelligent author. In all are found the conveniency and stability derived from gravitation. They all experience vicissitudes of days and nights, and changes of season. They all, at least Jupiter, Mars, and Venus, have the same advantages from their atmosphere as we have. In all the planets, the axes of rotation are permanent. Nothing is more probable than that the same attracting influence, acting according to the same rule, reaches to the fixed stars: but, if this be only probable, another thing is certain, *viz.* that the same element of light does. The light from a fixed star affects our eyes in the same manner, is refracted and reflected according to the same laws, as the light of a candle. The velocity of the light of the fixed stars is also the same, as the velocity of the light of the sun, reflected from the satellites of Jupiter. The heat of the sun, in kind, differs nothing from the heat of a coal fire.

In our own globe, the case is clearer. New countries are continually discovered, but the old laws of nature are always found in them: new plants perhaps, or animals, but always in company with plants and animals which we already know; and always possessing many of the same general properties. We never get amongst such original, or totally different, modes of existence, as to indicate, that we are come into the province of a different Creator, or under the direction of a different will. In truth, the same order of things attend us, wherever we go. The elements act upon one another, electricity operates, the tides rise and fall, the magnetic needle elects its position, in one region of the earth and sea, as well as in another. One atmosphere invests all parts of the globe, and connects all; one sun illuminates; one moon exerts its specific attraction upon all parts. If there be a variety in natural effects, as, *e. g.* in the tides of different seas, that very variety is the result of the same cause, acting under different circumstances. In many cases this is proved; in all, is probable.

The inspection and comparison of *living* forms, add to this argument examples without number. Of all large terrestrial animals, the structure is very much alike; their senses nearly the same; their natural functions and passions nearly the same; their viscera nearly the same, both in substance, shape, and office: digestion, nutrition, circulation, secretion, go on, in a similar manner, in all: the great circulating fluid is the same; for, I think, no difference has been discovered in the properties of *blood*, from whatever animal it be drawn. The experiment of transfusion proves, that the blood of one animal will serve for another. The *skeletons* also of the larger terrestrial animals, show particular varieties, but still under a great general affinity. The resemblance is somewhat less, yet sufficiently evident, between quadrupeds and birds. They are all alike in five respects, for one in which they differ.

In *fish*, which belong to another department, as it were, of nature, the points of comparison become fewer. But we never lose sight of our analogy, *e. g.* we still meet with a stomach, a liver, a spine; with bile and blood; with teeth; with eyes (which eyes are only slightly varied from our own, and which variation, in truth, demonstrates, not an interruption, but a continuance of the same exquisite plan; for it is the adaptation of the organ to the element, *viz.* to the different refraction of light passing into the eye out of a denser medium). The provinces, also, themselves of water and earth, are connected by the species of animals which inhabit both; and also by a large tribe of aquatic animals, which closely resemble the terrestrial in their internal structure; I mean the cetaceous tribe, which have hot blood, respiring lungs, bowels, and other essential parts, like those of land-animals. This similitude, surely, bespeaks the same creation and the same Creator.

Insects and *shell-fish* appear to me to differ from other classes of animals the most widely of any. Yet even here, beside many points of particular resemblance, there exists a general relation of a peculiar kind. It is the relation of inversion; the law of contrariety: namely, that, whereas, in other animals, the bones, to which the muscles are attached, lie *within* the body; in insects and shell-fish, they lie on the *outside* of it. The shell of a lobster performs to the animal the office of a *bone*, by furnishing to the tendons that fixed basis or immoveable fulcrum, without which, mechanically, they could not act. The crust of an insect is its shell, and answers the like purpose. The shell also of an oister stands in the place of a *bone;* the bases of the muscles being fixed to it, in the same manner, as, in other animals, they are fixed to the bones. All which (under wonderful varieties, indeed, and adaptations of form) confesses an imitation, a remembrance, a carrying on, of the same plan.

The observations here made, are equally applicable to plants; but, I think, unnecessary to be pursued. It is a very striking circumstance, and alone sufficient to prove all which we contend for, that, in this part likewise of organized nature, we perceive a continuation of the *sexual* system.

Certain however it is, that the whole argument for the divine unity, goes no further than to a unity of counsel.

It may likewise be acknowledged, that no arguments which we are in possession of, exclude the ministry of subordinate agents. If such there be, they act under a presiding, a controlling will; because they act according to certain general restrictions, by certain common rules, and, as it should seem, upon a general plan: but still such agents, and different ranks, and classes, and degrees of them, may be employed.

Chapter XXVI. The Goodness of the Deity....[214]

Chapter XXVII. Conclusion.

IN all cases, wherein the mind feels itself in danger of being confounded by variety, it is sure to rest upon a few strong points, or perhaps upon a single instance. Amongst a multitude of proofs, it is *one* that does the business. If we observe in any argument, that hardly two minds fix upon the same instance, the diversity of choice shows the strength of the argument, because it shows the number and competition of the examples. There is no subject in which the tendency to dwell upon select or single topics is so usual because there is no subject, of which, in its full extent, the latitude is so great, as that of natural history applied to the proof of an intelligent Creator. For my part, I take my stand in human anatomy: and the examples of mechanism I should be apt to draw out from the copious catalogue, which it supplies, are the pivot upon which the head turns, the ligament within the socket of the hip-joint, the pulley or trochlear muscles of the eye, the epiglottis, the bandages which tie down the tendons of the wrist and instep, the slit or perforated muscles at the hands and feet, the knitting of the intestines to the mesentery, the course of the chyle into the blood, and the constitution of the sexes as extended throughout the whole of the animal creation. To these instances, the reader's memory will go back, as they are severally set forth in their places; there is not one of the number which I do not think decisive; not one which is not strictly mechanical; nor have I read or heard of any solution of these appearances, which, in the smallest degree, shakes the conclusion that we build upon them.

But, of the greatest part of those, who, either in this book or any other, read arguments to prove the existence of a God, it will be said, that they leave off only where they began; that they were never ignorant of this great truth, never doubted

[214] Reader's note: this section appears at the end of the next chapter in this book.

of it; that it does not therefore appear, what is gained by researches from which no new opinion is learnt, and upon the subject of which no proofs were wanted. Now I answer that, by *investigation*, the following points are always gained, in favour of doctrines even the most generally acknowledged, (supposing them to be true), *viz.* stability and impression. Occasions will arise to try the firmness of our most habitual opinions. And upon these occasions, it is a matter of incalculable use to feel our foundation; to find a support in argument for what we had taken up upon authority. In the present case, the arguments upon which the conclusion rests, are exactly such, as a truth of universal concern ought to rest upon. "They are sufficiently open to the views and capacities of the unlearned, at the same time that they acquire new strength and lustre from the discoveries of the learned." If they had been altogether abstruse and recondite, they would not have found their way to the understandings of the mass of mankind; if they had been merely popular, they might have wanted solidity.

But, secondly, what is gained by research in the stability of our conclusion, is also gained from it in *impression*. Physicians tell us, that there is a great deal of difference between taking a medicine, and the medicine getting into the constitution. A difference not unlike which, obtains with respect to those great moral propositions, which ought to form the directing principles of human conduct. It is one thing to assent to a proposition of this sort; another, and a very different thing, to have properly imbibed its influence. I take the case to be this: perhaps almost every man living has a particular train of thought, into which his mind glides and falls, when at leisure from the impressions and ideas that occasionally excite it; perhaps, also, the train of thought here spoken of, more than any other thing, determines the character. It is of the utmost consequence, therefore, that this property of our constitution be well regulated. Now it is by frequent or continued meditation upon a subject, by placing a subject in different points of view, by induction of particulars, by variety of examples, by applying principles to the solution of phænomena, by dwelling upon proofs and consequences, that mental exercise is drawn into any particular channel. It is by these means, at least, that we have any power over it. The train of spontaneous thought, and the choice of that train, may be directed to different ends, and may appear to be more or less judiciously fixed, according to the purpose, in respect of which we consider it: but, in a *moral view*, I shall not, I believe, be contradicted when I say, that, if one train of thinking be more desirable than another, it is that which regards the phænomena of nature with a constant reference to a supreme intelligent Author. To have made this the ruling, the habitual sentiment of our minds, is to have laid the foundation of every thing which is religious. The world thenceforth becomes a temple, and life itself one continued act of adoration. The change is no less than this, that, whereas formerly God was seldom in our thoughts, we can now scarcely look upon any thing without perceiving its relation to him. Every organized natural body, in the provisions which it contains for its sustentation and propagation, testifies a care, on the part of the Creator, expressly directed to these purposes. We are on all sides surrounded by such bodies; examined in their parts, wonderfully curious; compared with one another, no less wonderfully diversified. So that the mind, as well as the eye, may either expatiate in variety and multitude, or fix itself down to the investigation of particular divisions of the science. And in either case it will rise up from its occupation, possessed by the subject, in a very different manner, and with a very different degree of influence, from what a mere assent to any verbal proposition which can be formed concerning the existence of the Deity, at least that merely complying assent with which those about us are satisfied, and with which we are too apt to satisfy ourselves, will or can produce upon the thoughts. More especially may this difference be perceived, in the degree of admiration and of awe, with which the Divinity is regarded, when represented to the understanding by its own remarks, its own reflections, and its own reasonings, compared with what is excited by any language that can be used by others. The works of nature want only to be contemplated. When contemplated, they have every thing in them which can astonish by their greatness: for, of the vast scale of operation, through which our discoveries carry us, at one end we see an intelligent Power arranging planetary systems, fixing, for instance, the trajectory of *Saturn*, or constructing a ring of two hundred thousand miles diameter, to surround his body, and be suspended like a magnificent arch over the heads of his inhabitants; and, at the other, bending a hooked tooth, concerting and providing an appropriate mechanism, for the clasping and reclasping of the filaments of the feather of the humming-bird. We have proof, not only of both these works proceeding from an intelligent agent, but of their proceeding from the same agent; for, in the first place, we can trace an identity of plan, a connexion of system, from Saturn to our own globe: and when arrived upon our globe, we can, in the second place, pursue the connexion through all the organized, especially the animated, bodies which it supports. We can observe marks of a common relation, as well to one another, as to the elements of which their habitation is composed. Therefore one mind hath planned, or at least hath prescribed, a general plan for all these productions. One Being has been concerned in all.

Under this stupendous Being we live. Our happiness, our existence, is in his hands. All we expect must come from him. Nor ought we to feel our situation insecure. In every nature, and in every portion of nature, which we can descry, we find attention bestowed upon even the minutest arts. The hinges in the wings of an *earwig*, and the joints of its antennæ, are as highly wrought, as if the Creator had nothing else to finish. We see no signs or diminution of care by multiplicity of objects, or of distraction of thought by variety. We have no reason to fear, therefore, our being forgotten, or overlooked, or neglected.

The existence and character of the Deity, is, in every view, the most interesting of all human speculations. In none, however, is it more so, than as it facilitates the belief of the fundamental articles of *Revelation.* It is a step to have it proved, that there must be something in the world more than what we see. It is a further step to know, that, amongst the invisible things of nature, there must be an intelligent mind, concerned in its production, order, and support. These points being assured to us by Natural Theology, we may well leave to Revelation the disclosure of many particulars, which our researches cannot reach, respecting either the nature of this Being as the original cause of all things, or his character and designs as a moral governor; and not only so, but the more full confirmation of other particulars, of which, though they do not lie altogether beyond our reasonings and our probabilities, the certainty is by no means equal to the importance. The true theist will be the first to listen to *any* credible communication of Divine knowledge. Nothing which he has learned from Natural Theology, will diminish his desire of further instruction, or his disposition to receive it with humility and thankfulness. He wishes for light: he rejoices in light. His inward veneration of this great Being, will incline him to attend with the utmost seriousness, not only to all that can be discovered concerning him by researches into nature, but to all that is taught by a revelation, which gives reasonable proof of having proceeded from him.

But, above every other article of revealed religion, does the anterior belief of a Deity bear with the strongest force upon that grand point, which gives indeed interest and importance to all the rest,--the resurrection of the human dead. The thing might appear hopeless, did we not see a power at work adequate to the effect, a power under the guidance of an intelligent will, and a power penetrating the inmost recesses of all substance. I am far from justifying the opinion of those, who "thought it a thing incredible, that God should raise the dead:" but I admit, that it is first necessary to be persuaded, that there *is* a God, to do so. This being thoroughly settled in our minds, there seems to be nothing in this process (concealed as we confess it to be) which need to shock our belief. They who have taken up the opinion, that the acts of the human mind depend upon *organization*, that the mind itself indeed consists in organization, are supposed to find a greater difficulty than others do, in admitting a transition by death to a new state of sentient existence, because the old organization is apparently dissolved. But I do not see that any impracticability need be apprehended even by these; or that the change, even upon their hypothesis, is far removed from the analogy of some other operations, which we know with certainty that the Deity is carrying on. In the ordinary derivation of plants and animals, from one another, a particle, in many cases, minuter than all assignable, all conceivable dimension; an aura, an effluvium, an infinitesimal; determines the organization of a future body: does no less than fix, whether that which is about to be produced, shall be a vegetable, a merely sentient, or a rational being: an oak, a frog, or a philosopher; makes all these differences; gives to the future body its qualities, and nature and species. And this particle, from which springs, and by which is determined a whole future nature, itself proceeds from, and owes its constitution to, a prior body: nevertheless, which is seen in plants most decisively, the incepted organization, though formed within, and through, and by a preceding organization, is not corrupted by its corruption, or destroyed by its dissolution: but, on the contrary, is sometimes extricated and developed by those very causes; survives and comes into action, when the purpose, for which it was prepared, requires its use. Now an œconomy which nature has adopted, when the purpose was to transfer an organization from one individual to another, may have something analogous to it, when the purpose is to transmit an organization from one state of being to another state: and they who found thought in organization, may see something in this analogy applicable to their difficulties; for, whatever can transmit a similarity of organization will answer their purpose, because, according even to their own theory, it may be the vehicle of consciousness, and because consciousness carries identity and individuality along with it through all changes of form or of visible qualities. In the most general case, that, as we have said, of the derivation of plants and animals from one another, the latent organization is either itself similar to the old organization, or has the power of communicating to new matter the old organic form. But it is not restricted to this rule. There are other cases, especially in the progress of insect life, in which the dormant organization does not much resemble that which encloses it, and still less suits with the situation in which the enclosing body is placed, but suits with a different situation to which it is destined. In the larva of the libellula, which lives constantly, and has still long to live, under water, are descried the wings of a fly, which two years afterwards is to mount into the air. Is there nothing in this analogy? It serves at least to show, that even in the observable course of nature, organizations are formed one beneath another; and, amongst a thousand other instances, it shows completely, that the Deity can mould and fashion the parts of material nature, so as to fulfil any purpose whatever which he is pleased to appoint.

They who refer the operations of mind to a substance totally and essentially different from matter, (as most certainly these operations, though affected by material causes, hold very little affinity to any properties of matter with which we are acquainted), adopt perhaps a juster reasoning and a better philosophy: and by these the considerations above suggested are not wanted, at least in the same degree. But to such as find, which some persons do find, an insuperable difficulty in shaking off an adherence to those analogies, which the corporeal world is continually suggesting to their thoughts; to such, I say, every consideration will be a relief, which manifests the extent of that intelligent power which is acting in nature, the fruitfulness of its resources, the variety, and aptness, and success of its means; most especially every consideration, which tends to show that, in the translation of a conscious existence, there is not, even in their own way of regarding it, any thing greatly beyond, or totally unlike, what takes place in such parts (probably small parts) of the order of nature, as are accessible to our observation.

Again; if there be those who think, that the contractedness and debility of the human faculties in our present state, seem ill to accord with the high destinies which the expectations of religion point out to us, I would only ask them, whether any one, who saw a child two hours after its birth, could suppose that it would ever come to understand *fluxions* (*Note:* See Search's Light of Nature, *passim.*); or who then shall say, what farther amplification of intellectual powers, what accession of knowledge, what advance and improvement, the rational faculty, be its constitution what it will, may not admit of, when placed amidst new objects, and endowed with a sensorium adapted, as it undoubtedly will be, and as our present senses are, to the perception of those substances, and of those properties of things, with which our concern may lie.

Upon the whole; in every thing which respects this awful, but, as we trust, glorious change, we have a wise and powerful Being, (the author, in nature, of infinitely various expedients for infinitely various ends), upon whom to rely for the choice and appointment of means, adequate to the execution of any plan which his goodness or his justice may have formed, for the moral and accountable part of his terrestrial creation. That great office rests with *him:* be it *ours* to hope and to prepare, under a firm and settled persuasion, that, living and dying, we are his; that life is passed in his constant presence, that death resigns us to his merciful disposal.

FINIS.

This is the same David Hume already employed for his argument for compatibilism in an earlier chapter of this book. Among other things, Hume was a consistent and serious skeptic with regard to the claims of religion. His Dialogues Concerning Natural Religion provides a critique of numerous arguments for God's existence, and the reliability of miracle testimony, among other things. The work was not published until after his death. The "Dialogues" features three characters: Demea, Cleanthes, and Philo. In our excerpt, Cleanthes offers a version of the design argument (by analogy) similar to the one Paley will provide several decades later. Philo then begins a systematic criticism of this argument, questioning the analogy itself, the sample on which it is based, and the scope and specificity of its conclusion even in the unlikely event that the argument survives the other criticisms. For these reasons, and others, Hume is often regarded as a philosophical mentor to those advocating skeptical philosophy in general, or agnosticism with regard to theism in particular.

David Hume
Dialogues Concerning Natural Religion

Treatise on The One God - Part II

...Not to lose any time in circumlocutions, said Cleanthes, addressing himself to Demea, much less in replying to the pious declamations of Philo; I shall briefly explain how I conceive this matter. Look round the world: contemplate the whole and every part of it: you will find it to be nothing but one great machine, subdivided into an infinite number of lesser machines, which again admit of subdivisions to a degree beyond what human senses and faculties can trace and explain. All these various machines, and even their most minute parts, are adjusted to each other with an accuracy which ravishes into admiration all men who have ever contemplated them. The curious adapting of means to ends, throughout all nature, resembles exactly, though it much exceeds, the productions of human contrivance; of human designs, thought, wisdom, and intelligence. Since, therefore, the effects resemble each other, we are led to infer, by all the rules of analogy, that the causes also resemble; and that the Author of Nature is somewhat similar to the mind of man, though possessed of much larger faculties, proportioned to the grandeur of the work which he has executed. By this argument a posteriori, and by this argument alone, do we prove at once the existence of a Deity, and his similarity to human mind and intelligence.

I shall be so free, Cleanthes, said Demea, as to tell you, that from the beginning, I could not approve of your conclusion concerning the similarity of the Deity to men; still less can I approve of the mediums by which you endeavour to establish it. What! No demonstration of the Being of God! No abstract arguments! No proofs a priori! Are these, which have hitherto been so much insisted on by philosophers, all fallacy, all sophism? Can we reach no further in this subject than experience and probability? I will not say that this is betraying the cause of a Deity: but surely, by this affected candour, you give advantages to Atheists, which they never could obtain by the mere dint of argument and reasoning.

What I chiefly scruple in this subject, said Philo, is not so much that all religious arguments are by Cleanthes reduced to experience, as that they appear not to be even the most certain and irrefragable of that inferior kind. That a stone will fall, that fire will burn, that the earth has solidity, we have observed a thousand and a thousand times; and when any new instance of this nature is presented, we draw without hesitation the accustomed inference. The exact similarity of the cases gives us a perfect assurance of a similar event; and a stronger evidence is never desired nor sought after. But wherever you depart, in the least, from the similarity of the cases, you diminish proportionably the evidence; and may at last bring it to a very weak analogy, which is confessedly liable to error and uncertainty. After having experienced the circulation of the blood in human creatures, we make no doubt that it takes place in Titius and Maevius. But from its circulation in frogs and fishes, it is only a presumption, though a strong one, from analogy, that it takes place in men and other animals. The analogical reasoning is much weaker, when we infer the circulation of the sap in vegetables from our experience that the blood circulates in animals; and those, who hastily followed that imperfect analogy, are found, by more accurate experiments, to have been mistaken.

If we see a house, Cleanthes, we conclude, with the greatest certainty, that it had an architect or builder; because this is precisely that species of effect which we have experienced to proceed from that species of cause. But surely you will not affirm, that the universe bears such a resemblance to a house that we can with the same certainty infer a similar cause, or that the analogy is here entire and perfect. The dissimilitude is so striking, that the utmost you can here pretend to is a guess, a conjecture, a presumption concerning a similar cause; and how that pretension will be received in the world, I leave you to consider.

It would surely be very ill received, replied Cleanthes; and I should be deservedly blamed and detested, did I allow, that the proofs of a Deity amounted to no more than a guess or conjecture. But is the whole adjustment of means to ends in a house and in the universe so slight a resemblance? The economy of final causes? The order, proportion, and arrangement of every part? Steps of a stair are plainly contrived, that human legs may use them in mounting; and this inference is certain and infallible. Human legs are also contrived for walking and mounting; and this inference, I allow, is not altogether so certain, because of the dissimilarity which you remark; but does it, therefore, deserve the name only of presumption or conjecture?

Good God! cried Demea, interrupting him, where are we? Zealous defenders of religion allow, that the proofs of a Deity fall short of perfect evidence! And you, Philo, on whose assistance I depended in proving the adorable mysteriousness of the Divine Nature, do you assent to all these extravagant opinions of Cleanthes? For what other name can I give them? or, why spare my censure, when such principles are advanced, supported by such an authority, before so young a man as Pamphilus?

You seem not to apprehend, replied Philo, that I argue with Cleanthes in his own way; and, by shewing him the dangerous consequences of his tenets, hope at last to reduce him to our opinion. But what sticks most with you, I observe, is the representation which Cleanthes has made of the argument a posteriori; and finding that that argument is likely to escape your hold and vanish into air, you think it so disguised, that you can scarcely believe it to be set in its true light. Now, however much I may dissent, in other respects, from the dangerous principles of Cleanthes, I must allow that he has fairly represented that argument; and I shall endeavour so to state the matter to you, that you will entertain no further scruples with regard to it.

Were a man to abstract from every thing which he knows or has seen, he would be altogether incapable, merely from his own ideas, to determine what kind of scene the universe must be, or to give the preference to one state or situation of things above another. For as nothing which he clearly conceives could be esteemed impossible or implying a contradiction, every chimera of his fancy would be upon an equal footing; nor could he assign any just reason why he adheres to one idea or system, and rejects the others which are equally possible.

Again; after he opens his eyes, and contemplates the world as it really is, it would be impossible for him at first to assign the cause of any one event, much less of the whole of things, or of the universe. He might set his fancy a rambling; and she might bring him in an infinite variety of reports and representations. These would all be possible; but being all equally possible, he would never of himself give a satisfactory account for his preferring one of them to the rest. Experience alone can point out to him the true cause of any phenomenon.

Now, according to this method of reasoning,

Demea, it follows, (and is, indeed, tacitly allowed by Cleanthes himself,) that order, arrangement, or the adjustment of final causes, is not of itself any proof of design; but only so far as it has been experienced to proceed from that principle. For ought we can know a priori, matter may contain the source or spring of order originally within itself as well as mind does; and there is no more difficulty in conceiving, that the several elements, from an internal unknown cause, may fall into the most exquisite arrangement, than to conceive that their ideas, in the great universal mind, from a like internal unknown cause, fall into that arrangement. The equal possibility of both these suppositions is allowed. But, by experience, we find, (according to Cleanthes,) that there is a difference between them. Throw several pieces of steel together, without shape or form; they will never arrange themselves so as to compose a watch. Stone, and mortar, and wood, without an architect, never erect a house. But the ideas in a human mind, we see, by an unknown, inexplicable economy, arrange themselves so as to form the plan of a watch or house. Experience, therefore, proves, that there is an original principle of order in mind, not in matter. From similar effects we infer similar causes. The adjustment of means to ends is alike in the universe, as in a machine of human contrivance. The causes, therefore, must be resembling.

I was from the beginning scandalized, I must own, with this resemblance, which is asserted, between the Deity and human creatures; and must conceive it to imply such a degradation of the Supreme Being as no sound Theist could endure. With your assistance, therefore, Demea, I shall endeavour to defend what you justly call the adorable mysteriousness of the Divine Nature, and shall refute this reasoning of Cleanthes, provided he allows that I have made a fair representation of it.

When Cleanthes had assented, Philo, after a short pause, proceeded in the following manner.

That all inferences, Cleanthes, concerning fact, are founded on experience; and that all experimental reasonings are founded on the supposition that similar causes prove similar effects, and similar effects similar causes; I shall not at present much dispute with you. But observe, I entreat you, with what extreme caution all just reasoners proceed in the transferring of experiments to similar cases. Unless the cases be exactly similar, they repose no perfect confidence in applying their past observation to any particular phenomenon. Every alteration of circumstances occasions a doubt concerning the event; and it requires new experiments to prove certainly, that the new circumstances are of no moment or importance. A change in bulk, situation, arrangement, age, disposition of the air, or surrounding bodies; any of these particulars may be attended with the most unexpected consequences: and unless the objects be quite familiar to us, it is the highest temerity to expect with assurance, after any of these changes, an event similar to that which before fell under our observation. The slow and deliberate steps of philosophers here, if any where, are distinguished from the precipitate march of the vulgar, who, hurried on by the smallest similitude, are incapable of all discernment or consideration.

But can you think, Cleanthes, that your usual phlegm and philosophy have been preserved in so wide a step as you have taken, when you compared to the universe houses, ships, furniture, machines, and, from their similarity in some circumstances, inferred a similarity in their causes? Thought, design, intelligence, such as we discover in men and other animals, is no more than one of the springs and principles of the universe, as well as heat or cold, attraction or repulsion, and a hundred others, which fall under daily observation. It is an active cause, by which some particular parts of nature, we find, produce alterations on other parts. But can a conclusion, with any propriety, be transferred from parts to the whole? Does not the great disproportion bar all comparison and inference? From observing the growth of a hair, can we learn any thing concerning the generation of a man? Would the manner of a leaf's blowing, even though perfectly known, afford us any instruction concerning the vegetation of a tree?

But, allowing that we were to take the

operations of one part of nature upon another, for the foundation of our judgment concerning the origin of the whole, (which never can be admitted,) yet why select so minute, so weak, so bounded a principle, as the reason and design of animals is found to be upon this planet? What peculiar privilege has this little agitation of the brain which we call thought, that we must thus make it the model of the whole universe? Our partiality in our own favour does indeed present it on all occasions; but sound philosophy ought carefully to guard against so natural an illusion.

So far from admitting, continued Philo, that the operations of a part can afford us any just conclusion concerning the origin of the whole, I will not allow any one part to form a rule for another part, if the latter be very remote from the former. Is there any reasonable ground to conclude, that the inhabitants of other planets possess thought, intelligence, reason, or any thing similar to these faculties in men? When nature has so extremely diversified her manner of operation in this small globe, can we imagine that she incessantly copies herself throughout so immense a universe? And if thought, as we may well suppose, be confined merely to this narrow corner, and has even there so limited a sphere of action, with what propriety can we assign it for the original cause of all things? The narrow views of a peasant, who makes his domestic economy the rule for the government of kingdoms, is in comparison a pardonable sophism.

But were we ever so much assured, that a thought and reason, resembling the human, were to be found throughout the whole universe, and were its activity elsewhere vastly greater and more commanding than it appears in this globe; yet I cannot see, why the operations of a world constituted, arranged, adjusted, can with any propriety be extended to a world which is in its embryo state, and is advancing towards that constitution and arrangement. By observation, we know somewhat of the economy, action, and nourishment of a finished animal; but we must transfer with great caution that observation to the growth of a foetus in the womb, and still more in the formation of an animalcule in the loins of its male parent. Nature, we find, even from our limited experience, possesses an infinite number of springs and principles, which incessantly discover themselves on every change of her position and situation. And what new and unknown principles would actuate her in so new and unknown a situation as that of the formation of a universe, we cannot, without the utmost temerity, pretend to determine.

A very small part of this great system, during a very short time, is very imperfectly discovered to us; and do we then pronounce decisively concerning the origin of the whole?

Admirable conclusion! Stone, wood, brick, iron, brass, have not, at this time, in this minute globe of earth, an order or arrangement without human art and contrivance; therefore the universe could not originally attain its order and arrangement, without something similar to human art.

But is a part of nature a rule for another part very wide of the former? Is it a rule for the whole? Is a very small part a rule for the universe? Is nature in one situation, a certain rule for nature in another situation vastly different from the former?

And can you blame me, Cleanthes, if I here imitate the prudent reserve of Simonides, who, according to the noted story, being asked by Hiero, What God was? desired a day to think of it, and then two days more; and after that manner continually prolonged the term, without ever bringing in his definition or description? Could you even blame me, if I answered at first, that I did not know, and was sensible that this subject lay vastly beyond the reach of my faculties? You might cry out sceptic and rallier, as much as you pleased: but having found, in so many other subjects much more familiar, the imperfections and even contradictions of human reason, I never should expect any success from its feeble conjectures, in a subject so sublime, and so remote from the sphere of our observation. When two species of objects have always been observed to be conjoined together, I can infer, by custom, the existence of one wherever I see the existence of the other; and this I call an argument from experience. But how this argument can have place, where the objects, as in the present case, are single, individual, without parallel, or specific resemblance, may be difficult to explain. And will any man tell me with a serious countenance, that an orderly universe must arise from some thought and art like the human, because we have experience of it? To ascertain this reasoning, it were requisite that we had experience of the origin of worlds; and it is not sufficient, surely, that we have seen ships and cities arise from human art and contrivance....

Part III

How he most absurd argument, replied Cleanthes, in the hands of a man of ingenuity and invention, may acquire an air of probability! Are you not aware, Philo, that it became necessary for Copernicus and his first disciples to prove the similarity of the terrestrial and celestial matter; because several philosophers, blinded by old systems, and supported by some sensible appearances, had denied that similarity? but that it is by no means necessary, that Theists should prove the similarity of the works of Nature to those of Art; because this similarity is self-evident and undeniable? The same matter, a like form; what more is requisite to shew an analogy between their causes, and to ascertain the origin of all things from a divine purpose and intention? Your objections, I must freely tell you, are no better than the abstruse cavils of those philosophers who denied motion; and ought to be refuted in the same manner, by illustrations, examples, and instances, rather than by serious argument and philosophy.

Suppose, therefore, that an articulate voice were heard in the clouds, much louder and more melodious than any which human art could ever reach: suppose, that this voice were extended in the same instant over all nations, and spoke to each nation in its own language and dialect: suppose, that the words delivered not only contain a just sense and meaning, but convey some instruction altogether worthy of a benevolent Being, superior to mankind: could you possibly hesitate a moment concerning the cause of this voice? and must you not instantly ascribe it to some design or purpose? Yet I cannot see but all the same objections (if they merit that appellation) which lie against the system of Theism, may also be produced against this inference.

Might you not say, that all conclusions concerning fact were founded on experience: that when we hear an articulate voice in the dark, and thence infer a man, it is only the resemblance of the effects which leads us to conclude that there is a like resemblance in the cause: but that this extraordinary voice, by its loudness, extent, and flexibility to all languages, bears so little analogy to any human voice, that we have no reason to suppose any analogy in their causes: and consequently, that a rational, wise, coherent speech proceeded, you know not whence, from some accidental whistling of the winds, not from any divine reason or intelligence? You see clearly your own objections in these cavils, and I hope too you see clearly, that they cannot possibly have more force in the one case than in the other.

But to bring the case still nearer the present one of the universe, I shall make two suppositions, which imply not any absurdity or impossibility. Suppose that there is a natural, universal, invariable language, common to every individual of human race; and that books are natural productions, which perpetuate themselves in the same manner with animals and vegetables, by descent and propagation. Several expressions of our passions contain a universal language: all brute animals have a natural speech, which, however limited, is very intelligible to their own species. And as there are infinitely fewer parts and less contrivance in the finest composition of eloquence, than in the coarsest organized body, the propagation of an Iliad or Aeneid is an easier supposition than that of any plant or animal.

Suppose, therefore, that you enter into your library, thus peopled by natural volumes, containing the most refined reason and most exquisite beauty; could you possibly open one of them, and doubt, that its original cause bore the strongest analogy to mind and intelligence? When it reasons and discourses; when it expostulates, argues, and enforces its views and topics; when it applies sometimes to the pure intellect, sometimes to the affections; when it collects, disposes, and adorns every consideration suited to the subject; could you persist in asserting, that all this, at the bottom, had really no meaning; and that the first formation of this volume in the loins of its original parent proceeded not from thought and design? Your obstinacy, I know, reaches not that degree of firmness: even your sceptical play and wantonness would be abashed at so glaring an absurdity.

But if there be any difference, Philo, between this supposed case and the real one of the universe, it is all to the advantage of the latter. The anatomy of an animal affords many stronger instances of design than the perusal of Livy or Tacitus; and any objection which you start in the former case, by carrying me back to so unusual and extraordinary a scene as the first formation of worlds, the same objection has place on the supposition of our vegetating library. Choose, then, your party, Philo, without ambiguity or evasion; assert either that a rational volume is no proof of a rational cause, or admit of a similar cause to all the works of nature.

Let me here observe too, continued Cleanthes, that this religious argument, instead of being weakened by that scepticism so much affected by you, rather acquires force from it, and becomes more firm and undisputed. To exclude all argument or reasoning of every kind, is either affectation or madness. The declared profession of every reasonable sceptic is only to reject abstruse, remote, and refined arguments; to adhere to common sense and the plain instincts of nature; and to assent, wherever any reasons strike him with so full a force that he cannot, without the greatest violence, prevent it. Now the arguments for Natural Religion are plainly of this kind; and nothing but the most perverse, obstinate metaphysics can reject them. Consider, anatomize the eye; survey its structure and contrivance; and tell me, from your own feeling, if the idea of a contriver does not immediately flow in upon you with a force like that of sensation. The most obvious conclusion, surely, is in favour of design; and it requires time, reflection, and study, to summon up those frivolous, though abstruse objections, which can support Infidelity. Who can behold the male and female of each species, the correspondence of their parts and instincts, their passions, and whole course of life before and after generation, but must be sensible, that the propagation of the species is intended by Nature? Millions and millions of such instances present themselves through every part of the universe; and no language can convey a more intelligible irresistible meaning, than the curious adjustment of final causes. To what degree, therefore, of blind dogmatism must one have attained, to reject such natural and such convincing arguments?...

Now, Cleanthes, said Philo, with an air of alacrity and triumph, mark the consequences. First, By this method of reasoning, you renounce all claim to infinity in any of the attributes of the Deity. For, as the cause ought only to be proportioned to the effect, and the effect, so far as it falls under our cognizance, is not infinite; what pretensions have we, upon your suppositions, to ascribe that attribute to the Divine Being? You will still insist, that, by removing him so much from all similarity to human creatures, we give in to the most arbitrary hypothesis, and at the same time weaken all proofs of his existence.

Secondly, You have no reason, on your theory, for ascribing perfection to the Deity, even in his finite capacity, or for supposing him free from every error, mistake, or incoherence, in his undertakings. There are many inexplicable difficulties in the works of Nature, which, if we allow a perfect author to be proved a priori, are easily solved, and become only seeming difficulties, from the narrow capacity of man, who cannot trace infinite relations. But according to your method of reasoning, these difficulties become all real; and perhaps will be insisted on, as new instances of likeness to human art and contrivance. At least, you must acknowledge, that it is impossible for us to tell, from our limited views, whether this system contains any great faults, or deserves any considerable praise, if compared to other possible, and even real systems. Could a peasant, if the Aeneid were read to him, pronounce that poem to be absolutely faultless, or even assign to it its proper rank among the productions of human wit, he, who had never seen any other production?

But were this world ever so perfect a production, it must still remain uncertain, whether all the excellences of the work can justly be ascribed to the workman. If we survey a ship, what an exalted idea must we form of the ingenuity of the carpenter who framed so complicated, useful, and beautiful a machine? And what surprize must we feel, when we find him a stupid mechanic, who imitated others, and copied an art, which, through a long succession of ages, after multiplied trials, mistakes, corrections, deliberations, and controversies, had been gradually improving?

Many worlds might have been botched and bungled, throughout an eternity, ere this system was struck out; much labour lost, many fruitless trials made; and a slow, but continued improvement carried on during infinite ages in the art of world-making. In such subjects, who can determine, where the truth; nay, who can conjecture where the probability lies, amidst a great number of hypotheses which may be proposed, and a still greater which may be imagined?

And what shadow of an argument, continued Philo, can you produce, from your hypothesis, to prove the unity of the Deity? A great number of men join in building a house or ship, in rearing a city, in framing a commonwealth; why may not several deities combine in contriving and framing a world? This is only so much greater similarity to human affairs. By sharing the work among several, we may so much further limit the attributes of each, and get rid of that extensive power and knowledge, which must be supposed in one deity, and which, according to you, can only serve to weaken the proof of his existence. And if such foolish, such vicious creatures as man, can yet often unite in framing and executing one plan, how much more those deities or demons, whom we may suppose several degrees more perfect!

To multiply causes without necessity, is indeed contrary to true philosophy: but this principle applies not to the present case. Were one deity antecedently proved by your theory, who were possessed of every attribute requisite to the production of the universe; it would be needless, I own, (though not absurd,) to suppose any other deity existent. But while it is still a question,

Whether all these attributes are united in one subject, or dispersed among several independent beings, by what phenomena in nature can we pretend to decide the controversy? Where we see a body raised in a scale, we are sure that there is in the opposite scale, however concealed from sight, some counterpoising weight equal to it; but it is still allowed to doubt, whether that weight be an aggregate of several distinct bodies, or one uniform united mass. And if the weight requisite very much exceeds any thing which we have ever seen conjoined in any single body, the former supposition becomes still more probable and natural. An intelligent being of such vast power and capacity as is necessary to produce the universe, or, to speak in the language of ancient philosophy, so prodigious an animal exceeds all analogy, and even comprehension.

But further, Cleanthes: men are mortal, and renew their species by generation; and this is common to all living creatures. The two great sexes of male and female, says Milton, animate the world. Why must this circumstance, so universal, so essential, be excluded from those numerous and limited deities? Behold, then, the theogony of ancient times brought back upon us.

And why not become a perfect Anthropomorphite? Why not assert the deity or deities to be corporeal, and to have eyes, a nose, mouth, ears, etc.? Epicurus maintained, that no man had ever seen reason but in a human figure; therefore the gods must have a human figure. And this argument, which is deservedly so much ridiculed by Cicero, becomes, according to you, solid and philosophical.

In a word, Cleanthes, a man who follows your hypothesis is able perhaps to assert, or conjecture, that the universe, sometime, arose from something like design: but beyond that position he cannot ascertain one single circumstance; and is left afterwards to fix every point of his theology by the utmost license of fancy and hypothesis. This world, for aught he knows, is very faulty and imperfect, compared to a superior standard; and was only the first rude essay of some infant deity, who afterwards abandoned it, ashamed of his lame performance: it is the work only of some dependent, inferior deity; and is the object of derision to his superiors: it is the production of old age and dotage in some superannuated deity; and ever since his death, has run on at adventures, from the first impulse and active force which it received from him. You justly give signs of horror, Demea, at these strange suppositions; but these, and a thousand more of the same kind, are Cleanthes's suppositions, not mine. From the moment the attributes of the Deity are supposed finite, all these have place. And I cannot, for my part, think that so wild and unsettled a system of theology is, in any respect, preferable to none at all.

Chapter 8: Philosophy of Religion II "Proving" that God does *not* Exist: The Problem of Evil

Comprehension questions you should be able to answer after reading this introduction:

1. *What is the "problem of evil (POE)?"*
2. *What is the difference between moral evil and natural evil?*
3. *What are the five claims that constitute an "inconsistent set," according to the POE?*
4. *What is the "free will defense?" Why do some believe that it is impossible for God to create humans with free will but without the risk of moral evil?*
5. *What is the "greater good defense?" What is the difference between a "general" and a "particular" greater good defense?*
6. *What is the "greater good" (chief purpose of life) according to Craig, Lewis, and Paley?*
7. *How does this greater good (#6) connect to the free will defense? The greater good defense?*
8. *How does Johnson criticize the free will defense? The greater good defense?*

In the late Spring of 2008, a friend of mine died.

When it actually happened, I barely mourned for Shirley. I believe that's because I had already mourned for her, deeply and intensely some months prior, when we first learned of her cancer. Although no cancer is "kind," hers seemed especially cruel. The tumor in her throat closed it off, making it impossible for her to eat solid food for several months. She was fed through a tube inserted into her stomach, and could only suck on ice chips to keep her mouth and throat moist. Intensive chemotherapy caused the tumor in her throat to shrink down to the point where she was able to ingest tiny pieces of solid food, and I remember one day when she told me that had eaten a piece of buttered bread the night before, and how amazingly good it had tasted. Just buttered bread...

Chemotherapy or not, the cancer had spread to several internal organs, and all of us knew that Shirley had only months, at most, to live. As best she could, she remained active, until she was so weak and sickened from the cancer and the chemotherapy itself, that she became completely bedridden. I think it fortunate that she only lasted a few days in that state before one night, in the company of several friends, she simply closed her eyes and stopped breathing. About one week before, I had spoken with her on the phone, and she told me that her problem had to be "dealt with" in one way or another. I knew, then, what she meant: she had reached the point where death was being viewed as a welcome release.

Shirley's story has many elements of sadness to it, but I've not yet mentioned the triumphant elements. I have rarely, if ever, been so impressed by such courage. Her calm, valiant approach to her illness and her own death inspired me. I hope that when it's my turn to die, that I can do so with even a fraction of the dignity she displayed.

Another important feature of her story, not

yet mentioned, is that she was a woman of faith. As death neared, her faith deepened and grew in ways that amazed me. Moreover, she testified to me (and others) that never in her life had she seen so clearly the power of love and friendship. Although the cancer had brought her body low, her spirit soared, borne up in part by her own courage, in part by the compassion and love of her friends, and perhaps even by Grace.

Shirley's story represents the antagonism behind the philosophical and theological problem known as the "Problem of Evil." The problem of evil (POE) is that it (viz., evil) seemingly should not exist—at least not if the God of the Western faith traditions exists. And yet, people like Shirley get cancer, suffer, and die.

Although this was not the case with Shirley, for many, the existence of (seemingly) unjustified suffering constitutes a challenge to theistic belief. The Christian writer and apologist C.S. Lewis wrote of his own experience and perspective as follows:

> *Not many years ago when I was an atheist, if anyone had asked me, 'Why do you not believe in God?' my reply would have run something like this:*
>
> *"Look at the universe we live in. By far the greatest part of it consists of empty space, completely dark and unimaginably cold. The bodies which move in this space are so few and so small in comparison with the space itself that even if every one of them were known to be crowded as full as it could hold with perfectly happy creatures, it would still be difficult to believe that life and happiness were more than a byproduct to the power that made the universe. As it is, however, the scientists think it likely that very few of the suns of space—perhaps none of them except our own— have any planets; and in our own system it is improbable that any planet except the Earth sustains life. And Earth herself existed without life for millions of years and may exist for millions more when life has left her. And what is it like while it lasts? It is so arranged that all the forms of it can live only by preying upon one another. In the lower forms this process entails only death, but in the higher there appears a new quality called consciousness which enables it to be attended with pain. The creatures cause pain by being born, and live by inflicting pain, and in pain they mostly die. In the most complex of all the creatures, Man, yet another quality appears, which we call reason, whereby he is enabled to foresee his own pain which henceforth is preceded with acute mental suffering, and to foresee his own death while keenly desiring permanence. It also enables men by a hundred ingenious contrivances to inflict a great deal more pain than they otherwise could have done on one another and on the irrational creatures. This power they have exploited to the full. Their history is largely a record of crime, war, disease, and terror, with just sufficient happiness interposed to give them, while it lasts, an agonised apprehension of losing it, and, when it is lost, the poignant misery of remembering. Every now and then they improve their condition a little and what we call a civilisation appears. But all civilisations pass away and, even while they remain, inflict peculiar sufferings of their own probably sufficient to outweigh what alleviations they may have brought to the normal pains of man. That our own civilisation has done so, no one will dispute; that it will pass away like all its predecessors is surely probable. Even if it should not, what then? The race is doomed. Every race that comes into being in any part of the universe is doomed; for the universe, they tell us, is running down, and will sometime be a uniform infinity of homogeneous matter at a low temperature. All stories will come to nothing: all life will turn out in the end to have been a transitory and senseless*

> *contortion upon the idiotic face of infinite matter. If you ask me to believe that this is the work of a benevolent and omnipotent spirit, I reply that all the evidence points in the opposite direction. Either there is no spirit behind the universe, or else a spirit indifferent to good and evil, or else an evil spirit."*[215]

Sometimes the POE is offered as some sort of "proof" that God doesn't exist. Other times, it is offered as a way to undermine *warrant* (justification) for theistic belief. In real life, some people literally lose their faith when grappling with seemingly unjustified suffering. In this way, the POE constitutes a negative theistic argument (i.e., an argument *against* God's existence).

With regard to Shirley, suffering captures the first part of the POE. The virtue she displayed, and the faith she enjoyed, represents a possible response to the POE. We'll begin with some conceptual clarification, then proceed to outline the nature of the POE in greater detail. Finally, we'll consider the sorts of defenses theists have made in the face of the POE.

Evil

What is meant by "evil?" Oftentimes, what is meant by evil is something like "villainy" or "depravity." We associate evil with the deplorable acts of persons. But, for the purposes of the POE, evil is defined simply as "unjustified suffering." This is a more general usage of the term "evil," obviously, but it's a necessary broadening of the term in order to account for the different types of "evil" we encounter—not all unjustified suffering comes at the hands of bad people, after all.

1. **Natural evil**: unjustified suffering attributed to "nature," as opposed to a moral agent.
2. **Moral evil**: unjustified suffering inflicted by moral agents.

Moral evil is fairly obvious: rape, murder, assault, abuse of all kinds—essentially, any of the many various horrible things humans can do to one another. If the unjustified suffering can be traced back to a moral agent, it's an example of moral evil.

Natural evil is all the unjustified suffering that's left over, that can't be attributed to a moral agent. Natural disasters are good candidates, as well as disease, or naturally occurring droughts or famines. The inevitable frailty and decay of the body and mind could count as natural evil as well.

It's important to note that for both moral and natural evil, in order for them to count *as* evil, the suffering must be unjustified. If there is some sort of justification for the suffering, it is no longer "evil." A child might "suffer," for example, if you punish her for serious misbehavior, but so long as the punishment is fair and proportionate to the misbehavior (and aims at correcting that behavior), most of us would not regard the "time out" as "evil."

The possibility that there might be a justification to suffering leads to another important distinction: the logical POE v. the evidential POE.

The logical POE claims that there is something logically inconsistent between the existence of an all-powerful, all-knowing, morally perfect God, and the existence of evil. That is, if evil exists, that sort of God *can't* exist. The idea behind this is captured well by Lewis:

> *If God were good, He would wish to make His creatures perfectly happy, and if God were almighty He would be able to do what He wished. But the creatures are not happy. Therefore God lacks either goodness, or power, or both. This is the problem of pain, in its simplest form.*[216]

---

215 C.S. Lewis, *The Problem of Pain*, Harper One, 1940/1996, pp. 1-3.

216 Lewis, *Problem of Pain*, p. 16. Note, what Lewis is calling the "problem of pain" is what we are calling the "problem of evil."

To be honest, very few people take seriously the logical version of the POE, since all that is necessary to deflate it is the acknowledgment that it's *possible* that God could have a morally sufficient reason to allow suffering to occur. Given how difficult (if not impossible) it would be to somehow prove that it's not even *possible* that God (if God exists) could have a morally sufficient reason to allow suffering, most people concerned with the POE focus on the evidential version.

The evidential version of the POE does not claim that it's impossible for God to exist alongside evil, but merely that it's unlikely—that the existence of evil counts as evidence against God's existence. In this way, the POE serves to undermine confidence in the belief that God exists, it undermines *warrant*. For the remainder of this chapter, assume that any reference to the POE is a reference to the evidential version.

As a final point of clarification, it's important to note that the POE isn't some vague and sentimental notion that it's "sad" that bad things happen to good people, nor is it (only) an intense, personally emotional response to an experience of suffering. The POE, understood in a philosophical context, is not a problem fit for counseling. This is not to disparage counseling, or minimize the significance of the "emotional" version of the POE—it's simply to point out that the emotional version of the POE is not an *argument*.

Sometimes, when confronted with tragedy and suffering, people of faith will have a "why God?" moment. Their pain and grief is real, and powerful—but they're not questioning God's *existence*. They might be questioning God's goodness, or faithfulness, or God's plan, or wondering (in general) why God would let such things happen to them, but they're not doubting the very existence of God, any more than a child who is upset with his parents for something is doubting his parents' existence. In those sorts of cases, what people need is a shoulder to cry on, some therapy, some support, and the like. They're not seeking a philosophical defense of the consistency of God's existence and the occurrence of suffering.

Within a philosophical context, the (evidential) POE is an *intellectual* problem, a problem of rationality and reasonableness. The problem only arises for theists. This is not to say that atheists don't suffer, of course, or that their suffering doesn't matter. Atheists and theists alike suffer, and die. The difference is that only theists might have any reason to be surprised by that fact.

If I am an atheist, I believe there is no God. Consequently, I believe that the origin and explanation for this universe is a naturalistic one. That we have *this* sort of universe is attributable to the laws of physics. That living things of various kinds and with various natures populate the Earth is explainable by appealing to evolution. There is no "plan" for the world, no way that the world is "supposed" to be.

If I believe that human beings are simply sophisticated animals, why should it surprise me when we sometimes turn against one another? As much as cancer or natural disasters might afflict me, why would I expect that the world would not have such things in it? Atheists might wish for a safer world with less suffering, but there should be no cause for surprise that we have a suffering-filled world in the first place. Why wouldn't we?

Theists, on the other hand, should have a different sort of problem with the POE. If one is a Christian, Jew, or Muslim, one believes (among other things) that there is an all-knowing, all-powerful, perfectly good God who created the entire universe. Given the presumed existence of such a God, the presence of unjustified suffering in the world poses an intellectual puzzle to be solved. Why would God permit such evil to exist and to occur?

The concern is this: if there is an all-knowing God, God knows about every instance of suffering in the entire world. God is never "surprised" by an occurrence of suffering. If God is all-powerful, God can do anything—including (it would seem) preventing any or all incidents of suffering. Finally, if God is perfectly good, it would seem that God would want there to be no unjustified suffering. So, if God is aware of suffering, and has the power to prevent it, and has the desire to prevent it, there should be no unjustified suffering.

And yet, we find it all around us, including in our own lives.

Imagine that I told you that the Earth was flat, and that I appear to be serious. Imagine, also, that you care enough to debate with me on this issue. Imagine, too, that you present to me all the many pieces of evidence that would seemingly prove me wrong. Say, for example, that you show me photos of the Earth taken from space. Suppose, also, that you show me images of the shadow of the Earth that's cast on the moon, and point out its curvature.

Imagine if, after all the compelling evidence you've presented to me, I nevertheless shake my head, roll my eyes, and insist that the Earth is flat anyway. Wouldn't I seem to be both irrational and unreasonable?

The threat behind the POE is that it might make theists appear to be irrational and unreasonable in the same sort of way. The fact of suffering is taken to be evidence against God's existence. If theists continue to claim God exists, in spite of this evidence, perhaps they're just as irrationally stubborn as those who insist that the Earth is flat, in spite of all the evidence to the contrary? Specifically, the concern is that you can't believe all five of the following claims to be true at the same time, and continue to be rational in your believing.

- God exists
- God is all-powerful (omnipotent)
- God is all-knowing (omniscient)
- God is morally perfect
- Evil exists

If we accept all of these claims, we appear to be accepting a contradiction—or at least a set of beliefs that are implausible, as a set. To resolve this problem and restore our rationality, we are supposed to deny the truth of at least one of those claims. In so doing, the intellectual puzzle is solved. Let us consider how denying each of these claims could "solve" the POE, and the consequences of each "solution."

- It is false that <u>God exists</u>

Atheism "solves" the POE. This is not to make the absurd claim that atheism somehow eliminates suffering, but merely to point out (as stated above) that the suffering is no longer puzzling if we eliminate the God that would (seemingly) not allow it to exist. Not surprisingly, this is not a popular strategy among theists! While atheism does eliminate the intellectual confusion concerning the existence of evil, it does so at the cost of one's faith.

- It is false that God is <u>all-powerful</u>

This "solves" the POE not by denying God's existence, but by denying one of the traditional properties of God thought to be inconsistent with the existence of evil. After all, if God is not powerful enough to prevent evil, it would explain why evil occurs even if God exists. The problem with this solution, however, is that this is certainly not the God of the Western theistic traditions! Even if there is room for legitimate theological debate as to whether God is truly *all*-powerful, God is clearly thought to be really, really powerful in all three Western theistic traditions. At the very least, God is powerful enough to create an entire universe without any material cause, and powerful enough to perform miracles from time to time. But, the God that is not powerful enough to prevent evil is, in some ways, not even as powerful as human beings. Human beings are powerful enough to prevent many cases of "evil." Human beings can be heroic and compassionate, can save lives, prevent bullying, heal wounds, etc. If God isn't even as powerful as a human fire fighter, or paramedic, how is God worthy of worship?

- It is false that God is <u>all-knowing</u>

Similar to the previous "solution," if God is unaware of the occurrence of evil, or unaware of how to stop it, it would explain why evil exists even if God exists. Also similarly to the previous "solution," however, this strategy will not work for theists, because it requires a radical revision of their concept of God. Human beings can be aware of unjustified suffering, and even predict it, in cases like hurricanes. Weather forecasters can predict hurricanes, sometimes days ahead of time, and predict with generally impressive accuracy where and when those hurricanes will strike—thereby giving residents sufficient warning to flee. Human law enforcement officers can profile serial killers or sexual predators and predict (and thereby prevent) their future crimes. What kind of God would God be if God didn't even know as much as a human weather forecaster? The local weather person can predict a hurricane, but God can't?

- It is false that God is morally perfect

If God is indifferent to our suffering, or perhaps even delights in it, it would explain why evil occurs even if God exists. After all, the existence of evil is puzzling on the assumption that God is opposed to evil, but what if this assumption is false? While technically "solving" the POE, this, too, will not be a satisfying strategy for theists. Without God's perfect goodness, God is simply a cosmic dictator, worshipped out of fear or awe rather than love. Perhaps this God exists, but if so, this is not the God of Judaism, Christianity, or Islam—at least as understood by most adherents of those traditions.

- It is false that evil exists

If it will be unsatisfying to theists to deny God's existence, or any of God's (essential) attributes, the only remaining option is to deny that "evil" exists. There are several ways in which this might be done.

- All suffering is deserved

This approach eliminates "evil" by denying that the suffering is unjustified. Instead, all suffering is deserved. There are no truly innocent people, no truly innocent "victims." Sometimes this strategy is explained by appealing to notions such as the doctrine of Original Sin. Perhaps all of us are born "sinful," and we all deserve whatever afflictions we face. Only by Grace alone are we spared from suffering. This view is coherent, but terribly harsh. It requires us to believe even that newborn infants deserve to suffer. Childhood cancer? Deserved. A toddler kidnapped, raped, and murdered? Deserved. Not surprisingly, very few theists adopt this strategy.

- Suffering is not deserved, but is "justified."

Most theists will attempt to solve the POE by claiming that although there truly are many (tragic) cases of undeserved suffering, such suffering is nevertheless justified. That is, there is a good, morally sufficient reason that the suffering is allowed (by God) to take place. What that good reason is, remains to be seen, and will occupy our focus for the remainder of the chapter.

"Solving" the Problem of Evil

The POE is thought to make it difficult for a theist to remain a theist without suffering from some intellectual embarrassment. That is, the POE alleges that there is something irrational about believing in an all-knowing, all-powerful, perfectly good God in spite of the tremendous amount of (seemingly) unjustified suffering in the world. What can a theist say in response, and in defense of the rationality of her faith?

Any defense of theistic belief in the face of the POE (sometimes referred to as a "theodicy") will amount to a claim that there is a justification, or at least a possible justification, for the suffering to occur. In other words, there is a sufficient reason for God, if God exists, to permit the world to be as it is.

The sorts of reasons available to the theist will, not surprisingly, vary depending upon the particular faith tradition of that theist. There are certain "generic" resources available to virtually any adherent of the three major Western theistic traditions (i.e., Christianity, Islam, Judaism), but then each particular religion will also have its own "tool box," its own resources with which to confront the POE. We will consider a "generic" theodicy provided by William Paley, and then (briefly) consider the specifically (Protestant) Christian approach as provided by the prominent Christian philosopher and apologist William Lane Craig, as well as that of C.S. Lewis.

Most theodicies will address the evidential version of the POE by claiming that there is (or at least could be) a "morally sufficient justification" for God to have created (and sustained) a world such as this one. If that is true, then it is no longer inconsistent (or somehow intellectually embarrassing) to acknowledge our world as it is, and continue to believe in God. Most of these theodicies include a combination of what is known as the "free will defense" and the "greater good defense." Paley's, Craig's, and Lewis' versions are no exception.

The Free Will Defense

> *The mischiefs of which mankind are the occasion to one another, by their private wickednesses and cruelties; by tyrannical exercises of power; by rebellions against just authority; by wars; by national jealousies and competitions operating to the destruction of third countries; or by other instances of misconduct either in individuals or societies, are all to be resolved into the character of man as a free agent.*[217]

Suppose that human beings have genuine free will. Suppose also that free will, in this context, is the "agency theorist" version of free will. That is, free will requires an "ability to do otherwise," genuine choice. If I have free will, and if I am responsible for my actions, then, at the time of a given action, I must have had a genuine choice. I must have an "ability to do otherwise." If I am to be responsible for knocking someone to the ground, it must have been the result of my choice, and it must have been within my power to do something other than knock that person down. If I knock someone down as a result of having a seizure, or as a result of unintentionally stumbling into that person, or (more bizarrely) as a result of having been hypnotized or mind-controlled, then it wouldn't seem fair to say that I am responsible for what I did. On the other hand, if I could have knocked the person down, and could have refrained from doing so, but chose to knock the person down, then I am responsible for my action, because it was my choice, and because I could have done otherwise.

If humans have free will, then we can make good choices, or bad choices. Many of our bad choices introduce suffering into the world. This is what we referred to earlier as "moral evil," or what Paley refers to as "civil evil." Murder is a choice, as is rape, as is dishonesty, as is abuse of all kinds. To put it bluntly, if we are upset about moral evil, we shouldn't misplace the blame. Don't blame God for rape or murder, blame the rapist or murderer! Blame and righteous indignation are appropriate responses to moral evil, but we should direct them to the proper source: the person who actually did the evil deed.

The free will defense, by itself, is almost never recognized as "enough" of a defense for a variety of reasons. For one, it does nothing to address "natural evil" (what Paley refers to as "physical evil"). Human free will does nothing to account for natural disasters, for example (except on some very specific theological interpretations). A theodicy that included only a free will defense would leave unaddressed a significant source of suffering. Moreover, even if we confine ourselves only to the category of moral evil, there is still room to object.

Imagine a case of child molestation. A young child is being molested by his or her stepfather. Naturally, we are outraged and blame the stepfather for this terrible example of moral evil. Now imagine that we discover that the child's mother, while not a participant in the abuse, nevertheless knew that it was taking place, and did nothing to stop it. It's possible to be sympathetic. After all, we might speculate, there might be any number of reasons why she didn't intervene? Maybe she was afraid. Maybe there's something we don't know. All the same, most of us,

---

217 Paley, *Natural Theology*, chapter xxvi (selection included at the end of this chapter)

while we place the blame overwhelmingly on the shoulders of the abuser, still have some blame left over for the mother. She might not have been personally responsible for the abuse, but she knew about it and did nothing to stop it, and that's bad as well. We think it would be a terrible thing for a person to shove a child into a swimming pool, resulting in the child's drowning. We also think it a terrible thing if some other people witnessed the child drowning, and didn't even try to help.

We might call this the "bystander-problem." B.C. Johnson raises problem with his hypothetical example of an infant trapped in a burning home, doomed to burn to death. Johnson asks, mostly rhetorically, "Could we possibly describe as "good" any person who had die power to save this child and yet refused to do so? God undoubtedly has this power and yet in many cases of this sort he has refused to help. Can we call God "good"? Are there adequate excuses for his behavior?"[218]

Note an important feature of this sort of example: it is not the arsonist who is being questioned, but the "innocent bystander" who, while not responsible for the fire, passively lets the infant die. Isn't such a bystander also, somehow, "responsible" for the death of the infant? If we would have concerns about the moral qualities of a person who wouldn't even *try* to save the infant, if she thought she could do so, shouldn't we have the same sorts of concerns about the moral qualities (or existence) of God?

This is a certainly a possible problem for Western theists. According to all three major Western religions, God is "everywhere" in the sense of being casually interactive with all points in space. God is also aware of what transpires in all places. God, then, is the perpetual "innocent bystander" who is there, and "does nothing" when any and every child is ever molested, when any and every child ever drowns. Indeed, for every occurrence of suffering, God is "right there" and does nothing to prevent the suffering from taking place. If we would hold a human being accountable for being an "innocent bystander" who refuses to help, why wouldn't we hold God accountable as well? Isn't it worse, actually, given the fact that, unlike a human being, God has nothing to fear from intervening? If I play the hero and intervene in a case of domestic violence, my own safety is endangered, but it's not as if God has to fear getting beat up, or shot, or stabbed—unlike me.

There are two basic ways to interpret this critique of the free will defense. The first is that it suggests that although humans do (and should) have free will, God shouldn't let us abuse it by making poor choices that cause harm to others. In the same way that a good parent presumably wouldn't let her child take a gun to school after he declared his intention to get revenge on some bullies, just for the sake of preserving his "autonomy," so too should God stop His "children" from harming one another as a result of poor free choices. Better yet, God should have created us so we never make such horrible choices in the first place!

Suppose that God is all-powerful, and can therefore do anything. God could have created a world in which we have free will, and choose to abuse it and inflict suffering on each other (moral evil). Or, God could have created a world in which we have free will, but such that we never actually make any wrong decisions, and therefore never inflict moral evil on one another. The atheist philosopher poses the question: "if God has made men such that in their free choices they sometimes prefer what is good and sometimes what is evil, why could he not have made men such that they always freely choose the good?"[219]

If we compare two possible worlds (e.g., one with free will and moral evil, and one with free will but no moral evil), it seems that a perfectly good God would have created the one without moral evil—and yet, the world *with* moral evil is the one we got stuck with. How can a theist explain that?

One way is to dismiss the complaint as incoherent. That is, to say that God could have

[218] From: B.C. Johnson, "The Problem of Good and Evil," *The Atheist Debater's Handbook*. Prometheus Books, 1983. Pp. 99-108.

[219] J. L. Mackie, "Evil and Omnipotence," *Mind*, New Series, Vol. 64, No. 254. (Apr., 1955), p.209.

created us with free will, but in such a way that we would never abuse it, actually involves a contradiction. In fact, it is conceptually impossible that God create persons who are truly free, but who could never "sin."

> *To be a person is to be a finite center of freedom, a (relatively) free and self-directing agent responsible for one's own decisions. This involves being free to act wrongly as well as to act rightly. The idea of a person who can be infallibly guaranteed always to act rightly is self-contradictory. There can be no guarantee in advance that a genuinely free moral agent will never choose amiss. Consequently, the possibility of wrongdoing or sin is logically inseparable from the creation of finite persons, and to say that God should not have created beings who might sin amounts to saying he should not have created people.*[220]

Free will requires the *ability to do otherwise.* A guarantee never to abuse free will is to deny that "ability to do otherwise." Critics like Mackie, however, disagree—seeing no inherent impossibility of creating free creatures who always choose rightly, or, if there is one, then interpreting this limitation as evidence that God would not truly be omnipotent.

> *If there is no logical impossibility in a man's freely choosing the good on one, or on several, occasions, there cannot be a logical impossibility in his freely choosing the good on every occasion. God was not, then, faced with a choice between making innocent automata and making beings who, in acting freely, would sometimes go wrong: there was open to him the obviously better possibility of making beings who would act freely but always go right. Clearly, his failure to avail himself of this possibility is inconsistent with his being both omnipotent and wholly good.*[221]

Most theists, however, understand "omnipotence" as something like the ability to do all and anything that is *possible* to do. Classic conundrums like "Can God create a rock so heavy that He can't lift it?" are exposed as being meaningless questions, rather than theological pitfalls.

> *His Omnipotence means power to do all that is intrinsically possible, not to do the intrinsically impossible. You may attribute miracles to Him, but not nonsense. There is no limit to His power. If you choose to say, 'God can give a creature free will and at the same time withhold free will from it,' you have not succeeded in saying anything about God: meaningless combinations of words do not suddenly acquire meaning simply because we prefix to them the two other words, 'God can.' It remains true that all things are possible with God: the intrinsic impossibilities are not things but nonentities. It is no more possible for God than for the weakest of His creatures to carry out both of two mutually exclusive alternatives; not because His power meets an obstacle, but because nonsense remains nonsense even when we talk it about God.*[222]

While the application to free will and moral evil might be less obvious than the "create a rock too heavy to lift" demand, Lewis would allege they

---

220 John Hick, "The Problem of Evil" in John Hick, *Philosophy of Religion* 4th. ed. (Upper Saddle Hill, N.J.: Prentice Hall, 1989. John Hick claims to offer a specifically Christian response to the POE, but this is a controversial claim, as there are numerous "unorthodox" elements of his full theodicy. His approach might more accurately be interpreted as "Unitarian," with some points of contact with Christianity

221 Mackie. Ibid.

222 Lewis, *Problem of Pain*, p. 18.

are of the same type: to propose that God create truly free persons who can be guaranteed never to choose to do wrong is akin to asking God to create a rock too heavy for God to lift, or to create a 4-sided triangle. In each case, the demand is for impossible, and omnipotence does not, and cannot, require the ability to do the intrinsically impossible—at least not without losing any coherent meaning.

How am I truly free if it is never within my power to choose to do something morally wrong? If it is not within my power to lie, how is it to my credit when I always tell the truth? To say that God should create persons who necessarily do no wrong is simply to say that God should not have created any persons at all!

"Agreed!" some of you might be thinking. "If moral evil is the price we have to pay for free will, then God shouldn't have created us with free will, and if people couldn't exists unless they had free will, then maybe there shouldn't be any people." This is the second way to interpret the critique of the free will defense. The theist must now explain why free will is "worth it," even though it comes at such a terrible price (moral evil).

The Greater Good Defense

Paley, Craig, Lewis, and Hick offer several reasons why God would not intervene to prevent suffering, most of which connect to a "greater good" defense. Any greater good defense is going to claim that a "greater good" is served by the occurrence of suffering than would have been possible without it. Some versions offer a "general justification" for suffering, while others offer a "particular justification" for suffering.

A general justification, or a general greater good defense, claims that a greater good is served by our living in a certain kind of world, namely, one in which we have free will (and therefore run the risk of moral evil), and one in which natural evils can occur. There is something so valuable about free will that it's "worth it" for humanity, even if moral evil is the price we must pay for it. Similarly, living in a dangerous, challenging environment is also worth it, despite the pains associated with natural evil. This general justification does not claim that every single event in human history serves this greater good, but merely that the basic conditions of this world do. As John Hick describes such general justifications:

> *It does not claim to explain, nor to explain away, every instance of evil in human experience, but only to point to certain considerations which prevent the fact of evil . . . From constituting a final and insuperable bar to rational belief in God.*
>
> *It is not possible to show positively that each item of human pain serves the divine purpose of good, but, on the other hand, it does seem possible to show that the divine purpose as understood in Judaism and Christianity could not be forwarded in a world which was designed as a permanent hedonistic paradise.*[223]

As stated, a general greater good defense will claim that the general conditions of this life and world serve a "greater good," and these general conditions include our possessing free will, and living in an environment that includes natural evil. Let us start with the possibly-bold assumption that God has a good reason to create people, in general. If there are to be people, what follows from that?

Lewis proposes that for me (or you) to be a person (a self-conscious creature) requires that others exist as well. After all, how can I understand "self" if there is no "other" with which to contrast? And, if I am to be a *free* self, then choice must be possible—and choice requires the existence of things from which to choose. "A creature with no environment would have no choices to make: so that freedom, like self-consciousness . . . again demands the presence to the self of something other than the self."[224]

If two or more selves are to be able to meet and interact, they will require an environment in

[223] John Hick, Philosophy of Religion.

[224] Lewis, Problem of Pain, p.20.

which to do so—an "external world," as it were.

> *People often talk as if nothing were easier than for two naked minds to 'meet' or become aware of each other. But I see no possibility of their doing so except in a common medium which forms their 'external world' or environment. Even our vague attempt to imagine such a meeting between disembodied spirits usually slips in surreptitiously the idea of, at least, a common space and common time, to give the co- in co-existence a meaning: and space and time are already an environment. But more than this is required. If your thoughts and passions were directly present to me, like my own, without any mark of externality or otherness, how should I distinguish them from mine? And what thoughts or passions could we begin to have without objects to think and feel about? Nay, could I even begin to have the conception of 'external' and 'other' unless I had experience of an 'external world'?*[225]

If there is to be an external world within which we will live and interact, what properties should this world have? The complaint against natural evil, of course, is that our actual world is filled with things that would not, or should not, exist if God exists. Our world shouldn't have diseases, natural disasters, droughts, famines, and the like. People shouldn't starve, or drown, or be crushed by earthquakes, or burned up in fires. Even if we can somehow account for moral evil by appealing to the free will defense, there is seemingly no justification for the dangerous and hostile world in which we live. Here, it is useful to quote Lewis' response at length.

> *If matter is to serve as a neutral field it must have a fixed nature of its own. If a "world" or material system had only a single inhabitant it might conform at every moment to his wishes — "trees for his sake would crowd into a shade." But if you were introduced into a world which thus varied at my every whim, you would be quite unable to act in it and would thus lose the exercise of your free will. Nor is it clear that you could make your presence known to me — all the matter by which you attempted to make signs to me being already in my control and therefore not capable of being manipulated by you.*
>
> *Again, if matter has a fixed nature and obeys constant laws, not all states of matter will be equally agreeable to the wishes of a given soul, nor all equally beneficial for that particular aggregate of matter which he calls his body. If fire comforts that body at a certain distance, it will destroy it when the distance is reduced. Hence, even in a perfect world, the necessity for those danger signals which the pain-fibres in our nerves are apparently designed to transmit. Does this mean an inevitable element of evil (in the form of pain) in any possible world? I think not: for while it may be true that the least sin is an incalculable evil, the evil of pain depends on degree, and pains below a certain intensity are not feared or resented at all. No one minds the process "warm — beautifully hot — too hot — it stings" which warns him to withdraw his hand from exposure to the fire: and, if I may trust my own feeling, a slight aching in the legs as we climb into bed after a good day's walking is, in fact, pleasurable.*
>
> *Yet again, if the fixed nature of matter prevents it from being always, and in all its dispositions, equally agreeable even to a single soul, much less is it possible for the matter of the universe at any moment to be distributed so that it is equally convenient and pleasurable to each member of a*

---

225 Lewis, *Problem of Pain*, pp. 20-21.

society. If a man traveling in one direction is having a journey down hill, a man going in the opposite direction must be going up hill. If even a pebble lies where I want it to lie, it cannot, except by a coincidence, be where you want it to lie. And this is very far from being an evil: on the contrary, it furnishes occasion for all those acts of courtesy, respect, and unselfishness by which love and good humor and modesty express themselves. But it certainly leaves the way open to a great evil, that of competition and hostility. And if souls are free, they cannot be prevented from dealing with the problem by competition instead of courtesy. And once they have advanced to actual hostility, they can then exploit the fixed nature of matter to hurt one another. The permanent nature of wood which enables us to use it as a beam also enables us to use it for hitting our neighbor on the head. The permanent nature of matter in general means that when human beings fight, the victory ordinarily goes to those who have superior weapons, skill, and numbers, even if their cause is unjust.[226]

This "neutral" environment in which we actually find ourselves is objective. It does not favor my desires or thoughts over yours, or vice-versa. Fire is impartial: it is always hot! Sometimes, the heat is enjoyable, and sometimes it burns, but the fire, at least, is consistent. The very same feature of the world (e.g., fire's hotness) is agreeable or disagreeable to us relative to context. This allows for acts of kindness and hospitality (e.g., inviting you into my home to warm yourself by my fire), but also for acts of outright hostility (e.g., burning someone's house to the ground, or, worse, burning someone alive!). For God to miraculously prevent harm and spare us and others from pain or loss would either be to create a world in which free will was impossible (e.g., one in which I can't choose to use fire to hurt you), or else one with a miraculously fluctuating environment and no serious consequences for our actions (e.g., one in which the hotness of fire fluctuates depending on its application).

The implications of such continuous "miraculous" interventions are both far-reaching, and mind boggling.

In a game of chess you can make certain arbitrary concessions to your opponent, which stand to the ordinary rules of the game as miracles stand to the laws of nature. You can deprive yourself of a castle, or allow the other man sometimes to take back a move made inadvertently. But if you conceded everything that at any moment happened to suit him — if all his moves were revocable and if all your pieces disappeared whenever their position on the board was not to his liking — then you could not have a game at all. So it is with the life of souls in a world: fixed laws, consequences unfolding by causal necessity, the whole natural order, are at once limits within which their common life is confined and also the sole condition under which any such life is possible. Try to exclude the possibility of suffering which the order of nature and the existence of free wills involve, and you find that you have excluded life itself.[227]

Later in this chapter, we will consider how such an unstable environment might (negatively) impact life's meaning and value, but here the claim is more blunt: a Nature not governed by predictable "rules" (e.g., fire is always hot) is not a "Nature" at all, and an environment in which life is immune to harm is one in which life is not actually possible. If there is to be life at all, it must exist in an environment at least similar to the actual world—and this means the possibility of natural evil. If some of those living creatures are to be free, responsible, and self-conscious persons, then we run the risk of moral evil. The "general greater

[226] Lewis, *Problem of Pain*, pp.22-24.

[227] Lewis, *Problem of Pain*, p.25.

good defense" claims that these (general) conditions serve a greater good, and are therefore justified.

Recall, however, that there exist both "general" as well as "particular" justifications. *A particular justification will claim that every event that occurs is permitted to occur because it serves that greater good.* In Christianity, this is usually based on a belief in Providence—the view that God is in control of the unfolding of history, according to God's own perfect plan. If one believes in Providence, it is not merely that this general sort of world serves the "greater good," but that everything that occurs, though not necessarily willed by God (e.g., sin) is nevertheless permitted to occur because it serves the grander purpose of God's Providence.

> *So when people ask, 'Why doesn't God just remove all the suffering from the world?', they really have no idea what they're asking for or what the consequences might be. The brutal murder of an innocent man or a child's dying of leukemia could send a ripple effect through history so that God's reason for permitting it might not emerge until centuries later or perhaps in another country. Only an omniscient mind could grasp the complexities of directing a world of free persons toward one's pre-visioned goals. You have only to think of the innumerable, incalculable contingencies involved in arriving at a single historical event, say, the Allied victory at D-day, in order to appreciate the point. We have no idea of the natural and moral evils that might be involved in order for God to arrange the circumstances and free agents in them necessary for some intended purpose, nor can we discern what reasons God might have in mind for permitting some instance of suffering to enter our lives. But He will have good reasons in light of the purposes of His Kingdom.*[228]

In this passage from Craig, we find another of his arguments: human beings are not in a good "epistemic position" to claim that it is unlikely that the world's suffering has a morally sufficient justification (e.g,. by serving a greater good), let alone that it is impossible. We often find ourselves surprised by the unfolding of events over just a short span of time, and about which we think we have much understanding. Paley raised a similar point centuries prior:

> *... with many of these laws we are not acquainted at all, or we are totally unable to trace them in their branches, and in their operation; the effect of which ignorance is, that they cannot be of importance to us as measures by which to regulate our conduct. The conservation of them may be of importance in other respects, or to other beings, but we are uninformed of their value or use; uninformed, consequently, when, and how far, they may or may not be suspended, or their effects turned aside, by a presiding and benevolent will, without incurring greater evils than those which would be avoided.*

I suspect many reading this chapter can think of events that, at the time, seemed disastrous, or at least very bad, but which, sometime later, turned out to have been "for the best." Many years ago, I applied for a full-time teaching position at a University where I had been teaching part-time, and was excited to get an interview. I was devastated when I didn't get the job and feared that it had been my "best shot" at being a tenured professor. Less than a year later I applied for the job I now have—a job I never would have applied for had I gotten the first one—and I am certain that I am much happier with the job I now have, than I would have been had I not been "devastated."

The chorus of a Garth Brooks song puts it this way:

[228]http://www.reasonablefaith.org/why-does-god-permit-suffering-to-continue

> *"Sometimes I thank God for unanswered prayers*
> *Remember when you're talkin' to the man upstairs*
> *That just because he doesn't answer doesn't mean he don't care*
> *Some of God's greatest gifts are unanswered prayers"*

"But," an objector might say, "this will only be convincing for someone who already believes in God! That is, an appeal to Providence, and a faith that there is a 'greater good' being served even if I'm in no position to perceive it, presupposes that God exists and is good. Such an appeal will fall on deaf ears if presented to an atheist!" Indeed it does. The aforementioned B.C. Johnson dismisses such an appeal by observing that "this argument does not explain why God allowed the child to burn to death. It merely claims that there is some reason discoverable in the long run. But the belief that such a reason is within our grasp must rest upon the additional belief that God is good. This is just to counter evidence against such a belief by assuming the belief to be true."

Correct—but the POE isn't a problem for atheists. The POE is precisely a problem for those people who already believe in God, and are wondering if the POE should cause them to reconsider. But, if I already believe in God, and if I already believe that God has Providentially ordered the unfolding of history in ways I couldn't possibly hope to comprehend, why should those beliefs not factor into my evaluation of the POE?

Those promoting the POE claim that suffering renders God's existence unlikely. Unlikely relative to what context? Probability assessments are always made against a set of background considerations. For example, suppose we want to know what the probability is that a particular person has a Bachelor's degree. Is it likely, or unlikely? If your answer is "I have no idea, I need more information," then you've got the right idea. If, for example, we're talking about an average person over the age of 25 in the United States, the probability is roughly 30%, but if the context is the entire world, then the probability is roughly 7%. These numbers vary further of course by gender and other demographic variables. Imagine if the particular person were a student in a kindergarten class!

When someone claims suffering renders God's existence improbable, what is our context? Is suffering the only thing being considered? In that case, the case for God might look bad, but why should suffering be the only evidence being considered? What happens to that probability assessment if we add to it the notion of Providence? What if we add various arguments for God's existence, such as the design, cosmological, or ontological arguments? What if we add the argument from miracles, or an appeal to the internal witness of the Holy Spirit?

For a person of faith (in other words, for a person for whom the POE is a problem), there is likely more to consider than just suffering. *Craig claims that when we consider the full scope of the evidence it is by no means obvious that God's existence is improbable.*

Finally, as one more component of a "full scope of evidence/greater good" appeal, Craig recommends that we consider what assumption is being made about the purpose of life, when grappling with the POE. If we assume, for example, that the purpose of this life is pleasure, happiness, safety, or the like, then it will be challenging to perceive in what way many experiences of suffering serve those ends. If the "greater good" intended by life itself is happiness, then it might be difficult to discern in what way great suffering conduces to happiness. But why should we assume that the purpose of this life or this world is happiness? Paley, after considering various possible purposes for this world, instead concludes that this life is best understood as a place of "probation."

> *Now we assert the most probable supposition to be, that it is a state of moral probation; and that many things in it suit with this hypothesis, which suit no other. It is not a state of unmixed happiness, or of happiness simply: it is not a state of*

designed misery, or of misery simply: it is not a state of retribution: it is not a state of punishment. It suits with none of these suppositions. It accords much better with the idea of its being a condition calculated for the production, exercise, and improvement of moral qualities, with a view to a future state, in which these qualities, after being so produced, exercised, and improved, may, by a new and more favouring constitution of things, receive their reward, or become their own.[229]

How should the theist regard herself, in her relationship to God? Like God's pet, or like God's child? The difference is significant, and relevant to the POE.

If we are God's pets, then we might well expect that our habitat should be a lot nicer than it actually is. Most of us who own pets, for example, try our best to make our pets happy, considering the resources we have at our disposal. That is, we generally feed our pets the best food we can afford. We try to provide a clean environment. We provide toys, and veterinary visits (when needed, and when affordable), and tummy rubs, and play time, and we try to make our pets as happy as we can, for as long as we're able. If a pet owner does not, we suspect there must be something morally wrong with her.

Imagine, for example, that we learn that a woman has dozens of cats, but keeps them in deplorable conditions. They don't have enough food. They live in filthy conditions, and many of them are injured or diseased and receive no medical care. Should we learn of a situation like that, as we sometimes do, we immediately infer several basic possible explanations.

- The woman can't afford to make things better.
- The woman doesn't know or understand how bad things are.
- The woman isn't actually there to take care of them (e.g., she has died, or moved away).
- The woman is cruel.

Now, apply this kind of reasoning to the POE. We are God's pets, and we're suffering. How can we explain this?

- [God] "can't afford" to make things better (i.e., God is not all-powerful).
- [God] doesn't know or understand how bad things are (i.e., God is not all-knowing).
- [God] isn't actually there to take care of them (i.e., God doesn't exist).
- [God] is cruel (i.e., God is not perfectly good).

You can see how this reasoning works. If we're God's pets, one might think we'd have a home that isn't so filled with danger and disease. One might think God wouldn't let so many of his pets starve, or hurt one another. Of course, this analogy is a bit problematic, since we "good and wise" humans often do things to and for our pets that are for their own good, but which, from their perspective, might seem "mean" or at least undesirable.

Lewis raises this analogy, using dogs as his specific example. Dogs are lovable, but humans interfere with the dog's nature to make them more so. We bathe dogs, house-train them, teach them not to steal food from the table, etc.—and in so doing enable ourselves to love the dog more completely. If the puppy could express its experience during the training phase, it might well question the goodness of humans, but (Lewis alleges), the fully-grown and well-trained dog who, by virtue of that, is healthier, longer-lived, and "admitted, as it were by Grace, to a whole world of affections, loyalties, interests, and comforts entirely beyond its animal destiny, would have no such doubts."[230] In my own case, I restrict my cat's access to food, and occasionally take her to the vet for check-ups, and she might well think that I am being "mean" (if such projections make any sense), but what I do is done

---

[229] Paley, Ibid.

[230] Lewis, *Problem of Pain*, p.36.

out of love, and concern for her overall well-being.

Another, more significant problem, though, according to both Craig and Lewis, is that we shouldn't be thinking of ourselves as God's pets! If we think of ourselves as pets, we form certain expectations of what sort of world we think we should have, and, not finding that world in real life, we call God into question. The solution to this problem is to realize that we're not pets, but "children"—children of God, specifically.

My cat is brilliant and sweet, but I don't think she's ever going to be any "better" than she is now. That is, I think "nature" has provided her with all the tools she needs to survive thanks to her natural instincts. I like to think that she enjoys my company, but I'm sure that what she really enjoys is all the stuff I do for her, such as giving her food that she doesn't need to hunt! I monitor how many treats I give my cat, but not because I think she needs to learn any sort of lesson about temperance (as if she could learn such a lesson), but instead because I want to keep her from gaining too much weight at the expense of her health. Ultimately, I don't believe my cat is a "moral" creature. That is not to say that she's immoral, but rather amoral. She's just not capable of being morally responsible. It's not the sort of creature she is, or ever can be.

The same can't be said of human children, and that's why I don't employ the same principles with my niece and nephews as I do with my cat. I monitor what I give to them, and what I do for them, not merely for the sake of their health, but, to be blunt, because I don't want to have any part in turning them into spoiled brats. One day, my niece and nephews will be adults, and will have to tackle life's challenges on their own. Their childhood is the training ground in which they are learning how to do that. Part of being a responsible parent (or care-giver) is facilitating that training. A parent who indulges his child's every desire can, in some cases, be killing that child with kindness. If the primary purpose of childhood, and the primary goal of childrearing, was "happiness," then we should expect a certain sort of (generally indulgent) behavior on the part of parents. But, if we switch the purpose and goal to something like "facilitating the child's maturing into a responsible adult," then our expectations of parent behavior changes as well.

In 2014, a drunk driving case made national headlines because of a peculiar defense argument: "affluenza." The driver (16 year old Ethan Couch, who drove drunk and caused an accident resulting in the deaths of four people) was defended in court by psychologist Dr. G. Dick Miller. Miller said the boy's parents gave him "freedoms no young person should have," that he was a product of "'affluenza"—which he described as his family thinking that wealth bought privilege, and not perceiving any rational link between behavior and consequences. As an example of this, Miller pointed out that Couch's parents allowed him to drive (illegally) starting at the age of 13, and that they did not punish him after police ticketed him (then 15) for being parked in a pickup truck with a naked, passed out, 14-year-old girl.[231] The implication, of course, legal defense strategy aside, is that we are not (ultimately) doing our children any favors if we fail to "set limits," or correct bad behavior.

> *Love between father and son, in this symbol (Father to Christ), means essentially authoritative love on the one side, and obedient love on the other. The father uses his authority to make the son into the sort of human being he, rightly, and in his superior wisdom, wants him to be. Even in our own days, though a man might say it, he could mean noting by saying "I love my son but don't care how great a blackguard he is provided he has a good time."*[232]

What kind of a parent is indifferent to what sort of person his or her child becomes? How is it "love" to either not care whether your child is good or bad, or, if you do care,

231 http://www.wfaa.com/story/local/2015/05/28/14140396/

232 Lewis, Problem of Pain, p.37.

to do nothing to promote the good? Indeed, Lewis argues, it is because of love that we care, and the same is true of God.

When Christianity says that God loves man, it means that God loves man: not that He has some "disinterested", because really indifferent, concern for our welfare, but that, in awful and surprising truth, we are the objects of His love. You asked for a loving God: you have one. The great spirit you so lightly invoked, the "lord of terrible aspect", is present: not a senile benevolence that drowsily wishes you to be happy in your own way, not the cold philanthropy of a conscientious magistrate, nor the care of a host who feels responsible for the comfort of his guests, but the consuming fire Himself, the Love that made the worlds, persistent as the artist's love for his work and despotic as a man's love for a dog, provident and venerable as a father's love for a child, jealous, inexorable, exacting as love between the sexes.[233]

A basic principle that we all presumably recognize is that growth (the kind we most value, at least), requires resistance. We know that this is so with respect to growing in physical strength. If I join a gym, and I do one set of 5 curls with ½ pound weights, I'm just never going to grow bigger and stronger. In terms of fitness and strength, growth requires resistance to be overcome.

We also understand this principle with respect to intellectual growth. This might sound shocking, but you don't want this material, or this class, to be easy—at least not if you actually care about learning something. We only grow, intellectually, when we are presented with an intellectual challenge to overcome.

Can we also add moral and spiritual growth to this same pattern? To grow with respect to my moral character requires challenges to overcome as well. Children must be allowed to take risks, and make mistakes. Children must be allowed to experience disappointment and frustration. Only then will they be able to learn how to grapple with such things themselves. A child who never learns how to deal with fear, disappointment, frustration, or loss, as a child, will not be able to function as an adult member of society. This means that parents, including wise, morally decent parents, can be justified in allowing their children to suffer, if the purpose of that suffering is to allow opportunities for growth. Love is not always identical to kindness, or leniency.

By the goodness of God we mean nowadays almost exclusively His lovingness; and in this we may be right. And by Love, in this context, most of us mean kindness—the desire to see others than the self happy; not happy in this way or in that, but just happy. What would really satisfy us would be a God who said of anything we happened to like doing, 'What does it matter so long as they are contented?' We want, in fact, not so much a Father in Heaven as a grandfather in heaven—a senile benevolence who, as they say, 'liked to see young people enjoying themselves' and whose plan for the universe was simply that it might be truly said at the end of each day, 'a good time was had by all'. Not many people, I admit, would formulate a theology in precisely those terms: but a conception not very different lurks at the back of many minds. I do not claim to be an exception: I should very much like to live in a universe which was governed on such lines. But since it is abundantly clear that I don't, and since I have reason to believe, nevertheless, that, God is Love, I conclude that my conception of love needs correction.

I might, indeed, have learned, even from the poets, that Love is something more stern and splendid than mere kindness: . . . Kindness consents very readily to the

233 Lewis, Problem of Pain, p.39.

removal of its object – we have all met people whose kindness to animals is constantly leading them to kill animals lest they should suffer. Kindness, merely as such, cares not whether its object becomes good or bad, provided only that it escapes suffering. As Scripture points out, it is bastards who are spoiled: the legitimate sons, who are to carry on the family tradition, are punished. (Hebrews 12:8) It is for people whom we care nothing about that we demand happiness on any terms: with our friends, our lovers, our children, we are exacting and would rather see them suffer much than be happy in contemptible and estranging modes. If God is Love, He is, by definition, something more than mere kindness. And it appears, from all the records, that though He has often rebuked us and condemned us, He has never regarded us with contempt. He has paid us the intolerable compliment of loving us, in the deepest, most tragic, most inexorable sense.[234]

If we believe the purpose of life is our own happiness, we might well expect a very pleasant environment in which to live, and question the qualities (or existence) of a God who failed to provide them. But, according to Lewis, Paley, and Craig, the chief purpose of life, according to Christianity, is not happiness, but knowledge of (and relation with) God. As Lewis puts it, "What we would here and now call our 'happiness' is not the end God chiefly has in view: but when we are such as He can love without impediment, we shall in fact be happy."[235]
According to Craig:

One reason that the problem of evil seems so puzzling is that we tend to think that if God exists, then His goal for human life is happiness in this world. God's role is to provide comfortable environment for His human pets. But on the Christian view this is false. We are not God's pets, and man's end is not happiness in this world, but the knowledge of God, which will ultimately bring true and everlasting human fulfillment. Many evils occur in life which may be utterly pointless with respect to the goal of producing human happiness in this world, but they may not be unjustified with respect to producing the knowledge of God. Innocent human suffering provides an occasion for deeper dependency and trust in God, either on the part of the sufferer or those around him. Of course, whether God's purpose is achieved through our suffering will depend on our response. Do we respond with anger and bitterness toward God, or do we turn to Him in faith for strength to endure?

In similar fashion (some centuries earlier), Paley points to the character-formation potential of the trials and tribulations of life (conceivable as the combination of natural/physical and moral/civic evils).

In the wide scale of human condition, there is not perhaps one of its manifold diversities, which does not bear upon the design here suggested. Virtue is infinitely various. There is no situation in which a rational being is placed, from that of the best-instructed Christian, down to the condition of the rudest barbarian, which affords not room for moral agency; for the acquisition, exercise, and display of voluntary qualities, good and bad. Health and sickness, enjoyment and suffering, riches and poverty, knowledge and ignorance, power and subjection, liberty and bondage, civilization and barbarity, have all their offices and duties, all serve for the formation of character: for when we speak of a state of trial, it must be remembered, that characters are not only tried, or proved, or detected, but that they

[234] Lewis, *Problem of Pain*, pp.31-33.

[235] Lewis, *Problem of Pain*, p. 41.

> *are generated also, and formed, by circumstances.*[236]

We can see the connection between this line of defense and the free will defense. According to the Christian tradition (as understood by Craig), God Providentially creates and orders a world that maximizes God's purposes. With respect to humans, this means a world best suited for bringing as many people as possible freely to knowledge of, and relationship with, God. To make it a genuine choice, we must have free will, and the possession of free will entails the risk of moral evil. What's more, one can imagine that a pain-free paradise (i.e., one without natural evil), while quite conducive to happiness, might not be as conducive to the purpose of bringing people to God. As Lewis describes:

> *My own experience is something like this. I am progressing along the path of life in my ordinary contentedly fallen and godless condition, absorbed in a merry meeting with my friends for the morrow or a bit of work that tickles my vanity today, a holiday or a new book, when suddenly a stab of abdominal pain that threatens serious disease, or a headline in the newspapers that threatens us all with destruction, sends this whole pack of cards tumbling down. At first I am overwhelmed, and all my little happinesses look like broken toys. Then, slowly and reluctantly, bit by bit, I try to bring myself into the frame of mind that I should be in at all times. I remind myself that all these toys were never intended to possess my heart, that my true good is in another world and my only real treasure is Christ. And perhaps, by God's grace, I succeed, and for a day or two become a creature consciously dependent on God and drawing its strength from the right sources. But the moment the threat is withdrawn, my whole nature leaps back to the toys: I am even anxious, God forgive me, to banish from my mind the only thing that supported me under the threat because it is now associated with the misery of those few days. Thus the terrible necessity of tribulation is only too clear. God has had me for but forty-eight hours and then only by dint of taking everything else away from me. Let Him but sheathe that sword for a moment and I behave like a puppy when the hated bath is over—I shake myself as dry as I can and race off to reacquire my comfortable dirtiness, if not in the nearest manure heap, at least in the nearest flower bed. And that is why tribulations cannot cease until God either sees us remade or sees that our remaking is now hopeless.*[237]

If the purpose of this life is to bring as many people as possible to a relationship with God, then a pain-free paradise might not serve that purpose well at all. Paley would add that such a paradise would likewise not be conducive to the formation of good character.

If life were a paradise free from pain, resistance, setbacks, struggle, or even toil, our "dependency upon supernatural aid" would produce undesirable results. No longer needing to "work" for anything, this would "introduce negligence, inactivity, and disorder, into the most useful occupations of human life; and thereby deteriorate the condition of human life itself." Some of you might be thinking that such a "deteriorated" condition sounds pretty good! So work? No struggle? No pain? No loss? But, according to Paley, such a life would lack numerous qualities that we deem valuable and important.

For one, virtue would be impossible. In the actual world, suffering is an occasion to develop and display virtue. "Again, one man's sufferings may be another man's trial. The family of a sick parent is a school of filial piety. . . . It is upon such

[236] Paley, Ibid.

[237] Lewis, *Problem of Pain*, pp.106-107.

sufferings alone that benevolence can operate."[238] In other words, virtues require "the existence of evil, without which it would have no object, no material to work upon, . . ."[239] Courage requires danger. Compassion requires that others suffer. Charity requires need. Justice requires that things sometimes occur that shouldn't.

Moreover, Paley argues that even our enjoyment of life, and its meaning, would be imperiled in a world without pain.

> *Of other external evils (still confining ourselves to what are called physical or natural evils), a considerable part come within the scope of the following observation:--The great principle of human satisfaction is engagement. It is a most just distinction, which the late Mr. Tucker has dwelt upon so largely in his works, between pleasures in which we are passive, and pleasures in which we are active. And, I believe, every attentive observer of human life will assent to his position, that, however grateful the sensations may occasionally be in which we are passive, it is not these, but the latter class of our pleasures, which constitute satisfaction; which supply that regular stream of moderate and miscellaneous enjoyments, in which happiness, as distinguished from voluptuousness, consists. Now for rational occupation, which is, in other words, for the very material of contented existence, there would be no place left, if either the things with which we had to do were absolutely impracticable to our endeavours, or if they were too obedient to our uses. A world, furnished with advantages on one side, and beset with difficulties, wants, and inconveniences on the other, is the proper abode of free, rational, and active natures, being the fittest to stimulate and exercise their faculties. The very refractoriness of the objects they have to deal with, contributes to this purpose. A world in which nothing depended upon ourselves, however it might have suited an imaginary race of beings, would not have suited mankind. Their skill, prudence, industry; their various arts, and their best attainments, from the application of which they draw, if not their highest, their most permanent gratifications, would be insignificant, if things could be either moulded by our volitions, or, of their own accord, conformed themselves to our views and wishes.*[240]

Here Paley is claiming that, as much as we enjoy "passive" pleasures, we value "active" pleasures, requiring our deliberate engagement, more so. We can imagine a world in which I don't have to "do" anything in order to be pleased.

- Why bother getting out of bed? Nothing "bad" can happen to you if you stay in bed all the time instead.
- Why bother eating? You can't starve, or even feel hungry (since hunger is an experience of suffering). Of course, you can't overeat either. . . .
- Why go to school? You can't suffer as a result of ignorance.
- Why go to work? You can't suffer as a result of not going to work. You can't lose your home, or your electricity, or anything else normally paid from your wages, since any of those outcomes would involve suffering. Of course, you don't need a house or electricity anyway, since being homeless and in the cold or dark can't produce any suffering. . . .
- Why socialize with other people? You can't experience the suffering of loneliness. Of course, nothing bad can ever happen from any socializing that you might do anyway.
- Why *not* get drunk and then drive home? Nothing bad can happen to me, or anyone

[238] Paley, Ibid.
[239] Paley, Ibid
[240] Paley, Ibid

else. Hell, get drunk, put on a blindfold, and drive home backwards! No one can get injured. I can't even damage my car.

- Why not go to work with a gun and fire it at people as many times as you can squeeze the trigger? Nothing bad can happen to them, or you. No injuries, no deaths. You can't even be disappointed by your failure to hurt someone, since disappointment is also a form of suffering.
- Why do anything, in fact? After all, nothing bad can result from you doing absolutely nothing at all for your entire existence.

Contrast this bizarre world without consequences to the one in which we actually live. In this world, there *are* consequences for our actions. Real consequences. Permanent ones. If I get drunk and then drive home, it's not only my own life I place in danger, but the lives of everyone else on the road. My choice to drink and drive has profound significance because of the serious and lasting consequences that might result. If you choose to stay in bed all day, and never go to work or school, there will be consequences with respect to the overall quality of your life, and your life prospects. It makes a difference whether you get out of bed each day. It makes a difference what you do. A difference to you, and to others. A world without challenge (and, therefore, the risk of suffering) is a world empty of growth potential, and even meaning itself. That sort of world might be acceptable for a "pet," but would *we* really desire such an existence? Isn't it possible that the conditions of our world, complete with natural and moral evils, actually serves a "greater good" (e.g., our character development)? If one can't imagine that to be so, Craig would remind us that we are not in a good epistemic position to assess whether the events and conditions of our world fail to serve such a greater good.

But, the critic might ask, why do we have *so much* "evil" in the world? Perhaps some amount of suffering is needed for to make existence meaningful, and to give us opportunity for "growth," but surely we don't need *all* the suffering that we actually find in this world. For example, an environment in which the most "challenging" natural evil was mild rain and the common cold would still produce suffering, and therefore opportunities for growth. Why do we need natural disasters that kill thousands, or diseases like cancer that kill millions? Surely we have more suffering than is needed, and any suffering in excess of what is needed will be *unjustified*.

A possible theistic response to this is to challenge our ability to assess the amount of suffering needed in the first place. How do we *know* that we have "too much" suffering? How could we possibly know? Perhaps we have exactly as much suffering as is needed, and not a bit more. How could you, or I, be in a position to make that judgment? Moreover, isn't it the case that our perception of suffering is relative? That is, based upon one's life experiences and expectations, what is deemed "unbearable" to one person is a part of daily life to someone else. Spoiled, wealthy teens might groan from the injustice of having to make the bed in the morning, while another teen working in an Asian sweatshop on the other side of the world is grateful to have a 5 minute break to stretch and use the bathroom during her 10 hour shift. The muscle pain that might put me out of a game might be shrugged off by a more rugged athlete.

As a thought experiment, imagine a world in which the worst thing that could ever happen to someone, is a tooth-ache. Now, imagine that you awake one morning to find yourself with a tooth-ache. In that world, wouldn't you be crying out, "Why God? Why do you allow me to suffer so?" From our perspective, that seems silly, because we can imagine far worse things than a tooth-ache. We have to contend with cancer, and rape, genocide, and Alzheimer's disease. Certainly, those things are far worse. Or so it seems, to us. Try a different thought experiment.

What do you think is the worst thing that could ever happen to anyone? Identify it, whether it's having a certain disease, or a certain injury, or being the victim of a certain crime. *That* (whatever it is), is too much to bear. If God exists, God would never allow *that*. Now, suppose that God agrees, and eliminates that thing (whatever it was), from the world.

What's number two on your list? It just got promoted to number one, didn't it? Isn't that new thing (whatever *it* is), now "the worst thing in the world," that which "no one should ever have to endure?" Shouldn't God eliminate that new thing from the world? And if God does, what was number three? And then number four, and number five, and so on. You probably get the point by now. *Any* amount of suffering might seem like "too much." We don't like to suffer! But, if the only amount of suffering that we'll think is acceptable is "none at all," and if a world without suffering is a world without potential for meaning and growth, then we're just asking for a world in which the most basic project of our existence isn't possible. If there's a good reason for God to permit our suffering, than quibbling over the precise amount of suffering that's justifiable for God to allow won't get us anywhere.

Another possible complaint against this kind of greater good defense is that God could at least be more selective with respect to *who* He permits to suffer. Why does God let bad things happen to good people? Perhaps suffering is necessary. Perhaps we need free will and the consequent risk of moral evil. Perhaps we need a challenging environment, too, and therefore run the risk of natural evil. But, why doesn't God just cause natural and moral evil to afflict bad people only? Why should good people get cancer? Or get molested as a child? If those things are needed, why not be a little more discriminating and only allow people who *deserve* to suffer, to suffer?

As a reply, imagine that you lived in a world in which every time anyone told a lie of any kind, that person was immediately struck dead by a bolt of lightning. Imagine, also, that in that world, any time anyone refuses to help another person in need (when able to do so), the one who refuses to help grows a cancerous tumor instantly. I'd bet that this imaginary world is filled with honest and generous people! I'm confident that if I lived in that world, I would be scrupulously honest—boorishly so. I'm sure you would be as well. Why? Isn't the answer obvious? To avoid the deadly lightning! Or, in the case of helping others, to avoid the tumor. In such a world, we have an obvious ulterior motive when it comes to telling the truth and being charitable: our very lives are at stake. We're not being honest and generous because we deem it the right thing to do, but we're doing so out of fear of immediate and negative consequences if we refuse. Contrast that with the real world.

In the real world, being a good person is no guarantee that bad things will never happen to you. It's possible to be a wonderful, honest, kind, generous human being, and still get cancer, still become homeless, still get raped and murdered, still be killed by a natural disaster, etc. Being a good person is no insurance policy against suffering in this world. For that reason, we know that when people *do* choose to do the right thing, it's not because they think it will spare them from suffering. It must be for some other reason—perhaps simply because it's the right thing to do. A world where suffering can afflict any one of us is a world in which our motives can be more pure, more morally valuable—and therefore more conducive to character growth.

Ultimately, Paley argues that the kind of world in which we live, with all its attendant pains, is "worth it"—not only on the presumption that "Heaven" awaits those who pass their "probation," but even with respect to what we value in this life alone. As regards pain, Paley reminds us that it is "seldom the object of contrivance; that when it is so, the contrivance rests ultimately in good."[241] Pain serves as a warning against greater harms or dangers. Pain is also capable of relief, and although pain may be violent or frequent, "it is seldom both violent and long-continued: and its pauses and intermissions become positive pleasures."[242] Paley even goes so far as to claim that existence of pain causes pleasure to be all the more pleasurable, as moments of pain or sadness make joy all the more meaningful to us. Even death (and our fear of it), perhaps the most infamous of

[241] Paley, Ibid

[242] Paley, Ibid

"pains," serves a positive function. Paley claims that the "horror of death proves the value of life."

> *Death implies separation: and the loss of those whom we love, must necessarily, so far as we can conceive, be accompanied with pain. To the brute creation, nature seems to have stepped in with some secret provision for their relief, under the rupture of their attachments. In their instincts towards their offspring, and of their offspring to them, I have often been surprised to observe how ardently they love, and how soon they forget. The pertinacity of human sorrow (upon which, time also, at length, lays its softening hand) is probably, therefore, in some manner connected with the qualities of our rational or moral nature. One thing however is clear, viz. that it is better that we should possess affections, the sources of so many virtues, and so many joys, although they be exposed to the incidents of life, as well as the interruptions of mortality, than, by the want of them, be reduced to a state of selfishness, apathy, and quietism.*[243]

Although this might be hard to accept in the depths of our grief, Paley claims that we are far better off being capable of all the depths of our emotions (including grief), necessitated by the kind of world in which we live, than if we were incapable of such feelings (including their depths, and contrasts) at all. Pain is "worth it." This world might not seem ideal from the standpoint of our comfort and pleasure, but Lewis suggests that it *shouldn't.*

> *The Christian doctrine of suffering explains, I believe, a very curious fact about the world we live in. The settled happiness and security which we all desire, God withholds from us by the nature of the world: but joy, pleasure, and merriment He has scattered broadcast...The security we crave would teach us to rest our hearts in this world and oppose an obstacle to our return to God...Our Father refreshes us on the journey with some pleasant inns, but will not encourage us to mistake them for home.*[244]

B.C. Johnson takes issue with this general line of reasoning, of course. He attempts to show the perils of these sorts of arguments by means of a "*reductio ad absurdum*" technique. A "*reductio*" involves showing that an argument or claim, when pushed to its "inevitable conclusions" produces absurd results, and therefore there must be something faulty with the argument or claim itself.

How might this apply to the greater good strategy considered above? Johnson considers three variants of the greater good justification: that God doesn't intervene to prevent suffering because to do so would (1) cause us to become dependent creatures, (2) remove our sense of moral urgency, and (3) eliminate opportunities to develop and display virtue. Note that these represent the same basic points offered by Paley and Craig above. Johnson interprets these arguments as concluding that our suffering is justified because it maximizes our independence, sense of moral urgency, and opportunities to develop/display virtue. He then responds to these claims in the same way, by means of a "*reductio.*"

1. If it is good to maximize X (independence/moral urgency/virtue building), then we ought to perform every action that promotes X.
2. We ought not to perform every action that promotes X.
3. Therefore, it is not good to maximize X

The key to Johnson's argument is the second premise: we ought not to perform every action that promotes X. To see why this is so, Johnson considers several extreme (and absurd) examples of actions that promote "X (i.e., independence/moral urgency/virtue building)."

243 Paley, Ibid

244 Lewis, *Problem of Pain*, p.116.

> *It is worthwhile to emphasize, however, that we encourage efforts to eliminate evils; we approve of efforts to promote peace, prevent famine, and wipe out disease. In other words, we do value a world with fewer or (if possible) no opportunities for the development of virtue (when "virtue" is understood to mean the reduction of suffering). If we produce such a world for succeeding generations, how will they develop virtues? Without war, disease, and famine, they will not be virtuous. Should we then cease our attempts to wipe out war, disease, and famine? If we do not believe that it is right to cease attempts at improving the world, then by implication we admit that virtue-building is not an excuse for God to permit disasters. For we admit that the development of virtue is no excuse for permitting disasters.*[245]

In other words, if we really believed that "we ought to perform every action that promotes X (independence/moral urgency/virtue building)," then rather than trying to eliminate sources of suffering in the world, we should be trying to *increase* suffering in the world. However, we all (presumably) think that is absurd. By implication, we don't *really* think that it is good to maximize "X (independence/moral urgency/virtue building)." Since the value of "maximizing X" was the force behind this version of the greater good defense, Johnson thinks the greater good defense fails.

Conclusion

The POE is a negative theistic argument that can serve to undermine justification for theistic belief. It is based on the claim that the sort of world in which we live (i.e., one filled with seemingly unjustified suffering) is unlikely to exist if there also exists a God who is all-knowing, all-powerful, and perfectly good. Given that our world *does* contain such suffering, that sort of God is unlikely to exist—and, even though the POE does not *refute* the existence of that God, it does (or can) serve to lessen the confidence that one might have that such a God really does exist.

The POE is a difficult problem, and not only for its intellectual properties, but also given the fact that the abstract observations about pain and suffering correspond to real-world occurrences. The POE hits people "at home." In their experiences of abuse. In their cancer. In their lost loved ones. For such reasons, the POE (literally) *feels* different than the "problem" posed by whether or not the universe had a cause of its existence, or whether the universe is actually infinite in the past.

For some, the POE is intractable, and they lose their faith from it, or never come to faith in the first place. It is, however, possible to offer "solutions" to the POE as we can see from Paley, Lewis, and Craig. Admittedly, these solutions threaten to be question-begging in that they are unlikely to be compelling except for those who already believe in the existence of that sort of God. On the other hand, unlike with most of cases of begging the question, this is not necessarily a problem. After all, the POE arises as a problem only for those who already believe that God exists (and who are trying to make sense of evil given that belief). It only makes sense that efforts to understand evil in that context would make use of elements of the worldview that is imperiled by the POE in the first place.

---

[245] Johnson, Ibid.

Exercises for Wisdom and Growth

1. Do you believe that suffering serves a purpose? Does it always serve a purpose, or only sometimes? What is this purpose? If only sometimes, what makes the difference between "purposeful" suffering and suffering with no purpose?
2. If you believe in God, has there even been a time in your life when your belief or confidence in that God was shaken by a tragic event? How did you resolve your concerns? Do Craig's arguments help? Lewis'? Paley's?
3. If you do not believe in God, to what extent (if any) does the POE contribute to that?
4. In epistemology, there are what is known as "undercutting defeaters," and "rebutting defeaters." A "defeater" is simply a claim that counts against a belief that you have (i.e., it serves as evidence against it). Undercutting defeaters are bits of evidence that cause you to *lose confidence* that your belief is true. Rebutting defeaters serve to cause you to flatly reject your belief (i.e., to conclude that your belief is false). Do you find the POE to be a defeater for belief in God? If so, is it an "undercutting" defeater, or a "rebutting" defeater?
5. Some might claim that Craig's claim that we are no epistemic position to conclude that suffering could serve a greater good is just a fancier sounding version of the more commonly expressed claim that "God works in mysterious ways." Some might dismiss this as an appeal to ignorance. In effect, Craig can't identify the "greater good" being served, but merely assumes, on faith, perhaps, that there must be one anyway. Not surprisingly, Craig disagrees with this characterization of his argument. With whom do you agree? How much do you think your own faith (or lack thereof) contributes to your assessment?

We have another offering from Hume, from the same "Dialogues" we encountered in a previous chapter. In this section, Demea, Cleanthes, and Philo are continuing their discussion of religious arguments, though the discussion now focuses on human suffering. They catalog a variety of sources of such suffering, both "natural" and that inflicted by the actions of other humans. After the dramatic and sobering listing of these "evils," Philo delivers the punch line by appealing to the ancient philosopher Epicurus, and, in so doing, calls into question the properties, or existence, of God. This excerpt is doubly excellent for its capacity to provide a sense of history to the problem of evil. Considered by many to be the most compelling evidentiary threat against theism today, the problem of evil is here traced back not only to Hume, but thousands of years earlier to the pre-Christian philosopher Epicurus.

David Hume
Dialogues Concerning Natural Religion

Part X

It is my opinion, I own, replied Demea, that each man feels, in a manner, the truth of religion within his own breast, and, from a consciousness of his imbecility and misery, rather than from any reasoning, is led to seek protection from that Being, on whom he and all nature is dependent. So anxious or so tedious are even the best scenes of life, that futurity is still the object of all our hopes and fears. We incessantly look forward, and endeavour, by prayers, adoration, and sacrifice, to appease those unknown powers, whom we find, by experience, so able to afflict and oppress us. Wretched creatures that we are! what resource for us amidst the innumerable ills of life, did not religion suggest some methods of atonement, and appease those terrors with which we are incessantly agitated and tormented?

I am indeed persuaded, said Philo, that the best, and indeed the only method of bringing every one to a due sense of religion, is by just representations of the misery and wickedness of men. And for that purpose a talent of eloquence and strong imagery is more requisite than that of reasoning and argument. For is it necessary to prove what every one feels within himself? It is only necessary to make us feel it, if possible, more intimately and sensibly.

The people, indeed, replied Demea, are sufficiently convinced of this great and melancholy truth. The miseries of life; the unhappiness of man; the general corruptions of our nature; the unsatisfactory enjoyment of pleasures, riches, honours; these phrases have become almost proverbial in all languages. And who can doubt of what all men declare from their own immediate feeling and experience?

In this point, said Philo, the learned are perfectly agreed with the vulgar; and in all letters, sacred and profane, the topic of human misery has been insisted on with the most pathetic eloquence that sorrow and melancholy could inspire. The poets, who speak from sentiment, without a system, and whose testimony has therefore the more authority, abound in images of this nature. From Homer down to Dr. Young, the whole inspired tribe have ever been sensible, that no other representation of things would suit the feeling and observation of each individual.

As to authorities, replied Demea, you need not seek them. Look round this library of Cleanthes. I shall venture to affirm, that, except authors of particular sciences, such as chemistry or botany, who have no occasion to treat of human life, there is scarce one of those innumerable writers, from whom the sense of human misery has not, in some passage or other, extorted a complaint and confession of it. At least, the chance is entirely on that side; and no one author has ever, so far as I can recollect, been so extravagant as to deny it.

There you must excuse me, said Philo: Leibnitz has denied it; and is perhaps the first who ventured upon so bold and paradoxical an opinion; at least, the first who made it essential to his philosophical system.

And by being the first, replied Demea, might he not have been sensible of his error? For is this a subject in which philosophers can propose to make discoveries especially in so late an age? And can any man hope by a simple denial (for the subject scarcely admits of reasoning), to bear down the united testimony of mankind, founded on sense and consciousness?

And why should man, added he, pretend to an exemption from the lot of all other animals? The whole earth, believe me, Philo, is cursed and polluted. A perpetual war is kindled amongst all living creatures. Necessity, hunger, want, stimulate the strong and courageous: fear, anxiety, terror, agitate the weak and infirm. The first entrance into life gives anguish to the new-born infant and to its wretched parent: weakness, impotence, distress, attend each stage of that life: and it is at last finished in agony and horror.

Observe too, says Philo, the curious artifices of Nature, in order to embitter the life of every living being. The stronger prey upon the weaker, and keep them in perpetual terror and anxiety. The weaker too, in their turn, often prey upon the stronger, and vex and molest them without relaxation. Consider that innumerable race of insects, which either are bred on the body of each animal, or, flying about, infix their stings in him. These insects have others still less than themselves, which torment them. And thus on each hand, before and behind, above and below, every animal is surrounded with enemies, which incessantly seek his misery and distruction.

Man alone, said Demea, seems to be, in part, an exception to this rule. For by combination in society, he can easily master lions, tigers, and bears, whose greater strength and agility naturally enable them to prey upon him.

On the contrary, it is here chiefly, cried Philo, that the uniform and equal maxims of Nature are most apparent. Man, it is true, can, by combination, surmount all his real enemies, and become master of the whole animal creation: but does he not immediately raise up to himself imaginary enemies, the demons of his fancy, who haunt him with superstitious terrors, and blast every enjoyment of life? His pleasure, as he imagines, becomes, in their eyes, a crime: his food and repose give them umbrage and offence: his very sleep and dreams furnish new materials to anxious fear: and even death, his refuge from every other ill, presents only the dread of endless and innumerable woes. Nor does the wolf molest more the timid flock, than superstition does the anxious breast of wretched mortals.

Besides, consider, Demea: this very society, by which we surmount those wild beasts, our natural enemies; what new enemies does it not raise to us? What woe and misery does it not occasion? Man is the greatest enemy of man. Oppression, injustice, contempt, contumely, violence, sedition, war, calumny, treachery, fraud; by these they mutually torment each other; and they would soon dissolve that society which they had formed, were it not for the dread of still greater ills, which must attend their separation.

But though these external insults, said Demea, from animals, from men, from all the elements, which assault us, form a frightful catalogue of woes, they are nothing in comparison of those which arise within ourselves, from the distempered condition of our mind and body. How many lie under the lingering torment of diseases? Hear the pathetic enumeration of the great poet.

> Intestine stone and ulcer, colic-pangs,
> Demoniac frenzy, moping melancholy,
> And moon-struck madness, pining atrohy,
> Marasmus, and wide-wasting pestilence.
> Dire was the tossing, deep the groans: DESPAIR
> Tended the sick, busiest from couch to couch.
> And over them triumphant DEATH his dart
> Shook: but delay'd to strike, though oft invok'd
> With vows, as their chief good and final hope.

The disorders of the mind, continued Demea, though more secret, are not perhaps less dismal and vexatious. Remorse, shame, anguish, rage, disappointment, anxiety, fear, dejection, despair; who has ever passed through life without cruel inroads from these tormentors? How many have scarcely ever felt any better sensations? Labour and poverty, so abhorred by every one, are the certain lot of the far greater number; and those few privileged persons, who enjoy ease and opulence, never reach contentment or true felicity. All the goods of life united would not make a very happy man; but all the ills united would make a wretch indeed; and any one of them almost (and who can be free from every one?) nay often the absence of one good (and who can possess all?) is sufficient to render life ineligible.

Were a stranger to drop on a sudden into this world, I would shew him, as a specimen of its ills, an hospital full of diseases, a prison crowded with malefactors and debtors, a field of battle strewed with carcases, a fleet foundering in the ocean, a nation languishing under tyranny, famine, or pestilence. To turn the gay side of life to him and give him a notion of its pleasures; whither should I conduct him? to a ball, to an opera, to court? He might justly think, that I was only shewing him a diversity of distress and sorrow.

There is no evading such striking instances, said Philo, but by apologies, which still further aggravate the charge. Why have all men, I ask, in all ages, complained incessantly of the miseries of life? .... They have no just reason, says one: these complaints proceed only from their discontented, repining, anxious disposition .... And can there possibly, I reply, be a more certain foundation of misery, than such a wretched temper?

But if they were really as unhappy as they pretend, says my antagonist, why do they remain in life? ....

Not satisfied with life, afraid of death.

This is the secret chain, say I, that holds us. We are terrified, not bribed to the continuance of our existence. . . .

And is it possible, Cleanthes, said Philo, that after all these reflections, and infinitely more, which might be suggested, you can still persevere in your Anthropomorphism, and assert the moral attributes of the Deity, his justice, benevolence, mercy, and rectitude, to be of the same nature with these virtues in human creatures? His power we allow is infinite: whatever he wills is executed: but neither man nor any other animal is happy: therefore he does not will their happiness. His wisdom is infinite: he is never mistaken in choosing the means to any end: but the course of Nature tends not to human or animal felicity: therefore it is not established for that purpose. Through the whole compass of human knowledge, there are no inferences more certain and infallible than these. In what respect, then, do his benevolence and mercy resemble the benevolence and mercy of men?

Epicurus's old questions are yet unanswered.

Is he willing to prevent evil, but not able? then is he impotent. Is he able, but not willing? then is he malevolent. Is he both able and willing? whence then is evil? . . .

Part XI

Did I shew you a house or palace, where there was not one apartment convenient or agreeable; where the windows, doors, fires, passages, stairs, and the whole economy of the building, were the source of noise, confusion, fatigue, darkness, and the extremes of heat and cold; you would certainly blame the contrivance, without any further examination. The architect would in vain display his subtilty, and prove to you, that if this door or that window were altered, greater ills would ensue. What he says may be strictly true: the alteration of one particular, while the other parts of the building remain, may only augment the inconveniences. But still you would assert in general, that, if the architect had had skill and good intentions, he might have formed such a plan of the whole, and might have adjusted the parts in such a manner, as would have remedied all or most of these inconveniences. His ignorance, or even your own ignorance of such a plan, will never convince you of the impossibility of it. If you find any inconveniences and deformities in the building, you will always, without entering into any detail, condemn the architect.

In short, I repeat the question: Is the world, considered in general, and as it appears to us in this life, different from what a man, or such a limited being, would, beforehand, expect from a very powerful, wise, and benevolent Deity? It must be strange prejudice to assert the contrary. And from thence I conclude, that however consistent the world may be, allowing certain suppositions and conjectures, with the idea of such a Deity, it can never afford us an inference concerning his existence. The consistence is not absolutely denied, only the inference. Conjectures, especially where infinity is excluded from the Divine attributes, may perhaps be sufficient to prove a consistence, but can never be foundations for any inference.

There seems to be four circumstances, on which depend all, or the greatest part of the ills, that molest sensible creatures; and it is not impossible but all these circumstances may be necessary and unavoidable. We know so little beyond common life, or even of common life, that, with regard to the economy of a universe, there is no conjecture, however wild, which may not be just; nor any one, however plausible, which may not be erroneous. All that belongs to human understanding, in this deep ignorance and obscurity, is to be sceptical, or at least cautious, and not to admit of any hypothesis whatever, much less of any which is supported by no appearance of probability. Now, this I assert to be the case with regard to all the causes of evil, and the circumstances on which it depends. None of them appear to human reason in the least degree necessary or unavoidable; nor can we suppose them such, without the utmost license of imagination.

The first circumstance which introduces evil, is that contrivance or economy of the animal creation, by which pains, as well as pleasures, are employed to excite all creatures to action, and make them vigilant in the great work of self-preservation. Now pleasure alone, in its various degrees, seems to human understanding sufficient for this purpose. All animals might be constantly in a state of enjoyment: but when urged by any of the necessities of nature, such as thirst, hunger, weariness; instead of pain, they might feel a diminution of pleasure, by which they might be prompted to seek that object which is necessary to their subsistence. Men pursue pleasure as eagerly as they avoid pain; at least they might have been so constituted. It seems, therefore, plainly possible to carry on the business of life without any pain. Why then is any animal ever rendered susceptible of such a sensation? If animals can be free from it an hour, they might enjoy a perpetual exemption from it; and it required as particular a contrivance of their organs to produce that feeling, as to endow them with sight, hearing, or any of the senses. Shall we conjecture, that such a contrivance was necessary, without any appearance of reason? and shall we build on that conjecture as on the most certain truth?

But a capacity of pain would not alone produce pain, were it not for the second circumstance, viz. the conducting of the world by general laws; and this seems nowise necessary to a very perfect Being. It is true, if every thing were conducted by particular volitions, the course of nature would be perpetually broken, and no man could employ his reason in the conduct of life. But might not other particular volitions remedy this inconvenience? In short, might not the Deity exterminate all ill, wherever it were to be found; and produce all good, without any preparation, or long progress of causes and effects?

Besides, we must consider, that, according to the present economy of the world, the course of nature, though supposed exactly regular, yet to us appears not so, and many events are uncertain, and many disappoint our expectations. Health and sickness, calm and tempest, with an infinite number of other accidents, whose causes are unknown and variable, have a great influence both on the fortunes of particular persons and on the prosperity of public societies; and indeed all human life, in a manner, depends on such accidents. A being, therefore, who knows the secret springs of the universe, might easily, by particular volitions, turn all these accidents to the good of mankind, and render the whole world happy, without discovering himself in any operation. A fleet, whose purposes were salutary to society, might always meet with a fair wind. Good princes enjoy sound health and long life. Persons born to power and authority, be framed with good tempers and virtuous dispositions. A few such events as these, regularly and wisely conducted, would change the face of the world; and yet would no more seem to disturb the course of nature, or confound human conduct, than the present economy of things, where the causes are secret, and variable, and compounded. Some small touches given to Caligula's brain in his infancy, might have converted him into a Trajan. One wave, a little higher than the rest, by burying Caesar and his fortune in the bottom of the ocean, might have restored liberty to a considerable part of mankind. There may, for aught we know, be good reasons why Providence interposes not in this manner; but they are unknown to us; and though the mere supposition, that such reasons exist, may be sufficient to save the conclusion concerning the Divine attributes, yet surely it can never be sufficient to establish that conclusion.

If every thing in the universe be conducted by general laws, and if animals be rendered susceptible of pain, it scarcely seems possible but some ill must arise in the various shocks of matter, and the various concurrence and opposition of general laws; but this ill would be very rare, were it not for the third circumstance, which I proposed to mention, viz. the great frugality with which all powers and faculties are distributed to every particular being. So well adjusted are the organs and capacities of all animals, and so well fitted to their preservation, that, as far as history or tradition reaches, there appears not to be any single species which has yet been extinguished in the universe. Every animal has the requisite endowments; but these endowments are bestowed with so scrupulous an economy, that any considerable diminution must entirely destroy the creature. Wherever one power is encreased, there is a proportional abatement in the others. Animals which excel in swiftness are commonly defective in force. Those which possess both are either imperfect in some of their senses, or are oppressed with the most craving wants. The human species, whose chief excellency is reason and sagacity, is of all others the most necessitous, and the most deficient in bodily advantages; without clothes, without arms, without food, without lodging, without any convenience of life, except what they owe to their own skill and industry. In short, nature seems to have formed an exact calculation of the necessities of her creatures; and, like a rigid master, has afforded them little more powers or endowments than what are strictly sufficient to supply those necessities. An indulgent parent would have bestowed a large stock, in order to guard against accidents, and secure the happiness and welfare of the creature in the most unfortunate concurrence of circumstances. Every course of life would not have been so surrounded with precipices, that the least departure from the true path, by mistake or necessity, must involve us in misery and ruin. Some reserve, some fund, would have been provided to insure happiness; nor would the powers and the necessities have been adjusted with so rigid an economy. The Author of Nature is inconceivably powerful: his force is supposed great, if not altogether inexhaustible: nor is there any reason, as far as we can judge, to make him observe this strict frugality in his dealings with his creatures. It would have been better, were his power extremely limited, to have created fewer animals, and to have endowed these with more faculties for their happiness and preservation. A builder is never esteemed prudent, who undertakes a plan beyond what his stock will enable him to finish.

In order to cure most of the ills of human life, I require not that man should have the wings of the eagle, the swiftness of the stag, the force of the ox, the arms of the lion, the scales of the crocodile or rhinoceros; much less do I demand the sagacity of an angel or cherubim. I am contented to take an increase in one single power or faculty of his soul. Let him be endowed with a greater propensity to industry and labour; a more vigorous spring and activity of mind; a more constant bent to business and application. Let the whole species possess naturally an equal diligence with that which many individuals are able to attain by habit and reflection; and the most beneficial consequences, without any alloy of ill, is the immediate and necessary result of this endowment. Almost all the moral, as well as natural evils of human life, arise from idleness; and were our species, by the original constitution of their frame, exempt from this vice or infirmity, the perfect cultivation of land, the improvement of arts and manufactures, the exact execution of every office and duty, immediately follow; and men at once may fully reach that state of society, which is so imperfectly attained by the best regulated government. But as industry is a power, and the most valuable of any, Nature seems determined, suitably to her usual maxims, to bestow it on men with a very sparing hand; and rather to punish him severely for his deficiency in it, than to reward him for his attainments. She has so contrived his frame, that nothing but the most violent necessity can oblige him to labour; and she employs all his other wants to overcome, at least in part, the want of diligence, and to endow him with some share of a faculty of which she has thought fit naturally to bereave him. Here our demands may be allowed very humble, and therefore the more reasonable. If we required the endowments of superior penetration and judgment, of a more delicate taste of beauty, of a nicer sensibility to benevolence and friendship; we might be told, that we impiously pretend to break the order of Nature; that we want to exalt ourselves into a higher rank of being; that the presents which we require, not being suitable to our state and condition, would only be pernicious to us. But it is hard; I dare to repeat it, it is hard, that being placed in a world so full of wants and necessities, where almost every being and element is either our foe or refuses its assistance . . . we should also have our own temper to struggle with, and should be deprived of that faculty which can alone fence against these multiplied evils.

The fourth circumstance, whence arises the misery and ill of the universe, is the inaccurate workmanship of all the springs and principles of the great machine of nature. It must be acknowledged, that there are few parts of the universe, which seem not to serve some purpose, and whose removal would not produce a visible defect and disorder in the whole. The parts hang all together; nor can one be touched without affecting the rest, in a greater or less degree. But at the same time, it must be observed, that none of these parts or principles, however useful, are so accurately adjusted, as to keep precisely within those bounds in which their utility consists; but they are, all of them, apt, on every occasion, to run into the one extreme or the other. One would imagine, that this grand production had not received the last hand of the maker; so little finished is every part, and so coarse are the strokes with which it is executed. Thus, the winds are requisite to convey the vapours along the surface of the globe, and to assist men in navigation: but how oft, rising up to tempests and hurricanes, do they become pernicious? Rains are necessary to nourish all the plants and animals of the earth: but how often are they defective? how often excessive? Heat is requisite to all life and vegetation; but is not always found in the due proportion. On the mixture and secretion of the humours and juices of the body depend the health and prosperity of the animal: but the parts perform not regularly their proper function. What more useful than all the passions of the mind, ambition, vanity, love, anger? But how oft do they break their bounds, and cause the greatest convulsions in society? There is nothing so advantageous in the universe, but what frequently becomes pernicious, by its excess or defect; nor has Nature guarded, with the requisite accuracy, against all disorder or confusion. The irregularity is never perhaps so great as to destroy any species; but is often sufficient to involve the individuals in ruin and misery.

On the concurrence, then, of these four circumstances, does all or the greatest part of natural evil depend. Were all living creatures incapable of pain, or were the world administered by particular volitions, evil never could have found access into the universe: and were animals endowed with a large stock of powers and faculties, beyond what strict necessity requires; or were the several springs and principles of the universe so accurately framed as to preserve always the just temperament and medium; there must have been very little ill in comparison of what we feel at present. What then shall we pronounce on this occasion? Shall we say that these circumstances are not necessary, and that they might easily have been altered in the contrivance of the universe? This decision seems too presumptuous for creatures so blind and ignorant. Let us be more modest in our conclusions. Let us allow, that, if the goodness of the Deity (I mean a goodness like the human) could be established on any tolerable reasons a priori, these phenomena, however untoward, would not be sufficient to subvert that principle; but might easily, in some unknown manner, be reconcilable to it. But let us still assert, that as this goodness is not antecedently established, but must be inferred from the phenomena, there can be no grounds for such an inference, while there are so many ills in the universe, and while these ills might so easily have been remedied, as far as human understanding can be allowed to judge on such a subject. I am Sceptic enough to allow, that the bad appearances, notwithstanding all my reasonings, may be compatible with such attributes as you suppose; but surely they can never prove these attributes. Such a conclusion cannot result from Scepticism, but must arise from the phenomena, and from our confidence in the reasonings which we deduce from these phenomena.

Look round this universe. What an immense profusion of beings, animated and organized, sensible and active! You admire this prodigious variety and fecundity. But inspect a little more narrowly these living existences, the only beings worth regarding. How hostile and destructive to each other! How insufficient all of them for their own happiness! How contemptible or odious to the spectator! The whole presents nothing but the idea of a blind Nature, impregnated by a great vivifying principle, and pouring forth from her lap, without discernment or parental care, her maimed and abortive children!

Here the Manichaean system occurs as a proper hypothesis to solve the difficulty: and no doubt, in some respects, it is very specious, and has more probability than the common hypothesis, by giving a plausible account of the strange mixture of good and ill which appears in life. But if we consider, on the other hand, the perfect uniformity and agreement of the parts of the universe, we shall not discover in it any marks of the combat of a malevolent with a benevolent being. There is indeed an opposition of pains and pleasures in the feelings of sensible creatures: but are not all the operations of Nature carried on by an opposition of principles, of hot and cold, moist and dry, light and heavy? The true conclusion is, that the original Source of all things is entirely indifferent to all these principles; and has no more regard to good above ill, than to heat above cold, or to drought above moisture, or to light above heavy.

There may four hypotheses be framed concerning the first causes of the universe: that they are endowed with perfect goodness; that they have perfect malice; that they are opposite, and have both goodness and malice; that they have neither goodness nor malice. Mixed phenomena can never prove the two former unmixed principles; and the uniformity and steadiness of general laws seem to oppose the third. The fourth, therefore, seems by far the most probable.

What I have said concerning natural evil will apply to moral, with little or no variation; and we have no more reason to infer, that the rectitude of the Supreme Being resembles human rectitude, than that his benevolence resembles the human. Nay, it will be thought, that we have still greater cause to exclude from him moral sentiments, such as we feel them; since moral evil, in the opinion of many, is much more predominant above moral good than natural evil above natural good.

This is another selection from Paley's "Natural Theology." In this section, Paley attempts to respond to the problem of evil, considering possible justifications for both moral and natural evil.

William Paley, D.D., Late Archdeacon of Carlisle
Natural Theology; or, Evidences of the Existence and Attributes of the Deity Collected from the Appearancs of Nature
The Twelfth Edition, 1809

CHAPTER XXVI. THE GOODNESS OF THE DEITY.

...

Of the ORIGIN OF EVIL, no universal solution has been discovered; I mean, no solution which reaches to all cases of complaint. The most comprehensive is that which arises from the consideration of *general rules.* We may, I think, without much difficulty, be brought to admit the four following points: first, that important advantages may accrue to the universe from the order of nature proceeding according to general laws: secondly, that general laws, however well set and constituted, often thwart and cross one another: thirdly, that from these thwartings and crossings, frequent particular inconveniencies will arise: and, fourthly, that it agrees with our observation to suppose, that some degree of these inconveniencies takes place in the works of nature. These points may be allowed; and it may also be asserted, that the general laws with which we are acquainted, are directed to beneficial ends. On the other hand, with many of these laws we are not acquainted at all, or we are totally unable to trace them in their branches, and in their operation; the effect of which ignorance is, that they cannot be of importance to us as measures by which to regulate our conduct. The conservation of them may be of importance in other respects, or to other beings, but we are uninformed of their value or use; uninformed, consequently, when, and how far, they may or may not be suspended, or their effects turned aside, by a presiding and benevolent will, without incurring greater evils than those which would be avoided. The consideration, therefore, of general laws, although it may concern the question of the origin of evil very nearly (which I think it does), rests in views disproportionate to our faculties, and in a knowledge which we do not possess. It serves rather to account for the obscurity of the subject, than to supply us with distinct answers to our difficulties. However, whilst we assent to the above-stated propositions as principles, whatever uncertainty we may find in the application, we lay a ground for believing, that cases of apparent evil, for which *we* can suggest no particular reason, are governed by reasons, which are more general, which lie deeper in the order of second causes, and which on that account, are removed to a greater distance from us....

Of *bodily pain*, the principal observation, no doubt, is that which we have already made, and already dwelt upon, *viz.* "that it is seldom the object of contrivance; that when it is so, the contrivance rests ultimately in good."

To which, however, may be added, that the annexing of pain to the means of destruction is a salutary provision; inasmuch as it teaches vigilance and caution; both gives notice of danger, and excites those endeavours which may be necessary to preservation. The evil consequence, which sometimes arises from the want of that timely intimation of danger which pain gives, is known to the inhabitants of cold countries by the example of frost-bitten limbs. I have conversed with patients who have lost toes and fingers by this cause. They have in general told me, that they were totally unconscious of any local uneasiness at the time. Some I have heard declare, that, whilst they were about their employment, neither their situation, nor the state of the air, was unpleasant. They felt no pain; they suspected no mischief; till, by the application of warmth, they discovered, too late, the fatal injury which some of their extremities had suffered. I say that this shows the use of pain, and that we stand in need of such a monitor. I believe also that the use extends further than we suppose, or can now trace; that to disagreeable sensations we, and all animals owe or have owed, many habits of action which are salutary, but which are become so familiar, as not easily to be referred to their origin.

PAIN also itself is not without its *alleviations.* It may be violent and frequent; but it is seldom both violent and long-continued: and its pauses and intermissions become positive pleasures. It has the power of shedding a satisfaction over intervals of ease, which, I believe, few enjoyments exceed. A man resting from a fit of the stone or gout, is, for the time, in possession of feelings which undisturbed health cannot impart. They may be dearly bought, but still they are to be set against the price. And, indeed, it depends upon the duration and urgency of the pain, whether they be dearly bought or not. I am far from being sure, that a man is not a gainer by suffering a moderate interruption of bodily ease for a couple of hours out of the four-and-twenty. Two very common observations favour this opinion: one is, that remissions of pain call forth, from those who experience them, stronger expressions of satisfaction and of gratitude towards both the author and the instruments of their relief, than are excited by advantages of any other kind; the second is, that the spirits of sick men do not sink in proportion to the acuteness of their sufferings; but rather appear to be roused and supported, not by pain, but by the high degree of comfort which they derive from its cessation, or even its subsidency, whenever that occurs: and which they taste with a relish, that diffuses some portion of mental complacency over the whole of that mixed state of sensations in which disease has placed them. . . .

Of *mortal* diseases, the great use is to reconcile us to death. The horror of death proves the value of life. But it is in the power of disease to abate, or even extinguish, this horror; which it does in a wonderful manner, and, oftentimes, by a mild and imperceptible gradation. Every man who has been placed in a situation to observe it, is surprised with the change which has been wrought in himself, when he compares the view which he entertains of death upon a sick-bed, with the heart-sinking dismay with which he should some time ago have met it in health. There is no similitude between the sensations of a man led to execution, and the calm expiring of a patient at the close of his disease. Death to him is only the last of a long train of changes; in his progress through which, it is possible that he may experience no shocks or sudden transitions.

Death itself, as a mode of removal and of succession, is so connected with the whole order of our animal world, that almost every thing in that world must be changed, to be able to do without it. It may seem likewise impossible to separate the fear of death from the enjoyment of life, or the perception of that fear from rational natures. Brutes are in a great measure delivered from all anxiety on this account by the inferiority of their faculties; or rather they seem to be armed with the apprehension of death just sufficiently to put them upon the means of preservation, and no further. But would a human being wish to purchase this immunity at the expense of those mental powers which enable him to look forward to the future?

Death implies *separation:* and the loss of those whom we love, must necessarily, so far as we can conceive, be accompanied with pain. To the brute creation, nature seems to have stepped in with some secret provision for their relief, under the rupture of their attachments. In their instincts towards their offspring, and of their offspring to them, I have often been surprised to observe how ardently they love, and how soon they forget. The pertinacity of human sorrow (upon which, time also, at length, lays its softening hand) is probably, therefore, in some manner connected with the qualities of our rational or moral nature. One thing however is clear, *viz.* that it is better that we should possess affections, the sources of so many virtues, and so many joys, although they be exposed to the incidents of life, as well as the interruptions of mortality, than, by the want of them, be reduced to a state of selfishness, apathy, and quietism.

Of other external evils (still confining ourselves to what are called physical or natural evils), a considerable part come within the scope of the following observation:--The great principle of human satisfaction is *engagement*. It is a most just distinction, which the late Mr. Tucker has dwelt upon so largely in his works, between pleasures in which we are passive, and pleasures in which we are active. And, I believe, every attentive observer of human life will assent to his position, that, however grateful the sensations may occasionally be in which we are passive, it is not these, but the latter class of our pleasures, which constitute satisfaction; which supply that regular stream of moderate and miscellaneous enjoyments, in which happiness, as distinguished from voluptuousness, consists. Now for rational occupation, which is, in other words, for the very material of contented existence, there would be no place left, if either the things with which we had to do were absolutely impracticable to our endeavours, or if they were too obedient to our uses. A world, furnished with advantages on one side, and beset with difficulties, wants, and inconveniences on the other, is the proper abode of free, rational, and active natures, being the fittest to stimulate and exercise their faculties. The very *refractoriness* of the objects they have to deal with, contributes to this purpose. A world in which nothing depended upon ourselves, however it might have suited an imaginary race of beings, would not have suited mankind. Their skill, prudence, industry; their various arts, and their best attainments, from the application of which they draw, if not their highest, their most permanent gratifications, would be insignificant, if things could be either moulded by our volitions, or, of their own accord, conformed themselves to our views and wishes. Now it is in this refractoriness that we discern the seed and principle of *physical* evil, as far as it arises from that which is external to us.

Civil evils, or the evils of civil life, are much more easily disposed of, than physical evils: because they are, in truth, of much less magnitude, and also because they result, by a kind of necessity, not only from the constitution of our nature, but from a part of that constitution which no one would wish to see altered. . . .

The mischiefs of which mankind are the occasion to one another, by their private wickednesses and cruelties; by tyrannical exercises of power; by rebellions against just authority; by wars; by national jealousies and competitions operating to the destruction of third countries; or by other instances of misconduct either in individuals or societies, are all to be resolved into the character of man as a *free agent*. Free agency in its very essence contains liability to abuse. Yet, if you deprive man of his free agency, you subvert his nature. You may have order from him and regularity, as you may from the tides or the trade-winds, but you put an end to his moral character, to virtue, to merit, to accountableness, to the use indeed of reason. To which must be added the observation, that even the bad qualities of mankind have an origin in their good ones. The case is this: human passions are either necessary to human welfare, or capable of being made, and, in a great majority of instances, in fact, made, conducive to its happiness. These passions are strong and general; and, perhaps, would not answer their purpose unless they were so. But strength and generality, when it is expedient that particular circumstances should be respected, become, if left to themselves, excess and misdirection. From which excess and misdirection, the vices of mankind (the causes, no doubt, of much misery) appear to spring. This account, whilst it shows us the principle of vice, shows us, at the same time, the province of reason and of self-government: the want also of every support which can be procured to either from the aids of religion; and it shows this, without having recourse to any native, gratuitous malignity in the human constitution. Mr. Hume, in his posthumous dialogues, asserts, indeed, of *idleness*, or aversion to labour (which he states to lie at the root of a considerable part of the evils which mankind suffer), that it is simple and merely bad. But how does he distinguish idleness from the love of ease? or is he sure, that the love of ease in individuals is not the chief foundation of social tranquillity? It will be found, I believe, to be true, that in every community there is a large class of its members, whose idleness is the best quality about them, being the corrective of other bad ones. If it were possible, in every instance, to give a right determination to industry, we could never have too much of it. But this is not possible, if men are to be free. And without this, nothing would be so dangerous, as an incessant, universal, indefatigable activity. In the civil world, as well as in the material, it is the *vis inertiœ* which keeps things in their places. . . .

Of *sensible* interposition we may be permitted to remark, that a Providence, always and certainly distinguishable, would be neither more nor less than miracles rendered frequent and common. It is difficult to judge of the state into which this would throw us. It is enough to say, that it would cast us upon a quite different dispensation from that under which we live. It would be a total and radical change. And the change would deeply affect, or perhaps subvert, the whole conduct of human affairs. I can readily believe, that, other circumstances being adapted to it, such a state might be better than our present state. It may be the state of other beings; it may be ours hereafter. But the question with which we are now concerned is, how far it would be consistent with our condition, supposing it in other respects to remain as it is? And in this question there seem to be reasons of great moment on the negative side. For instance, so long as bodily labour continues, on so many accounts, to be necessary for the bulk of mankind, any dependency upon supernatural aid, by unfixing those motives which promote exertion, or by relaxing those habits which engender patient industry, might introduce negligence, inactivity, and disorder, into the most useful occupations of human life; and thereby deteriorate the condition of human life itself.

As moral agents, we should experience a still greater alteration; of which, more will be said under the next article.

Although therefore the Deity, who possesses the power of winding and turning, as he pleases, the course of causes which issue from himself, do in fact interpose to alter or intercept effects, which without such interposition would have taken place; yet it is by no means incredible, that his Providence, which always rests upon final good, may have made a *reserve* with respect to the manifestation of his interference, a part of the very plan which he has appointed for our terrestrial existence, and a part conformable with, or, in some sort, required by, other parts of the same plan. It is at any rate evident, that a large and ample province remains for the exercise of Providence, without its being naturally perceptible by us: because obscurity, when applied to the interruption of laws, bears a necessary proportion to the imperfection of our knowledge when applied to the laws themselves, or rather to the effects which these laws, under their various and incalculable combinations, would of their own accord produce. And if it be said, that the doctrine of Divine Providence, by reason of the ambiguity under which its exertions present themselves, can be attended with no *practical* influence upon our conduct; that, although we believe ever so firmly that there is a. Providence, we must prepare, and provide, and act, as if there were none; I answer, that this is admitted: and that we further allege, that so to prepare, and so to provide, is consistent with the most perfect assurance of the reality of a Providence: and not only so, but that it is, probably, one advantage of the present state of our information, that our provisions and preparations are not disturbed by it. Or if it be still asked, Of what use at all then is the doctrine, if it neither alter our measures nor regulate our conduct? I answer again, that it is of the greatest use, but that it is a doctrine of sentiment and piety, not (immediately at least) of action or conduct; that it applies to the consolation of men's minds, to their devotions, to the excitement of gratitude, the support of patience, the keeping alive and the strengthening of every motive for endeavouring to please our Maker; and that these are great uses.

OF ALL VIEWS under which human life has ever been considered, the most reasonable in my judgement is that, which regards it as a state of *probation.* If the course of the world was separated from the contrivances of nature, I do not know that it would be necessary to look for any other account of it, than what, if it may be called an account, is contained in the answer, that events rise up by chance. But since the contrivances of nature decidedly evince *intention;* and since the course of the world and the contrivances of nature have the same author; we are, by the force of this connexion, led to believe, that the appearance, under which events take place, is reconcileable with the supposition of design on the part of the Deity. It is enough that they be reconcileable with this supposition; and it is undoubtedly true, that they may be reconcileable, though we cannot reconcile them. The mind, however, which contemplates the works of nature, and, in those works, sees so much of means directed to ends, of beneficial effects brought about by wise expedients, of concerted trains of causes terminating in the happiest results; so much, in a word, of counsel, intention, and benevolence: a mind, I say, drawn into the habit of thought which these observations excite, can hardly turn its view to the condition of our own species, without endeavouring to suggest to itself some purpose, some design, for which the state in which we are placed is fitted, and which it is made to serve. Now we assert the most probable supposition to be, that it is a state of moral probation; and that many things in it suit with this hypothesis, which suit no other. It is not a state of unmixed happiness, or of happiness simply: it is not a state of designed misery, or of misery simply: it is not a state of retribution: it is not a state of punishment. It suits with none of these suppositions. It accords much better with the idea of its being a condition calculated for the production, exercise, and improvement of moral qualities, with a view to a future state, in which these qualities, after being so produced, exercised, and improved, may, by a new and more favouring constitution of things, receive their reward, or become their own. If it be said, that this is to enter upon a religious rather than a philosophical consideration, I answer, that the name of Religion ought to form no objection, if it shall turn out to be the case, that the more religious our views are, the more probability they contain. The degree of beneficence, of benevolent intention, and of power, exercised in the construction of sensitive beings, goes strongly in favour, not only of a creative, but of a continuing care, that is, of a ruling Providence. The degree of chance which appears to prevail in the world, requires to be reconciled with this hypothesis. Now it is one thing to maintain the doctrine of Providence along with that of a future state, and another thing without it. In my opinion, the two doctrines must stand or fall together. For although more of this apparent chance may perhaps, upon other principles, be accounted for, than is generally supposed, yet a future state alone rectifies all disorders: and if it can be shown, that the appearance of disorder is consistent with the uses of life as a *preparatory* state, or that in some respects it promotes these uses, then so far as this hypothesis may be accepted the ground of the difficulty is done away.

In the wide scale of human condition, there is not perhaps one of its manifold diversities, which does not bear upon the design here suggested. Virtue is infinitely various. There is no situation in which a rational being is placed, from that of the best-instructed Christian, down to the condition of the rudest barbarian, which affords not room for moral agency; for the acquisition, exercise, and display of voluntary qualities, good and bad. Health and sickness, enjoyment and suffering, riches and poverty, knowledge and ignorance, power and subjection, liberty and bondage, civilization and barbarity, have all their offices and duties, all serve for the *formation* of character: for when we speak of a state of trial, it must be remembered, that characters are not only tried, or proved, or detected, but that they are generated also, and *formed*, by circumstances. The best dispositions may subsist under the most depressed, the most afflicted fortunes. A West-

Indian slave, who, amidst his wrongs, retains his benevolence, I for my part, look upon, as amongst the foremost of human candidates for the rewards of virtue. The kind master of such a slave, that is, he, who in the exercise of an inordinate authority, postpones, in any degree, his own interest to his slave's comfort, is likewise a meritorious character: but still he is inferior to his slave. All however which I contend for, is, that these destinies, opposite as they may be in every other view, are both *trials;* and equally such. The observation may be applied to every other condition; to the whole range of the scale, not excepting even its lowest extremity. *Savages* appear to us all alike; but it is owing to the distance at which we view savage life, that we perceive in it no discrimation of character. I make no doubt, but that moral qualities, both good and bad, are called into action as much, and that they subsist in as great variety, in these inartificial societies, as they are, or do, in polished life. Certain at least it is, that the good and ill treatment which each individual meets with, depends more upon the choice and voluntary conduct of those about him, than it does or ought to do, under regular civil institutions, and the coercion of public laws. So again, to turn our eyes to the other end of the scale, namely, that part of it which is occupied by mankind, enjoying the benefits of learning, together with the lights of revelation, there also, the advantage is all along *probationary.* Christianity itself, I mean the revelation of Christianity, is not only a blessing but a trial. It is one of the diversified means by which the character is exercised: and they who require of Christianity, that the revelation of it should be universal, may possibly be found to require, that one species of probation should be adopted, if not to the exclusion of others, at least to the narrowing of that variety which the wisdom of the Deity hath appointed to this part of his moral economy(*Note:* The reader will observe, that I speak of the revelation of Christianity as distinct from Christianity itself. The *dispensation* may already be universal. That part of mankind which never heard of CHRIST'S name, may nevertheless be redeemed, that is, be placed in a better condition, with respect to their future state, by his intervention; may be the objects of his benignity and intercession, as well as of the propitiatory virtue of his passion. But this is not "natural theology;" therefore I will not dwell longer upon it.)

Now if this supposition be well founded: that is, if it be true, that our ultimate, or our most permanent happiness, will depend, not upon the temporary condition into which we are cast, but upon our behaviour in it; then is it a much more fit subject of *chance* than we usually allow or apprehend it to be, in what manner, the variety of external circumstances, which subsist in the human world, is distributed amongst the individuals of the species. "This life being a state of probation, "it is immaterial, says Rousseau, "what kind of trials we experience in it, provided they produce their effects." Of two agents who stand indifferent to the moral Governor of the universe, one may be exercised by riches, the other by poverty. The treatment of these two shall appear to be very opposite, whilst in truth it is the same: for though, in many respects, there be great disparity between the conditions assigned, in one main article there may be none, *viz.* in that they are alike trials; have both their duties and temptations, not less arduous or less dangerous, in one case than the other; so that if the final award follow the character, the original distribution of the circumstances under which that character is formed, may be defended upon principles not only of justice but of equality. What hinders therefore, but that mankind may draw lots for their condition? They take their portion of faculties and opportunities, as any unknown cause, or concourse of causes, or as causes acting for other purposes, may happen to set them out; but the event is governed by that which depends upon themselves, the application of what they have received. In dividing the talents, no rule was observed; none was necessary: in rewarding the use of them, that of the most correct justice. The chief difference at last appears to be, that the right use of more talents, *i. e.* of a greater trust, will be more highly rewarded, than the right use of fewer talents, *i. e.* of a less trust. And since for other purposes, it is expedient, that there be an inequality of concredited talents here, as well, probably, as an inequality of conditions hereafter, though all remuneratory, can any rule, adapted to that inequality, be more agreeable, even to our apprehensions of distributive justice, than this is?

We have said, that the appearance of *casualty*, which attends the occurrences and events of life, not only does not interfere with its uses, as a state of probation, but that it promotes these uses.

Passive virtues, of all others the severest and the most sublime; of all others, perhaps, the most acceptable to the Deity; would, it is evident, be excluded from a constitution, in which happiness and misery regularly followed virtue and vice. Patience and composure under distress, affliction, and pain; a steadfast keeping up of our confidence in God, and of our reliance upon his final goodness, at the time when every thing present is adverse and discouraging; and (what is no less difficult to retain) a cordial desire for the happiness of others, even when we are deprived of our own: these dispositions, which constitute, perhaps, the perfection of our moral nature, would not have found their proper office and object in a state of avowed retribution; and in which, consequently, endurance of evil would be only submission to punishment.

Again: one man's sufferings may be another man's trial. The family of a sick parent is a school of filial piety. The charities of domestic life, and not only these, but all the social virtues, are called out by distress. But then, misery, to be the proper object of mitigation, or of that benevolence which endeavours to relieve, must be really or apparently casual. It is upon such sufferings alone that benevolence can operate. For were there no evils in the world, but what were punishments, properly and intelligibly such, benevolence would only stand in the way of justice. Such evils, consistently with the administration of moral government, could not be prevented or alleviated, that is to say, could not be remitted in whole or in part, except by the authority which inflicted them, or by an appellate or superior authority. This consideration, which is founded in our most acknowledged apprehensions of the nature of penal justice, may possess its weight in the Divine councils. Virtue perhaps is the greatest of all ends. In human beings, relative virtues form a large part of the whole. Now relative virtue presupposes, not only the existence of evil, without which it could have no object, no material to work upon, but that evils be, apparently at least, *misfortunes;* that is, the effects of apparent chance. It may be in pursuance, therefore, and in furtherance of the same scheme of probation, that the evils of life are made *so* to present themselves.

I have already observed, that, when we let in religious considerations, we often let in light upon the difficulties of nature. So in the fact now to be accounted for, the degree of happiness, which we usually enjoy in this life, may be better suited to a state of trial and probation, than a greater degree would be. The truth is, we are rather too much delighted with the world, than too little. Imperfect, broken, and precarious as our pleasures are, they are more than sufficient to attach us to the eager pursuit of them. A regard to a future state can hardly keep its place as it is. If we were designed therefore to be influenced by that regard, might not a more indulgent system, a higher, or more uninterrupted state of gratification, have interfered with the design? At least it seems expedient, that mankind should be susceptible of this influence, when presented to them: that the condition of the world should not be such, as to exclude its operation, or even to weaken it more than it does. In a religious view (however we may complain of them in every other) privation, disappointment, and satiety, are not without the most salutary tendencies.

Chapter 9
Death and the Meaning of Life

Comprehension questions you should be able to answer after reading this introduction:

1. *Explain each of the following terms: atomism, hedonism, intrinsically good/bad, extrinsically good/bad.*
2. *Explain why Epicurus thinks that death isn't "bad."*
3. *What is the "deprivationist" view of the possible badness of death? What is a "negative evil?"*
4. *Explain why Nagel thinks that death can be bad.*
5. *Explain how Feldman argues that death can be bad.*
6. *What is a "project," as the term is employed by Nussbaum? Using this notion of projects, explain why she thinks death can be bad.*
7. *What is Williams' "identity condition?" What is the "attractiveness condition?"*
8. *Why does Williams think that living forever would be undesirable?*
9. *What are "self-exhausting" pleasures? What are "repeatable pleasures?" Why does Fischer think that Williams is mistaken about the inevitable boredom of living forever?*
10. *What is the difference between quality of life, and quantity of life?*
11. *How might death be valuable (a "good" thing), according to Lucretius? According to Nussbaum?*

Socrates, in Plato's *Phaedo*, claims that philosophy is a preparation for death. While this might be perceived as a melodramatic statement, it is certainly true that the contemplation of death is a staple of philosophical activity.

The philosophical issues raised by death are numerous and deep. What *is* death in the first place? What constitutes the state of being dead from that of being alive? Is death a state that can be experienced at all, or is death "nothing?" Does the "self" persist beyond death? When (if ever) is it morally permissible to bring about death? Is death a bad thing, or a good thing, or neither? In what sense?

While all these questions are interesting and worthy of pursuit, we will focus on death in an indirect way. I believe that by examining death, by considering what it is about death that we fear, that is good or bad or desirable, we actually gain insight into what is good and bad about *life*. Finally, having understood what makes both death, and life, valuable, we will be presented with an imperative to live well.

Death is Not Bad

According to Epicurus (341 BCE-270 BCE), death not only isn't bad, but it cannot be bad.

> *So death, the most frightening of bad things, is nothing to us; since when we exist, death is not yet present, and when death is present, then we do not exist. Therefore, it is relevant neither to the living nor to the dead, since it does not affect the former, and the latter do not exist. (Letter to Menoeceus)*

Death is nothing to us: for that which is dissolved is without sensation; and that which lacks sensation is nothing to us. (Principle Doctrine II)

In these two quotations, Epicurus summarizes his infamous death argument. In order to understand it, we need to understand two key premises held by Epicurus: atomism, and hedonism.

Atomism

Atomism is a school of thought that comes in several varieties, but the basic assumption behind ancient Greek atomism is that reality is composed of atoms, and void. Atoms are indivisible particles that combine to form all the objects in the universe, and some versions of atomism additionally held that these atoms move through the void in regular, law-like ways. Ancient atomists included Epicurus, Lucretius, Democritus, and Leucippus. Atomism was eclipsed by Aristotelian thought until it was revived many centuries later. Later neo-atomists included Rene Descartes, Robert Boyle, Francis Bacon, Thomas Hobbes, and Galileo Galilei. Whatever one thinks of atomism, it is remarkable that this idea that became so prominent in physics as of the Renaissance was originally conceived well over a thousand years prior through philosophical speculation.

The significance of atomism with regard to Epicurus' death argument is that it entailed (for Epicurus) that there was no afterlife. Human beings are particular collections of atoms. When we die, those atoms separate and are recycled and recombined to create new objects. If one agrees with this premise—if one agrees that we are purely physical beings composed of a vast number of tiny particles—then it's hard to imagine how one could continue to exist in any meaningful, identity-preserving fashion, after the death of the body. For this reason, Epicurus believes that we simply cease to exist when we die. No identity is preserved, no self remains to experience being dead. When he said "death is nothing to us," he meant that literally. Death is nothing. Not-a-thing. This is what is known as the "annihilationist" account of death, because the self is "annihilated" at death.

Think of it this way: at any particular moment of time, you are either alive, or dead. If you are alive, you are not experiencing being dead—because you're not dead! Pretty obvious, right? What about when you're dead? Well, according to Epicurus, "you" cease to exist as soon as you're dead. So, there is no "you" to experience "you" being dead. Therefore, you don't experience being dead when you're alive, or when you're dead. In other words, neither you, nor anyone else, ever experiences being dead. Why would this mean that death isn't bad? To understand that, we need Epicurus' second key premise: hedonism.

Hedonism

Hedonism conjures up all sorts of associations. Drunkenness. Over-eating. Narcotics. Wanton sexual activity. For many people, to say that someone is a hedonist is not a compliment. Indeed, it's an allegation that someone pursues sensual pleasures too much. This understanding has almost nothing in common with the notion of hedonism that forms a key premise in Epicurus' death argument.

Hedonism, in the Epicurean sense, was simply a recognition that pleasure and pain are our most fundamental value judgments. That is, everything that we claim is "good" is good because, in some way or another, it can be traced back to pleasure. Everything that we claim is "bad" is bad because we can, in some way or another, trace it back to pain. Why is friendship a good thing? Ultimately, because it's pleasurable. Why is betraying a friend a bad thing? Ultimately, because it's painful.

Pleasure and pain are taken to be our most fundamental value judgments because our ability to ask "why" seems to stop once we reach pleasure or pain.

Would it be a good thing or a bad thing if I were to set you on fire?

"Bad."

Why is it bad?

"Because you shouldn't set people on fire. It's

wrong."

Why would it be bad for me to do something wrong to you?

"Because I don't want to be set on fire!"

Why don't you want to be set on fire?

"Because it would hurt!"

Why is it bad to hurt?

(Awkward silence.)

How exactly would one answer that? How does one explain *why* pain is bad, or pleasure is good? For hedonists, in the classical sense, pleasure *just is* good, as a brute fact of our nature, and pain *just is* bad, as a brute fact of our nature. I sometimes refer to this as "cave man ethics." Pain bad. Pleasure good.

Cave man ethics needn't be crude or simple, of course. Hedonists (in the classical sense) recognize the complexity of situations. For example, you might choose to forego a pleasure—but when you do it is presumed that is for the sake of a greater pleasure, or the avoidance of a worse pain. For example, I might resist the pleasure of a second piece of cake for dessert, but presumably I'm doing so to avoid the pains of indigestion, or obesity. We also might voluntarily submit to pain, but for similar reasons. I go to the dentist a couple times each year. Invariably, it is painful—even if I'm only getting my teeth cleaned. Yet, I go to the dentist anyway because, in doing so, I'm avoiding the greater pains of tooth decay.

A further layer of complexity can be added when we recognize the distinction between "intrinsic" and "extrinsic" goods (or evils). Something is intrinsically good if it is, itself, pleasurable, at that moment. Conversely, something is intrinsically bad if it is, itself, painful, at that moment. Stepping on a nail is intrinsically bad because it hurts, right then and there. Something is extrinsically good if it *leads* to pleasure, or extrinsically bad if it leads to pain. Poverty, for example, is not itself painful—but it might well lead to pain (e.g., the pain of hunger, exposure to the elements due to homelessness, or even just the pain of worrying over how to pay your bills). For classical hedonists, the only way something can be bad is if it is either intrinsically or extrinsically bad, in other words, if it is either painful or leads to pain. If neither, then it is not "bad."

This recognition of the obvious (that pain is bad and pleasure is good), and the judgment that this recognition should inform our decision making [i.e., that we ought to pursue pleasure (good) and avoid pain (bad)] is a very early precursor to the ethical theory known as utilitarianism. For our purposes, however, we need only see how it applies to Epicurus' death argument.

If we combine atomism and hedonism, we get the following:

1. Each person stops existing at the moment of death.
2. If each person stops existing at the moment of death, then no one feels any pain while dead, nor does that person feel any pain later, as a result of being dead.
3. If no one feels any pain while dead, then death (being dead) is not intrinsically bad for the one who is dead.
4. If death does not lead to any later state of pain, then death (being dead) is not extrinsically bad for the one who is dead.
5. Therefore, death is neither intrinsically nor extrinsically bad for the one who is dead.
6. Therefore, death is not bad for the one who is dead.

Exercise Break

Think about death. Contemplate your own, and that of others. What is it about death (if anything) that makes it "bad"—or at least something you would generally prefer to avoid? It's a good idea to make a list of the various aspects or consequences of death that make it seem "bad" or at least generally undesirable.

I have a prediction: if you actually did the "exercise break" just now, I doubt you find Epicurus' argument convincing. Even if you agree with him about our ceasing to exist when dead, and even if you agree with his assumptions concerning pleasure and pain, my prediction is that you still have a "problem" with death. If so, you are not alone.

Death Can be bad

Lots of people, including numerous philosophers, disagree with the Epicurean claim that death can't be bad for the one who is dead. There are a variety of reasons for this, but we will focus on one type of rebuttal known as a "deprivationist" account of the badness of death.

Deprivationism

As a classical hedonist, Epicurus believed that the only way something could be bad is if it was painful (intrinsically bad) or caused pain (extrinsically bad). Either way, pain is a necessary ingredient for something to be bad. Deprivationists disagree. They claim that something can be bad not only if it is painful (or causes pain), but also if it *deprives* you of something that would have been good. A very simple example can illustrate this idea.

Imagine you have been invited to a wedding. You know the couple very well, and like them very much. Suppose also that you enjoy parties, in general, and weddings in particular. You are confident that you are going to experience a lot of pleasure as a result of having a good time at the wedding, and reception, and that you will likely form many pleasant memories as a result of having attended.

Now imagine that you get in your car to head to the wedding, and your car won't start. Suppose also that no one is available to give you a ride. Suppose that it's a Sunday and no mechanic is available to try to fix your car. Suppose, in other words, that it is no longer possible for you to attend the wedding.

Many of us would say that it is a "bad thing" (for you) that your car wouldn't start. We would say this not because your car not starting literally caused you pain, or even contributed to pain later, but because your car not starting caused you to miss out on the good time you otherwise would have had. In other words, your car not starting "deprived" you of something that would have been good. This is the deprivationist sense of something being "bad." If one is a deprivationist with regard to the badness of death, the idea is that death is (or at least can be) bad by virtue of deprivation.

Exercise Break

Take a moment to think, and then write down at least 20 things that you enjoy in life, things that make life worth living. There are no wrong answers here. Anything that you enjoy in life, from the greatest achievements to the simplest enjoyments, is a candidate for your list.

Epicurus claimed that death can't be bad for the one who is dead because being dead is neither painful, nor does it lead to pain (for the one who is dead). If the annihilationist understanding of death is correct, it is true that being dead is neither painful, nor leads to pain. Of course, some of you might believe that the annihilationist account is false, and that the self somehow survives the death of the body (perhaps to go to Heaven, or Hell, or to reincarnated, etc.). Either way, deprivationism poses a threat to the claim that death can't be bad.

If the anihilationists are right, and we cease to exist at death, then, rather obviously, death *deprives* us of all the countless things we would have been able to experience, had we continued to live. Think of all those things you enjoy in life. When you die, and cease to exist, you are no longer doing those things. After all, there is no longer any "you" to do those things, no matter what those things happened to be.

President Barack Obama's grandmother, Madelyne Payne Dunham, died at the age of 86 on November 3rd, 2008—*one day* before her grandson was elected President of the United States in what was undoubtedly an historic election. Death "deprived" her of the ability to experience what might well have been the proudest moment of her life. The event need not be so historic, of course.

Death threatens to deprive each one of us of the chance to experience things that are important to us, both big and small. Death deprives us of pleasures, hobbies, friendships, marriages, travel, and all the other things that might matter to us. "But," you might say, "death can also deprive us of pain, misery, loneliness, despair, oppression, torture, and all the other things that might make life unbearable to us." Indeed. This is why most deprivationists will be careful to say that death *can* be bad rather than that death *is* bad. Whether or not death is bad will depend on that of which we are being deprived. Sometimes, death is seen as a blessing, such as when a quick death spares someone from intense, lingering pain. Most of us, however, most of the time, are not facing torture and agony. Most of us, most of the time, are facing ordinary days—most of which are, on balance, filled with more pleasures than pains. This is why most of us, most of the time, would rather continue to live, than die. This is also why, for most of us, most of the time, death is usually regarded as a bad thing.

What if the anihilationists are wrong? What if there is an afterlife? Death still presents a deprivationist threat. Suppose there is a Heaven, and suppose President Obama's grandmother found herself there after her body died. She still missed the election. "But she's in Heaven! She's not worrying about missing the election!" Quite possibly true. Nevertheless, she still missed it—as well as every other earthly pleasure or goal she might have had. Even people of deep faith, who truly believe that the dead are "in a better place," can still lament when someone has died. Even if it is a source of great comfort to believe in an afterlife, it's still possible (and common) to think it regrettable that the deceased nevertheless missed out on something he or she would have enjoyed.

Deprivationists approach this conclusion in a variety of ways, and you should read the essay "Who Wants to Live Forever" at the end of this chapter for details. *<u>Nagel</u> claims that death can be bad because it deprives us of pleasurable experiences we otherwise would have enjoyed. <u>Feldman</u> claims death can be bad because it* *deprives us of lives that otherwise would have had greater value. Nussbaum claims that death can be bad because it deprives us of our ability to complete our subjectively meaningful life projects. In each case, however, death is seen as a deprivation.*

If we are sympathetic to the deprivationists, and agree that death is (or at least can be) bad, then are we implicitly (or even explicitly) yearning for immortality instead? After all, what are the alternatives to death? Never having been born? That seems melodramatic! Immortality, then? If death is bad, not dying (immortality) must be good, right?

Not so fast. Just as there are philosophers who argue that death is (or at least can be) bad, there are also those who caution us against a hasty wish for immortality. Continuous life, let alone immortality, they argue, might well be worse than death.

Boredom

What would it take for immortality to be desirable? Bernard Williams claims that at least two conditions would need to be satisfied. The first is the identity condition. This is actually pretty simple. The identity condition requires that, in order for immortality to be desirable for me, it has to be "me" that is continuing to exist. In other words, identity must be preserved in a meaningful, recognizable sort of way. It is no consolation, in the face of death, for me to hear that matter is neither created nor destroyed, but only changes state. Therefore, the matter that makes up my body will continue to exist in some form or another. How does that help me? I don't self-identify solely as a particular collection of sub-atomic particles. That matter and energy are (possibly) "immortal" does nothing to preserve "me." So, in order for immortality to be valuable to me, it has to be me that continues to exist.

The second condition that must be satisfied is the attractiveness condition. This doesn't mean that immortality is desirable only if one is physically attractive—though I wouldn't mind! What needs to be "attractive" is the condition of one's existence. Suppose I were to announce that I had been diagnosed with a terminal, incurable disease and had only weeks left to live. Suppose someone were to say to me, "even though your body might die, you will continue to exist forever—in Hell!" That's not the least bit comforting. Or suppose someone were to offer me some magical pill that granted me bodily immortality—and then encased my feet in concrete, wrapped me in chains, and dropped me off a boat in the middle of the Pacific Ocean. I would live forever, in the pitch black depths of the ocean. No thanks! The idea here is simple: most of us don't want to continue to live regardless of the condition of our life. An eternal life of suffering is not "attractive" to most of us.

Even if immortality satisfied the identity condition, would it satisfy the attractiveness condition? William's thinks not. He claims that life will, inevitably, become boring and thereby cease to satisfy the attractiveness condition. At some point, we will have "done it all," and "seen it all." Relationships will have become tedious. Life will have become a burden. At that point, death might be regarded as a sweet release. Death might be a bad thing, but it's better than the alternative.

I think Williams is mistaken, and so does John Fischer. We'll start with Fischer. Fischer distinguishes between two types of pleasures: self-exhausting, and repeatable. Self-exhausting pleasures are those pleasures that, once experienced, are pleasures we wouldn't seek to experience again. There was nothing wrong with them. It's just that we've "been there and done that," and have no need to do it again. I suspect for most of us, graduating from high school is a self-exhausting pleasure. It might have been a big deal at the time, and it might have been a pleasurable experience, but I doubt many would want to re-enroll in high school in order to graduate again. As another example, consider my own visit to the "Four Corners" monument (see photo). This is where four states (Colorado, Utah, New Mexico, and

Arizona) come together at one spot. There is a platform upon which one may stand, effectively standing in all four states simultaneously. There is also a bathroom, and some stands where Native Americans sell jewelry and crafts. I have no regrets that I visited Four Corners. In fact, I found some marginal pleasure in having done so. I also cannot imagine ever making it a point to go there again. Been there. Done that. For me, it was certainly a self-exhausting pleasure.

If self-exhausting pleasures were the only pleasures possible, then it seems likely that, if one lived long enough (let alone "forever"), eventually one would have checked off everything that was on one's list, and there would be nothing pleasurable left in life. But why should we think that the only pleasures in life are self-exhausting?

Fischer claims that there are also <u>repeatable pleasures.</u> These are pleasures that, once experienced, we would like to experience again. Examples abound. Your favorite food, by virtue of being your favorite, is probably something you would like to experience more than once. For most people, I doubt sexual activity is a "been there, done that, don't ever need to do that again" sort of pleasure. Friendships, by their very nature, are "repeatable" pleasures. Imagine the absurdity of a friendship in which, after enjoying each other's company one time, you have no desire to ever enjoy that person's company again? In what way was that even a friendship? If there really are repeatable pleasures in life, then even if one lived "forever," it's not obvious that one would run out of pleasurable activities to enjoy. After all, many of them are repeatable.

Exercise Break

Do you agree that there are repeatable pleasures? If you do, list at least 10 things that are, for you, repeatable pleasures. If you think that there are no repeatable pleasures, why not?

In addition, I think Williams seems to be presupposing that the world around us is somehow unchanging and static, and this just seems to be false. If life were like a video game in which, after one explored the entire "level," there was nothing left to discover, no new areas to explore, and no new creatures or people "spawning" to replace those already encountered, then life would be like those video games that have no "replay" value. Or, to use another example (for the benefit of those unfamiliar with video games), if life were like a house, with a limited number of rooms in which the furniture never changed, then, no matter how big the house, given enough time, you will have eventually completed the tour and have nothing left to see. But why assume that life is like either example? Isn't life constantly changing around us? New people are being born, new products and technologies are being invented, new books are being written, and new movies made.

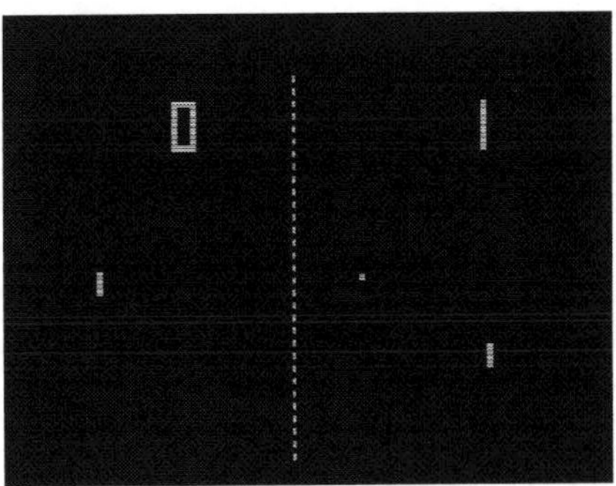

Continuing with the video game example, I remember when "Pong" was released. We had the Pong game in our basement, and it was amazing. It was a game, but also a video. It was a "video-game," as it were. It is no exaggeration to say that, at that time, I never could have imagined the game systems to come. Wii? X-box Kinect? Using just one medium of entertainment (video games), in my lifetime alone, there have already been staggering changes, and vastly new and different ways to enjoy gaming. The same reasoning could apply to all sorts of other categories of pleasures. There are always new books to read. There are always new songs to listen to, and even new musical genres.

To put it bluntly, Williams' claim that life would eventually and inevitably become boring says more about Williams than it does about life—or so it seems to me. If the world is constantly changing, and if repeatable pleasures exist, it is by no means obvious that life is destined to become boring. Some of us, at least, might find ourselves with plenty to do, and plenty of pleasures at our disposal.

Even though I disagree with Williams, I acknowledge that he and I (and others) are probably in agreement about at least one thing: the importance of quality of life.

Quality of Life

Williams claims that unending life would eventually fail to satisfy the attractiveness condition. In other words, our existence would eventually no longer be of sufficient quality to make life worth living. Death might be "bad," but a poor quality of existence would be worse. Quality of life should be emphasized more than quantity.

In some contexts, we easily recognize that quantity, by itself, does not equate to quality. We can use art for an example. Pick your favorite medium: painting, poetry, dance, sculpture, dance.... In each case, you have not necessarily made a work of art better simply by making it larger, or of greater duration. A good song is not necessarily made better by being made longer. Often, the song can be ruined if it's too long. A painting is not necessarily better simply because it is made larger. Or, consider this Haiku written by a 22-year-old Japanese kamikaze pilot from the "Seven Lives" unit before he went into combat in 1945:

"If only we might fall
like Cherry blossoms in the spring
so pure and radiant."

Part of the beauty, part of the *art,* of this poem, is that it conveys a powerful idea with so few words. If you turned this 15-word poem into a 15-page essay, you would destroy it as a poem.

Some philosophers (often, especially, those with existentialist leanings) like to think of life as a work of art. Your life, my life, each life—they are living works of art in progress. If you find this metaphor compelling, then perhaps a similar conclusion applies to our lives as applies to art: quality is more important than quantity.

One thing nearly every tombstone has in common is a set of dates indicating birth, and death. The span of years in-between varies, of course. For some the duration of life was 100 years, for others 60, for others 20, and so on. If one takes seriously the notion that quality is more important than quantity, then what will matter far more than the total number of years separating those dates is what one did with those years, no matter how many there were.

Each one of us is "dying" at the very moment we read this sentence. Life is a terminal condition. A verse from the Switchfoot song, "Where I Belong" includes the following:

"But I'm not sentimental
This skin and bones is a rental
And no one makes it out alive"

That is not meant to be morbid, but a plain statement of fact. Each one of us dies—the only difference (with regard to quantity) is how long it takes to do so. If we recognize that life, and therefore the time we have to experience it, is a finite resource, perhaps we can be motivated to seek the most quality from that life as is possible.

Exercise Break

If you knew, with 100% certainty, that you were going to die at the age of 30 (or 40 if you're already in your thirties, or 50, if already in your forties, etc.), would you do anything differently with your life right now? What if you knew you were going to die exactly 24 hours from this moment? Would you live the next 24 hours differently than you normally would?

If you actually performed the exercise break, I'm extraordinarily confident that you concluded that you would, indeed, live your life differently if you knew death was looming nearer than you had expected. Probably each of us would. So why don't we? None of us is guaranteed any particular span of life. We are not guaranteed even 30 years, nor even 30 more minutes. People die from car accidents, or have heart attacks, or are victims of workplace violence, or suffer from any number of unexpected calamities. None of us is immune to such things, as much as we might wish otherwise.

Should we curl up in despair, then, and bemoan our fate? Not at all. Just the opposite, actually. Let death be an inspiration to us. Another Switchfoot song asks the simple but poignant question in its title verse: "This is your life, are you who you want to be?"

Are you who you want to be? Is this the life you want for yourself? If not, then, recognizing that this is the *only* life (at least on this Earth) you will have, and recognizing that you don't have "forever" ahead of you on this Earth, do something about it!

If we know that we don't have "forever" in this world, then let us try to make the most of however much time we have. If I might die on my fortieth birthday, then let me live the next couple years well and fully, with as few regrets as possible. If I might die in a car accident later today, then let me live the next few hours well.

There is nothing glorious about dying young. To emphasize quality is not to disdain quantity. An excellent *long* life would be a wonderful thing. However, a miserable long life is probably something far less desirable.

The Value of Death

If deprivationists are right, then death can be bad because it deprives us of things we would otherwise enjoy and value. Is death all and only bad, though? Does death serve any purpose, have any value?

I will not address practical considerations, such as population control, or limited natural resources. I will focus only on more obviously "philosophical" considerations. Here is one: if not for death, those very things we value would not be so valuable.

Consider the value of time. If we can be certain of anything, we should be certain that the amount of time we have with which to experience this (Earthly) life is finite.

According to the U.S. Census Bureau (2012), the average life expectancy for a man born the same year I was born is 69.1 years. I'll just round down to 69. If I have correctly assumed the average age of the readers of this book, your life expectancy is 73 years if male, and 79 if female (rounded to nearest whole number). There are 525,600 minutes in a year. So, the *average* number of minutes available for someone like me is 36,266,400. That's an average, of course, so I might find myself with more, or less, by large or small margins. Thirty six million minutes sounds like a lot of time (even though I've used up more than half!), but whether it sounds like a lot, or a little, one thing that it is not, is *infinite*. This Earthly life of mine has a finite duration, a limit to which I am always drawing closer—and you and I are just the same in that regard.

Remember the exercise break from earlier? What if you knew you were going to die at the age of 30? What if you knew you were going to die in 24 hours? What if you knew that your time is limited?

It is.

This realization could be crushing, but it doesn't need to be, and therein lies a possible value of death. Perhaps death, by guaranteeing a finite limit to life, makes that life, and the time with which we live, all the more valuable than it otherwise would, or could, have been?

Maybe it's as simple as the "law" of supply and demand? When something is a limited, and desired, resource, we tend to value it more highly. For each one of us, time is a limited resource. For most of us, more time is something we desire. Therefore, we should value time more highly (than if time were unlimited for us). The challenge is that most of us are in a state of denial with regard to the temporal limit of our lives. It's a cliché, but no less truthful because of that fact: most of us sleepwalk through life, living as though we had "forever" at our disposal, and we don't think, or act, otherwise unless and until some event forces us to do so—usually in traumatic fashion.

- Someone has a near-death experience and is (at least temporarily) filled with a newfound appreciation for life, and a motivation to live life to the fullest.
- A loved one dies, and one thinks:
- "I never realized how much so-and-so meant to me until he/she was gone."
- "I wish I had said 'I love you' one more time."
- "I had always meant to say 'I'm sorry.'"
- "All so-and-so ever wanted from me was some time, and I was always too busy—and now it's too late."

As a "professional philosopher," and someone who thinks about these sorts of things much more than most, I would like to think I am better prepared than most to handle death and appreciate life. The fact is, each one of us, myself included, always has something to learn. Early in 2012, my father took a "stress test" to determine if he had any heart problems. His doctor wasn't pleased with the results, and scheduled him for a more invasive procedure to determine if his arteries had any blockage. While he was undergoing this second procedure, he began to have a heart attack. He was very fortunate (or perhaps it was Providence) that he began to have a heart attack in the cardiology unit of a hospital, with the head of that program present in the room. They were able to administer nitro glycerin in time to prevent him from having damage to his heart, and scheduled him for emergency double-bypass surgery later that day. I was in my office, preparing to teach a class, when I got the phone call. I was soon on my way to the hospital, where I spent the next dozen hours or so, and where I would return each day for the next several days.

For those of you with relevant experience, you will likely agree with me that hospitals are not very pleasant places. While I was visiting my father, another patient (no more than 30 feet away) "crashed." Alarms sounded, and at least a half-dozen hospital staff rushed to his room to try to resuscitate him while his stunned and crying family waited outside his room. After a couple minutes of intervention, his heart began beating again. A few minutes later, he crashed again. This process repeated a total of four times in less than one hour. At that point, his family told the staff to stop. They let him go.

If you've never been in that sort of situation, it's difficult to convey what it feels like, but it connects very much to several of the themes of this chapter. What price should we be willing to pay for a little bit of an extension to a life? I don't know how many more times that man could have been revived. Perhaps the process of him dying, and being brought back, could have continued for days longer, or weeks, or months. If one believes that quality is more important than quantity, however, it's not obvious that it would be a good thing to keep reviving him just for the sake of a few more hours, or even days—not to mention the fact that he was unconscious the whole time, and being kept alive only by virtue of machines and those interventions. Painful though it undoubtedly was for his family, I understand why they decided to "let him go."

I didn't know that man, or his family, so I don't know the kind of relationships he had with them, and whether or not his loved ones were at peace with how they had enjoyed that relationship, or whether they had regrets. I couldn't help but think of my own father, and my relationship with him, however, as I sat in his hospital room, seeing him pale and recovering from major surgery, while watching another man die across the hall.

As a philosopher, I've thought about death and its meaning quite a lot, but my experiences in that hospital, and with my father, brought death into focus for me more acutely than had any book. It became so much more obvious to me, so undeniable, that my father was a mortal man who would one day die.

If I hadn't understood before, I understand now: I have only a finite amount of time left with my father. Perhaps I should make more effort not to squander it? It was hard not to imagine myself in the place of those other family members. Did they have regrets? Would I? There is nothing magical about this particular gesture, but it is a concrete act: I now make it a point to have lunch with my parents each week. I enjoy my time with them, and, to be blunt, I don't know how many lunches we've got left. In its own cold way, death has given my relationship with them more value than it otherwise would have had, and given me a greater sense of urgency to appreciate the time I have with them

Exercise Break

Though it might be painful to contemplate, is there someone important from your life that has died? Did you have any regrets? Were there things you wish you had done or said when you had the chance? Are there people in your life who are important to you now? If one of them were to die suddenly, would you have regrets? Would there be things you would wish you had said or done? If so, are these things that you could address "now" if you so choose?

I mentioned that it was hard not to imagine myself in the place of those other family members. Well, it was also hard not to imagine myself in the place of the dying man—especially after I learned that he was only a few years older than I. My father isn't going to live forever, but neither am I! Neither is anyone in my life. If a relationship is important to you, then it's a good idea to enjoy it and appreciate it while you can. If a project or goal is important to you, it's a good idea to pursue it while you can.

The fact that time on this Earth is a limited resource for each one of us could be a crushing revelation—or it could be a source of great inspiration. Death can be bad if for no other reason than deprivation: it deprives the one who is dead, but who would have been alive, of any number of valuable and pleasurable experiences, and of the ability to fulfill his or her subjectively valuable life projects. On the other hand, the badness of death will depend on quality of life issues. For one whose life is abject misery, death will not seem so bad, when it comes.[246] In any case, bodily death is the inevitable fate for each one of us. It can't be

[246] At the end of 2014, a close friend's mother died. She suffered for six months from cancer, and, for the last few weeks, was in constant and agonizing pain, was completely bed-ridden, and was

prevented, but only postponed, at best. Perhaps the best we can do is to try to live a life such that death, whenever it comes, is as "least bad" as possible. This requires that we live authentic lives, providing as few opportunities for regret as is possible. All the while, by virtue of death reminding us all that our time is a limited resource, our projects and relationships, and even life itself, can have a greater value, a greater significance, and provide us with a greater sense of urgency and motivation to live life well, while we still can.

Live well!

Exercises for Wisdom and Growth

1. When you think about death, what is it about death that makes it "bad," or "good?" It is entirely appropriate to generate a list of each.
2. This probably informs your answers to #1 above, but what do you believe death *is* for the one who is dead? Do you believe in some sort of afterlife, or do you believe death is "annihilation" and we simply cease to exist?
3. If you could be given the gift of bodily immortality, at the time of your choosing, and your body would "freeze" in the shape and health it's in at that moment, would you desire to live forever? Why, or why not?
4. The 2007 film, "The Bucket List" popularized the idea of having a list of things you want to do before you "kick the bucket." If you haven't already made one, take some time and do so. Come up with at least 10 things you would like to do before you die.
5. Does the fact that you will not live forever, but will one day die, give you any motivation to pursue those items on your bucket list (#4 above)? Why, or why not?

---

delirious and confused for those few hours each day when she was not unconscious from all the sedatives and pain-killers. The last time I saw her, she was literally screaming in pain, for over an hour, before she lost consciousness. I'm not afraid to admit that I was grateful when she finally died. Although her life had ended, so had her pain.

This reading is slightly awkward to introduce as I am its co-author. My colleague (Professor Dixon) and I wrote this several years ago. Though neither of us is remotely as famous as any of the other philosophers I have provided access to in this book, we like to think that our writing is accessible and relevant. Life has continued and changed for us since we first wrote the article. One of us has experienced the death of his mother, providing a deeper personal perspective on death, especially with regard to the very first paragraph of the essay. The other of us has gone through a painful divorce, providing all the more perspective on the value of life projects (including relationships) provided by virtue of their limited duration. In this reading, we consider death and its value as a way to understand life and its value. We consider claims that death is not bad (or that it can be), and also whether continued existence is always good. After considering the significance of quality of life issues to the value of death, we conclude with a simple (but, we hope, compelling) imperative: live well.

Ted M. Preston and Scott Dixon

Who Wants to Live Forever? Immortality, Authenticity, and Living Forever in the Present

[Originally Published in the *International Journal for Philosophy of Religion*, Vol. 61(2), April 2007: 99-117. Reprinted with the kind permission of Springer Publishing]

We began writing this paper immediately after returning home from a memorial service. The service was for the mother of a friend, and she died at the age of eighty-nine. We had only met the deceased once, so her death was not a deeply personal loss for *us*. Something that struck us, during the eulogies, was how both of her children relied upon stories. Her son stuck mainly with stories about his childhood, in which his mother would appear as an interesting supporting character. Her daughter tried to give a quick narrative of some of the major events of her mother's life, such as her place of birth, when she moved from England to Canada, and then to the United States, when she met the man she would marry, and so on. Not knowing the deceased well at all, and not being "in" on the jokes and references, the narrative was a bit boring, from our perspective—but we knew full well that it was not from the perspective of those telling the stories, nor to those who were personally connected to them.

Our memorial experience articulates what Thomas Nagel refers to as the subjective / objective distinction. Subjectively, her death meant very little to us, largely due to a lack of specific relations with her. For instance, we had no stories to tell, as we were not connected with her in any sort of significant way. Objectively, however, we could understand why all of this was meaningful to the appropriate persons. As sons, we empathized with her children enough to appreciate what they were saying, but still, the meaning of it all was limited. It was not either of *our* moms after all, it was theirs.

Whether bodily death is a bad thing is hardly a new topic for discussion, but we do hope to provide a different outlook. After having examined and clarified some key elements of the debate, our claim will be that death is, subjectively, a bad thing—though not necessarily the worst of all options one might face. Our further claim is that just how bad death is, both subjectively and objectively, will depend overwhelmingly on the quality of life that someone has led. At that stage, we will borrow somewhat from broadly existentialist notions of authenticity and existentialism's focus on living consciously, and intentionally. At the same time, we will argue that, for many of us, our notions of quality of life come from an overly narrow and, frankly, *elitist* strain of philosophy. We will end by pointing to implications for living generated by these findings.

Death is *not* bad

Get used to believing that death is nothing to us. For all good and bad consists in sense-experience, and death is the privation of sense-experience. Hence, a correct knowledge of the fact that death is nothing to us makes the mortality of life a matter for contentment, not by adding a limitless time [to life] but by removing the longing for immortality. For there is nothing fearful in life for one who has grasped that there is nothing fearful in the absence of life. Thus he is a fool who says that he fears death not because it will be painful when present but because it is painful when it is still to come. For that which while present causes no distress causes unnecessary pain when merely anticipated. So death, the most frightening of bad things, is nothing to us; since when we exist, death is not yet present, and when death is present, then we do not exist. Therefore, it is relevant neither to the living nor to the dead, since it does not affect the former, and the latter do not exist.[i]

Most philosophers are familiar with Epicurus's famous argument for why death is not a bad thing (at least to the one who is dead), but for the benefit of the uninitiated, a very brief summary will be supplied.

1. Each person stops existing at the moment of death.
2. If (1), then no one feels any pain while dead.
3. If no one feels any pain while dead, then death does not lead to anything intrinsically bad for the one who dies.
4. If death does not lead to anything intrinsically bad for the one who is dead, then death is not extrinsically bad for the one who is dead.
5. Therefore, death is not extrinsically bad for the one who is dead.[ii]

This summary, taken from Feldman, distinguishes intrinsic and extrinsic goods in recognition of Epicurus's hedonistic assumptions according to which pain is the only thing intrinsically bad (i.e., bad in itself). Other sorts of things can be bad (e.g., poverty, sickness, ignorance), but such things are derivatively bad—"evil only because they happen to be connected to pain."[iii] The assumption, expressed in what Feldman calls the "causal hypothesis," is the following: "If something is extrinsically bad for a person, then it is bad for him or her because it leads to later intrinsic bads for him or her."[iv]

Assuming that all of the premises are true, it would appear that being dead really is nothing extrinsically bad for the dead.[247] When we weep for them, we are really weeping for ourselves. When we lament their passing, we are really acknowledging that we, not they, have been somehow diminished. In other words, being dead is nothing subjectively to the one dead; yet, objectively it influences those around the deceased in varying ways. Nevertheless, one must wonder why humanity has struggled, psychologically, philosophically, and religiously, with death for the subject, if the "problem" had been so neatly solved millennia ago. We frequently teach this argument to our students, and once it appears that the argument is at least understood, we ask them if they feel any better about their impending future demise. In other words, knowing that death is a certainty, do they still fear death, in spite of Epicurus's labors? The answer is

[247]Though the word "death" is ambiguous, what is meant here is that the state of being dead is not bad for the one who is dead. Rosenbaum, in "How to Be Dead and Not Care: A Defense of Epicurus," articulates three concepts: dying, death, and being dead. *Dying* is the period leading up to death, it can occur over a period of time or momentarily. *Death* is the time or first instance of someone being dead. *Being dead* is the (irreversible) state after death in which there is no longer an experiencing subject.

invariably, and overwhelmingly, *yes*—and it would be more than uncharitable to write this off as a mere student reaction. Indeed, most people we know—professional philosophers included—regard the argument as a "good" argument, but also as unpersuasive for some reason outside of the scope of the argument. Arguably, since death is not something we experience in life, the air of mysteriousness takes hold of even the most learned on the subject. This just may be a feature of one's psychology; yet, should we dismiss it so easily? If so many remain without consolation from Epicurus' argument, perhaps we have good reason to believe that death is a bad thing after all.

Death *is* bad

If we take the previous anecdotal claims seriously, to a good number of people, it is just *obvious* that death is a bad thing. Maybe it is just the mysterious nature of it again doing too much work. Of course, it is also possible that a variety of metaphysical assumptions are lurking beneath the surface of such a judgment, and, perhaps, if unearthed and challenged, one might have a change of mind. A very basic distinction one may make is between those who believe that the self is annihilated at bodily death, and those who believe the self "survives" bodily death.[248]

If one believes that the self persists beyond death, then whether death is a bad thing depends largely on what one anticipates will follow it. If you anticipate an eternity of torment, then it is hard to imagine how death could fail to be a bad thing, no matter how rotten one's earthly existence is. If, on the other hand, one is at least optimistic, let alone convinced, that something better (e.g., "paradise") awaits, then death could conceivably be a welcome release from a presently less-than-ideal existence. At the same time, even those who are ostensibly convinced that a better existence awaits beyond the grave still lament the approach of death—at least sometimes. They objectively lament the approach of others' death, because of what is lost in their own lives. They even subjectively lament the approach of their own death out of a sense of what they assume will be lost to them: earthly experiences. In this sense, they share, to a certain extent, the perspective of those who believe they will no longer exist, upon their death. Death of the body is, or at least can be, a bad thing because of that which it takes away from us: the ability to experience.

To better articulate this notion, consider Feldman. After constructing what he takes to be the most plausible Epicurean argument for why death is not a bad thing, Feldman proceeds to dispute it. He claims, for example, that the causal hypothesis is false, and that some things are extrinsically bad though they cause no pain. To illustrate this, he imagines a girl born in a country in which girls are not allowed to learn to read and write, but are taught to do laundry and raise children instead. Having grown up in this country, the girl is reasonably satisfied, and thinks she has lived as she ought to have. To her dying day, she never realizes what might have been. Feldman imagines further that she has some natural gift for poetry, and would have excelled at it had she been allowed to learn to read and write, and would likely have grown to become a successful and happy poet, if given a chance. "I would want to say that it is a great pity that this woman had not been born in another country. I would say that something very bad happened to her, even though she never suffered any pains as a result."[v]

As a result of such reflections, Feldman proposes an alternative to the "causal hypothesis: "Something is extrinsically bad for a person if and only if he or she would have been intrinsically better off if it had not taken place."[vi] If one no longer exists upon death, obviously death cannot be a bad thing subjectively in terms of pain, or sadness, or being roasted over coals and poked with pointy sticks, or the like. Instead, if death is an "evil," it is a negative one: an evil of deprivation—and what might have been. For example, upon dying, we can no longer experience pleasurable activities of any kind, nor even enjoy the mere possibility of enjoying such activities

[248] Throughout this essay, "death" should be taken to mean "bodily death."

ever again.

> *Death might be very bad for the one who is dead. If death deprives him of a lot of pleasure—the pleasure he would have enjoyed if he had not died—the death might be a huge misfortune for someone. More explicitly, death might be extrinsically bad for the one who is dead even though nothing intrinsically bad happens to him as a result. In my view, death would be extrinsically bad for him if his life would have contained more intrinsic value if he had not died then.*[vii]

This is a tricky issue. On the one hand, someone might claim that even a negative evil has to happen to *someone*, and the dead person who no longer exists is no longer a "somebody" to experience the evil, so there shouldn't be any subjective harm. On the other hand, it is a powerful intuition that death deprives the *dead* of something, somehow. Nagel tries to resolve this problem by claiming that the person who *used* to exist can be benefited or harmed by death, and tries to show that our intuitions are in harmony with this idea. For instance, he claims we could and would say of someone trapped in a burning building who died instantly from being hit on the head rather than burning to death, that the person was lucky, or better off, for having died quickly. Of course, after dying from the head trauma, there was no one in existence who was spared the pain of burning to death, but Nagel claims that the "him" we refer to in such an example refers to the person who *was* alive and who *would have* suffered.[viii] Nagel believes the person subjectively benefited, although no subject was there to receive the benefit. It would be easier to understand this objectively in terms of the qualitative assessment of Feldman; however, that is not Nagel's position.

Similarly, if someone dies before seeing the birth of a grandchild, and there is no life after death, there is no person in existence who is presently being deprived of anything at all, including, of course, births of grandchildren. But the person who *was* alive and who *would have* seen it, if not for death, has counterfactually and subjectively missed out on something.

> *The same kind of thing could be said about death as a negative evil. When you die, all the good things in your life come to a stop: no more meals, movies, travel, conversation, love, work, books, music, or anything else. If those things would be good, their absence is bad. Of course, you won't miss them: death is not like being locked up in solitary confinement. But the ending of everything good in life, because of the stopping of life itself, seems clearly to be a negative evil for the person who was alive and is now dead. When someone we know dies, we feel sorry not only for ourselves but for him, because he cannot see the sun shine today, or smell the bread in the toaster.*[ix]

This is admittedly a confusing concept: the idea that one can be negatively harmed or benefited even when one does not exist, but it is a concept Nagel claims is intuitively powerful for us, and which Feldman supports. It is confusing because of its counterfactual base; that a subject experiences harm or good even though there is no subject. It is intuitive because we do talk and think in terms of what it would have been for someone to experience. What these two articulations may show is that counterfactuals are being used in different ways, with the intuitive version masking a lot of the work of the counterfactual harm version.

In response to the problem of locating *when* death is a problem for someone, Feldman claims that a state of affairs can be bad for someone regardless of when it occurs: "The only requirement is that the value of the life he leads if it occurs is lower than the value of the life he leads if it does not occur."[x] The comparison is between the respective values of two possible lives. The state of affairs pertaining to someone dying at some particular time, is bad for that person, if "the value-for-her of the life she leads where [that state of affairs] occurs is lower than the value-for-her of the life she would have led if [that state of affairs] had not taken place."[xi] *When* is it the case that the value-for-her of her life would be comparatively lower? Eternally. Eternally, as opposed to at any particular moment, because "when we say that her death is a bad for her, we are really expressing a complex fact about the relative values of two possible lives."[xii] Lives taken as a whole, that is. It seems that Feldman is offering an objective qualitative analysis here, which may be addressing a different component than Nagel's subjective argument does. If we take the two arguments together, they may offer a rather compelling account of why deprivation is a bad thing in an abstracted sense. We should not forget, however, that a possible life is not a life that is lived or being lived. In that way, they both lose a bit of their intuitive force.

In another attempt to undermine the Epicurean argument that death is not a bad thing but one that focuses upon one's actual desires and interests, we may turn to Nussbaum's work. Adding to an argument already developed by David Furley, Nussbaum argues that death is bad for the one who dies because it renders "empty and vain the plans, hopes, and desires that this person had during life."[xiii] As an example, consider someone dying of a terminal disease. Subjectively, the terminally ill person is unaware of this fact, though some friends and family do know. This person plans for a future that, unbeknownst to him, will be denied him, and, to the friends and relatives who objectively know, "his hopes and projects for the future seem, right now, particularly vain, futile, and pathetic, since they are doomed to incompleteness."[xiv] Moreover, the futility is not removed by removing the knowing spectators. "Any death that frustrates hopes and plans is bad for the life it terminates, because it reflects retrospectively on that life, showing its hopes and projects to have been, at the very time the agent was forming them, empty and meaningless."[xv]

Nussbaum is making an interesting move here. She is collapsing the subjective and objective views, such that if the agent were aware, his projects would change and mirror reality. He would realize that his interests cannot be realized, and would change his interests, and live out his days with an accurate assessment of his interests and mortality.

Nussbaum appreciates this argument because it shows how death reflects back on an actual life, and our intuitions do not depend on "the irrational fiction of a surviving subject."[xvi] This argument is in harmony with Nagel's claim that death can be bad for someone—even if that someone no longer exists. And, because it is rooted in the feared futility of our current projects, it is not vulnerable to the "asymmetry problem" (i.e., the alleged irrationality of lamenting the loss of possible experience in the future due to "premature" death, but not lamenting the loss of possible experience in the past due to not having been born sooner) since the unborn do not yet have any projects subject to futility. Nussbaum adds, to this argument, however, by appealing to the temporally extended structure of the relationships and activities we tend to cherish.

> *A parent's love for a child, a child's for a parent, a teacher's for a student, a citizen's for a city: these involve interaction over time, and much planning and hoping. Even the love or friendship of two mature adults has a structure that evolves and deepens over time; and it will centrally involve sharing future-directed projects. This orientation to the future seems to be inseparable from the value we attach to these relationships; we cannot imagine them taking place in an instant without imagining them stripped of much of the human value they actually have....Much the same, too, can be said of individual forms of virtuous activity. To act justly or courageously, one must undertake complex projects that develop over time; so too for intellectual and creative work; so too for athletic achievement....So death, when it comes, does not only frustrate projects and desires that just happen to be*

> *there. It intrudes upon the value and beauty of temporally evolving activities and relations. And the fear of death is not only the fear that present projects are right now empty, it is the fear that present value and wonder is right now diminished.*[xvii]

This argument also helps to explain our intuition that death is especially tragic when it comes prematurely. While we might grieve the death of someone at any age, it seems especially bad when it is a child, or a young adult, that died. We sometimes explicitly state this in terms of the deceased having "so much left to do," or having their "whole lives ahead of them." It is not that death is unimportant when it is the elderly who die, but that, in many cases, the elderly have already had a chance to accomplish goals they have set for themselves. Indeed, many times those who face impending death with tranquility are those who can say, of themselves, that they have already lived a long, full life—while the elderly who most lament death are those who regret what they have failed to do in the time they had. "It is those who are most afraid of having missed something who are also most afraid of missing out on something when they die."[xviii]

Note that this is a statement about when death is *most* terrible; the superlative draws out an intuitive comparison. The elderly also have lives of value, and can leave projects unfulfilled. Indeed, if we understand the evil of death in terms of rendering our current projects futile, it explains how death can be a bad thing for *anyone*. "Even if there should be a person for whom death arrives just as all current projects are, for the moment, complete and at a standstill—if such a thing ever happens for a person who loves living—still, the bare project to form new projects is itself interrupted; and it seems that this project is itself a valuable one in a human life."[xix] It is important to note that the sorts of projects referred to are not necessarily isolated, but can also be complex projects involving plans to do something, or certain sorts of things, repeatedly over the course of a complete life. Projects such as having a good marriage, or being a good philosopher, or a wine enthusiast are subject to frustration by death not because some particular activity is interrupted, but because of the interruption of "a pattern of daily acting and interacting, extended over time, in which the temporal extension, including the formation of patterns and habits, is a major source of its value and depth."[xx] In short, death interrupts the most basic project of living a complete human life. That completeness includes realization of one's *own* interests, but also realization of interests that anyone might have given a certain history. Death then interrupts both one's particular subjective interests, and objective interests that anyone might have living as a human being.

To sum up thus far: we have good reasons to believe both that death can be, and typically is, a bad thing, regardless of whether or not death is annihilation, and that some deaths are worse than others.

Immortality is *Worse* than Death

In fairness, it is now time for a counter-point. Epicurus, it should be granted, has a response to the sorts of maneuvers we have considered above: true pleasure is not additive (i.e., not made "better" by being prolonged or experienced more often). If your life is a good one, and worth living, it is not made better, or more worthwhile, for having a greater duration. Kaufmann makes a similar point through an artistic metaphor, claiming that "a superb short poem would not gain by being made longer and longer, and still longer and, if possible, endless," and that a "Rembrandt self-portrait would not become better by being made larger and ever larger."[xxi] Indeed, though many believe death, as termination of experience, to be a bad thing, many others believe the *alternative*, immortality, or never-ending experience, to be so.

According to Williams, the value of immortality must be measured against the "identity" and "attractiveness" conditions. The identity condition claims that for immortality to be desirable it must be such that it is one's own self that persists over time. In other words, if one's identity is not maintained, if it is not "I" who am immortal, then an eternal extension of my life would no longer involve "me" and thus would be of no interest to "me." The attractiveness condition simply states that eternal life would be desirable only if that life appears appealing (i.e., not an eternity of ceaseless torment, ceaseless boredom, etc.). Williams primary foci seems to be on the subjective aspect of immortality. For something to be meaningful for Williams it has to be you, the same you that has subjectively experienced things in the past, and you have to find those experiences attractive and worthwhile. Moreover, being "you" is not enough on its own. "You" need to that continuation of self appealing. Williams claims that indefinitely many experiences will necessarily produce boredom, and thus the attractiveness condition will not be satisfied.

In general, we can ask, what is it about the imaged activities of an eternal life which would stave off the principle hazard . . . boredom. The Don Juan in Hell joke, that heaven's prospects are tedious and the devil has the best tunes, though a tired fancy in itself, at least serves to show up a real and (I suspect) a profound difficulty, of proving and model of an unending, supposedly satisfying, state or activity which would not rightly prove boring to anyone who remained conscious of himself and who had acquired a character, interests, tastes and impatiences in the course of living, already, a finite life.[xxii]

Like Williams, Kaufmann too is concerned with what might most generally be referred to as "quality" of life. He argues against what he takes to be our cultural focus on *quantity* of life in his essay, "Death Without Dread." Kaufmann's essay is challenging due to its radically different style. This is no standard argumentative essay, but a series of poems, with some commentary here and there. Nevertheless, aside from the opportunity to appreciate some good poems, the essay also provides a powerful, non-standardly conveyed challenge to the idea that death is something terrible, to be feared and postponed as long as possible. What follows is what we find to be the most powerful poem found in his essay.

To the Parcae

A single summer grant me, great powers, and
a single autumn for fully ripened song
that, sated with the sweetness of my
playing, my heart may more willingly die.

That soul that, living, did not attain its divine
right cannot repose in the nether world.
But once what I am bent on, what is
holy, my poetry, is accomplished:

Be welcome then, stillness of the shadow's world!
I shall be satisfied though my lyre will not
accompany me down there. Once I
lived like the gods, and more is not needed [xxiii]

The view expressed here is that if one lives the right sort of life, death does not have to be seen as a deprivation. Who needs more life if you have lived well and done it right already?[249] As Kaufmann writes, "It is those who are most afraid of having missed something who are also most afraid of missing out on something when they die."[xxiv]

This outlook is expressed by Nietzsche, and by a variety of Romantic poets. Kaufmann claims that the most intense love of life takes the sting out of death ("Once I lived like the gods, and more is not needed"). There is a motivating sentiment running through such examples that an especially long life, let alone an eternal one, could be far from a blessing, but in fact, a curse. If one's life is already as vibrant and beautiful as it could be, it is not improved upon by making it longer. In fact,

---

[249] We should point out that it seems Kaufmann has to assume an objective perspective to make this claim meaningful, because 'doing it right' is a normative judgment about one's whole life, and, by extension, one is dead at the time one has the perspective to make this claim. The significance of an objective v. subjective perspective will be amplified later.

longevity might spoil it.

> *In life, as in art, it is not quantity that counts, but quality. To associate happiness with a long life is a colossal stupidity, led to the absurd by the miseries of extreme old age. Our culture has long made the mistake of going in for a mindless cult of quantity, counting the ever-growing life expectancy as a self-evident success, as if death were the only enemy of man. This folly depends on the withering of intensity and meaning. It is only when life has lost its sense that no standards remain to evaluate it except length. But a superb short poem would not gain by being made longer and longer, and still longer and, if possible, endless. A Rembrandt self-portrait would not become better by being made larger and ever larger. Perfection lies in intensity, and what is most intense cannot be endured long.*[xxv]

Kaufmann's points are that we should not automatically and mindlessly strive to live as long as is possible, that we should not teach that life is necessarily a boon and death a curse, nor that suicide is a sin, that we should try to live well rather than long, and that we should not dread death—and the best insurance against this is to have lived rich, intense lives in which we use our time well. To help us achieve that sort of life, Kaufmann offers the following recommendations.

> *We should impress on ourselves how young so many great composers, painters, poets, writers died, and in our youth we ought to make a rendezvous with death, pledging to be ready for it at the age of thirty, and then, if we live that long, make another date at forty. Granted that much life, one might well feel that anything beyond that is a present and that henceforth one ought to be ready any time. At the very least one ought to feel that way before one reaches fifty.*[xxvi]

At this stage, though we might believe (contra Epicurus) that death is generally a bad thing, we might also find ourselves thinking that immortality does not sound so great either. In such a case, though death might be bad, it might prove to be better than the alternative—a lesser of the available evils. Indeed, to the extent death does appear to us a bad thing, it might be due to unfortunate standards of value, unrealistic expectations, and ultimately, lives not lived as fully as they might have been. While this seems to have some merit, we shall maintain that there are good reasons to believe that death is, nevertheless, at least often, though not always, worse than its alternative.

Immortality is not *Necessarily* Worse than Death

Williams has argued that immortality would become boring, but Fischer criticizes him for employing standards to evaluate the value of an eternal life that we do not use for evaluating our mortal lives, and, in so doing, for making needless demands of eternality. First, Fischer points to Williams' demand for "an unending, supposedly satisfying state or activity" as odd. Why must it be *one*, single satisfying state? He then points to Williams' claim that "nothing less will do for eternity than something that makes boredom *unthinkable*."[xxvii] Fischer finds this claim to be further evidence that Williams expects a single state of satisfaction from eternal life.[xxviii] Fischer then rightly asks why an eternal life could not be valuable by virtue of amounting to a package of activities that is satisfying overall.

> *Certainly, an immortal life could consist in a certain mix of activities, possibly including friendship, love, family, intellectual, artistic, and athletic activity, sensual delights, and so forth. We could imagine that any one of these would be boring and alienating, pursued relentlessly and without some combination of the others. In general, single-minded and*

> *unbalanced pursuit of any single kind of activity will be unattractive. But of course from the fact that one's life is unending it does not follow that it must be unitary or unbalanced. That one's life is endless clearly does not have the implication that one must endlessly and single-mindedly pursue some particular sort of activity.*[xxix]

In short, it appears that Williams employs asymmetrical demands. Eternal life must be utterly absorbing at every moment, or else it would be unendurable. But, of course, our *actual* lives are not utterly absorbing at every moment. Are they then unendurable? Clearly not. Perhaps, though, the amount of time involved really does make a difference. Perhaps we can endure our mortal lives because our lives are so short as to ensure a certain potential for novel experiences. We do experience boredom from time to time, but it is a boredom that can be cured. If we live for an eternity, perhaps we will soon do everything that we could ever wish to do, experience everything worth experiencing, and then all we have left is repetition of the same things, which simply gets boring after enough time—and we will certainly have plenty of *that*.

To combat this line of reasoning, Fischer distinguishes between different sorts of pleasures. Some are "self-exhausting," such that one experience (or a few) of something is enough, and one no longer desires more of that experience.[xxx] Perhaps completing a degree program (e.g., a Ph.D. in philosophy) is thought desirable in order to prove that one has what it takes to complete all the necessary coursework, and write and defend a dissertation. After a successful defense, perhaps one would have no desire to ever again pursue another graduate degree since one had already proved that one has "what it takes." But, there are also "repeatable" pleasures—pleasures that are satisfying when experienced, but such that one would desire to repeat the experience in the future—though not necessarily right away.[xxxi] Candidates for such pleasures are sexual and gustatory experiences, experiencing fine art, pleasant conversation, etc. If an immortal lived in a static environment, becoming bored would be a more serious threat, but reality is far from static. Whether one can ever step into the same river twice, it is certainly the case that the environment changes. Is this not what we all (usually) experience when we return to our home towns after years of absence? Even if an immortal has visited every city on the planet, those cities will have changed (if nothing else, than with respect to the particular people occupying them) before the immortal can cycle through them again. Will there not always be something to read? After all, writers keep writing, and how many of us have an eidetic memory such that we can never enjoy a book again, once read, no matter how long ago? Given an imperfect memory, and sufficient time between readings, "old" books should seem like new. Will beautiful views not change over time, for better or for worse? Even wine made by the same winery and maker, with the same varietal, will change subtly from one vintage to the next. In summary, unless we make some rather profound, and utterly implausible, assumptions such that the world is effectively unchanging, repeatable pleasures allow for novel experiences, no matter how long one lives. On the very plausible assumption that there are a great many repeatable pleasures (admittedly relative to each person), Fischer concludes that Williams' boredom thesis becomes very implausible.[250]

---

[250] If we look at the boredom condition objectively, as experience simpliciter, it may be true that a sufficiently long finite life, let alone an infinite one, lacks a significant meaning. However, once value is added in any form, it looks as if life can be attractive, possibly indefinitely. Williams seems to have confused what might count objectively and what might count subjectively as meaningful. More so, Williams's use of "prove" draws into question what might actually count as a meaningful life at all. Williams has begged the question here in a pernicious way. He has assumed that a long life cannot be meaningful and has assumed that no one, in principle, will find it

Though boredom and a lack of meaning are not identical, we think there are some important similarities—at the very least with respect to the perspectives adopted by those who presume immortality to be unendurable, or a wrong-headed pursuit at the very least. It is difficult to imagine someone disagreeing with the claim that we ought to be concerned with the quality of our lives, and that we ought to recognize that longevity ought not to be our sole, or even our primary concern. However, we find ourselves taking issue with the assumption that a life lived well is not made better by lasting longer. Kaufmann appeals to artistic metaphors, and this, we believe, leads to trouble. While it might be true that "a superb short poem would not gain by being made longer and longer, and still longer and, if possible, endless," and that a "Rembrandt self-portrait would not become better by being made larger and ever larger," it is not clear that the claim that "perfection lies in intensity, and what is most intense cannot be endured long" applies equally well to human lives.[xxxii] We can certainly regard ourselves as works of art, perhaps as artist and artwork in one, and such a conception, we will grant, can be helpful, but the analogy between artwork and human lives can be misleading, given a certain focus.

The vision of a human life as a work of art, as an effort at self-creation is certainly not Kaufmann's alone. Foucault refers to the "asceticism of the dandy who makes of his body, his behavior, his feelings and passions, his very existence, a work of art. Modern man, . . . is not the man who goes off to discover himself, his secrets and his hidden truth; he is the man who tries to invent himself."[xxxiii] Elsewhere, he writes, "we have to create ourselves as a work of art."[xxxiv] This is certainly in harmony with Nietzsche's famous claim that it is only as an aesthetic phenomenon that life is justified.[xxxv]

> *To "give style" to one's character--a great and rare art! It is practiced by those who survey all the strengths and weaknesses of their nature and fit them into an artistic plan until every one of them appears as art and reason and even weaknesses delight the eye.*[xxxvi]

When Rorty discusses Nietzsche and self-creation, he refers to a quotation from Coleridge that admonishes us "to create the taste by which [we] will be judged."[xxxvii] In discussion, what this amounts to is the creation of one's *own* "final vocabulary.' That is, the "set of words which [we] employ to justify [our] actions, [our] beliefs, and [our] lives. . . . They are the words in which we tell, sometimes prospectively and sometimes retrospectively, the story of our lives."[xxxviii]

Shusterman, however, criticizes Rorty for allegedly presenting both the curious, intellectual "ironist" and the "strong poet" as aiming at the same thing: self-creation, and as employing the same means: novel redescriptions of the self. But, Shusterman claims that "the aims of self-creation and of enrichment through endlessly curious self-redescription are not at all identical."[xxxix] Not only can we achieve one without the other, but that they are even in tension. "Boundless seeking for change can threaten the concentration necessary for creating oneself in a strong and satisfying way."[xl]

> *Even if the ethical goal of narrative self-creation be modeled on the creation of an aesthetic work of art, it still does not follow that such creation must be radically novel and altogether unique. For neither do artworks require such radical and idiosyncratic originality in order to be aesthetically satisfying, as we can see most clearly in classical and medieval art. To*

---

meaningful. The first assumption is specious enough; yet, the second, in principle, is beyond the scope of any argument. There is no way to eliminate the subjective aspect of a life. Fischer's conclusion supports that an irreducible element of subjectivity makes one's life meaningful, either finitely or infinitely.

> *think that true artistic creation precludes established types and variations on familiar formulas is to confuse art with the artistic ideology of romantic individualism and the modernist avant-garde, a historically parochial confusion to which Rorty falls victim. One can style oneself aesthetically, create one's life as a work of art, by adopting and adapting familiar roles and life-styles, adjusting these generic forms to one's individual contingent circumstances.*[xli]

Shusterman claims this is the aesthetic construction of life recognized by Foucault in his description of the Greeks. One was to follow an art of living that was based upon already socially entrenched formulas and ideals. "There was no need to invent an entirely new formula; there was nothing inartistic about elegant variations on the familiar."[xlii] Though there is much less consensus on appropriate life-styles today, "this merely provides us with more materials and models for artistic self-fashioning."[xliii]

We can take from this argument not only that "originality" is not essential for a "work-of-art-self," but also (perhaps) that not only can a quality life consist in "elegant variations on the familiar," so too can experiences be satisfying and repeatable though they be "mere" elegant variations on the familiar. That is, repetition need not be stifling. How meaningful or satisfying an experience is must be regarded as a subjective experience, and we expect that some philosophical and artistic aesthetes (perhaps, such as Williams) are presuming an objective perspective from which they can conclude that a considerably longer life would invariably turn tedious. Subjectively, however, it certainly seems possible that doing the same sorts of things over and over can be enjoyable, fulfilling, and meaningful.

Much turns on our conception of what renders life meaningful. Nagel begins his essay addressing the possibility that life is meaningless by drawing out some of the implicit assumptions behind the thoughts and questions that plague us. "The idea seems to be that we are in some kind of rat race, struggling to achieve our goals and make something of our lives, but that this makes sense only if those achievements will be permanent. But they won't be."[xliv]

Given death, and the ultimate destruction of everything that is, if there is to be any overall purpose in what we do, that purpose will have to be found *within* our lives rather than from outside of it. While we can explain the purpose and meaning behind particular acts in our lives (e.g., coming to class a certain day, taking a particular course, getting a certain degree, accepting an invitation to dinner, etc.), none of the explanations we provide explain the point of one's life taken as a whole. We might explain coming to class a certain day by appealing to a desire not to miss the material, but "not missing the material" does not give an explanation for one's life itself. We might explain pursuing a degree by appealing to a desire to make more money, but against the backdrop of a dying universe, "making more money" seems to fail to give a purpose for one's whole life.

From within the perspective of our own lives, it seems to us like our decisions, our lives, and even our very existence matters. Can we say the same thing from the outside perspective, from the perspective of eternity? Arguably not, as Nagel states that when the subjective and objective views collide, the result is absurdity. Given that we are self-conscious beings, we can reflect on our lives, and with this reflection comes detachment. The detachment is the source of a lack of meaning, as one gets away from specific subjective pursuits and interests, the very value of those pursuits comes into question. *Mattering* is a subjective concept and if we want our lives to matter, we must learn to recognize where our own reflection causes a loss of meaning. Otherwise, objectivity takes too strong of a hold and our lives are meaningless *sub species aeternitatis*. Of course, none of us actually lives a life employing only an objective perspective. The meaning of our lives is subjectively measured, and, for that reason, refreshingly in our own hands. Experiences that might appear to some as objectively tedious might appear to one as subjectively fulfilling. It is presumptuous, then, to conclude that a long life, or even an eternal one, must inevitably prove itself to be less desirable than demise.

Implications

It would appear, then, that there are good reasons to regard death as a *prima facie* bad thing, but we all, of course, recognize instances in which death would be regarded as a welcome release. The most obvious cases are those in which the deceased had long-suffered, either physically or mentally—or perhaps both. Such cases can range from the oppressive (e.g., cases of systematic torture and imprisonment, as experienced by political prisoners of tyrants throughout history), to the surreally tragic (e.g., the case of "Johnny" from Dalton Trumbo's "Johnny Got his Gun," in which the protagonist loses both legs, both arms, his face, his eyes, his ears, and his voice during WWI), to the disturbingly common (e.g., the experience of any one of the millions who die, slowly, from cancer, emphysema, Alzheimer's etc.).

Beyond such examples where death is regarded as a welcome release, we might make a more general observation that despite death being (generally) a bad thing, it might be an *essential* thing for a variety of reasons. Consider the following from Lucretius:

> *Death has stolen upon you unawares, before you are ready to retire from life's banquet filled and satisfied. Come now, put away all that is unbecoming to your ears and compose your mind to make way for others....The old is always thrust aside to make way for the new, and one thing must be built out of the wreck of others....There is need of matter, so that later generations may arise; when they have lived out their spans, they will all follow you. Bygone generations have taken your road, and those to come will take it no less. So one thing will never cease to spring from another. To none is life given in freehold; to all on lease.*[xlv]

Imagining a world of limited resources, if none ever dies, the resources will eventually run out. In a world where none dies, but some continue to be born, the burden will fall most heavily on the young, "for the people already around, who already command resources, will cling to them tenaciously. Life will be like a university faculty with no retirements, in which the old, tenaciously clinging to their tenured posts, will prevent the entry of an entire generation of young people."[xlvi]

Nussbaum appreciates this approach because, rather than claiming that death is nothing bad whatsoever, it instead focuses on the importance of individual death in the grander needs of all. "It does not ask us not to think untimely death a tragedy; or even to stop fearing our death, as a loss, at any time. It reminds us, however, that this loss is someone else's good, that what you wish most to avoid is necessary and good for unborn others, that nature's structure contains an always tragic tension between the desires of the part and the requirements of the whole."[xlvii]

Of course, one might offer in rebuttal that a way to eliminate or reduce this tension exists other than the necessity of life: reduce births. In a world with limited resources, why not favor those already existing, those who already have lives and projects and relationships, those who would be missed, and who would counterfactually be missing out, on all the things they used to enjoy? If it becomes possible to drastically prolong life, let alone make persons immortal, why should we resist doing so rather than curbing population growth?

Nussbaum replies that although death is a loss, so too is an absence of birth. Many of the things we value about the world and our lives involve new births, the relationships that emerge from them, the injection of new ideas, perspectives, and energy into our lives and cultures, and so on. More so, Nussbaum claims that someone who would wish to prolong her life, at the expense of additional births "is a parasite on the very system she seeks to subvert."[xlviii]

> *For in growing up to the point of frozenness that she now proposes, she has profited from the old system, from the love and care of parents, the concern of teachers. In opting for a world that no longer contains these structures, she seems to be opting for a world in which she could never have come to be exactly as she is.*[xlix]

Beyond the pains of inconsistency, Nussbaum makes what we take to be a much stronger argument against the allure of immortality: that it would "bring about the death of value as we know it."[l] For this argument, Nussbaum is clearly assuming not simply long-lived persons, or even persons who could live indefinitely long lives, but persons who *cannot* die by any means.[251] Such persons would be like the Olympian gods. While this might seem desirable on the surface, Nussbaum claims that, by removing death, we would introduce two substantial changes to ourselves: one concerns risk, and the other, time.[li]

If one can *never* die, under any circumstances, it is doubtful that such a person could have the virtue of courage, "for courage consists in a certain way of acting and reacting in the face of death and the risk of death."[lii] By extension, any aspect of love and friendship stemming from a willingness to die for one's friend or lover would be lost as well. Heroic self-sacrifice would be necessarily limited. One could never make the "ultimate" sacrifice. Would there be any need for temperance, in a world in which one could never drink oneself to death, and in which there is always time to correct for obesity, or drunkenness (or any vice, for that matter)? What would justice be in a world without death? "Political justice and private generosity are concerned with the allocation of resources like food, seen as necessary for life itself, and not simply for play or amusement. The profound seriousness and urgency of human thought about justice arises from the awareness that we all really need the things that justice distributes, and need them for life itself."[liii] Parents would not be necessary for the survival and growth of children, nor cities for citizens. Without the possibility of genuine altruistic sacrifice, relationships would lose their seriousness, and take on an optional, playful tone.

In a world populated by immortals, the loss of genuine risk produces a loss of things we seemingly value—but the absence of limits to the time we have to live would allegedly produce a loss as well. Nussbaum claims that the intensity and dedication with which we pursue certain of our tasks is necessarily related to the awareness we have of our temporal limitations. We do not have the luxury of an eternity. "In raising a child, in cherishing a lover, in performing a demanding task of work or thought or artistic creation, we are aware, at some level, of the thought that each of these efforts is structured and constrained by finite time."[liv] If we had (literally) forever ahead of us, would we ever have gotten around to writing this paper? Could not we have always put it off, knowing that we could always come back to it? It was a recognition that we are getting older, and that we do not have too many decades left (at best!), that inspired one of us recently to return to martial arts training in preparation for opening a dojo when ready to retire from academia. Without the limits set by mortality and declining health and vigor, would there be any perceived pressing need to resume training?

If the preceding is correct, then for reasons of scarce resources, as well as for reasons of the very things we value in the first place, death might be an *unfortunate necessity*. The terminology is important. Death is unfortunate because it really is a bad thing, an evil. Yet, it might simultaneously be a necessary evil. Immortality is less desirable than mortality not because an eternal life would be insufferably boring, but because of the loss of temporally-contingent value immortality would bring about. If that is true, then perhaps *rather*

---

[251]If, on the other hand, we imagine an "immortality" that comes about by ceasing the aging process, and conquering disease, but that does not protect us against violent death, much of her argument is inapplicable.

than immortality, we should simply hope for enough life to have lived well, and the chance to prepare for a good end.

"Neo-Epicureans"

Luper-Foy describes a mentality he attributes to "neo-Epicureans" that would facilitate not only life of quality, but an easier transition from life into death. Because "neo-Epicureans" recognize that it is foolish to yearn for more life than could be expected from the average person, given the state of technology and medicine at the time, they engineer themselves so that their happiness does not require more than that anticipated span. They recognize they will not live forever, so, for obvious practical reasons, they limit themselves to projects that could come to fruition with the normal span of a life, and, for any project likely to last beyond their lives (e.g., organizations, businesses, even raising and fostering family), they make appropriate preparations to make themselves "dispensable."

For example, if they plan to have children, neo-Epicurean parents will see to it that the youngsters grow into relatively self-sufficient adults, or at least that the children's well-being does not depend on the survival of their parents beyond a normal lifetime. Neo-Epicureans know that they cannot expect to survive beyond a normal lifetime, and so make sure that well before then they have fully equipped their children for life....In short, as their final years approach, neo-Epicureans make themselves completely dispensable to everything they care about. Not worried that the concerns of their lifetimes will come to a bad end with their deaths, they do not regret passing away.[lv]

This does *not* mean taking life lightly, or regarding death with indifference. Indeed, a death that comes before one can properly prepare will be met with regret. Such persons are in no hurry to become dispensable. Early on in life, they begin to take the responsible steps towards becoming dispensable, "but—like a coffin—dispensability is something they want only when they die."[lvi]

For having our lives deeply intertwined with those of others is part of what makes life worthwhile. What neo-Epicureans want is not that their lives should have made no difference to anybody or anything. What they want is that their *deaths* should make no difference. . . . It is the fact that we are indispensable to people and projects we care about that motivates us to live another day; we should undermine this motivation, therefore, only when we are prepared to die.[lvii]

Kaufmann urges us to live life well and beautifully, and to focus on quality of life rather than quantity. But, whereas he seems to deny the problem of death, Luper-Foy acknowledges it—though with much the same message.

If we are doomed to undergo the misfortune of dying, we can at least make our destiny as tolerable as possible. We can allow ourselves to live life passionately, but according to a plan whereby everything we propose to do can be accomplished within the span of a normal lifetime. Concerns which transcend those limits we should occasionally allow ourselves as well, but only if we plan to render them invulnerable to our deaths. If we succeed in moulding the scheme of our desires in this way, and if we die only after accomplishing what we have set out to do, then for us dying will not be such a bad thing. Whether we can say that it will not be a bad thing at *all* depends on what we think we could do with more time than is granted us.[lviii]

Conclusion

Death is not the worst thing that can happen to us, but it is a bad thing. At the very least, it puts to an end our objective, bare project of forming and pursuing subjective projects. But, it also puts an end, temporally, to one's *own* projects—those that I identify with as "mine." The quality and quantity of subjective projects are a good part of the calculation of the value of a life. If we are lucky, we live long enough to satisfy a great many of those projects, and, while there is always more that could be done, we will feel mostly satisfied. Our identities, to a large part, come from our projects, and a satisfaction of projects, leads to a satisfaction of identity when the question of a good life arises. A recurring theme throughout is satisfaction—and rightly so, as it is teleological in nature. We live life for a purpose, and maybe Aristotle was right; *eudaimonia*, or flourishing, seems to be what we all are really after, regardless of our ages and places in life. What Aristotle left out is the subjective aspect, or one's *own* flourishing, and what counts as that is going to be inherently individualistic. If one's own conception of one's life is not satisfactory and one no longer cares about it, and the end comes, then death might not be *that* bad after all—perhaps even relatively welcome given what one perceives to be the other options. However, if one *is* satisfied with life, and the end comes, then death, while perhaps necessary, will nevertheless be regarded as a necessary *evil*.

The sting of death can be reduced if one lives life well, and prepares in the right sort of ways (e.g., as a "neo-epicurean").[lix] In such an ideal case, perhaps one could even "go gentle into that good night." Unfortunately, death often catches us unaware, and unprepared. Especially in those cases, typically when death comes to the young, death is a very bad thing due to a lack of satisfaction and flourishing. Given that very few us know the day and hour of our deaths, it is urgent, then, that we live rich and robust lives at all times, young or old. This style of living requires awareness of oneself and one's projects at the level of the moment, the day, and the future—with each eventually representing something about *eudaimonia*.

This style of living can be applied to immortality. Identities, as such, seek completion or closure, whether one is mortal, or immortal. Bodily death seems most tragic when the deceased lacked the time needed to come to a good end, to write a good conclusion for his life story, as it were. Although death is not an issue in the same way for immortals, the death of *identities* does possibly occur. For instance, for 100 years someone is a philosopher, for the next 100 years the same person is a video game maker, and so on. Though technically the same person (or else Williams' "identity condition" will be violated), there is nevertheless a sense in which one's projects can be such as to create a sub-identity, through which we are capable of flourishing, and for which closure is both possible and desirable. We mortals experience something similar as we live through the typical phases of our own bodily lives. As a child, we may live well or poorly. Failure to achieve proper "closure" in childhood contributes to developmental and social challenges in later stages of life. We can live well or poorly as working adults. We can achieve a satisfying closure to our careers, or we can be laid off, forced into retirement, die before finishing our *magnum opus*, etc. We can live well or poorly as parents. We can live well or poorly in our senior years, and so on. Whether we are speaking of mortal lives or immortal lives, we can understand phases defined, at least in part, by virtue of the projects pertaining to them. A proper closure to each project, or cluster of projects, is indicative of *eudaimonia*. Thus, there is a type of "death" even in immortality, or so it seems to us. Though not a death of the body, it is quite possibly a more important death: *the end of being identified with certain projects, and a rebirth into new ones.* Whether end-and-rebirth makes immortality attractive to some, we can only suppose, but in principle it articulates how an immortal life can have meaning through *repeatable eudaimonistic "lives" based on different consecutive projects.*[252]

---

252 Our anonymous reviewer posits an interesting question about the nature of immortality and if it shares any similarities with the nature of resurrection. We find the reviewer's idea interesting that a future resurrection may have an impact on the kind of life that is being led and the value of that life. For instance, suppose that my current pursuits in life are being thwarted due to a lack of resources that may not allow me to flourish in this lifetime. However, if it is the case that I will be resurrected upon bodily death, and have all sorts of pursuits available including the one thwarted, then my pursuits being thwarted now do not seem to harm me in any substantive manner. Of course, we would agree with that because it seems to be a logical outcome. One

Can *eudaimonia* become boring over an infinite span of time? We have no reason to suppose that, if we take our own finite lives as analogies. We cannot beg the question and assume that flourishing over many life times would become boring. It seems a simple truth is missed here: life is what you make of it. The subjective element of experience cannot be so easily disregarded in favor of an objective element like a boredom condition. Nevertheless, perhaps some of us would not want to live *forever.* We, however, suspect a great many of us would at least want to live a lot longer than we probably will, especially if we do not know the timing of our deaths and are not presently flourishing in the right sort of ways. Thus, it is imperative to live forever in the present, with flourishing always in mind.

---

[i] Epicurus (1926). Letter to Menoeceus. (In The Extant Remains. Cyril Bailey (Trans.) Oxford: Clarendon Press.), sections 124-125.
[ii] Feldman, Fred (1992). Confrontations with the Reaper. A Philosophical Study on the Nature and Value of Death. (Oxford: Oxford University Press.), 132.
[iii] Ibid., 33.
[iv] Ibid., 135.
[v] Ibid., 138.
[vi] Ibid.
[vii] Ibid., 140.
[viii] Nagel, Thomas (1987). What Does it all Mean? (Oxford: Oxford University Press.), 92.
[ix] Ibid., 93.
[x] Feldman, 152.
[xi] Ibid., 155.
[xii] Ibid., 154.
[xiii] Nussbaum, Martha C (1994). The Therapy of Desire. Theory and Practice in Hellenistic Ethics. (Princeton: Princeton University Press.), 207.
[xiv] Ibid.
[xv] Ibid.
[xvi] Ibid., 208.
[xvii] Ibid., 208-209.
[xviii] Kaufmann, Walter (1976). Death without Dread. (In Existentialism, Religion, and Death: Thirteen Essays (pp. 224-248). New York: Meridian.), 231.
[xix] Nussbaum, 210.
[xx] Ibid.
[xxi] Kaufmann, 244.
[xxii] Williams, Bernard (1973). The Makropulos Case. (In Problems of the Self. Philosophical Papers 1956-1972 (pp. 82-100). Cambridge: Cambridge University Press.), 94-95.
[xxiii] Hölderlin, quoted in Kaufmann, 231.
[xxiv] Kaufmann, 231.
[xxv] Ibid., 244.
[xxvi] Ibid., 248.
[xxvii] Williams, 95.
[xxviii] Fischer, John Martin (2004). Why Immortality is Not So Bad. (In David Benatar (Ed.), Life, Death, and Meaning (pp. 349-363) Lanham: Rowman & Littlefied, Inc.), 353.
[xxix] Ibid., 353-354.
[xxx] Ibid., 355.
[xxxi] Ibid., 356.
[xxxii] Kaufmann, 244.
[xxxiii] Foucault, Michel (1984). The Foucault Reader (Paul Rabinow (Ed.))(New York: Pantheon Books.), 41-42.
[xxxiv] Ibid., 351.
[xxxv] Nietzsche, Friedrich (1967). The Birth of Tragedy (In The Birth of Tragedy and the Case of Wagner (Trans. Walter Kaufmann.))(New York: Vintage Books.), section 5.
[xxxvi] Nietzsche, Friedrich (1974). The Gay Science. (Trans. Walter Kaufmann.)(New York: Vintage Books.), section 290.

---

response to this is that we have no guarantee that in any future stage the current harm will be rectified. Resurrection only potentially makes rectifying harm possible but it does not guarantee it. A resurrected body is not necessarily one that has unlimited powers and abilities. Indeed, barring very specific theological assumptions, a resurrected body could be a deficient one, and even one more limited than the current one. Nor necessarily does resurrection entail immortality. All it entails is survival after death, which may be terminated in the future. So resurrection to a new life does not necessarily solve the problem of projects thwarted in the current life.

[xxxvii] Rorty, Richard (1989). Contingency, Irony, and Solidarity. (Cambridge University Press.), 97.
[xxxviii] Ibid., 73.
[xxxix] Shusterman, Richard (2000). Pragmatist Aesthetics. Living Beauty, Rethinking Art. 2nd edition. (New York: Rowman & Littlefield Publishers, Inc.), 247.
[xl] Ibid.
[xli] Ibid., 253.
[xlii] Ibid., 245.
[xliii] Ibid.
[xliv] Nagel, 95.
[xlv] Lucretius (1994). On the Nature of the Universe. (Trans. R.E. Latham. Introduction and notes by John Godwin.)(London: Penguin Books.), book 3, lines 962-971.
[xlvi] Nussbaum, 223.
[xlvii] Ibid.
[xlviii] Ibid., 225.
[xlix] Ibid.
[l] Ibis., 226.
[li] Ibid., 227.
[lii] Ibid.
[liii] Ibid., 228.
[liv] Ibid., 229.
[lv] Luper-Foy, Steven (1987). Annihilation. The Philosophical Quarterly, 37(148), 233-252: 247-248.
[lvi] Ibid., 248.
[lvii] Ibid.
[lviii] Ibid., 252.
[lix] David Hume's death is good example of this view. From his own account he lived a good life and was prepared to die. Death seemed to have no real hold over him at all. See David Hume's *My Own Life,"* In spring, 1775, I was struck with a disorder in my bowels, which at first gave me no alarm, but has since, as I apprehend it, become mortal and incurable. I now reckon upon a speedy dissolution. I have suffered very little pain from my disorder; and what is more strange, have, notwithstanding the great decline of my person, never suffered a moment's abatement of my spirits; insomuch, that were I to name a period of my life, which I should most choose to pass over again, I might be tempted to point to this later period. I possess the same ardour as ever in study, and the same gaiety in company. I consider, besides, that a man of sixty-five, by dying, cuts off only a few years of infirmities; and though I see many symptoms of my literary reputation's breaking out at last with additional lustre, I knew that I could have but few years to enjoy it. It is difficult to be more detached from life than I am at present."

Chapter 10
Philosophical "Therapy"

Comprehension questions you should be able to answer after reading this introduction:

1. *Why is it unlikely that merely listening to a philosophy lecture would be sufficient to make it a "way of life?"*
2. *What are "spiritual exercises," and what is their purpose?*
3. *How do the Stoics understand human freedom? What is the difference between a "principle cause" and an "initiating cause?" How does this fit with their understanding of Fate?*
4. *According to Epictetus, what sorts of things are "up to us?" What things are not? Why should we focus on the things that are up to us?*
5. *What do the Stoics mean by each of the following?*
   a. *Representation*
   b. *Judgment*
   c. *Assent*
6. *Why do Stoics believe we should not "add to appearances?"*
7. *What are "externals?" Why is their value "indifferent?" In what way are some "indifferents" nevertheless to be "preferred?"*
8. *What does it mean to "act under reserve?"*
9. *What are some Stoic spiritual exercises, and what is their purpose? Be sure to be able to explain each of the following:*
   a. *Not "adding to appearances"*
   b. *Purely physical definitions*
   c. *Identifying what is up to us, and not up to us*
   d. *Understanding the "nature" of a thing*
   e. *Anticipating "evils"*
   f. *The "view from above"*

The final chapter of this book will bring us full circle, back to the beginning. In the introduction of this book, I described the ancient model of philosophy as a way of life, as a means of self-transformation—the goal of which being flourishing (*eudaimonia*).

In the intervening chapters, we have covered epistemological issues such as whether knowledge is possible, and how best to understand "truth." We have addressed metaphysical concerns such as the whether or not humans have free will, and whether or not God exists. We have also considered "axiological" concerns such as the nature of moral value judgments, and possible justifications for the State. In the preceding chapter, we even considered death and the meaning of life itself.

My hope, throughout, was that it would be obvious that considering these issues, the questions that arise from them, and the possible answers we might offer in response to them, is *useful, practical, meaningful.*

As one final effort to drive home that point, we will consider philosophy in its most blatantly "therapeutic" form, and, appropriately, we will draw on ancient sources to do so.

Since at least Pythagoras (571 - 495 BCE), there has been something "self-serving" about philosophy—just in the sense that doing philosophy was good for the philosopher. Wisdom was valued not just for the sake of knowing all kinds of cool things, but because it was believed that it contributed to, and was, indeed, necessary for, happiness. Pythagoras sought "salvation" in philosophy.

Socrates (470/469 - 399 BCE) used philosophy to cure ignorance and correct vice.

Plato (428/427 or 424/423 - 348/347 BCE) conceived of philosophy as the means by which we escape from the fluctuating world of appearance, purify our soul, and acquire true knowledge in contemplation of the Forms.

Aristotle (384 - 322 BCE) regarded philosophical contemplation as the peak of human activity and fulfillment. The practical value of philosophy was clear, but, up to this point, philosophy was often regarded as an exercise in abstraction and theorizing.

While all philosophers used arguments to establish their points, the Skeptics, such as Pyrrho (365 - 275 BCE), began to use philosophical arguments as a therapeutic technique. Their opposing arguments (for and against) a particular claim enabled them to suspend judgment, and achieve tranquility. These arguments could be honed, practiced, and put to use in systematic ways in daily life. This therapeutic, intentional application of philosophy reached new heights in the Hellenistic schools that will be our final subjects of inquiry. In these schools, more so than any other, the practical value of philosophy is evident. Philosophy had truly become a "way of life."

In a book of that name (Philosophy as a Way of Life), Pierre Hadot discusses this understanding of philosophy. Philosophy was not treated primarily, let alone exclusively, as an intellectual, academic, or analytical exercise. It was a spiritual (or, perhaps, existential) practice—a way of life. Becoming a member of a philosophical school was tantamount to a religious conversion involving one's entire self.

As tends to be the case with actual religious conversions, simply reading, analyzing, and discussing texts (e.g., the Bible) would not normally be sufficient for "conversion." To continue the analogy, it's one thing to merely *name* oneself a Christian, and quite another thing to *live* as one. So, too, with ancient philosophical schools.

Aristotle, for example, divided students of philosophy into two categories. One type is already predisposed to virtue, or at least has benefited from a good education. For these people, reading and listening to philosophical lectures can be helpful in transforming their "natural" predispositions into conscious, deliberate virtues.

The other type, though, is one who is not already virtuous and is, at the time, a slave to her passions. "He who is inclined to obey his passions will listen in vain and without profit, since the goal is not knowledge but practice."[253] For such persons, reading books and listening to lectures will not be enough. "The auditor's soul must be worked on for a long time, in order that it make good use of attractions and repulsions, just as we turn over the earth which will nourish the seeds."[254] This indicates that, for some of us—if not most of us, something more potent than mere "study" is needed to actually affect a change in behavior. To reuse vocabulary from our introductory chapter: acquiring an understanding of *logos*, essential though it might be, is unsufficient to change's one way of life. Philosophy can't be *merely* "theoretical" if it is to inspire a personal transformation.

In additional to theoretical understanding, the philosopher needs training, spiritual exercises (*askesis*).

[253]Aristotle. *Nicomachean Ethics*, 2nd edition. Translated by Terence Irwin (Indianapolis: Hackett, 1999), 1095a4-6.

[254]Ibid., 1179b24.

Spiritual Exercises[255]

The previously mentioned Pierre Hadot was arguably the foremost expert on these spiritual exercises as they were employed throughout the history of Western philosophy. Then, as now, it is usually not an easy thing to sincerely and authentically live according to one's system of beliefs and values. "Such a transformation of vision is not easy, and it is precisely here that spiritual exercises come in. Little by little, they make possible the indispensable metamorphosis of our inner self."[256]

In whatever system we find them, *spiritual exercises serve to transform the practitioner's life such that he can consistently live as his doctrines prescribe*. But just what are spiritual exercises? Hadot describes spiritual exercises as "practices which could be physical, as in dietary regimes [e.g., Epicurean moderation], or discursive, as in dialogue and meditation [e.g., Stoic death meditations], but which were all intended to effect a modification and transformation in the subject who practiced them."[257] Elsewhere, he defines spiritual exercises as *"voluntary, personal practices intended to cause a transformation of the self."*[258] This brief definition requires explanation, which I shall attempt to provide in the spirit of Hadot, if not in his own words.

Spiritual exercises are personal because they apply to oneself. One cannot perform spiritual exercises on behalf of someone else. They are voluntary because they must be deliberate and intended. While brainwashing might be an effective way to change behavior and perspective, brainwashing is not a spiritual exercise. Finally, they are transformative of the self because they involve a modification of one's behavior and perspective with respect to one's values (especially one's moral values). It is useful to quote Hadot at length.

> *"Spiritual exercises." The expression is a bit disconcerting for the contemporary reader. In the first place, it is no longer quite fashionable these days to use the word "spiritual." It is nevertheless necessary to use this term, I believe, because none of the other adjectives we could use—"psychic," "moral," "ethical," "intellectual," "of thought," "of the soul"—covers all the aspects of the reality we want to describe. Since, in these exercises, it is thought which, as it were, takes itself as its own subject-matter, and seeks to modify itself, it would be possible for us to speak in terms of "thought exercises." Yet the word "thought" does not indicate clearly enough that imagination and sensibility play a very important role in these exercises. For the same reason, we cannot be satisfied with "intellectual exercises," although such intellectual factors as definition, division, ratiocination, reading, investigation, and rhetorical amplification play a large role in them. "Ethical exercises" is a rather tempting expression, since, as we shall see, the exercises in question contribute in a powerful way to the therapeutics of the passions, and have to do with the conduct of life. Yet, here again, this would be too limited a view of things....these exercises in fact correspond to a transformation of our vision of the world, and to a metamorphosis of our personality.*[259]

---

255 Much of the content of this section comes from, or is adapted from, my doctoral dissertation. It is available (in limited fashion) here:

http://search.proquest.com/docview/305002711/abstract

256 Pierre Hadot. *Philosophy as a Way of Life. Spiritual Exercises from Socrates to Foucault.* Edited by Arnold I. Davidson. Translated by Michael Chase (Oxford: Blackwell Publishers, 1995), 83.

257 Pierre Hadot, *What is Ancient Philosophy?* Translated by Michael Chase (Cambridge: Harvard University Press, 2002), 6.

258 Ibid., 179-180.

259 Hadot, Philosophy as a Way of Life, 81-82.

Spiritual exercises may involve thought experiments, meditations, and discourse (especially with oneself), but are identical to none of these things. Spiritual exercises are concerned with "the conduct of life," but not merely with behavior *per se*. Spiritual exercises aim at nothing less than self-transformation, at transforming one's perspective, behavior, and character.

Spiritual exercises, then, are not identical with behavior modification in general—though behavior is modified in both cases. For example, a convicted sex offender who volunteers to undergo chemical castration in order to suppress his deviant sexual impulses will (allegedly) display a change in behavior as a result of the medication, but we would not claim that the chemical castration was therefore a spiritual exercise.

Spiritual exercises require deliberate, self-reflective effort on the part of the practitioner. The practitioner must know what she is doing, and why. Spiritual exercises must be "mental" exercises. This, of course, is not to say that they must be *exclusively* mental (e.g., imaginative exercises), but that they necessarily involve the mind's conscious efforts. Hadot says of Socrates that he was a master of dialogue with himself, and "therefore, a master of the practice of spiritual exercises."[260] He says that the same thing happens in *every* spiritual exercise: "we must *let* ourselves be changed, in our point of view, attitudes, and convictions. This means that we must dialogue with ourselves, and hence we must do battle with ourselves."[261] A key *feature* of spiritual exercises, then (though not the only feature), is speaking with oneself—where "speaking" is understood to include "inner" dialogues.

Having provided a general account of what spiritual exercises are, we will now put them to use in a therapeutic context. The "problem" that we will address in this chapter is an extension of our focus from the previous chapter: death.

Death is the inevitable end of life, but most of us dread it all the same, and most of us grieve when those we love die. So, fear of death and the grief and loss that we experience when death comes are the problems which we will attempt to solve using philosophy.

Before we can get to the "therapy" (*askesis*), we must first understand the philosophical context in which the problem is to situated, understood, and addressed. In other words, we must acquire theoretical understanding (*logos*). In this case, we will consider death and grief from within the Stoic system/worldview.

Finally, because mere theoretical understanding is insufficient for self-transformation, we will then apply Stoic principles to the problems at hand (i.e., death and grief), using the Stoic philosopher Seneca as our mentor.

The Stoic "system" (worldview)

Stoicism was named for a porch.

That's right. The word "stoicism" comes from "*stoa*," meaning a covered walkway (similar to the *peripatoi* from which Aristotle's followers acquired their name: "*peripatetics*."). Specifically, the "*stoa*" at the Agora in Athens is where the philosophers later to be named "stoics" would loiter and lecture.

Stoicism can be divided into two rough periods: First, there was the (Greek) "theoretical" period of its founder Zeno of Citium in Cyprus (344 –262 BCE, as well as his successors: Cleanthes (330 – 230 BCE), and Chrysippus (279 – 206 BCE)(all dates are approximate). Then, there was the (Roman) "therapeutic" period represented by Seneca (4 BCE–65 CE), Musonius Rufus (20-101 CE[262]), Epictetus (55–135 CE) and the Emperor Marcus Aurelius (121–180 CE).

Early Stoicism was heavily theoretical, abstract, detailed, and painstakingly developed. The Stoic system may be divided into three disciplines: logic, "physics," and "ethics." Although Aristotle is often credited for his development of what we now call "logic," a strong case can be made that the Stoics were more important and influential in this field. They developed what we

260Ibid., 90.

261Ibid., 91.

262 These dates are largely speculative.

now call "propositional logic," tests for validity, and several rules of inference including *modus ponens* and *modus tollens*. They also developed careful analyses of concepts, and language in general—all of which was intended to be put to use in their pursuit of *eudaimonia*.

The second category ("physics") involves the Stoic understanding of the cosmos and how it operates. This can get very complicated, but we will consider just enough detail (I hope) to motivate our understanding of the therapeutic application of Stoicism. The two most central ideas (for our purposes) from this category are the Stoic concepts of Fate and Freedom.

Fate and Freedom

The Stoics believed that "God," or "Zeus" (or Nature, or Fate, depending on which Stoic is writing) is immanent throughout the cosmos. To avoid confusing their concept of the divine with the Judeo-Christian concept, I will hereafter use the term "Fate."

The physical universe is Fate's "body." Fate is identical with the cosmos. This view is often referred to as "pantheism." The universe itself is Fate's body, and matter was thought to be inert. *Fate is recognized not only as the "body" (to which the cosmos is identical), but also as the "logos" (eternal Reason) that moves and governs all the operations of the universe and the unfolding of history.* All events, therefore, are manifestations of Fate's "will." Moreover, Fate is perfectly rational. As such, all events transpire in accordance with perfect Reason. This assumption allows the Stoics to go from mere determinism, to "Providence." *All that happens is fated to happen, but all that happens is for the best, and couldn't have turned out any better way.*

Although the transition from this Stoic concept of Fate to the Western theistic (e.g., Christian, Muslim, or Jewish) concept of Providence is an easy transition to make (and an appealing one, for some contemporary Stoics), we must be careful not to impose contemporary views of the divine onto the ancient Stoics.

Fate, unlike the Judeo-Christian God, is identical to creation, not its transcendent Creator. And, while Fate is perfectly rational (and therefore a mind), Fate is not "personal" in the way the Judeo-Christian God is thought to be, nor is Fate responsive to human needs or prayers. All events occur (and will occur) as they *must* occur, according to the perfectly rational will of Fate. Praying that events might turn out a certain way is a futile effort—if your hope is to bring about an event that is contrary to the will of Fate. Instead, the Stoics thought we should attempt to align our own will with Fate (more on that later).

Because *all* events are the manifestation of Fate's will, human events are no exception. All the events in your life, and all the actions you take, are fated to occur exactly as they do, and could not have turned out any other way. Nevertheless, Stoics believed that there is something different and special about human beings, and a sense in which we are "free" and accountable for our actions, even though all events are the product of Fate.

It is generally recognized that the Stoics (specifically, Chrysippus) were the first "compatibilists" with regard to determinism and free will. *That is to say that the Stoics believed that all events are determined (fated) to occur exactly as they do, but there is, nevertheless, a sense in which we are "free"—and that freedom (and responsibility) is "compatible" with determinism (Fate).*

As you might recall from the previous free will chapter, contemporary compatibilists identify free actions (i.e., those for which we may rightfully be held responsible) as being the effects of "internal causes." An easier way to think about this is to ask, of any action you take, "did I do it because I wanted to?" If the answer is yes, you acted on an internal cause (i.e., something about *you*). If the answer is no, you likely acted on an external cause (i.e., something "outside" of you).

For an obvious example, consider the difference between murder and suicide. Imagine that a person is standing on a balcony, twenty stories up in a tall building. Imagine that this person falls from that balcony to his death below. Now consider two different versions of that story. In one, the person is seriously depressed and wants to end his life. As a result, he leaps over the balcony. In the other version, he is simply admiring the view when another person (for some reason) rushes up behind him and tosses him over the edge. In the first case, the cause was "internal" (the man's own desire to die). In the second, the cause was "external" (the shove from the murderer).

Note that we interpret these events very differently, even though the physical descriptions are quite similar (i.e., a body falling to its death). The first example is an example of suicide, and we say (with however much sympathy and compassion we might be able to generate) that it is his own fault that he's dead. He's responsible for his actions. The second example is an example of murder, and we do not claim that it's his own fault that he's dead. Instead, the responsibility is found with the person who pushed him. Why? Because the murderer is the one who was acting from an internal cause (in this case, apparently, a desire to kill).

Although the Stoics didn't describe their compatibilism in exactly the same way, their system involves the same basic idea: we are responsible for our actions when those actions stem from something about ourselves, as opposed to something wholly external to ourselves. To use the Stoic vocabulary, "externals" can be "initiating causes" (antecedent causes), but are not "principle causes."

Their most famous example used to illustrate this was that of a cylinder rolling down a hill. To make it a bit more visually appealing, instead of a cylinder, think of a tire. If you are standing atop the hill with that tire, and you give it a shove, you have provided the "initiating cause." However, that tire isn't going to roll down the hill unless it has a shape that is conducive to rolling. The "principle cause," therefore, of the tire rolling down the hill is its own shape. After all, you could provide the same initiating cause to an anvil and that anvil won't roll down the hill. Because not all objects will respond to the initiating cause in the same way, the "responsibility" for the event lies in the primary cause, rather than the initiating cause—though, to be sure, the event wouldn't have taken place if not for that initiating cause.

Now, apply this same kind of reasoning to people, and our own behavior. Events that occur around us serve as initiating causes for events. However, to the extent that our own actions are the result of ourselves (as a principle cause), we are responsible for those actions. Consider your reaction to the image here.

The sight of that model was an initiating cause of whatever reaction you had. Your reaction would not have occurred if not for that initiating cause. However, I'm confident that not every reader responded in exactly the same way. Let's break it down to just one (and perhaps the most obvious) response: attraction (or not). Some of you might have deemed the model to be physically attractive, but others did not. The model is the same initiating cause for both groups of responses, so the difference must be found not in the model but in *you.*

Although the sight of the model was the initiating cause of your response, the principle cause was something about *you* that facilitated attraction, or not. Rather obviously, if you are heterosexual female (or a gay male) you're presumably much more likely to find that model sexually attractive than if you are heterosexual male (or gay female). Even if the sexuality "lines up," there are still matters of personal taste. Perhaps that model just isn't "your type?" The point, of course, is that your response to that model is "up to you" in the sense that your actions stem from something about you, as opposed to something wholly external to you.

As another example, consider two politicians both being offered an identical bribe by the same lobbyist. One politician accepts the bribe, the offer refuses. Both experienced the same initiating cause (the bribe), but their reactions were different. Wherein is to be found the difference? In *them*, of course! There is something about the one that makes him susceptible to bribes, and something about the other that makes him resistant. Their actions, therefore, are attributable to themselves, as principle causes, rather than the bribes, as initiating causes.

Just to be clear, compatibilists (include Stoics) acknowledge that the sort of person we are (i.e., our nature as a principle cause) is also the product of Fate—in other words, the sort of person we are, just like everything else in the cosmos, is the will of Fate, and couldn't have been any other way. Nevertheless, when it comes to personal responsibility, what we seek (according to compatibilists) is *not* some ability to somehow defy Fate (or causal determinism, in less "spiritualized" versions of compatibilism), but simply the ability to be able to trace our actions back to our own character, as opposed to something wholly external to us. We blame someone for having an extra million dollars in her bank account when it's the result of accepting a bribe. We don't blame that person if it was the result of an error in a bank computer. The first example can be traced back to her character, the second cannot.

The Roman Stoic, Epictetus, famously delineates those things that are "up to us" from those that are not in the very first paragraph of the *Encheiridion*.

> *There are things which are within our power, and there are things which are beyond our power. Within our power are opinion, aim, desire, aversion, and, in one word, whatever affairs are our own. Beyond our power are body, property, reputation, office, and, in one word, whatever are not properly our own affairs.*

Notice that those few things "within our power" are all "internal," all mental activities stemming from the sort of person we are: "opinion, aim, desire, aversion." Notice also that those things described as being "beyond our power" are all "external" to us: body, property, reputation, office. You might immediately wonder how your own body is listed as being beyond your power. After all, it seems obvious that one can control one's body to make it do as we wish. Tell that to someone with cerebral palsy, or a broken leg, or arthritis, or who is suffering from a stroke, or in the midst of a heart attack, or who is pinned underneath the rubble of a collapsed building. You can "will" any number of things, but whether or not those things come to be depends upon the cooperation of things not under your control—including the operations of your own body.

You might wonder how "property" is not under your control. After all, your property is *your* property, to dispose of as you see fit—unless someone *steals* it. Or it's destroyed in an earthquake, or eaten by termites. "But isn't my reputation under my own control?" No. Your reputation is always the product of your actions as interpreted and judged by *others*. Those judgments are not under your control. Your behavior might be interpreted as "confidence" by one person and "arrogance" by another. What if the person judging you is racially biased, or sexist?

While traditional ("orthodox") Stoics believed that all events are fated to occur exactly as they do, some contemporary readers might be uncomfortable with the idea of Fate, or Providence, or even the plainly secular notion of causal determinism. Indeed, some contemporary Stoics offer a revised version of what is "up to us" that doesn't place so much emphasis on Fate.

William Irvine, for example, suggests that we should interpret Epictetus' "dichotomy of control" as a "trichotomy of control," instead.[263] A traditional reading of Epictetus' passage above would delineate those things over which we have complete control (e.g., opinion, desire, goal-setting, etc.), from those over which we do not have complete control (e.g., the outcome of events). Irvine, however, thinks these divisions are not sufficiently subtle (or accurate). Instead,

[263] See William Irvine's book, *A Guide to the Good Life*—and specifically his chapter entitled "The Dichotomy of Control."

he proposes three categories:

1. Things over which we have complete control (e.g. goal-setting).
2. Things over which we have no control at all (e.g., whether or not the sun will rise tomorrow, or events in the past).
3. Things over which we have some control, but not complete control (e.g., whether we win a competition).

Some things are obviously completely beyond our control, and it seems futile to worry about them. It is in no way "up to me" whether the sun rises tomorrow. Similarly, events that have already occurred are obviously beyond my control. Obsessing over something that happened yesterday, or a few years ago, is a waste (except, perhaps, if all we're talking about is learning a lesson so as to be less likely to repeat a similar mistake in the future). Wringing our hands over what happened in the past is not a good use of time or resources, as nothing can be done to change the past.

Other things are things of which we are in complete control. Although Epictetus includes desires and aversions in this category, Irvine thinks him mistaken, if we assume the common understanding of those terms. In a great many cases, desires and aversions simply occur, rise up within us whether we would want them to, or not. If I am hungry, and see some food, it doesn't seem fully under my control whether or not I desire to eat. Similarly, if I am uncomfortable around spiders (as I am), it doesn't seem fully under my control whether or not I will be startled and uncomfortable (to say the least) should a big spider drop onto my face while I'm sleeping. Irvine thinks that desires and aversions actually belong in the third category (see below). If so, what remains for this category? Irvine's answer is goal-setting and personal values.

Goal-setting is completely under our control in the sense that although we are not in full control over whether we achieve our goals, we are in control of what goals we set for ourselves in the first place. If my goal is to win a sparring match in a martial arts tournament, I have set for myself a goal that is not fully under my control. After all, my opponent is going to have some say as to the outcome of our match! He might be much more skilled than I. My body might not cooperate. I might twist an ankle, or have a heart attack in the middle of the fight. I can't guarantee that I will win the fight, as "winning the fight" is a goal that exceeds my control. But, if my goal is, instead, to fight as well as I'm able, given the circumstances, it seems I have a set a goal that is within my control. After all, my own effort seems "up to me," even in the compatibilist sense favored by traditional Stoics.

Values are also under my control, according to Irvine. Whether or not I become wealthy is not fully up to me, but whether or not I value wealth is—at least in the compatibilist sense that it stems from my character as a principle cause. To the extent that our values stem from, and define, our character, our own character is fully up to us as well.

What remains are all those things that are "somewhat" up to us—neither wholly beyond our control, nor wholly under our control. Let's return to the sparring match, as it illustrates precisely the sorts of actions Irvine thinks belong to this category. As mentioned, the outcome of the match is not fully under my control, but it's also not wholly outside of my control, according to Irvine. After all, my own preparation and effort surely play some causal role in determining the outcome of the match. Needless to say, if I have trained hard, and if I fight to the best of my ability, I am more likely to win the match than if I hadn't trained at all, or if I half-heartedly compete.[264]

To summarize, (orthodox) Stoics believed

[264] I feel it important to point out that this trichotomy is *not* orthodox Stoic thought, but Irvine's own, modified, version. A traditional Stoic would likely counter that the outcome of that match (for example) is not even partially under my control, as I could get in a car accident on the way to the tournament, or have a heart attack moments before it begins, etc.

that all events are fated to occur exactly as they do by virtue of the perfectly rational will of Fate. Nevertheless, there is a sense in which we are responsible for our actions, and our proper focus should be on those things that are "up to us" rather than those that are not. Even a more contemporary (less "fatalistic") interpretation acknowledges that there are degrees of control we can exercise over various things. Recognizing this, and regulating our mental life on that basis, leads us to the final category of Stoic theory: "ethics."

This final category has a misleading name. Most of us, today, when we think of "ethics," think either of a list of moral commandments ("thou shalts" and "thou shalt nots") or else a formalized study of moral concepts. Stoic ethics didn't so much address moral rules governing our behavior with others (though such things were certainly derived from their system) as it addressed an understanding of how best to achieve *eudaimonia* ("happiness"—understood by the Stoics as "tranquility"). Stoicism was more "self-help" than "ethics" (as most understand the term today).

"Ethics" involved the proper use of what is "up to us"—namely, the judgments we make concerning events as they transpire. According to orthodox Stoicism, given Fate, whatever happens was fated to occur, and could not have turned out any other way. Similarly, whatever *will* happen is also the unavoidable will of Fate. What is up to us is the extent to which we align our will with Fate. What is at stake is our own tranquility.

The Stoics offered what would become a famous analogy to illustrate our relationship to Fate. Imagine a dog leashed to a cart (or, today, a slow-moving car). The dog is being pulled, and will be pulled, in whatever direction the cart (or car) goes. Resistance is futile. The cart (or car) *will* "win." In other words, the dog is going to end up wherever he is taken. Now consider the difference between the dog that is being dragged, and the one that is happily following the cart. Both end up at the same destination, but one has a miserable trip. So too with us, and Fate.

Our lives will transpire however Fate wills them to unfold. There is nothing we can do about *that*. What is up to us, however, is whether we align our will with Fate and walk, or get dragged. It makes no difference to Fate, but it makes a lot of difference to us. Needless to say, our lives will be much more pleasant if we avoid getting dragged.

Why is it that so many of us get "dragged" along by Fate? Largely because of an improper use of our faculties of "assent" and "desire." Stoicism claims that most of us suffer from false beliefs (judgments) and improper desires. To understand the process by which we form false judgments, we need to understand how the Stoics thought we formed judgments in the first place. Our minds process information in the following steps:

- Representation: the mind receives the images (impressions) that come through our bodily sensations.
- Judgment: An almost involuntary/ unconscious judgment concerning the representation, shaped by the person's dispositions, preconceptions, and mental habits.
- Presentation: Presentation of the impression and judgment to the conscious mind. In effect, the soul tells itself what a given impression *is*.
- Assent: Formation of desires and impulses to action based upon our judgments about a thing. We give "assent" to the representation by acting upon it in a certain way.

Imagine that someone returns to a parking lot to discover her car has been keyed. As might be typical, she gets very upset. What has happened here? First, she received an "impression"—namely, the sight of her car with a scratch across its paint. Then, she has a (presumably quick) "conversation" with herself in which she interprets that impression. Judging from her reaction, it's obvious that she formed some sort of negative judgment in response to that impression. "Someone keyed my car? This sucks!" She then "assents" to that judgment by virtue of her actions (e.g., swearing, physiological responses such as an increased pulse rate or a headache, throwing her purse down, etc.).

One of Epictetus' most famous saying is that people "are disturbed not by things, but by the views which they take of things." In other words, things and events are not good or bad, in themselves. They take on the quality of good or bad by virtue of the judgments that we *add* to them. The controversial rejection of emotion attributed to Stoicism stems from this.

Emotions are thought to be our "assent" to judgments. When we cry in response to an event, we have assented to the judgment that there is something "bad" about what happened. When we fume in anger, that anger *is* our assent to the judgment that some event is worthy of our anger. Traditional Stoics believe that that is simply not true.

If I get angry at the sight of my keyed car, my anger is my assent to the judgment that it's a bad thing that my car has been keyed. *Stoics believe that we should not "add" to appearances, but accept them as they are presented to us.* As Epictetus says, "Right from the start, get into the habit of saying to every harsh appearance, 'You are an appearance, and not the only way of seeing the thing that appears.' Then examine it and test it by the yardsticks you have."

Being angry that my car was keyed implies that I have added a judgment ("this is bad") to an appearance (the literal sight of my car, now with an irregular line through the paint). There is nothing inherently bad about a car with a line scratched through its paint. What makes it bad is my own belief that it is bad. If I don't add that judgment to the appearance, I won't be angered by the sight of it, and my tranquility will be preserved.

"But it *is* a bad thing that your car got keyed!" you might respond. "Now it is worth less, and it doesn't look as good, and you'll have to pay to get the paint fixed, or at least fix it yourself, and that will be a hassle. Some jerk vandalized your property, and he didn't have that right."

So, I should give him control over my mind, in addition to control over my paint job? According to Stoicism, externals are not up to me. My car is an external. I can't control whether or not it remains in pristine condition. Even accepting Irvine's trichotomy of control, at best the appearance of my car is something over which I have some, but not total, control.

For example, I might make it a point to park it only in "good" areas, with ample lighting, and in so doing try to reduce the risk of vandalism. Even then, the best I can achieve is risk reduction, not risk elimination. In an obvious, common-sense, sort of way, I am not in control of the other 7 billion (or so) people in the world. If someone wants to key my car, there is no way I can guarantee it won't happen unless I don't have a car—in which case the person could just vandalize other of my property instead.

Stoicism holds that externals (my car) are not under my control, but my response to events is (at least in the sense that it's based on my character). A vandal has sufficient power to damage my car, but that vandal doesn't have sufficient power to make me upset. I must give him that power. Again we can appeal to Epictetus: "For another cannot hurt you, unless you please. You will then be hurt when you consent to be hurt." When a vandal damages my car, he damages an external—something that was never under my control to begin with. When I become upset at the vandalism, I have let the vandal damage my virtue. "If a person had delivered up your body to some passer-by, you would certainly be angry. And do you feel no shame in delivering up your own mind to any reviler, to be disconcerted and confounded?"

Remember that the primary function of philosophy, of all these efforts, according to Stoicism, is *eudaimonia*—happiness, understood as a state of tranquility that we can achieve when we live "according to Nature." We live according to Nature when we are governed by Reason, when we employ what is up to us (our judgments) properly, by recognizing what is up to us and what is not, and by aligning our will with that of "Fate" with regard to those things not up to us.

If your goal is something different, their advice and strategies are unlikely to make much sense. If, for example, your goal in life is to maintain a car with an unblemished surface, you will probably not agree with their advice. Good luck with that. Vandals are numerous—as are branches, rocks tossed by other cars, birds, wind and other erosive elements, etc. If your happiness is based on whether or not you can keep your car sufficiently pretty, you are setting yourself up for a lifetime of challenge and frustration. If, on the other hand, you prefer tranquility to an impeccably painted car, then the Stoic strategy might be right for you.

While specific exercises will be addressed in the next section, we can presently outline how Stoics believed we should exercise that which is up to us: our judgments.

In the first place, there is the process of disciplining our assent. Recall that for Stoics, "assent" occurs when we accept an appearance as true. However, most of us, much of the time, do not merely accept the appearance as it is presented to us, but "add" to the appearance (e.g., the mere sight of my now-scratched car transforms into the angrily entertained thought that my car has been scratched—with the anger indicating the addition of the judgment that it's a bad thing for my car to have been scratched). Generally speaking, then, we should resist adding to appearances.

In addition to regulating our assent to appearances, we ought to regulate our desires. Given the Stoic belief in Fate, the proper use of desire is to desire whatever is fated to occur. As Epictetus says, "Demand not that events should happen as you wish; but wish them to happen as they do happen, and you will go on well."

We have already discussed the Stoic notions of freedom and Fate above. If you accept the doctrine of Fate, the Stoic advice seems like common sense. If there is a conflict between your desires, and reality, there are only two ways to resolve that conflict: either change reality, or change your desires. But, given the Stoic doctrine of Fate, it is not within our power to change reality. Events will transpire as they have been fated to transpire. So, the only remedy within my power is to change my desires instead.

What should I desire? Whatever it is that actually transpires! If I "embrace fate" and desire things to happen as they do, in fact, happen, then my desires will always be satisfied, and I will never be frustrated. Even if one accepts Irvine's modified Stoicism with its trichotomy of control instead, and acknowledge that there are things that are up to us (e.g., judgments), other things not at all up to us (i.e., externals, in general), and other things that are not fully up to us (e.g., externals to which we contribute, such as the outcome of a competition), we can still recognize that there is a way to regulate our desires so as to promote our own tranquility.

Imagine that I am going to participate in a sparring match with another fighter. Suppose my desire is to win the fight. If one believes in Fate, I am either fated to win the fight, or not. If I am not fated to win the fight, and I desire to win, then I desire something not under my control, and am setting myself up for frustration. So, a safer (and more appropriate) desire would be to desire whichever outcome is fated to happen. In that way, I will be satisfied either way.

Even if we are reluctant to accept the doctrine of Fate, there is still a plausible sense in which desiring victory is unwise. Even if the outcome is not fated, it nevertheless remains not fully under my control. Using Irvine's categories, I contribute to the outcome of the fight by virtue of my preparation and performance, but it's not fully under my control by any stretch of the imagination. My opponent will presumably want to win, too.

Desiring to "win" is to desire something beyond my control, but desiring something like "doing my best, under the circumstances" is more realistic. Even if I "lose," I can still satisfy my desire if only I do the best I can. This is similar to the folk wisdom behind encouraging someone to "do your best."

At this point, some of you might rightly be wondering if this strategy doesn't just amount to paralysis in the face of life. "Desire what happens? How does anyone *do* anything, then? It's not as if I can sit back and watch my own sparring match to see its outcome, and then quickly desire that particular outcome. It's not as if, when I get sick, I can just wait to see what happens so I know which outcome (recovery, or death) to desire."

According to Stoicism, "externals" have no

true value. Only that which is up to us (our own virtue) has any value. All other things (all externals) are, strictly speaking, "indifferent." Cars are indifferent, having no value (positive or negative). This is why a proper Stoic will not be disturbed if his car gets scratched. It had no value to begin with! All "things" in our lives (e.g., clothes, furniture, iphones, etc.) are indifferent, in this sense. More controversially, even such things as friends, health, and reputation, in that they are externals, are likewise "indifferent."

That being said, some externals, while being "indifferent," are nevertheless "preferred." Things that are "preferred" are those things that are consistent with our nature as rational animals and that are generally conducive to flourishing (though not necessary for it). Eating, for example, is "preferred" over starving. Being healthy is preferred to being sick. Being financially secure is preferable to desperate poverty. Having good friends is preferable to being lonely. Having a good reputation is preferable to being slandered. With regard to things that are preferred, in this sense, it is appropriate for us to pursue them—though we should recognize that they remain "indifferent," remember that our happiness does not depend on them, and "embrace Fate" with regard to them.

How does a Stoic do this? By acting "under reserve." Stoics, like everyone else, have to make plans, have to make decisions, have to actually live their lives. Yet, Stoics are supposed to desire that things happen as they are fated to happen. A Stoic reconciles these demands by forming conditional desires in the following general form: "I want X, if Fate permits" (where "X" is something to be preferred).

Before delving into this notion in greater detail, please note the obvious similarity between "*acting under reserve*" and the Muslim and Christian notion of "God willing." Muslims will often say, of some future event they intend, "insha'Allah" (God willing)."And never say of anything, 'I shall do such and such thing tomorrow. Except (with the saying): 'If God wills!'"[265] In the Christian New Testament, we find the same idea: "Now listen, you who say, 'Today or tomorrow we will go to this or that city, spend a year there, carry on business and make money.' Why, you do not even know what will happen tomorrow. What is your life? You are a mist that appears for a little while and then vanishes. Instead, you ought to say, 'If it is the Lord's will, we will live and do this or that.'"[266]

What the Muslim, Christian, and Stoic systems have in common in this respect is that each recognizes a power far greater that controls what transpires, and each recognizes the value of aligning your own will with that power. *A Stoic, then, will pursue preferable things, but recognize that those things are not under her control (at least not fully), and will also recognize that not even those things have true value.* Health is preferable to sickness, and I will pursue it as such. I will even desire health—if Fate permits (or, God willing). If I find myself sick instead of healthy, I will pursue recovery and desire it—if Fate permits. Whatever happens, sickness or health, recovery or decline, is beyond my control, and none of those outcomes is a prerequisite for the only thing of true value: virtue. I can be virtuous (by regulating my assent, and aligning my will with Nature) whether I am sick or healthy—though it's preferable to be healthy.

So, there is no need to think that Stoics must curl up into a fetal position, awaiting Fate and unsure of what they should desire. They will live and choose in ways outwardly similar to everyone else. They will pursue friendship and health, prosperity and love. When they do so, however, they recognize what is up to them, and what it not, and they regulate their desire so as to desire only what Fate permits. They guard themselves from attachment to "indifferents," and they discipline themselves in ways that preserve and promote their own tranquility in the face of whatever Fate has in store. Admittedly, however, this is easier said, than done. Accordingly, Stoicism had numerous exercises with which to make such a life possible.

Now that we have shifted our emphasis to

[265]Surat Al Kahf (18):23-24.

[266]James 4:13-15.

living a pleasant life, and now that we have acquired a proper theoretical understanding of the world (*logos*), we can (gradually) shift from theory, to therapy, and begin to employ some exercises to address death.

Stoic Spiritual Exercises

Perhaps no other school has a more documented usage of spiritual exercises than Stoicism. We find multiple and lengthy examples of exercises in Epictetus, Marcus Aurelius, and Seneca. In each, the fundamental assumption is the same: spiritual exercises are to be used so that the Stoic may successfully and sincerely digest and express his values through his acts.

One of the reasons why humans suffer is because we "add to appearances." We've already discussed this earlier in this chapter, but it's important enough to warrant some review. As Epictetus famously claimed, "Men are disturbed not by things, but by the views which they take of things. Thus death is nothing terrible, else it would have appeared so to Socrates. But the terror consists in our notion of death, that it is terrible."[267] An important exercise, then, will be one which serves to correct our judgments.

One way of correcting our judgments is to continually remind ourselves of the "nature" of a thing.

> *With regard to whatever objects either delight the mind, or contribute to use, or are tenderly beloved, remind yourself of what nature they are, beginning with the merest trifles: if you have a favorite cup, that it is but a cup of which you are fond, – for thus, if it is broken, you can bear it; if you embrace your child, or your wife, that you embrace a mortal, – and thus, if either of them dies, you can bear it.*[268]

In this example, Epictetus first considers a cup. Part of the nature of a cup is that it is fragile. Cups are the sorts of things that can be (and often are, eventually) broken. If you expect your cup to never break, you have forgotten the kind of thing that it is. If you get upset that there is heavy traffic on the freeway, you have forgotten the "nature" of freeways (namely, that they tend to suffer from heavy traffic, at least here in Southern California!). Perhaps shockingly, Epictetus uses the examples of one's own wife and child, and reminds us that it is part of the nature of mortals that we die. In a certain sense, then, if you are shocked and grief-stricken that a loved one dies, you have forgotten the kind of thing that that person was (i.e., mortal). He continues this same line of thought by observing that "If you wish your children and your wife and your friends to live forever, you are foolish; for you wish things to be in your power which are not so; and what belongs to others to be

---

267 Epictetus, *Encheiridion*, section V.

268 Ibid., section III.

your own."[269]

Exercise Break

Identify a physical object in your life that holds great value to you. It could be anything: a house, a car, a piece of jewelry, a photo album, or even a human being. Now, construct a "purely physical" definition of that thing in the style Marcus provides above. Try to eliminate any judgments or emotional investments in your description, and describe it the way a scientist might, or perhaps the way an utterly alien being from another world might.

To help us understand the nature of a thing, and to not "add" to it, *Marcus Aurelius advises us to construct purely "physical" definitions of objects that present themselves to us.* "Look at the object itself as it is in its essence, in its nudity, and tell yourself the name which is peculiar to it."[270] Sometimes shocking in its blunt results, this exercise serves to strip things of any imposed values. For example, "sexual union is the rubbing together of abdomens, with the spasmodic ejaculation of a sticky fluid."[271]

We also suffer because we attribute a greater value to things or events than they deserve. This understanding doesn't even require that accept the Stoic doctrine that only virtue is (truly) "good," and all other things are (technically) "indifferent." Even if you reject this Stoic value system, we can still recognize that we sometimes take things "too seriously," or blow things "out of proportion."

To correct this tendency, another exercise employed by the Stoics involves adopting a "cosmopolitan" view, or a "view from above," in order to achieve proper perspective. We do this through an exercise of the imagination in which we picture ourselves rising up and seeing the things and events of the world from an ever-higher perspective. The idea behind this exercise is that the significance of many of our problems can be diminished if we keep the long view in mind. If we consider the event or problem against the backdrop of our whole life, let alone against the backdrop of history, we will likely realize that the problem just isn't as serious as we initially judged it to be.

Exercise Break

Cognitive Behavioral Therapy is a contemporary approach to therapy that draws heavily and unmistakably from Stoic insights and exercises. Donald Robertson provides an excellent example of this exercise in his 2010 book, The Philosophy of Cognitive-Behavioural Therapy: Stoic Philosophy as Rational and Cognitive Psychotherapy. It is provided below. It is a little lengthy, but remember that it is meant as an exercise. This isn't something you merely read, it is something you read and *do*. I encourage you to not only read the exercise, but to actually give it a try.

---

[269] Ibid., section XIV.

[270] Marcus Aurelius Antonius, *The Meditations.* Translated, with an introduction, by G.M.A. Grube (Indianapolis: Hackett, 1983), III.11.

[271] Ibid., VI.13.

...imagine your own feet are gently leaving the ground. You begin floating serenely upwards, slowly and continuously, rising upwards. All the while your gaze keeps returning to your own body, now seated there below you as you rise above it. Keep looking down toward your body as you float higher and higher.... The roof and ceiling disappear, allowing you to float freely upward. Gazing down you see yourself seated comfortably below in the building, looking contented and contemplative. You see all the rooms, and any other people around.

As you continue to float gently higher and higher, your perspective widens more and more until you see the whole surrounding area. You see all the buildings nearby from above. You see the people in buildings and in the streets and roads. You observe people far below working, or walking along the pavement, people cycling or driving their cars, and those travelling on buses and trains. You begin to contemplate the whole network of human lives and how people everywhere are interacting with each other, influencing each other, encountering each other in different ways...

Floating higher, people become as small as ants below. Rising up into the clouds, you see the whole of the surrounding region beneath you. You see both towns and countryside, and gradually the coastline comes into view as your perspective becomes more and more expansive... You float gently up above the clouds, above the weather, and through the upper atmosphere of the planet Earth... So high that you eventually rise beyond the sphere of the planet itself, and into outer space... You look toward planet Earth and see it suspended in space before you, silently turning... resplendent in all its majesty and beauty...

You see the whole of your home planet... the blue of the great oceans... and the brown and green of the continental land masses... You see the white of the polar ice caps, north and south... You see the grey wisps of cloud that pass silently across the surface of the Earth... Though you can no longer see yourself from so far above, you know and feel that you are down there on Earth below, and that your life is important, and what you make of your life is important. Your change in perspective changes your view of things, your values and priorities...

You contemplate all the countless living beings upon the Earth. The population of the planet is over six billion people... You realise that your life is one among many, one person among the total population of the Earth... You think of the rich diversity of human life on Earth. The many languages spoken by people of different races, in different countries... people of all different ages... newborn infants, elderly people, people in the prime of life... You think of the enormous variety of human experiences... some people right now are unhappy, some people are happy... and you realise how richly varied the tapestry of human life before you seems.

And yet as you gaze upon the planet Earth you are also aware of its position within the rest of the universe... a tiny speck of stardust, adrift in the immeasurable vastness of cosmic space... This world of ours is merely a single planet, a tiny grain of sand by comparison with the endless tracts of cosmic space... a tiny rock in space, revolving around our Sun... the Sun itself just one of countless billions of stars which punctuate the velvet blackness of our galaxy...

You think about the present moment on Earth and see it within the broader context of your life as a whole. You think of your lifespan as a whole, in its totality... You think of your own life as one moment in the enormous lifespan of mankind... Hundreds of generations have lived and died before you... many more will live and die in the future, long after you yourself are gone... Civilisations too have a lifespan; you think of the many great cities which have arisen and been destroyed throughout the ages... and your own civilisation as one in a series... perhaps in the future to be followed by new cities, peoples, languages, cultures, and ways of life...

You think of the lifespan of humanity itself... Just one of countless billions of species living upon the planet... Mankind arose as a race roughly two hundred thousand years ago... animal life itself first appeared on Earth over four billion years ago... Contemplate time as follows... Realise that if the history of life on Earth filled an encyclopaedia a thousand pages long... the life of the entire human race could be represented by a single sentence somewhere in that book... just one sentence...

And yet you think of the lifespan of the planet itself... Countless billions of years old... the life of the planet Earth too has a beginning, middle, and end... Formed from the debris of an exploding star, unimaginably long ago... one day in the distant future its destiny is to be swallowed up and consumed by the fires of our own Sun... You think of the great lifespan of the universe itself... the almost incomprehensible vastness of universal time... starting with a cosmic explosion, a big bang they say, immeasurable ages ago in the past... Perhaps one day, at the end of time, this whole universe will implode upon itself and disappear once again... Who can imagine what, if anything, might follow, at the end of time, in the wake of our own universe's demise...

Contemplating the vast lifespan of the universe, remember that the present moment is but the briefest of instants... the mere blink of an eye... the turn of a screw... a fleeting second in the mighty river of cosmic time... Yet the "here and now" is important... standing as the centre point of all human experience... Here and now you find yourself at the centre of living time... Though your body may be small in the grand scheme of things, your imagination, the human imagination, is as big as the universe... bigger than the universe... enveloping everything that can be conceived... From the cosmic point of view, your body seems small, but your imagination seems utterly vast...

You contemplate all things, past, present and future... You see your life within the bigger picture... the total context of cosmic time and space... The totality is absolute reality... You see yourself as an integral part of something much bigger, something truly vast, the "All" itself... Just as the cells of your own body work together to form a greater unity, a living being, so your body as a whole is like a single cell in the organism of the universe... Along with every atom in the universe you necessarily contribute your role to the unfolding of its grand design...

As your consciousness expands, and your mind stretches out to reach and touch the vastness of eternity... Things change greatly in perspective... and shifts occur in their relative importance... Trivial things seem trivial to you... Indifferent things seem indifferent... The significance of your own attitude toward life becomes more apparent... you realise that life is what you make of it... You learn to put things in perspective, and focus on your true values and priorities in life... One stage at a time, you develop the serenity to accept the things you cannot change, the courage to change the things you can, and the wisdom to know the difference... You follow nature... your own true nature as a rational, truth-seeking human being... and the one great nature of the universe as a whole...

Now in a moment you are beginning to sink back down to Earth, toward your place in the here and now... Part of you can remain aware of the view from above, and always return to and remember that sense of serenity and perspective.

Now you begin your descent back down to Earth, to face the future with renewed strength and serenity... You sink back down through the sky... down... down... down... toward the local area... down... down... down... into this building... down... down... down... You sink back gently into your body... all the way now... as your feet slowly come to rest upon the floor once again..."

If, as an exercise, we try to adopt that "view from above," and we observe the world and our lives from afar, we can also imagine how we would observe change occurring.

To use a cinematic analogy, as we rise "above" our lives it's as though the camera is pulling away from the scene. We can also imagine the film speeding up, in which case we would see persons born, maturing, dying, and decaying in a matter of moments; buildings being constructed, weathering, and crumbling to ruin in mere moments; entire civilizations rising and falling before our eyes. "Acquire a method for contemplating how all things transform themselves into one another. Concentrate your attention on this without ceasing, and exercise yourself on this point. Observe every object, and imagine that it is dissolving and in full transformation; it is rotting and wasting away."[272]

The idea is the same: by situating a problem or event in the "grand scheme of things," against the backdrop of the entire cosmos and all of time, whatever problem we're facing is likely to appear as an infinitesimal speck against such a backdrop. If we just adopt the long view, nothing is truly very bad.

Yet another Stoic exercise *involved preparing ourselves in advance for "unpleasantries" by imagining them happening to us.* By *not* making use of such exercises, we make ourselves vulnerable to emotional upset. "Because we never anticipate any evil before it actually arrives, but, imagining that we ourselves are exempt and are travelling a less exposed path, we refuse to be taught by the mishaps of others that such are the lot of all. So many funerals pass our doors, yet we never think of death!"[273] So, too, with respect to wealth. We never imagine losing ours, even though others lose theirs all the time. "Of necessity, therefore, we are more prone to collapse; we are struck, as it were, off our guard; blows that are long foreseen fall less violently."[274] Epictetus offers examples ranging from anticipating being splashed at a public bath,[275] to the much more shocking example of whispering to yourself, while kissing your child goodnight, "tomorrow you will die."[276] Morbid though it might sound, Epictetus is not advocating that we dwell on death as though we want the person to die! Rather, it's an extension of remembering the nature of a thing (e.g., human nature is to be mortal), and also building up resilience to

---

[272]Ibid., X.11,18.

[273]Seneca, "To Marcia on Consolation." Section VIII.

[274]Ibid.

[275]Epictetus, *Encheiridion*, section IV.

[276]Epictetus. *The Discourses Books III-IV.Fragments.Encheiridion.*Vol. 2. Translated by W.A. Oldfather (Cambridge: Harvard University Press, 2000), III.24.

unpleasant events by having already contemplated them beforehand. "Let death and exile, and all other things which appear terrible, be daily before your eyes, but death chiefly; and you will never entertain any abject thought, nor too eagerly covet anything."[277]

We are to remind ourselves constantly that all "fortuitous things" such as children, honors, fame, wealth, and noble and beautiful spouses are "not our own but borrowed trappings; not one of them is given to us outright."[278] Employing the same metaphors used by Epictetus, Seneca describes such things as lent "properties that adorn life's stage" and which must "go back to their owners."[279] A one-time mention of this will prove insufficient. "Often must the heart be reminded—it must remember that loved objects will surely leave, nay, are already leaving."[280] *Repetition, then, is key to self-transformation.*

For most of us, the mere anticipation (let alone the experience) of sickness, injury, poverty, ridicule, loss, and death causes us to suffer and be afraid.

> *Will you, then, realize that this epitome of all the ills that befall man, of his ignoble spirit, and his cowardice, is not death, but it is rather the fear of death? Against this fear, then, I would have you discipline yourself, toward this let all your reasoning tend, your exercises, your reading; and then you will know that this is the only way in which men achieve freedom.*[281]

Another powerful and well-known use of Spiritual Exercises by the Stoics was designed to provide one with tranquility specifically in the face of death. Epictetus advises us to closely consider that nature of death, to uncover what it is, without adding to appearances. We are encouraged to "turn it about" as if we held it in our hand and see that death "does not bite."[282]

The description of what occurs at death is meant to diminish the gravity of dying. The inevitability of death is stressed. "The paltry body must be separated from the bit of spirit, either now or later, just as it existed apart from it before."[283] The Stoic can argue that, given death's inevitability, it seems to make little sense to be concerned with whether one dies sooner rather than later. "Why are you grieved, then, if it be separated now? For if it be not separated now, it will be later."[284] Epictetus also provides a concrete example of a death-scenario to picture in one's mind. Imagine being on a ship that is sinking into the ocean.

> *What, then, have I to do? What I can; that is the only thing I do; I drown without fear, neither shrieking nor crying out against God, but recognizing that what is born must also perish...What difference, then, is it to me how I pass away, whether by drowning or by a fever? For by something of the sort I must needs pass away.*[285]

Put another way, "what concern is it to you by which road you descend to the House of Hades? They are all equal."[286]

In the face of a perceived loss, such as the death of a son, we can combat our initial grief by pointing out to ourselves, based on the Stoic belief in Fate, that grieving his death means placing blame "back to the time when he was born, for his death was proclaimed at birth; into this condition was he begotten, this fate attended him

[277] Epictetus, *Encheiridion*, section XXI.
[278] Seneca, "To Marcia on Consolation." Section X.
[279] Ibid.
[280] Ibid.
[281] Epictetus. *The Discourses Books III-IV.Fragments.Encheiridion.*Vol. 2. Translated by W.A. Oldfather (Cambridge: Harvard University Press, 2000), III.26.
[282] Epictetus, *The Discourses as Reported by Arrian.* Vol. 1.Translated by W.A. Oldfather. Reset and reprinted edition (Cambridge: Harvard University Press, 1998), II.1.
[283] Ibid., II.1.
[284] Ibid.
[285] Ibid., II.5.
[286] Ibid., II.6.

straightway from the womb."[287] The assumption is that to lament one aspect of someone's life (e.g., the time and manner of their death) is to lament their entire life. Given Fate, the son could not have died at any time other than he did. To wish otherwise would be to wish he had not been born when he was, or have been the person that he was. By reminding ourselves of these claims time and again, we can actually come to express sincerely (through our behavior) the belief that death is not a bad thing.

By reframing each of these so-called hardships through continual spiritual exercises, the Stoic learns how to change his reaction to them. Given perseverance, it is claimed that the Stoic will achieve inner calm even in the face of what the rest of us would fear.

What all such exercises have in common is their presumed practicality. These are not esoteric practices with abstract aims. Rather, they serve to prepare one's character for transformation and, little by little, to transform it. They reinforce core principles in the adherent's mind. They make the relevant beliefs more "actionable," more "efficacious." The point of all such exercises is to *train* oneself to adopt certain attitudes and make certain judgments. The nature of the training is designed such that through constant repetition, the desired response becomes second-nature to the adherent.

An analogy may be taken from the martial arts (or from any athletic activity for that matter). A martial artist does not become a proficient fighter by looking at pictures of techniques, or by listening to his *Sensei* describe how to punch and kick. Essential to martial training is exhausting repetition. After having punched with the correct form thousands of times, the artist has trained his body to automatically punch correctly. A theoretical discussion of how to block a punch to the face is useless to the fighter when a punch is actually thrown. However, by practicing with a partner thousands of times, the fighter's body will automatically react when a punch is thrown and execute the block. In this case, practice really does make perfect.

The same line of thought extends to spiritual exercises, and from their earliest inception, such exercises had an apt comparison in physical exercises. The Stoic philosopher Musonius Rufus says that we will exercise both the body and soul "if we accustom ourselves to the cold, to heat, to hunger, to frugal nourishment, to hard beds, to abstinence from pleasant things, and to tolerance of unpleasant things."[288] The body will become hardened to pain, while the soul becomes more temperate and steadfast. Pierre Hadot says that "just as the athlete gave strength and form to his body by means of repeated bodily exercises, so the philosopher developed his strength of soul by means of philosophical exercises, and transformed himself. This analogy was all the more clear because it was precisely in the gymnasium—the place where physical exercises were practiced—that philosophy lessons were often given as well."[289]

After being told one time that death should not be feared, it is doubtful that the Stoic will have experienced the inner transformation such that, when confronted with death, he will truly be unafraid. For example, according to Tacitus' account, when Seneca was committing suicide by the order of Nero, his friends became upset (reminiscent of the death of Socrates). "Where had their philosophy gone, [Seneca] asked, and that resolution against impending misfortunes which they had devised over so many years?'" Even in the presence of a great Stoic philosopher, it was difficult (apparently) for his like-minded friends to *act* as if they truly believed death was not a terrible thing.

---

[287] Seneca, "To Marcia on Consolation," section X.

[288] Quoted in Hadot, What is Ancient Philosophy?, 189.

[289] Hadot, What is Ancient Philosophy?, 189.

Exercise Break

Read the following account of Seneca's death. Do you think you could face your own death with the same calm and dignity? What sorts of exercises from above do you think might have prepared Seneca for his own death?

Then followed the destruction of Annaeus Seneca,...

Seneca, quite unmoved, asked for tablets on which to inscribe his will, and, on the centurion's refusal, turned to his friends, protesting that as he was forbidden to requite them, he bequeathed to them the only, but still the noblest possession yet remaining to him, the pattern of his life, which, if they remembered, they would win a name for moral worth and steadfast friendship. At the same time he called them back from their tears to manly resolution, now with friendly talk, and now with the sterner language of rebuke. "Where," he asked again and again, "are your maxims of philosophy, or the preparation of so many years' study against evils to come? Who knew not Nero's cruelty? After a mother's and a brother's murder, nothing remains but to add the destruction of a guardian and a tutor.

Having spoken these and like words, meant, so to say, for all, he embraced his wife; then softening awhile from the stern resolution of the hour, he begged and implored her to spare herself the burden of perpetual sorrow, and, in the contemplation of a life virtuously spent, to endure a husband's loss with honourable consolations. She declared, in answer, that she too had decided to die, and claimed for herself the blow of the executioner. There upon Seneca, not to thwart her noble ambition, from an affection too which would not leave behind him for insult one whom he dearly loved, replied: "I have shown you ways of smoothing life; you prefer the glory of dying. I will not grudge you such a noble example. Let the fortitude of so courageous an end be alike in both of us, but let there be more in your decease to win fame.

Then by one and the same stroke they sundered with a dagger the arteries of their arms. Seneca, as his aged frame, attenuated by frugal diet, allowed the blood to escape but slowly, severed also the veins of his legs and knees. Worn out by cruel anguish, afraid too that his sufferings might break his wife's spirit, and that, as he looked on her tortures, he might himself sink into irresolution, he persuaded her to retire into another chamber. Even at the last moment his eloquence failed him not; he summoned his secretaries, and dictated much to them which, as it has been published for all readers in his own words, I forbear to paraphrase.

Nero meanwhile, having no personal hatred against Paulina and not wishing to heighten the odium of his cruelty, forbade her death. At the soldiers' prompting, her slaves and freedmen bound up her arms, and stanched the bleeding, whether with her knowledge is doubtful. For as the vulgar are ever ready to think the worst, there were persons who believed that, as long as she dreaded Nero's relentlessness, she sought the glory of sharing her husband's death, but that after a time, when a more soothing prospect presented itself, she yielded to the charms of life. To this she added a few subsequent years, with a most praise worthy remembrance of her husband, and with a countenance and frame white to a degree of pallor which denoted a loss of much vital energy.

Seneca meantime, as the tedious process of death still lingered on, begged Statius Annaeus, whom he had long esteemed for his faithful friendship and medical skill, to produce a poison with which he had some time before provided himself, same drug which extinguished the life of those who were condemned by a public sentence of the people of Athens. It was brought to him and he drank it in vain, chilled as he was throughout his limbs, and his frame closed against the efficacy of the poison. At last he entered a pool of heated water, from which he sprinkled the nearest of his slaves, adding the exclamation, "I offer this liquid as a libation to Jupiter the Deliverer." He was then carried into a bath, with the steam of which he was suffocated, and he was burnt without any of the usual funeral rites. So he had directed in a codicil of his will, when even in the height of his wealth and power he was thinking of his life's close.[290]

Seneca's own death provides a perfect example of philosophy in practice. Due to his philosophical views and *training*, Seneca faced death with dignity. Let us use the example of death for one final application of Stoic *askesis.*

Seneca's "Letter to Marcia, on Consolation," is a letter offering philosophical therapy, but also an opportunity to promote Stoic principles. The letter begins with Seneca reminding Marcia that she has been grief-stricken for three years already. Although she has faced, and recovered from grief in the past (e.g., the death of her father), she is currently seemingly inconsolable in the face of the death of her son. All other attempts at consolation, including the ministrations of friends, diversions such as literature, and even the passage of time, had failed to help her overcome her grief.

All means have been tried in vain : the consolations of your friends, who are weary of offering them, and the influence of great men who are related to you: literature, a taste which your father enjoyed and which you have inherited from him, now finds your ears closed, and affords you but a futile consolation, which scarcely engages your thoughts for a moment. Even time itself, nature's greatest remedy, which quiets the most bitter grief, loses its power with you alone.

Seneca will now apply philosophy to the task of unburdening Marcia from her grief. To begin with, he provides examples of two different grieving mothers: Octavia (the sister of Augustus Caesar), and Livia (the wife of Augustus Caesar). Octavia became a grief-stricken recluse, while Livia faced grief with a dignified (Stoic) resolve.

Choose, therefore, which of these two examples you think the more commendable: if you prefer to follow the former, you will remove yourself from the number of the living; you will shun the sight both of other people's children and of your own, and even of him whose loss you deplore; you will be looked upon by mothers as an omen of evil; you will refuse to take part in honourable, permissible pleasures, thinking them unbecoming for one so afflicted; you will be loath to linger above ground, and will be especially angry with your age, because it will not straightway bring your life abruptly to an end. I here put the best construction on what is really most contemptible and foreign to your character. I mean that you will show yourself unwilling to live, and unable to die. If, on the other hand, showing a milder and better regulated

---

290 Tacitus: **Annals**, Book 15, Translated by Alfred John Church and William Jackson Brodribb. Slightly adapted. Full text online at: http://classics.mit.edu/Tacitus/annals.html

> *spirit, you try to follow the example of the latter most exalted lady, you will not be in misery, nor will you wear your life out with suffering. Plague on it! what madness this is, to punish one's self because one is unfortunate, and not to lessen, but to increase one's ills!*

Seneca's treatment goes far beyond merely encouraging Marcia to emulate the more "noble" example of grieving, however. He proceeds to evaluate her grief with a series of exercises drawing upon basic Stoic principles. Many of his exercises and encouragements involve challenging "appearances," and offering new and different perspectives.

He points out, for example, that her friends don't know to behave around her, implying that she should consider the perspectives of those friends.

> *In the next place, I pray and beseech you not to be self-willed and beyond the management of your friends. You must be aware that none of them know how to behave, whether to mention Drusus in your presence or not, as they neither wish to wrong a noble youth by forgetting him nor to hurt you by speaking of him. When we leave you and assemble together by ourselves, we talk freely about his sayings and doings, treating them with the respect which they deserve: in your presence deep silence is observed about him, and thus you lose that greatest of pleasures, the hearing the praises of your son, which I doubt not you would be willing to hand down to all future ages, had you the means of so doing, even at the cost of your own life.*

Seneca suggests that grief can become, in some people (such as Marcia herself?) a perverse form of pride, that people can take an odd sort of pride or pleasure in demonstrating their misery. "Do not, I implore you, take a perverse pride in appearing the most unhappy of women." Nor should Marcia force herself to continue to grieve, as opposed to letting time (if nothing else) ease her sorrows.

> *Yet there is a great difference between allowing and forcing yourself to grieve. How much more in accordance with your cultivated taste it would be to put an end to your mourning instead of looking for the end to come, and not to wait for the day when your sorrow shall cease against your will: dismiss it of your own accord.*

If Marcia is ready to "dismiss" her grief, then, instead of taking pride in misery, Marcia should keep in mind that adversity is an opportunity to display her virtue and strength.

> *...there is no great credit in behaving bravely in times of prosperity, when life glides easily with a favouring current-neither does; a calm sea and fair wind display the art of the pilot . some foul weather is wanted to prove his courage.*

Not only is adversity an opportunity to display virtue, but there is nothing to be gained from grieving—it's not as if her tears and misery will bring her son back from the dead!

> *...if fate can be overcome by tears, let us bring tears to bear upon it: let every day be passed in mourning, every night be spent in sorrow instead of sleep: let your breast be torn by your own hands, your very face attacked by them, and every kind of cruelty be practised by your grief, if it will profit you. But if the dead cannot be brought back to life, however much we may beat our breasts, if destiny remains fixed and immoveable forever, not to be changed by any sorrow, however great, and death does not loose his hold of anything that he once has taken away, then let our futile grief be brought to an end.*

As another example of questioning judgments, and considering different perspectives, Seneca asks Marcia about the nature of her complaint. Is she upset because she received no pleasure from her son's life, or just that she would have received more if he had lived longer? If she received no pleasure at all from him, then why is she complaining? She lost something that was of no value to her anyway! If she did receive pleasure from knowing him, then she should be grateful rather than resentful. If her complaint is that she would have preferred to receive more pleasure (by virtue of him living longer), then what would have been "long enough?"

> *"But," say you, "it might have lasted longer." True, but you have been better dealt with than if you had never had a son, for, supposing you were given your choice, which is the better lot, to be happy for a short time or not at all? It is better to enjoy pleasures which soon leave us than to enjoy none at all.*

It is better to have had a son than to have had none at all, and better to have lost a son (at a young age) who was good and virtuous, than see a son live longer, and perhaps suffer a lesser quality of life or character. Besides, her son (like all humans) was mortal. This entailed that he would die someday. If he had not died the day he did, he would have died some other day instead. Which day would have been acceptable to her? Indeed, if Marcia accepts the Stoic doctrine of Fate, then no other day was possible.

> *To each man a varying length of days has been assigned: no one dies before his time, because he was not destined to live any longer than he did. Everyone's end is fixed, and will always remain where it has been placed: neither industry nor favour will move it on any further. . . . so you need not burden yourself with the thought, "He might have lived longer." His life has not been cut short, nor does chance ever cut short our years: every man receives as much as was promised to him: the Fates go their own way, and neither add anything nor take away anything from what they have once promised. Prayers and endeavours are all in vain : each man will have as much life as his first day placed to his credit: from the time when he first saw the light he has entered on the path that leads to death, and is drawing nearer to his doom: those same years which were added to his youth were subtracted from his life.*

Even if Marcia didn't want to accept the Stoic doctrine of Fate, other exercises might be useful. Even if we reject "Fate," it is nevertheless useful to keep in mind the "nature" of a thing—in this case, a human being.

Humans are, by their very nature, *mortal*. We are each making "progress" towards death from the day we are born.

> *If you grieve for the death of your son, the fault lies with the time when he was born, for at his birth he was told that death was his doom: it is the law under which he was born, the fate which has pursued him ever since he left his mother's womb.*

In a sense, to lament the death of her son is to lament his birth, since he was dying from the moment he was born, and because he was born a mortal man, it was his "destiny" to die. For Marcia to wish he would not die is, in effect, to wish he not be born—since it is in the nature of anything born that it must die. Seneca repeats this theme numerous times throughout his letter.

> *Your son has died: in other words he has reached that goal towards which those whom you regard as more fortunate than your offspring are still hastening. this is the point towards which move at different rates all the crowds which are squabbling in the law courts, sitting in the theatres, praying in the temples. Those whom you love and those whom you despise will both be made equal in the same ashes. This is the meaning of that command, KNOW

> *THYSELF, which is written on the shrine of the Pythian oracle. What is man? a potter's vessel, to be broken by the slightest shake or toss: it requires no great storm to rend you asunder: you fall to pieces wherever you strike.*

The language here is perhaps disturbingly poetic. Humans are "a potter's vessel to be broken by the slightest shake or toss." In other words, it is in our nature to be fragile, mortal, subject to disease, injury, and death. If Marcia expected her son to live forever, she had forgotten what kind of thing her son was: a mortal man.

> *"Still, it is a sad thing to lose a young man whom you have brought up, just as he was becoming a defence and a pride both to his mother and to his country." No one denies that it is sad: but it is the common lot of mortals.*

Here Seneca softens for a moment, and acknowledges that it might well be a sad experience to lose a loved on. But, sad or not, it is inevitable, and to be expected of each and every one of us.

> *...all our relatives, both those who by the order of their birth we hope will outlive ourselves, and those who themselves most properly wish to die before us, ought to be loved by us as persons whom we cannot be sure of having with us forever, nor even for long. We ought frequently to remind ourselves that we must love the things of this life as we would what is shortly to leave us, or indeed in the very act of leaving us.*

Having focused on the nature of human beings (i.e., our mortality), Seneca now sneaks in some advice: given that every human is mortal, and that it is in our nature to die, we should remind ourselves that every person important to us will "shortly leave us"—if not "today," then "someday." This reminder might inspire us to cherish and appreciate them more while they remain in our lives, but also connects to another important Stoic exercise: anticipating "evils."

> *It is because we never expect that any evil will befall ourselves before it comes, we will not be taught by seeing the misfortunes of others that they are the common inheritance of all men, but imagine that the path which we have begun to tread is free from them and less beset by dangers than that of other people. How many funerals pass our houses? yet we do not think of death. How many untimely deaths?...When, therefore, misfortune befalls us, we cannot help collapsing all the more completely, because we are struck as it were unawares: a blow which has long been foreseen falls much less heavily upon us...."I never thought it would happen!" How can you think that anything will not happen, when you know that it may happen to many men, and has happened to many? That is a noble verse, and worthy of a nobler source than the stage:—"What one hath suffered may befall us all." That man has lost his children: you may lose yours.*

Drawing an analogy from physical combat, Seneca observes that unexpected blows strike us more severely. Suppose that someone sucker-punches you in the stomach. Because you didn't see the blow coming, you had no chance to prepare yourself, and will likely get the wind knocked out of you. But now imagine that you know, in advance, that someone is about to punch you. You have time to tighten your abdominal muscles, control your breathing, and receive the blow. Even better, suppose you have been exercising your abdominal muscles for years, in preparation, and they are now rock-hard as a result? In such a case, perhaps the punch doesn't even hurt you at all? Similarly, with regard to life events, Seneca observes that we are more vulnerable when taken by surprise. This is commonsense, I suspect, in certain cases. If a loved one dies suddenly, without warning, it is a shocking event—but if that loved one dies from cancer, several months after being diagnosed, and having informed his family members, there is nothing "shocking" about the death. Everyone saw it coming. They might still be sad, but the "blow" is presumably "lessened."

Seneca explains Marcia's grief, in part, by claiming that had not adequately prepared, in advance, for her don's death. Did she have any specific reason to believe he was going to die? None of which we (the readers) are aware—but she had a *general reason* to believe he was going to die: he was mortal! In the future, then, Marcia can strengthen herself against grief by reminding herself (in advance) that all other loved ones in her life are equally mortal, and that they too will one day die.

> *My Marcia, all these adventitious circumstances which glitter around us, such as children, office in the state, wealth, large halls, vestibules crowded with clients seeking vainly for admittance, a noble name, a well-born or beautiful wife, and every other thing which depends entirely upon uncertain and changeful fortune, are but furniture which is not our own, but entrusted to us on loan: none of these things are given to us outright: the stage of our lives is adorned with properties gathered from various sources, and soon to be returned to their several owners: some of them will be taken away on the first day, some on the second, and but few will remain till the end. We have, therefore, no grounds for regarding ourselves with complacency, as though the things which surround us were our own: they are only borrowed: we have the use and enjoyment of them for a time regulated by the lender, who controls his own gift...*

Finally, Seneca offers an exercise of perspective that will be made even more famous by the emperor Marcus Aurelius: the "view from above."

> *Born for a very brief space of time, we regard this life as an inn which we are soon to quit that it may be made ready for the coming guest. Do I speak of our lives, which we know roll away incredibly fast? Reckon up the centuries of cities: you will find that even those which boast of their antiquity have not existed for long. All human works are brief and fleeting; they take up no part whatever of infinite time. Tried by the standard of the universe, we regard this earth of ours, with all its cities, nations, rivers, and sea-board as a mere point: our life occupies less than a point when compared with all time, the measure of which exceeds that of the world, for indeed the world is contained many times in it. Of what importance, then, can it be to lengthen that which, however much you add to it, will never be much more than nothing? We can only make our lives long by one expedient, that is, by being satisfied with their length: you may tell me of long-lived men, whose length of days has been celebrated by tradition, you may assign a hundred and ten years apiece to them: yet when you allow your mind to conceive the idea of eternity, there will be no difference between the shortest and the longest life, if you compare the time during which any one has been alive with that during which he has not been alive.*

Marcia laments that her son died "young." But, Seneca asks, against the backdrop of eternity, whose life is *long*? When compared to the age of the universe, and the span of all time, *every* human life is but the briefest, infinitesimal "specks." In the grand scheme of things, what difference does it make if someone lives 20 years, or 40 years, or a hundred years, when we're dealing in the scale of billions of years? Or eternity? A facet of our nature as human beings is not only that we're mortal, but that our life spans are very brief, if we expand our perspective. It should come as no surprise, then, when someone dies "young." We all do.

Seneca had at least two ambitions in his Letter

to Marcia: demonstrate Stoic philosophy, and help Marcia deal with her grief. To that end, he reframes her judgments concerning her son's death, and offers several exercises to help her conquer her grief with "stoic" resolve. Seneca did not merely seek to take away some of the sting of death, however. He also sought to use our knowledge of the inevitability of death to live a better life. For those of you interested in those lessons, I encourage you to read the second letter included at the end of this chapter: "On the Shortness of Life."

Conclusion

Philosophy, as it is perceived and practiced by most today, conjures associations of abstract and esoteric conversations that are, at best, intellectually stimulating, and, at worst, a waste of time better spent on more practical pursuits. What I hope to have demonstrated by the end of this final chapter of this work is that such need not be the only interpretation of philosophy available, and that such an interpretation bears no resemblance to philosophy as it was practiced amongst its ancient Greek and Roman developers.

Although I personally find great solace in Stoicism and Stoic spiritual exercises, and can attest to the positive transformations they have brought to my life, it is not my goal to have converted all (or even any) of you readers to a Stoic mindset. Instead, I hope merely to have brought to your attention the practical value of philosophy, and demonstrated how philosophy can be put to work in our lives through the example of Stoicism.

Philosophy was once regarded as the means by which we may strive to live an excellent life, to flourish as a human being. It allows us to fulfill our potential, to be more fully awake and engaged with our lives, and to achieve a measure of the happiness that so often eludes us. Regardless of whether you continue to study philosophy in the formal sense, my sincere hope is that your exposure to philosophy, and your continued use of it (even as an "amateur"), will help you to achieve *eudaimonia*.

EXERCISES FOR WISDOM AND GROWTH

1. Identify a "problem" in your life. Using the Stoic exercises covered in this chapter, analyze and treat that "problem." Use the following questions or instructions to help you with this process:
   a. What is the problem?
   b. Describe the problem in "purely physical" terms, as an "appearance," without adding any judgments.
   c. What judgments, if any, had you added to the appearance *before* this exercise?
   d. Try to look at your problem from the perspective of all of space and time, using the "view from above" exercise. In the "grand scheme of things," how serious is this problem? Imagine how you (or others) will view this problem a day from now, a week from now, a month from now, a year from now, a decade from now, fifty years from now, one hundred years from now, and a thousand years from now. How "big" is your problem, ultimately?
   e. With regard to your problem: what is under your control, and what is not under your control? List them.
      i. Under my control:
      ii. Not under my control:
   f. How much "good" is it doing you, or will it do you, to worry about or to focus on the parts of your problem that are not under your control?
   g. Is your problem unique, or have others faced it (or something like it) as well? Do you live in a world where things like this happen? Should it surprise you that you could experience such a problem? If others have had to deal with such things before, do you think you can as well?

The following work from Epictetus, "The Enchiridion" is provided in its entirety. It provides a brief and helpful survey of key stoic themes, especially those that were emphasized in the Roman period of stoicism. Epictetus (55 CE – 135 CE) was a former "house slave" of Epaphroditos—a secretary to the Emperor Nero. Indeed, we don't know "Epictetus'" real name, as Epictetus (epíktetos/(ἐπίκτητος) literally means "acquired" in Latin—undoubtedly a reference to his slave status. His owner allowed him to study philosophy under the Stoic Musonius Rufus. He was freed after Nero's death in 68 CE, and began to teach philosophy in Rome, but migrated to Nicopolis in Greece after the Emperor Domitian banished philosophers from Rome in 93 CE. That both a slave (Epictetus) and a Roman Emperor (Marcus Aurelius) would both be devoted to stoicism is a testimony to its broad appeal.

Epictetus
The Enchiridion[291]
("The Manual" or "The Handbook")

Translated by Thomas Wentworth Higginson.

I.

There are things which are within our power, and there are things which are beyond our power. Within our power are opinion, aim, desire, aversion, and, in one word, whatever affairs are our own. Beyond our power are body, property, reputation, office, and, in one word, whatever are not properly our own affairs.

Now, the things within our power are by nature free, unrestricted, unhindered; but those beyond our power are weak, dependent, restricted, alien. Remember, then, that if you attribute freedom to things by nature dependent, and take what belongs to others for you own, you will be hindered, you will lament, you will be disturbed, you will find fault both with gods and men. But if you take for your own only that which is your own, and view what belongs to others just as it really is, then no one will ever compel you, no one will restrict you, you will find fault with no one, you will accuse no one, you will do nothing against your will; no one will hurt you, you will not have an enemy, nor will you suffer any harm.

Aiming therefore at such great things, remember that you must not allow yourself any inclination, however slight, towards the attainment of the others; but that you must entirely quit some of them, and for the present postpone the rest. But if you would have these, and possess power and wealth likewise, you may miss the latter in seeking the former; and you will certainly fail of that by which alone happiness and freedom are procured.

Seek at once, therefore, to be able to say to every unpleasing semblance, "You are but a semblance and by no means the real thing." And then examine it by those rules which you have; and first and chiefly, by this: whether it concerns the things which are within our own power, or those which are not; and if it concerns anything beyond our power, be prepared to say that it is nothing to you.

II.

Remember that desire demands the attainment of that of which you are desirous; and aversion demands the avoidance of that to which you are averse; that he who fails of the object of his desires is disappointed; and he who incurs the object of his aversion is wretched. If, then, you shun only those undesirable things which you can control, you will never incur anything you shun; but if you shun sickness, or death, or poverty, you

291 http://www.davemckay.co.uk/philosophy/epictetus/epictetus.php?name=enchiridion.higginson

will run the risk of wretchedness. Remove [the habit of] aversion, then, from all things that are not within our power, and apply it to things undesirable, which are within our power. But for the present altogether restrain desire; for if you desire any of the things not within our own power, you must necessarily be disappointed; and you are not yet secure of those which are within our power, and so are legitimate objects of desire. Where it is practically necessary for you to pursue or avoid anything, do even this with discretion, and gentleness, and moderation.

III.

With regard to whatever objects either delight the mind, or contribute to use, or are tenderly beloved, remind yourself of what nature they are, beginning with the merest trifles: if you have a favorite cup, that it is but a cup of which you are fond, - for thus, if it is broken, you can bear it; if you embrace your child, or your wife, that you embrace a mortal, - and thus, if either of them dies, you can bear it.

IV.

When you set about any action, remind yourself of what nature the action is. If you are going to bathe, represent to yourself the incidents usual in the bath, - some persons pouring out, others pushing in, others scolding, others pilfering. And thus you will more safely go about this action, if you say to yourself, "I will now go to bathe, and keep my own will in harmony with nature." And so with regard to every other action. For thus, if any impediment arises in bathing, you will be able to say, "It was not only to bathe that I desired, but to keep my will in harmony with nature; and I shall not keep it thus, if I am out of humor at things that happen."

V.

Men are disturbed not by things, but by the views which they take of things. Thus death is nothing terrible, else it would have appeared so to Socrates. But the terror consists in our notion of death, that it is terrible. When, therefore, we are hindered, or disturbed, or grieved, let us never impute it to others, but to ourselves; that is, to our own views. It is the action of an uninstructed person to reproach others for his own misfortunes; of one entering upon instruction, to reproach himself; and of one perfectly instructed, to reproach neither others or himself.

VI.

Be not elated at any excellence not your own. If a horse should be elated, and say, "I am handsome," it might be endurable. But when you are elated, and say, "I have a handsome horse," know that you are elated only on the merit of the horse. What then is your own? The use of phenomena of existence. So that when you are in harmony with nature in this respect, you will be elated with some reason; for you will be elated at some good of your own.

VII.

As in a voyage, when the ship is at anchor, if you go on shore to get water, you may amuse yourself with picking up a shell-fish or a truffle in your way, but your thoughts ought to be bent towards the ship, and perpetually attentive, lest the captain should call, and then you must leave all these things, that you may not have to be carried on board the vessel, bound like a sheep; thus likewise in life, if, instead of a truffle or shell-fish, such a thing as a wife or a child be granted you, there is not objection; but if the captain calls, run to the ship, leave all these things, and never look behind. But if you are old, never go far from the ship, lest you should be missing when called for.

VIII.

Demand not that events should happen as you wish; but wish them to happen as they do happen, and you will go on well.

IX.

Sickness is an impediment to the body, but not to the will, unless itself pleases. Lameness is an impediment to the leg, but not to the will; and say this to yourself with regard to everything that happens. For you will find it to be an impediment to something else, but not truly to yourself.

X.

Upon every accident, remember to turn towards yourself and inquire what faculty you have for its use. If you encounter a handsome person, you will find continence the faculty needed; if pain, then fortitude; if reviling, then patience. And when thus habituated, the phenomena of existence will not overwhelm you.

XI.

Never say of anything, "I have lost it;" but, "I have restored it." Has your child died? It is restored. Has your wife died? She is restored. Has your estate been taken away? That likewise is restored. "But it was a bad man who took it." What is it to you by whose hands he who gave it has demanded it again? While he permits you to possess it, hold it as something not your own; as do travellers at an inn.

XII.

If you would improve, lay aside such reasonings as these: "If I neglect my affairs, I shall not have a maintenance; if I do not punish my servant, he will be good for nothing." For it were better to die of hunger, exempt from grief and fear, than to live in affluence with perturbation; and it is better that your servant should be bad than you unhappy.

Begin therefore with little things. Is a little oil spilt or a little wine stolen? Say to yourself, "This is the price paid for peace and tranquillity; and nothing is to be had for nothing." And when you call your servant, consider that it is possible he may not come at your call; or, if he does, that he may not do what you wish. But it is not at all desirable for him, and very undesirable for you, that it should be in his power to cause you any disturbance.

XIII.

If you would improve, be content to be thought foolish and dull with regard to externals. Do not desire to be thought to know anything; and though you should appear to others to be somebody, distrust yourself. For be assured, it is not easy at once to keep your will in harmony with nature, and to secure externals; but while you are absorbed in the one, you must of necessity neglect the other.

XIV.

If you wish your children and your wife and your friends to live forever, you are foolish; for you wish things to be in your power which are not so; and what belongs to others to be your own. So likewise, if you wish your servant to be without fault, you are foolish; for you wish vice not to be vice, but something else. But if you wish not to be disappointed in your desires, that is in your own power. Exercise, therefore, what is in your power. A man's master is he who is able to confer or remove whatever that man seeks or shuns. Whoever then would be free, let him wish for nothing, let him decline nothing, which depends on others; else he must necessarily be a slave.

XV.

Remember that you must behave as at a banquet. Is anything brought round to you? Put out your hand, and take a moderate share. Does it pass by you? Do not stop it. Is it not come yet? Do not yearn in desire towards it, but wait till it reaches you. So with regard to children, wife, office, riches; and you will some time or other be worthy to feast with the gods. And if you do not so much as take the things which are set before you, but are able even to forego them, then you will not only be worthy to feast with the gods, but to rule with them also. For, by thus doing, Diogenes and Heraclitus, and others like them, deservedly became divine, and were so recognized.

XVI.

When you see any one weeping for grief, either that his son has gone abroad, or that he has suffered in his affairs, take care not to be overcome by the apparent evil; but discriminate, and be ready to say, "What hurts this man is not this occurrence itself, – for another man might not be hurt by it, – but the view he chooses to take of it." As far as conversation goes, however, do not disdain to accommodate yourself to him, and if need be, to groan with him. Take heed, however, not to groan inwardly too.

XVII.

Remember that you are an actor in a drama of such sort as the author chooses, – if short, then in a short one; if long, then in a long one. If it be his pleasure that you should enact a poor man, see that you act it well; or a cripple, or a ruler, or a private citizen. For this is your business, to act well the given part; but to choose it, belongs to another.

XVIII.

When a raven happens to croak unluckily, be not overcome by appearances, but discriminate, and say, – "Nothing is portended to *me*; but either to my paltry body, or property, or reputation, or children, or wife. But to *me* all portents are lucky, if I will. For whatsoever happens, it belongs to me to derive advantage therefrom."

XIX.

You can be unconquerable, if you enter into no combat in which it is not in your own power to conquer. When, therefore, you see any one eminent in honors or power, or high esteem on any other account, take heed not to be bewildered by appearances and to pronounce him happy; for if the essence of good consists in things within our own power, there will be no room for envy or emulation. But, for your part, do not desire to be a general, or a senator, or a consul, but to be free; and the only way to this is a disregard of things which lie not within our own power.

XX.

Remember that it is not he who gives abuse or blows who affronts; but the view we take of these things as insulting. When, therefore, any one provokes you, be assured that it is your own opinion which provokes you. Try, therefore, in the first place, not to be bewildered by appearances. For if you once gain time and respite, you will more easily command yourself.

XXI.

Let death and exile, and all other things which appear terrible, be daily before your eyes, but death chiefly; and you will never entertain any abject thought, not too eagerly covet anything.

XXII.

If you have an earnest desire towards philosophy, prepare yourself from the very first to have the multitude laugh and sneer, and say, "He is returned to us a philosopher all at once;" and "Whence this supercilious look?" Now, for your part, do not have a supercilious look indeed; but keep steadily to those things which appear best to you, as one appointed by God to this particular station. For remember that, if you are persistent, those very persons who at first ridiculed will afterwards admire you. But if you are conquered by them, you will incur a double ridicule.

XXIII.

If you ever happen to turn your attention to externals, for the pleasure of any one, be assured that you have ruined your scheme of life. Be contented, then, in everything, with being a philosopher; and if you with to seem so likewise to any one, appear so to yourself, and it will suffice you.

XXIV.

Let not such considerations as these distress you: "I shall live in discredit, and be nobody anywhere." For if discredit be an evil, you can no more be involved in any evil through another, than in baseness. Is it any business of yours, then, to get power, or to be admitted to an entertainment? By no means. How, then, after all, is this discredit? And how is it true that you will be nobody anywhere; when you ought to be somebody in those things only which are within your own power, in which you may be of the greatest consequence? "But my friends will be unassisted." What do you mean by unassisted? They will not have money from you; nor will you make them Roman citizens. Who told you, then, that these are among the things within our own power, and not rather the affair of others? And who can give to another the things which he has not? "Well, but get them, then, that we too may have a share." If I can get them with the preservation of my own honor and fidelity and self-respect, show me the way, and I will get them; but if you require me to lose my own proper good, that you may gain what is no good, consider how unreasonable and foolish you are. Besides, which would you rather have, a sum of money, or a faithful and honorable friend? Rather assist me, then, to gain this character, than require me to do those things by which I may lose it. Well, but my country, say you, as far as depends upon me, will be unassisted. Here, again, what assistance is this you mean? It will not have porticoes nor baths of your providing? And what signifies that? Why, neither does a smith provide it with shoes, or a shoemaker with arms. It is enough if every one fully performs his own proper business. And were you to supply it with another faithful and honorable citizen, would not he be of use to it? Yes. Therefore neither are you yourself useless to it. "What place, then," say you, "shall I hold in the state?" Whatever you can hold with the preservation of your fidelity and honor. But if, by desiring to be useful to that, you lose these, how can you serve your country, when you have become faithless and shameless?

XXV.

Is any one preferred before you at an entertainment, or in courtesies, or in confidential conversation? If these things are good, you ought to rejoice that he has them; and if they are evil, do not be grieved that you have them not. And remember that you cannot be permitted to rival others in externals, without using the same means to obtain them. For how can he who will not haunt the door of any man, will not attend him, will not praise him, have an equal share with him who does these things? You are unjust, then, and unreasonable, if you are unwilling to pay the price for which these things are sold, and would have them for nothing. For how much are lettuces sold? An obolus, for instance. If another, then, paying an obolus, takes the lettuces, and you, not paying it, go without them, do not imagine that he has gained any advantage over you. For as he has the lettuces, so you have the obolus which you did not give. So, in the present case, you have not been invited to such a person's entertainment, because you have not paid him the price for which a supper is sold. It is sold for praise; it is sold for attendance. Give him, then, the value, if it be for your advantage. But if you would at the same time not pay the one, and yet receive the other, you are unreasonable, and foolish. Have you nothing, then, in place of the supper? Yes, indeed, you have: not to praise him whom you do not like to praise; not to bear the insolence of his lackeys.

XXVI.

The will of Nature may be learned from things upon which we are all agreed. As, when our neighbor's boy has broken a cup, or the like, we are ready at once to say, "These are casualties that will happen;" be assured, then, that when your own cup is likewise broken, you ought to be affected just as when another's cup was broken. Now apply this to greater things. Is the child or wife of another dead? There is no one who would not say, "This is an accident of mortality." But if any one's own child happens to die, it is immediately, "Alas! how wretched am I!" It should be always remembered how we are affected on hearing the same thing concerning others.

XXVII.

As a mark is not set up for the sake of missing the aim, so neither does the nature of evil exist in the world.

XXVIII.

If a person had delivered up your body to some passer-by, you would certainly be angry. And do you feel no shame in delivering up your own mind to any reviler, to be disconcerted and confounded?

XXIX.

In every affair consider what precedes and follows, and then undertake it. Otherwise you will begin with spirit indeed, careless of the consequences, and when these are developed, you will shamefully desist. "I would conquer at the Olympic games." But consider what precedes and follows, and then, if it be for your advantage, engage in the affair. You must conform to rules, submit to a diet, refrain from dainties; exercise your body, whether you choose it or not, at a stated hour, in heat and cold; you must drink no cold water, and sometimes no wine, – in a word, you must give yourself up to your trainer as to a physician. Then, in the combat, you may be thrown into a ditch, dislocate your arm, turn your ankle, swallow abundance of dust, receive stripes [for negligence], and, after all, lose the victory. When you have reckoned up all this, if your inclination still holds, set about the combat. Otherwise, take notice, you will behave like children who sometimes play wrestlers, sometimes gladiators, sometimes blow a trumpet, and sometimes act a tragedy, when they have seen and admired these shows. Thus you too will be at one time a wrestler, at another a gladiator; now a philosopher, now an orator; but nothing in earnest. Like an ape you mimic all you see, and one thing after another is sure to please you, but is out of favor as soon as it becomes familiar. For you have never entered upon anything considerately, nor after having surveyed and tested the whole matter; but carelessly, and with a half-way zeal. Thus some, when they have seen a philosopher, and heard a man speaking like Euphrates, – though indeed who can speak like him? – have a mind to be philosophers too. Consider first, man, what the matter is, and what your own nature is able to bear. If you would be a wrestler, consider your shoulders, your back, your thighs; for different persons are made for different things. Do you think that you can act as you do, and be a philosopher; that you can eat, drink, be angry, be discontented, as you are now? You must watch, you must labor, you must get the better of certain appetites; must quit your acquaintance, be despised by your servant, be laughed at by those you meet; come off worse than others in everything, – in offices, in honors, before tribunals. When you have fully considered all these things, approach, if you please; if, by parting with them, you have a mind to purchase serenity, freedom, and tranquillity. If not, do not come hither; do not, like children, be now a philosopher, then a publican, then an orator, and then one of Caesar's officers. These things are not consistent. You must be one man either good or bad. You must cultivate either your own Reason or else externals, apply yourself either to things within or without you; that is, be either a philosopher, or one of the mob.

XXX.

Duties are universally measured by relations. Is a certain man your father? In this are implied, taking care of him; submitting to him in all things; patiently receiving his reproaches, his correction. But he is a bad father. Is your natural tie, then, to a *good* father? No, but to a father. Is a brother unjust? Well, preserve your own just relation towards him. Consider not what *he* does, but what *you* are to do, to keep your own will in state conformable to nature. For another cannot hurt you, unless you please. You will then be hurt when you consent to be hurt. In this manner, therefore, if you accustom yourself to contemplate the relations of neighbor, citizen, commander, you can deduce from each the corresponding duties.

XXXI.

Be assured that the essential property of piety towards the gods lies in this, to form right opinions concerning them, as existing, and as governing the universe justly and well. And fix yourself in this resolution, to obey them, and yield to them, and willingly follow them amidst all events, as being ruled by the most perfect wisdom. For thus you will never find fault with the gods, nor accuse them of neglecting you. And it is not possible for this to be effected any other way than by withdrawing yourself from things which are not within our own power, and by making good or evil to consist only in those which are. For if you suppose any of the things to be either good or evil, it is inevitable that, when you are disappointed of what you wish, or incur what you would avoid, you should reproach and blame their authors. For every creature is naturally formed to flee and abhor things that appear hurtful, and that which causes them; and to pursue and admire those which appear beneficial, and that which causes them. It is impractical, then, that one who supposes himself to be hurt should rejoice in the person who, as he thinks, hurts him; just as it is impossible to rejoice in the hurt itself. Hence, also, a father is reviled by his son, when he does not impart the things which seem to be good; and this made Polynices and Eteocles mutually enemies, that empire seemed good to both. On this account the husbandman reviles the gods; the sailor, the merchant, or those who have lost wife or child. For where our interest is, there too is piety directed. So that whoever is careful to regulate his desires and aversions as he ought is thus made careful of piety likewise. But it also becomes incumbent on every one to offer libations and sacrifices and first-fruits, according to the customs of his country, purely, and not heedlessly nor negligently; nor avariciously, nor yet extravagantly.

XXXII.

When you have recourse to divination, remember that you know not what the event will be, and you come to learn it of the diviner; but of what nature it is you knew before coming; at least, if you are of philosophic mind. For if it is among the things not within our power, it can by no means be either good or evil. Do not, therefore, bring with you to the diviner either desire or aversion, – else you will approach him trembling, – but first clearly understand that every event is indifferent, and nothing to *you*, of whatever sort it may be; for it will be in your power to make a right use of it, and this no one can hinder. Then come with confidence to the gods as your counsellors; and afterwards, when any counsel is given you, remember what counsellors you have assumed, and whose advice you will neglect, if you disobey. Come to divination, as Socrates prescribed, in cases of which the whole consideration relates to the event, and in which no opportunities are afforded by reason, or any other art, to discover the matter in view. When, therefore, it is our duty to share the danger of a friend or of our country, we ought not to consult the oracle as to whether we shall share it with them or not. For though the diviner should forewarn you that the auspices are unfavorable, this means no more than that either death or mutilation or exile is portended. But we have reason within us; and it directs, even with these hazards, to stand by our friend and country. Attend, therefore, to the greater diviner, the Pythian god, who once cast out of the temple him who neglected to save his friend.

XXXIII.

Begin by prescribing to yourself some character and demeanor, such as you may preserve both alone and in company.

Be mostly silent; or speak merely what is needful, and in few words. We may, however, enter sparingly into discourse sometimes, when occasion calls for it; but let it not run on any of the common subjects, as gladiators, or horse-races, or athletic champions, or food, or drink, – the vulgar topics of conversation; and especially not on men, so as either to blame, or praise, or make comparisons. If you are able, then, by your own conversation, bring over that of your company to proper subjects; but if you happen to find yourself among strangers, be silent.

Let not your laughter be loud, frequent, or abundant.

Avoid taking oaths, if possible, altogether; at any rate, so far as you are able.

Avoid public and vulgar entertainments; but if ever an occasion calls you to them, keep your attention upon the stretch, that you may not imperceptibly slide into vulgarity. For be assured that if a person be ever so pure himself, yet, if his companion be corrupted, he who converses with him will be corrupted likewise.

Provide things relating to the body no farther than absolute need requires; as meat, drink, clothing, house, retinue. But cut off everything that looks towards show and luxury.

Before marriage, guard yourself with all your ability from unlawful intercourse with women; yet be not uncharitable or severe to those who are led into this, not frequently boast that you yourself do otherwise.

If any one tells you that such a person speaks ill of you, do not make excuses about what is said of you, but answer: "He was ignorant of my other faults, else he would not have mentioned these alone."

It is not necessary for you to appear often at public spectacles; but if ever there is a proper occasion for you to be there, do not appear more solicitous for any other than for yourself; that is, wish things to be only just as they are, and only the best man to win: for thus nothing will go against you. But abstain entirely from acclamations and derision and violent emotions. And when you come away, do not discourse a great deal on what has passed, and what contributes nothing to your own amendment. For it would appear by such discourse that you were dazzled by the show.

Be not prompt or ready to attend private recitations; but if you do attend, preserve your gravity and dignity, and yet avoid making yourself disagreeable.

When you are going to confer with any one, and especially with one who seems your superior, represent to yourself how Socrates or Zeno would behave in such a case, and you will not be at a loss to meet properly whatever may occur.

When you are going before any one in power, fancy to yourself that you may not find him at home, that you may be shut out, that the doors may not be opened to you, that he may not notice you. If, with all this, it be your duty to go, bear what happens, and never say to yourself, "It was not worth so much." For this is vulgar, and like a man bewildered by externals.

In society, avoid a frequent and excessive mention of your own actions and dangers. For however agreeable it may be to yourself to allude to risks you have run, it is not equally agreeable to others to hear your adventures. Avoid likewise an endeavor to excite laughter. For this may readily slide you into vulgarity, and, besides, may be apt to lower you in the esteem of your acquaintance. Approaches to indecent discourse are likewise dangerous. Therefore when anything of this sort happens, use the first fit opportunity to rebuke him who makes advances that way; or, at least, by silence and blushing and a serious look, show yourself to be displeased by such talk.

XXXIV.

If you are dazzled by the semblance of any promised pleasure; guard yourself against being bewildered by it; but let the affair wait your leisure, and procure yourself some delay. Then bring to your mind both points of time, – that in which you shall enjoy the pleasure, and that in which you will repent and reproach yourself, after you have enjoyed it, – and set before you, in opposition to these, how you will rejoice and applaud yourself, if you abstain. And even though it should appear to you a seasonable gratification, take heed that its enticements and allurements and seductions may not subdue you; but set in opposition to this, how much better it is to be conscious of having gained so great a victory.

XXXV.

When you do anything from a clear judgment that it ought to be done, never shrink from being seen to do it, even though the world should misunderstand it; for if you are not acting rightly, shun the action itself; if you are, why fear those who wrongly censure you?

XXXVI.

As the proposition, *either it is day, or it is night,* has much force in a disjunctive argument, but none at all in a conjunctive one; so, at a feast, to choose the largest share is very suitable to the bodily appetite, but utterly inconsistent with the social spirit of the entertainment. Remember, then, when you eat with another, not only the value to the body of those things which are set before you, but also the value of proper courtesy toward your host.

XXXVII.

If you have assumed any character beyond your strength, you have both demeaned yourself ill that, and quitted one which you might have supported.

XXXVIII.

As in walking you take care not to tread upon a nail, or turn your foot, so likewise take care not to hurt the ruling faculty of your mind. And if we were to guard against this in every action, we should enter upon action more safely.

XXXIX.

The body is to every one the proper measure of its possessions, as the foot is of the shoe. If, therefore, you stop at this, you will keep the measure; but if you move beyond it, you must necessarily be carried forward, as down a precipice; as in the case of a shoe, if you go beyond its fitness to the foot, it comes first to be gilded, then purple, and then studded with jewels. For to that which once exceeds the fit measure there is no bound.

XL.

Women from fourteen years old are flattered by men with the title of mistresses. Therefore, perceiving that they are regarded only as qualified to give men pleasure, they begin to adorn themselves, and in that to place all their hopes. It is worth while, therefore, to try that they may perceive themselves honored only so far as they appear beautiful in their demeanor, and modestly virtuous.

XLI.

It is a mark of want of intellect, to spend much time in things relating to the body; as to be immoderate in exercises, in eating and drinking, and in the discharge of other animal functions. These things should be done incidentally and our main strength be applied to our reason.

XLII.

When any person does ill by you, or speaks ill of you, remember that he acts or speaks from an impression that it is right for him to do so. Now, it is not possible that he should follow what appears right to you, but only what appears so to himself. Therefore, if he judges from false appearances, he is the person hurt; since he too is the person deceived. For if any one takes a true proposition to be false, the proposition is not hurt, but only the man is deceived. Setting out, then, from these principles, you will meekly bear with a person who reviles you; for you will say upon every occasion, "It seemed so to him."

XLIII.

Everything has two handles: one by which it may be borne, another by which it cannot. If your brother acts unjustly, do not lay hold on the affair by the handle of his injustice, for by that it cannot be borne; but rather by the opposite, that he is your brother, that he was brought up with you; and thus you will lay hold on it as it is to be borne.

XLIV.

These reasonings have no logical connection: "I am richer than you; therefore I am superior." "I am more eloquent than you; therefore I am your superior." The true logical connection is rather this: "I am richer than you; therefore my possessions must exceed yours." "I am more eloquent than you; therefore my style must surpass yours." But you, after all, consist neither in property nor in style.

XLV.

Does any one bathe hastily? Do not say that he does it ill, but hastily. Does any one drink much wine? Do not say that he does ill, but that he drinks a great deal. For unless you perfectly understand his motives, how should you know if he acts ill? Thus you will not risk yielding to any appearances but such as you fully comprehend.

XLVI.

Never proclaim yourself a philosopher; nor make much talk among the ignorant about your principles, but show them by actions. Thus, at an entertainment, do not discourse how people ought to eat; but eat as you ought. For remember that thus Socrates also universally avoided all ostentation. And when persons came to him, and desired to be introduced by him to philosophers, he took them and introduced them; so well did he bear being overlooked. So if ever there should be among the ignorant any discussion of principles, be for the most part silent. For there is great danger in hastily throwing out what is undigested. And if any one tells you that you know nothing, and you are not nettled at it, then you may be sure that you have really entered on your work. For sheep do not hastily throw up the grass, to show the shepherds how much they have eaten; but, inwardly digesting their food, they produce it outwardly in wool and milk. Thus, therefore, do you not make an exhibition before the ignorant of your principles; but of the actions to which their digestion gives rise.

XLVII.

When you have learned to nourish your body frugally, do not pique yourself upon it; nor, if you drink water, be saying upon every occasion, "I drink water." But first consider how much more frugal are the poor than we, and how much more patient of hardship. If at any time you would inure yourself by exercise to labor and privation, for your own sake and not for the public, do not attempt great feats; but when you are violently thirsty, just rinse your mouth with water, and tell nobody.

XLVIII.

The condition and characteristic of a vulgar person is that he never looks for either help or harm from himself, but only from externals. The condition and characteristic of a philosopher is that he looks to himself for all help or harm. The marks of a proficient are that he censures no one, praises no one, blames no one, accuses no one; says nothing concerning himself as being anybody, or knowing anything. When he is in any instance hindered or restrained, he accuses himself; and if he is praised, he smiles to himself at the person who praises him; and if he is censured, he makes no defence. But he goes about with the caution of a convalescent, careful of interference with anything that is doing well, but not yet quite secure. He restrains desire; he transfers his aversion to those things only which thwart the proper use of our own will; he employs his energies moderately in all directions; if he appears stupid or ignorant, he does not care; and, in a word, he keeps watch over himself as over an enemy and one in ambush.

XLIX.

When any one shows himself vain, on being able to understand and interpret the works of Chrysippus, say to yourself: "Unless Chrysippus had written obscurely, this person would have had nothing to be vain of. But what do I desire? To understand Nature, and follow her. I ask, then, who interprets her; and hearing that Chrysippus does, I have recourse to him. I do not understand his writings. I seek, therefore, one to interpret *them*." So far there is nothing to value myself upon. And when I find an interpreter, what remains is to make use of his instructions. This alone is the valuable thing. But if I admire merely the interpretation, what do I become more than a grammarian, instead of a philosopher, except, indeed, that instead of Homer I interpret Chrysippus? When any one, therefore, desires me to read Chrysippus to him, I rather blush, when I cannot exhibit actions that are harmonious and consonant with his discourse.

L.

Whatever rules you have adopted, abide by them as laws, and as if you would be impious to transgress them; and do not regard what any one says of you, for this, after all, is no concern of yours.

LI.

How long, then, will you delay to demand of yourself the noblest improvements, and in no instance to transgress the judgments of reason? You have received the philosophic principles with which you ought to be conversant; and you have been conversant with them. For what other master, then, do you wait as an excuse for this delay in self-reformation? You are no longer a boy, but a grown man. If, therefore, you will be negligent and slothful, and always add procrastination to procrastination, purpose to purpose, and fix day after day in which you will attend to yourself, you will insensibly continue to accomplish nothing, and, living and dying, remain of vulgar mind. This instant, then, think yourself worthy of living as a noun grown up and a proficient. Let whatever appears to be the best, be to you an inviolable law. And if any instance of pain or pleasure, glory or disgrace, be set before you, remember that now is the combat, now the Olympiad comes on, nor can it be put off; and that by one failure and defeat honor may be lost – or won. Thus Socrates became perfect, improving himself by everything, following reason alone. And though you are not yet a Socrates, you ought, however, to live as one seeking to be a Socrates.

LII.

The first and the most necessary topic in philosophy is the practical application of principles, as, *We ought not to lie*; the second is that of demonstrations, as, *Why it is that we ought not to lie*; the third, that which gives strength and logical connection to the other two, as, *Why this is a demonstration*. For what is demonstration? What is a consequence; what a contradiction; what truth; what falsehood? The third point is then necessary on account of the second; and the second on account of the first. But the most necessary, and that whereon we ought to rest, is the first. But we do just the contrary. For we spend all our time on the third point, and employ all our diligence about that, and entirely neglect the first. Therefore, at the same time that we lie, we are very ready to show how it is demonstrated that lying is wrong.

LIII.

Upon all occasions we ought to have these maxims ready at hand: –

"Conduct me, Zeus, and thou, O Destiny,
Wherever your decrees have fixed my lot.
I follow cheerfully; and, did I not,
Wicked and wretched, I must follow still."[1]

"Whoe'er yields properly to Fate is deemed
Wise among men, and knows the laws of Heaven."[2]

And this third: –

"O Crito, if it thus pleases the gods, thus let it be.
Anytus and Melitus may kill me indeed; but hurt me they cannot."[3]

---

[1] Cleanthes, *Hymn to Zeus*, quoted by Seneca, Epistle 107.

[2] Euripides, Fragment 965 Nauck.

[3] Plato, *Crito* 43d; *Apology* 30c–d.

We end the book as we began it: with some selections from Seneca. In what follows, you will find selections from two more of Seneca's letters. One is entitled "On the Shortness of Life," and addresses both the sting of death as well as providing inspiration to live fully while we still can. The other, entitled "To Marcia, On Consolation," is an application of Stoic philosophy to the problem of grief.

L. Annaeus Seneca

The Sixth Book of the Dialogues of L. Annaeus Seneca, Addressed to Marcia. Of Consolation.

I.

DID I not know, Marcia, that you have as little of a woman's weakness of mind as of her other vices, and that your life was regarded as a pattern of antique virtue, I should not have dared to combat your grief, which is one that many men fondly nurse and embrace, nor should I have conceived the hope of persuading you to hold fortune blameless, having to plead for her at such an unfavorable time, before so partial a judge, and against such an odious charge. I derive confidence, however, from the proved strength of your mind, and your virtue, which has been proved by a severe test. All men know how well you behaved towards your father, whom you loved as dearly as your children in all respects, save that you did not wish him to survive you: indeed, for all that I know you may have wished that also: for great affection ventures to break some of the golden rules of life. You did all that lay in your power to avert the death of your father, Aulus Cremutius Cordus ;[1] but when it became clear that, surrounded as he was by the myrmidons of Sejanus, there was no other way of escape from slavery, you did not indeed approve of his resolution, but gave up all attempts to oppose it; you shed tears openly, and choked down your sobs, yet did not screen them behind a smiling face; and you did all this in the present century, when not to be unnatural towards one's parents is considered the height of filial affection. When the changes of our times gave you an opportunity, you restored to the use of man that genius of your father for which he had suffered, and made him in real truth immortal by publishing as an eternal memorial of him those books which that bravest of men had written with his own blood. You have done a great service to Roman literature: a large part of Cordus's books had been burned; a great service to posterity, who will receive a true account of events, which cost its author so dear; and a great service to himself, whose memory flourishes and ever will flourish, as long as men set any value upon the facts of Roman history, as long as any one lives who wishes to review the deeds of our fathers, to know what a true Roman was like—one who still remained unconquered when all other necks were broken in to receive the yoke of Sejanus, one who was free in every thought, feeling, and act. By Hercules, the state would have sustained a great loss if you had not brought him forth from the oblivion to which his two splendid qualities, eloquence and independence, had consigned him: he is now read, is popular, is received into men's hands and bosoms, and fears no old age: but as for those who butchered him, before long men will cease to speak even of their crimes, the only things by which they are remembered. This greatness of mind in you has forbidden me to take into consideration your sex or your face, still clouded by the sorrow by which so many years ago it was suddenly overcast. See; I shall do nothing underhand, nor try to steal away your sorrows: I have reminded you of old hurts, and to prove that your present wound may be healed, I have shown you the scar of one which was equally severe. Let others use soft measures and caresses; I have determined to do battle with your grief, and I will dry those weary and exhausted eyes, which already, to tell you the truth, are weeping more from habit than from sorrow. I will effect this cure, if possible, with your goodwill: if you disapprove of my efforts, or dislike them, then you must continue to hug and fondle the grief which you have adopted as the survivor of your son. What, I pray you, is to be the end of it? All means have been tried in vain : the consolations of your friends, who are weary of offering them, and the influence of great men who are related to you: literature, a taste which your father enjoyed and which you have inherited from him, now finds your ears closed, and affords you but a futile consolation, which scarcely engages your thoughts for a moment. Even time itself, nature's greatest remedy, which quiets the most bitter grief, loses its power with you alone. Three years have already passed, and still your grief has lost none of its first poignancy, but renews and strengthens itself day by day, and has now dwelt so long with you that it has acquired a domicile in your mind, and actually thinks that it would be base to leave it. All vices sink into our whole being, if we do not crush them before they gain a footing; and in like manner these sad, pitiable, and discordant feelings end by feeding upon their own bitterness, until the unhappy mind takes a sort of morbid delight in grief. I should have liked, therefore, to have attempted to effect this cure in the earliest stages of the disorder, before its force was fully developed; it might have been checked by milder remedies, but now that it has been confirmed by time it cannot be beaten without a hard struggle. In like manner, wounds heal easily when the blood is fresh upon them: they can then be cleared out and brought to the surface, and admit of being probed by the finger: when disease has turned them into malignant ulcers, their cure is more difficult. I cannot now influence so strong a grief by polite and mild measures: it must be broken down by force.

II.

I am aware that all who wish to give any one advice begin with precepts, and end with examples: but it is sometimes useful to alter this fashion, for we must deal differently with different people. Some are guided by reason, others must be confronted with authority and the names of celebrated persons, whose brilliancy dazzles their mind and destroys their power of free judgment. I will place before your eyes two of the greatest examples belonging to your sex and your century: one, that of a woman who allowed herself to be entirely carried away by grief; the other, one who, though afflicted by a like misfortune, and an even greater loss, yet did not allow her sorrows to reign over her for a very long time, but quickly restored her mind to its accustomed frame. Octavia and Livia, the former Augustus's sister, the latter his wife, both lost their sons when they were young men, and when they were certain of succeeding to the throne. Octavia lost Marcellus, whom both his father-in-law and his uncle had begun to depend upon, and to place upon his shoulders the weight of the empire—a young man of keen intelligence and firm character, frugal and moderate in his desires to an extent which deserved especial admiration in one so young and so wealthy, strong to endure labour, averse to indulgence, and able to bear whatever burden his uncle might choose to lay, or I may say to pile upon his shoulders. Augustus had well chosen him as a foundation, for he would not have given way under any weight, however excessive. His mother never ceased to weep and sob during her whole life, never endured to listen to wholesome advice, never even allowed her thoughts to be diverted from her sorrow. She remained during her whole life just as she was during the funeral, with all the strength of her mind intently fixed upon one subject. I do not say that she lacked the courage to shake off her grief, but she refused to be comforted, thought that it would be a second bereavement to lose her tears, and would not have any portrait of her darling son, nor allow any allusion to be made to him. She hated all mothers, and raged against Livia with especial fury, because it seemed as though the brilliant prospect once in store for her own child was now transferred to Livia's son. Passing all her days in darkened rooms and alone, not conversing even with her brother, she refused to accept the poems which were composed in memory of Marcellus, and all the other honours paid him by literature, and closed her ears against all consolation. She lived buried and hidden from view, neglecting her accustomed duties, and actually angry with the excessive splendour of her brother's prosperity, in which she shared. Though surrounded by her children and grandchildren, she would not lay aside her mourning garb, though by retaining it she seemed to put a slight upon all her relations, in thinking herself bereaved in spite of their being alive.

III.

Livia lost her son Drusus, who would have been a great emperor, and was already a great general: he had marched far into Germany, and had planted the Roman standards in places where the very existence of the Romans was hardly known. He died on the march, his very foes treating him with respect, observing a reciprocal truce, and not having the heart to wish for what would do them most service. In addition to his dying thus in his country's service, great sorrow for him was expressed by the citizens, the provinces, and the whole of Italy, through which his corpse was attended by the people of the free towns and colonies, who poured out to perform the last sad offices to him, till it reached Rome in a procession which resembled a triumph. His mother was not permitted to receive his last kiss and gather the last fond words from his dying lips: she followed the relics of her Drusus on their long journey, though every one of the funeral pyres with which all Italy was glowing seemed to renew her grief, as though she had lost him so many times. When, however, she at last laid him in the tomb, she left her sorrow there with him, and grieved no more than was becoming to a Caesar or due to a son. She did not cease to make frequent mention of the name of her Drusus, to set up his portrait in all places, both public and private, and to speak of him and listen while others spoke of him with the greatest pleasure: she lived with his memory ; which none can embrace and consort with who has made it painful to himself.[2] Choose, therefore, which of these two examples you think the more commendable: if you prefer to follow the former, you will remove yourself from the number of the living; you will shun the sight both of other people's children and of your own, and even of him whose loss you deplore; you will be looked upon by mothers as an omen of evil; you will refuse to take part in honourable, permissible pleasures, thinking them unbecoming for one so afflicted; you will be loath to linger above ground, and will be especially angry with your age, because it will not straightway bring your life abruptly to an end. I here put the best construction on what is really most contemptible and foreign to your character. I mean that you will show yourself unwilling to live, and unable to die. If, on the other hand, showing a milder and better regulated spirit, you try to follow the example of the latter most exalted lady, you will not be in misery, nor will you wear your life out with suffering. Plague on it! what madness this is, to punish one's self because one is unfortunate, and not to lessen, but to increase one's ills! You ought to display, in this matter also, that decent behaviour and modesty which has characterised all your life: for there is such a thing as self-restraint in grief also. You will show more respect for the youth himself, who well deserves that it should make you glad to speak and think of him, if you make him able to meet his mother with a cheerful countenance, even as he was wont to do when alive. . . .

V.

"In the next place, I pray and beseech you not to be self-willed and beyond the management of your friends. You must be aware that none of them know how to behave, whether to mention Drusus in your presence or not, as they neither wish to wrong a noble youth by forgetting him nor to hurt you by speaking of him. When we leave you and assemble together by ourselves, we talk freely about his sayings and doings, treating them with the respect which they deserve: in your presence deep silence is observed about him, and thus you lose that greatest of pleasures, the hearing the praises of your son, which I doubt not you would be willing to hand down to all future ages, had you the means of so doing, even at the cost of your own life. Wherefore endure to listen to, nay, encourage conversation of which he is the subject, and let your ears be open to the name and memory of your son. You ought not to consider this painful, like those who in such a case think that part of their misfortune consists in listening to consolation. As it is, you have altogether run into the other extreme, and, forgetting the better aspects of your lot, look only upon its worse side: you pay no attention to the pleasure you have had in your son's society and your joyful meetings with him, the sweet caresses of his babyhood, the progress of his education: you fix all your attention upon that last scene of all: and to this, as though it were not shocking enough, you add every horror you can. Do not, I implore you, take a perverse pride in appearing the most unhappy of women: and reflect also that there is no great credit in behaving bravely in times of prosperity, when life glides easily with a favouring current-neither does; a calm sea and fair wind display the art of the pilot . some foul weather is wanted to prove his courage. Like him, then, do not give way, but rather plant yourself firmly, and endure whatever burden may fall upon you from above; scared though you may have been at the first roar of the tempest. There is nothing that fastens such a reproach [3] on Fortune as resignation." After this he points out to her the son who is yet alive: he points out grandchildren from the lost one.

VI.

It is your trouble, Marcia, which has been dealt with here: it is beside your couch of mourning that Areus has been sitting: change the characters, and it is you whom he has been consoling. But, on the other hand, Marcia, suppose that you have sustained a greater loss than ever mother did before you: see, I am not soothing you or making light of your misfortune: if fate can be overcome by tears, let us bring tears to bear upon it: let every day be passed in mourning, every night be spent in sorrow instead of sleep: let your breast be torn by your own hands, your very face attacked by them, and every kind of cruelty be practised by your grief, if it will profit you. But if the dead cannot be brought back to life, however much we may beat our breasts, if destiny remains fixed and immoveable forever, not to be changed by any sorrow, however great, and death does not loose his hold of anything that he once has taken away, then let our futile grief be brought to an end. Let us, then, steer our own course, and no longer allow ourselves to be driven to leeward by the force of our misfortune. He is a sorry pilot who lets the waves wring his rudder from his grasp, who leaves the sails to fly loose, and abandons the ship to the storm: but he who boldly grasps the helm and clings to it until the sea closes over him, deserves praise even though he be shipwrecked.

VII.

"But," say you, "sorrow for the loss of one's own children is natural." Who denies it? provided it be reasonable? for we cannot help feeling a pang, and the stoutest-hearted of us are cast down not only at the death of those dearest to us, but even when they leave us on a journey. Nevertheless, the mourning which public opinion enjoins is more than nature insists upon. Observe how intense and yet how brief are the sorrows of dumb animals: we hear a cow lowing for one or two days, nor do mares pursue their wild and senseless gallops for longer: wild beasts after they have tracked their lost cubs throughout the forest, and often visited their plundered dens, quench their rage within a short space of time. Birds circle round their empty nests with loud and piteous cries, yet almost immediately resume their ordinary flight in silence; nor does any creature spend long periods in sorrowing for the loss of its offspring, except man, who encourages his own grief, the measure of which depends not upon his sufferings, but upon his will. You may know that to be utterly broken down by grief is not natural, by observing that the same bereavement inflicts a deeper wound upon women than upon men, upon savages than upon civilized and cultivated persons, upon the unlearned than upon the learned: yet those passions which derive their force from nature are equally powerful in all men: therefore it is dear that a passion of varying strength cannot be a natural one. Fire will burn all people equally, male and female, of every rank and every age: steel will exhibit its cutting power on all bodies alike: and why? Because these things derive their strength from nature, which makes no distinction of persons. Poverty, grief, and ambition,[4] are felt differently by different people, according as they are influenced by habit: a rooted prejudice about the terrors of these things, though they are not really to be feared, makes a man weak and unable to endure them.

VIII.

Moreover, that which depends upon nature is not weakened by delay, but grief is gradually effaced by time. However obstinate it may be, though it be daily renewed and be exasperated by all attempts to soothe it, yet even this becomes weakened by time, which is the most efficient means of taming its fierceness. You, Marcia, have still a mighty sorrow abiding with you, nevertheless it already appears to have become blunted: it is obstinate and enduring, but not so acute as it was at first: and this also will be taken from you piecemeal by succeeding years. Whenever you are engaged in other pursuits your mind will be relieved from its burden: at present you keep watch over yourself to prevent this. Yet there is a great difference between allowing and forcing yourself to grieve. How much more in accordance with your cultivated taste it would be to put an end to your mourning instead of looking for the end to come, and not to wait for the day when your sorrow shall cease against your will: dismiss it of your own accord.

IX.

"Why then," you ask, "do we show such persistence in mourning for our friends, if it be not nature that bids us do so?" It is because we never expect that any evil will befall ourselves before it comes, we will not be taught by seeing the misfortunes of others that they are the common inheritance of all men, but imagine that the path which we have begun to tread is free from them and less beset by dangers than that of other people. How many funerals pass our houses? yet we do not think of death. How many untimely deaths? we think only of our son's coming of age, of his service in the army, or of his succession to his father's estate. How many rich men suddenly sink into poverty before our very eyes, without its ever occurring to our minds that our own wealth is exposed to exactly the same risks? When, therefore, misfortune befalls us, we cannot help collapsing all the more completely, because we are struck as it were unawares: a blow which has long been foreseen falls much less heavily upon us. Do you wish to know how completely exposed you are to every stroke of fate, and that the same shafts which have transfixed others are whirling around yourself? Then imagine that you are mounting without sufficient armour to assault some city wall or some strong and lofty position manned by a great host, expect a wound, and suppose that all those stones, arrows, and darts which fill the upper air are aimed at your body: whenever anyone falls at your side or behind your back, exclaim, "Fortune, you will not outwit me, or catch me confident and heedless: I know what you are preparing to do: you have struck down another, but you aimed at me." Whoever looks upon his own affairs as though he were at the point of death? which of us ever dares to think about banishment, want, or mourning? who, if advised to meditate upon these subjects, would not reject the idea like an evil omen, and bid it depart from him and alight on the heads of his enemies, or even on that of his untimely adviser? "I never thought it would happen!" How can you think that anything will not happen, when you know that it may happen to many men, and has happened to many? That is a noble verse, and worthy of a nobler source than the stage:—

"What one hath suffered may befall us all."

That man has lost his children: you may lose yours. That man has been convicted: your innocence is in peril. We are deceived and weakened by this delusion, when we suffer what we never foresaw that we possibly could suffer: but by looking forward to the coming of our sorrows we take the sting out of them when they come.

X.

My Marcia, all these adventitious circumstances which glitter around us, such as children, office in the state, wealth, large halls, vestibules crowded with clients seeking vainly for admittance, a noble name, a well-born or beautiful wife, and every other thing which depends entirely upon uncertain and changeful fortune, are but furniture which is not our own, but entrusted to us on loan: none of these things are given to us outright: the stage of our lives is adorned with properties gathered from various sources, and soon to be returned to their several owners: some of them will be taken away on the first day, some on the second, and but few will remain till the end. We have, therefore, no grounds for regarding ourselves with complacency, as though the things which surround us were our own: they are only borrowed: we have the use and enjoyment of them for a time regulated by the lender, who controls his own gift: it is our duty always to be able to lay our hands upon what has been lent us with no fixed date for its return, and to restore it when called upon without a murmur: the most detestable kind of debtor is he who rails at his creditor. Hence all our relatives, both those who by the order of their birth we hope will outlive ourselves, and those who themselves most properly wish to die before us, ought to be loved by us as persons whom we cannot be sure of having with us forever, nor even for long. We ought frequently to remind ourselves that we must love the things of this life as we would what is shortly to leave us, or indeed in the very act of leaving us. Whatever gift Fortune bestows upon a man, let him think while he enjoys it, that it will prove as fickle as the goddess from whom it came. Snatch what pleasure you can from your children, allow your children in their turn to take pleasure in your society, and drain every pleasure to the dregs without any delay. We cannot reckon on tonight, nay, I have allowed too long a delay, we cannot reckon on this hour: we most make haste: the enemy presses on behind us: soon that society of yours will be broken up, that pleasant company will be taken by assault and dispersed. Pillage is the universal law: unhappy creatures, know you not that life is but a flight? If you grieve for the death of your son, the fault lies with the time when he was born, for at his birth he was told that death was his doom: it is the law under which he was born, the fate which has pursued him ever since he left his mother's womb. We have come under the dominion of Fortune, and a harsh and unconquerable dominion it is: at her caprice we must suffer all things whether we deserve them or not. She maltreats our bodies with anger, insult, and cruelty: some she burns, the fire being sometimes applied as a punishment and sometimes as a remedy: some she imprisons, allowing it to be done at one time by our enemies, at another by our countrymen: she tosses others naked on the changeful seas, and after their struggle with the waves will not even cast them out upon the sand or the shore, but will entomb them in the belly of some huge sea-monster: she wears away others to a skeleton by diverse kinds of disease, and keeps them long in suspense between life and death: she is as capricious in her rewards and punishments as a fickle, whimsical, and careless mistress is with those of her slaves.

XI.

Why need we weep over parts of our life? the whole of it calls for tears: new miseries assail us before we have freed ourselves from the old ones. You, therefore, who allow them to trouble you to an unreasonable extent ought especially to restrain yourselves, and to muster all the powers of the human breast to combat your fears and your pains. Moreover, what forgetfulness of your own position and that of mankind is this? You were born a mortal, and you have given birth to mortals: yourself a weak and fragile body, liable to all diseases, can you have hoped to produce anything strong and lasting from such unstable materials? Your son has died: in other words he has reached that goal towards which those whom you regard as more fortunate than your offspring are still hastening. this is the point towards which move at different rates all the crowds which are squabbling in the law courts, sitting in the theatres, praying in the temples. Those whom you love and those whom you despise will both be made equal in the same ashes. This is the meaning of that command, KNOW THYSELF, which is written on the shrine of the Pythian oracle. What is man? a potter's vessel, to be broken by the slightest shake or toss: it requires no great storm to rend you asunder: you fall to pieces wherever you strike. What is man? a weakly and frail body, naked, without any natural protection, dependent on the help of others, exposed to all the scorn of Fortune; even when his muscles are well trained he is the prey and the food of the first wild beast he meets, formed of weak and unstable substances, fair in outward feature, but unable to endure cold, heat, or labour, and yet falling to ruin if kept in sloth and idleness, fearing his very victuals, for he is starved if he has them not, and bursts if he has too much. He cannot be kept safe without anxious care, his breath only stays in the body on sufferance, and has no real hold upon it; he starts at every sudden danger, every loud and unexpected noise that reaches his ears. Ever a cause of anxiety to ourselves, diseased and useless as we are, can we be surprised at the death of a creature which can be killed by a single hiccup? Is it a great undertaking to put an end to us? why, smells, tastes, fatigue and want of sleep, food and drink, and the very necessaries of life, are mortal. Whithersoever he moves he straightway becomes conscious of his weakness, not being able to bear all climates, falling sick after drinking strange water, breathing an air to which he is not accustomed, or from other causes and reasons of the most trifling kind, frail, sickly, entering upon his life with weeping: yet nevertheless what a disturbance this despicable creature makes! what ideas it conceives, forgetting its lowly condition! It exercises its mind upon matters which are immortal and eternal, and arranges the affairs of its grandchildren and great-grandchildren, while death surprises it in the midst of its far-reaching schemes, and what we call old age is but the round of a very few years.

XII.

Supposing that your sorrow has any method at all, iIs it your own sufferings or those of him who is gone that it has in view? Why do you grieve over your lost son? is it because you have received no pleasure from him, or because you would have received more had he lived longer? If you answer that you have received no pleasure from him you make your loss more endurable: for men miss less when lost what has given them no enjoyment or gladness. If, again, you admit that you have received much pleasure, it is your duty not to complain of that part which you have lost, but to return thanks for that which you have enjoyed. His rearing alone ought to have brought you a sufficient return for your labours, for it can hardly be that those who take the greatest pains to rear puppies, birds, and such like paltry objects of amusement derive a certain pleasure from the sight and touch and fawning caresses of these dumb creatures, and yet that those who rear children should not find their reward in doing so. Thus, even though his industry may have gained nothing for you, his carefulness may have saved nothing for you, his foresight may have given you no advice, yet you found sufficient reward in having owned him and loved him. "But," say you, "it might have lasted longer." True, but you have been better dealt with than if you had never had a son, for, supposing you were given your choice, which is the better lot, to be happy for a short time or not at all? It is better to enjoy pleasures which soon leave us than to enjoy none at all. Which, again, would you choose? to have had one who was a disgrace to you, and who merely filled the position and owned the name of your son, or one of such noble character as your son's was? a youth who soon grew discreet and dutiful, soon became a husband and a father, soon became eager for public honours, and soon obtained the priesthood, winning his way to all these admirable things with equally admirable speed. It falls to scarcely any one's lot to enjoy great prosperity, and also to enjoy it for a long time: only a dull kind of happiness can last for long and accompany us to the end of our lives. The immortal gods, who did not intend to give you a son for long, gave you one who was straightway what another would have required long training to become. You cannot even say that you have been specially marked by the gods for misfortune because you have had no pleasure in your son. Look at any company of people, whether they be known to you or not: everywhere you will see some who have endured greater misfortunes than your own. Great generals and princes have undergone like bereavements: mythology tells us that the gods themselves are not exempt from them, its aim, I suppose, being to lighten our sorrow at death by the thought that even deities are subject to it. Look around, I repeat, at every one: you cannot mention any house so miserable as not to find comfort in the fact of another being yet more miserable. I do not, by Hercules, think so ill of your principles as to suppose that you would bear your sorrow more lightly were I to show you an enormous company of mourners: that is a spiteful sort of consolation which we derive from the number of our fellow-sufferers: nevertheless I will quote some instances, not indeed in order to teach you that this often befalls men, for it is absurd to multiply examples of man's mortality, but to let you know that there have been many who have lightened their misfortunes by patient endurance of them. I will begin with the luckiest man of all. Lucius Sulla lost his son, yet this did not impair either the spitefulness or the brilliant valour which he displayed at the expense of his enemies and his countrymen alike, nor did it make him appear to have assumed his well-known title untruly that he did so after his son's death, fearing neither the hatred of men, by whose sufferings that excessive prosperity of his was purchased, nor the ill-will of the gods, to whom it was a reproach that Sulla should be so truly The Fortunate. What, however, Sulla's real character was may pass among questions still undecided: even his enemies will admit that he took up arms with honour, and laid them aside with honour: his example proves the point at issue, that an evil which befalls even the most prosperous cannot be one of the first magnitude....

XVII.

"Still, it is a sad thing to lose a young man whom you have brought up, just as he was becoming a defence and a pride both to his mother and to his country." No one denies that it is sad: but it is the common lot of mortals. You were born to lose others, to be lost, to hope, to fear, to destroy your own peace and that of others, to fear and yet to long for death, and, worst of all, never to know what your real position is. If you were about to journey to Syracuse, and someone were to say :—"Learn beforehand all the discomforts, and all the pleasures of your coming voyage, and then set sail. The sights which you will enjoy will be as follows: first, you will see the island itself, now separated from Italy by a narrow strait, but which, we know, once formed part of the mainland. The sea suddenly broke through, and

'Sever'd Sicilia from the western shore.' [9]

Next, as you will be able to sail close to Charybdis, of which the poets have sung, you will see that greediest of whirlpools, quite smooth if no south wind be blowing, but whenever there is a gale from that quarter, sucking down ships into a huge and deep abyss. You will see the fountain of Arethusa, so famed in song, with its waters bright and pellucid to the very bottom, and pouring forth an icy stream which it either finds on the spot or else plunges it under ground, conveys it thither as a separate river beneath so many seas, free from any mixture of less pure water, and there brings it again to the surface. You will see a harbor which is more sheltered than all the others in the world, whether they be natural or improved by human art for the protection of shipping; so safe, that even the most violent storms are powerless to disturb it. You will see the place where the power of Athens was broken, where that natural prison, hewn deep among precipices of rock, received so many thousands of captives: you will see the great city itself, occupying a wider site than many capitals, an extremely warm resort in winter, where not a single day passes without sunshine: but when you have observed all this, you must remember that the advantages of its winter climate are counterbalanced by a hot and pestilential summer: that here will be the tyrant Dionysius, the destroyer of freedom, of justice, and of law, who is greedy of power even after conversing with Plato, and of life even after he has been exiled; that he will burn some, flog others, and behead others for slight offences; that he will exercise his lust upon both sexes You have now heard all that can attract you thither, all that can deter you from going: now, then, either set sail or remain at home!" If, after this declaration, anybody were to say that he wished to go to Syracuse, he could blame no one but himself for what befell him there, because he would not stumble upon it unknowingly, but would have gone thither fully aware of what was before him. To everyone Nature says: "I do not deceive any person. If you choose to have children, they may be handsome, or they may be deformed; perhaps they will be born dumb. One of them may perhaps prove the saviour of his country, or perhaps its betrayer. You need not despair of their being raised to such honour that for their sake no one will dare to speak evil of you: yet remember that they may reach such a pitch of infamy as themselves to become curses to you. There is nothing to prevent their performing the last offices for you, and your panegyric being spoken by your children: but bold yourself prepared nevertheless to place a son as boy, man, or greybeard, upon the funeral pyre: for years have nothing to do with the matter, since every sort of funeral in which a parent buries his child must alike be untimely.[10] If you still choose to rear children, after I have explained these conditions to you, you render yourself incapable of blaming the gods, for they never guaranteed anything to you."

XVIII.

You may make this simile apply to your whole entrance into life. I have explained to you what attractions and what drawbacks there would be if you were thinking of going to Syracuse: now suppose that I were to come and give you advice when you were going to be born. "You are about," I should say, "to enter a city of which both gods and men are citizens, a city which contains the whole universe, which is bound by irrevocable and eternal laws, and wherein the heavenly bodies run their unwearied courses: you will see therein innumerable twinkling stars, and the sun, whose single light pervades every place, who by his daily course marks the times of day and night, and by his yearly course makes a more equal division between summer and winter. You will see his place taken by night by the moon, who borrows at her meetings with her brother a gentle and softer light, and who at one time is invisible, at another hangs full faced above the earth, ever waxing and waning, each phase unlike the last. You will see five stars, moving in the opposite direction to the others, stemming the whirl of the skies towards the West: on the slightest motions of these depend the fortunes of nations, and according as the aspect of the planets is auspicious or malignant, the greatest empires rise and fall: you will see with wonder the gathering clouds, the falling showers, the zigzag lightning, the crashing together of the heavens. When, sated with the wonders above, you turn your eyes towards the earth, they will be met by objects of a different yet equally admirable aspect: on one side a boundless expanse of open plains, on another the towering peaks of lofty and snow-clad mountains: the downward course of rivers, some streams running eastward, some westward from the same source: the woods which wave even on the mountain tops, the vast forests with all the creatures that dwell therein, and the confused harmony of the birds: the variously-placed cities, the nations which natural obstacles keep secluded from the world, some of whom withdraw themselves to lofty mountains, while others dwell in fear and trembling on the sloping banks of rivers: the crops which are assisted by cultivation, and the trees which bear fruit even without it: the rivers that flow gently through the meadows, the lovely bays and shores that curve inwards to form harbours: the countless islands scattered over the main, which break and spangle the seas. What of the brilliancy of stones and gems, the gold that rolls amid the sands of rushing streams, the heaven-born fires that burst forth from the midst of the earth and even from the midst of the sea; the ocean itself, that binds land to land, dividing the nations by its three-fold indentations, and boiling up with mighty rage? Swimming upon its waves, making them disturbed and swelling without wind, you will see animals exceeding the size of any that belong to the land, some clumsy and requiring others to guide their movements, some swift and .moving faster than the utmost efforts of rowers, some of them that drink in the waters and blow them out again to the great perils of those who sail near them: you will see here ships seeking for unknown lands: you will see that man's audacity leaves nothing unattempted, and you will yourself be both a witness and a sharer in great attempts. You will both learn and teach the arts by which men's lives are supplied with necessaries, are adorned, and are ruled: but in this same place there will be a thousand pestilences fatal to both body and mind, there will be wars and highway robberies, poisonings and shipwrecks, extremes of climate and excesses of body, untimely griefs for our dearest ones, and death for ourselves, of which we cannot tell whether it will be easy or by torture at the hands of the executioner. Now consider and weigh carefully in your own mind which you would choose. If you wish to enjoy these blessings you must pass through these pains. Do you answer that you choose to live? 'Of course.' Nay, I thought you would not enter upon that of which the least diminution causes pain. Live, then, as has been agreed on. You say, "No one has asked my opinion." Our parents' opinion was taken about us, when, knowing what the conditions of life are, they brought us into it. . . .

XXI.

"Yet," say you, "he perished too soon and untimely." In the first place, suppose that he had lived to extreme old age: let him continue alive to the extreme limits of human existence: how much is it after all? Born for a very brief space of time, we regard this life as an inn which we are soon to quit that it may be made ready for the coming guest. Do I speak of our lives, which we know roll away incredibly fast? Reckon up the centuries of cities: you will find that even those which boast of their antiquity have not existed for long. All human works are brief and fleeting; they take up no part whatever of infinite time. Tried by the standard of the universe, we regard this earth of ours, with all its cities, nations, rivers, and sea-board as a mere point: our life occupies less than a point when compared with all time, the measure of which exceeds that of the world, for indeed the world is contained many times in it. Of what importance, then, can it be to lengthen that which, however much you add to it, will never be much more than nothing? We can only make our lives long by one expedient, that is, by being satisfied with their length: you may tell me of long-lived men, whose length of days has been celebrated by tradition, you may assign a hundred and ten years apiece to them: yet when you allow your mind to conceive the idea of eternity, there will be no difference between the shortest and the longest life, if you compare the time during which any one has been alive with that during which he has not been alive. In the next place, when he died his life was complete: he had lived as long as he needed to live: there was nothing left for him to accomplish. All men do not grow old at the same age, nor indeed do all animals: some are wearied out by life at fourteen years of age, and what is only the first stage of life with man is their extreme limit of longevity. To each man a varying length of days has been assigned: no one dies before his time, because he was not destined to live any longer than he did. Everyone's end is fixed, and will always remain where it has been placed: neither industry nor favour will move it on any further. Believe, then, that you lost him by advice: he took all that was his own,

"And reached the goal allotted to his life,"

so you need not burden yourself with the thought, "He might have lived longer." His life has not been cut short, nor does chance ever cut short our years: every man receives as much as was promised to him: the Fates go their own way, and neither add anything nor take away anything from what they have once promised. Prayers and endeavours are all in vain : each man will have as much life as his first day placed to his credit: from the time when he first saw the light he has entered on the path that leads to death, and is drawing nearer to his doom: those same years which were added to his youth were subtracted from his life. We all fall into this mistake of supposing that it is only old men, already in the decline of life, who are drawing near to death, whereas our first infancy, our youth, indeed every time of life leads thither. The Fates ply their own work: they take from us the consciousness of our death, and, the better to conceal its approaches, death lurks under the very names we give to life: infancy changes into boyhood, maturity swallows up the boy, old age the man: these stages themselves, if you reckon them properly, are so many losses.

XXII.

Do you complain, Marcia, that your son did not live as long as he might have done? How do you know that it was to his advantage to live longer? whether his interest was not served by this death? Whom can you find at the present time whose fortunes are grounded on such sure foundations that they have nothing to fear in the future? All human affairs are evanescent and perishable, nor is any part of our life so frail and liable to accident as that which we especially enjoy. We ought, therefore, to pray for death when our fortune is at its best, because so great is the uncertainty and turmoil in which we live, that we can be sure of nothing but what is past. Think of your son's handsome person, which you had guarded in perfect purity among all the temptations of a voluptuous capital. Who could have undertaken to keep that clear of all diseases, so that it might preserve its beauty of form unimpaired even to old age? Think of the many taints of the mind: for fine dispositions do not always continue to their life's end to make good the promise of their youth, but have often broken down: either extravagance, all the more shameful for being indulged in late in life, takes possession of men and makes their well-begun lives end in disgrace, or they devote their entire thoughts to the eating-house and the belly, and they become interested in nothing save what they shall eat and what they shall drink. Add to this conflagrations, falling houses, shipwrecks, the agonizing operations of surgeons, who cut pieces of bone out of men's living bodies, plunge their whole hands into their entrails, and inflict more than one kind of pain to effect the cure of shameful diseases. After these comes exile; your son was not more innocent than Rutilius: imprisonment; he was not wiser than Socrates: the piercing of one's breast by a self-inflicted wound; he was not of holier life than Cato. When you look at these examples, you will perceive that nature deals very kindly with those whom she puts speedily in a place of safety because there awaited them the payment of some such price as this for their lives. Nothing is so deceptive, nothing is so treacherous as human life; by Hercules, were it not given to men before they could form an opinion, no one would take it. Not to be born, therefore, is the happiest lot of all, and the nearest thing to this, I imagine, is that we should soon finish our strife here and be restored again to our former rest....

XXIV.

Begin to reckon his age, not by years, but by virtues: he lived long enough. He was left as a ward in the care of guardians up to his fourteenth year, and never passed out of that of his mother: when he had a household of his own he was loath to leave yours, and continued to dwell under his mother's roof, though few sons can endure to live under their father's. Though a youth whose height, beauty, and vigour of body destined him for the army, yet he refused to serve, that he might not be separated from you. Consider, Marcia, how seldom mothers who live in separate houses see their children: consider how they lose and pass in anxiety all those years during which they have sons in the army, and you will see that this time, none of which you lost, was of considerable extent: he never went out of your sight: it was under your eyes that he applied himself to the cultivation of an admirable intellect and one which would have rivaled that of his grandfather, had it not been hindered by shyness, which has concealed many men's accomplishments: though a youth of unusual beauty, and living among such throngs of women who made it their business to seduce men, he gratified the wishes of none of them, and when the effrontery of some led them so far as actually to tempt him, he blushed as deeply at having found favour in their eyes as though he had been guilty. By this holiness of life he caused himself, while yet quite a boy, to be thought worthy of the priesthood, which no doubt he owed to his mother's influence; but even his mother's influence would have had no weight if the candidate for whom it was exerted had been unfit for the post. Dwell upon these virtues, and nurse your son as it were in your lap: now he is more at leisure to respond to your caresses, he has nothing to call him away from you, he will never be an anxiety or a sorrow to you. You have grieved at the only grief so good a son could cause you: all else is beyond the power of fortune to harm, and is full of pleasure, if only you know how to make use of your son, if you do but know what his most precious quality was. It is merely the outward semblance of your son that has perished, his likeness, and that not a very good one; he himself is immortal, and is now in a far better state, set free from the burden of all that was not his own, and left simply by himself: all this apparatus which you see about us of bones and sinews, this covering of skin, this face, these our servants the hands, and all the rest of our environment, are but chains and darkness to the soul: they overwhelm it, choke it, corrupt it, fill it with false ideas, and keep it at a distance from its own true sphere: it has to struggle continually against this burden of the flesh, lest it be dragged down and sunk by it. It ever strives to rise up again to the place from whence it was sent down on earth: there eternal rest awaits it, there it will behold what is pure and clear, in place of what is foul and turbid.

XXV.

You need not, therefore, hasten to the burial-place of your son : that which lies there is but the worst part of him and that which gave him most trouble, only bones and ashes, which are no more parts of him than clothes or other coverings of his body. He is complete, and without leaving any part of himself behind on earth has taken wing and gone away altogether: he has tarried a brief space above us while his soul was being cleansed and purified from the vices and rust which all mortal lives must contract, and from thence he will rise to the high heavens and join the souls of the blessed: a saintly company will welcome him thither, — Scipios and Catos; and among the rest of those who have held life cheap and set themselves free, thanks to death, albeit all there are alike akin, your father, Marcia, will embrace his grandson as he rejoices in the unwonted light, will teach him the motion of the stars which are so near to them, and introduce him with joy into all the secrets of nature, not by guesswork but by real knowledge. Even as a stranger is grateful to one who shows him the way about an unknown city, so is a searcher after the causes of what he sees in the heavens to one of his own family who can explain them to him. He will delight in gazing deep down upon the earth, for it is a delight to look from aloft at what one has left below. Bear yourself, therefore, Marcia, as though you were placed before the eyes of your father and your son, yet not such as you knew them, but far loftier beings, placed in a higher sphere. Blush, then, to do any mean or common action, or to weep for those your relatives who have been changed for the better. Free to roam through the open, boundless realms of the ever-living universe, they are not hindered in their course by intervening seas, lofty mountains, impassable valleys, or the treacherous flats of the Syrtes: they find a level path everywhere, are swift and ready of motion, and are permeated in their turn by the stars and dwell together with them.

XXVI.

Imagine then, Marcia, that your father, whose influence over you was as great as yours over your son, no longer in that frame of mind in which he deplored the civil wars, or in which he forever proscribed those who would have proscribed him, but in a mood as much more joyful as his abode now is higher than of old, is saying, as he looks down from the height of heaven, "My daughter, why does this sorrow possess you for so long? why do you live in such ignorance of the truth, as to think that your son has been unfairly dealt with because he has returned to his ancestors in his prime, without decay of body or mind, leaving his family flourishing? Do you not know with what storms Fortune unsettles everything? how she proves kind and compliant to none save to those who have the fewest possible dealings with her? Need I remind you of kings who would have been the happiest of mortals had death sooner withdrawn them from the ruin which was approaching them ?or of Roman generals, whose greatness, had but a few years been taken from their lives, would have wanted nothing to render it complete? or of men of the highest distinction and noblest birth who have calmly offered their necks to the stroke of a soldier's sword? Look at your father and your grandfather: the former fell into the hands of a foreign murderer: I allowed no man to take any liberties with me, and by abstinence from food showed that my spirit was as great as my writings had represented it. Why, then, should that member of our household who died most happily of all be mourned in it the longest? We have all assembled together, and, not being plunged in utter darkness, we see that with you on earth there is nothing to be wished for, nothing grand or magnificent, but all is mean, sad, anxious, and hardly receives a fractional part of the clear light in which we dwell. I need not say that here are no frantic charges of rival armies, no fleets shattering one another, no parricides, actual or meditated, no courts where men babble over lawsuits for days together, here is nothing underhand, all hearts and minds are open and unveiled, our life is public and known to all, and that we command a view of all time and of things to come. I used to take pleasure in compiling the history of what took place in one century among a few people in the most out-of-the-way corner of the world: here I enjoy the spectacle of all the centuries, the whole chain of events from age to age as long as years have been. I may view kingdoms when they rise and when they fall, and behold the ruin of cities and the new channels made by the sea. If it will be any consolation to you in your bereavement to know that it is the common lot of all, be assured that nothing will continue to stand in the place in which it now stands, but that time will lay everything low and bear it away with itself: it will sport, not only with men—for how small a part are they of the dominion of Fortune? — but with districts, provinces, quarters of the world: it will efface entire mountains, and in other places will pile new rocks on high: it will dry up seas, change the course of rivers, destroy the intercourse of nation with nation, and break up the communion and fellowship of the human race: in other regions it will swallow up cities by opening vast chasms in the earth, will shake them with earthquakes, will breathe forth pestilence from the nether world, cover all habitable ground with inundations and destroy every creature in the flooded world, or burn up all mortals by a huge conflagration. When the time shall arrive for the world to be brought to an end, that it may begin its life anew, all the forces of nature will perish in conflict with one another, the stars will be dashed together, and all the lights which now gleam in regular order in various parts of the sky will then blaze in one fire with all their fuel burning at once. Then we also, the souls of the blest and the heirs of eternal life, whenever God thinks fit to reconstruct the universe, when all things are settling down again, we also, being a small accessory to the universal wreck,[13] shall be changed into our old elements. Happy is your son, Marcia, in that he already knows this."

Endnotes

[1] See Merivale's "History of the Romans under the Empire," ch. Xiv

[2] If it is a pain to dwell upon the thought of lost friends, of course you do not continually refresh the memory of them by speaking of them

[3] See my note on *invidiam facere alicui* in Juv. 15.—J. E. B. Mayor

[4] Koch declares that this cannot be the true reading, and suggests *deminutio*, 'degradation.'

[5] This seems to have been part of the ceremony of dedication. Pulvillus was dedicating the Temple of Jupiter in the Capitol. See Livy ii. 8; Cic.Pro Domo, paragraph cxxi.

[6] Lucius -Æmilius Paullus conquered Perses, the last King of Macedonia, B.C. 168

[7] "For he had four sons, two, as has been already related, adopted into other families, Scipio and Fabius; and two others, who were still children, by his second wife, who lived in his own house. Of these, one died five days before Æmilius's triumph, at the age of fourteen, and the other, twelve years old, died three days after it: so that there was no Roman that did not grieve for him," &e.—Plutarch, "Life of Æmilius, *ch. xxxv.*

[8] A. U. C. 695, B.C. 59

[9] Virg. XL. III. 418

[10] See Mayor's note on Juv. i., and above, c. 16, § 4

[11] Lipsius points out that this idea is borrowed from the comic poet Antipbanes. See Meineke's "Comic Fragments," p. 3

[12] This I believe to be the meaning of the text, but Koch reasonably conjectures that the true reading is *editur subscriptio* "an indictment was made out against him." See "On Benefits," iii. 26.

[13] *Ruinae*; Koch's *urinae* is a misprint

Lucius Annaeus Seneca
On the Shortness of Life

I. The majority of mortals, Paulinus,[1] complain bitterly of the spitefulness of Nature, because we are born for a brief span of life, because even this space that has been granted to us rushes by so speedily and so swiftly that all save a very few find life at an end just when they are getting ready to live. Nor is it merely the common herd and the unthinking crowd that bemoan what is, as men deem it, an universal ill; the same feeling has called forth complaint also from men who were famous. It was this that made the greatest of physicians exclaim that "life is short, art is long;"[2] it was this that led Aristotle,[3] while expostulating with Nature, to enter an indictment most unbecoming to a wise man—that, in point of age, she has shown such favour to animals that they drag out five or ten lifetimes,[4] but that a much shorter limit is fixed for man, though he is born for so many and such great achievements. It is not that we have a short space of time, but that we waste much of it. Life is long enough, and it has been given in sufficiently generous measure to allow the accomplishment of the very greatest things if the whole of it is well invested. But when it is squandered in luxury and carelessness, when it is devoted to no good end, forced at last by the ultimate necessity we perceive that it has passed away before we were aware that it was passing. So it is—the life we receive is not short, but we make it so, nor do we have any lack of it, but are wasteful of it. Just as great and princely wealth is scattered in a moment when it comes into the hands of a bad owner, while wealth however limited, if it is entrusted to a good guardian, increases by use, so our life is amply long for him who orders it properly.

II. Why do we complain of Nature? She has shown herself kindly; life, if you know how to use it, is long. But one man is possessed by an avarice that is insatiable, another by a toilsome devotion to tasks that are useless; one man is besotted with wine, another is paralyzed by sloth; one man is exhausted by an ambition that always hangs upon the decision of others, another, driven on by the greed of the trader, is led over all lands and all seas by the hope of gain; some are tormented by a passion for war and are always either bent upon inflicting danger upon others or concerned about their own; some there are who are worn out by voluntary servitude in a thankless attendance upon the great; many are kept busy either in the pursuit of other men's fortune or in complaining of their own; many, following no fixed aim, shifting and inconstant and dissatisfied, are plunged by their fickleness into plans that are ever new; some have no fixed principle by which to direct their course, but Fate takes them unawares while they loll and yawn—so surely does it happen that I cannot doubt the truth of that utterance which the greatest of poets delivered with all the seeming of an oracle: "The part of life we really live is small."[5] For all the rest of existence is not life, but merely time. Vices beset us and surround us on every side, and they do not permit us to rise anew and lift up our eyes for the discernment of truth, but they keep us down when once they have overwhelmed us and we are chained to lust. Their victims are never allowed to return to their true selves; if ever they chance to find some release, like the waters of the deep sea which continue to heave even after the storm is past, they are tossed about, and no rest from their lusts abides. Think you that I am speaking of the wretches whose evils are admitted? Look at those whose prosperity men flock to behold; they are smothered by their blessings. To how many are riches a burden! From how many do eloquence and the daily straining to display their powers draw forth blood! How many are pale from constant pleasures! To how many does the throng of clients that crowd about them leave no freedom! In short, run through the list of all these men from the lowest to the highest—this man desires an advocate,[6] this one answers the call, that one is on trial, that one defends him, that one gives sentence; no one asserts his claim to himself, everyone is wasted for the sake of another. Ask about the men whose names are known by heart, and you will see that these are the marks that distinguish them: A cultivates B and B cultivates C; no one is his own master. And then certain men show the most senseless indignation—they complain of the insolence of their superiors, because they were too busy to see them when they wished an audience! But can anyone have the hardihood to complain of the pride of another when he himself has no time to attend to himself? After all, no matter who you are, the great man does sometimes look toward you even if his face is insolent, he does sometimes condescend to listen to your words, he permits you to appear at his side; but you never deign to look upon yourself, to give ear to yourself. There is no reason, therefore, to count anyone in debt for such services, seeing that, when you performed them, you had no wish for another's company, but could not endure your own.

III. Though all the brilliant intellects of the ages were to concentrate upon this one theme, never could they adequately express their wonder at this dense darkness of the human mind. Men do not suffer anyone to seize their estates, and they rush to stones and arms if there is even the slightest dispute about the limit of their lands, yet they allow others to trespass upon their life—nay, they themselves even lead in those who will eventually possess it. No one is to be found who is willing to distribute his money, yet among how many does each one of us distribute his life! In guarding their fortune men are often closefisted, yet, when it comes to the matter of wasting time, in the case of the one thing in which it is right to be miserly, they show themselves most prodigal. And so I should like to lay hold upon someone from the company of older men and say: "I see that you have reached the farthest limit of human life, you are pressing hard upon your hundredth year, or are even beyond it; come now, recall your life and make a reckoning. Consider how much of your time was taken up with a moneylender, how much with a mistress, how much with a patron, how much with a client, how much in wrangling with your wife, how much in punishing your slaves, how much in rushing about the city on social duties. Add the diseases which we have caused by our own acts, add, too, the time that has lain idle and unused; you will see that you have fewer years to your credit than you count. Look back in memory and consider when you ever had a fixed plan, how few days have passed as you had intended, when you were ever at your own disposal, when your face ever wore its natural expression, when your mind was ever unperturbed, what work you have achieved in so long a life, how many have robbed you of life when you were not aware of what you were losing, how much was taken up in useless sorrow, in foolish joy, in greedy desire, in the allurements of society, how little of yourself was left to you; you will perceive that you are dying before your season!"[7] What, then, is the reason of this? You live as if you were destined to live forever, no thought of your frailty ever enters your head, of how much time has already gone by you take no heed. You squander time as if you drew from a full and abundant supply, though all the while that day which you bestow on some person or thing is perhaps your last. You have all the fears of mortals and all the desires of immortals. You will hear many men saying: "After my fiftieth year I shall retire into leisure, my sixtieth year shall release me from public duties." And what guarantee, pray, have you that your life will last longer? Who will suffer your course to be just as you plan it? Are you not ashamed to reserve for yourself only the remnant of life, and to set apart for wisdom only that time which cannot be devoted to any business? How late it is to begin to live just when we must cease to live! What foolish forgetfulness of mortality to postpone wholesome plans to the fiftieth and sixtieth year, and to intend to begin life at a point to which few have attained!

IV. You will see that the most powerful and highly placed men let drop remarks in which they long for leisure, acclaim it, and prefer it to all their blessings. They desire at times, if it could be with safety, to descend from their high pinnacle; for, though nothing from without should assail or shatter, Fortune of its very self comes crashing down.[8]

The deified Augustus, to whom the gods vouchsafed more than to any other man, did not cease to pray for rest and to seek release from public affairs; all his conversation ever reverted to this subject—his hope of leisure. This was the sweet, even if vain, consolation with which he would gladden his labours—that he would one day live for himself. In a letter addressed to the senate, in which he had promised that his rest would not be devoid of dignity nor inconsistent with his former glory, I find these words: "But these matters can be shown better by deeds than by promises. Nevertheless, since the joyful reality is still far distant, my desire for that time most earnestly prayed for has led me to forestall some of its delight by the pleasure of words." So desirable a thing did leisure seem that he anticipated it in thought because he could not attain it in reality. He who saw everything depending upon himself alone, who determined the fortune of individuals and of nations, thought most happily of that future day on which he should lay aside his greatness. He had discovered how much sweat those blessings that shone throughout all lands drew forth, how many secret worries they concealed. Forced to pit arms first against his countrymen, then against his colleagues, and lastly against his relatives, he shed blood on land and sea.

Through Macedonia, Sicily, Egypt, Syria, and Asia, and almost all countries he followed the path of battle, and when his troops were weary of shedding Roman blood, he turned them to foreign wars. While he was pacifying the Alpine regions, and subduing the enemies planted in the midst of a peaceful empire, while he was extending its bounds even beyond the Rhine and the Euphrates and the Danube, in Rome itself the swords of Murena, Caepio, Lepidus, Egnatius, and others were being whetted to slay him. Not yet had he escaped their plots, when his daughter[9] and all the noble youths who were bound to her by adultery as by a sacred oath, oft alarmed his failing years—and there was Paulus, and a second time the need to fear a woman in league with an Antony.[10] When be had cut away these ulcers[11] together with the limbs themselves, others would grow in their place; just as in a body that was overburdened with blood, there was always a rupture somewhere. And so he longed for leisure, in the hope and thought of which he found relief for his labours. This was the prayer of one who was able to answer the prayers of mankind.

V. Marcus Cicero, long flung among men like Catiline and Clodius and Pompey and Crassus, some open enemies, others doubtful friends, as he is tossed to and fro along with the state and seeks to keep it from destruction, to be at last swept away, unable as he was to be restful in prosperity or patient in adversity—how many times does he curse that very consulship of his, which he had lauded without end, though not without reason! How tearful the words he uses in a letter[12] written to Atticus, when Pompey the elder had been conquered, and the son was still trying to restore his shattered arms in Spain! "Do you ask," he said, "what I am doing here? I am lingering in my Tusculan villa half a prisoner." He then proceeds to other statements, in which he bewails his former life and complains of the present and despairs of the future. Cicero said that he was "half a prisoner." But, in very truth, never will the wise man resort to so lowly a term, never will he be half a prisoner—he who always possesses an undiminished and stable liberty, being free and his own master and towering over all others. For what can possibly be above him who is above Fortune?...

VII.

...

Finally, everybody agrees that no one pursuit can be successfully followed by a man who is busied with many things—eloquence cannot, nor the liberal studies—since the mind, when its interests are divided, takes in nothing very deeply, but rejects everything that is, as it were, crammed into it. There is nothing the busy man is less busied with than living: there is nothing that is harder to learn. Of the other arts there are many teachers everywhere; some of them we have seen that mere boys have mastered so thoroughly that they could even play the master. It takes the whole of life to learn how to live, and—what will perhaps make you wonder more—it takes the whole of life to learn how to die. Many very great men, having laid aside all their encumbrances, having renounced riches, business, and pleasures, have made it their one aim up to the very end of life to know how to live; yet the greater number of them have departed from life confessing that they did not yet know—still less do those others know. Believe me, it takes a great man and one who has risen far above human weaknesses not to allow any of his time to be filched from him, and it follows that the life of such a man is very long because he has devoted wholly to himself whatever time he has had. None of it lay neglected and idle; none of it was under the control of another, for, guarding it most grudgingly, he found nothing that was worthy to be taken in exchange for his time. And so that man had time enough, but those who have been robbed of much of their life by the public, have necessarily had too little of it.

And there is no reason for you to suppose that these people are not sometimes aware of their loss. Indeed, you will hear many of those who are burdened by great prosperity cry out at times in the midst of their throngs of clients, or their pleadings in court, or their other glorious miseries: "I have no chance to live." Of course you have no chance! All those who summon you to themselves, turn you away from your own self. Of how many days has that defendant robbed you? Of how many that candidate? Of how many that old woman wearied with burying her heirs?[16] Of how many that man who is shamming sickness for the purpose of exciting the greed of the legacy-hunters? Of how many that very powerful friend who has you and your like on the list, not of his friends, but of his retinue? Check off, I say, and review the days of your life; you will see that very few, and those the refuse. have been left for you. That man who had prayed for the fasces,[17] when he attains them, desires to lay them aside and says over and over: "When will this year be over!" That man gives games,[18] and, after setting great value on gaining the chance to give them, now says: "When shall I be rid of them?" That advocate is lionized throughout the whole forum, and fills all the place with a great crowd that stretches farther than he can be heard, yet he says: "When will vacation time come?" Everyone hurries his life on and suffers from a yearning for the future and a weariness of the present. But he who bestows all of his time on his own needs, who plans out every day as if it were his last, neither longs for nor fears the morrow. For what new pleasure is there that any hour can now bring? They are all known, all have been enjoyed to the full. Mistress Fortune may deal out the rest as she likes; his life has already found safety. Something may be added to it, but nothing taken from it, and he will take any addition as the man who is satisfied and filled takes the food which he does not desire and yet can hold. And so there is no reason for you to think that any man has lived long because he has grey hairs or wrinkles; he has not lived long—he has existed long. For what if you should think that that man had had a long voyage who had been caught by a fierce storm as soon as he left harbour, and, swept hither and thither by a succession of winds that raged from different quarters, had been driven in a circle around the same course? Not much voyaging did he have, but much tossing about.

VIII. I am often filled with wonder when I see some men demanding the time of others and those from whom they ask it most indulgent. Both of them fix their eyes on the object of the request for time, neither of them on the time itself; just as if what is asked were nothing, what is given, nothing. Men trifle with the most precious thing in the world; but they are blind to it because it is an incorporeal thing, because it does not come beneath the sight of the eyes, and for this reason it is counted a very cheap thing—nay, of almost no value at all. Men set very great store by pensions and doles, and for these they hire out their labour or service or effort. But no one sets a value on time; all use it lavishly as if it cost nothing. But see how these same people clasp the knees of physicians if they fall ill and the danger of death draws nearer, see how ready they are, if threatened with capital punishment, to spend all their possessions in order to live! So great is the inconsistency of their feelings. But if each one could have the number of his future years set before him as is possible in the case of the years that have passed, how alarmed those would be who saw only a few remaining, how sparing of them would they be! And yet it is easy to dispense an amount that is assured, no matter how small it may be; but that must be guarded more carefully which will fail you know not when.

Yet there is no reason for you to suppose that these people do not know how precious a thing time is; for to those whom they love most devotedly they have a habit of saying that they are ready to give them a part of their own years. And they do give it, without realizing it; but the result of their giving is that they themselves suffer loss without adding to the years of their dear ones. But the very thing they do not know is whether they are suffering loss; therefore, the removal of something that is lost without being noticed they find is bearable. Yet no one will bring back the years, no one will bestow you once more on yourself. Life will follow the path it started upon, and will neither reverse nor check its course; it will make no noise, it will not remind you of its swiftness. Silent it will glide on; it will not prolong itself at the command of a king, or at the applause of the populace. Just as it was started on its first day, so it will run; nowhere will it turn aside, nowhere will it delay. And what will be the result? You have been engrossed, life hastens by; meanwhile death will be at hand, for which, willy nilly, you must find leisure.

IX. Can anything be sillier than the point of view of certain people—I mean those who boast of their foresight? They keep themselves very busily engaged in order that they may be able to live better; they spend life in making ready to live! They form their purposes with a view to the distant future; yet postponement is the greatest waste of life; it deprives them of each day as it comes, it snatches from them the present by promising something hereafter. The greatest hindrance to living is expectancy, which depends upon the morrow and wastes to-day. You dispose of that which lies in the hands of Fortune, you let go that which lies in your own. Whither do you look? At what goal do you aim? All things that are still to come lie in uncertainty; live straightway! See how the greatest of bards cries out, and, as if inspired with divine utterance, sings the saving strain:

The fairest day in hapless mortals' life
Is ever first to flee.[19]

"Why do you delay," says he, "Why are you idle? Unless you seize the day, it flees." Even though you seize it, it still will flee; therefore you must vie with time's swiftness in the speed of using it, and, as from a torrent that rushes by and will not always flow, you must drink quickly. And, too, the utterance of the bard is most admirably worded to cast censure upon infinite delay, in that he says, not "the fairest age," but "the fairest day." Why, to whatever length your greed inclines, do you stretch before yourself months and years in long array, unconcerned and slow though time flies so fast? The poet speaks to you about the day, and about this very day that is flying. Is there, then, any doubt that for hapless mortals, that is, for men who are engrossed, the fairest day is ever the first to flee? Old age surprises them while their minds are still childish, and they come to it unprepared and unarmed, for they have made no provision for it; they have stumbled upon it suddenly and unexpectedly, they did not notice that it was drawing nearer day by day. Even as conversation or reading or deep meditation on some subject beguiles the traveller, and he finds that he has reached the end of his journey before he was aware that he was approaching it, just so with this unceasing and most swift journey of life, which we make at the same pace whether waking or sleeping; those who are engrossed become aware of it only at the end.

X. Should I choose to divide my subject into heads with their separate proofs, many arguments will occur to me by which I could prove that busy men find life very short. But Fabianus,[20] who was none of your lecture-room philosophers of to-day, but one of the genuine and old-fashioned kind, used to say that we must fight against the passions with main force, not with artifice, and that the battle-line must be turned by a bold attack, not by inflicting pinpricks; that sophistry is not serviceable, for the passions must be, not nipped, but crushed. Yet, in order that the victims of them nay be censured, each for his own particular fault,

I say that they must be instructed, not merely wept over.

Life is divided into three periods—that which has been, that which is, that which will be. Of these the present time is short, the future is doubtful, the past is certain. For the last is the one over which Fortune has lost control, is the one which cannot be brought back under any man's power. But men who are engrossed lose this; for they have no time to look back upon the past, and even if they should have, it is not pleasant to recall something they must view with regret. They are, therefore, unwilling to direct their thoughts backward to ill-spent hours, and those whose vices become obvious if they review the past, even the vices which were disguised under some allurement of momentary pleasure, do not have the courage to revert to those hours. No one willingly turns his thought back to the past, unless all his acts have been submitted to the censorship of his conscience, which is never deceived; he who has ambitiously coveted, proudly scorned, recklessly conquered, treacherously betrayed, greedily seized, or lavishly squandered, must needs fear his own memory. And yet this is the part of our time that is sacred and set apart, put beyond the reach of all human mishaps, and removed from the dominion of Fortune, the part which is disquieted by no want, by no fear, by no attacks of disease; this can neither be troubled nor be snatched away—it is an everlasting and unanxious possession. The present offers only one day at a time, and each by minutes; but all the days of past time will appear when you bid them, they will suffer you to behold them and keep them at your will—a thing which those who are engrossed have no time to do. The mind that is untroubled and tranquil has the power to roam into all the parts of its life; but the minds of the engrossed, just as if weighted by a yoke, cannot turn and look behind. And so their life vanishes into an abyss; and as it does no good, no matter how much water you pour into a vessel, if there is no bottom[21] to receive and hold it, so with time—it makes no difference how much is given; if there is nothing for it to settle upon, it passes out through the chinks and holes of the mind. Present time is very brief, so brief, indeed, that to some there seems to be none; for it is always in motion, it ever flows and hurries on; it ceases to be before it has come, and can no more brook delay than the firmament or the stars, whose ever unresting movement never lets them abide in the same track. The engrossed, therefore, are concerned with present time alone, and it is so brief that it cannot be grasped, and even this is filched away from them, distracted as they are among many things.

XI. In a word, do you want to know how they do not "live long"? See how eager they are to live long! Decrepit old men beg in their prayers for the addition of a few more years; they pretend that they are younger than they are; they comfort themselves with a falsehood, and are as pleased to deceive themselves as if they deceived Fate at the same time. But when at last some infirmity has reminded them of their mortality, in what terror do they die, feeling that they are being dragged out of life, and not merely leaving it. They cry out that they have been fools, because they have not really lived, and that they will live henceforth in leisure if only they escape from this illness; then at last they reflect how uselessly they have striven for things which they did not enjoy, and how all their toil has gone for nothing. But for those whose life is passed remote from all business, why should it not be ample? None of it is assigned to another, none of it is scattered in this direction and that, none of it is committed to Fortune, none of it perishes from neglect, none is subtracted by wasteful giving, none of it is unused; the whole of it, so to speak, yields income. And so, however small the amount of it, it is abundantly sufficient, and therefore, whenever his last day shall come, the wise man will not hesitate to go to meet death with steady step.

XII. Perhaps you ask whom I would call "the engrossed "? There is no reason for you to suppose that I mean only those whom the dogs[22] that have at length been let in drive out from the law-court, those whom you see either gloriously crushed in their own crowd of followers, or scornfully in someone else's, those whom social duties call forth from their own homes to bump them against someone else's doors, or whom the praetor's hammer[23] keeps busy in seeking gain that is disreputable and that will one day fester. Even the leisure of some men is engrossed; in their villa or on their couch, in the midst of solitude, although they have withdrawn from all others, they are themselves the source of their own worry; we should say that these are living, not in leisure, but in busy idleness.[24] Would you say that that man is at leisure[25] who arranges with finical care his Corinthian bronzes, that the mania of a few makes costly, and spends the greater part of each day upon rusty bits of copper? Who sits in a public wrestling-place (for, to our shame I we labour with vices that are not even Roman) watching the wrangling of lads? Who sorts out the herds of his pack-mules into pairs of the same age and colour? Who feeds all the newest athletes? Tell me, would you say that those men are at leisure who pass many hours at the barber's while they are being stripped of whatever grew out the night before? while a solemn debate is held over each separate hair? while either disarranged locks are restored to their place or thinning ones drawn from this side and that toward the forehead? How angry they get if the barber has been a bit too careless, just as if he were shearing a real man! How they flare up if any of their mane is lopped off, if any of it lies out of order, if it does not all fall into its proper ringlets! Who of these would not rather have the state disordered than his hair? Who is not more concerned to have his head trim rather than safe? Who would not rather be well barbered than upright? Would you say that these are at leisure who are occupied with the comb and the mirror? And what of those who are engaged in composing, hearing, and learning songs, while they twist the voice, whose best and simplest movement Nature designed to be straightforward, into the meanderings of some indolent tune, who are always snapping their fingers as they beat time to some song they have in their head, who are overheard humming a tune when they have been summoned to serious, often even melancholy, matters? These have not leisure, but idle occupation. And their banquets, Heaven knows! I cannot reckon among their unoccupied hours, since I see how anxiously they set out their silver plate, how diligently they tie up the tunics of their pretty slave-boys, how breathlessly they watch to see in what style the wild boar issues from the hands of the cook, with what speed at a given signal smooth-faced boys hurry to perform their duties, with what skill the birds are carved into portions all according to rule, how carefully unhappy little lads wipe up the spittle of drunkards. By such means they seek the reputation of being fastidious and elegant, and to such an extent do their evils follow them into all the privacies of life that they can neither eat nor drink without ostentation. And I would not count these among the leisured class either—the men who have themselves borne hither and thither in a sedan-chair and a litter, and are punctual at the hours for their rides as if it were unlawful to omit them, who are reminded by someone else when they must bathe, when they must swim, when they must dine; so enfeebled are they by the excessive lassitude of a pampered mind that they cannot find out by themselves whether they are hungry! I hear that one of these pampered people—provided that you can call it pampering to unlearn the habits of human life—when he had been lifted by hands from the bath and placed in his sedan-chair, said questioningly: "Am I now seated?" Do you think that this man, who does not know whether he is sitting, knows whether he is alive, whether he sees, whether he is at leisure? I find it hard to say whether I pity him more if he really did not know, or if he pretended not to know this. They really are subject to forgetfulness of many things, but they also pretend forgetfulness of many. Some vices delight them as being proofs of their prosperity; it seems the part of a man who is very lowly and despicable to know what he is doing. After this imagine that the mimes[26] fabricate many things to make a mock of luxury! In very truth, they pass over more than they invent, and such a multitude of unbelievable vices has come forth in this age, so clever in this one direction, that by now we can charge the mimes with neglect. To think that there is anyone who is so lost in luxury that he takes another's word as to whether he is sitting down! This man, then, is not at leisure, you must apply to him a different term—he is sick, nay, he is dead; that man is at leisure, who has also a perception of his leisure. But this other who is half alive, who, in order that he may know the postures of his own body, needs someone to tell him—how can he be the master of any of his time?...

XIV. Of all men they alone are at leisure who take time for philosophy, they alone really live; for they are not content to be good guardians of their own lifetime only. They annex ever age to their own; all the years that have gone ore them are an addition to their store. Unless we are most ungrateful, all those men, glorious fashioners of holy thoughts, were born for us; for us they have prepared a way of life. By other men's labours we are led to the sight of things most beautiful that have been wrested from darkness and brought into light; from no age are we shut out, we have access to all ages, and if it is our wish, by greatness of mind, to pass beyond the narrow limits of human weakness, there is a great stretch of time through which we may roam. We may argue with Socrates, we may doubt[32] with Carneades, find peace with Epicurus, overcome human nature with the Stoics, exceed it with the Cynics. Since Nature allows us to enter into fellowship with every age, why should we not turn from this paltry and fleeting span of time and surrender ourselves with all our soul to the past, which is boundless, which is eternal, which we share with our betters?

Those who rush about in the performance of social duties, who give themselves and others no rest, when they have fully indulged their madness, when they have every day crossed everybody's threshold, and have left no open door unvisited, when they have carried around their venal greeting to houses that are very far apart—out of a city so huge and torn by such varied desires, how few will they be able to see? How many will there be who either from sleep or self-indulgence or rudeness will keep them out! How many who, when they have tortured them with long waiting, will rush by, pretending to be in a hurry! How many will avoid passing out through a hall that is crowded with clients, and will make their escape through some concealed door as if it were not more discourteous to deceive than to exclude. How many, still half asleep and sluggish from last night's debauch, scarcely lifting their lips in the midst of a most insolent yawn, manage to bestow on yonder poor wretches, who break their own slumber[33] in order to wait on that of another, the right name only after it has been whispered to them a thousand times!

But we may fairly say that they alone are engaged in the true duties of life who shall wish to have Zeno, Pythagoras, Democritus, and all the other high priests of liberal studies, and Aristotle and Theophrastus, as their most intimate friends every day. No one of these will be "not at home," no one of these will fail to have his visitor leave more happy and more devoted to himself than when he came, no one of these will allow anyone to leave him with empty hands; all mortals can meet with them by night or by day.

XV. No one of these will force you to die, but all will teach you how to die; no one of these will wear out your years, but each will add his own years to yours; conversations with no one of these will bring you peril, the friendship of none will endanger your life, the courting of none will tax your purse. From them you will take whatever you wish; it will be no fault of theirs if you do not draw the utmost that you can desire. What happiness, what a fair old age awaits him who has offered himself as a client to these! He will have friends from whom he may seek counsel on matters great and small, whom he may consult every day about himself, from whom he may hear truth without insult, praise without flattery, and after whose likeness he may fashion himself.

We are wont to say that it was not in our power to choose the parents who fell to our lot, that they have been given to men by chance; yet *we* may be the sons of whomsoever we will. Households there are of noblest intellects; choose the one into which you wish to be adopted; you will inherit not merely their name, but even their property, which there will be no need to guard in a mean or niggardly spirit; the more persons you share it with, the greater it will become. These will open to you the path to immortality, and will raise you to a height from which no one is cast down. This is the only way of prolonging mortality—nay, of turning it into immortality. Honours, monuments, all that ambition has commanded by decrees or reared in works of stone, quickly sink to ruin; there is nothing that the lapse of time does not tear down and remove. But the works which philosophy has consecrated cannot be harmed; no age will destroy them, no age reduce them; the following and each succeeding age will but increase the reverence for them, since envy works upon what is close at hand, and things that are far off we are more free to admire. The life of the philosopher, therefore, has wide range, and he is not confined by the same bounds that shut others in. He alone is freed from the limitations of the human race; all ages serve him as if a god. Has some time passed by? This he embraces by recollection. Is time present? This he uses. Is it still to come? This he anticipates. He makes his life long by combining all times into one.

XVI. But those who forget the past, neglect the present, and fear for the future have a life that is very brief and troubled; when they have reached the end of it, the poor wretches perceive too late that for such a long while they have been busied in doing nothing. Nor because they sometimes invoke death, have you any reason to think it any proof that they find life long. In their folly they are harassed by shifting emotions which rush them into the very things they dread; they often pray for death because they fear it. And, too, you have no reason to think that this is any proof that they are living a long time—the fact that the day often seems to them long, the fact that they complain that the hours pass slowly until the time set for dinner arrives; for, whenever their engrossments fail them, they are restless because they are left with nothing to do, and they do not know how to dispose of their leisure or to drag out the time. And so they strive for something else to occupy them, and all the intervening time is irksome; exactly as they do when a gladiatorial exhibition\b is been announced, or when they are waiting for the appointed time of some other show or amusement, they want to skip over the days that lie between. All postponement of something they hope for seems long to them. Yet the time which they enjoy is short and swift, and it is made much shorter by their own fault; for they flee from one pleasure to another and cannot remain fixed in one desire. Their days are not long to them, but hateful; yet, on the other hand, how scanty seem the nights which they spend in the arms of a harlot or in wine! It is this also that accounts for the madness of poets in fostering human frailties by the tales in which they represent that Jupiter under the enticement of the pleasures of a lover doubled the length of the night. For what is it but to inflame our vices to inscribe the name of the gods as their sponsors, and to present the excused indulgence of divinity as an example to our own weakness? Can the nights which they pay for so dearly fail to seem all too short to these men? They lose the day in expectation of the night, and the night in fear of the dawn.

XVII. The very pleasures of such men are uneasy and disquieted by alarms of various sorts, and at the very moment of rejoicing the anxious thought comes over them: How long will these things last?" This feeling has led kings to weep over the power they possessed, and they have not so much delighted in the greatness of their fortune, as they have viewed with terror the end to which it must some time come. When the King of Persia,[34] in all the insolence of his pride, spread his army over the vast plains and could not grasp its number but simply its measure,[35] he shed copious tears because inside of a hundred years not a man of such a mighty army would be alive.[36] But he who wept was to bring upon them their fate, was to give some to their doom on the sea, some on the land, some in battle, some in flight, and within a short time was to destroy all those for whose hundredth year he had such fear. And why is it that even their joys are uneasy from fear? Because they do not rest on stable causes, but are perturbed as groundlessly as they are born. But of what sort do you think those times are which even by their own confession are wretched, since even the joys by which they are exalted and lifted above mankind are by no means pure? All the greatest blessings are a source of anxiety, and at no time is fortune less wisely trusted than when it is best; to maintain prosperity there is need of other prosperity, and in behalf of the prayers that have turned out well we must make still other prayers. For everything that comes to us from chance is unstable, and the higher it rises, the more liable it is to fall. Moreover, what is doomed to perish brings pleasure to no one; very wretched, therefore, and not merely short, must the life of those be who work hard to gain what they must work harder to keep. By great toil they attain what they wish, and with anxiety hold what they have attained; meanwhile they take no account of time that will never more return. New engrossments take the place of the old, hope leads to new hope, ambition to new ambition. They do not seek an end of their wretchedness, but change the cause. Have we been tormented by our own public honours? Those of others take more of our time. Have we ceased to labour as candidates? We begin to canvass for others. Have we got rid of the troubles of a prosecutor? We find those of a judge. Has a man ceased to be a judge? He becomes president of a court. Has he become infirm in managing the property of others at a salary? He is perplexed by caring for his own wealth. Have the barracks[37] set Marius free? The consulship keeps him busy. Does Quintius[38] hasten to get to the end of his dictatorship? He will be called back to it from the plough. Scipio will go against the Carthaginians before he is ripe for so great an undertaking; victorious over Hannibal, victorious over Antiochus, the glory of his own consulship, the surety for his brother's, did he not stand in his own way, he would be set beside Jove[39]; but the discord of civilians will vex their preserver, and, when as a young man he had scorned honours that rivalled those of the gods, at length, when he is old, his ambition will lake delight in stubborn exile.[40] Reasons for anxiety will never be lacking, whether born of prosperity or of wretchedness; life pushes on in a succession of engrossments. We shall always pray for leisure, but never enjoy it....

XIX. Do you retire to these quieter, safer, greater things! Think you that it is just the same whether you are concerned in having corn from oversea poured into the granaries, unhurt either by the dishonesty or the neglect of those who transport it, in seeing that it does not become heated and spoiled by collecting moisture and tallies in weight and measure, or whether you enter upon these sacred and lofty studies with the purpose of discovering what substance, what pleasure, what mode of life, what shape God has; what fate awaits your soul; where Nature lays us to rest When we are freed from the body; what the principle is that upholds all the heaviest matter in the centre of this world, suspends the light on high, carries fire to the topmost part, summons the stars to their proper changes—and ether matters, in turn, full of mighty wonders? You really must leave the ground and turn your mind's eye upon these things! Now while the blood is hot, we must enter with brisk step upon the better course. In this kind of life there awaits much that is good to know—the love and practice of the virtues, forgetfulness of the passions, knowledge of living and dying, and a life of deep repose.

The condition of all who are engrossed is wretched, but most wretched is the condition of those who labour at engrossments that are not even their own, who regulate their sleep by that of another, their walk by the pace of another, who are under orders in case of the freest things in the world—loving and hating. If these wish to know how short their life is, let them reflect how small a part of it is their own.

XX. And so when you see a man often wearing the robe of office, when you see one whose name is famous in the Forum, do not envy him; those things are bought at the price of life. They will waste all their years, in order that they may have one year reckoned by their name.[44] Life has left some in the midst of their first struggles, before they could climb up to the height of their ambition; some, when they have crawled up through a thousand indignities to the crowning dignity, have been possessed by the unhappy thought that they have but toiled for an inscription on a tomb; some who have come to extreme old age, while they adjusted it to new hopes as if it were youth, have had it fail from sheer weakness in the midst of their great and shameless endeavours. Shameful is he whose breath leaves him in the midst of a trial when, advanced in years and still courting the applause of an ignorant circle, he is pleading for some litigant who is the veriest stranger;

disgraceful is he who, exhausted more quickly by his mode of living than by his labour, collapses in the very midst of his duties; disgraceful is he who dies in the act of receiving payments on account, and draws a smile from his long delayed[45] heir. I cannot pass over an instance which occurs to me. Sextus[46] Turannius was an old man of long tested diligence, who, after his ninetieth year, having received release from the duties of his office by Gaius Caesar's own act, ordered himself to be laid out on his bed and to be mourned by the assembled household as if he were dead. The whole house bemoaned the leisure of its old master, and did not end its sorrow until his accustomed work was restored to him. Is it really such pleasure for a man to die in harness? Yet very many have the same feeling; their desire for their labour lasts longer than their ability; they fight against the weakness of the body, they judge old age to be a hardship on no other score than because it puts them aside. The law does not draft a soldier after his fiftieth year, it does not call a senator after his sixtieth; it is more difficult for men to obtain leisure from themselves than from the law. Meantime, while they rob and are being robbed, while they break up each other's repose, while they make each other wretched, their life is without profit, without pleasure, without any improvement of the mind. No one keeps death in view, no one refrains from far-reaching hopes; some men, indeed, even arrange for things that lie beyond life—huge masses of tombs and dedications of public works and gifts for their funeral-pyres and ostentatious funerals. But, in very truth, the funerals of such men ought to be conducted by the light of torches and wax tapers,[47] as though they had lived but the tiniest span.

[1] It is clear from chapters 18 and 19 that, when this essay was written (in or about A.D. 49), Paulinus was *praefectus annonae*, the official who superintended the grain supply of Rome, and was, therefore, a man of importance. He was, believably, a near relative of Seneca's wife, Pompeia Paulina, and is usually identified with the father of a certain Pompeius Paulinus, who held high public posts under Nero (Pliny, *Nat. Hist.* xxxiii. 143; Tacitus, *Annals*, xiii. 53. 2; xv.

[2] The famous aphorism of Hippocrates of Cos: ὁ βίος βραχύς, ἡ δὲ τέχνη μακρή.

[3] An error for Theophrastus, as shown by Cicero, Tusc. Disp. iii. 69: "Theophrastus autem moriens accusasse naturam dicitur, quod cervis et cornicibus vitam diuturnam, quorum id nihil interesset, hominibus, quorum maxime interfuisset, tam exiguam vitam dedisset; quorum si aetas potuisset esse longinquior, futurum fuisse ut omnibus perfectis artibus omni doctrina hominum vita erudiretur."

[4] *i.e.*, of man. *Cf.* Hesiod, *Frag.* 183 (Rzach):'Εννέα τοι ζώει γενεὰς λακέρυζα κορώνη ἀνδρῶν γηράντω· ἔλαφος δέ τε τετρακόρωνος.

[5] A prose rendering of an unknown poet. *Cf.* the epitaph quoted by Cassius Dio, lxix. 19: Σίμιλις ἐνταῦθα κεῖται βιοὺς μὲν ἔτη τόσα, ζήσας δὲ ἔτη ἑπτά.

[6] Not one who undertook the actual defense, but one who by his presence and advice lent support in court.

[7] Literally, "unripe." At 100 he should "come to his grave in a full age, like as a shock of corn cometh in in his season" (Job v. 26); but he is still unripe.

[8] The idea is that greatness sinks beneath its own weight. *Cf.* Seneca, *Agamemnon*, 88 *sq.*: Sidunt ipso pondere magna ceditque oneri Fortuna suo.

[9] The notorious Julia, who was banished by Augustus to the island of Pandataria.

[10] In 31 B.C. Augustus had been pitted against Mark Antony and Cleopatra; in 2 B.C. Iullus Antonius, younger son of the triumvir, was sentenced to death by reason of his intrigue with the elder Julia.

[11] The language is reminiscent of Augustus's own characterization of Julia and his two grandchildren in Suetonius (*Aug.* 65. 5): "nec (solebat) aliter eos appellare quam tris vomicas ac tria carcinomata sua" ("his trio of boils and trio of ulcers").

[12] Not extant.

[13] As tribune in 91 B.C. he proposed a corn law and the granting of citizenship to the Italians.

[14] Throughout the essay *occupati*, "the

engrossed," is a technical term designating those who are so absorbed in the interests of life that they take no time for philosophy.

15 *i.e.*, the various types of *occupati* that have been sketchily presented. The looseness of the structure has led some editors to doubt the integrity of the passage.

16 *i.e.*, she has become the prey of legacy-hunters.

17 The rods that were the symbol of high office.

18 At this time the management of the public games was committed to the praetors.

19 Virgil, *Georgics*, iii. 66 *sq*.

20 A much admired teacher of Seneca.

21 An allusion to the fate of the Danaids, who in Hades forever poured water into a vessel with a perforated bottom.

22 Apparently watch-dogs that were let in at nightfall, and caught the engrossed lawyer still at his task.

23 Literally, "spear," which was stuck in the ground as the sign of a public auction where captured or confiscated goods were put up for sale.

24 *Cf.* Pliny, *Epistles*, i. 9. 8: "satius est enim, ut Atilius noster eruditissime simul et facetissime dixit, otiosum esse quam nihil agere."

25 For the technical meaning of *otiosi*, "the leisured," see Seneca's definition at the beginning of chap. 14.

26 Actors in the popular mimes, or low farces, that were often censured for their indecencies.

27 The ancient codex was made of tablets of wood fastened together.

28 Such, doubtless, as Marius, Sulla, Caesar, Crassus.

29 Pliny (*Nat. Hist.* viii. 21) reports that the people were so moved by pity that they rose in a body and called down curses upon Pompey. Cicero's impressions of the occasion are recorded in *Ad Fam.* vii. 1. 3: "extremus elephantorum dies fuit, in quo admiratio magna vulgi atque turbae, delectatio nulla exstitit; quin etiam misericordia quaedam consecuta est atque opinio eiusmodi, esse quandam illi beluae cum genere humana societatem."

30 *i.e.*, *Magnus*.

31 A name applied to a consecrated space kept vacant within and (according to Livy, i. 44) without the city wall. The right of extending it belonged originally to the king who had added territory to Rome.

32 The New Academy taught that certainty of knowledge was unattainable.

33 The *salutatio* was held in the early morning.

34 Xerxes, who invaded Greece in 480 B.C.

35 On the plain of Doriscus in Thrace the huge land force was estimated by counting the number of times a space capable of holding 10,000 men was filled (Herodotus, vii. 60).

36 Herodotus, vii. 45, 46 tells the story.

37 *Caliga*, the boot of the common soldier, is here synonymous with service in the army.

38 His first appointment was announced to him while he was ploughing his own fields.

39 He did not allow his statue to be placed in the Capitol.

40 Disgusted with politics, he died in exile at Liternum.

41 Probably an allusion to the mad wish of Caligula: "utinam populus Romanus unam cervicem haberet!" (Suetonius, *Calig.* 30), cited in *De Ira*, iii. 19. 2. The logic of the whole passage suffers from the uncertainty of the text.

42 Three and a half miles long, reaching from Baiae to the mole of Puteoli (Suetonius, *Calig.* 19).

43 Xerxes, who laid a bridge over the Hellespont.

44 The Roman year was dated by the names of the two annual consuls.

45 *i.e.*, long kept out of his inheritance.

46 Tacitus (*Annals*, i. 7) gives the *praenomen* as Gaius.

47 *i.e.*, as if they were children, whose funerals took place by night (Servius, *Aeneid*, xi. 143).

NOTES

Determinism

- d'Holbach
- humans are purely physical
- All events are determined
- No choice, only one path
- There is no free will

compatibilism

- Hume
- " "
- " "
- " "
- free will is to act from internal causes

Agency Theory

- Reid
- Humans are not purely physical
- Some events are not determined.
- Choice; multiple "paths"
- Free will is to be "self-caused" (choice, agent causation)

NOTES

NOTES

NOTES

NOTES

Made in the USA
San Bernardino, CA
27 December 2016